CW01497745

ENDURING THE WHIRLWIND

Enduring the Whirlwind

The German Army and the Russo-German War 1941-1943

Wolverhampton Military Studies No.21

Gregory Liedtke

Helion & Company Limited

Helion & Company Limited
26 Willow Road
Solihull
West Midlands
B91 1UE
England
Tel. 0121 705 3393
Fax 0121 711 4075
Email: info@helion.co.uk
Website: www.helion.co.uk
Twitter: @helionbooks
Visit our blog http://blog.helion.co.uk/

Published by Helion & Company 2016
Designed and typeset by Mach 3 Solutions Ltd (www.mach3solutions.co.uk)
Cover designed by Paul Hewitt, Battlefield Design (www.battlefield-design.co.uk)
Printed by Gutenberg Press Limited, Tarxien, Malta

Text © Gregory Liedtke 2016
Maps drawn by George Anderson © Helion & Company Ltd 2016

ISBN 978-1-910777-75-6

British Library Cataloguing-in-Publication Data.
A catalogue record for this book is available from the British Library.

For details of other military history titles published by Helion & Company Limited contact the above address, or visit our website: http://www.helion.co.uk.

We always welcome receiving book proposals from prospective authors.

Contents

List of Maps

List of Tables

Glossary of Terms and Abbreviations

Abgänge	Departure
Armee	Army; An organizational formation consisting of at least two *Korps*.
Aufklärungs	Reconnaissance
Beflpz., Befpz.	Abbreviation for *Befehlpanzer* (command tank)
Bewegungskrieg	A war of, or characterized by, movement
Einsatzstärke	Action strength; see definition of *Einsatzstarke*.
Eisenbahntruppen	Railway troops.
Ersatz	Replacement.
Ersatzheer	Replacement Army; organization responsible for training and supplying the *Feldheer* with personnel replacements, and for raising new formations.
Fallschirmjäger	Parachute troops.
Feldausbildung Division	Field training division; formation created to provide advanced training to new recruits, but deployed in occupied territories to also conduct garrison duties.
Feldersatz	Field replacement.
Feldheer	Field army.
FHO	Abbreviation for *Fremde Heere Ost*.
Flak	Abbreviation for *Flakartillerie*.
Flakartillerie	Anti-aircraft artillery.
Flivos	German slang for *Flieger Verbindungsoffizier* (Air Liaison Officer).
Fremde Heere Ost	Foreign Armies East; the department within OKH responsible for military intelligence operations focused upon the Soviet Union and eastern Europe.

Gefechtsstärke	Translated as fighting strength, this indicates the overall number of fit and available personnel within the combat units (infantry, artillery, armoured, engineer, anti-tank, reconnaissance, etc.) of a given formation, including headquarters staff, and administration and supply personnel.
Gesamtstärke	Total strength; see definition of *Tagesstärke*.
Geschwader	Literally squadron; usually used in conjunction with a *Luftwaffe* organization comparable to a British air wing and composed of 100-150 aircraft.
Grabenstärke	Translated literally as trench strength this is a somewhat confusing term because its definition is the same as either *Kampfstärke* or *Infanteriestärke*, depending upon the specific context.
Grenzschutz	Border guard.
GrW	Abbreviation for *Granatwerfer*, or mortar.
Heer	Army; denoting the broader land component of the German armed forces.
Heeres Flakartillerie	Army anti-aircraft artillery.
Heeresgruppe	Army group
Hilfswillige	Volunteer helpers; Soviet citizens who volunteered or were conscripted into the German Army or *Luftwaffe* to serve in an auxiliary (non-combat) capacity.
Hiwis	German slang for *Hilfswillige*.
IG	Abbreviation for *Infanteriegeschütz*.
Infanterie	Infantry
Infanteriegeschütz	Infantry gun; a 7.5 cm or 15 cm artillery piece usually intended for direct fire support.
Infanteriestärke	Refers to the frontline infantry strength. Usually this just relates to the number of infantrymen within infantry companies, but when related to the strength of a division this can sometimes also include the combat strength of the divisional reconnaissance and engineer battalions.
Iststärke	The actual or available strength on a specific day. This includes all the personnel belonging to a given unit and includes those who were on leave or otherwise temporarily absent. Also included are any sick or wounded personnel who were expected to return within eight weeks.
Jagdstaffeln	Single-engine fighter squadrons
Kampfstaffeln	Bomber squadrons

Kampfstärke	Meaning combat strength, this refers to all the frontline combat personnel of a combat unit (such as riflemen, tank crews, mortar teams, anti-tank gunners, etc.). It does not encompass artillery personnel, or the administration and supply elements of combat units, since these are not actually or normally assigned to combat duties in the front line.
Kavallerie	Cavalry
Kommando der Panzertruppen	Armoured Troops Command
Kopfstärke	Literally means headcount and relates to the same definition as *Verpflegungsstärke*.
Korps	Corps; organization consisting of two or more divisions plus support troops.
Kriegsakademie	German Army (formerly Prussian) War Academy.
Kriegsmarine	Germany's wartime navy.
Kriegsstärkenach-weisungen	Wartime table of organization and equipment, this provides the official number of personnel and equipment for any given type of unit.
KStN	Abbreviation for *Kriegsstärkenachweisungen*.
Landwehr	Reservists, usually composed of older age classes.
le.FH	Light field howitzer (usually 10.5 cm).
le.IG	Light infantry gun (usually 7.5 cm).
Leichte	Light
Luftkriegsak-ademie	Luftwaffe War Academy
Luftwaffe	Air Force
Machinegewehr	Machine-gun
Marder	A series (I-III) of *ad-hoc* tank destroyers utilizing a variety of tank chassis and mounting a 7.5 cm or 7.62 cm anti-tank gun.
Maskirovka	Soviet military doctrine that encompasses concealment, simulation, decoys, and disinformation, all for a purpose of deceiving an opponent.
MG	Abbreviation for machine-gun.
Mitte	Centre
Nachrichten-helferinnen	Female communications auxiliaries.
NbW	Abbreviation for *Nebelwerfer*.
Nebelwerfer	Literally fog thrower; a variety of rocket launchers ranging in size from 15 cm to 32 cm.
Nord	North

Oberkommando des Heeres	High Command of the German Army.
Oberkommando der Luftwaffe	High Command of the German Air Force.
Oberkommando der Wehrmacht	High Command of the German Armed Forces.
OKH	Abbreviation for *Oberkommando des Heeres*.
OKL	Abbreviation for *Oberkommando der Luftwaffe*.
OKW	Abbreviation for *Oberkommando der Wehrmacht*.
Osoaviakhim	Soviet paramilitary organization responsible for providing civil defence and some military training.
Ostfront	Eastern front
Ostheer	That part of the German Army deployed on the Eastern front.
Ostlegionen	Eastern Legions; umbrella term used to group the various battalions (Armenians, Azerbaijani, North Caucasus, Georgian, Turcoman, Volga Tartar) of volunteers raised by the German Army from amongst the populations of the Caucasus.
Osttruppen	Eastern Troops; umbrella term used to define all troops raised by the German Army from amongst the population of the Soviet Union.
Pak	Abbreviation for *Panzerabwehrkanone* (anti-tank gun)
Panzer	Tank
Panzerarmee	Tank army; initially these were composed exclusively of panzer and motorised divisions, but increasingly included infantry formations.
Panzergrenadier	Motorised or mechanized infantry, usually that belonging to panzer or (from 1945) *panzergrenadier* divisions.
Panzergruppe	Tank group; the forerunner of *Panzerarmee*.
Panzerjäger	Tank hunters; refers to anti-tank units.
Panzerspahwagen	Armoured reconnaissance vehicle.
Panzertruppen	Tank Troops
Pionier	Combat engineers
PSW	Abbreviation for *Panzerspahwagen*.
Radfahr	Bicycle
Raupenschlepper Ost	Caterpillar Tractor East; fully tracked lightweight vehicle introduced in 1942 in response to the poor performance of wheeled and half-tracked vehicles in the mud and snow experienced on the Eastern front.

Reichsbahn	German national railway
Reichsluft-ministerium	Reich Air Ministry
Reichswehr	'Imperial Defence Force'; title of the German armed forces between 1919 and 1935.
s.FH	Heavy field howitzer (usually 15 cm)
s.IG	Heavy infantry gun (usually 15 cm)
Schützen	Originally described infantrymen armed with a rifled musket or performing a light infantry role; this term was the title given to the motorized or mechanized infantry components of panzer divisions until replaced by the term *panzergrenadier* in June 1942.
Schützen-panzerwagen	Armoured half-tracked vehicle usually employed to carry infantry.
Schutzpolizei	Federal or State Police
Schwadron	Squadron
Schwere	Heavy
Sollstärke	Designates the number of personnel a unit is authorized to posses according to its current tables of organization (or KStN).
SPW	Abbreviation for *Schutzenpanzerwagen*.
Stabshelferinnen	Female Staff Auxiliary.
STAVKA	Abbreviation for the 'Main Command of the Armed Forces of the USSR'; the high command of the Soviet armed forces.
StuG	Abbreviation of Sturmgeschütz.
Sturmgeschütz	Assault gun (equipped with a 7.5 cm gun).
StuH	Abbreviation for *Sturmhaubitze*, a variant of the *Sturmgeschutz* equipped with a 10.5 cm howitzer.
Süd	South
Tagesstärke	Literally meaning 'daily strength', this relates to the actual number of personnel present with a unit on a specific date, including anyone temporarily attached from other formations and organizations.
TOE	Table of Organization and Equipment
Verpflegungsstärke	The total ration strength of a given unit on a specific date, and includes everyone, including sick and wounded personnel, prisoners of war, non-military manpower, and personnel attached from other military organizations and services, that drew rations from that particular unit.
VVS	Abbreviation of *Voenno-Vozdushnye Sily*; the Red Army Air Force.

Wehrmacht	'Armed Force'; the German Armed Forces, including all branches and services.
Wehrmacht-helferinnen	Female Armed Forces Auxiliaries.
Wehrmacht-transportchef	Commander of Armed Forces Transport
Welle	Wave
Westwall	An extensive system of fortifications built along Germanys' western border between 1938 and 1940.
Zugmaschine	A half-tracked towing vehicle.

Table of Military Ranks

German Army/Luftwaffe	British Army	U.S. Army
Generalfeldmarschall	Field Marshal	General of the Army
Generaloberst	General	General
General	Lieutenant-General	Lieutenant-General
der Infanterie (of Infantry)		
der Artillerie (of Artillery)		
der Flakartillerie (of Flak Artillery)		
der Flieger (of Aviation)		
der Kavallerie (of Cavalry)		
der Panzertruppen (of Panzer Troops)		
der Pioniere (of Engineers)		
Generalleutnant	Major-General	Major-General
Generalmajor	Brigadier	Brigadier-General
Oberst	Colonel	Colonel
Oberstleutnant	Lieutenant-Colonel	Lieutenant-Colonel
Major	Major	Major
Hauptmann	Captain	Captain
Oberleutnant	Lieutenant	First Lieutenant
Leutnant	Second Lieutenant	Second Lieutenant

The Wolverhampton Military Studies Series
Series Editor's Preface

As series editor, it is my great pleasure to introduce the *Wolverhampton Military Studies Series* to you. Our intention is that in this series of books you will find military history that is new and innovative, and academically rigorous with a strong basis in fact and in analytical research, but also is the kind of military history that is for all readers, whatever their particular interests, or their level of interest in the subject. To paraphrase an old aphorism: a military history book is not less important just because it is popular, and it is not more scholarly just because it is dull. With every one of our publications we want to bring you the kind of military history that you will want to read simply because it is a good and well-written book, as well as bringing new light, new perspectives, and new factual evidence to its subject.

In devising the *Wolverhampton Military Studies Series*, we gave much thought to the series title: this is a *military* series. We take the view that history is everything except the things that have not happened yet, and even then a good book about the military aspects of the future would find its way into this series. We are not bound to any particular time period or cut-off date. Writing military history often divides quite sharply into eras, from the modern through the early modern to the mediaeval and ancient; and into regions or continents, with a division between western military history and the military history of other countries and cultures being particularly marked. Inevitably, we have had to start somewhere, and the first books of the series deal with British military topics and events of the twentieth century and later nineteenth century. But this series is open to any book that challenges received and accepted ideas about any aspect of military history, and does so in a way that encourages its readers to enjoy the discovery.

In the same way, this series is not limited to being about wars, or about grand strategy, or wider defence matters, or the sociology of armed forces as institutions, or civilian society and culture at war. None of these are specifically excluded, and in some cases they play an important part in the books that comprise our series. But there are already many books in existence, some of them of the highest scholarly standards, which cater to these particular approaches. The main theme of the *Wolverhampton Military Studies Series* is the military aspects of wars, the preparation for wars or their prevention, and their aftermath. This includes some books whose main theme is the technical details of how armed forces have worked, some books on wars and battles, and some books that re-examine the evidence about the existing stories, to show in a different light what everyone thought they already knew and understood.

As series editor, together with my fellow editorial board members, and our publisher Duncan Rogers of Helion, I have found that we have known immediately and almost by instinct the kind of books that fit within this series. They are very much the kind of well-written and challenging books that my students at the University of Wolverhampton would want to read. They are books which enhance knowledge, and offer new perspectives. Also, they are books for anyone with an interest in military history and events, from expert scholars to occasional readers. One of the great benefits of the study of military history is that it includes a large and often committed section of the wider population, who want to read the best military history that they can find; our aim for this series is to provide it.

Stephen Badsey
University of Wolverhampton

Introduction

> ...myths, once buttressed by public credibility, assume a veneer of historical truth and are more easily enlarged upon than refuted.
>
> Charles W. Sydnor, Jr.[1]

Despite a mountain of literature and the availability of a wide range of archival material, many aspects of the Second World War remain poorly or, at best, partly understood. In particular, North American and Western European perceptions of the ferocious struggle between Germany and the Soviet Union between 1941 and 1945 continue to be clouded by a combination of their own distinct historiographical development, a near fetish amongst the general public for anything related to the military forces of the Third Reich, and a host of interminable fallacies that even decades of scholarship appear unable to overcome.[2] Seemingly the most impermeable of these perceptions relates to the notion that the military forces of Germany were not really defeated by the Soviet Red Army on the battlefield at all, at least not in terms of operational or tactical level proficiency. One of the crucial facets underpinning this argument is the belief that Germany was simply unable to provide adequate personnel and equipment replacements to maintain the German Army as a viable military machine capable of defeating, or at least fending off, the massive armies fielded by its Soviet adversary. Instead, the German forces on the Eastern Front became progressively weaker as their ranks were thinned by years of relentless battle. Ultimately, the depleted formations of the once vaunted German Army were merely overwhelmed by vastly superior Soviet 'hordes' of men and machines, but only after an extremely bloody, hard fought and heroic struggle. As succinctly expressed by one British military historian:

---

1   Charles W. Sydnor, Jr. "The History of the SS Totenkopfdivision and the Postwar Mythology of the Waffen-SS." *Central European History*, Vol. 6, No. 4 (December 1973), pp. 341.
2   For a broader discussion of these issues, see David M. Glantz, "American Perspectives on Eastern Front Operations in the Second World War with Soviet Commentary." *Journal of Slavic Military Studies*, Vol. 1, No. 1 (1995), pp. 108-132, and Ronald Smelser & Edward Davies II, *The Myth of the Eastern Front: The Nazi-Soviet War in American Popular Culture.* (Cambridge, MA: 2007).

[The German Army] ...in the east was simply inundated. From now on the Russians were able to marshal huge forces at whatever point of the front they chose and smash through the German lines almost with impunity. Offensive followed offensive, up and down the front, swamping the defenders and inexorably pushing them back, first out of the Soviet Union and then to the gates of Berlin itself.[3]

Similarly, in his immensely popular work, *Panzer Battles: A Study in the Employment of Armour in the Second World War* (now in its seventh edition), former German *Generalmajor* Friedrich von Mellenthin observed: "...the weak German forces were like rocks in the ocean, surrounded by endless waves of men and tanks which surged around and finally submerged them."[4] This argument of a German Army possessing generally superior leadership and near-flawless operational and tactical skill but starved of sufficient men and equipment that doomed it to defeat became one of the main pillars upon which Western perceptions of the Russo-German War were constructed.[5] However, despite the preponderance of this numerical-weakness argument within the historiography, and its centrality as an explanation for Germany's defeat by the Soviet Union, no systematic examination has yet been undertaken to reveal just how well Germany was able to make good the losses of men and equipment it sustained on the Eastern Front, and how this was reflected in the strength and capabilities of its field divisions deployed there.

The primary goal of this study is to address the perception of numerical-weakness in terms of Germany's ability to replace its losses and regenerate its military strength, and assess just how accurate this argument was during the first half of the Russo-German War (June 1941 – June 1943). Specifically it asks the questions: to what extent was Germany able to provide the reinforcements and replacements needed to maintain the strength of the *Ostheer*? And to what extent was this reflected in the fighting capabilities of the German field divisions committed to the Eastern Front during 1941-1943?[6] In contrast to the notions found within both academic and popular studies of the conflict, this study finds that numerical-weakness as the primary factor

---

3   John Ellis, *Brute Force: Allied Strategy and Tactics in the Second World War*. (New York: 1990), p. 102.
4   Friedrich von Mellenthin, *Panzer Battles: A Study of the Employment of Armour in the Second World War*. (New York: 1971), p. 365.
5   For discussions regarding German numerical inferiority as it relates to the notion of superior German military performance, see Roger A. Beaumont, "On the Wehrmacht Mystique." *Military Review*, Vol. 66, No. 7 (July 1986), Martin van Crevald, *Fighting Power: German and U.S. Army Performance, 1939-1945*. (Westport, CT: 1982), Martin van Crevald, "On Learning from the Wehrmacht and Other Things." *Military Review*, Vol. 68, No. 1 (January 1988), and Kurt Pätzold, *Ihr waren die besten Soldaten: Ursprung und Geschichte einer Legende*. (Leipzig: 2000).
6   The term *Ostheer* (literally translated as Eastern Army) refers to that portion of the German Army engaged along Germany's Eastern Front in the period of 1941-1945, as

in the defeat of the *Ostheer* at the hands of the Red Army – specifically as it relates to the strength and condition of the German units involved – has been overemphasized and frequently exaggerated. In fact, Germany was actually able to regenerate its forces to a remarkable degree with a steady flow of fresh men and equipment, and German field divisions on the Eastern Front were usually far stronger than the accepted narratives of the war would have one believe.

While historians have increasingly questioned the veracity of much of what was considered to be true about the Russo-German War in recent decades, the historiographical development of the literature makes any attempt at revision an extremely difficult process. Until the end of the 1950s, very few English-language monographs directly addressed the Eastern Front. The earliest accounts tended to either be narrow in their timeframe or they were otherwise confined to specific events, thereby providing Western audiences with some details, but little real sense of the true immensity of the conflict.[7] The first general history, *The War in Eastern Europe*, was published by the United States Army, followed a few years later by Wladyslaw Anders *Hitler's Defeat in Russia*.[8] Shortly thereafter, the British War Office published *Germany's Defeat in the East: The Soviet Armies at War, 1941-1945* and *The German Russian War, 1941-1945*.[9] These general accounts, now almost forgotten, established the broad methodologies and thematic patterns that continue to dominate Eastern Front historiography to the present day. Specifically, they portrayed the German Army (and indeed, the German Armed Forces, or *Wehrmacht*, as a whole) as being unassociated with the brutalities committed by the functionaries and organizations of the Nazi Party and Adolf Hitler's government. According to these early accounts, the *Wehrmacht* was an extremely professional and competent organization whose defeat was solely attributable to the combination of Hitler's amateurish meddling in military affairs and the overwhelming strength of Germany's enemies.

In creating this montage of *Wehrmacht* superiority, the initial monographs concerning the Russo-German War relied predominately upon German accounts, particularly those written by former German officers. Reliance on Russian materials was comparatively rare. There are several reasons for this over-reliance on German

---

opposed to the *Westheer* that fought against the Western Allies in France during 1944-1945.

7   W.E.D. Allen & Paul Muratoff, *The Russian Campaigns of 1944-1945*. (New York: 1946); Alexander Werth, *The Year of Stalingrad*. (New York: 1947); Ronald Seth, *Stalingrad: Point of No Return. The Story of the Battle, August 1942 – February 1943*. (New York: 1959), Werth, a Russian-born, naturalized British writer who worked for the British Broadcasting Company as its Russia correspondent and who based his writing upon his extensive wartime experiences, produced the first complete English-language account of the fighting around Stalingrad.

8   United States Army, *The War in Eastern Europe*. (West Point, NY: 1949); Wladyslaw Anders, *Hitler's Defeat in Russia*. (Chicago: 1953).

9   E. Lederrey, *Germany's Defeat in the East: The Soviet Armies at War, 1941-1945*. (London: 1955); A. Guillaume, *The German Russian War, 1941-1945*. (London: 1956).

sources. First, within the Soviet Union, the authoritarian nature of Joseph Stalin's regime meant that Russian historians were severely restricted as to how and what they could say in their histories of The Great Patriotic War, a circumstance that only moderately improved when Nikita Khrushchev assumed leadership of the Soviet Union after 1953. Russian studies of this period, while factually correct in most cases, tended to glorify the actions of the Soviet state and its leadership and extol the virtues of the communist system. Indeed, the language of the narratives is burdened by ideological phraseology that makes them appear excessively propagandistic, something that in turn reduces perceptions of their validity as credible historical accounts. Moreover, they focus their attention upon the principal Soviet victories (mainly the fighting around Moscow, Stalingrad, Kursk, and Berlin), while mention of the Red Army's numerous battlefield defeats, to say nothing of the true scale and cost of the massive struggle, are notable only for their absence.[10] Exacerbating the tendencies of

10   For an overview of recent discussions within Russia regarding the re-evaluation of many long-held beliefs, see Frank Ellis, "The Great Fatherland War in Soviet and Post-Soviet Literature." *Journal of Slavic Military Studies*, Vol. 20, No. 4 (2007), pp. 609-632. An insightful, though Cold War-era, look into Soviet perceptions can be found in Matthew P. Gallagher, *The Soviet History of World War II: Myths, Memories, and Realities*. (New York: 1963). A more recent treatment of popular perceptions in Russia is Nina Tumarkin, *The Living and the Dead: The Rise and Fall of the Cult of World War II in Russia*. (New York: 1994). For discussions regarding the scale of Russia's wartime losses, see Edwin Bacon, "Soviet Military Losses in World War II." *Journal of Slavic Military Studies*, Vol. 6, No. 4 (1993), pp. 613-633, V.E. Korol, "The Price of Victory: Myths and Realities." *Journal of Slavic Military Studies*, Vol. 9, No. 2 (1996), pp. 417-426, S.A. Il'Enkov, "Concerning the Registration of Soviet Armed Forces' Wartime Irrecoverable Losses, 1941-1945." *Journal of Slavic Military Studies*, Vol. 9, No. 2 (1996), pp. 440-442, and Boris V. Sokolov, "The Cost of War: Human Losses for the USSR and Germany, 1941-1945." *Journal of Slavic Military Studies*, Vol. 9, No. 1 (1999), pp. 152-193. For a narrow treatment of the subject of Soviet losses, see Tatiana M. Tver, "The Battle for Rzhev: Ideology Instead of Statistics." *Journal of Slavic Military Studies*, Vol. 18, No. 3 (2005), pp. 359-368. Although his methodology is still the subject of intense debate, the foremost resource regarding Soviet losses is G.F. Krivosheev, *Soviet Casualties and Combat Losses in the 20th Century*. (Mechanicsburg, PA: 1997). For an idea of just how much of the Russo-German War has been overlooked until relatively recently, see David M. Glantz, "The Failures of Historiography: The Forgotten Battles of the German-Soviet War." *Journal of Slavic Military Studies*, Vol. 8, No. 4 (1995), pp. 768-808. Glantz later expanded this paper into a series of privately published manuscripts that currently total sex separate volumes. See David M. Glantz, *Forgotten Battles of the German-Soviet War, 1941-1945. Volume One: The Summer-Fall Campaign, 22 June – 4 December 1941*. (Carlisle, PA: 1999), *Forgotten Battles of the German-Soviet War, 1941-1945. Volume Two: The Winter Campaign, 5 December 1941 – April 1942*. (Carlisle, PA: 1999), *Forgotten Battles of the German-Soviet War, 1941-1945. Volume Three: The Summer Campaign, 12 May – 18 November 1942*. (Carlisle, PA: 1999), *Forgotten Battles of the German-Soviet War, 1941-1945. Volume Four: The Winter Campaign, 19 November 1942 – 21 March 1943*. (Carlisle, PA: 1999), *Forgotten Battles of the German-Soviet War, 1941-1945. Volume Five: The Summer-Fall Campaign, 1 July – 31 December 1943, Parts One & Two*. (Carlisle, PA: 2000), and *Forgotten Battles of the German-Soviet*

Western scholars to ignore Russian sources was the emergence by the late 1940s of the Cold War between the liberal democratic states of North America and Europe, on the one side, and the Soviet Union and its communist allies, on the other. The deep suspicions and antagonisms aroused during this long confrontation were directly transposed upon the perceptions of Western scholars and the broader public, rendering many to believe that Russian sources were dubious at best, especially since Western academics were denied access to Soviet archives.[11] Moreover, linguistic ignorance also appears to have hampered many Western scholars from making much use of Russian-language sources, while only a relatively small number of published Soviet accounts and memoirs were ever translated into English.[12]

The second factor behind the peculiar development of this early stage of the historiography, and arguably the most significant, was the abundance of published German accounts. These German accounts ranged from the general histories of the Second World War written by Kurt von Tippelskirch and Walter Görlitz to a host of treatise directly related to the Eastern Front and its various operations, the majority of which were written by officers who had been directly involved.[13] A supplementary array of

War, 1941-1945. Volume Six: The Winter Campaign, 24 December 1943 – April 1944, Parts One & Two. (Carlisle, PA: 2004).

11   The first Western academics did not gain access to Soviet archival materials until the late 1970s, and even then what they could examine was tightly controlled and restricted. This changed for some time after the end of the Cold War, when access was virtually unlimited. Currently, Western usage of the Russian archives is hampered by newly levied regulations, which has again imposed restrictions upon a good deal of previously declassified material, and by the underfunded and poorly organized nature of the archives themselves. For a sense of the problems of simply determining the locations of the archival material and even just what these might contain, see George C. Browder, "Captured German and Other Nations' Documents in the Osoby (Special) Archive, Moscow." *Central European History*, Vol. 24, No. 4 (1991), pp. 424-445.

12   In comparison with their German counterparts, the memoirs of senior Soviet officers did not appear in English until many years after the war. The very first was Vasily I. Chuikov's, *The Battle for Stalingrad.* (New York: 1964), followed by Andrei I. Eremenko, *The Arduous Beginning.* (Moscow: 1966) and Ivan S. Konev, *Year of Victory.* (Moscow: 1969). Written thereafter was Konstantin K. Rokossovskii, *A Soldier's Duty.* (Moscow: 1970), Kirill A. Meretskov, *City Invincible.* (Moscow: 1970), Sergei M. Shtemenko, *The Soviet General Staff at War, 1941-1945.* (Moscow: 1970), Kirill A. Meretskov, *Serving the People.* (Moscow: 1971), and Ivan S. Konev, *The Great March of Liberation.* (Moscow: 1972). Some years later there also emerged Sergei M. Shtemenko, *The Last Six Months: Russia's Final Battles with Hitler's Armies in World War II.* (New York: 1977) and Aleksandr M. Vasilevsky, *The Matter of My Whole Life.* (Moscow: 1978).

13   The general histories of the war produced by Tippelskirch and Görlitz appear to have been amongst the very first produced in any language. Kurt von Tippelskirch, *Geschichte des Zweiten Weltkrieg.* (Bonn: 1951) and Walter Görlitz, *Der Zweite Weltkrieg, 1939-1945. Band I & II.* (Stuttgart: 1951-1952). Of the operational and tactical level monographs, of particular note are Friedrich Hossbach, *Die Schlacht um Ostpreussen. Aus der kampfender deutschen 4. Armee um Ostpreussen in der zeit von 19.7.1944 – 30.1.1945.* (Uberlingen/Bodensee: 1951), Otto Heidenkämpfer, *Witebsk: Kampf und Untergang der 3. Panzerarmee.*

compendia addressed Germany's larger strategic situation during the war, criticized Hitler's leadership, or else argued how the German Army as an institution was separate from the policies and objectives of the Nazi Party and government.[14] Several of these studies had previously been published in the numerous German military and historical journals that were themselves laden with copious numbers of additional articles regarding the Eastern Front.[15] Further supplementing the German literature

(Heidelberg: 1954), Hans Steets, *Gebirgsjäger bei Uman: Die Korpsschlacht des XXXXIX. Gebirgs-Armeekorps bei Podwyssokoje, 1941.* (Heidelberg: 1955), Hans Doerr, *Der Feldzug nach Stalingrad: Versuch eines Operativen Überblickes.* (Darmstadt: 1955), Hans Friessner, *Verratene Schlachten: Die Tragödie der Deutschen Wehrmacht in Rumänien und Ungarn.* (Hamburg: 1956), Hermann Hoth, *Panzer-Operationen: Die Panzergruppe 3 und der Operative Gedanke der Deutschen Führung, Sommer 1941.* (Heidelberg: 1956), Hans Steets, *Gebirgsjäger in der nogaischen Steppe: Von Dnjepr zum Asowschen Meer, August-October 1941.* (Heidelberg: 1956), Horst Scheibert, *Nach Stalingrad – 48 Kilometer! Der Entsatzvorstoss der 6. Panzerdivision, Dezember 1942.* (Heidelberg: 1956), Hans Steets, *Gebirgsjäger zwischen Dnjepr und Don: Von Tschernigowka zum Mius, October-Dezember 1941.* (Heidelberg: 1957), Edgar Röhricht, *Probleme der Kesselschlacht. Dargestellt an Einkreisungs-Operationen im Zweiten Weltkrieg.* (Karlsruhe: 1958), Oscar Munzel, *Panzer Taktik: Raids gepanzerter Verbände im Ostfeldzug, 1941/1942.* (Neckargemund: 1959), F.M. von Senger und Etterlin, *Der Gegenschlag.* (Neckargemund: 1959), and Cajus Bekker, *Ostsee – Deutsches schicksal 1944/1945: Der Authentische Bericht von letzten Einsatz der Kriegsmarine.* (Oldenburg: 1959). Of these authors, Friessner commanded an army group, while Tippelskirch, Hoth, and Hossbach directed armies. Röhricht and Etterlin were corps commanders, Steets and Munzel led divisions, and Heidenkampfer and Doerr were staff officers. Horst Scheibert led a company of the *6. Panzer Division* during its efforts to relieve the German forces trapped at Stalingrad in 1942, and later rose to become a Brigadier General in the *Bundeswehr.* For the most comprehensive biographical study of Germans officers yet to emerge, see Dermot Bradley, et. al., *Generale des Heeres, 1921-1945. Band 1-7.* (Osnabruck: 1993-2002).

14   For discussions on strategy, see Adolf Heusinger, *Befel im Widerstreit: Schicksalsstunden der deutschen Armee, 1923-1945.* (Tubingen: 1950) and Eike Middeldorf, *Taktik im Russlandfeldzug: Erfahrungen und Folgerungen.* (Darmstadt: 1956). Critiques of Hitler as a military leader or of his use of the German Army in Russia can be found in, respectively, Gert Buchheit, *Hitler der Feldherr: Die Zerstörung einer Legende.* (Rastatt/Baden: 1958) and Maximilian Fretter-Pico, *Missbrauchte Infanterie: Deutsche Infanteriedivisionen in Osteuropaischen Grossraum, 1941-1944.* (Frankfurt am Main: 1957). Interestingly, a very early effort was made to illustrate the resistance found within the German Army against Hitler's rule, as seen in Fabian von Schlabrendorff, *Offiziere gegen Hitler.* (Zurich: 1946), or else to show how German officers were torn between their oath to Hitler, and either their own moral sensibilities or the broader notion of their responsibility to Germany, as portrayed in Friedrich Hossbach, *Zwischen Wehrmacht und Hitler, 1934-1938.* (Wolfenbuttel: 1949).

15   In terms of containing contributions from former members of the *Wehrmacht,* the most popular and academically respectable was *Wehrwissenschaftliche Rundschau* (1951-1982). *Alte Kameraden* (1950s-1960s), *Feldgrau* (1953-1964), and *Der Frontsoldat Erzählt* (1953-1965) were small pocket magazines supported by various German veterans associations that mostly contained firsthand recollections were also very popular though far from bookish. The more scholarly articles found their way into *Wehrkunde* (1953-1964),

was the publication of a host of German divisional and regimental histories. While these analyses contained more detailed accounts of the fighting on the Eastern Front, they also contributed to the dominance of the German perspective in the historiography, both through their absolute numbers and by buttressing the credibility of the narrative found in the broader studies that tended to emphasize German defeat in terms of numerical weakness.[16]

While the sheer number of German accounts in the 1950s was itself imposing, what made them truly appealing and seemingly invaluable was the credulity with which Anglo-American audiences received them. This popularity followed two separate, though usually overlapping paths. The first relates to the reception, especially amongst the general public, of the memoirs and biographies written by the more illustrious senior German officers. Those published in English came from such notable figures as Heinz Guderian, Erich von Manstein, Karl Rudolf Gerd von Rundstedt, and Friedrich von Mellenthin.[17] This reception was itself a consequence of the successful

---

Vierteljahrshefte für Zeitgeschichte (1953 to present), and *Militärgeschichliche Mitteilungen* (1967-1999). Although not widely available in the West, historians in East Germany also produced *Zeitschrift für Militärgeschichte* (1962-1971).

16   As many of these unit histories were either written by former commanding officers or were published by the respective veterans associations, it is likely that regimental pride played a significant role in this. For the primary examples of German divisional histories published until 1960, see Werner Conze, *Die Geschichte der 291. Infanterie Division, 1940-1945.* (Bad Nauheim: 1953), Hennecke Kardel, *Die Geschichte der 170. Infanterie Division, 1939-1945.* (Bad Nauheim: 1953), Albert Benary, *Die Berliner Bären-Division: Geschichte der 257. Infanterie Division, 1939-1945.* (Bad Nauheim: 1955), Julian Braun, *Enzian und Edelweiss: Die 4. Gebirgs Division 1940-1945.* (Bad Nauheim: 1955), Rudolf Gschöpf, *Mein Weg mit der 45. Infanterie Division.* (Linz: 1955), Ludwig Merker, *Das Buch der 78. Sturmdivision.* (Tubingen: 1955), Walter Schelm & Hans Mehrle, *Von den Kämpfen der 215. Wurttembergisch-badenischen Infanterie Division.* (1955), Hans Breithaupt, *Die Geschichte der 30. Infanterie Division, 1939-1945.* (Bad Nauheim: 1956), Jürgen Schröder & Joachim Schultz-Haumann, *Die Geschichte der Pommerschen 32. Infanterie Division, 1935-1945.* (Bad Nauheim: 1956), Hans von Tettau, *Geschichte der 24. Infanterie Division, 1935-1945.* (Stolberg: 1956), Rolf Grams, *Die 14. Panzer Division, 1940-1945.* (Bad Nauheim: 1957), Gerhardt Lohse, *Geschichte der Rheinisch-Westfälischen 126. Infanterie Division, 1940-1945.* (Bad Nauheim: 1957), Günther Nitz, *Die 292. Infanterie Division.* (Berlin: 1957), Horst Grossmann, *Geschichte der Rheinisch-Westfälischen 6. Infanterie Division, 1939-1945.* (Bad Nauheim: 1958), Paul Klatt, *Die 3. Gebirgs Division, 1939-1945.* (Bad Nauheim: 1958), Otto von Knobelssdorf, *Geschichte der Niedersächsischen 19. Panzer Division.* (Bad Nauheim: 1958), Hellmuth Spaeter, *Die Geschichte des Panzerkorps Grossdeutschland, Band I-III.* (Bielefeld: 1958), Hartwig Pohlman, *Geschichte der 96. Infanterie Division, 1939-1945.* (Bad Nauheim: 1959), and Josef Bauer, *290. Infanterie Division, 1940-1945.* (Delmenhorst: 1960).

17   Heinz Guderian, *Panzer Leader.* (London: 1952), Günther Blumentritt, *Von Rundstedt: The Soldier and the Man.* (London: 1952), Mellenthin, *Panzer Battles*, and Erich von Manstein, *Lost Victories.* (Chicago, IL: 1958). Of those published in German, see Franz Halder, *Hitler als Feldherr.* (Munich: 1949), Berhard von Lossberg, *Im Wehrmachtführungsstab: Bericht eines Generalstabsoffiziers.* (Hamburg: 1949), Wolfgang Foerster, *Ein General Kampft gegen*

public response to Basil Liddell Hart's *The Other Side of the Hill* published in 1948.[18] Utilizing personal interviews, Liddell Hart recounted the experiences of senior German generals, presenting the notion of a largely innocent and almost militarily infallible *Wehrmacht* that built on previous interpretations of the same ilk and, in a way, inoculated the Anglo-American public against contrary views.[19]

The second avenue by which German perspectives of the Eastern Front gained popularity with Western audiences was the German Military History Program, a

den Krieg: Aus nachgelassenen Papieren des Generalstabschefs Ludwig Beck. (Munchen: 1949), Franz Halder, *Gespräche mit Halder.* (Wiesbaden: 1950), Heinz Guderian, *Errinerungen eines Soldaten.* (Heidelberg: 1951), Erich von Manstein, *Verlorene Sieg.* (Bonn: 1955), and Erich von Manstein, *Aus einem Soldatenleben.* (Bonn: 1958). Interestingly, when asked by friends why he did not write any memoirs, *Generalfeldmarschall* Georg von Küchler is supposed to have responded, "The German generals should remain silent, since they had done nothing to avoid the catastrophe." In this, von Küchler appears to have mimicked the dictum of one of his predecessors, Constantin von Alvensleben. A prominent Prussian general of the Franco-Prussian War of 1870-1871, von Alvensleben apparently stated: "A Prussian general dies, he does not write memoirs." See reference in Marcel Stein, *Field Marshal von Manstein. A Portrait – The Janus Head.* (West Midlands, UK: 2006), p. 217.

18   Basil H. Liddell Hart, *The Other Side of the Hill.* (London: 1948). Published in condensed form within the United States as Basil H. Liddell Hart, *The German Generals Talk.* (New York: 1948). Although still retaining its immense popularity and having gone through at least six editions, Liddell Hart's study, and more importantly his motivations for writing it, has increasingly become the subject of scathing academic rebuke. In particular, see Alaric Searle, "A Very Special Relationship: Basil Liddell Hart, Wehrmacht Generals and the Debate on West German Rearmament, 1945-1953." *War in History*, Vol. 5, No. 3 (1998), pp. 327-357. For a broader examination of Liddell Hart, see John J. Mearsheimer, *Liddell Hart and the Weight of History.* (Ithaca, NY: 1988).

19   Shortly after the publication of Liddell Hart's work, this image of the *Wehrmacht* was again implanted upon English speaking audiences through the writing of Reginald Paget. Paget was the attorney for *Generalfeldmarschall* Erich von Manstein, one of Germany's most famous military leaders, at the latter's trial in 1949 regarding his role in war crimes committed in the Soviet Union. Paget's book, which largely mirrored the arguments used during the trial, stressed that Manstein was a brilliant officer reflective of the impeachable character and professionalism of the German Army, and that he was innocent of any involvement in any war crimes or atrocities. See Reginald T. Paget, *Manstein: His Campaigns and His Trials.* (London: 1951). For a recent treatment of Manstein's trial and Paget's defence, see Stein, *Field Marshal von Manstein. A Portrait – The Janus Head*, pp. 48-52. For a broader examination of the difficulties of prosecuting German generals as war criminals in the immediate postwar period, see J.H. Hoffmann, "German Field Marshals as War Criminals? A British Embarrassment." *Journal of Contemporary History*, Vol. 23 (1988), pp. 17-35 and Alaric Searle, "Revising the 'Myth' of a 'Clean Wehrmacht': Generals Trials, Public Opinion, and the Dynamics of Vergangenheitsbewaltung in West Germany, 1948-1960." *German Historical Institute London*, Vol. 25, No. 2 (November 2003), pp. 17-48. An excellent study detailing the transformation of British public opinion regarding their erstwhile German enemies can be found in Patrick Major, " 'Our Friend Rommel': The Wehrmacht as 'Worthy Enemy' in Postwar British Culture." *German History*, Vol. 26, No. 4 (2008), pp. 520-535.

project run and administered by the United States Army Historical Division during the period 1945-1961. The program itself ultimately entailed the production of approximately 2,500 manuscripts covering a wide range of topics, all of which were written by former officers of the *Wehrmacht*. Initially, the goal of the project was simply to facilitate the production of a comprehensive U.S. Army official history of the Second World War by creating a reservoir of detailed German accounts and perspectives, all relating specifically to those campaigns in which the United States had been engaged. However, the Cold War meant that a demobilized U.S. Army was confronted by the prospect of having to defend Europe from a numerically more powerful Red Army, something for which it was both physically and doctrinally unprepared to do. To develop appropriate strategies and doctrine, as well as to gain some insight into the character and nature of the Red Army, the Americans turned to the former German officers now in their employ.[20] Led by the former chief of staff of the German Army High Command (*Oberkommando des Heeres*, or OKH), *Generaloberst* Franz Halder, these officers produced a wide array of manuscripts. Their work ranged from specific campaigns and battles, to more general discussions regarding the nature of Soviet combat personnel and their fighting techniques and strategies, to surveys of the environmental conditions found within Russia and their impact upon modern armies.[21] The general tenor of these accounts mirrored that of the literature already mentioned above, specifically that the German Army was a paragon of military excellence whose defeat on the Eastern Front was solely attributable to a combination of Hitler's interference in military affairs and the Red Army's numerical superiority.[22]

While these studies were not immediately available to the general public, they did receive a warm reception within American military circles eager for any advice or information regarding the new Soviet adversary. In doing so, the U.S. Army as an institution seems to have wholeheartedly embraced the German account of the

---

20   For the impact of the German Military History Program upon U.S. Army doctrine, see Kevin Souter, "To Stem the Red Tide: The German Report Series and Its Effect on American Defense Doctrine, 1948-1954." *Journal of Military History*, Vol. 57, No. 4 (October 1993), pp. 653-688.

21   Initially, these officers wrote from memory or from whatever personal papers they still retained. Eventually, however, the Allied authorities provided them with German archival documents. This means that, while the insight they offer is not without its uses, the information they contain must be treated with caution and checked against other sources. The original manuscripts themselves are held at the U.S. Army War College in Carlisle, Pennsylvania, while microfilmed versions are available from the National Archives Records Administration in Washington, D.C. Some 250 of the manuscripts were published in Donald S. Detwiler (Ed.), *World War II German Military Studies*. (New York: 1979). For their more recent usage, see Peter G. Tsouras (Ed.), *Fighting in Hell: The German Ordeal on the Eastern Front*. (Mechanicsburg, PA: 1994).

22   Wolfram Wette, *The Wehrmacht: History, Myth, Reality*. (Cambridge, MA: 2006), pp. 229-233. A more detailed treatment of the role of Franz Halder in the development of the German Military History Program can be found in Smelser & Davies, *The Myth of the Eastern Front*, pp. 64-70.

Russo-German War. Indeed, in November 1961, the United States awarded Halder the Meritorious Civilian Service Award, the highest award a foreigner in American employ could obtain, for his role in directing the German Military History Program.[23] When made available for public consumption during the 1960s, the manuscripts' association as the product of an official program of the U.S. Army reinforced the legitimacy of their image of the war on the Eastern Front. In turn, this apparent legitimacy was implied upon the broader German literature by both academics and the general public, further cementing the notion that the German account of the Russo-German War was both accurate and unbiased.

As a consequence of these developments, by 1960 the German description of what had transpired during the savage contest between Germany and the Soviet Union had become firmly ensconced within Western consciousness. Certainly, the German memoir material played a central role in the formation of this narrative, as James Wood later noted:

> By committing their views to paper, the German officer corps had the last word on the Wehrmacht's performance in World War II and used it to the best of their abilities. The resulting body of work therefore came to be characterized by the absence of war crimes (with the exception of those committed by the Red Army), an unquestioning admiration of the professional skill of the German soldier, and an explanation of the loss of the war that is almost invariably linked to Allied material strength and/or the interference of a certain Austrian corporal.[24]

23   Some sense of the popularity amongst American military officers for the German manuscripts can be found in Ibid, pp. 70-73. For American treatment and views of German officers, see Arnold Krammer, "American Treatment of German Generals during World War II." *Journal of Military History*, Vol. 54, No. 1 (January 1990), pp. 27-46. A broader discussion of the development and impact of the German Military History Program, including its relationship to the establishment of the Bundeswehr and rearmament of Germany, can be found in Charles Burdick, "Deutschland und die Entwicklung der amtlichen amerikanischen Militargeschichtsforschung, 1920-1960." in K.D. Bracher, (Ed.), *Deutschland zwischen Krieg und Frieden.* (Dusseldorf: 1991), pp. 99-107, Christian Greiner, "'Operational History (German) Section' und 'Naval Historical Team.' Deutsches militärstrategisches Denken im Dienst der amerikanischen Streitkrafte von 1946 bis 1950." in Manfred Messerschmidt, et. al. (Ed.), *Militärgeschichte. Problem-Thesen-Wege.* (Stuttgart: 1982), pp. 409-435, Bernd Wegener, "Erschriebene Siege. Franz Halder, die 'Historical Division' und die Rekonstruktion des Zweiten Weltkrieges im Geiste des deutschen Generalstabs." in Ernst Willi Hansen, et. al. (Ed.), *Politischer Wandel, organisierte Gewalt und nationale Sicherheit. Beiträge zur neuren Geschichte Deutschlands und Frankreich.* (Munich: 1995), pp. 287-302, and Christina Marina, "Vernichtungskrieg, Kalter Krieg und Politisches Gedachtnis: Zum Umgang mit dem Krieg gegen die Sowjetunion in geteilten Deutschland." *Geschichte und Gessellschaft*, Vol. 34, No. 2 (2008), pp. 252-291.
24   James A. Wood, "Captive Historians, Captivated Audience: The German Military History Program, 1945-1961." *Journal of Military History*, Vol. 69 (January 2005), p. 127.

However, the frequency of this view in the German accounts needed the assistance of a number of unique circumstances to ensconce itself fully in the Western consciousness. Indeed, what actually transpired was a kind of historiographical perfect storm, whereby the large number of German accounts, produced in the context of the Cold War, complacently accepted by eager Western audiences, and largely left unchallenged by competing narratives, practically ensured the dominance of the German perspective.

Sporadic challenges to this dominant view appeared during the second phase of the historiography, which may generally be construed as falling within the period of the early 1960s to the mid-1980s. Facilitated by the return of captured German archival documents to West Germany, these new studies were written by German academics who questioned the notion that the *Wehrmacht* was almost isolated from the policies and crimes of Hitler and the Nazi Party.[25] Simultaneous with this development, a smattering of Russian memoirs began to appear, together with a limited number of more topical studies. These received a more hospitable welcome in the West than had previously been the case, largely because of the rapprochement that developed between the United States and the Soviet Union in the early 1970s.[26] Moreover, some of the broader English-language histories of the Eastern Front that are hallmarks of this period also contributed to these challenges through more balanced representations of the conflict. The first was Alexander Werth's *Russia at War, 1941-1945*, which employed an impressive array of Soviet sources and thereby produced the first alternative Soviet view of the war to reach Western audiences on a large scale.[27] One of the first accounts to recognize that not all was right within the historiography was *Barbarossa: The Russo-German Conflict, 1941-1945*, written by Alan Clark, who noted in his preface: "The Germans… have evolved a variety of excuses" that centred upon notions of numerical inferiority and Hitler's mishandling of military strategy.[28]

---

25 Foremost amongst these studies are Andreas Hillgruber, *Hitlers Strategie: Politik und Kriegführung, 1940-1941*. (Frankfurt am Main: 1965), Manfred Messerschmidt, *Die Wehrmacht im NS-Staat: Zeit der Indoktrination*. (Hamburg: 1969), and Klaus Jürgen Muller, *Das Heer und Hitler: Armee und nationalsozialistisches Regime, 1933-1940*. (Stuttgart: 1969). For the German Army's treatment of Soviet prisoners of war, see Christian Streit, *Keine Kameraden: Die Wehrmacht und die Sowjetischen Kriegsgefangen, 1941-1945*. (Stuttgart: 1978) and Alfred Streim, *Behandlung Sowjetischer Krieggefangenen im 'Fall Barbarossa'*. (Heidelberg: 1981).

26 Of the foremost of these more particular monographs, see John Erickson, *The Soviet High Command: A Military-Political History, 1918-1941*. (Boulder, CO: 1962), John A. Armstrong (Ed.), *Soviet Partisans in World War II*. (Madison, WS: 1964), V.I. Achlasov & N.B. Pavlovich, *Soviet Naval Operations in the Great Patriotic War, 1941-1945*. (Annapolis, MD: 1973), Martin Caiden, *The Tigers are Burning*. (New York: 1973), Ray Wagner, *The Soviet Air Force in World War II: The Official History*. (Garden City, NY: 1973), and Alexander Dallin, *German Rule in Russia, 1941-1945: A Study of Occupation Policies*. (New York: 1980).

27 Alexander Werth, *Russia at War, 1941-1945*. (New York: 1964).

28 Alan Clark, *Barbarossa: The Russo-German Conflict, 1941-1945*. (London: 1965), p. xix.

Providing a more human appraisal of the Red Army was William Craig's *Enemy at the Gates: The Battle for Stalingrad* that illuminated the bravery and skill of the common Soviet soldier as an individual rather than a simple cog in a massive military machine.[29] Then came John Erickson's monumental *The Road to Stalingrad* and, later, *The Road to Berlin*, which, by describing military actions at the operational level of war, postulated that the ultimate Soviet victory could not be attributed to numbers alone.[30]

But the myth of German military superiority still persisted. While Werth, Erickson, Clark and others challenged the German-centric view of the conflict and provided Western audiences with far more information on the Red Army than had previously been available, their impact upon overall Western perceptions of the Russo-German War was limited. The revisionist arguments of German academics, such as Andreas Hillgruber and Manfred Messerschmidt, remained virtually unknown outside of Germany to all but a handful of specialized scholars, and the few Russian memoirs and studies that appeared in English were drowned by fresh waves of German monographs.[31] Other factors conspired against new interpretations of the Russo-German War. The U.S. Army, eager to reinvent itself following the debacle in Vietnam and still having to deal with a potential clash with Warsaw Pact forces in Europe, again turned to German military history.[32] Even Clark's study, while it is certainly more critical

---

29   William Craig, *Enemy at the Gates: The Battle for Stalingrad.* (New York: 1973).

30   John Erickson, *The Road to Stalingrad: Stalin's War with Germany.* (New York: 1975), and John Erickson, *The Road to Berlin: Stalin's War with Germany.* (London: 1983).

31   Amongst the most significant of the German accounts produced during this period are Hans von Ahlfen & Hermann Niehoff, *So Kämpfte Breslau.* (Stuttgart: 1960), Kurt Dieckert & Horst Grossmann, *Der Kampf um Ostpreussen.* (Stuttgart: 1960), Hans-Adolf Jacobsen & Jürgen Rohwer (Ed.), *Entscheidungsschlachten des Zweiten Weltkrieg.* (Frankfurt: 1960), Hans von Ahlfen, *Der Kampf um Schlesien.* (Munchen: 1961), Walter Chales de Beaulieu, *Der Vorstoss der Panzergruppe 4 auf Leningrad.* (Neckargemund: 1961), Hans Meier-Welcker (Ed.), *Abwehrkämpfe am Nordflügel der Ostfront, 1944-1945.* (Stuttgart: 1961), Militärgeschichtliches Forschungamt (Ed.), *Operationsgebiet Ostliche Ostsee und der finnischbaltische Raum, 1944.* (Stuttgart: 1961), Alfred Philippi & Ferdinand Heim, *Der Feldzug gegen Sowjetrussland, 1941-1945.* (Stuttgart: 1962), Werner Haupt, *Demjansk 1942: Ein Bollwerk im Osten.* (Bad Nauheim: 1963), Peter Erlau, *Flucht aus der Weissen Hölle: Errinerungen an die Grosse Kesselschlacht der 1. Panzerarmee Hube in Raum um Kamenz-Podolsk von 8. März bis 9. April 1944.* (Stuttgart: 1968), Friedrich Burgmaier, *Der Ostfeldzug, 1941-1945. Band I-III.* (Munich: 1969), Gert Fricke, *'Fester Platz' Tarnopol 1944.* (Freiburg: 1969), and Hermann Geyr, *Das IX. Armeekorps im Ostfeldzug, 1941.* (Neckargemund: 1969). For just a few of the German divisional histories that continued to emerge, see Werner Haupt, *Die 260. Infanterie Division, 1939-1944.* (Bad Nauheim: 1970), Anton von Plato, *Die Geschichte der 5. Panzer Division, 1938-1945.* (Regensburg: 1978), Hans-Jochen Pflanz, *Geschichte der 258. Infanterie Division, Band I-III.* (Hamburg: 1979), Anton Donnhauser, *Der Weg der 11. Panzer Division, 1939-1945.* (Germany: 1982), and Helmut Breymayer, *Das Wiesel: Geschichte der 125. Infanterie Division, 1940-1944.* (Boblingen: 1983).

32   The majority of the speakers at the U.S. Army's Art of War Symposium during 1984 to 1986 were former *Wehrmacht* officers who spoke of their experiences fighting the Red

of the *Wehrmacht* than those of his predecessors, proceeds along the same general line as the conventional German-based narrative. Moreover, the works of Werth and Clark were quickly superseded by the considerably more popular English-language accounts that followed, specifically those written by Paul Carell, Earl Ziemke, and Albert Seaton.[33] In particular, Carell's lively and readable prose garnered widespread appeal with Anglo-American audiences.[34] In contrast, the massive length and prodigious detail of Erickson's accounts are, unfortunately, esoteric. This is reflected in their not having been republished until recently, and it explains why they never appealed to more than a narrow academic community.[35] Overall, while works such as Erickson's certainly created some ripples within the historiography, and thereby raised the first doubts as to the veracity of many long-held assumptions, the unrelenting dominance and popularity of the German narrative prevented any significant re-interpretations to the broader understanding of the conflict, especially amongst the general public.

Only recently, during the current third stage of the historiography, have Western perceptions of the Russo-German War begun to change significantly. The end of the Cold War and subsequent collapse of the Soviet Union resulted in Western researchers finally gaining access to the former Soviet archives. What is more, Russian scholars have been able to produce far more candid and critical accounts than had previously been the case.[36] These developments have led to a surge in interest, both academically and publicly, regarding Soviet experiences and perceptions of the conflict.[37] By far

Army. See David Glantz (Ed.), *From the Dnepr to the Vistula: Soviet Offensive Operations – November 1943-August 1944. 1985 Art of War Symposium.* (Carlisle, PA: 1985). For some examples that reflect this renewed fascination, see Trevor Dupuy, *A Genius for War: The German Army and the General Staff, 1807-1945.* (London: 1977) and Timothy A. Wray, *Standing Fast: German Defensive Doctrine on the Russian Front during World War II – Prewar to March 1943.* (Fort Leavenworth, KS: 1986).

33   Paul Carell, *Hitler Moves East.* (New York: 1965), Paul Carell, *Scorched Earth: The Russo-German War, 1943-1944.* (Toronto: 1966), Earl Ziemke, *Stalingrad to Berlin: The German Defeat in the East.* (Washington, DC: 1968), and Albert Seaton, *The Russo-German War, 1941-1945.* (London: 1971).

34   For example, Aberdeen Books published the latest edition of *Hitler's War on Russia* in 2009. It should also be noted that Paul Carell is a pseudonym. The author's real name in Paul Karl Schmidt, who during the Second World War worked as the chief press spokesman for Germany's Foreign Minister, Joachim von Ribbentrop. For a critical examination of Schmidt and his actions after the war, see Wigbert Benz, *Paul Carell: Ribbentrop's Presschef Paul Karl Schmidt vor und Nach 1945.* (Berlin: 2005).

35   Smelser & Davies, *The Myth of the Eastern Front*, p. 215. Also noted in Glantz, "American Perspectives on Eastern Front Operations in the Second World War with Soviet Commentary.", p. 121.

36   For an abbreviated study of the Russian literature, see Frank Ellis, "The Great Fatherland War in Soviet and Post-Soviet Literature." *Journal of Slavic Military Studies*, Vol. 20, No. 4 (2007), pp. 609-632.

37   For one of the first English-language presentations of junior Soviet officers who were till then virtually unknown in the west, see Richard N. Armstrong, *Red Army Tank Commanders: The Armoured Guards.* (Atglen, PA: 1994). The best sociological treatment

the most prominent author of this period is the American historian David Glantz, whose multitudinous studies of the Eastern Front dominate the current literature, so much so that noted military historian Robert Citino refers to the current historiographical stage as the "Glantz era."[38] While emphasizing the Soviet side of the war, Glantz makes prodigious use of *both* Russian and German source material, particularly archival documents.[39] In this manner, his highly-detailed studies have both

of the rank and file of the Red Army can be found in Mark von Hagen, *Soldiers in the Proletarian Dictatorship: The Red Army and the Soviet Socialist State, 1917-1930.* (Ithaca, NY: 1996), Roger R. Reese, *Stalin's Reluctant Soldiers: A Social History of the Red Army, 1925-1941.* (Lawrence, KS: 1996) and David R. Stone, *Hammer and Rifle – The Militarization of the Soviet Union, 1926-1933.* (Lawrence, KS: 2000). Soviet economic planning and industrial production during the war can be found in Mark Harrison, *Accounting for War: Soviet Production, Employment, and Defence Burden, 1940-1945.* (Cambridge: 1996), Richard Overy, *Russia's War: A History of the Soviet War Effort, 1941-1945.* (London: 1997) and Lennart Samuelson, *Plans for Stalin's War Machine: Tukhachevski and Military-Economic Planning, 1925-1941.* (Basingstoke: 2000). While laden with inaccuracies and factual errors, some insight into the experiences of the average Soviet soldier and citizen can be gleamed from Catherine Merridale, *Ivan's War: The Red Army 1939-1945.* (London: 2005), though a more scholarly account can be found in Robert W. Thurston & Berd Bonwetsch (Ed.), *The People's War: Responses to World War II in the Soviet Union.* (Chicago: 2000). For the participation of Soviet women in combat, see Reina Pennington, *Wings, Women, and War: Soviet Airwomen in World War II Combat.* (Lawrence, KS: 2001) and the somewhat more dated Bruce Myles, *Night Witches: The Untold Story of Soviet Women in Combat.* (Novato, CA: 1981). In terms of the postwar impact of the conflict upon the Soviet Union, see Elena Zubkova, *Russia After the War: Hopes, Illusions and Disappointments.* (Armonk, NY: 1998).

38   Robert M. Citino, *The German Way of War: From the Thirty Years War to the Third Reich.* (Lawrence, KS: 2005), p. 371.

39   Aside from a very numerous list of articles and manuscripts, his published books include David M. Glantz, *August Storm: The Soviet 1945 Strategic Offensive in Manchuria.* (Leavenworth, KS: 1983), *Soviet Military Deception in the Second World War.* (Totowa, NJ: 1989), *The Role of Intelligence in Soviet Military Strategy in World War II.* (Novato, CA: 1990), *From the Don to the Dnepr: Soviet Offensive Operations, December 1942 – August 1943.* (Portland, OR: 1991), *The Initial Period of War on the Eastern Front, 22nd June – August 1941.* (London: 1993), *A History of Soviet Airborne Forces.* (London: 1994), *Kharkov 1942: Anatomy of a Military Disaster.* (Rockville Centre, NY: 1998), *Stumbling Colossus: The Red Army on the Eve of World War II.* (Lawrence, KS: 1998), *Zhukov's Greatest Defeat: The Red Army's Epic Disaster in Operation Mars, 1942.* (Lawrence, KS: 1999), *Barbarossa: Hitler's Invasion of Russia.* (Charleston, SC: 2001), *The Battle for Leningrad, 1941-1944.* (Lawrence, KS: 2002), *Colossus Reborn: The Red Army at War, 1941-1943.* (Lawrence, KS: 2005), *Red Storm over the Balkans: The Failed Soviet Invasion of Romania, Spring 1944.* (Lawrence, KS: 2007), *After Stalingrad: The Red Army's Winter Offensive 1942-1943.* (Solihull, UK: 2008), *To the Gates of Stalingrad: Soviet-German Combat Operations, April-August 1942. The Stalingrad Trilogy. Volume One.* (Lawrence, KS: 2009), *Armageddon in Stalingrad, September-November 1942. The Stalingrad Trilogy. Volume Two.* (Lawrence, KS: 2009), and *Barbarossa Derailed: The Battle for Smolensk, 10 July – 10 September 1941. Volume One.* (Solihull, UK: 2010). For a complete accounting of his work, readers are referred to the bibliography.

broadened and deepened Western perceptions by revealing numerous aspects of the conflict that had been largely unknown or ignored, and also by challenging established views through the presentation of new information and alternative perspectives. Indeed, *When Titans Clashed*, co-authored with Jonathan M. House, was the first truly balanced general account of the Russo-German War, as it employed a wide range of sources and focused on how the Red Army won the war, rather than sticking with the traditional narrative to explain how the Germans lost it.[40] Although the voluminous monographs produced by Glantz dominate this cycle of the historiography, many other writers, likewise employing archival material and the most reliable of the secondary literature, have also produced an array of important works.[41] In aggregate, these efforts have increased dramatically the literature available to English-speaking audiences. They also reveal a far more sophisticated picture of the Soviet war effort than had previously been presented.

Complementing this reappraisal of the Red Army and the Soviet Union has been a parallel re-examination of the German side of the story. This re-examination is generally characterized by a much greater, indeed almost exclusive, employment of German archival documents. Secondary accounts and memoir material is not altogether ignored, but rather scrupulously referenced against the relevant and available archival information. This re-examination also treads down a wide range of thematic and topical avenues. While this process had already emerged by the mid-1960s, the effect of this steady accumulation of specific details required a long period of fermentation before reaching more than a very small audience of specialist scholars. Overall, the result has been the publication of numerous works of scrupulous detail. Foremost

---

40 David M. Glantz & Jonathan M. House, *When Titans Clashed: How the Red Army Stopped Hitler*. (Lawrence, KS: 1995).

41 Other authors that have added considerably to Western conceptions of both the Russo-German War and the Red Army include, James F. Gebhardt, *The Petsamo-Kirkenes Operation: Soviet Breakthrough and Pursuit in the Arctic, October 1944*. (Leavenworth, KS: 1990), James M. Goff, "Evolving Soviet Force Structure, 1941-1945: Process and Impact." *Journal of Soviet Military Studies*, Vol. 5, No. 3 (September 1992), pp. 363-404, Raymond W. Leonard, "Studying the Kremlin's Secret Soldiers: A Historiographical Essay on the GRU, 1918-1945." *Journal of Military History*, Vol. 56, No. 3 (July 1992), pp. 403-422, Walter Dunn, *Hitler's Nemesis: The Red Army, 1930-1945*. (New York: 1994), Carl van Dyke, *The Soviet Invasion of Finland*. (London: 1997), Bryan Fugate & Lev Dvoretsky, *Thunder on the Dnepr: Zhukov-Stalin and the Defeat of Blitzkrieg*. (Novato, CA: 1997), Walter Dunn, *Soviet Blitzkrieg: The Battle for White Russia, 1944*. (Boulder, CO: 2000), Albert L. Weeks, *Stalin's Other War: Soviet Grand Strategy, 1941-1945*. (Lauham, MD: 2002), Robert W. Stephan, *Stalin's Secret War: Soviet Counterintelligence Against the Nazi, 1941-1945*. (Lawrence, KS: 2004), Alexander Hill, "British Lend-Lease Aid and the Soviet War Effort, June 1941-June 1942." *Journal of Military History*, Vol. 17, No. 3 (July 2007), pp. 773-808, Roger R. Reese, "Lessons of the Winter War: A Study in the Effectiveness of the Red Army, 1939-1940." *Journal of Military History*, Vol. 72 (July 2008), pp. 825-852, and Arthur G. Volz, "A Soviet Estimate of German Tank Production." *Journal of Slavic Military Studies*, Vol. 21, No. 3 (2008), pp. 588-590.

have been the ten volume *Germany and the Second World War* series. Produced under the auspices of the *Militärgeschichtliches Forschungsamt* (initially the German Armed Forces Military History Research Office, but now the German Research Institute for Military History), these massive works, addressing a full spectrum of military, economic, social, and political aspects, represent Germany's *de facto* official history. Intensively researched and well documented, this body of work has produced a more multi-faceted appreciation of Germany's actions during the Second World War than had been presented in previous German accounts. In a similar fashion, a steadily increasing body of meticulously researched literature has added to this trend towards more detailed information. As such, this elaborate attention to detail has contributed to the creation of more refined considerations of the pertinent German efforts in the Russo-German War and, in some cases, has directly challenged many of the longest held tenets.[42]

Within large portions of academia, the combination of more detailed German studies together with the deluge of works regarding the Soviet perspective has begun to alter perceptions of the Russo-German War, as scholars begin to grasp fully its immense complexity. It is now clear that many of the assumptions made during the earlier, German-dominated period of the historiography are either inaccurate or

42 Contesting the long-held belief that the 1943 Battle of Kursk represented the swansong of the Panzer divisions is Niklas Zetterling & Anders Frankson, *Kursk 1943: A Statistical Analysis*. (Portland, OR: 2000). Likewise, the works of Geoffrey Megargee and David Stahel have addressed notions regarding the almost mythical excellence of senior German military leadership by focusing upon its innermost workings. See Geoffrey P. Megargee, *Inside Hitler's High Command*. (Lawrence, KS: 2005) and David Stahl, *Operation Barbarossa and Germany's Defeat in the East*. (Cambridge: 2009). In terms of enhancing scholarly appreciations of the German *Luftwaffe* and its operations on the Eastern Front, the most important works to date are Richard Muller, *The German Air War in Russia*. (Baltimore, MD: 1992), E.R. Hooten, *Phoenix Triumphant: The Rise and Rise of the Luftwaffe*. (London: 1994), James S. Corum, *The Luftwaffe: Creating the Operational Air War, 1918-1940*. (Lawrence, KS: 1997), E.R. Hooten, *Eagle in Flames: The Fall of the Luftwaffe*. (London: 1997), and Joel S.A. Hayward, *Stopped at Stalingrad: The Luftwaffe and Hitler's Defeat in the East, 1942-1943*. (Lawrence, KS: 1998). Utilizing both Soviet and German material, the best studies of the air war on the Eastern Front can be found in Christer Bergstrom's, *Barbarossa: The Air Battle, July – December 1941*. (Surrey, UK: 2007), *Stalingrad: The Air Battle, 1942 through January 1943*. (Surrey, UK: 2007), *Kursk: The Air Battle, July 1943*. (Surrey, UK: 2007), and *Bagration to Berlin: The Final Air Battles in the East, 1944-1945*. (Surrey, UK: 2008). Important detailed works covering various aspects of land operations include, Steven Newton, *Retreat from Leningrad: Army Group North, 1944-1945*. (Atglen, PA: 1995), Tony Le Tissier, *Zhukov at the Oder*. (Westport, CA: 1996), Tony Le Tissier, *Race for the Reichstag*. (London: 1999), Douglas E. Nash, *Hell's Gate: The Battle of the Cherkassy Pocket, January to February 1944*. (Southbury, CT: 2002), Steven Newton, *Kursk: The German View*. (Cambridge, MA: 2002), Niklas Zetterling & Anders Frankson, *The Korsun Pocket: The Encirclement and Breakout of a German Army in the East, 1944*. (Philadelphia, PA: 2008), and Robert M. Citino, *Death of the Wehrmacht: The German Campaigns of 1942*. (Lawrence, KS: 2007).

only provide a very limited understanding. Indeed, the credibility of the German memoir material has come under scathing academic rebuke, as illustrated by Gerhard Weinberg's argument that, "closer examination of these works with reference to contemporary evidence has shown the memoirs to be almost invariably inaccurate, distorted, and, in some instances, simply faked."[43]

However, old habits tend to die hard and many of the long-established assumptions regarding the Eastern Front remain solidly entrenched within Western consciousness, especially the general public. Large numbers of English-language monographs adhering to the German-centric view of the conflict continue to be published every year, most of which are of marginal value to the broader historiographical development since they rely almost exclusively upon secondary accounts and the memoir material.[44] Likewise, German memoirs continue to emerge at a steady pace.[45] It would seem that the ongoing production of such works is linked to the broad popularity of the *Wehrmacht* among the public at large.[46] In consequence, most trade publishing companies welcome these manuscripts because they are marketable. Cost matters. Academic studies tend to be larger and less accessible to the general public. Quite simply, they do not sell well, so publishers look more readily to popular histories. Ultimately, the attractiveness of the popular accounts may be perceived as a double-edged sword – on one side, keeping the field of study alive and thereby making the publication of the more academic accounts possible; and on the other, hindering the historiographical development by impairing scholarly efforts to challenge long-held, but increasingly obsolescent Western perceptions of the Russo-German conflict. Essentially, this is where the historiography at present stands – between a relatively small, but growing, community of academics and specialists espousing a broader, more sophisticated, view

43   Gerhard L. Weinberg, "Some Thoughts on World War II." *Journal of Military History*, Vol. 56, No. 4 (October 1992), p. 659.
44   Such populist works include James Lucas, *Battlegroup! German Kampfgruppen Action of World War Two.* (London: 1993), Peter G. Tsouras (Ed.), *The Anvil of War: German Generalship in Defense on the Eastern Front.* (Mechanicsburg, PA: 1994), Paul Adair, *Hitler's Greatest Defeat.* (London: 1994), Rolf Hinze, *East Front Drama – 1944: The Withdrawal Battle of Army Group Center.* (Winnipeg: 1996), Werner Haupt, *Army Group North: The Wehrmacht in Russia, 1941-1945.* (Atglen, PA: 1997), Christopher Duffy, *Red Storm on the Reich.* (London: 1997), Werner Haupt, *Army Group Centre: The Wehrmacht in Russia, 1941-1945.* (Atglen, PA: 1998), Samuel W. Mitcham, *Crumbling Empire: The German Defeat in the East, 1944.* (Westport, CT: 2001), and Rolf Hinze, *To the Bitter End: The Final Battles of Army Groups North Ukraine, A, Centre, Eastern Front, 1944-45.* (Solihull, UK: 2005).
45   For example, see Gottlob H. Bidermann, *In Deadly Combat: A German Soldier's Memoir of the Eastern Front.* (Lawrence, KS: 2000), Gunter K. Koschorrek, *Blood Red Snow: The Memoirs of a German Soldier on the Eastern Front.* (London: 2002), and Erhard Raus, *Panzer Operations: The Eastern Front Memoir of Erhard Raus, 1941-1945.* (New York: 2003).
46   For elaboration of this popularity, see Smelser & Davies, *The Myth of the Eastern Front* pp. 157-246.

of the war, and a steadily-refuted, but still-prevalent conception that maintains its appeal with Anglo-American audiences.

Under such historiographical circumstances, it is not really surprising that many of the pillars upon which Western perceptions of the Russo-German War rest have yet to be torn down, or even properly addressed. Despite the wealth of materials outlined above, assumptions regarding the role of Germany's numerical weakness continue to dominate the discourse of the German defeat on the Eastern Front. Certainly, thanks to the efforts of Glantz and other scholars, this point no longer resonates within the literature to the degree it once did. Yet, two questions remain unanswered, namely: to what extent was Germany able to provide the reinforcements and replacements needed to maintain the strength of the *Ostheer*? And to what extent is this reflected in the actual condition of the field divisions committed to the Eastern Front during 1941-1943?

To address these questions, one must carefully examine the monthly strength reports submitted by various divisions to OKH. These provide crucial details regarding authorized and actual strengths, losses and replacements, and the current availability of equipment unique to their own individual tables of organization and equipment. While a relatively small number of monographs have examined Germany's manpower situation and armaments production, they have generally done so only in the broadest sense, by focusing on overall strength and loss figures.[47] This form of big picture analysis is at best problematic, as there exist wide discrepancies amongst the various sources, even when those sources refer to the same topic and time. As noted within the semi-official German history of the Second World War:

> A study of how personnel numbers in Wehrmacht units developed in the Second World War is bedevilled with a great deal of uncertainty, and made very difficult on the one hand by the Wehrmacht's reporting system becoming increasingly inconsistent as the war progressed, and on the other by the disparate availability of sources due to the loss and destruction of documents.[48]

---

47   For what has been the standard work on the subject of German manpower since its publication, see Burkhart Müller-Hillebrand, *Das Heer 1933-1945, Band I-III.* (Darmstadt/Frankfurt: 1954-1969). For more recent and detailed examinations, see Bernhard R. Kroener, et. al. *Germany and the Second World War. Volume V: Organization and Mobilization of the German Sphere of Power, Part Two.* (Oxford: 2003), pp. 878-890, and Horst Boog, et. al. *Germany and the Second World War. Volume VI: The Global War.* (Oxford: 2003), pp. 863-878. (Henceforth, after the first full mention regarding a particular volume, references to the *Germany and the Second World War* series will be abbreviated to *GSWW*.) Also, see Bernhard Kroener, "Squaring the Circle: Blitzkrieg Strategy and Manpower Shortage, 1938-1942." in William Deist, (Ed.) *The German Military in the Age of Total War.* (Dover, NH: 1985).

48   Ralf Blank, et. al. *Germany and the Second World War. Volume IX/1: German Wartime Society 1939-1945: Politicization, Disintegration, and the Struggle for Society.* (Oxford: 2008), p. 694. For an excellent discussion of the problems regarding sources and accounting

Partly this bedevilment is attributable to different departments within OKH employing different accounting methods. It is also the result of personal, bureaucratic, and departmental rivalries, both within OKH and between OKH and all the other agencies of the High Command of the Armed Forces (*Oberkommando der Wehrmacht*, or OKW). Each of these entities fought for a greater share of the available resources and they did so in the context of the byzantine machinations within the upper echelons of the Third Reich.[49] Indeed, the chaos produced was such that even Hitler became exasperated, as noted by his Army adjutant, Gerhard Engel: "How was he to conduct the war, if he was counting on 1,000 additional tanks and then someone told him there were actually only 500? He had assumed that the people in the Ordnance Office could at least count."[50] Additionally, such statistics as those provided by general historical surveys give little or no indication of the actual state of particular German divisions in the field, either in terms of their actual strength or combat worthiness.[51]

Exacerbating this situation is the fact that the methodology adopted by the Organization Department of the Army General Staff for determining the replacement requirements of the field divisions was inaccurate, which in turn contributes to the confusion regarding the actual strength of the German Army at any given time. The head of the Organization Department from April to October 1942, Burkhart Müller-Hillebrand, admits as much in a study of German replacement and statistical systems that he produced for the U.S. Army after the war. Rather than assessing needs by comparing the authorized (*Sollstärke*) and actual (*Iststärke*) strengths of the divisions in the field, he admits that replacements requirements were based upon the 10-day casualty reports forwarded by the field armies. These reports only indicated losses due to enemy action and did not include casualties sustained through other means, such as sickness, suicide, or personnel transfers to other formations and

methodologies, see Niklas Zetterling & Anders Frankson, "Analyzing World War II Eastern Front Battles." *Journal of Slavic Military Studies*, Vol. 11, No. 1 (March 1998), pp. 176-203.

49   For elaboration of the various relationships, scheming, and power struggles that occurred within Germany's senior leadership circles, see Geoffrey P. Megargee, "Triumph of the Null: Structure and Conflict in the Command of German Land, 1939-1945." *War in History*, Vol. 4, No. 1 (1997), pp. 60-80, and Megargee, *Inside Hitler's High Command*. Also, see Mathew Cooper, *The German Army, 1933-1945: Its Political and Military Failure*. (London: 1978), Gordon A. Craig, *Politics of the Prussian Army, 1640-1945*. (London: 1975), Albert Speer, *Inside the Third Reich*. (New York: 1970), and Walter Warlimont, *Inside Hitler's Headquarters, 1939-1945*. (Novato, CA: 1964).

50   Diary entry for 4 October 1941. Gerhard Engel, *Heeresadjutant bei Hitler 1938-1943: Aufzeichnungen des Majors Engel*. (Stuttgart: 1974), p. 112. For an analysis of how this problem affected military operations and decision making, see Horst Boog, et. al. *Germany and the Second World War. Volume IV: The Attack on the Soviet Union*. (Oxford: 1998), p. 1131-1132.

51   Ibid, p. 1128.

branches of the army.[52] Likewise, such an assessment does not take into account the many different types of divisions that existed within the German Army, that these were raised in mobilization waves (*Welle*), each with their own specific structures, or that during the course of the was some 3,000 changes were made to the various wartime tables of organization (*Kriegsstärkenachweisungen*, or KStN).[53] As a result, no two German divisions had precisely identical organizational structures or establishment strengths, even if they were of the same type. While broader assessments of manpower and equipment strengths of the German Army have their uses and can certainly be of some benefit to any scholarly study, for the reasons noted above, they must be handled with care. This state of affairs dictates that the focus upon specifics, such as the previously mentioned monthly divisional reports, is not only wise but also essential in determining the actual strength of German forces committed to the Eastern Front.

In detailing the condition of German field formations, there exists a prodigious and seemingly pedantic German military terminology, especially that related to definitions of unit strength. This terminology is significant since the Germans employed what amounts to a small dictionary of terms when referring to various types of personnel and equipment statistics. Understanding them is vital to produce an accurate analysis. Indeed, a lack of precision in this regard, resulting in the inflation or deflation of German strength depending upon the specific example, has littered the historiography of the Second World War as a whole with a series of errors and misrepresentations. In turn, these faults have had serious repercussions for the accuracy of broader scholarly treatments of various battles, campaigns, strategies and policies, and of subsequent assessments of the exact impact or significance these issues may have

---

52   As Müller-Hillebrand himself notes: "In actual practice the exact authorized strength of the wartime army could no longer be ascertained at short notice, for at any time it meant several weeks of calculation..." Burkhart Müller-Hillebrand, "Statistics Systems." (March 1949). NARA FMS P-011, p. 10 & 40.

53   The figure for the number of KStN produced is an approximate estimate. Ibid, p. 38. For the most comprehensive examination yet to be produced regarding the individual organization and structure of German divisions, see Georg Tessin, *Verbände und Truppen der Deutschen Wehrmacht und Waffen-SS im Zweiten Weltkrieg, 1933-1945. Bande 1-17.* (Frankfurt am Main: 1966-2002). For the best treatment of Germany's armoured divisions, see Kamen Nevenkin, *Fire Brigades: The Panzer Divisions, 1943-1945.* (Winnipeg: 2008). There is also George F. Nafziger's, *The German Order of Battle - Panzers and Artillery in World War II.* (Mechanicsburg, PA: 1999) and *The German Order of Battle – Infantry in World War II.* (Mechanicsburg, PA: 2000). While dated, note should also be taken of the useful organizational information found in James F. Dunnigan, *The Russian Front: Germany's War in the East, 1941-1945.* (London: 1978), pp. 119-133. For the most recent monographs illustrating the importance of examining the structure and numerical strengths of individual German divisions, and the effect this can have in altering long-held scholarly perceptions of specific events, see Niklas Zetterling, *Normandy 1944: German Military Organization, Combat Power and Organization.* (Winnipeg: 2000) and Zetterling & Frankson, *Kursk 1943: A Statistical Analysis.*

had.[54] As explained by historians Nikolas Zetterling and Anders Frankson, "Numbers constitute a very important part of military history and analyses, but if they are not close to reality they can be very misleading."[55] Many of these terms do not render easily to English translation, which makes the use of the German phraseology advisable. For example, the terms *Gefechtsstärke*, *Kampfstärke*, and *Einsatzstärke* could all too easily be mistranslated into English as combat strength, yet all three have unique definitions, the significance of which is not embraced by the English term. Similarly, when examining reports of equipment losses, one needs to note the difference between *Ausfälle* (loss) and *Totalausfalle* (total loss). The former indicates equipment that has been damaged or somehow has become non-operational, but which can be salvaged, repaired, and returned to serviceability, whereas the latter refers to equipment that, for a variety of reasons, has been destroyed or permanently lost.

The following lists the primary terminology employed within German accounts to designate personnel strengths:

Sollstärke: This term is used to designate the number of personnel a unit is authorized to posses according to its current tables of organization (or KStN).

Verpflegungsstärke: Refers to the total ration strength of a given unit on a specific date and includes everyone, including sick and wounded personnel, prisoners of war, non-military manpower, and personnel attached from other military organizations and services, who drew rations from that particular unit. Similarly, the term *Kopfstärke* literally means headcount and relates to the same definition as *Verpflegungsstärke*.

Iststärke: The actual or available strength on a specific day. This includes all the personnel belonging to a given unit and includes those who were on leave or otherwise temporarily absent. Also included are any sick or wounded personnel who were expected to return within eight weeks.

Tagesstärke: Literally meaning daily strength, this relates to the actual number of personnel present with a unit on a specific date, including anyone temporarily attached from other formations and organizations. Some sources also employ the term *Gesamtstärke* (total strength), which has an identical definition.

---

54 For instance, Zetterling's employment of detailed statistics reveals that, despite a mythology to the contrary, the notion of numerical superiority actually played a greater role in terms of the Anglo-American breakout from Normandy in July 1944 than was ever the case for the Red Army on the Eastern Front. Likewise, Zetterling has shown that German casualties during the fighting in Normandy were far less severe than is usually stated. Zetterling, *Normandy 1944*, pp. 27-35 & 77-86.
55 Zetterling & Frankson, "Analyzing World War II Eastern Front Battles.", p. 198.

Gefechtsstärke: Translated as fighting strength, this indicates the overall number of fit and available personnel within the combat units (infantry, artillery, armoured, engineer, anti-tank, reconnaissance, etc.) of a given formation, including headquarters staff, and administration and supply personnel. Found occasionally within archival documents, the term *Einsatzstärke* (action strength) has a similar meaning.

Kampfstärke: Meaning combat strength, this refers to all the frontline combat personnel of a combat unit (such as riflemen, tank crews, mortar teams, anti-tank gunners, etc.). It does not encompass artillery personnel, or the administration and supply elements of combat units, since these are not actually or normally assigned to combat duties in the front line.

Infanteriestärke: Though occasionally related to the term *Kampfstarke*, this only refers to the frontline infantry strength. Usually this just relates to the number of infantrymen within infantry companies, but when related to the strength of a division this can sometimes also include the combat strength of the divisional reconnaissance and engineer battalions.

Grabenstärke: While translated literally as trench strength this is a somewhat confusing term because its definition is the same as either *Kampfstärke* or *Infanteriestärke*, depending upon the specific context.[56]

The strength figures to which these terms refer can vary considerably. For example, on 1 June 1944 *Heeresgruppe Mitte* reported an *Iststärke* of 644,396 personnel, but this does not mean that this number of personnel were physically with the army group on that date. This is instead listed as its *Tagesstärke*, which amounted to 486,493 personnel. It should also be understood that the given *Iststärke* figure does not include personnel from non-combat GHQ units or from formations within the army group area that were under OKH control. When these are added, the *Iststärke* of *Heeresgruppe Mitte* increases to approximately 849,000. However, these numbers cannot be interpreted as being representative of the army group's combat strength, since they only reveal how many men belonged to it or how many were actually present. Rather, wherever possible, it is important to discern the figures for *Gefechtsstärke* and *Kampfstärke*, which are listed, respectively, as 316,200 and 236,772.[57] As this illustrates, given the

---

56   *OKH GenStdH/Org.Abt. Nr. I/2000/44 geh.H.Qu., den 25.4.44. Betr: Festlegung der Starkebegriffe.* Bundesarchiv-Militarchiv (Henceforth referred to as BA-MA) RH 2/60, as quoted in Zetterling & Frankson, "Analyzing World War II Eastern Front Battles.", pp. 176-177. Also, see Kroener, et. al. *GSWW. Vol. V, Part Two.*, p. 897.
57   Zetterling, *Normandy 1944*, p. 13.

wide range of figures they represent, understanding and distinguishing these terms is crucial.

For reasons of space and because it encapsulates the timeframe during which the Third Reich reached the zenith of its power and thereby its potential to win the Second World War, this study will be limited to the first half of the Russo-German War (June 1941-July 1943) and the years preceding it. Specifically, chapter one outlines the background development of the German Army from 1919 until the fall of France in 1940. This includes a review of the various measures undertaken to circumvent the limitations imposed by the Treaty of Versailles, as well as the period following Hitler's ascension to power in 1933 that witnessed fierce inter-service rivalries over resource allocations as Germany's military capabilities were rebuilt. It also provides precise details concerning the evolution of the German Army during the first ten months of the Second World War, particularly to see how well the Army's material needs were met. Finally, this chapter also includes a cursory review of the military operations between September 1939 and June 1940 to illustrate the costly nature of modern warfare and how well Germany was able to deal with these costs at this early stage in the war.

The second chapter focuses upon Germany's decision to attack the Soviet Union and how the German Army went about preparing for this task between July 1940 and June 1941. This encompasses the various hurdles the Army experienced as it sought to significantly expand its force structure, and an assessment of how successfully the manpower and equipment requirements of this expansion were attained. The chapter concludes by laying out the size of the forces Germany assembled for the operation.

The third chapter details the course of the Russo-German War from the time of the invasion in June 1941 until German offensive operations came to a halt that December. Along with illustrating the size of the opposing Red Army, this chapter charts the flow of German personnel and material strengths. It also provides details concerning how well these strengths were maintained and assesses the condition of German forces at key moments in the campaign.

The fourth chapter begins with the Soviet winter counteroffensive that heralded the failure of the German invasion. Together with specifics concerning the extent of the losses sustained by the German Army till that point, this chapter also discusses the various crises that suddenly confronted Germany during the winter of 1941-1942. It then details efforts to rehabilitate the size and strength of the German Army in time for the resumption of its offensive operations in June 1942.

The fifth chapter outlines the development of German offensive operations in Russia between June and November 1942 and illustrates the Germans' renewed ability to inflict staggering losses upon the Red Army. It also draws attention to the faulty conduct of the summer campaign as the principal reason for its eventual failure, and shows how German strength was gradually depleted as the campaign progressed because of both the intensity of operations and the German own misuse of their available resources. This chapter concludes with a summary of the condition of German formations by late 1942.

The sixth chapter covers the period of November 1942 until July 1943. Included are explanations for the Soviet successes around Stalingrad that, rather than being focused upon German numerical weakness, centre upon German command failures and improvements in the leadership and capabilities of the Red Army. It then shows how the Germans continued ability to generate strength impacted the course of subsequent events and eventually brought the Soviet offensive to a halt. The chapter ends by summarizing just how well Germany was still able to muster fresh strength, and restore its badly depleted field forces to nearly their full authorized establishments.

This chronological approach is the most logical way of charting the various structural changes in the German forces while simultaneously tracking the ebb and flow of personnel and material resources. It also permits a host of mitigating factors to be included within the analysis. These elements include Germany's industrial war effort, strategic policy and planning, logistics, ideology, the war against partisans, power struggles within the Nazi Party and government and their concern for maintaining tranquillity on the home front, and the perception and attitude of the German Army itself as to what kind of war it was actually fighting in Russia. A chronological analysis allows these factors to be taken into account together with the actual ebb and flow of the military engagements, campaigns, and battles. Both the chronology of military actions and the additional factors just mentioned are interconnected in terms of their influence upon one another, representing the context in which the issue of force maintenance existed.

In some respects, the minutiae of detailing just how many tanks a particular German panzer division had at a given point, or determining if a nearly-forgotten infantry division received enough personnel replacements, may appear arcane. But nothing could be further from the truth. Such details provide the crucial foundations upon which the great contest between Germany and the Soviet Union, the largest and most costly land campaign in the history of civilization, is constructed and understood. They give meaning both to the sheer scale of the conflict, and to the efforts and sacrifices of the Red Army, as it recoiled in the face of invasion and gradually transformed itself into an organization that ultimately drove back and defeated the German invader. Such an analysis also reveals much more in terms of the specific strengths and weaknesses of the German Army as a military force, a bureaucratic organization, and as part of Germany's larger war effort. Finally, testing the validity of one of the most firmly entrenched tenets of the Russo-German War is itself a worthy endeavour because it contributes to our understanding of events and carries with it the possibility of creating tertiary effects because of how perceptions of numerical weakness have become interwoven with notions of German military professionalism and battlefield excellence. Such notions form the basis of much of the discourse concerning the Anglo-American campaigns of the Second World War, especially as a means of explaining the slow pace of operations, the lack of greater military success, or even serving as an excuse to justify battlefield defeats.

1

Prequel to Götterdämmerung. Rebuilding the German Army: From Rearmament to the fall of France, 1919 to June 1940

Although Prussian strategists appreciate the value of initiative, the rash deed and an exploited victory, they do not understand the critical, nay, decisive importance of lines of communication. They are incorrigible optimists, and have failed to organize life-sustaining arteries to the rear in the course of their tumultuous, forward operations.

Colonel Ferenc Vlasits
Austrian observer during the Second Schleswig War, 1864.[1]

Contrary to general perceptions, the Russo-German War was not the cause of the difficulties faced by the German Army in procuring sufficient manpower and equipment resources for its armies in the field. Rather, the relentless struggle between Germany and the Soviet Union during 1941 and 1945 exacerbated an already precarious situation. Despite the dramatic images of screaming Stuka dive-bombers and swirling columns of apparently invincible panzers that tends to dominate the accepted narrative of the early military victories of the *Wehrmacht*, it is vital to remember that Germany's military machine had modest roots and that its pre-war rearmament was driven and sometimes constrained by a host of competing and occasionally contradictory factors, individuals, and organizations. Indeed, German shortages of manpower and military equipment actually predated the outbreak of hostilities in 1939 and were largely the result of the competition over resources between the Army on one side, and industry and the other branches of the *Wehrmacht* on the other. These competitions would endure throughout the entire course of the war, but were considerably muted during its earliest stages because the speed of the German victories of 1939-1940 kept losses within manageable limits. Germany's civilian, military, and industrial leadership remained preoccupied with the appropriate scale of manpower distribution and

1   As quoted in Geoffrey Wawro, *The Austro-Prussian War: Austria's War with Prussia and Italy in 1866.* (New York: 1996), p. 31.

equipment allocation, but in the wake of the initial dramatic victories the issue was precluded from reaching crisis proportions.

In the aftermath of Imperial Germany's defeat in the First World War, the disarmament clauses of the Treaty of Versailles severely limited the size and capabilities of the post-war German Army. From a total strength of 350,000 personnel in June 1919, the new *Reichswehr* would be reduced to 100,000 men, including 4,000 officers, by January 1921.[2] To prevent the accumulation of trained manpower reserves, it was to consist of long-term volunteers, with officers serving twenty-five years and enlisted men enrolled for twelve. The Great General Staff was abolished, the *Kriegsakademie* was closed, and conscription was prohibited. The possession of tanks, aircraft, chemical weapons, anti-aircraft guns and heavy artillery by the *Reichswehr* was also forbidden.[3] An Inter-Allied Control Commission was to ensure that the seven infantry and three cavalry divisions of the *Reichswehr* were equipped with no more than 102,000 rifles and carbines, 1,926 machine guns, 204 7.7 cm and 84 10.5 cm artillery pieces, and 252 mortars. To maintain internal security and stability the *Reichswehr* was eventually allowed to retain 105 armoured cars, while the state police forces were permitted to have 150 such vehicles.[4] To ensure that these equipment levels could not be rapidly increased during any future crisis and to forestall the development of modern weapons, the industries of the great German armaments manufacturers, such as Krupp and Rheinmetall, were to be severely scaled down and their output closely monitored, especially in terms of the development and production of aircraft.[5]

From the outset, the leading personalities of the German government, industry, and the *Reichswehr* attempted to circumvent these restrictions as best they could. Between 1926 and 1932 the German Transport Ministry provided subsidies worth 321 million RM to various German aircraft manufacturers for research and development to provide some basic foundation for future aerial rearmament. More covertly, starting in 1925 the *Reichswehr* annually spent 10 million RM on training aircrew and developing aircraft.[6] With the signing of the Treaty of Rapallo between Germany and

---

2   James S. Corum, *The Roots of Blitzkrieg: Hans von Seeckt and German Military Reform.* (Lawrence, KS: 1992), p. 34. With the collapse of Imperial Germany in October 1918, the old Imperial German Army (*Kaiserlich Deutsches Armee*) was dissolved and replaced in January 1919 by the *Friedensheer* (Peace Army). In March 1921, in order to comply with the restrictions imposed at Versailles, the latter was folded into the *Reichswehr* (or National Defence Force), which would remain the premier military force of the Weimar Republic until replaced in October 1935 by the *Wehrmacht* (Defence Force or Armed Forces).

3   Citino, *The German Way of War*, p. 239.

4   Corum, *The Roots of Blitzkrieg*, p. 97.

5   Hooten, *Phoenix Triumphant*, pp. 27-42.

6   Edward L. Homze, *Arming the Luftwaffe: The Reich Air Ministry and the German Aircraft Industry, 1919-1939.* (Lincoln, NE: 1976), p. 31. In addition, throughout the 1920s the German Navy spent over 1 million RM per year on its own clandestine air training and development program. Corum, *The Luftwaffe*, p. 80.

the Soviet Union in April 1922, the *Reichswehr* was able secretly to establish a number of testing facilities in Russia, allowing Germany to retain a modest level of expertise in the use and development of modern weapons systems, such as tanks and aircraft.[7] These and other programs were fully supported by Germany's political leaders, who provided funding via camouflaged appropriations in the *Reichstag*.[8] Officially, the German defence budget grew from 409 million RM in 1924, to a peak of 827 million RM by 1928-1929.[9]

The significance of this funding is difficult to quantify given that a considerable, but unknown, amount of additional financing was covert or done via private individuals and commercial enterprises. However, in February 1927 *Generaloberst* Wilhelm Heye, commander of the *Reichswehr*, was able to report in a Cabinet meeting that secret reserve weapons stocks amounted to 350,000 rifles, 12,000 light and heavy machine-guns, 400 trench mortars, and 600 light and 75 heavy field artillery pieces.[10] Likewise, by 1933 the training facilities at Lipetsk in Russia had provided the *Reichswehr* with a small cadre of 120 fighter pilots and 100 observers, while a further 300 aircrew had been trained in Germany.[11] One estimate of the German air rearmament effort places expenditures for training and aircraft development between 1925 and 1933 at 100 million RM ($24 million U.S.), with another 70 million RM ($16.5 million U.S.) spent on developing the industrial infrastructure. By comparison, during this time the French spent approximately FFr 12,000 million ($49 million U.S.) on military, civilian, and colonial aviation.[12] Certainly, these figures show that Germany in no way possessed a real air force, or that the *Reichswehr* was in any way prepared for a major war. Nonetheless, with the foundation of the future *Luftwaffe* having been laid and with the German Army possessing a considerable stockpile of equipment, it is clear

---

7   For elaboration regarding the co-operation between the *Reichswehr* and the Soviet Union, see Edward H. Carr, *German–Soviet Relations between the Two World Wars, 1919-1939*. (Baltimore, MD: 1951), Lionel Kocham, *Russia and the Weimar Republic*. (Cambridge: 1954), Hans W. Gatzke, "Russo-German Military Collaboration during the Weimar Republic." *American Historical Review*, Vol. 63, No. 3 (1958), pp. 565-597, and Sergej A. Gorlow, "Geheimsache Moskau-Berlin: Die militärpolitische Zusammenarbeit zwischen der Sowjetunion und dem Deutschen Reich, 1920-1933." *Vierteljahrshefte für Zeitgeschichte*, Vol. 44, No. 1 (1996), pp. 133-165. A more recent treatment, despite its rather sensationalist approach, can be found in Yuri Dyakov, *The Red Army and the Wehrmacht: How the Soviets Militarized Germany, 1922-33, and Paved the Way for Fascism*. (Amherst: 1994).

8   For one of the best studies of the rearmament efforts of Weimar Germany, see Barton Whaley, *Covert German Rearmament, 1919-1939: Deception and Perception*. (Frederick, MD: 1984). For the participation of Germany's civilian leadership, see Hans W. Gatzke, *Stresemann and the Rearmament of Germany*. (Baltimore, MD: 1954).

9   F.L. Carsten, *The Reichswehr and Politics 1918-1933*. (Oxford: 1996), pp. 274-275.

10   Corum, *The Roots of Blitzkrieg*, p. 176.

11   Corum, *The Luftwaffe*, p. 115.

12   Hooten, *Phoenix Triumphant*, p. 62.

that the German rearmament efforts of the 1930s were certainly not starting from scratch.

Of far great significance to Germany's future military endeavours was the failure to create a sizeable pool to trained reservists. While the lengthy periods of service imposed by the Treaty of Versailles were themselves a significant obstacle since these placed the number of militarily trained men within Germany in irrevocable decline, the post-war decisions regarding the role and nature of the *Reichswehr* as an institution were equally important. This was established by its first Chief of the Army Command (*Chef der Heeresleitung*), Hans von Seeckt, who insisted that the *Reichswehr* would be a small elite force doctrinally focused on the conduct of manoeuvre warfare. Partly, this stemmed from Seeckt's belief that the complexities of modern warfare were simply beyond the abilities of poorly trained mass armies, and that only a highly disciplined and professional army could conduct such operations successfully. He would later write: "The mass becomes immobile, it can no longer manoeuvre, and therefore it cannot win. It can only crush." Given Germany's shortcomings for prosecuting large-scale, lengthy wars, especially in terms of strategic resources and industrial production, such a force presented the only possibility for conducting short, decisive campaigns against any potential French, Polish or Czech adversaries.[13] Seeckt concluded: "The goal of modern strategy will be to achieve a decision with highly mobile, highly capable forces, before the masses have even begun to move."[14] A large militia-type system would simply prove ineffective and therefore be a fruitless dispersion of valuable military equipment. As evidenced by the various paramilitary organizations that emerged in Germany after 1918, such as the notoriously uncontrollable Freikorps, Seeckt also worried that such a force would be ill disciplined and thereby be both politically and militarily unreliable.[15] Any reserves had to be strictly controlled by the German Army, rather than by local and regional authorities or any government agency other than the Ministry of Defence. Seeckt's views regarding paramilitary organizations and mass-based territorial forces was itself a reflection of a much older tenet within the German Army that was wary of any such armed forces and which rejected any kind of Peoples War and its associated *levee en masse* outright.[16]

---

13 In 1925, the peacetime strength of the French Army was 750,000 men; Poland had 300,000 men, and the Czech Army could muster 150,000 men. Wilhelm Deist, "The Road to Ideological War: Germany, 1918-1945." in Williamson Murray, et. al. *The Making of Strategy: Rulers, States, and War.* (New York: 1994), p. 357.

14 Hans von Seeckt, *Gedanken eines Soldaten.* (Leipzig: 1935), p. 54, as quoted in Citino, *The German Way of War*, p. 243. Also, see Matthias Strohn, "Hans von Seeckt and His Vision of a 'Modern Army'." *War in History*, Vol. 12, No. 3 (2005), pp. 318-337.

15 Walter Görlitz, *History of the German General Staff, 1657-1945.* (New York: 1966), pp. 219-246. As Görlitz notes, the chief concern for both the *Reichswehr* and the various Weimar governments was that they could never be certain that the weapons they distributed to the paramilitary and militia groups would not one day be used against them.

16 This concern for anything other than tightly controlled armies of professionals' dates to Germany's experience with mercenaries during the Thirty Years War (1618-1648) and

This institutional disdain for a broadly based militia-system, faithfully adhered to by Seeckt's successors after his dismissal in October 1926, did not mean that the leadership of the *Reichswehr* was ignorant of Germany's need for trained manpower.[17] Despite the terms of service dictated by the Treaty of Versailles, by 1926 the rate of discharges from the Reichswehr had increased to 25 percent, while officers were encouraged to leave the regular army and enter the reserves. Starting in 1923, under the cover of a national labour service, the army was able to provide military training to young volunteers. Preceding these measures was the establishment in 1921 of the *Grenzschutz*. Mainly deployed along Germany's eastern frontiers, these paramilitary border guards received military training from army instructors and were equipped with small arms and machine-guns. Yet the most effective of the various reserve forces available to the *Reichswehr* was the national Security Police (*Schutzpolizei*). Given basic military training, led by former army NCOs and officers, and equipped with small arms and armoured cars, the Security Police were also motorised and well-disciplined. They provided the *Reichswehr* with valuable supplementary manpower in times of crisis. For example, in the event of war the Bremen Security Police could be mobilized within eight hours and were assigned the task of manning western border defences.[18]

Prussia's resounding defeats in 1806 at the battles of Jena and Auerstadlt during the Napoleonic Wars. In terms of the debates regarding military reform following the latter, see Citino, *The German Way of War*, pp. 128-131, and Görlitz, *History of the German General Staff, 1657-1945*, pp. 28-43. For a thorough study, see Peter Paret, *The Cognitive Challenge of War: Prussia 1806.* (Princeton, NJ: 2009). The ultimate result of Prussia's defeat in 1806 was the adoption of universal conscription and the formation of a territorial militia, or *Landwehr*. For debates regarding the effectiveness of the *Landwehr* and its uncomfortable relationship with Prussia's conservative military and civilian leadership, see Denis E. Showalter, "The Prussian Landwehr and Its Critics, 1813-1819." *Central European History*, Vol. 14, No. 1 (March 1971), pp. 3-33, and Dierk Walter, "Roon, the Prussian Landwehr and the Reorganization of 1859-1860." *War in History*, Vol. 16, No. 3 (2009), pp. 269-297. For additional information concerning the problematical historical relationship between the German Army and the concept of 'People's War', see Stig Forster, "Facing 'People's War': Moltke the Elder and Germany's Military Options after 1871." *Journal of Strategic Studies*, Vol. 10, No. 2 (1987), pp. 209-230, Michael Geyr, "Insurrectionary Warfare: The German Debate about a Levee en Masse in October 1918." *Journal of Modern History*, Vol. 73, No. 3 (September 2001), pp. 459-527, and Beatrice Heuser, "Small War in the Age of Clausewitz: The Watershed Between Partisan War and People's War." *Journal of Strategic Studies*, Vol. 33, No. 1 (2010), pp. 139-162.

17   It should be noted that not all officers of the *Reichswehr* agreed with Seeckt's views on the utility of mass armies or how future wars would transpire. For example, see Corum, *The Roots of Blitzkrieg.*, pp. 53-54 & 63-64, and Gil-li Vardi, "Joachim von Stülpnagel's Military Thought and Planning." *War in History*, Vol. 17, No. 2 (2010), pp. 193-216.

18   It should be noted that the *Schutzpolizei* stood apart from the normal police (*Ordnungspolizei*). While the latter remained under local jurisdictions, the former was under central state control. Craig, *The Politics of the Prussian Army 1640-1945*, pp. 404-405.

Even so, at best the various means and measures available to create reserves ultimately produced mixed results. The number of reservists created through the establishment of a national labour service or by the premature discharge of army servicemen, collectively referred to as the Black Reichswehr because of its clandestine nature, probably only numbered in the tens of thousands. Similarly, the most reliable estimates place the effective strength of the *Grenzschutz* at around 40,000 men, while during the 1920s there may have been 70,000 security police.[19] In the 1920s, these efforts did provide the *Reichswehr* with a modicum ability to supplement its numbers of regular personnel in the advent of war. It also provided a small cadre of semi-trained personnel that the *Wehrmacht* was later able to draw upon during its expansion in the 1930s. However, these figures do not represent a substantial reservoir of trained manpower. Rather, they illustrate the abject failure of the *Reichswehr* to establish a coherent program capable of producing the large numbers of trained reservists needed for any large-scale or long-term conflict. As a result, the *Wehrmacht* ultimately went to war in 1939 with a dire shortage of trained manpower, as it was able to produce only four classes of trained reservists after 1933. In contrast, the Imperial Army had gone to war in 1914 with no fewer than forty reservist classes.[20] Certainly, this was largely the result of the restrictions imposed upon Germany in 1919 and thereby perhaps the most successful aspect of the disarmament provisions of the Treaty of Versailles. Yet it was also a consequence of a military culture within the German Army that concentrated upon the operational and tactical levels of war as a means of solving Germany's larger strategic dilemmas. Seeckt's focus upon mobile operations conducted by small armies is a case in point. Ultimately, long-range planning tended to be neglected, while uncomfortable strategic and logistical circumstances were marginalized or ignored, frequently within an atmosphere of wishful thinking.[21]

In a Cabinet meeting of 9 February 1933 – mere days after his appointment as chancellor – Adolf Hitler signalled that the era of modest German rearmament was at an end. Outlining his priorities, Hitler declared: "The future of Germany depends exclusively and only on the reconstruction of the Wehrmacht. All other tasks must cede precedence to the task of rearmament."[22] The scale of this new emphasis was made clear on 8 June when the president of the Reichsbank, Hjalmar Schacht, unveiled to

---

For the best explanation of the various measures undertaken by the *Reichswehr* to create a pool of trained manpower, see Corum, *The Roots of Blitzkrieg*, pp. 177-182.

19   Ibid, pp. 179 & 181.

20   Kroener, "Squaring the Circle: Blitzkrieg Strategy and Manpower Shortage, 1938-1942", p. 297.

21   This attitude and its relationship to German military culture is best illustrated in Robert Citino's *The German Way of War*, as well as his *Death of the Wehrmacht: The German Campaigns of 1942*. (Lawrence, KS: 2007) and *The Wehrmacht Retreats: Fighting a Lost War, 1943*. (Lawrence, KS: 2012). Also see Megargee, *Inside Hitler's High Command*, and Stahel, *Operation Barbarossa and Germany's Defeat in the East*.

22   Adam Tooze, *The Wages of Destruction: The Making and Breaking of the Nazi Economy*. (London: 2006), p. 38.

the Cabinet an ambitious plan to spend 35 billion RM on rearmament over the next eight years. Averaging almost 4.5 billion RM per year, this represented approximately five to ten percent of Germany's gross domestic product.[23]

But German rearmament faced significant obstacles. The greatest of these was the shortage of foreign capital brought on by a combination of the Great Depression, the steady worsening of Germany's international reputation that drove off foreign buyers, and the conundrum of having to allocate resources and production for domestic consumption instead of selling them to boost foreign currency reserves. Given that considerable quantities of strategic resources had to be purchased on the global market, as illustrated in Table 1.1, the shortage of foreign currency reserves proved to be a significant factor in determining the pace and scale of German rearmament.[24] Many of the industries needed for rearmament would have to be built or significantly expanded, and that would require massive investments and infrastructure development. To achieve autarky and relieve Germany's reliance upon foreign imports, immense resources would also have to be committed to establishing synthetic fuel and Buna rubber production facilities.[25] Aside from the economic difficulties, rearmament also threw the German Army, Navy, and newly created *Luftwaffe* into competition with each other over everything from manpower and equipment, to the allocation of raw materials and manufacturing capacities. This competition would only be exacerbated by the relentless pace at which Germany marched towards war, and by the lack, other than Hitler himself, of any central authority capable of distributing resources based upon strategic priorities. Finally, given the size of Germany's military forces in 1933, for the moment rearmament also had to remain secret in order not to alarm the other powers of Europe, particularly Great Britain and France. Abrogation of the

23   Ibid, pp. 53-54. Hjalmar Schacht would be appointed Minister of Economics in March 1934, and General Plenipotentiary for the War Economy the following month. After a number of disagreements with both Hitler and Hermann Göring, he resigned in November 1937.

24   By the autumn of 1935 the Reichsbank forecast that Germany would face a net foreign currency shortfall amounting to 400 million RM, for which the Reichsbank held reserves amounting to only 88 million RM. The tight situation regarding the availability of foreign currency was only exacerbated by public awareness of Germany's treatment of its Jewish population and its increasingly bellicose foreign policy, both of which served to drive off international consumers of German goods. For example, in 1928 German exports to the United States totalled 796 million RM, but shrank to only 150 million RM by 1936. Ibid., pp. 88 & 209. The most recent comprehensive examination of Germany's pre-war economic circumstances may be found in Tooze, *The Wages of Destruction*. Other important studies include Richard Overy's, *The Nazi Economic Recovery, 1932-1938*. (London: 1982) and *War and Economy in the Third Reich*. (Oxford: 1994). Also, see Kroener, et. al. *GSWW. Vol. V, Part Two.*

25   According to the final estimates of the Four Year plan announced by Hitler in August 1936, almost 9.5 billion RM were to be spent developing infrastructure and capacity, of which 35.2 percent were allotted towards oil and synthetic rubber facilities. Tooze, *The Wages of Destruction*, p. 226.

Treaty of Versailles and the public announcement of the existence of the *Luftwaffe* would have to wait until March 1935.

From the flimsy foundations established during the Weimar Republic, the political and military leadership of Germany committed themselves to the task of rapid rearmament without delay. The German Army finalized its initial plan by December 1933 and foresaw expansion proceeding in two four-year phases.[26] The first was to last until 1937 and was largely defensive in nature, entailing the breaking-up of the ten divisions of the *Reichswehr* into cadres around which 21 infantry and three cavalry divisions would be built. In the event of war, this number was to be increased to 63 divisions through the addition of volunteers and reservists. The second stage envisioned the establishment of an army capable of conducting an offensive war by 1941. While planners believed that this force level could only be accomplished through the re-introduction of conscription within two year, during 1934 the size of the Army had already increased to 240,000 men, most of whom were volunteers. To oversee the training and development of armoured formations, the *Inspektion der Kraftfahrkampftruppen* (Mechanized Troops Inspectorate) under *Generalleutnant* Oswald Lutz was established in June 1934.[27] The following month Krupp began delivering the first 150 *Panzerkampfwagen* Model I (Pz I) tanks that in October formed the first armoured training units. A further 650 of these training vehicles were scheduled for production during the following year together with the first of the next three models (Pz II-IV) intended for actual combat.[28]

Dissatisfied that Germany's military build-up wasn't progressing fast enough, on 16 March 1935 Hitler publicly announced the abrogation of the Treaty of Versailles, the reintroduction of compulsory military service and Germany's intention to expand its peacetime army to 36 divisions distributed between twelve army corps. Shortly thereafter, he enacted the *Wehrgesetz* (Defence Law) of 21 May, whereby the Ministry of Defence was renamed the *Reichskriegsministerium* (Reich War Ministry), the office of the *Chef der Heeresleitung* became the *Oberkommando des Heeres* (OKH) and the Army

---

26 Ibid, p. 57.
27 The first armoured training unit, consisting of personnel trained in Russia, had already been secretly formed on 1 November 1933. Thomas L. Jentz, *Panzertruppen: The Complete Guide to Creation and Employment of Germany's Tank Force, 1933-1942*. (Atglen, PA: 1996), p. 11.
28 Actual delivery of the first production models of the Pz III and IV would ultimately be delayed until 1936. Whaley, *Covert German Rearmament, 1919-1939*, p. 50. Whereas the Pz I had very thin armour and was armed with only twin machine guns, the Pz II possessed a 2 cm gun, the Pz III was equipped with a 3.7 cm gun, and the Pz IV had a 7.5 cm gun. The most detailed study of German armoured vehicles during the Second World War can be found in F.M. von Senger und Etterlin, *German Tanks of World War II: The Complete Illustrated History of German Armoured Fighting Vehicles, 1926-1945*. (New York: 1969).

General Staff was formally re-established. On 1 June the *Reichswehr* was officially renamed the *Wehrmacht*.[29]

Coming as it did within two years of the initial expansion of the Army, this latest push for an even larger force compounded already critical shortages of trained officers. From the initial pool of 4,000 officers who had belonged to the *Reichswehr*, 450 were veterinary or medical personnel while 500 others were transferred to the *Luftwaffe* in 1933. Aside from personnel required for staff and administrative appointments and all the various independent corps and army level units, the new target of 36 divisions alone would need 19,224 officers.[30] As the *Kriegsakademie* was only reopened on 15 October 1935, a variety of expedients were employed to attain the required numbers. These included the immediate granting of commissions to 1,500 non-commissioned officers, the drafting of 300 legal officials from the Ministry of Justice, and the transfer of 2,500 police officers from the *Landespolizei*. Supplementing these were officers who had been discharged since 1918, but who were now brought back into service. Allowances were also made for those no longer fit for front-line service, but who could still be useful in training and administrative establishments. Following the *Anschluss* with Austria in 1938, a further 1,800 Austrian officers were also taken on strength.[31] While these emergency measures mitigated the worst shortages, they could do little to alleviate the lack of trained General Staff officers or the concern amongst several senior commanders that the rapid expansion had diluted the high standards of the officer corps.[32]

Despite such concerns, the German Army continued its relentless growth. By August 1935 its ranks had swelled to approximately 350,000 men now equipped with 353 panzers, while the training manoeuvres of the preceding month had involved the participation of an improvised panzer division.[33] The success of these manoeuvres resulted in the creation of the *Kommando der Panzertruppen* (Armoured Troops Command) on 27 September, which established the panzer arm as its own distinct part of the German Army.[34] The formation of the first three panzer divisions followed on 15 October. That December the Chief of the Army General Staff, *General der Artillerie* Ludwig Beck, added three *leichte* (light mechanized) divisions and a further 44 panzer battalions to the projected expansion to hasten the development of the

---

29   Concurrently, the *Reichsmarine* (navy) was also renamed *Kriegsmarine*. The Army was referred to simply as the *Heer*.
30   Estimated number based upon the 534 officers required by the 1939 TOE of the infantry divisions belonging to the *1. Welle*. According to David Stone, *Fighting for the Fatherland: The Story of the German Soldier from 1648 to the Present Day*. (Washington, DC: 2006), p. 451, the Army was short of 12,000 of its required 30,000 officers in March 1937.
31   Cooper, *The German Army, 1933-1945*, pp. 159-160.
32   Ibid, p. 136. Also see Görlitz, *History of the German General Staff, 1657-1945*, p. 299.
33   Whaley, *Covert German Rearmament, 1919-1939*, p. 69.
34   Oswald Lutz was appointed the first head of *Kommando der Panzertruppen* after being promoted to *General der Panzertruppen* on 1 November 1935, while on 15 October 1935 *Oberst* Heinz Guderian was assigned to command the newly formed *2. Panzer Division*.

Army's offensive capabilities.[35] Completed in June 1936, the finalized plan for this latest phase of expansion set the targeted strength of the peacetime army at 43 active divisions, including three panzer and four motorised divisions, supported by 21 *Landwehr* (territorial) divisions. The development of infrastructure and the accumulation of equipment were to be accelerated in order to be able to mobilize 102 divisions and 3.6 million men by October 1940. By that point Army planners anticipated that the panzer divisions would be able to field, in addition to light models, some 1,812 Pz III and Pz IV.[36]

While struggling to fulfil its own ambitious expansion programmes, the German Army was in constant competition with the other branches of the armed services over the allocation of industrial and raw material resources.[37] In March 1934 the conventionally minded Commander-in-Chief of the German Navy, Admiral Erich Raeder, submitted an ambitious plan to Hitler for the establishment of a large ocean-going surface fleet that included the construction of eight battleships, three aircraft carriers, eight cruisers, 48 destroyers, and 72 U-boats by 1949.[38] Hitler approved the plan and construction of the first of the 32,000-ton Scharnhorst-class battlecruisers started in March 1935, together with the first of four Admiral Hipper-class heavy cruisers and some 13 destroyers. The commissioning of Germany's first U-boat followed on 28 June and a further eleven would enter service during the remainder of the year.[39] In 1936 construction started on the 42,000-ton battleships *Bismarck* and *Tirpitz*, along with the first of the aircraft carriers. Between 1936 and 1939, a further 13 destroyers and 15 torpedo boats would also be laid down.[40] Raeder followed this extensive initial effort with an even grander programme in December 1938. Referred to as Plan Z, this called for the construction of an imposing fleet totalling 797 vessels, including six giant battleships, eight cruisers, and 249 U-boats. Scheduled for completion by 1948, this plan entailed expenditures totalling 33 billion RM. With little consideration for how this latest plan for naval expansion would affect the other services, Hitler approved it on 27 January 1939 and assigned it absolute priority over all other industrial projects within the Reich.[41]

---

35   These panzer battalions were intended to form seven independent panzer brigades, capable of either providing infantry support or of forming the basis of a future panzer division. The first of these brigades was formed in October 1937, followed by a second in 1938. See Cooper, *The German Army, 1933-1945*, p. 154 and Tooze, *The Wages of Destruction*, p. 211.

36   Ibid, p. 211-212.

37   Deist, "The Road to Ideological War: Germany, 1918-1945.", pp. 375-378.

38   Tooze, *The Wages of Destruction*, pp. 58-59.

39   Interestingly, the signing of the Anglo-German Navy Treaty, which allowed Germany to build submarines and that was supposed to limit future battleships to 25,000-tons, occurred only ten days prior to the launch of *U-1*. Whaley, *Covert German Rearmament, 1919-1939*, p. 105.

40   See E. Groner, *Die Schiffe der deutschen Kriegsmarine*. (München: 1976).

41   Tooze, *The Wages of Destruction*, p. 288-289. Overall German naval expenditures increased from 312 million RM in 1933 to 2.39 billion RM by 1939, for a grand total spent during

Ultimately, given Germany's strategic situation, the entire scheme of creating an ostentatious surface fleet capable of challenging Great Britain and the United States was both unrealistic and a serious misallocation of resources. To conduct effective operations, the fleet forecast in Plan Z would have required the annual allocation of six million tons of oil and two million tons of diesel fuel by 1948 – an entirely illusionary figure given that the most optimistic assessments estimated that German domestic production would reach only two million tons of oil and 1.34 million tons of diesel by that time.[42] Moreover, throughout the course of the Second World War, the impact of those German capital ships actually completed was marginal. Overall, German surface warships and auxiliary cruisers sank 897,971 tons of merchant shipping between September 1939 and March 1941. During the same period, aircraft accounted for 864,239 tons, mines claimed 827,256 tons, and U-boats sank 3,453,394 tons. Of the tonnage sunk by the surface fleet, a greater portion was due to the operations of nine auxiliary cruisers, which sank or captured 138 ships of 857,533 tons between April 1940 and October 1943.[43] Perhaps the greatest drawback was that the resources required to produce these warships also impaired the growth of the pre-war U-boat fleet by tying up scarce shipyard space and raw material allocations. As a result, by September 1939 the German Navy possessed a mere 57 U-boats, of which only 32 were capable of operating on the high seas.[44] In exchange for the 200 million RM spent on the battleship *Bismarck* alone, the *Kriegsmarine* could have possessed an additional 30-50 U-boats, which cost between six and four million RM each.[45] Considering the havoc inflicted upon Allied shipping lanes during the first years of the war by Germany's existing submarine fleet, the impact of these additional U-boats would most likely have been very significant.[46]

this period of 8.289 billion RM. In comparison, British and American naval expenditures during this same period amounted to the equivalent of 10,061 billion RM and 13,278 billion RM, respectively. Ibid, p. 251.

42 Ibid, p. 295.

43 Boog, et. al. *GSWW., Vol. VI*, pp. 404 & 431.

44 The size of the U-boat fleet expanded very slowing during the early years of the war. By April 1941 the number available had only reached 108, of which a mere 28 were front-line boats. Ibid, p. 348.

45 Considering the shortages of raw materials Germany faced, the exchange of the brand-new battleship *Bismarck* for the aged British battlecruiser HMS *Hood* in May 1941 represented a very poor rate of return, even though this was far better than the accomplishments of the battleship *Tirpitz*, which sank in a Norwegian fjord during October 1944 having hardly ever fired a shot in anger. Tooze, *The Wages of Destruction*, p. 740.

46 Between July 1940 and March 1941, the exchange rate was 148,032 tons of Allied shipping for every U-boat lost. Boog, et. al. *GSWW., Vol. VI*, p. 404. For insight into the development of German naval strategy during the first years of the war, especially as this pertained to dealing with the United States, see Holger H. Herwig, "Prelude to Weltblitzkrieg: Germany's Naval Policy toward the United States of America, 1939-1941." *Journal of Modern History*, Vol. 43, No. 4 (December 1971), pp. 649-668.

While the steel requirements of the *Kriegsmarine* were never overly large, the redistribution of priorities in January 1939 came at a time when the efforts of the Army to create offensive capabilities were already in jeopardy of being derailed by the steel mills having reached the maximum capacity of production and by the increasingly serious shortages of iron ore. Having already been informed in November 1938 that the monthly steel ration allotted to the *Wehrmacht* as a whole would have to be reduced from 530,000 tons to only 300,000 tons, the Army had to relinquish an even greater share – this at a time when its expansion and preparations for war were reaching their zenith.[47] By July 1939, the Army was compelled to scale down its projected 1939-1940 programme: anticipated production of the MG 34 machine-gun had to be reduced from 61,000 to 13,000 units, while the target of 840 10.5 cm field howitzers was lowered to 460. In terms of the development of the Army's offensive capabilities, even worse was the decision that the scheduled production of 1,200 Pz III and Pz IV between October 1939 and October 1940 would have to be cut by one-half.[48] Although Plan Z never produced any surface warships, capricious decisions about naval production severely affected the Army and its armament programmes during 1939.

However irksome the diversion of resources to naval matters may have been for the senior leadership of the German Army, their greatest competitor throughout the pre-war period was always the *Luftwaffe*. From the outset, the establishment of a large air force was a top priority for Hitler and his government because it was a potent symbol of great power status, industrial and economic modernity, and could serve as a deterrent to cow Germany's neighbours until rearmament was complete. During the Cabinet meeting of 9 February 1933 – well before Schacht presented the finalized rearmament budget in June – Hitler ordered that a preliminary 40 million RM immediately be allotted to hasten the creation of an air force.[49] From this initial allocation, the portion assigned to the expansion of the *Luftwaffe* would consistently average between 30-40 percent of the entire defence budget throughout the period of 1934-1939, well ahead of proportion spent by its later adversaries on their air forces (see Table 1.2). To coordinate its development, armament, and expansion, the *Reichsluftministerium* (Reich Air Ministry or RLM) was created in March 1933 under the leadership of State Secretary Erhard Milch. While Hermann Göring, a former fighter pilot during the First World War and long-time member of the Nazi Party, was given oversight of all aerial development within Germany and ultimately made Commander-in-Chief of the *Luftwaffe*, Milch was the driving force behind the development and expansion of the air force during its formative years.

---

47   Alongside the shortages of steel, the allocation of aluminium had to be cut by 20 percent, rubber by 30 percent, and cement from 25 to 45 percent. Williamson Murray, *Strategy for Defeat: The Luftwaffe, 1933-1945.* (Secaucus, NJ: 1986), p. 31.
48   Tooze, *The Wages of Destruction*, pp. 302-303.
49   Hooten, *Phoenix Triumphant*, p. 95.

In September 1933 Milch unveiled his plan to create an air force of 2,000 aircraft within two years, hoping thereby rapidly to increase domestic aircraft manufacturing through a speedy injection of capital.[50] Within a month, the first combat air units had been formed and by May 1934 the *Luftwaffe* possessed two bomber and one fighter *geschwader* (wing) with a total of 34 air squadrons.[51]

When the existence of the *Luftwaffe* was publically revealed on 1 March 1935, it already had some 800 aircraft on strength.[52] Although these were entirely first-generation aircraft of dubious quality, this first phase had accomplished two important objectives. The first had been to create an air force and, more importantly, develop the necessary infrastructure and training establishments required for future growth.[53] The second objective was to inject sufficient capital into Germany's aircraft industries to develop their research and development facilities and expand production capabilities. The result was dramatic. In May 1933, the German aviation industry consisted of just 3,200 workers scattered across eight factories. By the end of that year it had already expanded to 11,000 factory workers, with a further 5,700 employed in engine plants. By December 1934, the industry was producing 160 aircraft per month and had already supplied the *Luftwaffe* with 1,900 aircraft, including some 1,300 training and communication planes. A year later monthly production had increased to 300 and the development and testing of improved second-generation aircraft, such as the Bf 109 fighter, the Ju 87 dive-bomber, and He 111 and Do 17 bombers, was well underway. During 1935 the industry grew to 61,000 workers, a figure that doubled by the following year. By the outbreak of war, approximately 2.35 billion RM had been invested into the aircraft industry, just under one-half of which had been provided by the German government. Ultimately, this massive scale of investment resulted in the production of the aircraft detailed in Table 1.3, and created an aircraft industry that, by 1939, employed at least 250,000 workers and was capable of producing 10,000 world-class aircraft per year.[54] At this point, aircraft production averaged almost 700 per month, of which almost 400 were combat aircraft.[55]

Not surprisingly, the *Luftwaffe*'s strength, capabilities and infrastructure increased in tandem. During 1935, it opened the *Luftkriegsakademie* to produce its own trained

50   Tooze, *The Wages of Destruction*, p. 57.
51   Corum, *The Luftwaffe*, p. 156. For the relentless pace of the *Luftwaffe*'s peacetime expansion, see Richard J. Overy, "The German Pre-War Aircraft Production Plans: November 1936 – April 1939." *English Historical Review*, Vol. 90, No. 357 (1975), pp. 778-797.
52   Corum, *The Luftwaffe*, p. 164.
53   By 1936 a total of 36 modern, fully equipped air bases had been established, each costing the equivalent of one infantry division. Hooten, *Phoenix Triumphant*, p. 98. As of the summer of 1934, some 30 training schools were in existence. Corum, *The Luftwaffe*, p. 156.
54   Tooze, *The Wages of Destruction*, p. 125, Hooten, *Phoenix Triumphant*, pp. 102 & 104-105, and Corum, *The Luftwaffe*, pp. 165-166.
55   Richard Overy, "German Air Strength, 1933 to 1939: A Note." *Historical Journal*, Vol. 27, No. 2 (June 1984), p. 468.

General Staff officers, and soon established seven officer training schools that by the end of the 1930s were producing 2,500 newly commissioned lieutenants every year.[56] The first *Fallschirmjäger* units were scheduled to begin formation in late 1936, although this was later delayed until the middle of the following year. Meanwhile, on 18 March 1935, responsibility for the 12 existing battalions of flak artillery was transferred from the German Army to the *Luftwaffe*. Entirely motorised and possessing the latest equipment, including the now famous 8.8 cm flak gun, within a year the flak arm grew to seven regiments controlling 32 mixed and nine light flak battalions. To enhance its ability to conduct ground-support, teams of *Flivos* (air liaison officers) were trained and equipped for assignment to army corps and divisional headquarters. To enable *Luftwaffe* air units to keep up with rapidly advancing Army formations, 117 motorised supply columns were created.[57] Although faced with the identical raw material shortages that confronted the Army, the number of aircraft also continued to increase.[58] By 1 April 1936 the *Luftwaffe* possessed 2,680 aircraft, including 1,000 bombers and 700 fighters, now organized into 114 air squadrons. As of 1 October 1938, the number of squadrons grew to a total of 272. Similarly, the total number of personnel increased from 178,000 in 1937 to 370,000 by April 1939.[59] In the wake of the Sudetenland Crisis of 1938, Hitler and Göring ordered a further expansion of the peacetime *Luftwaffe* to a total strength of 21,750 aircraft by January 1942.[60] Although such fantastic figures would never be achieved, by the time the *Luftwaffe* went to war in 1939 the extremely rapid pattern of growth and development of the preceding years, at a cost of 17.2 billion RM, had nonetheless ensured that it was the most modern air force on the European continent.[61]

---

56   From the extremely small cadre maintained by the *Reichswehr*, by April 1939 the *Luftwaffe* officer corps had grown to 16,600 active and 4,900 reserve officers. Hooten, *Phoenix Triumphant*, p. 170.

57   Corum, *The Luftwaffe*, p. 168 & 249-250. For a treatise concerning the development of *Luftwaffe* ground-support organizations and doctrine, see James S. Corum, "The Luftwaffe's Army Support Doctrine, 1918-1941." *Journal of Military History*, Vol. 59, No. 1 (January 1995), pp. 53-76.

58   The exhaustion of foreign currency reserves during 1937 and the resulting steel shortages caused the senior leadership of the *Luftwaffe* to consider a 25 percent reduction in aircraft production and a 66 percent reduction in the programme to expand manufacturing capacity. However, global trade increased by 25 percent during that year, resulting in an increased demand for exports, allowing Germany's leadership to weather the crisis, albeit with reductions to the production of training aircraft and spare parts. Tooze, *The Wages of Destruction*, pp. 232-233.

59   Hooten, *Phoenix Triumphant*, pp. 112 & 277.

60   Included in this figure were to be 7,000 of the newly designed Ju 88 medium bombers, and 800 four-engine He 177 heavy bombers, which were still in development. The projected cost of this massive increase was estimated at 60 billion RM. Tooze, *The Wages of Destruction*, p. 288 & 294.

61   Hooten, *Phoenix Triumphant*, p. 172.

Although the *Luftwaffe* played a key role in Germany's victories during 1939-1941, its establishment and the priority given it did have adverse consequences for the development of the Army. The creation of an air force required vast quantities of capital, industrial plant, raw materials and labour resources that otherwise would have been allotted to the Army. Motor vehicles needed to maintain the mobility of the Army's panzer and motorised divisions were instead allocated to the *Luftwaffe*'s ground organizations. The thousands of available flak guns could have significantly increased the Army's firepower, but the majority were assigned to air defence duties within the Reich where their usefulness was at best debatable. The technical requirements inherent within much of the *Luftwaffe* demanded a disproportionate number of intelligent, highly educated or skilled recruits while romanticized notions of service in the air force attracted large cohorts of young, enthusiastic volunteers.[62] Despite its much larger and equally technical requirements, the Army was forced to make do with whatever personnel remained after the *Luftwaffe* had taken its share.

The competition between the military services for men and resources was exacerbated by the fact that authority regarding rearmament resided with both the *Wehrmacht*'s Office of Economics and Armaments (*Wirtschafts und Rüstungs Amt*) and the civilian Reich Ministry of Economics (*Reichswirtschaftsministerium*) under Schacht, both of which had differing concerns, priorities, and objectives. In 1935, Göring was put in charge of the completing the Four Year Plan, adding yet another competing agency. Finally, the Ministry of Armaments and Munitions was created in 1940 under the leadership of Dr. Fritz Todt. All these agencies ostensibly had their own areas of responsibility, which invariably overlapped with one another and generated considerable antagonism between them, creating stresses between and producing an unnecessary amount of chaos within the overall rearmament effort.

Nonetheless, while the *Luftwaffe* basked in its newly-found strength and prestige, and as the *Kriegsmarine* frantically endeavoured to create an effective surface fleet, the expansion of the German Army had continued at a hectic pace. By the time of the Sudetenland Crisis in 1938, some 42 active divisions of 550,000 men had been established and the formation of an additional two panzer divisions had begun. While consisting principally of light Pz I and Pz II tanks, German armoured formations could nevertheless muster an imposing 2,608 panzers of all types.[63] Although the crisis highlighted glaring deficiencies that illustrated just how unprepared for a major conflict the *Wehrmacht* in fact was, it also had the effect of stimulating war preparations to an even greater degree.[64] On 14 October Göring announced plans for

---

62   From 1939 to 1944 approximately 24 percent of all German males who volunteered for military service joined the *Luftwaffe*; those enlisting with the Army totaled only 29 percent. Kroener, et. al. *GSWW. Vol. V, Part Two*, p. 919.

63   On 1 October 1938, this figure consisted of 1,468 Pz I, 823 Pz II, 182 Befelpanzer, 59 Pz III, and 76 Pz IV. Jentz, *Panzertruppen, Vol. One*, p. 48.

64   For assessments of the opposing military forces and their capabilities during the Sudetenland Crisis, see Williamson Murray, "Munich 1938: The Military Confrontation."

an even greater expansion of the *Wehrmacht*, which included the massive increase of *Luftwaffe* strength mentioned above. For its part, the Army was to accelerate its own production programmes, especially that concerning tanks and heavy artillery, and begin stockpiling reserves of strategic raw materials.[65] Although shortages of steel and other materials during 1939 precluded the possibility of production ever attaining the goals outlined by Göring, the annexation of Austria in 1938 and the occupation of the rump of Czechoslovakia in 1939 resulted in the acquisition of those countries gold and foreign currency reserves. Together with other expedients, this injection of new finance allowed German armament production to continue, at least in the short term.[66] In consequence, despite daunting economic problems and gloomy forecasts of the future, by June 1939 the Army had grown to 51 active divisions with 730,000 personnel.

Emphasis upon the scale of growth experienced by the German Army during the 1930s does not imply that no extremely serious deficiencies existed when it went to war in 1939. Of the 3,195 panzers on strength with the existing 33 panzer battalions on 1 September, there were only 98 Pz III and 211 Pz IV.[67] The remainder were vulnerable light tanks of limited utility, which meant that the panzer arm was forced to play a game of perpetual catch up throughout the war as it struggled to equip its panzer divisions with modern vehicles. While production shortfalls certainly had a role in this development, uncertainty within the Army regarding armour-heavy forces – quite natural given their unproven nature – was also partially to blame. Of the 35.6 billion RM budgeted for the Army's 1937-1941 expansion programme, only 4.7 percent was for the production of tanks and motor vehicles, while guns, artillery, and ammunition was allotted 32 percent. Fortification construction alone received 8.7 percent.[68] Despite the fact that the panzers became the iconic symbol of the German Army among the general public in the post-war period, during the 1930s most of its senior officers remained unconvinced regarding the significance of armour, what its proper role on the battlefield was, and the amount of investment Germany should commit to its development.[69] There was also confusion regarding what type of war

Journal of Strategic Studies, Vol. 2, No. 3 (1979), pp. 282-302, and Peter Gryner, "Czechoslovakia '38: What if They'd Fought." in Command Magazine, (Ed.) *Hitler's Army: The Evolution and Structure of German Forces*. (Conshohocken, PA: 1996), pp. 165-196.

65   Tooze, *The Wages of Destruction*, p. 288.

66   Before the annexation of Austria, German foreign currency reserves had fallen to 90 million RM ($36.15 million U.S.), sufficient to maintain imports for about one month. Absorbing Austria's gold and foreign currency reserves netted Germany 305 million RM ($122.5 million U.S.), while the equivalent of a further $115.75 million U.S. was garnered from the occupation of Czechoslovakia. Hooten, *Phoenix Triumphant*, pp. 162 & 170.

67   Cooper, *The German Army, 1933-1945*, p. 155. Jentz provides the somewhat higher figure of 3,472 panzers of all types. Jentz, *Panzertruppen, Vol. One*, p. 48.

68   Tooze, *The Wages of Destruction*, p. 212.

69   For a synopsis of the various factors and personalities involved in this, see Russell A. Hart, *Guderian: Panzer Pioneer or Myth Maker?* (Washington, DC: 2006), pp. 33-45.

Germany would ultimately fight – offensive or defensive? Limited or total? What role should armour-centric panzer divisions play?[70] Finally, it is important to note that in 1939, 46 out of the 51 active formations were not panzer divisions, and that these required huge amounts of equipment other than tanks.

An even more serious problem for Germany was manpower. By September 1939, the German Army had available 500,000 fully trained and 600,000 partially trained reservists, most of whom were recalled to the colours that same month.[71] With the reserves mobilized, the future expansion of the *Wehrmacht* and the replacement of its personnel casualties would depend upon the number of suitable males that could be obtained from among the civilian population. However, the immense rearmament programs of the 1930s ultimately meant that the German economy was already on a fully mobilized war footing by the end of the decade. While virtually eliminating unemployment, severe shortages of labour already existed by 1938 when the Labour Ministry reported that there were only 293,327 unemployed, barely one percent of the entire available workforce. Of these, no more than 28,000 were fully fit for work.[72] On 31 May 1939, the entire German workforce amounted to 24.5 million German men, 14.6 million German women, and 300,000 people labelled as foreigners or Jews. In consequence, any further withdrawal of males from the civilian sector would result in corresponding shortages of labour within the German economy. In turn, this would have a detrimental effect upon the manufacture of armaments, especially as 50.2 percent of the German workforce was employed on *Wehrmacht* contracts by 1940.[73] As well, the induction of rural conscripts would exacerbate already noticeable shortages of agricultural workers, thereby threatening to resurrect the same food shortages that plagued Germany during the First World War. Making matters worse, many of the males of the optimal recruiting classes, specifically those aged 20-25, were skilled industrial workers, which exempted them from military service. To gain the personnel it needed during the war, the Army would have to conscript large numbers of 35 to 45 year-old veterans of 1914-1918, whose age and previous experiences hardly made them fit the image of youthful, aggressive stormtroopers of post-war public memory.[74]

Few options were available to alleviate the shortages of labour. Despite the widespread belief that the Nazi regime was reluctant or incapable of mobilizing women for work because of societal or ideological concerns, by 1939 a third of all married women and more than one-half of all women between the ages of 15 and 60 were economically

---

70 Deist, "The Road to Ideological War: Germany, 1918-1945", pp. 378-385.
71 Cooper, *The German Army, 1933-1945*, p. 161. For a sense of the parallel Polish military preparations, see Michael Peszke, "Poland's Preparation for World War Two." *Military Affairs*, Vol. 43, No. 1 (February 1979), pp. 18-25.
72 Tooze, *The Wages of Destruction*, p. 260.
73 Ibid, pp. 358-359.
74 Cooper, *The German Army, 1933-1945*, p. 162. Also, see Kroener, "Squaring the Circle: Blitzkrieg Strategy and Manpower Shortage, 1938-1942", pp. 290-291.

active.[75] This represented more than one-third of the entire workforce, whereas the corresponding figure in Great Britain was only one-quarter.[76] With German women already heavily employed, the only real solution was to employ foreign workers and prisoners of war. Even before the invasion of France and the Low Countries in May 1940, 350,000 prisoners of war and 800,000 foreign workers were already employed across Germany.[77] As the manpower squeeze worsened during the war, these figures expanded accordingly.

Regardless of the limitations imposed because of manpower shortages, on 1 September 1939 the mobilized German Army totalled 3,706,104 men, including 105,394 officers – an immense achievement considering the size of the *Reichswehr* less than six years earlier. This would indicate that almost three million German males were withdrawn from the economic workforce for service in the Army. Simultaneously, the *Luftwaffe* and *Kriegsmarine* expanded to 677,000 and 122,000 men, respectively.[78] Continued expansion of the armed forces meant that the number of inducted German males totalled approximately 4.4 million by May 1940.[79] As their husbands were drafted and generous state run family support mechanisms were initiated, the number of employed women also dropped by nearly 300,000 by December 1939.[80] Despite some anxious moments, this huge withdrawal of labour from the civilian economy did not result in a collapse of production. As indicated in Table 1.4, most armament figures actually increased in the months following the outbreak of the war. By closing non-essential industries and services, and transferring the available labour to those areas where it was most needed, and by increasing working hours and efficiency, the number of workers lost to the economy was reduced to 2.4 million. This was further alleviated by the increased use of foreign workers and prisoners of war.[81] Although these measures meant that the most easily accessible labour sources had now been tapped and that henceforth manpower would increasingly become difficult to find,

75　For but one largely overlooked aspect of the participation of women in Germany's war effort, see Evelyn Zegenhagen, "German Women Pilots at War, 1939 to 1945." *Air Power History*, Vol. 10, No. 4 (Winter 2009), pp. 11-27.

76　Tooze, *The Wages of Destruction*, p. 358.

77　Ibid, p. 358. Also, see Richard Overy, " 'Blitzkriegwirtschaft'? Finanzpolitik, Lebensstandard und Arbeitseinsatz in Deutschland, 1939-1942." *Vierteljahrshefte für Zeitgeschichte*, Vol. 36, No. 3 (1988), p. 426.

78　Kroener, et. al. *GSWW. Vol. V: Part One*, p. 959.

79　Of these, some three quarters of a million worked in agriculture, 1.3 million were industrial workers, 930,000 were from the craft sector, 600,000 were shop workers, 600,000 were clerks and civil servants, while a further 200,000 men came from the transport sector. Tooze, *The Wages of Destruction*, p. 360.

80　Kroener, et. al. *GSWW. Vol. V: Part One*, pp. 881-882. Financial support for the families of servicemen amounted to 3.2 billion RM in 1940, and 4.2 billion RM in 1941. Richard Overy, "Mobilization for Total War in Germany 1939-1941." *English Historical Review*, Vol. 103, No. 408 (July 1988), p. 619.

81　Kroener, et. al. *GSWW. Vol. V: Part One*, p. 880.

they nonetheless permitted Germany to manage the problem for the first period of the war.

Confronted by constraints of both personnel and equipment, the German Army was forced to raise its formations in separate *Welle* (mobilization waves), rather than *en masse*. Upon mobilization, the Army was functionally divided into two groups: the *Feldheer* (Field Army), consisting of that part of the Army engaged in operations, and the *Ersatzheer* (Replacement Army), which was responsible for training replacement personnel and raising new formations. A total of 103 divisions were initially mobilized, including six panzer, four *leichte*, four motorised infantry, three *Gebirgs*, and 86 infantry divisions.[82] Of the infantry divisions, these were raised in four distinct *Welle*. The first consisted of the 35 active infantry divisions that had comprised the peacetime army, supplemented by fully trained reservists to fill out their authorized complement. The 16 divisions belonging to the second wave were activated upon mobilization and consisted of fully trained reservists with a cadre of personnel from the existing active divisions. Totalling 21 divisions, the formations of the third wave drew their manpower from the ranks of the partially trained reservists and required four to eight weeks before becoming fully operational. The fourth wave, comprising 14 divisions, was also formed from reservists and stiffened by a smattering of active personnel.[83] As indicated in Table 1.5, the required personnel strengths of these divisions varied considerably.

Ultimately, by the end of the Second World War the German Army had activated no fewer than 35 *Welle*, each of which possessed its own unique Table of Organization and Equipment (TOE). The formations created in each of these *Welle* were tailored to both personnel and equipment availability, and operational requirements. During the Polish Campaign, the bulk of the divisions of the second to fourth waves guarded western Germany against a possible French offensive. As noted above, the training and quality of the personnel of these formations were below those of the active divisions (those of the first wave), while their equipment holdings also tended to be lower, rendering them incapable of major offensive tasks. However, ensconced within the completed fortifications of the *Westwall*, these divisions were perfectly suited to the limited defensive duty to which they were assigned. Moreover, their existence allowed all but eleven of the active divisions, which were fully capable of conducting offensive operations, to be available for the rapid offensive against Poland. Nineteen divisions of the second to fourth waves were also committed to operations in the east where they guarded secondary sectors, flanks, or else served as reserves, thereby releasing the

---

82   In addition, at the start of the Polish Campaign, the improvised *Panzer Division Kempf* was organized from a series of independent Army and *Waffen-SS* units in East Prussia. There also existed a single cavalry brigade. Other ground combat formations included four fully motorised *Waffen-SS* regiments and two *Fallschirmjäger* regiments, the latter organized into the 7. *Flieger Division*.

83   Cooper, *The German Army, 1933-1945*, p. 164, and Kroener, et. al. *GSWW. Vol. V: Part One*, pp. 810-811.

active divisions for more important tasks.[84] While the *Welle* system tended to create an army of diverse capabilities and organizations, it also allowed the Germans to maximize the efficiency of their available resources.[85]

The specific equipment requirements of the various divisions that constituted the German Army on 1 October 1939 are detailed in Table 1.6. This designates the respective equipment consignments (per division) for each of the infantry divisions belonging to the first five waves, the motorised infantry divisions, and the *1. Kavallerie Brigade* based upon their assigned TOE. The needs of the mountain, *leichte*, and panzer divisions are also indicated, but are instead listed as total equipment requirements because of the wide organizational variations that existed amongst these formations.

In terms of material requirements, most sources concur that in September 1939 the German Army faced major shortages of arms and equipment.[86] There is little doubt that some shortages in fact existed – very few armies have ever gone to war equipped with everything they wanted or needed. This was especially true for the Germans given the context and speed of the "Wehrmacht's great leap forward."[87] And yet, despite the universal acceptance of this notion, no comprehensive statistical evaluation of the German Army's material status upon the outbreak of war has ever been produced.

While an exact determination of German material requirements is difficult to ascertain because of a lack of detailed information, it is nonetheless possible to construct a reasonably accurate estimate based upon the available information. Assessing the needs of German field divisions is relatively straightforward, since the material requirements listed in Table 1.6 need only be multiplied by the number of divisions that were then in existence.[88] As noted above, the total equipment requirements of the mountain, *leichte*, and panzer divisions are already known. Ascertaining the needs of the various independent army- and corps-level units is possible by examining the organization of the field army (*Kriegsgliederung des Feldheer*) of 15 January 1940 and then establishing

---

84   Ibid, pp. 813-813.
85   The French Army had a somewhat similar system, whereby the quality of their reserve divisions were assigned the designation 'Category A' or 'Category B' depending upon the training of their reservists and the proportion of the cadre provided by the regular army. J.E. Kaufmann & H.W. Kaufmann, *Hitler's Blitzkrieg Campaigns: The Invasion and Defense of Western Europe, 1939-1940.* (Conshohocken, PA: 1993), p. 50.
86   For example, see Cooper, *The German Army, 1933-1945*, p. 164.
87   Deist, "The Road to Ideological War: Germany, 1918-1945", p. 374.
88   On 1 October 1939 this included 35 infantry divisions belonging to the first wave, some 16 infantry divisions of the second wave, the 25 infantry divisions of the third wave, 14 infantry divisions of the fourth wave, five infantry divisions belonging to the fifth wave, and the four motorised infantry divisions. The *50., 60., 72. Infanterie Divisions* and the *14. Landwehr Division* were formed outside the *Welle* system but were organized and equipped along *3. Welle* lines and have thereby been included in that category.

which of these units existed on 1 October 1939 (see Appendix One).[89] The total equipment requirements of the field army may then be compared to the amount of equipment in stock with the German Army on 1 October 1939 to determine surpluses or shortages. The results of these calculations are illustrated in Table 1.7.

Naturally, large portions of the surplus stocks indicated in Table 1.7 were actually with the various training units and establishments of the *Ersatzheer*. It has not been possible to ascertain precisely what these were because of a lack of the requisite KStN. However, from information that was available, a reasonable estimation can again be made. On 1 October 1939, at least 293 infantry-type (including *Infanterie*, *Schützen*, and *Machinegewehr*) replacement battalions were in existence. According to KStN Nos. 6011 and 6021, each of these generally would have been equipped with three 5 cm mortars and 36 machine-guns, for a total of 879 mortars and 10,548 machine-guns.[90] In terms of units performing reconnaissance duties, KStN No. 6131 indicates that each bicycle replacement squadron (*Radfahr Ersatz Schwadron*) be equipped with 11 machine-guns and three 5 cm mortars. If we apply the same equipment level to all units training to conduct reconnaissance functions, and assume that each battalion had at least four squadrons, the 12 cavalry (*Kavallerie*), reconnaissance (*Aufklärungs*), and bicycle (*Radfahr*) replacement battalions would have needed 528 machine-guns and 144 5 cm mortars. Although KStN No. 6581 actually dates from 1 April 1941, and assuming its requirement of 12 3.7 cm Pak and six machine-guns for each anti-tank replacement (*Panzerjäger Ersatz*) company held true for the same units in 1939, then the 15 four-company *Panzerjäger Ersatz Bataillonen* would have claimed another 720 Pak and 360 machine-guns. No KStN for pioneer units was available, but by substituting in KStN No. 6021 the 22 *Pionier Ersatz Bataillonen*, each of three companies, would need 594 machine-guns. In October 1939 there also existed a total of 90 infantry-type (*Infanterie*, *(Mot.) Infanterie*, *Schützen*, *Landesschützen*) regimental headquarters to control the various replacement battalions, most of which were assigned one infantry anti-tank (*Infanterie Panzerjäger*) and one infantry gun (*Infanteriegeschütz*) company. Again, no exact KStN was available for these units, but by substituting in KStN Nos. 6581 and 6555 these units would have required 1,080 3.7 cm Pak, 720 7.5 cm light

---

89   For the *Kriegsgliederung des Feldheer* of 15 January 1940, see NARA T78 Rolls 402 and 403. For determining when certain units existed, see Tessin, *Verbände und Truppen der Deutschen Wehrmacht und Waffen-SS im Zweiten Weltkrieg, 1933-1945. Bande 1-17*, and the website "Lexikon der Wehrmacht" at http://lexikon-der-wehrmacht.de/

90   KStN No. 6011 specifies that each battalion headquarters be assigned three 5 cm mortars, while KStN No. 6021 requires each infantry replacement company be equipped with nine machine-guns. The estimated battalion total is based on the assumption that each battalion possessed four companies. For a complete list of KStN, see Georg Tessin, *Verbände und Truppen der deutschen Wehrmacht und Waffen-SS im Zweiten Weltkrieg, 1939-1945: Funfzehnter Band – Kriegsstärkenachweisungen (KStN), Taktische Zeichen, Traditionspflege*. (Osnabruck: 1988). The KStN referred to in the text may be found in NARA T78 Rolls 391 to 397.

infantry guns, and 900 machine-guns.[91] The 1939 equipment requirements of the 126 artillery replacement (*Artillerie Ersatz*) battalions are also unknown. Precisely where the artillery pieces used for training purposes were kept is a mystery, as later KStN for these units indicate that each of their three batteries was equipped with two machine-guns apiece and that none were assigned any integral guns.[92] With training units being constantly reshuffled around Germany, it is possible that these were kept by the various artillery training schools or at firing ranges to preclude having to move them, thereby saving vital trucks, fuel, and tires. While the number of guns needed for training purposes is therefore unknown, it would seem that the artillery training battalions would likely have needed at least 756 machine-guns. Based upon all these calculations, the *Ersatzheer* required approximately 13,686 machine-guns, 1,023 mortars, 1,800 Pak, and 720 infantry guns.

Comparing the estimated requirements of the *Ersatzheer* with the surpluses outlined in Table 1.7, the German Army in October 1939 would have been faced with shortages of roughly 300 Pak and 80 infantry guns. However, its leftover equipment would have included about 23,000 machine-guns and 1,400 mortars, as well as a fair proportion of the surplus 307 2 cm flak guns and 2,214 artillery pieces. Germany's circumstances, at least in terms of military equipment, were not entirely as dire as is usually presumed. At the very least, it would seem that upon the outbreak of war the German Army actually possessed enough equipment to at least bring its mobilized field divisions to their assigned levels of TOE.

Fortunately for Germany, its use of *Bewegungskrieg* (a war of movement) meant the campaign against Poland was short and only resulted in moderate personnel and equipment losses. During all its operations in September 1939, the frontline formations of the *Luftwaffe* reported that 330 of their aircraft had been destroyed or written-off and that a further 280 had been severely damaged. These were fully replaced by the acquisition of 640 replacement aircraft received from the factories or repair shops.[93] Although sources vary, the *Wehrmacht* as a whole sustained some 40,000-50,000 casualties.[94] Of the 2,675 panzers committed to the operation, 218

---

91   As noted, KStN No. 6581 (dated 1 April 1941) specified 12 3.7 cm Pak and six machine-guns per *Infanterie Panzerjäger* company. KStN No. 6555 (dated 1 February 1942) indicated that each *(Mot.) Infanterie Geschütz* company be equipped with eight 7.5 cm light infantry and four machine-guns.

92   For instance, KStN No. 6231 (dated to 1 April 1941) indicates only two machine-guns per heavy artillery replacement battery.

93   Kroener, et. al. *GSWW. Vol. V: Part One*, p. 733. *Luftwaffe* personnel losses during the Polish Campaign amounted to 759 men, of whom 539 were aircrew. Hooten, *Phoenix Triumphant*, p. 188.

94   For example, Cooper cites a total of 10,572 killed, 30,322 wounded, and 3,409 missing. Cooper, *The German Army, 1933-1945*, p. 169. Pat McTaggart quotes 8,082 killed, 27,278 wounded, and 5,029 missing. Pat McTaggart, "Poland '39", in Command Magazine, (Ed.) *Hitler's Army*, p. 220. The highest figures for German casualties, which state that 16,000

were listed as being *Totalausfalle* (totally lost), of which 167 were Pz I and Pz II.[95] During September to November, these losses were slowly replaced by the production of 253 new tanks. However, it should be noted that all but 15 of the newly produced panzers were the more battle-worthy medium models, thereby representing a significant improvement to the overall punch of the panzer divisions.[96]

While most German divisions committed to the invasion of Poland endured only moderate casualties, some – principally those engaged in the most intense fighting – had actually sustained heavy losses in a relatively short period of time (see Table 1.8). Of the 164 panzers on strength with the *7. Panzer Regiment*, some 72 were destroyed or disabled during the fighting around Mlawa on the very first day of the campaign.[97] The attempt by the *4. Panzer Division* to storm Warsaw on 8 September resulted in 57-63 of the 120 panzers of its *36. Panzer Regiment* being knocked-out by the Polish defenders within three hours.[98] Consisting of the *1.* and *4. Panzer Divisions*, the *XVI. (Motorisierte) Armeekorps*, which led the advance of *Heeresgruppe Süd* through Poland to the gates of Warsaw, reported the *Totalausfalle* of 166 of its panzers during the campaign, representing 76 percent of the total number of tanks lost by the German Army during the conquest of Poland.[99] Early on 9 September twelve Polish infantry divisions and three cavalry brigades attacked eastwards towards the Bzura River to escape the pocket forming in the Kutno region and reach Warsaw. The three infantry divisions and two cavalry brigades leading the advance slammed into the defending *24.* and *30. Infanterie Divisions* of the *X. Armeekorps*, and in savage fighting quickly managed to overwhelm parts of the latter.[100] The Germans responded rapidly by moving in additional divisions, including the *10., 17.* and *18. Infanterie Divisions*,

were killed, 32,000 wounded, and 5,000 were missing, can be found in Kaufmann & Kaufmann, *Hitler's Blitzkrieg Campaigns*, p. 92.

95   Ibid, p. 91. Kroener, et. al. *GSWW. Vol. V: Part One*, p. 728, cites a somewhat higher number (243), but this appears to include damaged panzers, mainly of the lighter models, which were deemed not worth repairing. The number of panzers committed to the invasion of Poland can be broken down as follows: 993 Pz I, 1,107 Pz II, 167 Pz 35(t) and 38(t), 87 Pz III, 192 Pz IV, and 129 *Befelpanzer* (command tanks). Jentz, *Panzertruppen, Vol. One*, p. 88, presents different figures for the total number of panzers present with the *Feldheer* as a whole.

96   Kroener, et. al. *GSWW. Vol. V: Part One*, p. 728.

97   Jentz, *Panzertruppen, Vol. One*, p. 93.

98   Kaufmann & Kaufmann, *Hitler's Blitzkrieg Campaigns*, p. 85, McTaggart, "Poland '39", p. 215, and Stone, *Fighting for the Fatherland*, p. 322. For an account of this action, see Jentz, *Panzertruppen, Vol. One*, pp. 93-99.

99   *XVI. Armeekorps Meldung – Kraftfahrzeugausfalle von 1-25.9.1939*. NARA T314 Roll 568, Frame 000178.

100 The Poznan Army commanded by General Tadeusz Kutrzeba controlled the Polish vanguard, consisting of the 14th, 17th, and 25th Infantry Divisions and the Podolska and Wielkopolska Cavalry Brigades. Robert Citino, "Beyond Fire and Movement: Command, Control, and Information in the German Blitzkrieg." *Journal of Strategic Studies*, Vol. 27, No. 2 (2004), p. 339.

containing the assault and ultimately destroying the Polish forces trapped around Kutno. The result was the capture of some 150-180,000 Polish prisoners.[101] However, the desperation of the Poles to escape encirclement produced intense combat that lasted until 19 September, and in the process inflicted severe casualties on the participating German divisions, specifically the five infantry divisions noted above. For the German Army this episode of fierce combat in the Kutno-Bzura area, resulting as it did in the rapid accumulation of casualties within a short period of time, was a potent harbinger of worse to come.

With the subjugation of Poland complete, the German Army turned to its next task – the conquest of Western Europe. Between September 1939 and April 1940, training was intensified to address some of the problems that had come to light during the operations in Poland. Some of the older personnel within combat units were exchanged for younger men, and a serious effort was made to improve the quality and quantity of equipment holdings, all which was mainly intended to enhance the combat proficiency of the infantry divisions.[102] Concurrently, five more *Welle* totalling 45 infantry divisions were called up, the existing cavalry brigade was expanded into a division, and the *leichte* divisions were converted into full panzer divisions.[103]

Overall, despite severe manpower and material constraints the Army nevertheless managed to expand the number of its divisions by 45 percent. Simultaneously, the *Luftwaffe* also raised an additional 30 *Kampfstaffeln* and 16 *Jagdstaffeln*, resulting in a 20 percent growth of its frontline aircraft strength between September 1939 and March 1940.[104] In turn, such increases were only possible because of the continued, albeit sometimes irregular, increases in armaments production (see Table 1.9). Although partially mitigated by trade agreements with the Soviet Union, the increase in armaments production is even more remarkable given that German imports had still fallen approximately 80 percent from their pre-war levels.[105] Considering that

101 McTaggart, "Poland '39", p. 217.
102 For instance, the existing *14. Landwehr Division* was upgraded to the *205. Infanterie Division* and assigned to the *3. Welle*. For a full account of these measures, see Williamson Murray, "The German Response to Victory in Poland: A Case Study in Professionalism." *Armed Forces & Society*, Vol. 7, No. 2 (Winter 1981), pp. 285-298.
103 As well, the various units of the *Waffen-SS* and *SS-Totenkopfverbande* were combined into two motorised divisions, while a number of serving and reservist police were formed into the *Polizei Division*. Three infantry divisions (*50., 60.,* and *72. Infanterie Divisions*) were formed from various police, frontier guard and reservist personnel and assigned to the *3. Welle*. Contrary to what is stated in most accounts, the decision to convert the *leichte* divisions into panzer divisions had already been made well before the Polish Campaign. Jentz, *Panzertruppen, Vol. One*, p. 105. The improvised *Panzer Division Kempf* was disbanded and its armoured elements transferred to the *10. Panzer Division*.
104 During the first quarter of 1940, the total number of aircrew increased by 25 percent and that of fully operational aircrew by 34 percent. Hooten, *Phoenix Triumphant*, p. 205 & 207.
105 During 1940 the Soviet Union would supply the following percentages of Germany's raw material requirements: phosphates 74 percent, asbestos 67 percent, chrome ore 65 percent, manganese 55 percent, nickel 40 percent, and 34 percent of all imported oil. Small wonder

armaments production continued to expand at a significant pace, this would seem to validate the assertion made by Adam Tooze that, contrary to the notion that its war effort was purposely constrained because of domestic considerations, by 1939-1940 the German economy was actually "going for broke."[106] As noted in Table 1.10, the result was that the Army's stock of equipment rose dramatically.

Considering the circumstances and shortages under which Germany laboured, the country's production of armaments is truly incredible. But how did these increases in weapons production and equipment stocks impact the divisions of the German Army in the field? By employing the methodology already explained above, it is possible to estimate the requirements of the *Feldheer* on 1 May 1940 and discover the extent to which new production met these needs. Illustrated in Table 1.11 are the individual divisional requirements of all of the various infantry and motorised divisions, the cumulative requirements of all the panzer and mountain divisions, and the material needs of the *1. Kavallerie Division*. Multiplying these requirements by the respective number of divisions shown in Table 1.12 produces the total amount of equipment needed by the German Army's field divisions, while the estimated requirements of the various independent units is derived from the *Kriegsgliederung des Feldheer* dated to 15 January 1940 and from determining which of these smaller units existed four months later (see Appendix Two).[107] The calculations from these estimates are shown in Table 1.13. In terms of the equipment needs of the *Ersatzheer*, by employing the corresponding methodology also explained previously and by adjusting for units that were subsequently created or disbanded, its requirements totalled roughly 14,841 machine-guns, 1,083 5 cm mortars, 1,884 Pak, 48 rocket launchers and 744 infantry guns.[108]

that *Oberst* Eduard Wagner, the Quartermaster General of the German Army, would later remark that, "the conclusion of this [Russo-German] treaty has saved us." Tooze, *The Wages of Destruction*, p. 321.

106   Ibid, pp. 333-338 & 347. For the best synopsis of the contending academic views, see Brett Gore, "Blitzkrieg under Fire: German Rearmament, Total Economic Mobilization, and the Myth of the 'Blitzkrieg' Strategy, 1933-1942." M.A. Thesis. (Calgary, Alberta: 2000), pp. 1-28.

107   For the *Kriegsgliederung des Feldheer* of 15 January 1940, see NARA T78 Rolls 402 and 403. For determining when certain units existed, see Tessin, *Verbände und Truppen der Deutschen Wehrmacht und Waffen-SS im Zweiten Weltkrieg, 1933-1945. Bande 1-17,* and the website "Lexikon der Wehrmacht" at http://lexikon-der-wehrmacht.de/

108   On 1 May 1940, the *Ersatzheer* included 313 infantry-type replacement battalions, 12 reconnaissance-type replacement battalions, 16 *panzerjäger* replacement battalions, 120 artillery replacement battalions, 37 *pionier* replacement battalions, and 93 infantry-type replacement regimental headquarters. For a full listing of these units, see Tessin, *Verbände und Truppen der Deutschen Wehrmacht und Waffen-SS im Zweiten Weltkrieg, 1933-1945. Bande 1-17,* and the website "Lexikon der Wehrmacht" at http://lexikon-der-wehrmacht. de/. The most significant addition at this point was the creation of two *Nebel Ersatz* (rocket-launcher replacement) battalions, each of three batteries. According to KStN No. 6294 (dated 1 April 1941) each of these batteries was to be equipped with two machine-

After deducting the requirements of the *Ersatzheer* from the surpluses indicated in Table 1.13, the result is not the picture of dire shortages and impending doom that is presented within most historical accounts. Instead, it would appear that, in May 1940, the German Army actually possessed a large pool of excess equipment, including 53,220 machine-guns, 7,806 mortars, 2,454 anti-tank guns, 120 infantry guns, and 78 *Nebelwerfer*. Additionally, a large portion of the 2,613 field artillery pieces, 262 light flak guns and 973 armoured cars listed as surpluses would have been in excess of the requirements of the *Ersatzheer* and thereby also part of the pool of extra equipment. This reservoir would have provided the German Army with a ready stock of replacement equipment. Yet given the organization of many of the German divisions committed against Western Europe, questions emerge regarding peculiarities within this excess stock. No fewer than 81 of the 135 infantry divisions fielded by the German Army in May 1940 lacked mortars; another nine had only a small number. Considering that many senior German officers viewed the offensive against Western Europe as akin to a forlorn hope, why were almost eight thousand mortars not issued when so few divisions were lavished with such a vital piece of kit? Furthermore, German divisions were assigned 922 field artillery pieces of either Czech or Polish make, which only exacerbated the logistical difficulties of an operation dependent upon speed. Why German-made guns were not assigned from the surplus stock, or why the foreign-made pieces were not assigned to the *Ersatzheer*, is a mystery.

While many divisions went short or had to make due, it is nonetheless evident that the German Army had considerable stocks of equipment at its disposal, although perhaps not where it actually needed them. This would seem to point to an administrative failure somewhere within the German Army General Staff, its Organizational Branch or the offices of the Chief of Army Equipment, rather than an acute shortage of material. One can only postulate if this was somehow related to the fear and trepidation that permeated the highest echelons of the Army's leadership as it embarked upon a campaign that many of its senior officers viewed as, at best, a risky gamble. Its most vehement critics included *Generaloberst* Fedor von Bock, who commanded one of the three participating army groups and was one of Germany's most reputable commanders:

> [Bock] stopped in on Halder… and implored him to drop that absurd plan. In the process, he reproached Halder for playing with Germany's destiny. The arguments he cited in this connection sounded entirely plausible: "You will be creeping by 10 miles from the Maginot Line with the flank of your breakthrough and hope the French will watch inertly! You are cramming the mass of the tank units together into the sparse roads of the Ardennes mountain country, as if there were no such thing as air power! And, you then hope to be able to lead an

guns and eight rocket launchers. See *OKH Kriegsstarkenachweisungen, Band 13a, Ersatz Einheiten 6105-6549*. NARA T78 Roll 394.

operation as far as the coast with an open southern flank 200 miles long, where stands the mass of the French Army!" He declared that this transcended "the frontiers of reason."[109]

It is possible that equipment was held back simply in case the attack degenerated into a disaster, or that this was some kind of bureaucratic error. More deviously, it could also be related to the anti-Nazi officers scattered about the German Army who may have wanted the offensive in the West to fail to discredit Hitler and his regime, thereby paving the way to a possible *putsch*.[110] All that can be truly argued is that such ambiguities point to the need for greater research into the inner-workings of the German Army and the mechanisms that distributed its military equipment.

Ultimately, these resources were to be vital because the fighting in France and the Low Countries in May to June 1940 actually entailed a great deal of fierce combat and heavy casualties for the *Wehrmacht*. At Gembloux on the 12-15 May and along the Somme and Aisne Rivers on 5-7 June, for example, Allied forces halted the advancing Germans and inflicted severe losses, particularly upon the vaunted panzer divisions (see Table 1.14 for the initial strength of the German panzer divisions).[111] During the period of 10-29 May, as it led the German advance through the Ardennes and into northern France to the English Channel, *Panzergruppe Kleist* sustained 6,052 casualties.[112] By the end of this first phase of the campaign, the *1. Panzer Regiment* (one of the two armoured regiments belonging to the *1. Panzer Division*) had been reduced to just 53 operational panzers from its original 111, while the *7. Panzer Division* was left with just 86 operational panzers from its initial strength of 225.[113] Overall German armour

---

109 Karl-Heinz Frieser, *The Blitzkrieg Legend: The 1940 Campaign in the West*. (Annapolis, MD: 2005), pp. 94-95.

110 Arguments regarding the impact of the German resistance upon Germany's military fortunes may be found in F.L. Carston, "A Bolshevik Conspiracy in the Wehrmacht." *Slavonic and East European Review*, Vol. 47, No. 109 (April 1974), pp. 483-509, and Walter Dunn, *Heroes or Traitors: The German Replacement Army, the July Plot, and Adolf Hitler*. (Westport, CT: 2003). For the resistance to Hitler within the *Wehrmacht*, see Pierre Galante, *Operation Valkyrie: The German Generals Plot Against Hitler*. (New York: 1981), and Peter Hoffmann, *The History of the German Resistance, 1933-1945*. (Cambridge, MA: 1977).

111 See Jeffrey A. Gunsburg "The Battle of the Belgian Plain, 12-14 May 1940: The First Great Tank Battle." *Journal of Military History*, Vol. 56, No. 2 (April 1992), pp. 207-244, and "The Battle of Gembloux, 14-15 May 1940: The 'Blitzkrieg' Checked." *Journal of Military History*, Vol. 64, No. 1 (January 2000), pp. 97-140. For the stand made by the French Army along the Aisne and Somme, see Martin S. Alexander, "After Dunkirk: The French Army's Performance against 'Case Red', 25 May to 25 June 1940." *War in History*, Vol. 14, No. 2 (2007), pp. 219-264.

112 Haupt, *Die 8. Panzer Division im Zweiten Weltkrieg*, p. 80.

113 Stoves, *Die 1. Panzer Division, 1935-1945*, p. 818, and Hasso von Manteuffel, *Die 7. Panzer Division im Zweiten Weltkrieg: Einsatz und Kampf der 'Gespenster Division', 1939-1945*. (Friedberg: 1986), p. 87.

losses (total write-offs or damaged beyond repair) during the campaign amounted to 753 of the committed 2,580 panzers and assault guns, a total of approximately 29 percent (see Table 1.15). Of the losses sustained by the panzers, 81.3 percent occurred during the first phase of the campaign (10-31 May), during which time a total of 217 replacement panzers were dispatched from Germany.[114]

Other equipment losses were moderate when compared to overall stocks, but astoundingly heavy given the dramatic success of the campaign and its short time frame. Between 10 May and 20 June 1940, the German Army sustained the following material losses: 6,198 pistols, 1,103 submachine guns, 14,778 rifles, 4,421 machine-guns, 636 3.7 cm Pak, 531 5 cm and 331 8.1 cm mortars, 154 7.5 cm and 23 15 cm infantry guns, 24 2 cm flak, and 137 10.5 cm FH, 88 15 cm FH, 27 10 cm K, and 6 21 cm field artillery pieces.[115] German industries largely compensated for such losses through the manufacture in May and June of 33,740 pistols, 9,510 submachine guns, 224,051 rifles, 9,610 machine-guns, 520 3.7 cm Pak, 2,000 mortars, 201 infantry guns, 1,115 2 cm flak, and 300 10.5 cm FH, 97 15 cm FH, and 87 heavier field artillery pieces.[116] While vividly illustrating the cost entailed by modern combat, such figures also show that the Germans were certainly capable of making good such material losses, as long as the fighting was kept to a short timeframe and the rate of loss did not climb to catastrophic proportions.

The same could be said for Army personnel losses, which amounted to 154,754 casualties, including 4,906 officers, between 10 May and 20 June (an average of 3,774 per day).[117] With the strength of the Army totalling 4.12 million on 15 April 1940, this represented a casualty rate of 3.8 percent. However, the *Feldheer* amounted to only 3.18 million men and hundreds of thousands of these were deployed to Norway or on occupation duty in Poland. Moreover, only 93 of the 135 divisions committed to the campaign actually saw combat, and many of these were only lightly engaged.[118] As a result, many of the divisions spearheading the German advance endured severe

114 Boog, et. al. *GSWW. Vol. IV*, p. 219, and Klaus Maier, et. al. *Germany and the Second World War. Volume II: Germany's Initial Conquests in Europe.* (Oxford: 1991), p. 290. The replacements dispatched in May consisted of 48 Pz I, 71 Pz 35(t) and 38(t), 71 Pz III, 19 Pz IV, and 8 Befelpanzer. The last of these had arrived at their designated units by 3 June. Jentz, *Panzertruppen, Vol. One*, pp. 134-135.

115 Hans-Adolf Jacobsen, (Ed.) *Kriegstagebuch des Oberkommandos der Wehrmacht (Wehrmachtfuhrungsstab). Band I: 1 August 1940 – 31 Dezember 1941.* (Frankfurt am Main: 1965), p. 1115, henceforth referred to as *KTB OKW, Band I*.

116 Kroener, et. al. *GSWW. Vol. V: Part One*, pp. 725-727.

117 These casualties included 26,455 killed (including 1,253 officers), 111,640 wounded (3,324 officers), and 16,659 missing (329 officers). Jacobsen, (Ed.) *KTB OKW, Band I*, pp. 1121-1122. Other accounts cite alternate specifics in their statistics, but are generally within the same range. See Cooper, *The German Army, 1933-1945*, p. 242, and Maier, et. al. *GSWW. Vol. II*, p. 304.

118 Frieser, *The Blitzkrieg Legend*, p. 36, and Cooper, *The German Army, 1933-1945*, pp. 212-213.

casualties (see Table 1.16). However, sufficient replacements were available to cover the losses sustained during the first stage of the campaign, which one source claims amounted to 61,238 between 10 May and 1 June.[119] Although the actual number dispatched to the front is unknown, prior to the outset of operations the *Ersatzheer* held 88 *Marsch* battalions with 80,000 replacement personnel in readiness to cover any losses.[120] These would have been more than sufficient to allow the Germans to make good their casualties and successfully conduct the second stage of the campaign. Conversely, had casualties been any greater or if the fighting had gone on for longer than it did, given Germany's manpower constraints and the limited pool of replacements available at the start of the campaign, the German Army would doubtlessly have experienced a situation similar to the one it would eventually find itself in when it went to war against the Soviet Union.

Fortunately for the *Wehrmacht*, the campaign in Western Europe successfully concluded before material or personnel losses became a major problem. Indeed, the first phase of the war from September 1939 to June 1940 succeeded beyond the wildest hopes of Germany's military planners and civilian leadership. For the moment, they could relish their achievements with some satisfaction. Despite the odds, Germany had defeated its immediate enemies or else had driven them from the continent. Starting from a very small foundation in 1933, and in spite of inter-service competition for material resources and manpower, the *Wehrmacht* had been developed to formidable proportions. In the face of daunting limitations for labour and raw materials, the production of weapons and equipment had sufficed and continued to increase in quantity. Thanks to the rapidity with which the campaigns of 1939-1940 were successfully concluded, losses of personnel and equipment had stayed within manageable levels. However, as illustrated during particular episodes of the Polish and French campaigns, the very essence of the German way of war – with its focus upon operational manoeuvre and speed to rapidly defeat an adversary – also imposed a level of intensity upon operations that quickly incurred a heavy toll of men and equipment. What might happen when used in a different operating environment, in a conflict of considerably longer duration or against a more robust adversary, remained to be seen.

---

119 Ibid, p. 236.
120 Ibid, p. 212. It should be noted that at least some German divisions possessed organic *Feldersatz* (field replacement) battalions, from which they could draw replacements, including all of the divisions comprising the first wave.

Table 1.1 German Import and Domestic Production of Rubber and Iron Ore, 1932-1939 (Thousands of tons)[1]

Year	Rubber		Iron Ore	
	Natural Rubber Imports	Buna Production	Iron Ore Imports	Domestic Production
1932	50	–	3,254	442
1933	61	–	4,104	828
1934	72	–	6,822	1,372
1935	74	0	9,995	1,849
1936	83	1	8,430	2,259
1937	100	4	9,690	2,759
1938	92	6	10,470	3,360
1939	77	22	10,043	3,928

1 Tooze, *The Wages of Destruction*, p. 228.

Table 1.2 Air Force Expenditures of the Great Powers of Europe, 1933-1939. (Expenses/budget in equivalent US dollars)[1]

Year	Germany		France		Great Britain	
	Expenses (millions)	% Defence Budget	Air Budget (millions)	% Defence Budget	Air Budget (millions)	% Defence Budget
1933	18.09	10.0	5.82	12.7	66.45	15.55
1934	24.59	32.9	9.88	15.9	88.15	15.48
1935	422.57	37.4	13.09	19.2	135.56	19.50
1936	897.17	38.2	17.39	18.5	247.16	26.10
1937	1,313.71	39.4	18.17	18.7	404.04	31.38
1938	2,420.08	34.9	22.12	22.9	669.00	34.89
1939	1,583.13	33.1	97.24	33.1	489.40	36.20
Total	6,679.34		183.71		2,099.76	

1 German expenses for 1939 only represent those funds spent by September. Hooten, *Phoenix Triumphant*, p. 276.

Table 1.3 European Aircraft Production and Proportion of Combat Aircraft, 1933-1939[1]

Year	Germany Combat			Great Britain Combat			Soviet Union Military Aircraft
	Total	Aircraft	%	Total	Aircraft	%	Total
1933	368	197	53.5	1,102	?	?	2,952
1934	1,968	840	42.7	1,108	?	?	3,109
1935	3,183	1,823	57.2	893	499	55.9	2,529
1936	5,112	1,530	30.0	1,830	871	47.6	3,578
1937	5,606	2,651	47.3	2,218	1,294	58.3	4,769
1938	5,235	3,350	64.0	2,828	1,393	49.3	5,469
1939	8,295	4,733	57.1	7,940	3,731	47.0	10,382
Totals	29,767	15,124	50.8	15,709	7,788	49.6	32,788

1 Note that the German figure for aircraft produced in 1939 only includes planes built by 31 August. The number shown for British production in 1939 represents aircraft constructed during the entire year. Hooten, *Phoenix Triumphant*, p. 279.

Table 1.4 German Armament Production, August to December 1939[1]

	August	September	October	November	December
Rifles (K98)	77,677	87,243	88,883	81,016	79,767
SMG	700	960	1,300	1,400	3,550
MG 34	4,101	3,526	2,948	3,300	3,018
2 cm Flak	210	326	510	362	413
8.8 cm Flak	24	41	40	62	40
Mortars	715	719	835	764	835
3.7 cm Pak	289	300	271	287	371
Infantry Guns	50	80	89	81	88
10.5 cm FH	47	83	137	134	137
15 cm FH	62	51	64	35	40
Pz III	20	40	40	35	42
Pz 38(t)	18	21	30	11	–
Pz IV	10	-	20	11	14
PSW	30	48	39	60	43
Trucks	2,167	1,743	2,099	2,039	2,062

1 Kroener, et. al. *GSWW. Vol. V: Part One*, pp. 725-727 & 742-743.

Table 1.5   Authorized Personnel Requirements of German Army Divisions, September 1939[1]

	1 *Welle*	2 *Welle*	3 *Welle*	4 *Welle*	Mtn. Div.	Mot. Div.	Panzer Div.	Leichte Div.	Kav. Bde.
Officers	534	491	578	491	459	492	394	332	192
Officials	102	98	94	99	85	133	115	105	29
NCOs	2,701	2,273	2,722	2,165	2,128	2,456	1,962	1,616	893
Other Ranks	14,397	12,411	14,507	12,264	14,516	13,364	9,321	8,719	5,570
Total	17,734	15,273	17,901	15,019	17,188	16,445	11,792	10,772	6,684

1   Kroener, et. al. *GSWW. Vol. V: Part One*, pp. 814-815.

Table 1.6   Equipment Requirements of German Army Field Divisions based upon assigned TOE, 1 October 1939[1]

		Mortars		Infantry Guns				Howitzers		
Welle	MG	5 cm	8.1 cm	7.5 cm	15 cm	Pak	Flak	10.5 cm	15 cm	PSW
1.	492	81	54	20	6	75	12	36	12	3
2.	466	–	–	26	–	75	–	36	12	3
3.	601	–	–	26	–	75	–	36	12	–
4.	466	–	–	26	–	75	–	36	12	–
5.	534	–	24	–	–	72	–	48[2]		
Mot. Inf. Div.	723	84	54	24	–	72	12	36	12	25
1. Kav. Bde.	136	9	18	12	–	21	–	8	–	6
Mtn. Div. Total	1,027	198	126	42	–	168	12	68	28	–
Leichte & Panzer Div. Total	2,951	321	192	122	–	471	108	212	80	700

1   Specific divisional equipment requirements taken from 1939 German Army and Waffen-SS TOE schematics detailed on the website of Dr. Leo Niehorster, "World War II Armed Forces – Orders of Battle and Organizations." at http://niehorster.orbat.com

2   Instead of artillery of German make, the divisions of the fifth wave were each authorized to have 12 8 cm FK 30(t), 24 10 cm le. FH 30(t), and 12 15 cm s. FH 25(t), all the Czech manufacture.

Table 1.7 Estimated German Field Army Equipment Requirements versus Existing Stock, 1 October 1939

	Army Stock 1.10.1939[1]	Actual Div. Requirements 1939 TOE	Army Troops Requirements 1939 TOE[2]	Total Requirements	Surplus Stock
MG	103,300	55,901	11,200	67,101	36,199
5 cm GrW	5,062	3,699	186	3,885	1,177
8.1 cm GrW	3.959	2,562	120	2,682	1,277
7.5 cm IG	2,931	2,402	42	2,444	487
15 cm IG	367	210	2	212	155
Pak	10,560	8,058	990	9,048	1,512
10 cm NbW	179	–	54	54	125
2 cm Flak	895	588	–	588	307
10.5 cm FH	4,919	3,604	132	3,736[3]	1,183
15 cm FH	2,434	1,164	528	1,692	742
Mountain Guns	213	68	–	68	145
10 cm K 18	400	8	252	260	140
15 cm K 18	25	–	21	21	4
21 cm to 42 cm guns	47	–	47	47	–
PSW	1,076	959	100	1,059	17

1 Kroener, et. al. *GSWW. Vol. V: Part One*, pp. 636-637.

2 A detailed breakdown of the various army- and corps-level units figured into this calculation is illustrated in Appendix One.

3 It should be noted that the guns illustrated as in stock or as requirements only indicates equipment of German manufacture. The previously mentioned requirement of 240 Czech artillery pieces for the divisions of the fifth wave is thereby not included in these estimates.

Table 1.8 Personnel Losses of German Divisions committed to the Polish Campaign, 1939[1]

Division	Killed	Wounded	Missing	Total	Sollstärke	% of Sollstärke
1. Panzer Div.	233	398	–	631	11,792	5.4
4. Panzer Div.	316	547	78	941	11,792	8.0
3. Leichte Div.	103	365	–	468	10,772	4.3
13. (Mot.) Inf. Div.	84	226	121	431	16,445	2.6
1. Gebirgs Div.	484	918	–	1,402	17,188	8.1
2. Gebirgs Div.	188	385	44	617	17,188	3.6
7. Infanterie Div.	170	402	21	593	17,734	3.3
10. Infanterie Div.	352	956	–	1,310	17,734	7.4
17. Infanterie Div.	276	767	–	1,043	17,734	5.9
18. Infanterie Div.	717	1,278	10	2,005	17,734	11.3
21. Infanterie Div.	231	636	–	867	17,734	4.9
24. Infanterie Div.	390	1,017	82	1,489	17,734	8.4
30. Infanterie Div.	795	794	–	1,589	17,734	9.0
44. Infanterie Div.	121	270	44	435	17,734	2.5
221. Infanterie Div.	125	235	–	360	17,901	2.0

1 Rolf Stoves, *Die 1. Panzer Division, 1935-1945.* (Bad Nauheim: 1961), p. 29, Joachim Neumann, *Die 4. Panzer Division, 1938-1943: Bericht und Betrachtung zu zwei Blitzfeldzugen und zwei Jahren Krieg in Russland.* (Bonn: 1989), Werner Haupt, *Die 8. Panzer Division im Zweiten Weltkrieg.* (Friedberg: 1987), p. 58, Dieter Hoffmann, *Die Magdeburger Division: Zur Geschichte der 13. Infanterie und 13. Panzer Division, 1935-1945.* (Magdeburg: 1999), p. 83, Roland Kalteneggar, *Die Stammdivision der deutsche Gebirgstruppe: Weg und Kampf der 1. Gebirgs Division, 1935-1945.* (Graz: 1981), p. 107, Wilhelm Hertlein, *Chronik der 7. Infanterie Division.* (Munchen: 1984), p. 38, August Schmidt, *Geschichte der 10. Division, 10. (Mot.) Infanterie Division, 10. Panzergrenadier Division, 1933-1945.* (Bad Nauheim: 1963), p. 55, Christoph Freiherr von Allmayer-Beck, *Die Geschichte des 21. Infanterie Division.* (Munchen: 1990), p. 636, Tettau, *Geschichte der 24. Infanterie Division, 1935-1945.*, p. 28, Breithaupt, *Die Geschichte der 30. Infanterie Division, 1939-1945.*, p. 62, Anton Schimak, et. al., *Die 44. Infanterie Division: Tagebuch der Hoch und Deutschmeister.* (Wien: 1969), p. 44. Also see *8. AOK Meldung – Gesamtverluste der 8. Armee 1-23.9.1939.* NARA T312 Roll 44, Frame 7556018, and *XVIII. Armeekorps Meldung 25.9.1939.* NARA T314 Roll 594, Frame 000373.

Table 1.9 German Monthly Armaments Production, December 1939 to April 1940[1]

	December 1939	January	February	March	April	Total Production Sept. 39-April 40
MG	3,018	3,801	3,522	3,821	3,828	27,764
3.7 cm Pak	371	251	271	271	277	2,299
5 cm Pak	–	2	–	4	16	22
2 cm Flak	413	370	320	617	676	3,594
8.8 cm Flak	40	99	54	78	74	488
Mortars	835	1,015	915	1,105	1,005	7,193
Infantry Guns	88	92	72	66	75	643
10.5 cm FH/FK	137	122	92	121	139	965
15 cm FH	40	33	28	50	65	366
Pz II	–	2	–	4	19	40
Pz III	42	42	49	51	51	350
Pz IV	14	20	20	24	20	119
Pz 38(t)	–	10	24	31	30	167
StuG III	–	–	3	6	10	19
PSW	43	24	5	16	12	247
Trucks	2,062	1,842	3,467	3,673	3,909	20,834
Towing vehicles	200	203	353	266	585	2,542

1 Kroener, et. al. *GSWW. Vol. V: Part One*, p. 725-727 & 742-743.

Table 1.10 Equipment in Stock with the German Army, 1 October 1939 and 1 May 1940[1]

	1.10.1939	1.5.1940	Percentage increase/decrease
MG	103,300	150,400	+45.6
2 cm Flak	895	1,487	+66.1
3.7 cm Pak	10,560	14,427	+36.6
5 cm GrW	5,062	9,967	+96.9
8 cm GrW	3,959	7,091	+79.1
10 cm NbW	179	288	+60.9
7.5 cm le. IG 18	2,931	3,365	+14.8
15 cm s. IG 33	367	491	+33.8
10.5 cm K18	20	44	+120
10.5 cm FH 16 & 18	4,919	5,538	+12.6
15 cm FH 18	2,434	2,383	- 2.1
10 cm K18	400	709	+77.3
15 cm K 18 & 39	25	177	+608
21 cm – 42 cm guns	47	163	+246.8
Pz I	1,305	1,266	- 3.0
Pz II	991	1,110	+12
Pz III	151	785	+419.9
Pz IV	143	290	+102.8
Pz 35(t)	125	143	+14.8
Pz 38(t)	122	238	+95.0

1 Kroener, et. al. *GSWW. Vol. V: Part One*, pp. 636-637.

Table 1.11 Equipment Requirements of German Army Field Divisions based upon assigned TOE, 1 May 1940[1]

Welle	MG	Mortars		Infantry Guns		Pak	Flak	Howitzers[2]		PSW
		5 cm	8.1 cm	7.5 cm	15 cm			10.5 cm	15 cm	
1.	549	84	54	20	6	75	12	36	12	3
2.	468	–	–	26	–	75	–	36	12	3
3.	549	–	–	26	–	75	–	36	12	–
4.	466	–	–	26	–	75	–	36	12	–
5.	534	–	24	–	–	72	–	48		–
6.	534	–	24	–	–	72	–	48		–
7.	509	–	–	12	–	48	–	24	–	–
8.	521	81	54	18	–	48	–	12		–
9.	439	–	–	–	–	9	–	18		–
Static Inf. Div.	288	–	–	–	–	–	–	48		–
Mot. Inf. Div.	357	57	36	16	–	48	–	24	12	10
1. Kav. Div. Mtn. Div.	317	9	30	22	–	30	–	24	–	13
Total Panzer Div.	1,136	204	138	42	–	171	–	40	8	–
Total	3,365	393	252	146	–	490	120	240	28	510

1 Specific divisional equipment requirements taken from 10 May 1940 German Army and Waffen-SS TOE schematics detailed on the website of Dr. Leo Niehorster, "World War II Armed Forces – Orders of Battle and Organizations." at http://niehorster.orbat.com. Also see *Kriegsgliederung des Feldheer* of 15 January 1940 and of 15 April 1940 in NARA T78, Rolls 402 and 403.

2 At the outset of operations in Western Europe during May 1940, many German divisions were equipped with foreign artillery. The divisions belonging to the fifth and sixth waves each required 12 7.5 cm FK(t), 24 10.5 cm le. FH(t), and 12 15 cm s. FH 25(t), while those of the eighth wave each needed 12 15 cm s. FH 25(t), all of which were of Czech design. The *Sollstärke* of the ninth wave required its formations each be equipped with 18 7.5 cm FK97(p), while that of the static infantry divisions dictated they be equipped with 36 7.5 cm FK97(p) and 12 10 cm K29/36(p). These latter were recently captured Polish artillery pieces. Other artillery not included in this table includes a total of 68 7.5 cm GK15 belonging to the mountain divisions, and 8 10 cm K of the panzer divisions.

Table 1.12 Divisions of the German Army by Type, 1 May 1940

1. Welle	35 infantry divisions
2. Welle	19 infantry divisions
3. Welle	22 infantry divisions
4. Welle	14 infantry divisions
5. Welle	5 infantry divisions
6. Welle	4 infantry divisions
7. Welle	13 infantry divisions
8. Welle	10 infantry divisions
9. Welle	9 infantry divisions
Static	4 infantry divisions
Total Infantry Divisions	135 infantry divisions
Other Divisions	10 panzer divisions
	4 motorised infantry divisions
	3 mountain divisions
	1 cavalry division
Total Number of Divisions	153 divisions

Table 1.13 German Field Army Equipment Requirements versus Existing Stock, 1 May 1940

	Army Stock 1.5.1940[1]	Actual Div. Requirements 1940 TOE[2]	Army Troops Requirements 1940 TOE	Total Requirements	Surplus Stock
MG	150,400	74,691	7,648	82,339	68,061
5 cm GrW	9,967	4,584	227	4,811	5,156
8.1 cm GrW	7,091	3,210	128	3,338	3,753
7.5 cm IG	3,365	2,740	38	2,778	587
15 cm IG	491	210	4	214	277
Pak	14,293	9,466	529	9,995	4,338
2 cm Flak	1,487	540	685	1,225	262
10 cm NbW	288	–	162	162	126
10.5 cm FH 18	5,538	4,284	72	4,356[3]	1,182
15 cm FH 18	2,383	1,164	504	1,668	715
Mountain Guns	354	68	–	68	286
10 cm K 18	709	8	464	472	237
15 cm K 18	177	–	42	42	135
21 cm to 42 cm	163	–	105	105	58
PSW	1,710	712	25	737	973

1 Kroener, et. al. *GSWW. Vol. V: Part One*, pp. 636-637.

2 It should be noted that the equipment requirements of the *Waffen-SS* are not included in these estimates or in the Army's total stock. The three divisions and one regiment of the *Waffen-SS* in existence on 1 May 1940 were authorized the following equipment: 1,737 MG, 213 5 cm GrW, 150 8.1 cm GrW, 54 7.5 cm and 4 15 cm IG, 237 Pak, 36 2 cm Flak, 57 PSW, 72 le. FH, 12 s. FH, and 36 various Czech guns. See 10 May 1940 German Army and Waffen-SS TOE schematics detailed on the website of Dr. Leo Niehorster, "World War II Armed Forces – Orders of Battle and Organizations." at http://niehorster.orbat.com

3 In addition, German divisions and independent units required 576 Czech, 346 Polish, and 28 various German guns that are not included in the figures for artillery shown here.

Table 1.14 Strength of German Panzer Divisions at the Outset of the French Campaign, 10 May 1940[1]

	Pz I	Pz II	Pz 35(t)	Pz 38(t)	Pz III	Pz IV	Befl.	Total
1. Panzer Division	52	98	–	–	58	40	8	256
2. Panzer Division	45	115	–	–	58	32	16	266
3. Panzer Division	117	129	–	–	42	26	27	341
4. Panzer Division	135	105	–	–	40	24	10	314
5. Panzer Division	97	120	–	–	52	32	26	327
6. Panzer Division	–	60	118	–	–	31	14	223
7. Panzer Division	34	68	–	91	–	24	8	225
8. Panzer Division	–	58	–	116	–	23	15	212
9. Panzer Division	30	54	–	–	41	16	12	153
10. Panzer Division	44	113	–	–	58	32	18	265

1 Jentz, *Panzertruppen, Vol. One*, pp. 120-121.

Table 1.15 German Armoured Strength and Losses, May-June 1940[1]

	Total Strength 1.5.1940[2]	Committed in West 10.5.1940	Percentage Committed	Total Losses 10.5-20.6.1940
Pz I	1,077	523	48.6	181
Pz II	1,109	955	86.1	241
Pz 35(t)	143	106	74.1	} 98
Pz 38(t)	238	228	95.8	
Pz III	381	349	91.6	135
Pz IV	290	278	95.9	97
Befelpanzer	244	135	55.3	?
StuG III	23	6	26.1	?
Total	3,505	2,580	73.6	753

1 Maier, et. al. *GSWW. Vol. II*, p. 290, and Boog, et. al. *GSWW. Volume IV*, p. 219.

2 Senger und Etterlin, *German Tanks of World War II*, p. 193.

Table 1.16 Casualties Sustained by German Formations during the French Campaign, May-June 1940[1]

	Killed	Wounded	Missing	Sick	Total
5. Panzer Division	366	1,454	18	226	2,064
7. Panzer Division	682	1,591	285	–	2,558
10. Panzer Division	420	1,488	56	–	1,964
(Mot.) Inf. Regt. 'GD'	221	830	57	–	1,108
1. Gebirgs Division	446	1,362	18	–	1,826
5. Infanterie Division	282	706	17	–	1,005
7. Infanterie Division	280	997	52	–	1,329
10. Infanterie Division	371	1,414	18	–	1,964
21. Infanterie Division	265	801	26	–	1,092
24. Infanterie Division	347	1,086	57	–	1,490
30. Infanterie Division	467	1,301	–	–	1,768
44. Infanterie Division	402	1,192	178	–	1,772
50. Infanterie Division	446	1,106	12	–	1,564
71. Infanterie Division	630	1,911	12	–	2,533
79. Infanterie Division	246	?	?	–	?
208. Infanterie Division	331	1,032	59	–	1,422
258. Infanterie Division	493	?	?	–	?
269. Infanterie Division	224	704	26	–	954
290. Infanterie Division	236	969	92	–	1,297*
291. Infanterie Division	458	1,139	–	–	1,587
292. Infanterie Division	248	739	45	–	1,032
Polizei Division	137	527	45	–	704

* Only for the period of 4-8.6.1940.

1 Plato, *Die Geschichte der 5. Panzer Division, 1938-1945*, p. 106, Manteuffel, *Die 7. Panzer Division im Zweiten Weltkrieg*, p. 117, Albert Schick, *Die 10. Panzer Division 1939-1943*. (Koln: 1993), p. 237, Schmidt, *Geschichte der 10. Division, 10. (Mot.) Infanterie Division, 10. Panzergrenadier Division, 1933-1945*, p. 237, Spaeter, *Die Geschichte des Panzerkorps Grossdeutschland, Vol. I*, p. 194, Kalteneggar, *Die Stammdivision der deutsche Gebirgstruppe*, p. 149, Adolf Reincke, *Die 5. Jager Division 1939-1945*. (Friedberg: 1980), p. 55, Hertlein, *Chronik der 7. Infanterie Division*, p. 49, Allmayer-Beck, *Die Geschichte des 21. Infanterie Division*, p. 90, Tettau, *Geschichte der 24. Infanterie Division, 1935-1945*, p. 28, Breithaupt, *Die Geschichte der 30. Infanterie Division, 1939-1945*, Schimak, et. al., *Die 44. Infanterie Division*, p. 108, Arbeitsgemeinschaft "Das Kleeblatt". *Die 71. Infanterie-Division im Zweiten Weltkrieg 1939 - 1945. Gefechts- und Erlebnisberichte aus den Kämpfen der "Glückhaften Division" von Verdun bis Stalingrad, von Monte Cassino bis zum Plattensee.* (Hildesheim: 1973), p. 102, Hans Sanger, *Die 79. Infanterie Division*. (Friedberg: 1979), p. 45, Pflanz, *Geschichte der 258. Infanterie Division, Band I*, p. 133, Helmut Romhild, *Geschichte der 269. Infanterie Division*. (Bad Nauheim: 1967), p. 83, Bauer, *290. Infanterie Division, 1940-1945*, p. 33, Conze, *Die Geschichte der 291. Infanterie Division, 1940-1945*, p. 33, Nitz, *Die 292. Infanterie Division*, p. 214, and Friedrich Husemann, *Die Guten Glaubens Waren: Geschichte der 4. SS-Polizei Panzergrenadier Division, Teile I.* (Osnabruck: 1971), p. 34.

2

Preparing for Barbarossa, June 1940 to June 1941

> You are certainly right to be anxious, based on your calculations, but…it takes a little luck, too, to conduct a war.
>
> Franz Halder, Chief of Staff of the German Army
> November 1941.[1]

As the German Army basked in the glow of its triumph following the capitulation of France, concerns regarding the availability of manpower and the production of war materials were temporarily forgotten. Of Germany's enemies, only Great Britain and its dominions remained and its situation was deemed so hopeless that many Germans considered peace to be imminent. On 23 June 1940, Hitler went so far as to order the disbandment of 35 of the Army's 155 divisions.[2] Older personnel, primarily veterans of the First World War, were to be discharged and sent home. This euphoria was both premature and short-lived. Despite his hopes to the contrary, by the beginning of July it was obvious to Hitler that Britain had no intention of agreeing to a negotiated peace with Germany.[3] Efforts to intimidate and bluff the British into an early peace through an aerial campaign (the famous Battle of Britain) and blatantly obvious invasion preparations (codenamed Operation Sealion) would continue until the autumn, but neither measure was really attractive or practicable, and both operations faced considerable institutional resistance from the *Luftwaffe* and the *Kriegsmarine*.[4] It was clear

1 Otto Eckstein, "Maschinenschriftliche Aufzeichnung von Oberst a. D. Otto Eckstein uber General E. Wagner, seine Arbeitsgebeit Quartiermeisterwesen und den Aufbau seiner Dienststelle," in BA-MA N 510/27 (Wagner papers), pp. 19-20, as quoted in Megargee, *Inside Hitler's High Command*, p. 137.
2 David Irving, *Hitler's War*. (New York: 1990), p. 300.
3 For a synopsis of Hitler's hopes and the various circumstances that influenced his strategic policy making, see Ibid, pp. 297-317. For a broader study, see Hillgruber, *Hitlers Strategie: Politik und Kriegsfuhrung 1940-41.*
4 Richard Muller notes that the *Kriegsmarine* in particular was "obstructionist and unenthusiastic", while the *Luftwaffe* viewed an aerial campaign against England as "an unpleasant aberration." Muller, *The German Air War in Russia*, p. 24. Hooton concludes

that Germany had to re-evaluate its long-term strategy versus Britain and prepare for a prolonged struggle of economic attrition.

The fundamental problem for Germany was that this was exactly the type of conflict it was the least capable of fighting. As the requisite naval and air forces were slowly accumulated and the impact of their operations was gradually felt, a protracted economic war against Great Britain could potentially take years before becoming effective. Moreover, the amplified production of aircraft and naval vessels entailed the increased use of raw materials that were already stretched thin. Although Germany had seized considerable quantities of raw materials through its conquests, these stockpiles were finite.[5] While the labour and industrial resources of Western Europe were currently at its disposal, this advantage was blunted by the fact that Germany now had to provide food, coal and oil to these same regions from its own constrained resources. Of these, the greatest concern was for the availability of food, especially after the poor European harvests of 1940-1941 witnessed a decline in the production of grain measured in the millions of tons. Caused by the removal of nitrogen-based fertilizers, manpower, and draught animals, the decline in grain production had the tertiary effect of causing farmers to cull their livestock for lack of animal feed. Prior to this, planners had already concluded in 1939 that Germany itself, even under optimal circumstances, could only produce 83 percent of its own food requirements.[6] Unless new sources of grain could be found, Germany's leaders were confronted by the same collapse of food production that had imperilled their forbearers during 1914-1918.[7]

that the *Luftwaffe* prepared for the Battle of Britain with "extraordinary lethargy" because of expectations that the British would agree to peace. In order to facilitate and encourage the British to negotiate, Hitler initially forbade terror attacks on English cities, while Göring stressed to the *Luftwaffe* command that "...every effort should be made to avoid unnecessary loss of life among the civilian population." See Hooton, *Eagle in Flames: The Fall of the Luftwaffe*, pp. 16-21. Also, see William L. Shirer, *The Rise and Fall of the Third Reich*. (New York: 1960), pp. 752-774. In contrast, Corum argues that the *Luftwaffe* leadership had no problem with having to conduct a strategic air war against Britain, but stresses that it lacked the force structure, intelligence information, and time needed to produce success. Corum, *The Luftwaffe*, pp. 280-284.

5   For example, approximately 790,000 tons of fuel had been captured during the occupation of Western Europe. Together with the lowered pace of operations following the capitulation of France, this permitted the accumulation of significant reserve stocks, which by 1 September 1940 totaled just over 2 million tons. In contrast, fuel stocks on 1 April had amounted to only 918,000 tons. Maier, et. al. *GSWW. Vol. II*, p. 264.

6   Jonathan Steinberg, "The Third Reich Reflected: German Civil Administration in the Occupied Soviet Union, 1941-1944." *English Historical Review*, Vol. 110, No. 437 (June 1995), p. 630.

7   Tooze, *Wages of Destruction*, pp. 411-420. Also, see Jason Crouthamel, "Nervous Nazis: War Neurosis, National Socialism and the Memory of the First World War." *War & Society*, Vol. 21, No. 2 (October 2003), pp. 55-75. For an indication of the role of food in the decision making process of Germany's previous leaders, see N.P. Howard, "The Social and Political Consequences of the Allied Food Blockade of Germany 1918-19." *German History*, Vol. 11, No. 2 (June 1993), pp. 161-188.

Ultimately, it was precisely this conundrum – the constricted availability of food, fuel and raw materials versus the prospect of a long, grinding war of economic attrition – that spurred Hitler's realization that Germany had to secure the resources it needed if the conflict was to be continued. Of those regions within reasonable reach of Germany's military capabilities, only the vast territories of the Soviet Union contained all the resources, and in sufficient quantity, that were required. Although the Soviets faithfully supplied considerable quantities of grain, oil, and other raw materials in accordance with the trade agreements established as part of the August 1939 non-aggression pact, Germany's dependence upon the Soviet Union in this regard was a continual cause for concern. The sheer scale of Soviet imports meant that Germany's wartime economy and industrial production was heavily dependent upon their continued availability, especially since it had no other sources of many of the specific raw materials being imported.[8]

However, the continued flow of this trade rested upon Soviet intentions and good will. These were thrown into question during the summer of 1940 when a succession of events led to increased tensions and a steady deterioration of Russo-German relations. On 23 May 1940, German intelligence agencies noted increased Soviet troop movements into the Baltic States and towards the Romanian border.[9] This was followed on 23 June by new Soviet demands upon Finland for territorial concessions in the vital nickel producing region of Petsamo, from which Germany obtained 60 percent of its nickel. Three days later, Soviet Foreign Minister and People's Commissar Vyacheslav Molotov presented the Romanian ambassador with an ultimatum demanding the immediate surrender of the provinces of Bessarabia and Northern Bukovina. Although the Romanians were inclined to fight, German diplomats pressured them to accede to Russian demands. Hostilities would threaten Romania's oil production, upon which Germany was utterly dependent, as this was its primary source of crude oil.[10] Moreover, conflict in Romania could potentially spread throughout the Balkans,

8   During the first twelve months following the signing of the pact, the Soviet Union supplied Germany with approximately 800 million RM worth of commodities, including 1 million tons of oil, one million tons of grain, 800,000 tons of iron ore, 500,000 tons of phosphate, 100,000 tons of cotton, 100,000 tons of chrome ore, 80,000 tons of manganese, 10,800 tons of copper, 1,575 tons of nickel, 985 tons of tin, and 1,300 tons of raw rubber. Boog, et. al. *GSWW. Vol. IV,* p. 115. Alternative statistics can be found in Edward E. Ericson, *Feeding the German Eagle: Soviet Economic Aid to Nazi Germany, 1933-1941.* (Westport, CT: 1999), pp. 195-199, and Geoffrey Roberts, *Stalin's Wars: From World War to Cold War, 1939-1953.* (New Haven, CT: 2006), p. 42.
9   In September and October 1939, the Soviet Union had forced the Baltic States into a series of mutual assistance treaties that permitted the Soviets to station troops at a number of sea and air bases throughout these countries.
10   Romanian oil deliveries to Germany amounted to 1,556,000 tons in 1939 and 1,304,800 tons in 1940. Of equal importance, during 1940 Romania food exports to Germany amounted to 979,866 tons. Mark Axworthy, *Third Axis – Fourth Ally: Romanian Armed Forces in the European War, 1941-1944.* (London: 1995), pp. 18-21 & 30.

which Germany was anxious to avoid given the key role the region played in sustaining its wartime economy.[11] Militarily, Germany was in no position to intervene as the preponderance of its ground forces were still stationed in Western Europe, while only a handful of low-grade formations guarded Poland.[12] In contrast, between September 1939 and December 1940, the size of the Red Army deployed in the western districts of the Soviet Union had expanded from two to four million men.[13] Without German assistance, Romania was forced to accept the Soviet demands and on 28 June the Red Army occupied the two provinces. This was followed by the incorporation of the Baltic States into the Soviet Union on 21 July. Although assigned to the Soviet sphere of influence under the protocols of the non-aggression pact, the complete absorption of the Baltic States into the Soviet Union entailed significant economic repercussions for Germany, since it had been the recipient of approximately 70 percent of all Baltic exports – including copious amounts of food and oil.[14] When combined, Soviet actions against Finland, Romania, and the Baltic States during the summer of 1940 appeared to represent a coherent effort to make Germany even more dependent upon Soviet exports through the control of vital resource areas. This economic dependence, and its potential to serve as a means of exerting political pressure (which some German diplomats had already taken to calling 'Soviet blackmail'), was highlighted in early August when the Soviet Union briefly suspended exports because of the dispute regarding the Balkans and by Germany's failure to pay for more than half of the materials it had thus far received.[15]

In response, Germany moved to forestall further Soviet encroachments into areas it viewed as being critical for both its economic independence and long-term survivability. On 25 August, OKW ordered the transfer of an additional ten divisions to Eastern Europe, "to demonstrate the presence of the German Army."[16] These included two panzer divisions whose task would be to secure the oilfields around Ploesti if the situation in the Balkans deteriorated any further. Five days later, Germany and Italy presided over the signing of the Second Vienna Arbitration Treaty that forced Romania to cede considerable territories to Hungary and Bulgaria in exchange for German and Italian security guarantees. Germany's assurances regarding the safety

11   See Gerhard Schreiber, et. al. *Germany and the Second World War. Volume III: The Mediterranean, South-East Europe, and North Africa, 1939-1941*, pp. 342-376.
12   In response, OKH issued instructions for the immediate transfer of 15 divisions to Poland from Western Europe on 26 June 1940. Stahel, *Operation Barbarossa and Germany's Defeat in the East*, p. 34.
13   H. Koch, "Hitler's 'Programme' and the Genesis of Operation 'Barbarossa'." *Historical Journal*, Vol. 26, No. 4 (December 1983), p. 911.
14   Ibid, p. 899. Estonia possessed a modest shale oil industry that produced approximately 120,000 tons of oil per year. Arnold Krammer, "Fueling the Third Reich." *Technology & Culture*, Vol. 19, No. 3 (July 1978), p. 409.
15   H. Koch, "Hitler's 'Programme' and the Genesis of Operation 'Barbarossa'.", p. 898, and Boog, et. al. *GSWW. Volume IV*, p. 131.
16   Barry A. Leach, *German Strategy against Russia, 1939-1941*. (Oxford: 1973), p. 56.

of its remaining territories effectively countered Soviet moves into Romania and the Balkans, for the first time, through the overt threat of military force.[17] This was followed on 22 September by an agreement with Finland allowing Germany to move troops to northern Norway through its territory. Simultaneously, the number of troops stationed in the far north of Norway was increased in case the need arose to rapidly intervene in the Petsamo region, while German weapons sales to Finland were also increased. On 27 September, the signing of the Tripartite Pact firmly established the alliance of Germany, Italy, and Japan, who were shortly thereafter joined by Hungary, Romania and Slovakia.[18] Back in Romania, the first elements of a German Military Mission began to arrive on 12 October, ostensibly to train the Romanian Army and Air Force, but with the main task of safeguarding the oilfields.

The initial bellicose response to Soviet moves towards Finland and the Balkans was then followed by an attempt to resolve Russo-German disagreements and bring the Soviet Union into a larger anti-British alliance, or continental bloc.[19] Following a Soviet request for discussions to reconcile Russo-German differences and clarify respective areas of influence, Molotov travelled to Berlin where he met with Hitler and the German Foreign Minister, Joachim von Ribbentrop. During the course of 12-13 November, Hitler and Ribbentrop endeavoured to convince Molotov of the opportunities, such as expansion into south-central Asia, which awaited the Soviet Union should it join the Tripartite Pact or if it at least increased its cooperation with Germany. Unimpressed with the vagueness of the German proposal, Molotov pressed for German recognition of Soviet interests in Finland and the Balkans, including the likely annexation of Finland and the establishment of Soviet air and naval bases in Bulgaria and Turkey. Hitler concluded the meeting by responding that, for economic reasons, Germany viewed the occupation of these regions, at least for the duration of the war with Great Britain, to be against its interests. On 25 November the Soviet Union formally replied to the German proposals, again reiterating that German recognition of its interests in Finland and the Balkans was a vital precondition for signing the Tripartite Pact. For Hitler this was unacceptable since a Soviet occupation of these areas would only increase Germany's dependence, and arguably marks the point at which he firmly resolved to invade the Soviet Union.[20]

---

17   H. Koch, "Hitler's 'Programme' and the Genesis of Operation 'Barbarossa'.", p. 907.
18   During 1941 Bulgaria, Yugoslavia, and Croatia also became signatories of the Tripartite Pact.
19   Hitler's meetings with Franco and Petain in late October had likewise attempted to bring Spain and Vichy France into such an alliance, but both proved inconclusive as neither Franco nor Petain were prepared to undertake such a step.
20   Currently, there are four interpretive threads regarding Hitler's motivations for invading the Soviet Union. The first, which has been detailed on the preceding pages, supposes that this stemmed from a largely rational assessment of Germany's strategic position following the surrender of France and Britain's refusal to come to terms. See H. Koch, "Hitler's 'Programme' and the Genesis of Operation 'Barbarossa'." and Tooze, *Wages of Destruction*, pp. 424-425.

By this point, German military planning for war with the Soviet Union was already well advanced. At a meeting at the Berghof with his service chiefs on 31 July, Hitler announced his intention to invade and crush the Soviet Union in a short campaign scheduled for the following year. The primary goal was to obtain resource-rich areas containing those items of which the Third Reich found increasingly scarce, particularly grain and oil. From the outset, German planners determined that the campaign would have to be of limited duration, lest Germany's own shortages of men, equipment, and raw materials made themselves felt, and before the Soviet Union had the opportunity to mobilize fully its own resources. To achieve this, the Red Army had to be quickly destroyed in a series of encirclement battles, preferably as close to the frontier as possible to mitigate the effects of time and space upon German logistics.[21] The invasion, codenamed Barbarossa, would hinge upon speed and the assumption that it was possible to annihilate Soviet military capabilities within a few months, if not weeks.

While contingency planning for a possible conflict with Russia had been in development prior to the meeting at the Berghof, Hitler's declaration signalled the beginning of an intense period of preparation as the *Wehrmacht* readied itself for the greatest

The second, which is frequently grouped together with the first, focuses upon the seemingly haphazard and opportunistic nature of Hitler's policies, and argues that the decision to attack Russia was a response to a perceived opportunity to do so. See Gerald Reitlinger, *The House Built on Sand: Conflicts of German Policy in Russia, 1939-1945*. (New York: 1960), A.J.P. Taylor, *The Origins of the Second World War*. (London: 1961), and E.M. Robertson, *Hitler's Pre-War Policy and Military Plans, 1933-1939*. (London: 1963).

A third interpretation primarily views the invasion of Russia as being part of a long-term program based upon Hitler's racial and ideological perceptions of an inevitable struggle against 'Jewish Bolshevism' and the acquisition of *Lebensraum*. For just a few works championing this argument, see Hillgruber, *Hitlers Strategie: Politik und Kriegführung, 1940-1941*, Gerd R. Ueberschar, "Hitlers Entschluss zum 'Lebensraum' – Krieg im Osten. Programmatisches Ziel oder militarstrategisches Kalkul?" in Gerd R. Ueberschar and Wolfram Wette, (ed.) *'Unternehmen Barbarossa': Der deutsche Uberfall auf die Sowjetunion 1941*. (Paderborn: 1984) and Norman Rich, *Hitler's War Aims, Volume One: Ideology, the Nazi State, and the Course of Expansion*. (New York: 1973).

The final interpretation, largely based upon German wartime propaganda and the postwar writing of senior German officials and officers, maintains that the invasion was undertaken to preempt an inevitable Soviet attack. This latter view has been resurgent in recent years, mainly because of the controversy and debate surrounding Victor Suvorov, *Icebreaker: Who Started the Second World War*. (London: 1990). For an indication of the controversy and contentiousness that still rages between these viewpoints, see H.W. Koch, "Operation Barbarossa: The Current State of the Debate." *Historical Journal*, Vol. 31, No. 2 (June 1988), pp. 377-390.

21   The best summaries detailing the evolution of the planning for the invasion of Russia may be found in Leach, *German Strategy against Russia, 1939-1941*, Boog, et. al. *GSWW. Vol. IV*, Gordon Grant, *Barbarossa: The German Campaign in Russia. Planning and Operations, 1940-1942*. (Victoria, BC: 2006), and Stahel, *Operation Barbarossa and Germany's Defeat in the East*.

challenge it had yet to face. The supreme challenge was to create the requisite number of divisions for the field army, which would require prodigious quantities of new men and equipment. To crush the Red Army and to ensure victory in a single campaign, Hitler ordered that the Army be expanded to a total of 180 divisions. This came only five weeks after his previous instructions of 23 June that ordered the reduction of the Army to 120 divisions. What is more, the number of armoured formations doubled from ten to 20 divisions, and the number of motorised infantry divisions increased from four to ten. Already having to cope with the creation of these new mechanized formations, the Army would now also have to create at least 40 new infantry divisions. All told, this meant that the Army would have to increase the number of its divisions by 38 percent within ten months.

Fortunately for German planners, the complex task of increasing the size of the Army in preparation for the war against Russia had already commenced with the expansion of the number of panzer and motorised divisions. In fact, the first of these had already been established prior to the meeting at the Berghof when the *60. Infanterie Division* was converted to the *60. (Motorisierte) Infanterie Division* on 17 July. Between October and November, a further seven infantry divisions were converted to motorised divisions.[22] Most elements redundant to the requirements of the TOE of motorised divisions transferred to the new panzer divisions to flesh out their ranks.[23] The creation of new panzer divisions began on 1 August with the formation of the *11. Panzer Division*. Two other panzer divisions were established later that month, followed by two in October and four in November. The last of the new armoured formations, the *12. Panzer Division*, was created on 10 January 1941. Cadres were drawn from two motorised and four infantry divisions that were disbanded, while additional personnel transfers, drafts of fresh recruits, and the incorporation of a number of smaller units them brought them up to full strength.[24] In North Africa, the *5. Leichte Division* was

---

22   These were the *3., 10., 14., 16., 18., 25.,* and *36. Infanterie Divisions.* The new motorised divisions they created retained their numerical designations. For detailed histories concerning the creation and organization of German divisions during the Second World War, see Tessin, *Verbande und Truppen der Deutschen Wehrmacht und Waffen-SS im Zweiten Weltkrieg, 1933-1945. Bande 1-17.*

23   Standard German infantry divisions at this stage of the war consisted of three infantry regiments of three battalions each, one artillery regiment with four battalions, and anti-tank, engineer, and reconnaissance battalions. Motorised divisions were based upon two motorised infantry regiments, each of three battalions, an artillery regiment of three battalions, and accompanying support elements. Hence, upon conversion to a motorised division, one infantry regiment and one artillery battalion from each disbanded infantry division remained leftover for service elsewhere.

24   The disbanded divisions were the *2.* and *13. (Mot.) Infanterie Divisions,* and the *4., 19., 27.,* and *33. Infanterie Divisions.* For additional details concerning the creation of new panzer divisions in 1940, see Jentz, *Panzertruppen, Vol. One,* pp. 142-150. Useful details concerning the evolution of German armoured units may also be found in W.J.K. Davis, *Panzer Regiments: Equipment and Organization.* (New Malden, Surrey: 1978).

created on 18 February from the various independent panzer and motorised units that had been transported to Libya to support the Italians.[25] Altogether, 19 new panzer or motorised divisions were established between the summer of 1940 and the spring of 1941.

Organizationally, the panzer divisions were reduced to a single panzer regiment consisting of either two or three battalions. While some historians have argued that this reduction represented a critical weakening of the armoured striking power of these divisions, the significance of this development has usually been exaggerated. Admittedly, the tank strength of panzer divisions decreased from an average of 258 tanks per division during the French campaign, to 206 at the outset of the invasion of Russia.[26] However, the addition of a second motorised infantry regiment increased the staying power of these divisions in combat. This augmentation was critical since, as Dennis Showalter, has noted, "There never seemed to be enough infantry... to cope with the near-simultaneous demands of breaking through defence lines, mopping up bypassed positions, securing exposed flanks, and consolidating captured ground in the face of counterattacks..."[27] Moreover, increased numbers of armoured half-tracks (*Schützenpanzerwagen*, or SPW) transported these infantrymen into battle. Although most infantry would still ride in trucks, the armour and ability of the SPW to move over rough terrain permitted at least some of the infantry to keep up with the advancing panzers off-road and therefore resulted in improved tank-infantry cooperation.[28] In addition, whereas the artillery regiments of most panzer divisions had previously possessed only two light artillery battalions, each was now assigned an additional heavy artillery battalion equipped with eight 15 cm howitzers and four 10 cm cannons as an organic element of its establishment. The panzer divisions were also provided with independent light anti-aircraft battalions and self-propelled infantry gun companies to supplement their firepower.

Similarly, the quality of the armour within the panzer divisions improved significantly. Of all the armour initially committed against France in May 1940, approximately 57 percent had been the lightly armed and armoured Pz I and Pz II. The more combat-worthy models (Pz 35t, 38t, III, IV and assault guns) had comprised only 38 percent of the tank force, with the balance being made up of command tanks.

---

25   On 1 August 1941 this division was converted into the *21. Panzer Division*.

26   Divisional averages derive from the comparison of figures provided in Jentz, *Panzertruppen, Vol. One*, pp. 120-121 & 206.

27   Dennis Showalter, *Hitler's Panzers: The Lightning Attacks that Revolutionized Warfare*. (New York: 2009), p. 135.

28   The actual number of SPW with each panzer division varied considerably and is difficult to establish with any certainty. The *1. Panzer Division* may have been equipped with sufficient numbers to outfit two full infantry battalions, while the *10. Panzer Division* may have had enough for one battalion. The *14., 16.,* and *19. Panzer Divisions* had no SPW at the outset of the campaign, while the remaining divisions only had enough to equip a single infantry company.

In contrast, at the outset of the invasion of Russia only 31 percent of the committed German tank fleet consisted of light Pz I and II, while the number of more combat capable models of panzers and assault guns now comprised 63 percent.[29] Further increasing the quality of German armour was the introduction of a new series of Pz III models (specifically series G to J), in which 30 mm of frontal armour was added and the more powerful 5 cm L/42 gun replaced the previous 3.7 cm main armament. As well, the stock of assault guns (*Sturmgeschütz*, or StuG), equipped with a 7.5 cm L/24 main gun, had increased substantially and 11 independent battalions (each with 21 StuG) were available at the outset of operations in the East. Further improvements in armour penetration came in April 1941, when orders were issued to equip the J series of the Pz III (and any other of the type undergoing overhaul in Germany) with the long-barrelled 5 cm L/60 main gun, which had twice the muzzle velocity of the short L/42.[30] By June 1941, 76 percent (1,090) of the total stock of 1,440 Pz III consisted of improved versions with better guns and armour.[31] As shown in Table 2.1, many of these improved versions had found their way into the panzer divisions by the time Barbarossa began.

Overall, the organizational transformation of the panzer divisions at this stage of the war was part of a longer, continuous evolution that sought to attain the optimal mix of infantry, artillery, and armour, as well as mobility and firepower.[32] The incorporation of improved armoured vehicles and increased firepower meant that the panzer divisions invading Russia were *qualitatively* stronger than their predecessors. Another factor to consider was the sheer geographic space that had to be covered in European Russia – operations against France had encompassed 80,500 square kilometres, while against Russia the total would be over 1.6 million square kilometres.[33] Increasing the number of available panzer divisions meant that German field commanders would now have more armoured formations with which to conduct their operations. This was

---

29   Sources vary as to the number of armoured vehicles initially deployed, but it would appear that at least the following were initially committed to Operation Barbarossa:

| Pz I | 337 | Pz 35t | 155 | Pz III | 973 | Befpz. | 225 | Total | 3,903 |
| Pz II | 890 | Pz 38t | 625 | Pz IV | 439 | StuG | 259 | | |

See Jentz, *Panzertruppen, Vol. One*, pp. 193 & 206. The total number was in fact greater since no statistics could be found for the *40. Panzer Battalion Z.b.V.* deployed in northern Finland, nor the *102. Panzer (Flamm) Btl.* that was at least partially equipped with captured French Char B1 tanks converted into flame-throwing vehicles. The number of assault guns shown represents the establishment of the 11 assault gun battalions participating in the offensive (231) and those assigned to *Waffen-SS* divisions and *(Mot.) Infanterie Regiment Grossdeutschland* (28).

30   Senger und Etterlin, *German Tanks of World War II*, p. 37.

31   Ibid, Appendix 2.

32   Showalter, *Hitler's Panzers*, p. 135. Also, see Jentz, *Panzertruppen, Vol. One*.

33   Cooper, *The German Army, 1933-1945*, p. 270.

especially vital given the key role encirclement operations had within German designs to secure victory in a single campaign.[34]

Concurrent with the formation of the armoured and motorised divisions was the creation of a large number of infantry divisions. Drawing upon cadres from existing divisions and supplemented by drafts of fresh recruits, this began in October 1940 with the establishment of ten infantry divisions belonging to the eleventh wave, and was followed by the creation of an additional 23 infantry and four light infantry divisions of the twelfth to fourteenth waves throughout November and December.[35] In addition, three *Gebirgs* divisions and one infantry division were created outside the *Welle* system during this same period.[36] These were followed by the formation of nine security divisions in March 1941 and the establishment of a further 15 infantry divisions of the fifteenth wave in April and May.[37] Overall, a total of 65 new infantry, light infantry, mountain, and security divisions were formed between October 1940 and May 1941.

Complicating the process of expansion outlined above was the simultaneous disbandment of some divisions and the temporary reduction of yet more to cadres. Between late June and early September 1940, some 26 infantry divisions were permanently disbanded. Of limited combat value, these were mainly from the ninth and tenth waves that had only begun forming in March, and which consisted primarily of older personnel, fortress troops, border guards, and police reservists equipped with obsolete or captured equipment. Some of these men were discharged from military service, while the remainder were transferred to rear-area security units or assigned to various administrative positions where they relieved younger men for frontline service.[38] Between mid-July and August an additional 18 infantry divisions were reduced to cadres while the bulk of their personnel were sent on extended leave to work in armaments factories. This "armaments holiday" was to facilitate the produc-

---

34   H.R. Trevor-Roper, ed. *Hitler's War Directives, 1939-1945.* (London: 1964), pp. 49-52.

35   The divisions formed were as follows: *11. Welle – 121., 122., 123., 125., 126., 129., 131., 132., 134.,* and *137. Infanterie Divisions*; *12. Welle – 102., 106., 110., 111., 112.,* and *113. Infanterie Divisions*; *97., 99., 100.,* and *101. Leichte Infanterie* (Light Infantry) *Divisions*; *13. Welle – 302., 304., 305., 306., 319., 320., 321., 323.,* and *327. Infanterie Divisions*; *14. Welle – 332., 333., 335., 336., 337., 339., 340.,* and *342. Infanterie Divisions*.

36   The *4., 5.,* and *6. Gebirgs Divisions* were formed from cadres of existing mountain divisions, while the *199. Infanterie Division* was created in Norway by drawing upon the personnel of divisions already stationed there.

37   These included the *702., 704., 707., 708., 709., 710., 711., 712., 713., 714., 715., 716.,* and *717. Infanterie Divisions* and the *207., 213., 221., 281., 285., 286., 403., 444.,* and *454. Sicherungs Divisions*.

38   These disbanded formations included three from the *3. Welle* (*209., 228.* and *231. Infanterie Divisions*), nine from the *9. Welle* (*351., 358., 365., 372., 379., 386., 393., 395.* and *399. Infanterie Divisions*), nine of the *10. Welle* (*270., 271., 273., 273., 276., 277., 278., 279.,* and *280. Infanterie Divisions*), and five divisions (*311., 554., 555., 556.,* and *557. Infanterie Divisions*) consisting of fortress troops, police and frontier guards formed outside the *Welle* system.

tion of equipment in preparation for the attack upon Russia.[39] Of these formations, 15 were later reconstituted as infantry divisions when their personnel were recalled in February 1941, while the men from the remainder were used to form the cadre of the nine security divisions established in March 1941.[40] It should also be noted that many existing divisions, from which cadres had been removed, had to incorporate substantial numbers of new recruits and, therefore, practically rebuild themselves.

When this complex period of expansion and development was over, the German Army had disbanded 43 of the 162 divisions that had existed on 10 May 1940. It then proceeded to create no fewer than 84 entirely *new* divisions, thereby increasing the total number of Army divisions to 203 by 22 June 1941. When all was said and done the net result was a 22 percent increase in the total number of divisions compared to those available on 10 May, but the actual increase when the disbanded formations are taken into account rises to 41 percent. In addition, a host of new command headquarters and corps- and army-level support units were formed, including one army group and four panzer group headquarters. Finally, four *Ersatz* brigades of the sixteenth wave were also established in 15 June 1941 with older personnel and minimal weapons and support services to provide garrison troops in occupied Poland and behind the imminent descent into Russia.

Such a massive expansion and reorganization presented monumental difficulties for Army planners, especially in terms of finding the requisite amounts of men and equipment. These difficulties were exacerbated by the Army's continuous fight with the other services over production priorities and manpower. Following his announcement regarding his intentions towards Russia at the Berghof, Hitler reversed his earlier decision of 12 July to assign production priority to the *Luftwaffe* and *Kriegsmarine* in conjunction with the struggle against Great Britain. However, while the requirements of the Army now took precedence, the other services were nonetheless instructed to continue their own expansion programmes.[41] Consequently, between 15 June 1940 and 15 June 1941, the personnel strength of the *Kriegsmarine* expanded from 189,000 to 404,000, while the *Luftwaffe* grew from 1,104,000 to 1,545,000. The *Waffen-SS* was also able to modestly swell its ranks from 125,000 to 160,000.[42] To replace its heavy losses of aircraft, expand its established strength and create the forces necessary for the air defence of Western Europe, the *Luftwaffe* in particular demanded

---

39   Tooze, *Wages of Destruction*, p. 437. This measure reduced the strength of the German Army from 4,347,000 personnel on 15 June 1940, to 3,994,000 by 15 August 1940. Kroener, et. al. *GSWW. Vol. V: Part One*, p. 1103.

40   The divisions sent on leave were from the third (*205., 206., 207., 209., 212., 213., 218., 221., 239.,* and *246. Infanterie Divisions*), fifth (*93., 94., 96.,* and *98. Infanterie Divisions*), and sixth waves (*81., 82., 83.,* and *88. Infanterie Divisions*). The personnel from the *207., 213.,* and *221. Infanterie Divisions* were later used to form the security divisions.

41   Boog, et. al. *GSWW. Vol. IV*, p. 200.

42   Kroener, et. al. *GSWW. Vol. V: Part One*, p. 1103.

vast increases to its assigned allotment of industrial plant and raw materials.[43] At the same time, the growing demands from the armed forces for more equipment and munitions in order to meet their individual expansion programmes entailed a simultaneous increase in the production of raw materials and in the output of German factories. In turn, this required ever-larger numbers of labourers. To meet the demands for increased production, in February 1941 analysts estimated that the economy was already short 1.09 million workers and that this figure would increase to 1.76 million by the summer.[44] Although 1.2 million prisoners of war and 1.3 million foreign civilians were employed within the borders of the Reich by the spring of 1941, German industry continued to require large numbers of German males.[45] By early 1941 a total of 4.8 million men, all of whom were fit for military service, were in reserved occupations that exempted them from being conscripted because of the their importance to the wartime economy.[46] Of these, approximately 640,000 were between 20 and 30 years of age.[47] In contrast, the number of deferments during the First World War had peaked at 2.4 million men in mid-1918, only half of whom had been considered fit for frontline service.[48]

Exacerbating German manpower difficulties further was the fact that many of the most highly skilled or technically proficient workers came from the younger age groups. On the one hand, their youth, vigour, and physical fitness made them the optimal recruits for a German Army whose operational doctrine demanded speed, endurance and aggression. Moreover, their proficiency with and enthusiasm for modern technologies meant they were an invaluable source of vehicle drivers, mechanical repair technicians, and radar and radio operators – niches that the German Army would always be hard pressed to fill. On the other hand, extracting them for military service would result in a corresponding shortage within industry, which would them be hard pressed to compensate for the lost skills and technical adeptness. The result was the very real danger that industrial output, and hence the production of military equipment and weaponry, might not only fall short of new manufacture goals: there was a real possibility that current production levels could falter and decline.

43   In addition to the heavy losses sustained during the French campaign, between July 1940 and May 1941 the frontline formations of the *Luftwaffe* lost 4,188 aircraft destroyed and a further 2,376 damaged. During the same period they received 9,563 new or refurbished aircraft. Ibid, p. 733. Simultaneously, the *Luftwaffe* had to expand its air defence assets and by June 1941 these totalled 1,206 heavy, and 887 medium and light flak batteries supported by 265 searchlight batteries. Boog, et. al. *GSWW. Vol. IV*, p. 376.
44   Overy, "Mobilization for Total War in Germany 1939-1941", p. 625.
45   Tooze, *The Wages of Destruction*, p. 517. Also, see Ulrich Herbert, *Hitler's Foreign Workers: Enforced Foreign Labour in Germany under the Third Reich*. (Cambridge: 1997).
46   Of these, some 1.5 million were in the armaments sector. Kroener, et. al. *GSWW. Vol. V: Part One*, p. 980.
47   A further 3.6 million men were categorized as being unfit for military service. Tooze, *The Wages of Destruction*, p. 437.
48   Kroener, et. al. *GSWW. Vol. V: Part One*, p. 796.

Despite such conundrums, the German Army was still able to tap into large reservoirs of manpower. Most of this appears to have been drawn from the civilian economy. One source puts the total number of workers called up between May 1940 and May 1941 at 1.4 million, although just how many of these men were released and then recalled under the "armaments holiday" program or were from the younger age groups detailed below, is unknown.[49] To mitigate the effects upon the armaments industries, a sizeable portion were men of the older age class (40-years and older) engaged in non-essential sectors of the economy. Many were employed within Germany as part of the *Ersatzheer*, or within the rear-area support services of the *Feldheer*, thereby releasing younger, more combat-fit men for frontline service. Others made up most of the personnel of the security divisions and the formations belonging to the fifteenth *Welle*. While the former safeguarded German lines of communication during the invasion of Russia, the latter were specifically created to defend Western Europe (and later newly conquered Yugoslavia), and thereby release more combat-worthy formations for service against Russia.[50] Other sources of manpower included the sizeable cohorts of the younger age groups: the 20-year olds of the 1920 class amounted to 748,204 and the first of these were inducted into the *Wehrmacht* on 1 October 1940.[51] The first of the 735,206 males comprising the 1921 class followed on 1 February 1941, but just how many were assigned to frontline combat formations or were held as replacements in the *Ersatzheer* at the time of the invasion of Russia is unknown. Not all of these young men would have been mentally or physically acceptable to the *Wehrmacht*, but estimates based upon later age groups indicates that anywhere from 81 to 86 percent would have been fully fit for combat, with a further three to four percent partially fit and therefore capable of some kind of less strenuous military activity.[52] Most would have been allotted to the Army, whose quota of the yearly intake of new recruits was set 72.5 percent in January 1941.[53] The last portion of the 1919 class, which seems to have amounted to approximately 68,000 men, were also called up during the autumn of 1940.[54] A final source of manpower consisted of 17-year olds who, though not

49   Tooze, *The Wages of Destruction*, p. 436. According to German historian Bernhard Kroener the actual number of men temporarily released by the Army never amounted to more than 100,000 because of internal Army opposition. Kroener, "Squaring the Circle: Blitzkrieg Strategy and Manpower Shortage, 1938-1942", p. 296. However, this estimate appears to be contradicted by the reduction experienced by the Army when its strength went from 4,347,000 personnel on 15 June 1940 to 3,994,000 by 15 August 1940. Kroener, et. al. *GSWW. Vol. V: Part One*, p. 1103.

50   Ibid, pp. 986-987.

51   Ibid, pp. 831-832.

52   Kroener, et. al. *GSWW. Vol. V: Part Two*, pp. 831-832.

53   Kroener, et. al. *GSWW. Vol. V: Part One*, p. 1043.

54   Jacobsen, (Ed.) *KTB OKW. Band I*, pp. 66-67.

eligible to be drafted, were permitted to volunteer. In 1940 and 1941 these volunteers totalled 348,000, of whom 102,000 entered the Army.[55] Despite all the difficulties it encountered and by drawing upon these varied sources of personnel, the German Army increased in strength from 4,347,000 on 15 June 1940 to 5,200,000 on 15 June 1941. During this same period the strength of the *Wehrmacht* as a whole expanded from 5,765,000 to 7,309,000 personnel.[56] Aside from some small shortages of specialized technical personnel, this enlargement meant the Army was able to man all of its front-line formations in time for Barbarossa. Of equal importance, the availability of manpower was such that the *Ersatzheer* was able to accumulate a considerable pool of 471,600 replacement personnel with at least three months training and thereby stood ready to replace casualties in the field forces as necessary. In addition, 114 of the 151 divisions committed to Barbarossa possessed a field replacement (*Feldersatz*) battalion as part of their internal structure that was intended to provide them with an immediate reservoir of replacement manpower in the field. These contained approximately 790 men apiece, for a total of 90,000 replacements that marched into Russia with the *Ostheer*. Together with those of the *Ersatzheer*, this meant that the German Army had the capability of sustaining 561,600 casualties.[57] This was 3.6 times greater than the losses that had been endured during the French campaign, which the Army's senior leadership had viewed with far greater trepidation than the forthcoming contest against the Russians. While the marshalling of this manpower represented what seemed to be a final maximum effort – 85 percent of all German males between the ages of 20 and 30 were already in the Wehrmacht by the summer of 1941 – most senior German military officers anticipated that this was sufficient given the timeframe in which Barbarossa was to take place. After all, it was expected that the "campaign against Russia would be a sand-table exercise in comparison [with the French campaign]."[58]

Alongside the need for personnel, preparing the German Army for the coming campaign against Russia required tremendous amounts of new arms and equipment. As noted above, the primary impediment to increasing armaments production for the Army remained the availability of the requisite labour force, a situation only aggravated by the simultaneous competing demands of the other services. By January 1941 tank production alone was short 6,000 skilled workers.[59] Other bottlenecks included the availability of raw materials and plant capacity, causing *Generaloberst* Friedrich

---

55   Of the remainder, 124,000 joined the *Kriegsmarine*, 73,000 entered the *Luftwaffe*, and 49,000 were enrolled into the *Waffen-SS*. Kroener, et. al. *GSWW. Vol. V: Part Two*, p. 920.

56   Kroener, et. al. *GSWW. Vol. V: Part One*, p. 1103.

57   Ibid, p. 980.

58   Andreas Hillgruber, "Noch einmal: Hitler's Wendung gegen die Sowjetunion 1940." *Geschichte in Wissenshaft und Unterricht*, Vol. 33, No. 4 (1982), p. 220. Also, see Geoffrey P. Megargee, *War of Annihilation: Combat and Genocide on the Eastern Front, 1941*. (New York: 2006), pp. 23-24.

59   Boog, et. al. *GSWW. Vol. IV*, p. 210.

Fromm, the Chief of Army Armaments and Commander of the *Ersatzheer*, to observe in April that seven million of the available 25 million shells for the Army's light field howitzer existed only as empty cartridges because of the lack of gunpowder and explosives.[60] Such problems were made worse by the transportation difficulties experienced by the *Reichsbahn*, which had consistently been neglected during the pre-war rearmament. While the capacity of Germany's rail system had managed to cope during the years of peace, when faced by massive increases in the dual requirements of both industry and the *Wehrmacht* both the system and its capacity came under increasing strain.[61] As will be seen, this strain upon the *Reichsbahn* eventually resulted in a near catastrophic collapse that affected Germany's armies in the field and its industrial production at home during the winter of 1941-1942. In the short term, as illustrated in Table 2.2, this combination of problems impaired the output efficiency of German armaments factories, which had the capacity to produce considerably more equipment than they actually did.

Nonetheless, despite the seemingly hopeless nature of its many systemic difficulties, German industry was able to meet most of the requirements of the Army's prodigious expansion program in time for the launch of Barbarossa. During the period of June 1940 to May 1941, weapons factories produced approximately 1.4 million rifles, 77,048 machine-guns, 12,471 mortars, 3,649 anti-tank and 1,475 infantry guns, 6,754 anti-aircraft guns, 1,083 rocket launchers, and 781 light and 361 heavy field howitzers.[62] Concurrently, the production of new vehicles included 2,122 panzers, 353 StuG, and 268 armoured cars (*Panzerspähwagen*, or PSW), as well as at least 138,806 new motorcycles, staff cars, trucks, and towing vehicles.[63] As illustrated in

---

60   Bernhard Kroener, "The 'Frozen Blitzkrieg': German Strategic Planning against the Soviet Union and the Causes of Its Failure." in Wegener (Ed.), *From Peace to War: Germany, Soviet Russia and the World, 1939-1941*, p. 144. For the total stock of shells on 1 April 1941, see Boog, et. al. *GSWW. Vol. IV*, pp. 218-219.

61   The most comprehensive examinations of the *Reichsbahn*'s wartime role are Hans Pottgiesser, *Die Deutsche Reichsbahn im Ostfeldzug, 1939-1944.* (Neckargemund: 1960), Horst Rohde, *Das deutsche Wehrmachttrasnportwesen im Zweiten Weltkrieg: Entstehung, Organisation, Aufgaben.* (Stuttgart: 1971), Eugen Kriedler, *Die Eisenbahnen im Machtbericht der Achsenmachte wahrend des Zweiten Weltkrieg.* (Gottingen: 1975), Klaus A. Friedrich Schuler, *Logistik im Russlandfeldzug: Die Rolle der Eisenbahn bei Planung, Vorbereitung und Durchfuhrung des deutschen Angriffs auf die Sowjetunion bis zur Krise vor Moskau im Winter, 1941-1942.* (Frankfurt: 1987), and Alfred A. Mierzejewski, *The Most Valuable Asset of the Reich: A History of the German National Railway, Vol. Two – 1933-1945.* (Chapel Hill, NC: 2000).

62   The number of anti-tank guns can be broken down as follows: 2,174 3.7 cm, 397 4.7 cm, and 1,078 5 cm Pak. The total for anti-aircraft guns includes 4,771 2 cm, 624 3.7 cm, and 1,359 8.8 cm Flak. Kroener, et. al. *GSWW. Vol. V: Part One*, pp. 725-727.

63   The number of new panzers produced includes 107 Pz II, 1,159 Pz III, 336 Pz IV, and 520 Pz 38(t). The figure for new vehicles includes 43,682 motorcycles, 27,826 staff cars, 46,203 trucks, 7,032 towing vehicles, and 14,063 other vehicles. Ibid, 742-743.

Table 2.3, this production translated into significant increases to the Army's existing stocks of weapons between May 1940 and June 1941.

Aside from German kit, the Army could also draw upon tremendous stocks of captured weapons and equipment. The occupation of Czechoslovakia in 1938 brought in at least 930 pieces of field artillery, and some 41,658 machine-guns, 901 anti-tank and 324 anti-aircraft guns, 3,366 mortars, and 7,295 artillery pieces were garnered from the successful campaigns of 1939 to 1941.[64] Given the speed and size of the expansion of the German Army between the summer of 1940 and spring of 1941, and the constraints upon domestic production, Germany pressed some of this equipment into service. Although most historical accounts deride the German employment of foreign weapons and equipment, much of this was of modern design and some was actually superior to their German counterparts. Moreover, most were assigned to formations of the *Ersatzheer*, the large number of army coastal artillery batteries formed in early 1941, or the divisions tasked with quiet garrison duties in Western Europe, Norway and the Balkans.[65] The divisions assigned to Barbarossa, on the other hand, were almost completely equipped with German weaponry, the only exception being the employment of a comparatively small number of Czech and French 4.7 cm anti-tank guns, the use of the excellent Czech-designed 15 cm FH 37(t) heavy field howitzer by three independent artillery battalions, and a number of Norwegian mountain guns utilized by two *Gebirgs* divisions located in northern Finland.

However, with the success of Barbarossa hinging upon the speedy destruction of the Red Army, large numbers of captured vehicles were employed with the divisions assigned to the East to increase their mobility. Exact figures have proven elusive, but this probably included the use of many of the available 4,930 Renault UE Chenillette tracked vehicles for towing anti-tank guns, as well as at least 13,000 French trucks that were requisitioned in early 1941.[66] Approximately 190 French Panhard armoured cars were employed with a variety of reconnaissance battalions, while an unknown percentage of the truck fleet belonging to the Army's vital supply services was also of foreign design. A total of 40 of the 151 divisions assigned to Barbarossa were equipped with captured vehicles, although nine of these were security divisions intended only

---

64 Ibid, p. 730. Aside from whatever they may have seized, the Germans also produced large quantities of ammunition in order to employ the weapons they captured. For instance, between 1939 and 1945 approximately 857,800 artillery rounds were manufactured for the Czech 15 cm s.FH 25(t) and 37(t) guns, while 1.35 million shells for the French 15.5 cm Gr 414/416(f) were produced from 1943 to 1945. For details on specific pieces of equipment, see Fritz Hahn, *Waffen und Geheimwaffen des deutschen Heeres, 1933-1945. Band I & II.* (Bonn: 1998).

65 The latter were only intended to release higher quality formations for operations in the East and provide a modicum of security to guard against the unlikely possibility of a British landing. Once matters had been successfully concluded in Russia, most were to be disbanded anyway.

66 Boog, et. al. *GSWW. Vol. IV*, pp. 211 & 310.

for rear-area policing.[67] Ultimately the use of these vehicles would prove to be a mixed blessing. Their use filled out authorized vehicles establishments and significantly increased overall mobility, but also added complications to maintenance and supply efforts. By the summer of 1941 the German Army employed about 2,000 different types of vehicles. For a single army group, this required stockpiling no less than one million different spare parts of all kinds.[68] Senior officers were fully aware of the problematic use of such equipment, but the overriding concern was to complete the campaign as quickly as possible and the use of these vehicles would facilitate that goal. In his diary entry of 20 January 1941, Halder illustrated the importance that the pace of operations would have upon the outcome of the campaign when he emphasized "Speed. No stopping!" and later added "No pause; that alone guarantees victory."[69] In short, OKH gambled that Barbarossa would be finished before the use of captured vehicles became a serious problem.

To determine the degree to which Army equipment needs were met, comparisons must be made between the total stocks of equipment with the German Army on 1 June 1941 and its actual requirements based upon specifically designated TOE. Ascertaining just what the latter amounted to is no easy task; by early June 1941 the German Army consisted of 203 field divisions, six brigades (or brigade-equivalent formations), and hundreds of smaller support units. As noted previously, considerable organizational differences existed between the field divisions. Based upon their specific type and to which particular *Welle* they belonged, some 20 different divisional schematics existed by the summer of 1941. Moreover, a great deal of individual variation existed within these specific organizational structures. For example, some panzer divisions had two panzer battalions while others had three; some had heavy infantry gun companies and others did not. Some infantry divisions had a full, partially motorised *Aufklärungs* battalion, while others had only a single company mounted on bicycles or horses.

Nonetheless, by employing the methodology already outlined in the previous chapter it is again possible to make some generalizations regarding equipment requirements. Detailed in Table 2.4 is the individual divisional TOE of the formations belonging to the first to fifteenth waves, the motorised, light infantry and security divisions, and the unique *1. Kavallerie* and *5. Leichte Divisions*. The equipment requirements of all the existing 20 panzer and six mountain divisions are also included, but these are listed as total (as opposed to individual) overall requirements because of the wide organizational discrepancies between the formations constituting their type. When the individual divisional requirements are multiplied by their respective number of

---

67   Ibid, pp. 222-224.
68   Kroener, "The 'Frozen Blitzkrieg': German Strategic Planning against the Soviet Union and the Causes of Its Failure", p. 146.
69   Franz Halder, *Kriegstagebuch: Tagliche Aufzeichnungen des Chefs des Generalstabes des Heeres 1939-1942. Band II.* (Ed.) Hans-Adolf Jacobsen & Alfred Philippi. (Stuttgart: 1962), p. 258.

formations (ten motorised infantry, four light infantry, nine security, and 152 various infantry divisions) and added together with the total numbers listed (for the panzer and mountain divisions, and the *1. Kavallerie* and *5. Leichte Divisions*), the overall amount of equipment required by the existing German divisions can then be approximated. A similar methodology has been used to determine the total equipment requirements of the various independent army- and corps-level units (the exact specifics of which are outlined in Appendix Three) by utilizing the *Kriegsgliederung des Feldheeres* dated 10 February 1941 and 15 May 1941.[70] The cumulative totals derived from these calculations are illustrated in Table 2.5.

Determining the extent of the material requirements of the *Ersatzheer* at the outset of Barbarossa remains problematic given the lack of information, but a supposition is possible. For certain, on 1 June 1941 the *Ersatzheer* was comprised of 334 various infantry-type (*Infanterie Ersatz, Infanterie Lehr, Schützen Ersatz*, etc.) replacement battalions, 91 infantry-type regimental headquarters, and 37 pioneer, 16 anti-tank, 128 artillery (or artillery demonstration), and five rocket launcher replacement battalions.[71] These numbers are then multiplied using the assigned organizations and strengths detailed for such units in the preceding chapter. The only significant addition is the *200. Sturmgeschütz Ersatz Abteilung*, created on 1 March 1941 to provide replacements to the burgeoning number of assault guns units. According to their corresponding KStN, each of its three batteries was to be equipped with seven StuG and nine machine-guns, while the headquarters battery was to have two machine-guns.[72] Based upon this accounting, the equipment requirements of the *Ersatzheer* can loosely be estimated as approximating 15,144 machine-guns, 1,002 mortars, 1,860 anti-tank guns, 128 *Nebelwerfer*, 728 infantry guns, and 21 StuG.

Based upon these calculations, just prior to the outset of Barbarossa the German Army possessed approximately 81,460 machine-guns, 5,968 mortars, 4,132 anti-tank guns, 386 infantry guns, and 678 rocket launchers that were surplus to all of its organizational requirements. Likewise, many of the 2,066 artillery pieces and 742 2 cm flak guns indicated as surplus in Table 2.5 would also have been in excess of its immediate

---

70 Confirmation of these numbers, by determining if and when a unit was actually in existence, has been derived by cross-referencing the information provided in *Anlage zu OKH, Generalstab des Heeres, Org. Abt. (I). Kriegsgliederung des Feldheeres 10 February 1941*, and *Anlage zu OKH, Generalstab des Heeres, Org. Abt. (I). Kriegsgliederung des Feldheeres 15 May 1941* found within NARA T78, Roll 404, Tessin, *Verbande und Truppen der Deutschen Wehrmacht und Waffen-SS im Zweiten Weltkrieg, 1933-1945. Bande 1-17*, and the website "Lexikon der Wehrmacht" at http://lexikon-der-wehrmacht.de/ For the specific organization and equipment of each of these units, see NARA T78 Roll 404.

71 Numbers ascertained by cross-referencing Tessin, *Verbände und Truppen der Deutschen Wehrmacht und Waffen-SS im Zweiten Weltkrieg, 1933-1945. Bande 1-17*, and the website "Lexikon der Wehrmacht" at http://lexikon-der-wehrmacht.de/

72 The organization of the batteries is taken from KStN No. 6249, while that of the headquarters battery may be found in KStN. No. 6247; both are dated to 1 April 1941. See NARA T78, Roll 394, Frames 6363537 and 6363543.

material needs. Given the dire impressions of the Army's material condition portrayed within the historiography, these figures are astounding. To be sure, some of this stock-pile would have been held as replacements to cover losses sustained during Barbarossa, or to outfit new armoured and motorised formations scheduled for creation upon its conclusion.[73] However, following the end of operations in the East, the Army was to be reduced in size by about 50 divisions.[74] Equipment from the disbanded formations would be transferred to those that remained, thus making surpluses of these propor-tions seemingly unnecessary. In any case, these figures point to the conclusion that the German Army possessed all the equipment it needed according to its designated TOE.

As Table 2.6 illustrates, surpluses also appear within the Army's armoured vehicle stocks. Admittedly, many of the vehicles indicated as surplus were deployed with the *Afrika Korps* in Libya (amounting to 314 tanks by early May), while the 14 panzer replacement battalions (each of three companies) and single assault gun replacement battalion would have required a further 861 vehicles for training purposes.[75] However, this still leaves a total surplus of 974 panzers and assault guns. Of these, 490 were of the more battle-worthy variety (Pz 35/38t, Pz III, Pz IV, and StuG). During the course of June, a further 312 newly manufactured armoured vehicles were delivered to the Army, of which only 30 were dispatched to the *Afrika Korps*.[76] In consequence, the German Army began Barbarossa with approximately 1,256 armoured vehicles (including 756 of the combat-worthy types) as surplus to its requirements and thereby available as replacements.

While the Army marshalled its forces and prepared for the forthcoming campaign, the *Luftwaffe* endeavoured to do likewise. However, unlike the Army, the *Luftwaffe* found itself continuously engaged throughout late 1940 and early 1941. In partic-ular, operations in the Balkans during the spring of 1941 proved both distracting and resulted in considerable aircraft losses.[77] This produced a great deal of anxiety amongst German military planners because of the key role the *Luftwaffe* was to perform in

---

73   Kroener, et. al. *GSWW. Vol. V: Part One*, p. 988-997.

74   Ibid, pp. 996 & 998.

75   The formations sent to North Africa possessed 25 Pz I, 90 Pz II, 142 Pz III, 40 Pz IV, and 17 command tanks. Jentz, *Panzertruppen, Vol. One*, p. 160. According to KStN No. 6561 (dated to 1 April 1941), each *leichte Panzer Ersatz Kompanie* was to be equipped with 11 Pz I, 3 Pz II, 3 Pz, III, and 3 Pz IV. The *panzer ersatz abteilungen* of the *Ersatzheer* would therefore have required 462 Pz I, 126 Pz II, 126 Pz III, and 126 Pz IV. See *OKH Kriegsstarkenachweisungen, Band 13b, Ersatz Einheiten.* NARA T78 Roll 395, Frame 6363860. As noted on page 101, the *200. Sturmgeschütz Ersatz Abteilung* required 21 StuG.

76   Boog, et. al. *GSWW. Vol. IV*, pp. 1120-1122, and Jentz, *Panzertruppen, Vol. One*, p. 167.

77   Between 1 April and 1 June 1941, at least 466 *Luftwaffe* aircraft were destroyed or written-off during operations over the Balkans and eastern Mediterranean. Christopher Shores, et. al. *Air War for Yugoslavia, Greece, and Crete 1940-1941.* (London: 1987), pp. 311 & 403.

ensuring that the strategic goal of Barbarossa, namely the destruction of Soviet military strength within three or four months, was met.[78] Nonetheless, although some units arrived in their assembly areas only hours before the commencement of operations, the *Luftwaffe* as a whole was well prepared. Hundreds of new airfields had been constructed across Poland and East Prussia, and to shield the Army from attacks by the Red Army Air Force and thereby facilitate its advance, the *Luftwaffe* provided 239 heavy and 125 medium and light flak batteries for air defence duties behind the *Ostheer*.[79] These batteries alone would have been equipped with 956 8.8 cm flak guns, and between 1,125 and 1,500 3.7 cm and 2 cm flak guns. Despite heavy commitments throughout Western Europe and the Mediterranean, the *Luftwaffe* was also able to assemble an impressive total of aircraft for Barbarossa. Significantly, in terms of the Russo-German War's established mythology regarding German numerical weakness, many of the most prominent accounts have long maintained that Germany deployed only about 2,000 aircraft to the East.[80] However, more recent scholarship has revealed this figure to be dramatically incorrect, and that the *Luftwaffe* actually committed 3,904 aircraft to Barbarossa (see Table 2.7), representing 69 percent of its total available strength.[81] Although long neglected within the literature, the contributions of the roughly 1,025 aircraft belonging to the air forces of Germany's European allies were also significant, with the Romanian Air Force itself conducting 17,368 sorties between 22 June and 16 October 1941, and thereby meriting consideration.[82] The result is a total Axis air fleet of about 5,000 aircraft of all types. In contrast, of a total air strength estimated at around 20,000 planes, approximately 9,912 Soviet aircraft were

---

78   The specific tasks of the *Luftwaffe* as noted in Hitler's Directive No. 21 'Case Barbarossa' were 1) "paralyse and eliminate the effectiveness of the Russian Air Force as far as possible" and 2) "support the main operations of the Army". Significantly, it also stressed that, "In order that we may concentrate all our strength against the enemy Air Force and for the immediate support of land operations, the Russian armaments industry will not be attacked during the main operations." See Trevor-Roper (Ed.), *Hitler's War Directives, 1939-1945*, pp. 49-53.

79   Boog, et. al. *GSWW. Vol. IV*, p. 376.

80   For example, see Seaton, *The Russo-German War, 1941-1945*, p. 62, Anders, *Hitler's Defeat in Russia*, p. 18, Carell, *Hitler Moves East, 1941-1943*, p. 19, and Cajus Bekker, *The Luftwaffe War Diaries*. (London: 1966), p. 219.

81   A further 1,766 *Luftwaffe* aircraft were deployed elsewhere. Boog, et. al. *GSWW. Vol. IV*, p. 372.

82   For the number of allied Axis aircraft, see Ibid, pp. 362, 371, & 464. Of the number of sorties conducted by the Romanians, see Axworthy, et. al. *Third Axis, Fourth Ally*, pp. 286 & 288. For further reading on the actions of Axis air forces, see James C. Corum, "The Luftwaffe and Its Allied Air Forces in World War II: Parallel War and the Failure of Strategic and Economic Cooperation." *Air Power History*, Vol. 51, No. 2 (Summer 2004), pp. 4-19, and Alexander Statiev, "Antonescu's Eagles against Stalin's Falcons: The Romanian Air Force, 1920-1941." *Journal of Military History*, Vol. 66, No. 4 (October 2002), pp. 1085-1113.

stationed throughout European Russia.[83] Thus the disparity in aircraft between the Axis and Soviet air forces declines from 1:4 (or 1:10 if counting all Russian aircraft) to a more accurate 1:2 (or 1:4). This illustrates that not only did the *Luftwaffe* concentrate a larger number of aircraft for Barbarossa, but also that its numerical odds versus its Russian adversary were considerably less daunting than have usually been claimed.

As dusk fell across the Soviet-German border on the evening of 21 June 1941, the final air and ground formations of the Wehrmacht were moved into their assembly areas. The code word DORTMUND, granting final authorization to proceed with Barbarossa, had already been sent out the previous day and the dawn would witness the beginning of the greatest land campaign in human history. Across 1,600 km of front, and supported by thousands of aircraft, 140 Army and *Waffen-SS* divisions stood posed for what Hitler was convinced would be Germany's "toughest struggle yet – by far the toughest!"[84] A further 12 divisions were allotted to Barbarossa but initially remained in OKH reserve. For the German Army, this marked the end of months of expansion and preparation. Despite substantial difficulties, the Army had managed to procure large numbers of men for the host of new divisions it had to create, and it still retained over half a million more men to serve as replacements. The doubling of the panzer divisions had been matched by corresponding increases to the quantity and quality of its fleet of armoured vehicles. German armaments industries had more than matched the increased size of the Army, with large reserve stocks of weapons and equipment remaining available as needed. Indeed, the size of these stocks had grown dramatically since the start of the war in 1939. With its personnel well trained and many having considerable combat experience, the Army had reached the apex of its existence in terms of tactical prowess and ability. Although some of its leaders, including Hitler, expressed anxiety at the prospect of war with the Soviet Union or how it was to be conducted, most German Army officers were confident that, whatever problems might emerge, the campaign would successfully be concluded in short order. Few would have been able to fathom that they were about to meet their match.

---

83 Note that the latter figure only includes aircraft belonging to the Soviet Air Force (*Voenno Vozdushnye Sily*, or VVS), the Long-Range (Strategic) Bomber Aviation, and the naval air assets of the Soviet Navy. Excluded are the aircraft of the Soviet Air Defence Forces (*ProtivoVozdushnaya Oborona Strany*, or PVO) for which no reliable figures could be found. Bergstrom, *Barbarossa: The Air Battle, July – December 1941*, pp. 131-132.

84 Irving, *Hitler's War*, p. 378. The frontage along the Finnish-Russian border would add a further 998 km, but not until three days after the beginning of Barbarossa.

Table 2.1 Armoured Strength of German Panzer Divisions committed to Barbarossa, 22 June 1941[1]

	Pz I	Pz II	Pz 35(t)	Pz 38(t)	Pz III*	Pz IV	Befl.	Total
1. Panzer Division	11	43	-	-	-/71	20	11	156
3. Panzer Division	13	59	-	-	29/81	32	15	229
4. Panzer Division	10	51	-	-	31/74	20	26	212
6. Panzer Division	11	47	155	-	-/-	30	13	256
7. Panzer Division	11	55	-	167	-/-	30	15	278
8. Panzer Division	11	49	-	118	-/-	30	15	223
9. Panzer Division	19	32	-	-	11/60	20	12	154
10. Panzer Division	11	47	-	-	-/105	20	17	200
11. Panzer Division	11	44	-	-	24/47	20	20	166
12. Panzer Division	51	34	-	109	-/-	30	8	232
13. Panzer Division	8	45	-	-	27/44	20	13	157
14. Panzer Division	11	45	-	-	23/45	20	10	154
16. Panzer Division	12	44	-	-	23/48	20	10	157
17. Panzer Division	22	45	-	-	-/106	30	13	216
18. Panzer Division	17	50	-	-	99/15	36	12	229
19. Panzer Division	53	35	-	110	-/-	30	11	239
20. Panzer Division	55	31	-	121	-/-	31	2	240
Total	337	756	155	625	267/696	439	223	3,498

* Pz III equipped with 3.7 cm gun/Pz III equipped with 5 cm gun.

1 Jentz, *Panzertruppen, Vol. One*, pp. 190-193 & 206.

Table 2.2 Armament Plant Capacity and Output for the German Army April 1941[1]

	Plant Capacity	Actual Output	Efficiency (%)
MG	14,650	9,000	61
Pak	320	280	88
Mortars	1,070	850	79
2 cm Flak	180	160	89
Rocket launchers	130	100	77
Infantry Guns	200	146	73
Light howitzers	150	120	80
Heavy artillery	149	133	89

1 Kroener, et. al. *GSWW. Vol. V: Part One*, p. 632.

Table 2.3 German Army Weapons Stocks, May 1940 and June 1941.[1]

	Total Stock 1.5.1940	Total Stock 1.6.1941	Increase of Total Stock
MG	150,400	203,250	35.1%
2 cm Flak	1,487	2,153	44.8%
3.7 cm Pak	14,257	15,522	8.9%
4.7 cm Pak (Czech)	36	785	2,080.5%
5 cm Pak	–	1,047	–
5 cm GrW	9,967	16,129	61.8%
8 cm GrW	7,091	11,767	65.9%
10 cm/15 cm NbW	288	1,112	268.1%
7.5 cm IG	3,365	4,176	24.1%
15 cm IG	491	867	76.6%
10.5 cm FH 16 & 18	5,538	7,076	27.8%
15 cm FH 18	2,383	2,867	20.3%
Pz I	1,266	966	-23.7%
Pz II	1,110	1,159	4.4%
Pz III	785	1,440	83.4%
Pz IV	290	572	97.2%
StuG	23	377	1,539.1%
Pz 35(t)	143	187	30.8%
Pz 38(t)	238	754	216.8%

1 Kroener, et. al. *GSWW. Vol. V: Part One*, pp. 636-637.

Table 2.4   Equipment Requirements of German Army Field Divisions based upon Assigned TOE, 22 June 1941[1]

Welle.	MG	Mortars		Infantry Guns		Pak[3]	Flak[4]	Howitzers[2]	
		5 cm	8.1 cm	7.5 cm	15 cm			10.5 cm	15 cm
1.	552	84	54	20	6	72	12	36	12
2.	549	84	54	20	6	72	–	36	12
3.	521	81	9	24	–	48	–	36	12
4.	547	87	54	20	6	73	–	36	12
5.	529	84	54	18	6	60	–	36	12
6.	521	81	54	18	–	48	–	36	12
7.	535	84	54	18	6	68	–	36	12
8.	523	84	54	18	6	68	–	36	12
11.	538	87	54	20	6	69	–	36	12
12.	550	84	54	20	6	75	–	36	12
13.	500	27	–	–	–	21	–	24	–
14.	500	27	–	–	–	21	–	24	–
15.	290	24	–	–	–	–	–	12	–
Mot. Inf. Div.	475	48	42	16	4	63	10	24	12
Sec. Div.	157	27	18	6	–	12	–	12	–
Light Inf. Div.	378	60	36	14	–	47	–	28	8
Kav. Div.	514	12	31	28	–	71	–	40	–
5. Light Div.	190	21	12	2	–	60	36	24	12
Mtn. Div. Total	2,504	363	204	71	–	307	–	192	36
Pz. Div. Total	9,798	960	600	412	108	1,020	174	480	216[5]

1   Figures drawn from NARA T78 Roll 404 and the 1941 German Army and Waffen-SS TOE schematics detailed on the website of Dr. Leo Niehorster, "World War II Armed Forces – Orders of Battle and Organizations." at http://niehorster.orbat.com

2   The amount of light field howitzers listed as total requirements for the mountain divisions includes a number of 7.5 cm GebG. 36 mountain guns.

3   This includes all 3.7 cm, 4.7 cm (Czech), and 5 cm Pak guns.

4   Figures for Flak include a number of 3.7 cm Flak and four-barrelled 2 cm *Vierlingsflak*.

5   In addition, the panzer divisions required 24 10 cm K 18 guns. At this point, one battery belonging to the artillery regiments of Panzer divisions was to have been outfitted with these guns, but by the time of Barbarossa only six panzer divisions were so equipped.

Table 2.5 Estimated German Field Army Equipment Requirements versus Existing Stocks, 1 June 1941

	Army Stock 1.6.1941[1]	Actual Div. Requirements 1941 TOE[2]	Army Troops Requirements 1941 TOE	Total Requirements	Surplus Stock
MG	203,250	98,269	8,377	106,646	96,604
5 cm GrW	16,129	13,233	219	13,452	2,677
8.1 cm GrW	11,767	7,370	114	7,474	4,293
7.5 cm IG	4,176	3,149	18	3,167	1,009
15 cm IG	867	754	8	762	105
Pak[3]	17,354	10,771	591	11,362	5,992
10/15 cm NbW	1,112	–	306[4]	306	806
2 cm Flak[5]	2,153	622	789	1,411	742
10.5 cm FH[6]	7,184	6,104	20	6,124	1,060
15 cm FH 18	2,867	1,856	504	2,360	507
10 cm K18	864	24	480	504	360
15 cm K18	68	–	65	65	3
21 cm to 42 cm guns	442	–	306	306	136
StuG	377	–	266*	266	111

*Includes 21 assigned to Waffen-SS.

1 Kroener, et. al. *GSWW. Vol. V: Part One*, pp. 636-637.

2 Not included in these figures are the equipment requirements of the five divisions and four brigades of the *Waffen-SS* since it is unclear whether its holdings are included within the Army's stock. In June 1941, the formations of the *Waffen-SS* required a total of 4,204 machine-guns, 612 5 cm and 390 8.1 cm mortars, 114 7.5 cm and 36 15 cm infantry guns, 439 Pak, 138 light Flak, 208 10.5 cm and 66 15 cm field howitzers. See the 1941 German Army and Waffen-SS TOE schematics detailed on the website of Dr. Leo Niehorster, "World War II Armed Forces – Orders of Battle and Organizations." at http://niehorster. orbat.com

3 This includes all 3.7 cm, 4.7 cm (Czech), and 5 cm Pak guns.

4 In June 1941 the *8. Nebelwerfer Battalion* was equipped with 24 of the new 28/32 cm NbW 41 launchers and is therefore not included in this figure.

5 Figures given as requirements for Flak include a number of 3.7 cm Flak and four-barrelled 2 cm *Vierlingsflak*, but stock only refers to single-barrelled 2 cm Flak.

6 Aside from 10.5 cm FH 16/18, stock includes a total of 108 mountain guns of various types.

Table 2.6 Overall Strength of German Armour Assets and Commitment to Barbarossa, 22 June 1941

	Overall Stock 1.6.1941[1]	With Army in East 22.6.1941	Percentage Committed	Surplus
Pz I	1,122	337	30.0	785
Pz II	1,204	890	73.9	314
Pz 35(t)	198	155	78.2	43
Pz 38(t)	779	625	80.2	154
Pz III	1,429	973	68.1	456
Pz IV	613	439	71.6	174
Beflpz.	330	225	68.2	105
StuG	377	259	68.7	118
Total	6,052	3,903	64.5	2,149

1 These figures include the following vehicles in repair or being upgraded: 245 Pz I, 45 Pz II, 11 Pz 35t, 25 Pz 38t, 104 Pz III, and 41 Pz IV. Hahn, *Waffen und Geheimwaffen des deutschen Heeres*, 1933-1945, *Band II*, p. 211.

Table 2.7 Strength and Operational Readiness of German Air Assets committed to Operation Barbarossa, 21 June 1941[1]

Under Luftwaffe control (Total/Operational)

Air Fleet	Strategic Recon	Bombers	Ju 87	Bf 109	Bf 110	Transport[2]	Other[3]	Total
Lft. 5[4]	–	22/17	40/37	12/12	4/4	–	20/12	98/82
Lft. 1	10/7	271/211	–	203/167	–	62/22	56/46	592/453
Lft. 2	–	299/222	425/323	384/284	98/60	115/69	46/36	1,367/994
Lft. 4	–	360/307	–	366/272	–	115/84	46/31	887/694
ObdL[5]	51/32	–	–	–	–	–	–	51/32
Total	61/39	952/757	465/360	965/735	102/64	292/175	168/125	2,995/2,255

Aircraft under Tactical Army Control (Total/Operational):

Army or Army Group	Long-Range Recon	Tactical Recon	Courier Aircraft	Total
20.	–	10/9	–	10/9
North	52/41	87/70	37/32	176/143
Centre	46/33	170/142	28/25	244/200
South	48/37	149/137	42/34	239/208
Total	146/111	416/358	107/91	669/560
Other Aircraft	240/217[6]			
Grand Total	3,904/3,052			

1　Boog, et. al. *GSWW. Vol. IV*, p. 364.

2　Includes both air corps transport squadrons (*Korpstransport Staffel*) and transport air groups (*Kampfgeschwader Z.b.V.*).

3　Includes weather (*Wekusta*) and maritime aircraft.

4　Only includes aircraft deployed against Russia, not total aircraft assigned to *Luftflotte 5* and stationed in Norway.

5　Refers to the specialised high-altitude, long-range reconnaissance planes of *Auklarungsgruppe ObdL* that was directly controlled by the Commander-in-Chief of the *Luftwaffe* (*Oberbefehlshaber der Luftwaffe*, or ObdL).

6　This includes various liaison aircraft and the transport aircraft assigned to both long- and short-range reconnaissance units.

3

Barbarossa Unleashed: The Invasion of Russia, June to October 1941

Your operations always hang by a thread!
Generalfeldmarschall Günther von Kluge to *Generaloberst* Heinz Guderian
9 July 1941[1]

During its first five months, the Russo-German War featured a German Army at the peak of its operational proficiency systematically destroying large portions of the opposing Soviet forces and rapidly advancing deep into the Soviet hinterland. Yet despite a string of victories Operation Barbarossa would eventually fail. In their search for why this transpired, historians have persistently argued that the Germans lacked the ability to make good their personnel and equipment losses and that, faced with swelling masses of Soviet troops, German forces simply became too weak to win the campaign.[2] To be sure, the size of the Red Army and the ability of the Soviet Union to muster fresh forces meant that there was always another series of Soviet armies to overcome; while badly led and facing a host of problems, these put up a ferocious resistance that imposed a relentless toll of men and machines upon the Germans. But the primary significance of this factor rests elsewhere, mainly in ensuring the long-term survivability of the Soviet Union, how it allowed the Red Army to endure the initial months of the war, and by the impact Soviet resistance had upon high-level German decision-making. While German personnel and material losses were heavy and this did lead to a gradual blunting of operational capabilities, the German Army was still able to maintain the strength of its field armies to a remarkable degree. In fact, the *Ostheer* received large numbers of replacement personnel, and the tank strengths of its panzer divisions generally remained high until late in the campaign. Frequently, German forces outnumbered their Soviet counterparts by significant margins. Operation Barbarossa would fail for a number of reasons – the resistance of the Red Army, poor German planning, logistical failures, the climate and terrain

---

1   Brian Fugate, *Operation Barbarossa: Strategy and Tactics on the Eastern Front, 1941.* (Novato, CA: 1984), p. 119.
2   See Ellis, *Brute Force*, p. 77, or Seaton, *The Russo-German War, 1941-1945*, pp. 171-175.

– but faltering unit strengths and personnel and equipment shortages only became a significant issue *after* the operation had already been lost.

In their explanations for the Germans initial successes, most narratives of the campaign tend to emphasize the utter confusion and unpreparedness experienced by the Russians during the first days of the war.[3] Stalin's abject refusal to face the reality of an impending German invasion unquestionably meant that many Soviet army and air force units were caught by surprise and suffered accordingly. However, the over-emphasis within the literature upon the level of the Russians' confusion and surprise tends to mask the fact that some (albeit comparatively few) units were prepared and responded as their pre-war training dictated, or that in general the Red Army fought back hard.[4] Although many border guard units were quickly overwhelmed, others fought with a tenacity born of desperation. Despite relentless *Luftwaffe* ground attacks, confusing orders, and shortages of all kinds, most regular Red Army forces immediately adjacent to the border moved to their assigned positions as quickly as they could, tried to establish coherent defence lines, or began launching local counter-attacks.[5] Recounting his experiences of that first day, one German officer belonging to the 6. *Panzer Division* later recalled, "Enemy resistance…was much stronger than expected."[6] As in the previous bouts of heavy fighting experienced by the *Wehrmacht*, the consequence was heavy casualties. In its failed attempt to capture the city of Brest on 22 June, the 45. *Infanterie Division* alone sustained 311 casualties, including 21 officers.[7] On both the ground and in the air, it quickly became evident that the Eastern campaign would extract a heavy toll from the *Wehrmacht*.[8]

At the outset of Barbarossa, the armed forces of the Soviet Union represented a mixture of both strengths and weaknesses. Mirroring the experience of the *Wehrmacht*, the Red Army had also undergone a massive force expansion during the years prior to 1941 (see Table 3.1). In only 36 months, the Red Army grew by almost four million men and 163 divisions, and a series of armoured, mechanized, and specialist units had been formed from scratch. Combined with Stalin's purges of the 1930s, this expansion placed tremendous demands upon the Soviet officer corps and resulted in crucial

3   For example, see Merridale, *Ivan's War*.
4   For Soviet preparations before the outbreak of hostilities, see Erickson, *The Road to Stalingrad*, pp. 101-122.
5   For the parlous state of Soviet communications, see Amnon Sella, " 'Barbarossa': Surprise Attack and Communication." *Journal of Contemporary History*, Vol. 13, No. 3 (July 1978), pp. 555-583.
6   Glantz, (Ed.) *The Initial Period of War on the Eastern Front, 22 June – August 1941*, p. 112.
7   Gschopf, *Mein Weg mit der 45. Infanterie Division*, p. 154.
8   A similar picture of Soviet resistance emerges in terms of air operations. Although the *Luftwaffe* inflicted extremely heavy losses upon its Soviet adversary, despite long-held beliefs within the literature to the contrary, it would never entirely control the skies over the Eastern Front. See Bergstrom, *Barbarossa: The Air Battle, July – December 1941*.

shortages of experienced, competent officers.[9] This deficiency had been vividly illustrated by the Red Army's poor performance during the Winter War with Finland (30 November – 13 March 1940) and would reappear during the summer of 1941.[10] The pace of expansion also meant that deficiencies in training and unit cohesion were almost universal. Whereas the German Army was fully equipped and possessed considerable surplus equipment stocks, significant portions of the Red Army were in a lamentable state. When the war began, many formations were under-strength in both men and equipment. Only four of the 29 mechanized corps possessed more than 75 percent of their authorized number of tanks, and few of the latest T-34 and KV series of tanks had managed to reach these formations by the time Germany attacked.[11] Most of the Soviet tank fleet consisted of older vehicles that, while still a match for their German counterparts, were rapidly approaching obsolescence. Moreover, on 15 June 1941, approximately 29 percent of these older models required major repairs and a further 44 percent needed some kind of lesser maintenance. Likewise, on 22 June the Red Army possessed only 314,200 of the 836,000 motor vehicles and tractors it needed, and 23 percent of these were listed as inoperable and in need of repair. Even Southwestern Front, whose formations ranked among the best equipped in the entire Red Army, faced significant equipment shortages, including 119,633 rifles and submachine guns, 9,278 machine-guns, 622 mortars, 222 anti-tank and 999 anti-aircraft guns, and 696 guns and howitzers.[12]

However, the great advantage held by the Soviet Union was the sheer size of its military resources and its pool of manpower. On 22 June, the Red Army fielded a total of 27 armies, 29 mechanized corps, 62 rifle corps, four cavalry corps, five airborne corps, 303 divisions (198 rifle, 61 tank, 31 mechanized, and 13 cavalry), 57 fortified regions, and a plethora of ancillary units. Further support came from the 165,000 men of the Border Guards Forces and 171,000 internal security personnel belonging to the People's Commissariat for Internal Affairs (NKVD). Including the Soviet Navy,

9   For an examination of the Soviet officer corps within the communist system, see Roger R. Reese, "Red Army Professionalism and the Communist Party, 1918-1941." *Journal of Military History*, Vol. 66, No. 1 (January 2002), pp. 71-102.

10   See Pavel Aptekar & Olga Dudorova, "The Unheeded Warning and the Winter War 1939-1940." *Journal of Slavic Military Studies*, Vol. 10, No. 1 (March 1997), pp. 200-209. For a challenge to the pervasive, long-standing belief of the Red Army's poor performance against Finland, see Reese, "Lessons of the Winter War: A Study in the Effectiveness of the Red Army, 1939-1940."

11   Louis Rotundo, "The Creation of Soviet Reserves and the 1941 Campaign." *Military Affairs*, Vol. 50, No. 1 (January 1986), p. 23. For instance, of the 1,031 medium and heavy tanks it was authorized, the 14th Mechanized Corps possessed 520 T-26 light tanks. Likewise, the 19th Mechanized Corps had only 280 tanks, of which a mere 11 were T-34's or KV-1's. Glantz & House, *When Titans Clashed*, p. 35. See also Michael Parrish, "Formation and Leadership of the Soviet Mechanized Corps in 1941." *Military Affairs*, Vol. 47, No. 2 (April 1983), pp. 63-66.

12   Glantz, *Stumbling Colossus*, p. 119, 177-178 & 182.

total Soviet military personnel numbered 5.7 million in mid-1941.[13] Replacement personnel and fresh drafts could be drawn from the 15-30 million men and women who had received paramilitary training through the *Osoaviakhim* during the 1930s. In material terms, the Red Army's stock of equipment by June 1941 included 248,900 machine-guns, 14,900 anti-tank and 8,600 anti-aircraft guns, 22,600 tanks, 33,200 artillery pieces, and 56,100 mortars.[14] Soviet military forces along Russia's western frontier were stationed in the Leningrad, Baltic, Western, and Kiev Special Military Districts, which were re-designated the Northern, Northwestern, Western, and Southwestern Fronts at the onset of hostilities. Including the Soviet 9th Army in the Odessa Military District, these contained 15 armies, 20 mechanized corps, 32 rifle corps, three cavalry and three airborne corps, and 163 divisions (97 rifle, 40 tank, 20 mechanized, and six cavalry) with 2.9 million men. Reinforcements could be drawn from formations stationed in the Soviet Far East and within the internal military districts, which possessed an additional six armies, 16 rifle corps, four mechanized corps, 83 divisions (59 rifle, seven cavalry, 11 tank and six mechanized), and 65 independent artillery regiments.[15] The quality of Soviet armoured forces was also improving with the introduction of advanced designs, and of the 1,684 tanks produced between January and June 1941, 1,503 were KV or T-34 tanks.[16] To alleviate the manpower shortages faced by under-strength Soviet formations, in April the People's Commissariat of Defence (NKO) ordered the activation of 900,000 reservists, of which 793,000 were called up in late May and early June. In consequence, most Soviet rifle divisions within the western military districts were increased in strength from their peacetime establishment of 6,000 men to 8,000-11,000 men (out of an authorized wartime strength of 14,500).[17]

In support of the ground forces, the various air contingents of the Soviet Union, including the VVS, training establishments, air defence forces, and naval air services, controlled a total of 20,978 aircraft, of which 13,211 were ready for combat.[18] The bulk of the aircraft equipping the air regiments of the VVS, such as the I-16 fighter and SB bomber, though usually derided as old or obsolete, were in actuality generally comparable to their contemporary British counterparts.[19] More significantly,

13   Ibid, pp. 11 & 107, and Goff, "Evolving Soviet Force Structure, 1941-1945: Process and Impact", p. 381.
14   Mawdsley, *Thunder in the East*, p. 47, and Bacon, "Soviet Military Losses in World War II.", p. 616.
15   Glantz, *Stumbling Colossus*, pp. 11.
16   Goff, "Evolving Soviet Force Structure, 1941-1945: Process and Impact.", p. 372. Bacon, "Soviet Military Losses in World War II.", p. 619, indicates that Soviet armour production between January and June 1941 amounted to 2,413 tanks, but he does not provide a breakdown according to type.
17   Glantz, *Stumbling Colossus*, p. 153.
18   Ibid, p. 21.
19   These included the Hawker Hurricane I, Spitfire V, and the Bristol Blenheim IV and Beaufort I.

improved designs comparable with the latest aircraft available to the *Luftwaffe*, such as MiG-3, Yak-1, and LaGG-5 fighters, Pe-2 light bombers, and Il-2 ground-attack aircraft, were reaching Soviet air units in increasing numbers. By late June, 1,448 (20 percent) out of the 7,133 aircraft stationed in the western military districts were of modern design.[20] Notable shortages of pilots existed, particularly for the newer models of aircraft, but this was slowly being rectified by the expansion of the number of pilot training schools.[21]

Even more detrimental to the prospects of Barbarossa's successful outcome was the Soviet pre-war accumulation of operational and strategic reserves. On 26 April 1941, one mechanized corps, two rifle corps, and two airborne brigades stationed in the Soviet Far East were ordered to redeploy to the western military districts. Within two weeks, four more rifle divisions were dispatched to the west from the Ural and Siberian Military Districts.[22] In consequence, the frontier districts were able to accumulate an operational reserve consisting of 17 corps (including six mechanized) and seven divisions. On 13 May, an NKO decree ordered the activation of a seven-army strategic reserve from amongst the forces stationed in the internal military districts. Totalling 14 rifle corps, five mechanized corps, 57 divisions (42 rifle, ten tank, and five mechanized), and 17 independent artillery regiments, this reserve was to deploy along the line of the Dvina and Dnepr Rivers, serving as a vital second echelon in support of the forces deployed along the western border. Admittedly, only nine divisions had completed their deployment by 22 June, with a further 19 divisions underway.[23] Nonetheless, by the time the *Wehrmacht* had overwhelmed the Soviet frontier armies most of these formations had moved into place and were ready to contest the next stage of the German advance.

In consequence, the first weeks of Barbarossa witnessed a series of dramatic German victories, but these were accompanied by heavy losses and a string of Soviet counterattacks.[24] Along the northern axis, the *LVI. (Mot.) Armee Korps* advanced 350 km in only four days.[25] At 0530 hours on 26 June, in cooperation with a team

---

20 These included at least 105 Yak-1 and 886 MiG-3 fighters, and a number of Pe-2 bombers. A total of 74 Il-2's had been produced during May 1941, but how many of these had reached Soviet air regiments at the time Barbarossa had begun is unknown. Glantz, *Stumbling Colossus*, p. 192.

21 The number of training schools expanded from 32 in 1939 to 111 by 1941. Ibid, p 187.

22 David M. Glantz, "Soviet Mobilization in Peace and War, 1924-1942: A Survey." *Journal of Slavic Military Studies*, Vol. 5, No. 3 (September 1992), pp. 343.

23 Glantz, *Stumbling Colossus*, pp. 10-11.

24 For the best synopsis yet produced regarding these early Soviet offensive operations, see Glantz, *Forgotten Battles of the German-Soviet War, 1941-1945. Vol. One*. Also see David Glantz, "Forgotten Battles of the German-Soviet War (1941-1945), Part One." *Journal of Slavic Military Studies*, Vol. 12, No. 4 (1999), pp. 149-197, and "Forgotten Battles of the German-Soviet War (1941-1945), Part Two." *Journal of Slavic Military Studies*, Vol. 13, No. 1 (2000), pp. 172-237.

25 Russel Stolfi, *Hitler's Panzers East: World War II Reinterpreted*. (Norman, OK: 1991), p. 45.

of *Brandenburgers*, the corps seized the critical road and rail bridges over the Dvina River at Daugavpils, which forced the Northwestern Front to abandon any notions it entertained of maintaining itself in Lithuania and retreat to the Dvina River line. Despite repeated Soviet counterattacks led by the fresh 21st Mechanized Corps and near suicidal efforts by Soviet bombers to destroy the bridges, the Germans managed to retain their bridgehead. Rather than continue its advance, the corps now had to mark time for several days to allow neighbouring units to catch up but Soviet armoured counterattacks were imposing significant delays. On 23 June, the Soviet 11th Mechanized Corps attacked the infantry divisions of the *I. Armee Korps* and in three days lost 704 of its original 749 tanks.[26] Further east, the 2nd Tank Division attacked the *6. Panzer Division* on 24 June and overran two of its bridge-heads over the Dubysa River around the town of Raseinai.[27] Faced by 300 Soviet tanks (including 50 heavy KV-1), the *6. Panzer Division* only just managed to hang on until the remaining divisions of the *XLI. (Mot.) Armee Korps* arrived. Three days of heavy fighting ensued until the Russian division was encircled and destroyed. This event constituted a significant psychological shock to many of the participating Germans, who watched as their best tanks and anti-tank guns were literally run over by seemingly impenetrable Soviet heavy tanks. "Our path to the east offered a dreadful picture of smashed vehicles of Motorised Rifle Regiment 114, rolled over by tanks[.] We also found our riflemen who had been cut-off two nights before. They had been killed and horribly mutilated."[28] After reorganizing itself, on 30 June the *XLI. (Mot.) Armee Korps* managed to seize its own bridgeheads across the Dvina at Jacobpils and Livany. On 2 July, both corps (as part of *4. Panzergruppe*) attacked out of their bridgeheads and began a concerted advance upon Leningrad via the cities of Ostrov and Pskov south of Lake Peipus. Notwithstanding fierce Soviet resistance, both cities had been captured by 8 July. However, despite a dramatic advance of 450 km, most of the Soviet Northwestern Front appears to have escaped, albeit without the bulk of its equipment.[29]

With Leningrad now only 250 km away, the *4. Panzergruppe* resumed its drive on 10 July. Three days later, elements of the *XLI. (Mot.) Armee Korps* had advanced an additional 140 km and seized bridgeheads over the Luga River. Here the advance stalled, having run into the hastily constructed Luga Defence Line, a 10-15 km deep barrier of minefields and fortified positions held by the Soviet Northern Front with a mixture of previously bloodied divisions, some newly created or transferred reserves, and three People's Militia Divisions. For the next six days, the Germans

26   Glantz, *The Battle for Leningrad, 1941-1944*, p. 32.
27   Glantz, *The Initial Period of War on the Eastern Front, 22nd June – August 1941*, p. 113.
28   Ibid, p. 116.
29   The strength of the Baltic Military District on 22 June amounted to 369,702 men, 7,019 guns and mortars, and 1,549 tanks. By 7 July, the Northwestern Front had sustained 90,000 casualties, and lost 1,000 tanks and 4,000 guns and mortars. Glantz, *The Battle for Leningrad, 1941-1944*, pp. 32 & 36.

endeavoured to overcome the Soviet defenders, but to no avail.[30] Support from the *LVI. (Mot.) Armee Korps*, advancing to the south, was not forthcoming because its own advance had slowed in the face of heavy Soviet resistance around the town of Soltsy. Moreover, on 14 July, this corps was hit by a powerful Soviet counter-attack consisting of one tank and five rifle divisions that encircled the *8. Panzer Division* for the next four days.[31] With the supporting infantry corps of the *16. Armee* trailing far to the southwest, mobile reserves had to be shifted from the main drive on Leningrad to rescue the *8. Panzer Division* from its predicament. Although it managed to fight its way out, heavy losses of men and equipment temporarily rendered the division *hors de combat*.[32] Although the Soviet counter-stroke had failed to destroy any of the encircled units, it was clear evidence that the Red Army, despite the damage it had taken, was still capable of offering surprisingly fierce resistance.

More significantly, the danger the Soviet counterstroke posed to the exposed flank of *4. Panzergruppe* precipitated a crisis that caused considerable anxiety amongst Hitler and the OKH. In its positions along the Luga River, the precious armoured spearhead of *Heeresgruppe Nord* was terribly exposed. The infantry corps of the *16. Armee* lingered far to the southwest as it slowly fought its way through difficult swamps and vast forests towards the city of Kholm. To the northwest, half of the *18. Armee* was preoccupied with the task of clearing Soviet forces from Estonia and the Baltic islands. Furthermore, the terrain around Leningrad was covered in large swaths of swamp and forest that had been buttressed by belts of formidable Soviet field fortifications, hardly an appropriate operating environment for panzer units unsupported by large amounts of infantry.[33] Mounting logistical problems exacerbated German concerns, as only one double-tracked rail line ran from the Nieman River to Leningrad, thereby limiting the pace at which supplies could be brought forward and stockpiled. Vital rail bridges at Riga and Petseri had also been destroyed and were not repaired until 17 and 24 July, respectively. The motorised supply columns belonging to *Heeresgruppe Nord*, whose serviceability levels had fallen to an average of 61 percent by 3 August, were forced to undertake 700 km roundtrip journeys between established supply dumps

---

30   In struggling to hold and expand its bridgehead over the Luga River between 14-22 July, the *6. Panzer Division* sustained 182 killed and 491 wounded. Around its bridgehead, the division reportedly counted 2,300 Russian dead and 71 destroyed tanks. *Kriegstagebuch der 6. Panzer Division (17.6-15.9.1941)*, NARA T315 Roll 323, Frames 000011-000124.
31   Glantz, *The Battle for Leningrad, 1941-1944*, pp. 43-45, and Glantz, *Forgotten Battles of the German-Soviet War, 1941-1945. Vol. One*, pp. 19-28.
32   By 18 July, the losses sustained by the *8. Panzer Division* thus far in the campaign amounted to 339 killed, 1,166 wounded, and 33 missing. Haupt, *Die 8. Panzer Division im Zweiten Weltkrieg*, p. 160. In the fighting around Soltsy, 70 of its 150 tanks were destroyed or damaged. Glantz, *Forgotten Battles of the German-Soviet War, 1941-1945. Vol. One*, p. 28.
33   See Jesse W. Miller Jr., "Forest Fighting on the Eastern Front in World War II." *Geographical Review*, Vol. 62, No. 2 (April 1972), pp. 186-202.

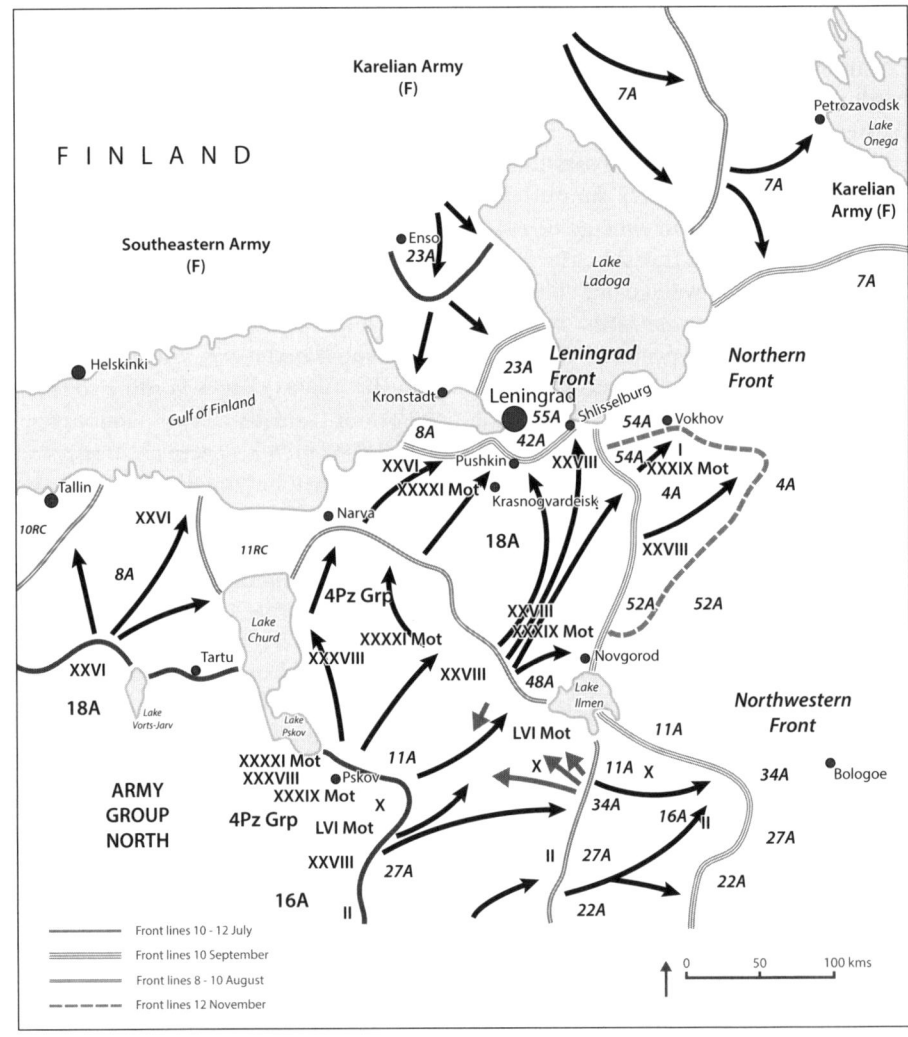

Map 3.1 Operations in the Leningrad Region, July to November 1941.

along the Dvina River and the panzer spearheads on the Luga.[34] In consequence, Hitler issued Directive No. 33 (19 July) and Supplement to Directive No. 33 (23 July) in which he ordered, "The advance on Leningrad will be resumed only when 18th Army has made contact with 4th Armoured Group and the extensive flank in the east is adequately protected by 16th Army." Before the drive upon Leningrad could be resumed, *Heeresgruppe Nord* was to assemble "strong forces of infantry...to avoid expending its mobile forces in frontal attacks over difficult terrain."[35] The immediate result was that the direct German advance upon Leningrad was brought to a halt for the next three weeks.

At this stage, personnel losses did not factor into the decision to halt the drive upon Leningrad. From 22 June to 20 July, *Heeresgruppe Nord* sustained at least 29,075 casualties, or an average of 1,038 per division.[36] These losses were partially mitigated by the fact that 24 of its 28 divisions possessed organic *Feldersatz* battalions containing an average of 790 men, or a total of 18,960 replacements. Although this still left *Heeresgruppe Nord* with 10,115 vacancies in the ranks, if the replacements were evenly distributed amongst its 264 combat battalions, this would have meant that every battalion was short only 38 men.[37] Given that, according to their assigned KStN, the established personnel strength of German infantry and motorised infantry battalions amounted to 861 and 1,089 men respectively (for more details, see Appendix Four), such a shortfall would have only represented a small reduction in fighting power.[38] To be sure, casualties were not evenly distributed amongst all the divisions: by 18 July the *8. Panzer Division* had sustained 1,538 casualties, while during 8-20 July the *30. Infanterie Division* took 1,033 casualties.[39]

---

34 The serviceability rate in some particular supply columns had been reduced to as much 44 percent. Schuler, *Logistik im Russlandfeldzug*, p. 314.

35 Trevor-Roper, ed. *Hitler's War Directives, 1939-1945*, pp. 89-93.

36 See Heeresarzt 10-Day Casualty Reports for *Heeresgruppe Nord* (22.6-20.7.41) in BA-MA RW 6/556 and 6/558.

37 The number of combat battalions includes all divisional infantry, motorized infantry, motorcycle and reconnaissance battalions. Three security divisions are not included since they were not involved in frontline combat and it is assumed their losses at this point were minor. The number of combat battalions is broken down as follows:

Three panzer divs. (x6 btls.)	= 18	22 infantry divisions (x10 btls.)	= 220
Two mot. inf. divs. (x8 btls.)	= 16	Total	= 264
One Waffen-SS mot. div. (x10 btls.)	= 10		

38 These battalion strengths are estimates based upon available KStN, some of which do not correspond to this specific time but which would have been roughly similar. The figure for infantry battalions is drawn from KStN Nr. 111, 131c, and 151c. The strength of the motorized infantry (*Schützen*) battalions is a composite drawn from KStN Nr. 1108, 1114, 1116, 1121, 1122, 1123, and 1124. It should also be noted that, given the variety of organizational differences already existing between divisions and that these translated into fluctuating personnel strengths, these battalion strengths only represent a general estimate.

39 Haupt, *Die 8. Panzer Division im Zweiten Weltkrieg*, p. 160, and Breithaupt, *Die Geschichte der 30. Infanterie Division, 1939-1945*, p. 87. The losses sustained by the *30. Infanterie*

Yet both these divisions possessed *Feldersatz* battalions, which meant their combat elements should have been short an actual total of 748 and 243 men, respectively. This translates into an average deficit of 125 men in each of the six combat battalions belonging to the *8. Panzer Division*, and 24 men in each of the ten battalions of the *30. Infanterie Division*, which would have been far from crippling. Moreover, approximately 65,000 replacements were dispatched to the *Ostheer* during July and presumably some of these were assigned to *Heeresgruppe Nord*.[40] Thus the shortages indicated above should have been even lower. This makes it evident that it was Soviet actions, as illustrated by the continued resistance on the flanks of *4. Panzergruppe* and the counterstroke at Soltsy, together with mounting logistical problems, and not personnel shortages, that were the primary rationale behind the decision to temporarily halt the advance on Leningrad.

Halting the drive upon Leningrad ultimately had significant consequences in that it allowed the Red Army to consolidate its defences around the city and bring up fresh reserves, especially in the area south of Lake Ilmen, which hampered the efforts of the *16. Armee* to clear the army group's right flank. In turn, this influenced Hitler in his decision to issue Directive No. 34 (30 July), which ordered *Heeresgruppe Mitte* to halt its advance upon Moscow and instead focus upon cooperating with *Heeresgruppe Nord* to clear out the Velikie Luki region and the area south of Lake Ilmen. On 8 August, he also ordered *Heeresgruppe Mitte* to transfer the *XXXIX. (Mot.) Armee Korps* (with one panzer and two motorised divisions) and half its available air support (in the form of the powerful *VIII. Fliegerkorps*) to its northern neighbour.[41] Just as the assault upon Leningrad resumed on 8 August, the Soviet Northwestern Front launched its own attacks around the cities of Staraia Russa and Kholm four days later. These attacks isolated a number of German infantry divisions and again threatened the flank of the forces moving upon Leningrad, forcing the Germans to shift two precious motorised divisions from their main effort to deal with them. Although the Northwestern Front was badly mauled in the ensuing German counterattack, the advance upon Leningrad was significantly weakened at a critical moment.[42]

Along the southern and southwestern approaches to the city, the outcome of the battle hung in the balance as the Germans fought their way through successive layers of Soviet defences at an agonizingly slow and costly pace. In just two days of fighting

  Division included 203 killed, 819 wounded, and 11 missing.

40 Kroener, et. al. *GSWW. Vol. V: Part One*, p. 1020.

41 The *VIII. Fliegerkorps* redeployed to the northern sector with five ground-attack, three bomber, and two fighter groups. The divisions transferred were the *12. Panzer, 18.*, and *20. (Mot.) Infanterie Divisions*.

42 From an original strength of 327,099 men, 541 tanks, and 1,667 machine-guns, the 11th, 27th, and 34th Armies of the Northwestern Front sustained 128,550 casualties and lost 481 tanks and 1,417 machine-guns between 10 August and 1 September. Glantz, *The Battle for Leningrad, 1941-1944*, p. 57.

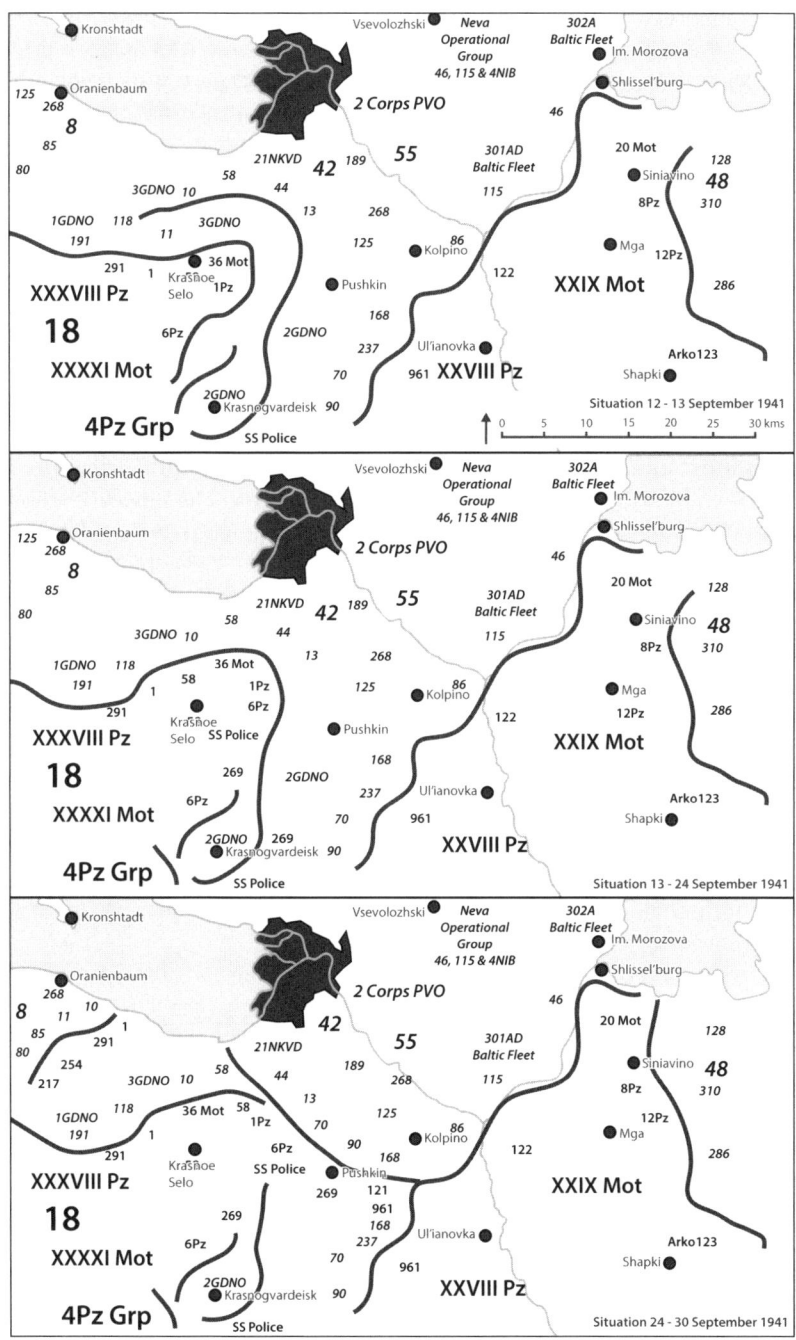

Map 3.2 The Slow German Advance on Leningrad, 12-30 September 1941.

(10-11 August) while breaking through the Luga Defence Line, the *121. Infanterie Division* sustained 937 casualties, including 43 officers.[43] The nearby *6. Panzer Division* had 1,197 casualties (8-20 August), including 282 on 8 August alone.[44] Both sides also enjoyed considerable air support: on 10 August, the VVS flew 908 sorties in the Leningrad region, while the *Luftwaffe* staged 1,126 sorties.[45] Soviet resistance on the ground was tenacious, having been galvanized on 9 September by the arrival of the tough and ruthless General of the Army Georgi Zhukov.[46] Nonetheless, during August and September, *Heeresgruppe Nord* slowly managed to isolate Leningrad from the rest of the Soviet Union by capturing Shlisselburg along the southern shore of Lake Ladoga and having literally advanced to within sight of the city. However, both combatants fought themselves to exhaustion and on 30 September *Generalfeldmarschall* Ritter Wilhelm von Leeb, the commander of *Heeresgruppe Nord*, ordered a halt to further attacks.

Casualties on both sides were staggering. Many Soviet formations were decimated in the fighting: on 20 August, the Soviet 48th Army reported its strength as only 6,235 men, 5,043 rifles, and 31 artillery pieces, while the 118th Rifle Division was reduced to 3,025 men, 17 artillery pieces, and 54 machine-guns by 9 September.[47] On 25 August, the Soviet 8th Army reported that it had lost 100 percent of its original regimental and battalion commanders.[48] Initially numbering some 517,000 personnel, the Soviet forces in the Leningrad region were reinforced during the course of operations by five additional army headquarters and 20 divisions, but between 10 July and 30 September total Soviet losses amounted to 344,926 casualties (including 214,078 killed or missing, and 130,848 wounded or sick), and included the loss of 1,492 tanks, and 9,885 guns and mortars.[49] By 30 September the VVS deployed in the Baltic region had also lost 2,692 aircraft since the start of the campaign.[50]

For *Heeresgruppe Nord* the fighting in August and September cost at least 92,532 casualties.[51] This translates into an average loss of 3,427 men in each of its 27 divisions, or 376 casualties for each of the 246 combat battalions that belonged to the army group.[52] During the period of 1 August to 20 September, the *121. Infanterie Division*

---

43   Traditionsverband der Division. *Geschichte der 121. Ostpreussischen Infanterie Division 1940-1945.* (Berlin: 1970), p. 87.
44   See *Kriegstagebuch der 6. Panzer Division (17.6-15.9.1941),* NARA T315 Roll 323.
45   Bergstrom, *Barbarossa: The Air Battle, July – December 1941,* pp. 57-58.
46   The most thorough account of this stage of the struggle around Leningrad can be found in Glantz, *The Battle for Leningrad, 1941-1944,* pp. 59-86.
47   Ibid, p. 61-62.
48   Erickson, *The Road to Stalingrad,* p. 189.
49   Krivosheev, *Soviet Casualties and Combat Losses in the 20th Century,* p. 115 & 260.
50   Bergstrom, *Barbarossa: The Air Battle, July – December 1941,* p. 88.
51   Heeresarzt 10-Day Casualty Reports for *Heeresgruppe Nord* (1.8-30.9.41) in BA-MA RW 6/556 and 6/558.
52   By late August, *Heeresgruppe Nord* consisted of 27 divisions whose combat battalions are broken down as follows:

alone sustained 4,327 casualties.[53] At first glance, losses on this scale would seem to have played the primary role in ultimately bringing the German assault on Leningrad to a standstill. However, according to Halder's war diary, 35,000 replacements had been dispatched to *Heeresgruppe Nord* since the start of the campaign or were due to arrive before the end of August. A further 20,000 replacements were scheduled to arrive in September.[54] Together with the men within the *Feldersatz* battalions, this meant that 73,960 replacements had been made available by the end of September to cover the 139,532 casualties the army group had sustained since June.[55] This would still have left a shortage of 65,572 men, but the exact implications of this are far from clear because of the shuffling of divisions between army groups. Still, if the replacements that arrived by the end of September (55,000) are counted against the losses sustained by *Heeresgruppe Nord* in August and September (92,532), the result is a deficit of 37,532. When divided by the number of combat battalions with the army group during the final advance upon Leningrad (246), the result is a shortage of 153 men per battalion. Adding the shortages that existed by the end of July (38), this means that the available combat battalions should have been short an average of 194 men by the end of September. Based upon their authorized strengths, infantry battalions (of 861 men) should still have retained an average of 667 men (78 percent).[56] For motorised battalions (with 1,089 men), the figure would have been 895 men (82 percent). Although these figures are speculative, this would seem to indicate that compared to the debilitated state of many Soviet units, *Heeresgruppe Nord* should have been in comparatively good shape in terms of manpower when von Leeb ordered it to halt.[57]

Four panzer divs. (x6 btls.)	= 24	18 infantry divisions (x10 btls.)	= 180
Four mot. inf. divs. (x8 btls.)	= 32	Total	= 246
One Waffen-SS mot. div. (x10 btls.)	= 10		

53 These losses included 805 killed, 3,136 wounded, and 387 missing. Previously, from 22 June to 30 July, the division had already suffered 2,201 casualties (480 killed, 1,584 wounded, and 137 missing). Traditionsverband. *Geschichte der 121. Ostpreussischen Infanterie Division 1940-1945*, p. 87.

54 Halder, *Kriegstagebuch. Band II*, p. 1201.

55 Heeresarzt 10-Day Casualty Reports for *Heeresgruppe Nord* (22.6-30.9.41) in BA-MA RW 6/556 and 6/558.

56 Significantly, reports submitted by the *18. Armee* indicate that by 19 October the average *Iststärke* of the (100) combat battalions within its ten infantry divisions amounted to 560 men, or 65 percent of their *Sollstärke*. Note that this army's combat losses during the first nineteen days of October amounted to 963 killed, 3,186 wounded, and 29 missing, for a total of 4,178 casualties. See *Heeresgruppe Nord, Abt. Ia. Lagebeurteilungen Nr. 1 (15 Juli – 24 November 1941)*. NARA T311 Roll 51, Frames 7064208 – 7064238. By evenly distributing the losses they had sustained thus far in October, this would seem to indicate that these battalions may have still retained about 70 percent of their *Sollstärke* by the end of September.

57 The figures shown for losses and replacements here represent a best guess based upon the material available. Not included in the German casualty figures are sick who were

While an assessment of the impact German personnel losses had upon the decision to stop operations around Leningrad is difficult to ascertain with any accuracy, it should be noted that von Leeb had laboured under considerable time constraints. On 6 September Hitler issued orders for the advance upon Moscow to be resumed by the end of the month. This entailed the transfer from von Leeb's command to *Heeresgruppe Mitte* of the headquarters of *4. Panzergruppe*, the headquarters of three motorised corps, and four panzer and motorised divisions starting on 15 September. The *VIII. Fliegerkorps* was also to be transferred south, taking with it most of the *Luftwaffe* formations that had been supporting *Heeresgruppe Nord*.[58] Although von Leeb still retained sizeable resources (including two panzer and two motorised divisions), the departure of these formations appear to have convinced him that his army group now lacked the resources to take Leningrad by direct assault or invest its environs more closely.[59]

Interestingly, while the German failure to capture Leningrad might be explained by a combination of Soviet resistance, heavy losses, Hitler's shifting strategic priorities and time constraints, it cannot be attributed to a lack of armour. By 10 September, the three original panzer divisions assigned to *4. Panzergruppe* had lost 131 tanks since the beginning of the campaign as *Totalausfälle* and had received only two replacements.[60] Nonetheless, together with the recently arrived *12. Panzer Division*, these divisions still retained a total of 637 panzers (or 73 percent of their initial strength) at the height of the push on Leningrad. As noted in Table 3.2, the majority (83 percent) of these vehicles were operational. As late as 26 September, the *8. Panzer Division* still had 93 panzers operational.[61] In contrast, by 1 September the Soviet defenders of Leningrad possessed significantly fewer tanks. The mainstay of Soviet armoured support had been the 10th Mechanized Corps, which had 1,348 tanks on 22 June.[62] However, by September this formation had been worn down by over two months of

transferred back to Germany for treatment. On the entire *Ostfront* these amounted to at least 127,800 men between June and September. Also excluded from the number of replacements are wounded personnel who remained in the army group rear area and were later directly returned to their units. These have been estimated at approximately 20,000 per month. Kroener, et. al. *GSWW. Vol. V: Part One*, p. 1020.

58   By early October, *Luftflotte 1* had been reduced to three fighter and six bomber groups. Bergstrom, *Barbarossa: The Air Battle, July – December 1941*, p. 94.

59   Hitler had long expressed his reluctance to storm Leningrad proper because of the losses he feared this would entail. Instead, the city was to be closely invested and reduced through starvation, artillery fire, and bombing. Although he had expressed this view to his advisors since July, the direct order was only issued on 22 September, by which time Soviet resistance had already brought the advance to a virtual halt. See Irving, *Hitler's War*, pp. 394-395, and Samuel W. Mitcham Jr. & Gene Mueller, *Hitler's Commanders: Officers of the Wehrmacht, the Luftwaffe, the Kriegsmarine, and the Waffen-SS*. (New York: 2000), p. 48.

60   Jentz, *Panzertruppen, Vol. One*, p. 206.

61   Haupt, *Die 8. Panzer Division im Zweiten Weltkrieg*, p. 176.

62   Steven J. Zaloga, "Technological Surprise and the Initial Period of War: The Case of the T-34 Tank in 1941." *Journal of Slavic Military Studies*, Vol. 6, No. 4 (1993), p. 638.

combat and its 21st and 24th Tank and 198th Motorised Divisions were operating separately across the front endeavouring to provide hard-pressed Soviet rifle formations with a modicum of armour support. By 1 August, the 24th Tank Division had already been reduced to 50 operational tanks.[63] During September this division was broken up into a separate tank brigade and an independent tank regiment, while the 198th Motorised Division was downgraded to a normal rifle division, which indicates that both formations had already lost most of their armour. The only other available Soviet armoured assets were the remnants of the 1st Tank Division and three weak independent tank battalions.[64]

To the south, German efforts in the sector of *Heeresgruppe Mitte* resulted in even greater successes than those initially witnessed in the Baltic region. In short order the *2.* and *3. Panzergruppe* smashed their way through Soviet border defences, fended off various Soviet counterattacks and by 30 June linked up west of Minsk to create a massive pocket enclosing most of the Soviet 3rd, 10th, 4th and 13th Armies. On 7 July, German panzer spearheads had already crossed the Berezina and pressed on to the Western Dvina and Dnepr Rivers. Although the reduction of the pocket entailed ferocious and time-consuming fighting, and large numbers of Soviet soldiers eventually managed to exfiltrate back to their own lines, the result was a tremendous victory. At the outset of operations, the Soviet Western Front had totalled 671,165 personnel, 14,171 guns and mortars, and 2,900 tanks.[65] On 9 July, *Wehrmacht* communiqués claimed that 323,898 prisoners had been taken, and that 1,809 artillery pieces and 3,332 tanks had been destroyed or captured.[66] Contemporary Russian sources quote Soviet losses in Belorussia during 22 June to 9 July as including 341,012 killed or missing, and 76,717 sick and wounded, for a total of 417,729 casualties.[67] Soviet material losses included 4,799 tanks, 9,427 guns and mortars, and 1,177 aircraft.[68] In only 18 days, *Heeresgruppe Mitte* had practically demolished the Soviet Western Front and advanced 460 kilometres into the Soviet Union.

---

63   See information regarding 10th Mechanized Corps on the website "RKKA in World War II." located at http://www.armchairgeneral.com/rkkaww2/formation/mechcorps/10mk.htm
64   On 18 August, the 1st Tank Division possessed 59 tanks, but this figure had been reduced to 20 KV tanks by 11 September. See information regarding "1st Tank Division" located at http://www.armchairgeneral.com/rkkaww2/formation/mechcorps/10mk.htm. At full strength, independent tank battalions were authorized to have 29 tanks. For the Soviet order of battle for 1 September 1941, see Glantz, *The Battle for Leningrad, 1941-1944*, pp. 497-500.
65   Glantz, *Barbarossa Derailed: The Battle for Smolensk, 10 July – 10 September 1941. Volume One*, p. 37.
66   Jacobsen, (Ed.) *KTB OKW. Band I*, p. 1217.
67   Krivosheev, *Soviet Casualties and Combat Losses in the 20th Century*, p. 111.
68   Glantz, *Barbarossa Derailed. Vol. One*, p. 33.

But this victory was not achieved without significant cost. The *10. (Mot.) Infanterie Division* lost 123 killed and 128 wounded on 6 July alone.[69] In the last days of June, the *5. Infanterie Division* sustained 230 casualties, the *7. Infanterie Division* lost 644 men, the *78. Infanterie Division* had 238 killed or wounded, and the *137. Infanterie Division* endured 705 casualties.[70] The worst hit was the *45. Infanterie Division* that lost 482 killed and 1,000 wounded between 22 and 30 June as it struggled to destroy the 3,000-4,500 Soviet defenders trapped within the citadel of Brest.[71] By 2 July, the *3. Panzergruppe* listed 1,769 men as casualties, while the *2. Panzergruppe* reported that its losses on 4 July had reached 7,089 casualties since the start of operations, and that these included the alarmingly high number of 367 officers.[72] While painful, for the moment such losses were still manageable, as the personnel held within divisional *Feldersatz* battalions would have replaced most of these losses. The three panzer and three motorised divisions belonging to the *3. Panzergruppe* each had their own *Feldersatz* battalion, and the 4,730 replacements these collectively held more than sufficed to cover their current losses. Although the 6,320 replacements held by the *Feldersatz* battalions of eight of *2. Panzergruppe*'s nine divisions did not entirely cover the 6,857 casualties they sustained, in most instances this resulted in small deficits that only marginally impaired their combat performance and abilities (see Table 3.3) The only possible exception may have been the *18. Panzer Division*, whose losses meant an average shortage of 121 men in each of its six combat battalions. Still, with each *schützen* or *kradschützen* battalion authorized 1,089 men, even this should have only had a minimal impact.

In material terms, the panzer divisions still retained the preponderance of their initial armoured strengths. Admittedly, by the end of operations around Minsk *operational* strengths had fallen, sometimes dramatically. However, most of the decline was due to mechanical breakdowns, mainly from the exertions of racing nonstop along hundreds of kilometres of rough dirt roads. Smaller numbers of tanks were rendered unserviceable because of damage they had taken in combat, but few vehicles had actually been destroyed of permanently lost.[73] From an initial strength of 218 tanks, the *18. Panzer Division* was left with merely 83 operational by 6 July, but only 16 panzers

69   Schmidt, *Geschichte der 10. Division, 10. (Mot.) Infanterie Division, 10. Panzergrenadier Division, 1933-1945*, p. 95.

70   Reincke, *Die 5. Jäger Division 1939-1945*, p. 69, Hertlein, *Chronik der 7. Infanterie Division*, p. 64, Merker, *Das Buch der 78. Sturmdivision*, p. 36, and Wilhelm Meyer-Detring, *Die 137. Infanterie Division im Mittelabschnitt der Ostfront.* (Niederosterreich: 1962), p. 28.

71   Gschopf, *Mein Weg mit der 45. Infanterie Division*, p. 158.

72   *Kriegstagebuch Nr. 1(25 May – 31 August 1941), Pz Gr. 3, Ia*. NARA T313 Roll 225, Frame 7489010, and *Anlagenband Nr. 2b zum KTB, PzAOK 2 Ia/IIa., Vom 22.7.1941. Verlustenmeldungen: Zahlmassige Verluste 5.7.1941 – 25.3.1942.*

73   During the entire month of June, operations in the East resulted in the *Totalausfalle* of only 118 panzers and StuG. Boog, et. al. *GSWW. Vol. IV*, p. 1120-1122.

had been registered as total losses.[74] Similarly, the *3. Panzergruppe* reported the *Totalausfälle* of 85 panzers by 4 July, but this represented only 8.3 percent of its total inventory of 1,015 panzers.[75] With roads choked by advancing infantry and logistical columns, and harassed by Soviet stragglers, maintenance units encountered considerable difficulties procuring spare parts from increasingly distant supply depots. Most importantly, the urgent need to continue operations before the Red Army regained its balance left precious little time in which to conduct needed maintenance and repairs. Still, given the availability of spare parts and time, operational readiness could be restored in relatively short order. On the evening of 28 June, the *7. Panzer Division* reported that half its Pz II and Pz 38t tanks (111 out of an initial 222) and 75 percent of its Pz IV (23 out of 30) were non-operational.[76] Nonetheless, having remained stationary as part of the encirclement ring around Minsk, the division could already report by 30 June that 149 of its panzers were ready for combat.[77] How many more were repaired by the time the division resumed its advance on 3 July is unknown.

Despite the dimensions of the German success along the central axis, the primary factor that would ultimately prove fatal to the outcome of Operation Barbarossa was already emerging. This was the sheer size of the Soviet response. By 1 July, the Soviet Union had mobilized 5.3 million reservists, of which 3,544,000 were deployed to the front by the end of the year.[78] During the course of the month the Red Army would form 13 new field armies, followed by another 14 field armies in August, five in September and October, eight in November and December, and ten more in the spring of 1942.[79] Especially along the Moscow axis, these armies were formed into successive echelons, capable of establishing yet another line of defence for the Germans to overcome, or else acting as reserves for counterstrokes. To complement these armies, throughout the second half of 1941 the Red Army established at least 286 new rifle divisions to replace the 124 divisions that were destroyed or disbanded. During this same period, the Soviets also managed to form 159 rifle brigades, 48 cavalry divisions, ten tank divisions, 68 independent tank brigades, 100 separate tank battalions, and a host of supporting artillery units.[80] Granted, the scale and speed of mobilization meant these formations faced shortages of men, equipment, leadership,

---

74   Wolfgang Paul, *Geschichte der 18. Panzer Division 1940-1943, mit Geschichte der 18. Artillerie Division 1943-1944, anhang Heeresartillerie Brigade 88, 1944-1945.* (Germany: 1989), p. 32-33.
75   These losses included 34 out of 302 Pz I/II (11 percent), 14 of 126 Pz III/IV (11 percent), and 37 of 507 Pz 35/38t (7 percent). *Kriegstagebuch Nr. 1(25 May – 31 August 1941), Pz Gr. 3, Ia.* NARA T313 Roll 225, Frame 7489040.
76   Stahl, *Operation Barbarossa and Germany's Defeat in the East,* p. 173.
77   Horst Scheibert, *Die Gespenster Division: Eine deutsche Panzer Division im Zweiten Weltkrieg.* (Friedberg: 1981), p. 54.
78   Rotundo, "The Creation of Soviet Reserves and the 1941 Campaign", p. 23.
79   Glantz & House, *When Titans Clashed,* p. 68.
80   At least 215 artillery, 72 anti-tank, and eight Guards Mortar regiments, as well as 73 independent battalions, were also formed. Rotundo, "The Creation of Soviet Reserves

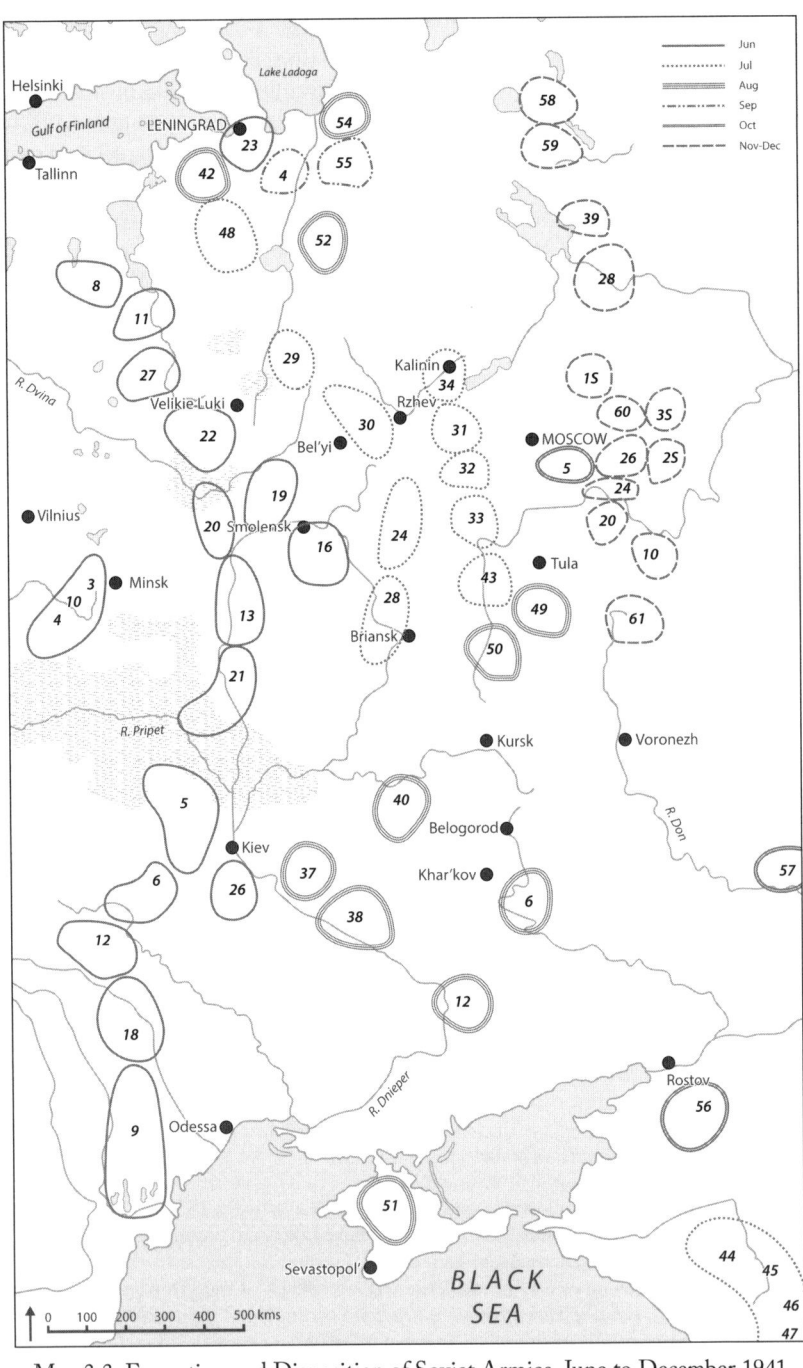

Map 3.3 Formation and Disposition of Soviet Armies, June to December 1941.

and training. Even so, despite the disruptions caused by the German invasion and the subsequent evacuation of 1,523 factories to safety behind the Ural Mountains, Soviet industry still managed to manufacture prodigious quantities of war material.[81] Between 22 June and 31 December 1941, this included approximately 4,177 tanks, 2,500 anti-tank and 3,400 anti-aircraft guns, 10,100 artillery pieces, 42,400 mortars, 1,000 Katyusha rocket launchers, and 9,900 combat aircraft.[82] The scale of this mobilization and its echeloning throughout the depths of the Soviet Union meant that the fundamental object of Operation Barbarossa, namely the destruction of the Red Army, could never possibly be achieved before the combination of the Germans own personnel and equipment losses, logistical problems, and sheer physical exhaustion reached their culmination point.

Conversely, by the time the vanguards of *Heeresgruppe Mitte* reached the line of the Western Dvina and Dnepr Rivers, the Soviet Western Front had only 24 divisions composed of 275,000 men, 135 tanks, and 3,416 guns and mortars immediately available to stop them, giving the Germans a considerable numerical edge in both men and equipment. However, a further 42 Soviet divisions were in the process of arriving, together with six fresh mechanized corps assigned to the region by STAVKA (High Command of the Armed Forces of the Soviet Union).[83] Equipped with 1,545 tanks, two of the latter conducted a hasty counterstroke, literally off the march, against advanced German positions east of Lepel. Poor preparations and a lack of reconnaissance doomed the Soviet attack to a costly failure, but the necessity of having to deal with it diverted the attention of four panzer divisions for the next three days.[84] Despite their cost, operations such as this did have a braking effect upon the Germans' advance by forcing them to respond. Moreover, these operations maintained the tempo and intensity of the fighting at a high level, gradually exhausting German forces and their capabilities, either through attrition, the physical exhaustion of personnel, or the wearing out of equipment.[85]

and the 1941 Campaign", p. 23. For somewhat different figures, see Glantz, "Soviet Mobilization in Peace and War, 1924-1942: A Survey", p. 352.

81   Glantz & House, *When Titans Clashed*, p. 72. Also see, Frederick Kagan, "The Evacuation of Soviet Industry in the wake of 'Barbarossa': A Key to the Soviet Victory." *Journal of Slavic Military Studies*, Vol. 8, No. 2 (June 1995), pp. 387-414.

82   Bacon, "Soviet Military Losses in World War II.", p. 619, and Mawdsley, *Thunder in the East*, p. 47.

83   Glantz, *Barbarossa Derailed. Vol. One*, p. 51.

84   While subjected to *Luftwaffe* attacks, the 5th and 7th Mechanized Corps began their operations immediately following road marches of, respectively, 135 and 126 kilometres. In the process, as many as half their tanks may have fallen out along the way because of mechanical breakdowns, damage, or lack of fuel. Glantz, *Barbarossa Derailed. Vol. One*, pp. 70-75. Also see Gary A. Dickson, "The Counterattack of the 7th Mechanized Corps, 5-9 July 1941." *Journal of Slavic Military Studies*, Vol. 26, No. 2 (June 2013), pp. 310-340.

85   For specific descriptions of the physical exhaustion being experienced by German soldiers by this point, see Stahl, *Operation Barbarossa and Germany's Defeat in the East*, pp. 202-203.

For the moment, concerns regarding the gradual dulling of the *Wehrmacht*'s offensive capabilities were muted by the success that *Heeresgruppe Mitte* achieved when it resumed its drive upon Moscow on 10 July. In short order, the armoured spearheads of *Generaloberst* Heinz Guderian's *2. Panzergruppe* stormed across the Dnepr River, swept past centres of Soviet resistance at Orsha and Mogilev, and drove hard for the city of Smolensk. Having captured Vitebsk on 9 July, the *3. Panzergruppe* to the north did likewise. By 16 July, the *29. (Mot.) Infanterie Division* had already captured most of Smolensk while the *7. Panzer Division* had seized the key road junction of Yartsevo, located 50 kilometres northeast of the city. As a result, the Soviet 19th, 20th, and 16th Armies were threatened with encirclement, and German spearheads were now positioned a mere 322 kilometres from Moscow.

At this stage, a number of problems emerged that hampered the development of a rapid German victory such as had occurred around Minsk. First, a significant number of German armoured and motorised divisions were not concentrated around Smolensk, but instead preoccupied by other tasks. The problems experienced by *Heeresgruppe Nord* regarding its right flank forced *Heeresgruppe Mitte* to divert one motorised and two infantry corps to the northeast towards Nevel and Velikie Luki, away from the main push on Smolensk. To the south, the entrapment of a sizeable body of Soviet troops around Mogilev meant that one-third of Guderian's forces, namely the entire *XXIV. (Mot.) Armee Korps*, was tied down for the rest of July fending off the repeated relief efforts of three Soviet armies. German infantry formations meant to relieve the panzer spearheads were taking longer to reach the front than expected, being either preoccupied mopping up pockets of Soviet resistance, delayed because of congested roads, or committed to guard the army group's steadily increasing southern flank.[86] Guderian exacerbated the dispersion of German armoured forces on 20 July, when, contrary to repeated orders to commit his forces to the northeast to seal the pocket around Smolensk, he dispatched most of the *XLVI. (Mot.) Armee Korps* (the second of this three corps – the third already having been committed around Smolensk) eastwards to capture a bridgehead across the Desna River at Yelnya.[87] Ultimately, this decision directly contributed to the Germans inability to fully seal the ring around Smolensk, and the pocket only ceased to exist on 6 August when Stalin finally permitted the evacuation of its 50,000 remaining Soviet defenders.

What made this troop dispersion problematic was the second factor inhibiting German operations around Smolensk, specifically the increasing scale and tenacity of Soviet resistance. Unlike the circumstances along the border in June, large amounts of Soviet reserves were now close at hand and able to conduct a series of fierce counterattacks. The primary recipients of these attacks were the already-overstretched German armoured and motorised divisions, which could do little more than – tenuously – hold their positions and wait for the infantry to catch up. Other Soviet forces

---

86   Ibid, pp. 261-264.
87   Ibid, p. 267.

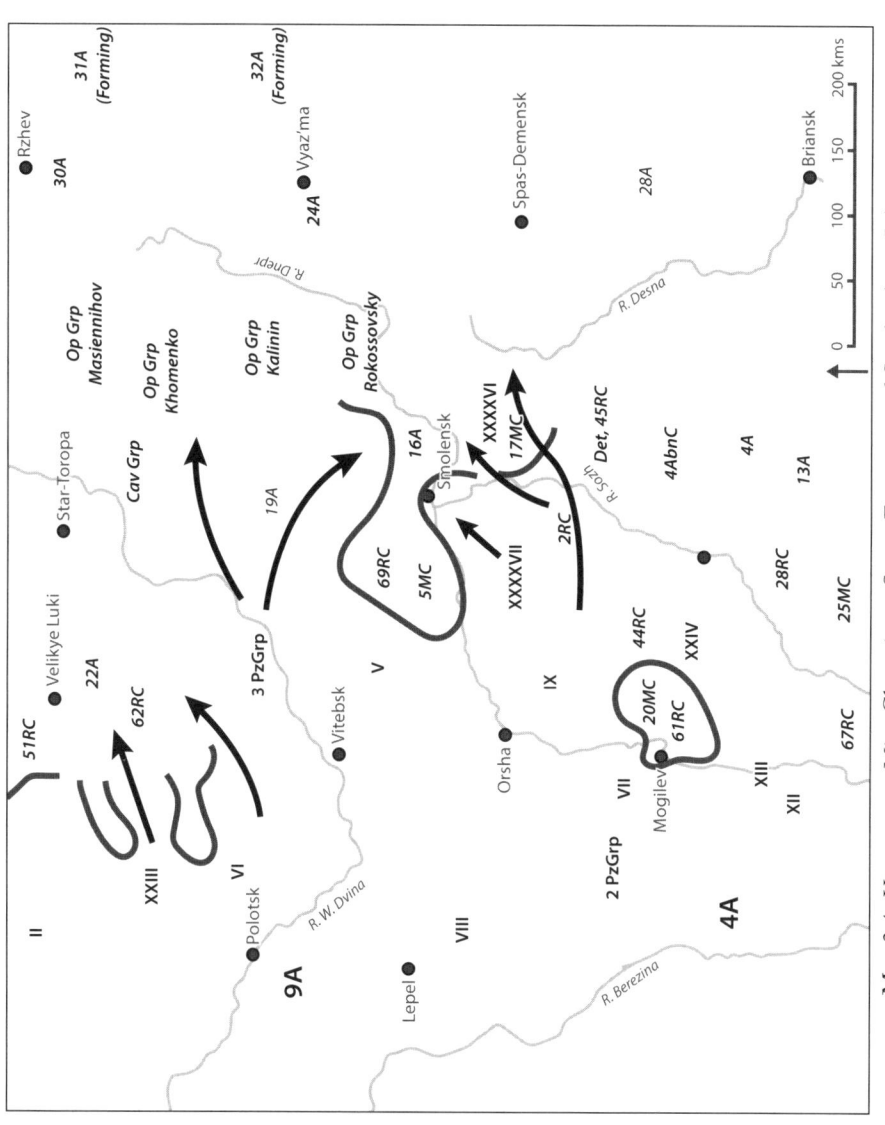

Map 3.4 *Heeresgruppe Mitte* Closes in on Soviet Forces around Smolensk, 20 July 1941.

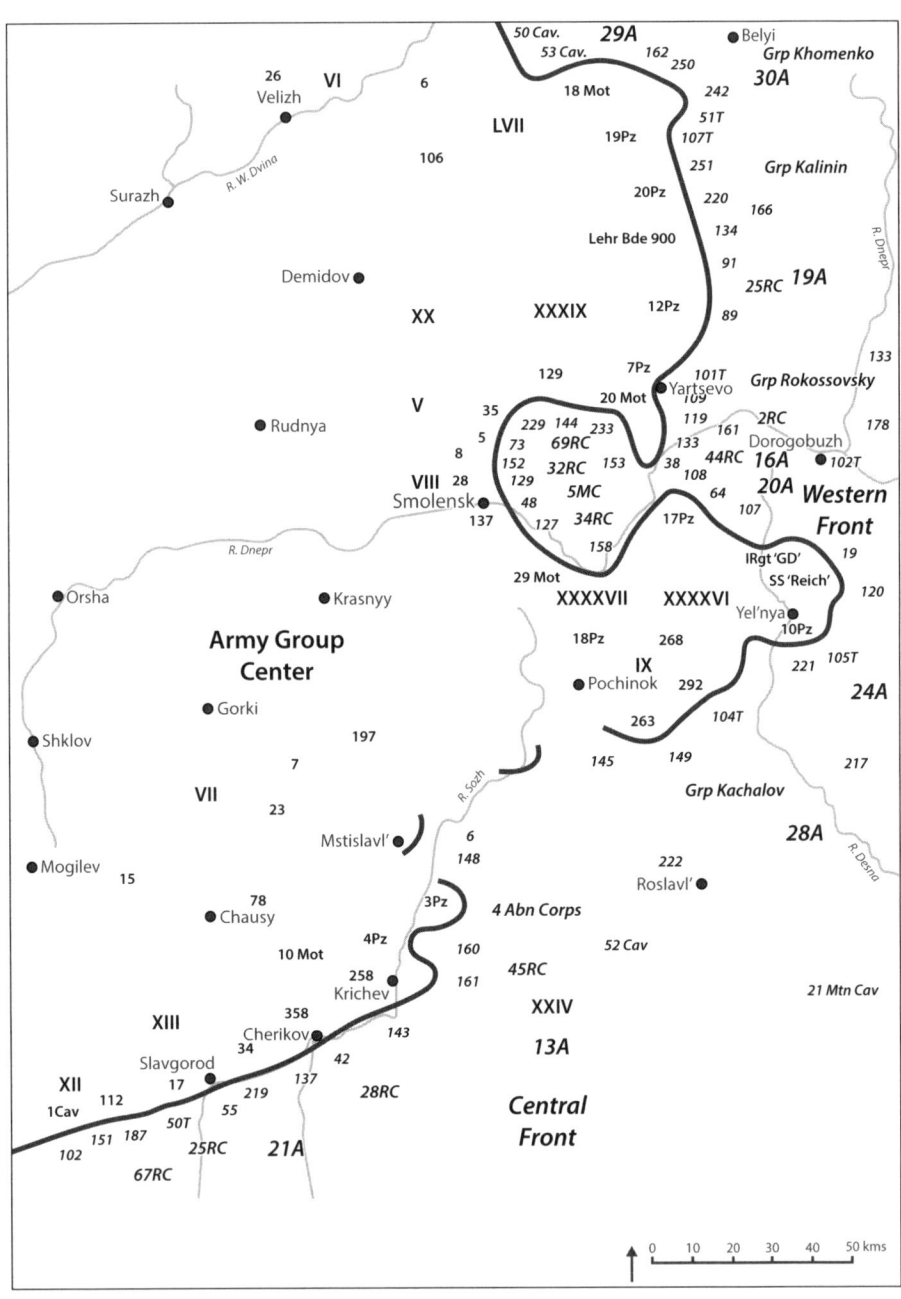

Map 3.5 The Smolensk Pocket, 28 July 1941.

staged seemingly continuous attacks to recapture Smolensk or relieve their comrades trapped around Mogilev. Still more tried to eject the *10. Panzer Division* from its bridgehead at Yelnya, or endeavoured to keep open the lifeline south of Yartsevo to the semi-encircled Soviet armies around Smolensk.[88] More ominously, in mid-August STAVKA ordered its armies along the Smolensk axis to stage more ambitious attacks in the sector stretching from Toropets to Yartsevo (17 August to 8 September) and to eliminate the German bridgehead at Yelnya (30 August to 8 September).[89]

For *Heeresgruppe Mitte*, the result was an uncomfortable number of anxious moments and a few outright setbacks. Although the *19. Panzer Division* captured Velikie Luki on 19 July it was compelled to abandon the city shortly thereafter when Soviet attacks threatened to overwhelm the *14. (Mot.) Infanterie Division* guarding its lines of communication to the southwest. While the city was recaptured by 26 August, it required the commitment of two panzer and seven infantry divisions.[90] Around Yartsevo, Soviet attacks pierced the lines of the *161. Infanterie Division* on 19 August, forcing the army group to commit the *7. Panzer Division*, which had only recently been relieved from the frontline for rest and refurbishment. Its counterattack on 21 August stabilized the situation, but failed to win back the lost ground and cost the division 30 panzers as *Totalausfalle*.[91] Nine days later, Soviet troops achieved a ten-kilometre deep penetration of the front held by the *23. Infanterie Division*; a counterattack the following day restored the German lines, but required the commitment of the *10. Panzer Division* and elements of another infantry division.[92] Most significantly, unrelenting Soviet attacks around Yelyna inflicted an unsustainable casualty rate upon the German formations deployed there. In consequence, OKH ordered the abandonment of the bridgehead and by 8 September German forces had pulled back across the Desna River, granting the Red Army its first clear victory.[93]

Admittedly, these events were overshadowed by the fact that *Heeresgruppe Mitte* had captured Smolensk, advanced hundreds of kilometres closer to Moscow, demolished yet another series of Soviet armies and, in the process, inflicted staggering losses upon the Red Army. German claims of Soviet losses during this stage of the campaign (10 July to 5 August) amounted to 310,000 prisoners, and the destruction or capture of 3,205 tanks and 3,120 artillery pieces. A smaller encirclement conducted around Roslavl by *2. Panzergruppe* (1-6 August) netted a further 38,568 prisoners,

---

88   For more details concerning individual Soviet attacks, see Glantz, *Forgotten Battles of the German-Soviet War, 1941-1945. Vol. One*.
89   Ibid, pp. 74-88.
90   See Glantz, *Barbarossa Derailed. Vol. One*, pp. 557-572.
91   *Kriegstagebuch Nr. 1(25 May – 31 August 1941), Pz Gr. 3, Ia*. NARA T313 Roll 225, Frame 7489183.
92   Jacobsen, (Ed.) *KTB OKW. Band I*, pp. 482-483.
93   See Fugate & Dvoretsky, *Thunder on the Dnepr*, Glantz, *Forgotten Battles of the German-Soviet War, 1941-1945. Vol. One*, pp. 82-88, and Pat McTaggart, "Smolensk-Yelnia: Blunting the Blitzkrieg." in Command Magazine, (Ed.) *Hitler's Army*, pp. 235-252.

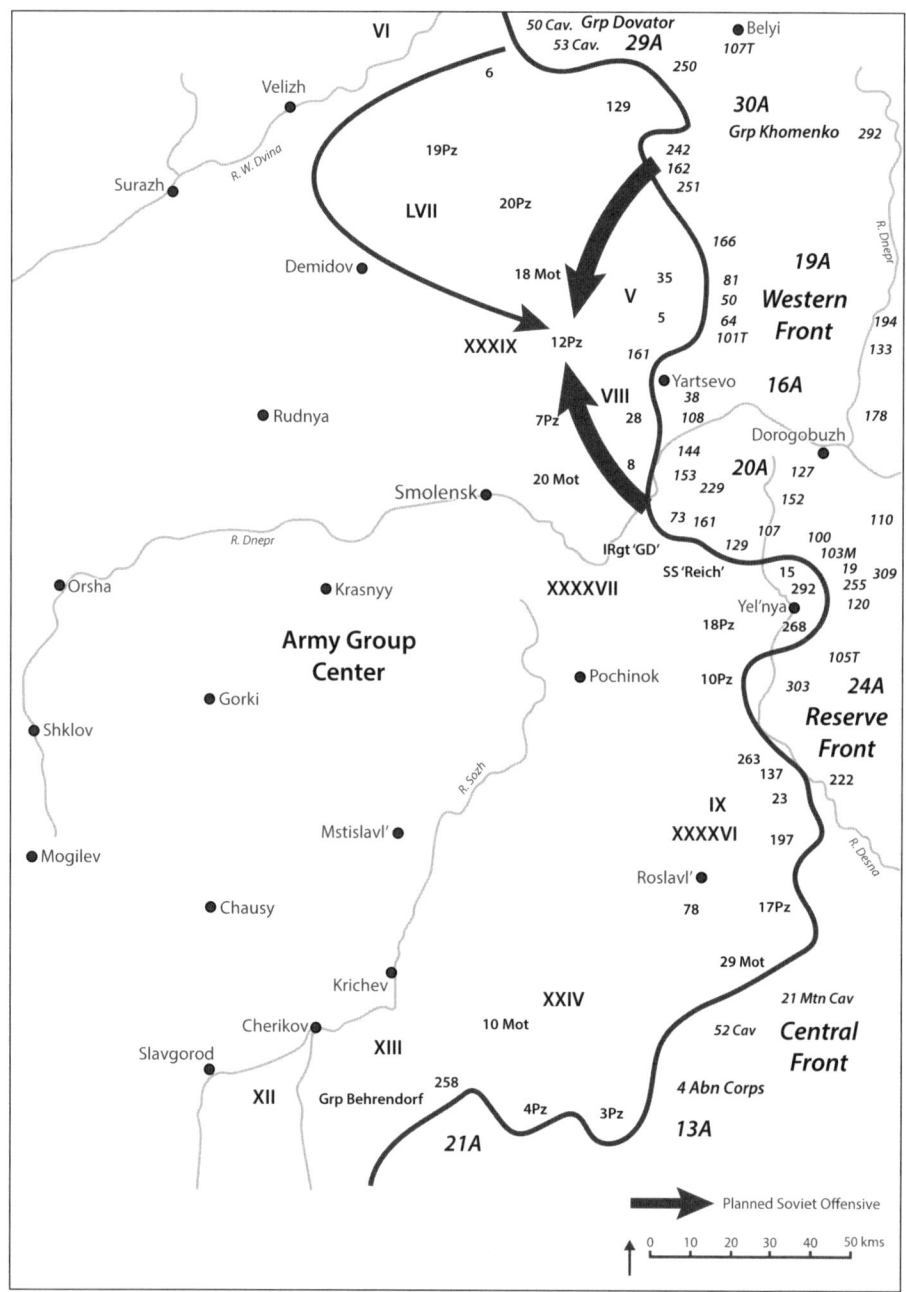

Map 3.6 *Heeresgruppe Mitte* Holds the Line, 15 August 1941.

250 tanks or armoured cars, 613 artillery pieces, 1,900 vehicles, and 942 machine-guns; another around Velikie Luki (22-26 August) produced 29,500 more prisoners and 393 captured artillery pieces.[94] Russian sources admit that between 10 July and 10 September the Soviet armies operating along the Smolensk axis sustained a total of 759,974 casualties, including 486,171 killed or missing, and that 1,348 tanks and 9,290 guns and mortars were lost.[95]

However dramatic the German victories seemed, the fighting did not end with the capture of Smolensk or the reduction of the pocket that bore its name. Instead, faced with persistent Soviet attacks across its front, *Heeresgruppe Mitte* was forced to endure two months of almost continuous operations that produced a debilitating number of casualties. Soviet pressure upon the army group was so great that on 28 August its commander, *Generalfeldmarschall* Fedor von Bock, telephoned Halder, "highly excited: Defenses of Army Grp. are near breaking point. Army Grp. cannot hold its eastern front if the Russians continue attacking."[96] Although the crisis passed, by the end of July the army group had sustained a total of 82,031 casualties. A further 75,849 casualties were incurred during August and 40,518 more in September, for a total of 198,398 casualties since the start of the campaign.[97] Specifically, the effort to reduce the Smolensk pocket cost the *5. Infanterie Division* some 1,565 casualties (20 July to 3 August) while the neighbouring *129. Infanterie Division* lost 1,011 men (26 July to 4 August).[98] For the *3. Panzergruppe* operating along the northeastern portion of the army group front, average losses rose from 161 men (22 June to 2 July) to about 396 men (3 July to 10 August) per day.[99] To the southeast, the fighting around Yelyna was especially bitter; holding the bridgehead cost the *XLVI. (Mot.) Armee Korps* a total of 4,252 men between 22 July and 8 August.[100] Relieving infantry formations fared no better; the *137. Infanterie Division* sustained 1,900 casualties (15 August to 5 September), while the *78. Infanterie Division* lost 1,155 men (21 August to 5

---

94   Jacobsen, (Ed.) *KTB OKW. Band I*, pp. 561, 593 & 1221.
95   Krivosheev, *Soviet Casualties and Combat Losses in the 20th Century*, pp. 116 & 260.
96   Halder, *Kriegstagebuch. Band II*, p. 1204.
97   Heeresarzt 10-Day Casualty Reports for *Heeresgruppe Mitte* (22.6-30.9.41) in BA-MA RW 6/556 and 6/558.
98   The *5. Infanterie Division* lost 378 killed, 1,114 wounded, and 73 missing, while the casualties sustained by the *129. Infanterie Division* included 233 killed, 668 wounded, and 110 missing. Reincke, *Die 5. Jäger Division 1939-1945*, p. 110, and Heinrich Boncsein, *Halten oder Sterben: Die hessisch-thüringische 129. Infanterie Division im Russland und Ostpreussen*. (Potsdam: 1999), p. 49.
99   *Kriegstagesbuch Nr. 1(25 May – 31 August 1941), Pz Gr. 3, Ia*. NARA T313 Roll 225, Frame 7489010 and *Tatigkeitsbericht (25 May – 31 August 1941), Pz Gr. 3, IIa*. NARA T313 Roll 231, Frame 7496139. By 10 August the *3. Panzergruppe* had lost a total of 4,975 killed, 11,740 wounded, and 486 missing, for a total of 17,209 casualties.
100 Otto Weidinger, *Division Das Reich. Der Weg der 2. SS-Panzer Division 'Das Reich'. Die Geschichte der Stammdivision der Waffen-SS. Band II*. (Osnabruck: 1972), pp. 339 & 349.

September).[101] Other divisions belonging to *Heeresgruppe Mitte* endured similar losses (see Table 3.4), with the invaluable armoured and motorised divisions sustaining an average of 29 percent more casualties than their infantry counterparts. Worst hit had been the *18. Panzer Division*. By 21 July this division had been reduced to an *Infanteriestärke* of approximately 600 men, forcing it to disband two of its four motorised infantry battalions. Three days later it possessed a mere 12 operational panzers. Total casualties (including sick and non-combat losses) since the start of the campaign amounted to 3,352 men by 28 July, and the following day the division reported a shortage of 3,353 men, 2,292 vehicles, 178 machine-guns, and 17 anti-tank guns. In contrast to its 21 June *Verpflegungsstärke* of 17,174 men, on 6 August the division possessed an *Iststärke* of 11,345 personnel.[102] In spite of the pressing need to pinch off the Smolensk pocket, *2. Panzergruppe* was forced to relieve the *18. Panzer Division* on 28 July and grant it an extended period of rest that lasted until at least 24 August.

Nonetheless, despite such losses, by late September the ranks of *Heeresgruppe Mitte* should largely have been replenished. Of the 55 combat divisions with the army group on 3 September, some 46 possessed *Feldersatz* battalions that should each have initially contained 790 men, or a total of 36,340 replacements.[103] To compensate for the 198,398 casualties sustained between 22 June and 30 September, some 125,000 replacements were dispatched to *Heeresgruppe Mitte* from Germany.[104] Together with men already present with the *Feldersatz* battalions, this meant that a total of 161,340 men were available to replace losses. Aside from the personnel now missing from the empty *Feldersatz* battalions, this should have meant that the army group was short only 37,058 men as it began its final offensive towards Moscow (Operation Typhoon) on 30 September. The impact of this shortage upon the available combat battalions should have been marginal. On 3 September, a total of 512 of these battalions would have been contained within the divisions present and, by evenly dividing the existing shortages, this represented an average shortfall of only 72 men per battalion.[105] Compared to their authorized *Sollstärke* (861 men per infantry battalion, and 1,089 men per motorised infantry, motorcycle or reconnaissance battalion), this theoretically meant that each combat battalion should have retained 92-93 percent of its authorized

---

101 Meyer-Detring, *Die 137. Infanterie Division im Mittelabschnitt der Ostfront*, p. 73, and
      Merker, *Das Buch der 78. Sturmdivision*, p. 67.
102 Paul, *Geschichte der 18. Panzer Division 1940-1943*, pp. 14, 40, 45-47.
103 Also present were three security divisions and two infantry divisions that were assigned
      rear area guard duties. Since these were not involved in frontline combat at this point,
      they have been excluded. For *Heeresgruppe Mitte*'s order of battle, see Jacobsen, (Ed.) *KTB
      OKW. Band I*, pp. 1140-1141.
104 *Anlage zum KTB AOK 2, Ia – Russland. Ersatzbewegung 13.9.1941*. T312 Roll 1249 Frame
      000812.
105 The number of combat battalions is broken down as follows:

Eight panzer divs. (x6 btls.)   = 48   One Waffen-SS mot. div. (x11 btls.)   = 11
Three mot. inf. divs. (x8 btls.) = 24   42 infantry divisions (x10 btls.)   = 420
One cavalry div. (x9 btls.)   = 9   Total   = 512

manpower strength. The precise distribution of replacements is unknown, and their impact is thereby difficult to ascertain, but most divisions appear to have been considerably restored. According to the divisional history of the *10. Panzer Division*, on 21 August its *Schützen* battalions retained 89 percent of their authorized *Kampfstärke*.[106] After the mauling around Yelnya, the divisional histories of the *78.* and *137. Infanterie Divisions* note that the injection of replacements restored the *Gefechtsstärke* of their infantry companies to an average of 113 and 100 men each.[107] Despite having sustained at least 1,541 casualties, the *(Mot.) Infanterie Regiment Grossdeutschland* still had a *Verpflegungsstärke* of 5,659 men on 1 October. Against its *Gesamtstärke* of 6,229 personnel on 21 June, this reflects a shortage of only nine percent.[108] More difficult to determine is just how many personnel were pirated from some divisions and reassigned to others. The divisional history of the *87. Infanterie Division* notes that during July it was forced to relinquish 350 men drawn from its infantry regiments and its entire *Feldersatz* battalion to the *2. Panzergruppe*.[109] Oddities such as this make an accurate accounting difficult at best, but whatever gaps still existed at this point should not have posed a significant obstacle to the successful outcome of Operation Typhoon, especially considering that the opposing Soviet divisions fared considerably worse.[110] In fact, when the operation commenced the Germans enjoyed a considerable numerical edge; while *Heeresgruppe Mitte* possessed a *Gesamtstärke* of 1,929,406 men on 1 October, the three Soviet Fronts deployed to defend Moscow fielded only 1,252,591 personnel.[111]

A similar regeneration occurred in terms of German armoured strength. Throughout July, the hectic pace of operations, Soviet resistance, abysmal roads, and logistical constraints played havoc with the operational armoured strength of the panzer divisions belonging to *Heeresgruppe Mitte*. By 21 July the *7. Panzer Division* possessed 118

---

106 Schick, *Die 10. Panzer Division 1939-1943*, p. 344.

107 Merker, *Das Buch der 78. Sturmdivision*, p. 67, and Meyer-Detring, *Die 137. Infanterie Division im Mittelabschnitt der Ostfront*, p. 77. At this stage of the war, rifle companies possessed an authorized *Gefechtsstärke* of 162 men each; in the case of these two divisions, this would mean that their rifle companies were at, respectively, 70 and 62 percent of their authorized *Gefechtsstärke*.

108 The losses only account for those sustained until 15 August. Weidinger, *Division Das Reich. Band II*, p. 371. For the strengths of this regiment, see *LVII. AK. Gefechts und Verpflegungsstärke (June 1941 – December 1941)*, NARA T314 Roll 761, Frames 000709 & 000761.

109 Martin Mann & Hermann Oehmichen, *Der Weg der 87. Infanterie Division*. (Germany: 1969), p. 81.

110 Against an authorized strength of 10,859 men, the Soviet divisions deployed to defend Moscow in late September appear to have been able to muster an average of only 5,000-7,000 men each. Klaus Reinhardt, *Die Wende vor Moskau: Das Scheitern der Strategie Hitlers im Winter 1941/42*. (Stuttgart: 1972), p. 61.

111 Michael Parrish, (Ed.) *Battle for Moscow: The 1942 Soviet General Staff Study*. (Toronto: 1989), p. 203. Other sources tend to quote even lower Soviet figures. See Erickson, *The Road to Stalingrad*, p. 213, and Seaton, *The Russo-German War, 1941-1945*, p. 179.

operational panzers and a further 96 in repair, and on the following day the *10. Panzer Division* reported that 74 of its panzers were ready for combat.[112] The *18. Panzer Division* was reduced to a lamentable 12 operational panzers by 24 July.[113] Six days later, the *4. Panzer Division* had 86 serviceable panzers and 50 more in workshops.[114] On 29 July, the *2. Panzergruppe* reported that only 286 of its original 1,086 panzers remained operational.[115] Yet by 8 August most of the panzer divisions belonging to the army group had been replaced by infantry divisions and were withdrawn into reserve. To be certain, many were soon recommitted, staging counterattacks against Soviet breakthroughs, as part of the operation to capture Velikie Luki, or else with the *2. Panzergruppe* in its drive south into the Ukraine. Nonetheless, as noted in Table 3.5, the operational armoured strength of *Heeresgruppe Mitte*'s panzer divisions had already increased by late August and early September. In contrast with their previous circumstances (on 22 and 24 July, respectively), the operational strength of the *10. Panzer Division* more than doubled, while that of the *18. Panzer Division* increased by 675 percent. Compared to its standing on 29 July and despite its continued operations, the number of serviceable tanks with *2. Panzergruppe* grew by 52 percent (from 286 operational panzers to 435). While the overall operational readiness within the army group stood at 41 percent of its initial complement, what is more significant is that the panzer divisions still retained over 71 percent of the tanks with which they started the campaign.[116] Aside from the *2. Panzergruppe* that campaigned in the Ukraine throughout September (minus the *10. Panzer Division*), the relative stability of the front during this period (August-September) meant that time was available to conduct needed repairs and servicing, consequently increasing the number of operational vehicles even further.[117] This was facilitated by a moderate easing of German logistics that would have permitted the dispatch of increased amounts of vital spare parts.[118]

---

112   Manteuffel, *Die 7. Panzer Division im Zweiten Weltkrieg*, p. 167, and Schick, *Die 10. Panzer Division 1939-1943*, p. 324.

113   Paul, *Geschichte der 18. Panzer Division 1940-1943*, p. 43.

114   Glantz, *The Initial Period of War on the Eastern Front, 22nd June – August 1941*, pp. 435-436.

115   Stahel, *Operation Barbarossa and Germany's Defeat in the East*, p. 316.

116   By this point the panzer divisions of *Heeresgruppe Mitte* had sustained a *Totalausfalle* of 641 tanks, and had received 67 replacements. Jentz, *Panzertruppen, Vol. One*, p. 206.

117   For a general survey of tank maintenance within the German Army, see Lukas Friedli, *Die Panzer-Instandsetzung der Wehrmacht.* (Uelzen, Germany: 2005). A detailed account of German field maintenance services during the early stages of the campaign in Russia is located within Burkhardt Müller-Hillebrand, "The Tank Repair Service in the German Army." (March 1951), NARA FMS P-040.

118   The average number of daily supply trains arriving at *Heeresgruppe Mitte* during August was about 22 (against a minimum requirement of 24). Though still inadequate, this did represent a modest improvement over the circumstances that had existed in July, when the number of daily supply trains had fluctuated between eight and fifteen. Schuler, *Logistik im Russlandfeldzug*, pp. 357 & 383.

The precise implications of this period of rehabilitation are difficult to quantify with any certainty. Within the literature, the presentation of German armoured strengths at the time of Typhoon are rather vague, lack credible sources, or else tend to focus upon German weaknesses rather than strengths.[119] Such somnolent historical analysis may be a reflection of the befuddlement that developed within OKH during September and October 1941, when it appears to have utterly lost track of the panzer divisions exact circumstances. In short, nobody in authority appears to have known just how many panzers remained in the field or how many had been lost.[120]

However, as postulated in Table 3.6, a more detailed accounting indicates that *Heeresgruppe Mitte* may have accumulated a considerably larger armoured contingent than most sources indicate.[121] Although the figures related to the four divisions (7., 10., 19. and 20. *Panzer Divisions*) that remained with the army group date from late August and early September, they are likely representative of the number of tanks available a month later since these formations remained relatively static, did not participate in extensive operations during the intervening period, and because they correspond to figures known for later periods.[122] The numbers given for the 1. and 6. *Panzer Divisions* are most likely also roughly accurate, as the former possessed 111 operational panzers on 28 September (versus the 99 on 10 September), while the latter still had an *Iststärke* of 142 tanks as late as 31 October.[123] The 11. *Panzer Division* was transferred from *Heeresgruppe Süd*, while the 2. and 5. *Panzer Divisions* were fresh formations having only just arrived from Germany. Replacement tanks were dispatched starting in September, but a number of these did not arrive until early October.[124] Exact figures for the number of assault guns is not known, but a total of 16

---

119 Many estimates are based upon percentages noted in Halder's war diary. See Halder, *Kriegstagebuch: Tagliche Aufzeichnungen des Chefs des Generalstabes des Heeres 1939-1942. Band II*, p. 1267. For nondescript estimates of German tank strength, see Showalter, *Hitler's Panzers*, p. 183, Seaton, *The Russo-German War, 1941-1945*, p. 172, and Ellis, *Brute Force*, p. 67. Cooper, *The German Army, 1933-1945*, p. 329, refers to Halder's estimates and states that 1,500 German tanks were committed to Typhoon, but otherwise provides no specific source for this figure.

120 See Boog, et. al. *GSWW. Vol. IV*, pp. 1131-1132.

121 For instance, Glantz & House, *When Titans Clashed*, p. 78, pegs German strength at 1,700 tanks. Fugate, *Operation Barbarossa*, p. 286, cites 1,216 panzers, but this actually refers to the number of operational vehicles at a later date. See Reinhardt, *Die Wende vor Moskau*, p. 317.

122 On 30 September, the *20. Panzer Division* fielded 83 operational panzers and as late as 16 October, the *19. Panzer Division* still had 125 panzers operational. Ibid, p. 317. The *10. Panzer Division* possessed 152 operational panzers on 1 October. Jentz, *Panzertruppen, Vol. One*, p. 210.

123 Ibid, pp. 208 & 211.

124 According to Wolfgang Paul, *Erfrorener Sieg: Die Schlacht um Moskau 1941/1942*. (Esslingen: 1975), p. 143, the *2. Panzergruppe* was assigned 100 replacement panzers, but half were still in transit when Typhoon began.

Sturmgeschütz battalions had been deployed to Russia by late September; at full strength (with 21 StuG per battalion), these would have totalled 336 guns. However, by the end of September a total of 52 StuG had been written-off and only four replacements had arrived.[125] Evenly dividing the remaining 288 StuG produces 18 per battalion, meaning that the 12 *Sturmgeschütz* battalions deployed with *Heeresgruppe Mitte* may have fielded a total of 216 StuG. The number of tanks fielded by *2. Panzergruppe* is based upon Halder's assertion that its panzer divisions still retained 50 percent (520) of their original tank strength (1,040).[126] This indicates that *Heeresgruppe Mitte* may have assembled as many as 2,572 armoured vehicles (2,356 tanks and 216 assault guns) for the final push on Moscow.

Admittedly speculative, this estimate may not be far off the mark. On 16 October, the panzer divisions arrayed with *Heeresgruppe Mitte* still fielded 1,217 operational panzers.[127] Considering that the autumn rains which began on the night of 6-7 October and quickly turned roads into almost impassable morasses, and that the near collapse of the German supply system and the preceding 17 days of ferocious combat all combined to inflict a heavy toll upon the panzer divisions operational readiness, the initial array of German armour must have been considerable.[128] An analysis of the overall armoured status of the *Ostheer* provides another means of gauging the accuracy of the grand total of panzers illustrated in Table 3.6. By the end of September, an additional 808 panzers had joined the 3,644 initially committed to Barbarossa.[129] Against this total of 4,452 tanks, some 1,693 were destroyed of permanently written-off

---

125   For assault gun losses and replacements, see Boog, et. al. *GSWW. Vol. IV*, pp. 1120-1122.

126   See Halder, *Kriegstagebuch. Band II*, p. 1267, and Jentz, *Panzertruppen, Vol. One*, p. 206. While giving no information regarding its overall number of tanks, David Stahel, *Kiev 1941: Hitler's Battle for Supremacy in the East*. (Cambridge, UK: 2012), p. 324, asserts that on 27 September the *2. Panzergruppe* possessed a mere 256 operational panzers.

127   Reinhardt, *Die Wende vor Moskau*, p. 317.

128   Contrary to historical perceptions, many German divisions endured very heavy casualties during the first weeks of Typhoon. The *2. SS-(Mot.) Division* alone sustained 1,607 casualties during 6-23 October. Otto Weidinger, *Division Das Reich. Der Weg der 2. SS-Panzer Division 'Das Reich'. Die Geschichte der Stammdivision der Waffen-SS. Band III.* (Osnabruck: 1972), p. 172. On 2 October alone the *18. Infanterie Regiment* of the *6. Infanterie Division* sustained 500 killed and wounded. Grossmann, *Geschichte der Rheinisch-Westfälischen 6. Infanterie Division, 1939-1945*, p. 70. In combat operations throughout October, the *78. Infanterie Division* reportedly suffered 2,400 casualties. Merker, *Das Buch der 78. Sturmdivision*, p. 121. Less than one week of fighting (2-7 October) cost the *129. Infanterie Division* some 1,039 casualties. Boncsein, *Halten Oder Sterben*, p. 77. During a similar period (2-10 October) some 1,200 killed and wounded were reported by the *137. Infanterie Division*. Meyer-Detring, *Die 137. Infanterie Division im Mittelabschnitt der Ostfront*, p. 83.

129   Some 380 panzers arrived with the *2.* and *5. Panzer Divisions*. For replacement vehicles sent to the *Ostheer*, including vehicles dispatched in September but which did not arrive until early October, see Boog, et. al. *GSWW. Vol. IV*, pp. 1120-1122.

between 22 June and 30 September, leaving the panzer divisions with 2,759.[130] By late September the remaining three panzer divisions with *1. Panzergruppe* probably possessed around 338 panzers, while the two panzer divisions still with *Heeresgruppe Nord* fielded between 167 and 318 panzers, meaning that 505 to 656 were not deployed with *Heeresgruppe Mitte*.[131] Subtracting these estimated figures from the total number of armoured vehicles remaining to the *Ostheer* still leaves 2,103 to 2,254 tanks with the 14 panzer divisions subordinated to *Heeresgruppe Mitte*. Adding the 216 assault guns of the *Sturmgeschütz* battalions with the army group, the total reaches 2,139 to 2,470 armoured vehicles. Even with the lowest of these figures, German forces committed to Typhoon possessed a better than two-to-one armour superiority over the opposing Soviet troops.[132] This superiority was vividly illustrated during the first days of the offensive, when German armoured spearheads shattered Soviet defences and largely destroyed the initial forces arrayed to defend Moscow during the double encirclement of Viazma-Briansk.[133] As Halder enthusiastically noted in his diary entry of 4 October, "Operation 'Teifun' [sic] is developing on a truly classical pattern."[134]

130 Ibid, pp. 1120-1122.
131 According to Jentz, *Panzertruppen, Vol. One*, p. 206, at the outset of the campaign the *13.*, *14.*, and *16. Panzer Divisions* of the *1. Panzergruppe* had possessed 472 panzers. By 22 September these divisions had sustained a *Totalausfalle* of 134 tanks. *Kriegstagebuch der Oberquartiermeisterabteilung der 1. Panzerarmee O.Qu. Panzergruppe 1 O.Qu. 2.5-31.10.1941*. NARA T313 Roll 15, Frame 7242291. The lower estimate for the *8.* and *12. Panzer Divisions* with *Heeresgruppe Nord* refers only to their combined operational armoured strength on 26 September and 1 October, respectively. Haupt, *Die 8. Panzer Division im Zweiten Weltkrieg*, p. 176, and Jentz, *Panzertruppen, Vol. One*, p. 210. The larger figure represents the combined *Iststärke* of both divisions on 10 September and 26 August. Ibid, p. 206.
132 Soviet forces around Moscow initially mustered 849 tanks. Reinhardt, *Die Wende vor Moskau*, p. 61.
133 Russian forces deployed amongst the Western, Briansk, and Reserve Fronts amounted to 83 rifle divisions, four motorized or tank divisions, nine cavalry divisions, and 14 tank or motorized brigades, totaling 1,252,591 personnel, 849 tanks, 20,665 field artillery pieces, anti-tank guns and mortars, and 739 anti-aircraft guns. Parrish, (Ed.) *Battle for Moscow*, p. 203. By 20 October, the Germans claimed to have taken 673,000 prisoners, and captured or destroyed 1,242 tanks and 5,412 artillery pieces. Jacobsen, (Ed.) *KTB OKW. Band I*, p. 1231. Russian sources conservatively maintain that, along the Moscow axis, Soviet personnel losses throughout 30 September to 5 December included 514,338 killed or missing, and 143,941 wounded, for a total of 658,279 casualties. Equipment losses during this period are given as 2,785 tanks, and 3,832 guns and mortars. Krivosheev, *Soviet Casualties and Combat Losses in the 20th Century*, pp. 118 & 261. Considering that 64 divisions, 11 tank brigades and 50 army artillery regiments were encircled at Viazma-Briansk, such figures are probably too low. Other sources state that Soviet losses during this first phase of Typhoon alone amounted to 346,800 killed or wounded, and 673,000 captured, or 1,019,800 casualties. See Glantz & House, *When Titans Clashed*, p. 336-337.
134 Halder, *Kriegstagebuch. Band II*, p. 138.

In contrast to the quick succession of victories achieved by the other two German army groups, the advance of *Heeresgruppe Süd* south of the Pripyat Marshes was far more difficult. The opposing formations belonging to the Soviet Southwestern Front were well-equipped, well-led, and far better prepared when compared with their compatriots to the north.[135] Its eight mechanized corps possessed 4,793 tanks, more than the other three Fronts combined.[136] Starting on 23 June, these staged fierce counterstrokes against the flanks of the *1. Panzergruppe* as it advanced upon the city of Dubno. Equipped with 638 tanks and supported by two battalions of assault guns (with 42 StuG), the one infantry (*57.*) and four panzer (*11., 13., 14.* and *16.*) divisions spearheading the advance quickly became bogged down in intense fighting with the arriving Soviet mechanized corps.[137] By 26 June, five mechanized corps and parts of two others had been committed, which placed intense pressure upon the now-defending German units in what would be the largest tank battle until the engagement at Kursk in 1943.[138] Massed Soviet armour achieved a number of penetrations, and on one occasion managed to drive the *57. Infanterie Division* back ten kilometres, but the more ably commanded and experienced panzer divisions, with intense air support, managed to eliminate breaches in the line, ward off most of the Soviet attacks, and slowly advance eastwards. By 30 June, the Soviet attacks finally petered out and the *1. Panzergruppe* resumed its advance upon Kiev. That same day the STAVKA authorized the Southwestern Front to withdraw to the defensive regions along the old pre-1939 border.

The Soviet effort to halt the German advance along the border had failed, and the vital armoured reserves had suffered debilitating losses.[139] Overall losses by 6 July

---

135 For the preparedness of the Southwestern Front, see Erickson, "The Soviet Response to Surprise Attack: Three Directives, 22 June 1941", especially p. 546.

136 In contrast, the two mechanized corps belonging to the Northwestern Front had 1,400 tanks, while the six mechanized corps of the Western Front fielded 2,502. The Southern Front (formed from the renaming of the Odessa Military District) possessed two mechanized corps containing 799 tanks. Glantz, *Stumbling Colossus*, p. 155.

137 Jentz, *Panzertruppen, Vol. One*, p. 206. The *9. Panzer*, *16.* and *25. (Mot.) Infanterie Divisions*, *SS-(Mot.) Division Wiking*, and *SS-(Mot.) Brigade Leibstandarte Adolf Hitler* (LSSAH) remained in reserve or were only committed later in the battle. The best account yet produced of the fighting in the Brody-Dubno region is Victor Kamenir, *The Bloody Triangle: The Defeat of Soviet Armour in the Ukraine, June 1941*. (Minneapolis, MN: 2008).

138 As noted, German armoured strength totalled 680 tanks and assault guns. On 22 June, the five Soviet mechanized corps (8th, 9th, 15th, 19th, and 22nd) entirely committed around Brody possessed 3,027 tanks, of which 345 were heavy KV or T-34 models. How many of these actually managed to make it to the battlefield is unknown, but of the 858 tanks initially assigned to the 8th Mechanized Corps, 152 were listed as non-operational. Ibid, pp. 36-46.

139 Exact Soviet tank losses in the Brody-Dubno engagement are not known, but were undoubtedly heavy. On 30 June, the 8th Mechanized Corps still possessed 207 out of its original complement of 858 tanks. Personnel losses included 635 killed and 1,673 wounded, although Kamenir believes this to be far too low. Ibid., p. 242. No figures were

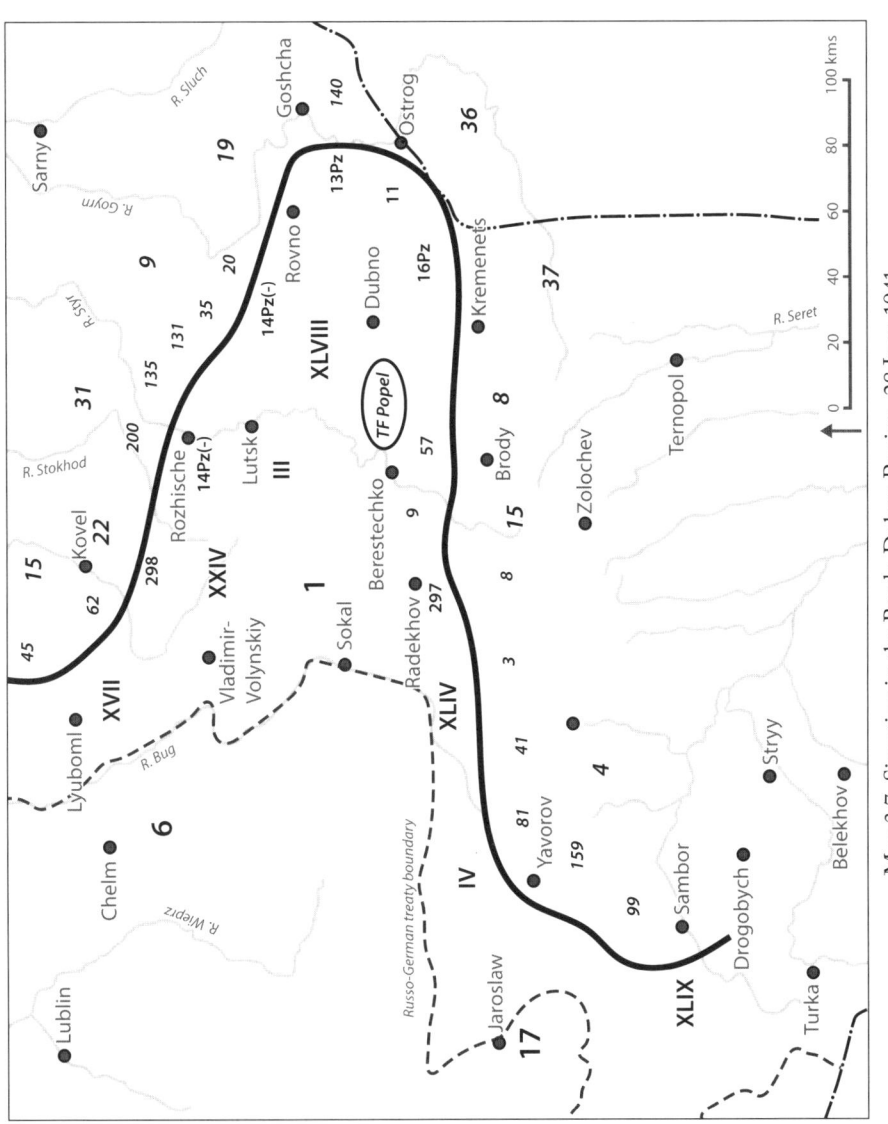

Map 3.7 Situation in the Brody-Dubno Region, 28 June 1941.

amounted to 231,207 casualties from the Southwestern Front's initial strength of 864,600 men, along with 4,381 tanks and 5,806 artillery pieces and mortars destroyed or captured.[140] Despite the intensity of the fighting, initial German personnel losses do not appear to have been excessive. Between 22-25 June the entire *XLIX. Gebirgs Korps* sustained only 872 casualties, while the *111. Infanterie Division* had lost 333 men by 27 June.[141] The *1. Panzergruppe* reported that its losses by 2 July amounted to 132 officers and 2,291 men. Equipment losses were more disconcerting; the *Totalausfalle* of equipment by 1 July included 89 panzers, 22 armoured cars (*Panzerspähwagen*, or PSW), 173 vehicles, and 90 motorcycles. Nonetheless, four days later 431 panzers were still listed as operational, while 200 more were in repair.[142]

Although Soviet defences along the border had crumbled, the STAVKA could at least take solace in the fact that the advance of *Heeresgruppe Süd* had been forestalled for a week, giving elements of three Soviet armies deployed west and southwest of Lvov time to retreat and thereby avoid encirclement. More importantly, despite inflicting heavy losses, *Heeresgruppe Süd* failed to disrupt the equilibrium of the Red Army in the Ukraine to the degree its compatriots had achieved in the Baltic or Belorussia. Consequently, Soviet resistance was far more coherent, forcing the Germans to fight their way slowly across the western Ukraine throughout July and August. Command disagreements as to how to proceed with operations resulted in the dispersal of German strength, slowing operations yet further.[143] Despite the sluggish pace of the German advance, by the end of August parts of three Soviet armies (24 divisions) were encircled and destroyed around Uman (2-8 August), another was besieged in Odessa, and the remaining Soviet forces had been driven from the western Ukraine.[144] The cost for this success was high. By 31 August, *Heeresgruppe Süd* had lost 27,710 killed, 103,608 wounded, and 7,186 missing, for a total of 138,504 casualties.[145] In terms of individual divisions, by the end of August the *198. Infanterie Division* had sustained 3,167 casualties, while the *44. Infanterie Division* had lost 2,147 men.[146] The *111. Infanterie*

available for the four other mechanized corps, but by 15 July these collectively retained a mere 194 tanks. On 22 June, they had possessed 2,169. Glantz, *Stumbling Colossus*, p. 232.

140 Krivosheev, *Soviet Casualties and Combat Losses in the 20th Century*, pp. 112 & 260.

141 Kalteneggar, *Die Stammdivision der deutsche Gebirgstruppe*, p. 216, and Friedrich Musculus, *Geschichte der 111. Infanterie Division, 1940-1944.* (Hamburg: 1980), pp. 431-433.

142 *Kriegstagebuch der Oberquartiermeisterabteilung der 1. Panzerarmee O.Qu. Panzergruppe 1 O.Qu. 2.5-31.10.1941.* NARA T313 Roll 15, Frames 7241708, 7241948 & 7241967.

143 See Boog, et. al. *GSWW. Vol. IV*, pp. 557-568.

144 German sources claim that 103,000 prisoners were taken, and 317 tanks, 858 artillery pieces, and 242 anti-tank and anti-aircraft guns were destroyed or captured around Uman. Jacobsen, (Ed.) *KTB OKW. Band I*, p. 1222.

145 See Heeresarzt 10-Day Casualty Reports for *Heeresgruppe Süd* (22.6-31.8.41) in BA-MA RW 6/556 and 6/558.

146 Gerhard Graser, *Zwischen Kattegat und Kaukasus: Weg und Kampfe der 198. Infanterie Division, 1939-1945.* (Tubingen: 1961), p. 379, and Schimak, et. al., *Die 44. Infanterie Division*, p. 179.

Division alone endured a staggering 5,457 casualties by 12 September.[147] During the fighting to clear the Uman pocket, the *125. Infanterie Division* lost 492 killed, 1,441 wounded, and 12 missing.[148] Equipment losses had also been serious: as of 30 August, the *1. Panzergruppe* reported the *Totalausfälle* of 174 panzers, 54 PSW, 2,405 motor vehicles, and 1,837 motorcycles. Some 767 machine-guns, 78 mortars, and 123 Pak were also lost, while only 245 machine-guns, 31 mortars, and 34 Pak had arrived as replacements.[149]

Despite such figures, *Heeresgruppe Süd* still retained the preponderance of its strength and operational capabilities. Together with the 34,760 personnel that were available within divisional *Feldersatz* battalions, till the end of August the army group received 54,000 replacements from Germany, so that a total of 88,760 men were available to redress losses.[150] Divided amongst the 451 combat battalions belonging to the army group, the 49,744 casualties not replaced translate into a shortage of 110 men per battalion.[151] Naturally, losses were not so evenly distributed; as noted in Table 3.7, some divisions suffered more than others. Conversely, with some divisions sustaining very heavy casualties, losses in others should have been relatively small. For the panzer divisions belonging to *1. Panzergruppe*, these still retained 78 percent of their initial armoured complement at the beginning of September (see Table 3.8). Although only 49 percent of the initial strength was operational, as previously noted this figure could increase quickly given the availability of spare parts and time. For example, by 10 September, the *14. Panzer Division* had managed to make 88 percent (120) of its remaining 136 panzers operational.[152]

The significance of these losses and replacements was dramatically demonstrated during September and October. Having secured bridgeheads over the Dnepr River, *1. Panzergruppe* drove northwards and on 15 September linked up with the *2. Panzergruppe* that had been diverted south into the Ukraine. In consequence, the preponderance of the Southwestern Front – four armies and parts of two others consisting of 43 divisions – was surrounded and had been destroyed by 26

147 Musculus, *Geschichte der 111. Infanterie Division, 1940-1944*, pp. 431-433.
148 Breymayer, *Das Wiesel*, p. 79.
149 *Kriegstagebuch der Oberquartiermeisterabteilung der 1. Panzerarmee O.Qu. Panzergruppe 1 O.Qu. 2.5-31.10.1941*. NARA T313 Roll 15, Frames 7242205-7242206.
150 On 1 September, *Heeresgruppe Süd* contained 52 divisions. Of these, 44 contained organic *Feldersatz* battalions with an estimated 790 men each. For the dispatch of replacements from Germany, see Halder, *Kriegstagebuch. Band II*, p. 1,201.
151 As previously noted, combat battalions refers to infantry, motorized infantry, motorcycle, and reconnaissance units. The number of combat battalions is broken down as follows:

Five panzer divisions (x6 btls.)	= 30	Six mtn. & light inf. divs. (x7 btls.)	=	42
Three mot. inf. divs. (x8 btls.)	= 24	34 infantry divisions (x10 btls.)	=	340
One SS div. & one SS bde.	= 15	Total	=	451

152 Jentz, *Panzertruppen, Vol. One*, p. 211.

September.[153] German forces committed to this operation sustained approximately 45,654 casualties, but Soviet losses were far greater.[154] Russian sources maintain that between 7 July and 26 September total Soviet losses in the Ukraine amounted to 700,544 casualties (616,304 killed or missing, and 84,240 wounded and sick), 411 tanks, and 28,419 guns and mortars.[155] Parallel German accounts stress that they took 665,212 prisoners, and destroyed or captured 884 tanks and 3,718 artillery pieces during the period of 25 August and 26 September alone.[156] Considering that Soviet sources admit that only 15,000 men remained with which to rebuild the Southwestern Front, the German claims are probably more accurate.[157]

While usually cited in retrospect to exemplify Hitler's interference with military operations and his role in the subsequent failure of Barbarossa, the Kiev encirclement served entirely rational economic and military ends. In terms of the former, it consolidated under German control the vast food producing regions of the Ukraine and obviated a mounting food crisis.[158] It also secured the vital manganese ore deposits around Nikopol, without which subsequent increases in steel production, and hence armaments production, would have been impossible.[159] Consequently, the destruction of the Soviet armies in the region also cleared the way for Germany rapidly to

153 For a detailed study of German operations, see Russel Stolfi, "The Greatest Encirclement in History: Link up of the German 3rd and 9th Panzer Divisions on 15 September 1941 in the Central Ukraine." *Royal United Services Institute Journal*, Vol. 141, No. 6 (December 1996), pp. 63-72. Also see Werner Haupt, *Kiew: Die Grosste Kesselschlacht*. (Bad Nauheim: 1964), and more recently Stahel, *Kiev 1941*.

154 Including losses sustained by divisions not directly participating in this operation, the *2. Panzergruppe* lost 2,635 killed, 9,770 wounded, and 134 missing between 21 August and 30 September. *Anlagenband Nr. 2b zum KTB, PzAOK 2 Ia/IIa., Vom 22.6.1941. Verlustenmeldungen: Zahlmassige Verluste 5.7.1941 – 25.3.1942.* BA-MA RH 21-2/757. The supporting *2. Armee* had 8,263 casualties during this same timeframe. During September, the *1. Panzergruppe* and *6. Armee* belonging to *Heeresgruppe Süd* sustained 7,365 and 17,487 casualties, respectively. See Heeresarzt 10-Day Casualty Reports for *2. Armee, 1. Panzergruppe*, and *6. Armee* (21.8-30.9.41) in BA-MA RW 6/556 and 6/558.

155 Krivosheev, *Soviet Casualties and Combat Losses in the 20th Century*, pp. 114 & 260.

156 The confusion regarding these conflicting claims reflects their differing time frames, and the fact that the German claims include estimates of Soviet losses during the fighting around the former's bridgeheads over the Dnepr River (31 August – 11 September: 52,811 prisoners, 285 tanks, 174 field guns, 21 anti-tank guns), and during the advance southwards of *2. Panzergruppe* and *2. Armee* (25 August – 15 September: 132,985 prisoners, 301 tanks, 1,121 field guns, 120 anti-tank guns). Actual German claims of the losses they inflicted once the Southwestern Front had been encircled (16-26 September) amounted to 479,416 prisoners, 238 tanks, 1,723 field guns, and 277 anti-tank guns. See Jacobsen, (Ed.) *KTB OKW. Band I*, pp. 661 & 1230.

157 Glantz & House, *When Titans Clashed*, p. 77.

158 Tooze, *The Wages of Destruction*, pp. 418-419. For the role of food in the decision to exterminate European Jewry and plans for the treatment of Slavs, see Ibid, pp. 476-480.

159 Kroener, et. al. *GSWW. Vol. V: Part Two*, p. 463.

gain control over the sprawling industrial and coal resources of the Donets region.[160] Militarily, the operation had dealt another tremendously costly defeat upon the Red Army. In doing so, it eliminated the serious threat these forces had posed to the deep rear of *Heeresgruppe Mitte*, shortened the army group's right flank by hundreds of kilometres, and thereby made possible the subsequent advance upon Moscow. Most importantly, the elimination of the massive bulge protruding around Kiev shortened German lines and freed three entire armies and parts of two armoured groups, containing at least 45 German and five Axis divisions, for employment elsewhere.[161]

Despite three months of continuous operations and having to transfer numerous divisions north for Operation Typhoon, *Heeresgruppe Süd* still had plenty of offensive combat power.[162] By 11 October, elements of *1. Panzergruppe* had isolated and destroyed two Soviet armies around Melitopol on the Azov Sea, and in the process captured another 106,332 prisoners, and destroyed or captured 212 tanks and 772 artillery pieces of all types.[163] Meanwhile, the *6.* and *17. Armee* cleared the vital industrial and coal-producing region along the Donets River basin and captured Kharkov on 24 October. In the process, the *6. Armee* alone claimed to have taken 21,574 prisoners, and destroyed 75 tanks.[164] Russian sources admit that, from an initial force numbering 541,600 personnel, Soviet losses between 29 September and 16 November amounted to 160,576 casualties (including 143,313 killed or missing, and 17,263 wounded or sick).[165] To the south, the *11. Armee* successfully breached the Soviet defences across the Perekop Isthmus and swept into the Crimean Peninsula. Except for the fortified city of Sevastopol, Soviet forces had been driven completely from the peninsula by 16 November. In doing so, *11. Armee* claimed that Soviet losses included 100,658 prisoners, 166 tanks and armoured cars, 1,297 guns and mortars, and 2,364 machine-guns.[166] Throughout October, these successes cost *Heeresgruppe Süd* a relatively modest total of 30,624 casualties.[167]

At this stage, however, the advance east finally began to sputter to a halt. Operable rail lines ended at the Dnepr River, from whence army group motorised supply columns had to take over. However, the number of operational vehicles in these units had

---

160 For the German exploitation of this region, see Tanja Penter, "Zwangsarbeit – Arbeit fur den Feind. Der Donbass unter deutscher Okkupation (1941-1943)", *Geschichte und Gesellschaft*, Vol. 31, No. 1 (2005), pp. 68-100.
161 The German forces included five panzer, five motorized, and 35 infantry divisions. Axis forces included the Slovak Mobile Division, the Hungarian Mobile Corps of three brigades, and the Italian *Corpo di Spedizione in Russe* (CSIR) with three divisions.
162 Two panzer, two motorized infantry, and four infantry divisions were transferred to *Heeresgruppe Mitte* following the reduction of the Kiev pocket.
163 Jacobsen, (Ed.) *KTB OKW. Band I*, p. 693.
164 Ibid, p. 721.
165 Krivosheev, *Soviet Casualties and Combat Losses in the 20th Century*, pp. 117 & 260.
166 Jacobsen, (Ed.) *KTB OKW. Band I*, p. 737.
167 See Heeresarzt 10-Day Casualty Reports for *Heeresgruppe Süd* (1-31.10.41) in BA-MA RW 6/556 and 6/558.

already fallen to 50 percent by 19 July.[168] Unlike its fellow army groups, *Heeresgruppe Süd* never enjoyed a significant operational pause, precluding any chance for large-scale vehicle maintenance or repair. Given what their circumstances were already like in July, by October the condition of the motorised supply units would certainly have been worse. The deterioration of the weather in early October exacerbated German supply difficulties by turning roads into swaths of seemingly bottomless mud. Trying to navigate through them placed even greater strain upon vehicles already in dire need of comprehensive overall, and even more became unserviceable. Others became hopelessly mired until the onset of frost, while overall supply deliveries were soon backlogged as columns made their way to their destinations with agonizing slowness. Horse-drawn wagons were increasingly used to replace motor vehicles, but these proved equally slow and their hauling capacity was limited.[169] *Heeresgruppe Süd* slowed down for want of adequate fuel and usable roads, not a lack of men or machines.

But OKH did not see it that way. Although fuel, ammunition, and food shortages increasingly plagued the frontline units, OKH still believed that *Heeresgruppe Süd* could at least reach the Don River, and maybe even Stalingrad and the Maikop oilfields, before halting for a prolonged period of rehabilitation.[170] Such optimism arose from the impression that the opposing Soviet forces, having sustained horrendous losses, were weak, in disarray, and were unable to offer effective resistance. It would also have been reinforced by the belief that the divisions of *Heeresgruppe Süd* still retained formidable offensive capabilities. By late September, for example, the three remaining panzer divisions still possessed an estimated total of 346 panzers.[171] Most of these would still have been available by early November.[172] The manpower situation also seemed manageable for the moment. To compensate for its losses of 216,954 men by 1 November, *Heeresgruppe Süd* had possessed or received a total of at least 128,760 replacements.[173] For the 356 combat battalions present, this meant

168 Schuler, *Logistik im Russlandfeldzug*, p. 314.

169 By 23 October, 2,500 wagon teams were being used in relays to haul 60 tons of supply from Zaporozhye to Mariupol per day. Boog, et. al. *GSWW. Vol. IV*, p. 615.

170 For the army group's increasing supply problems, command disagreements, and their effect upon operations, see Ibid, pp. 609-619.

171 Number determined by deducting *Totalausfalle* sustained by 22 September from initial strength plus replacements received. For losses, see *Kriegstagebuch der Oberquartiermeisterabteilung der 1. Panzerarmee O.Qu. Panzergruppe 1 O.Qu. 2.5-31.10.1941*. NARA T313, Roll 15, Frame 7242291. For initial strength, see Jentz, *Panzertruppen, Vol. One*, p. 206.

172 The *14. Panzer Division* possessed 58 operational panzers on 10 November, but how many were operational in the other two divisions could not be determined. Ibid, p. 211.

173 Casualties compiled from Heeresarzt 10-Day Casualty Reports for *Heeresgruppe Süd* (22.6-31.10.41) in BA-MA RW 6/556 and 6/558. According to Halder, *Kriegstagebuch. Band II*, p. 1201, some 94,000 replacements had been dispatched to *Heeresgruppe Süd* by the end of September. In addition, a total of 34,760 replacements were held within divisional *Feldersatz* battalions.

an average shortage of 218 men per battalion.[174] In general terms, infantry battalions should have retained an average of 75 percent of their *Sollstärke*, and motorised infantry battalions about 80 percent.[175] In reality, specific circumstances were not so balanced. As outlined in Table 3.9, by 1 November the combat battalions of the three panzer divisions within the *1. Panzerarmee* were at an average of 62 percent of their *Sollstärke*.[176] Other divisions were also below the average figure noted above. However, some were actually above average, such as the *60. (Mot.) Infanterie Division* and *4. Gebirgs Division*. Overall, the combat battalions of the *1. Panzerarmee* still retained an average of 71 percent of their *Sollstärke*. Considering that the army group had just endured over four months of continuous combat operations, and that *1. Panzerarmee* had been the forefront of these operations throughout, this was still a respectable figure. On 5 November, the advance upon Rostov and beyond was resumed.

Although the time was fast approaching when the divisions deployed on the *Ostfront* would need a substantial period of rest and rehabilitation, by October 1941 they had clearly not yet been bled white. The *Wehrmacht* had advanced to the very gates of Leningrad, Moscow, and the Caucasus, and in the process inflicted staggering losses upon the Red Army. Russian sources admit that Soviet losses from 22 June to 30 September totalled 2,817,303 personnel, 15,500 tanks, 66,928 guns and mortars, and 6,997 aircraft.[177] Despite engagement in combat on scales that had previously been unknown, and having suffered heavy casualties in the process, the formations of the *Ostheer* still remained formidable. In its preparations for Operation Typhoon, *Heeresgruppe Mitte* alone still marshalled between 2,103 and 2,572 tanks and assault guns. Although the number of operational vehicles would have been significantly less, this nonetheless indicates that German armoured strength was far from having been

---

174 Eight divisions were transferred to *Heeresgruppe Mitte* at the end of September. During October, the *71.* and *113. Infanterie*, and the *99. Leichte Infanterie Divisionen* were withdrawn and dispatched to the West. This left 38 divisions (excluding three security divisions) with *Heeresgruppe Süd*, whose combat battalions were as follows:

Three panzer divisions (x6 btls.)	= 18	Five mountain/leichte divs. (x7 btls)	= 35
One mot. infantry division (x8 btls.)	= 8	28 infantry divisions (x10 btls.)	= 280
One Waffen-SS div. plus one brigade	= 15	Total	= 356

By the end of September, the 451 combat battalions with the army group faced shortages of 132 men per battalion. During October casualties amounted to 30,624 men, adding a further shortage of 86 men to each of the remaining 356 combat battalions. All told, by early November average battalion shortages thereby amounted to 218 men. For losses in October, see Heeresarzt 10-Day Casualty Reports for *Heeresgruppe Süd* (1-31.10.41) in BA-MA 6/556 and 6/558.

175 The *Sollstärke* for infantry and motorized infantry battalions in 1941 were 861 and 1,089 men, respectively. For purposes of simplification, all combat battalions of infantry, mountain, and light infantry divisions have been allotted the former figure, while the combat battalions of all panzer, motorized infantry and *Waffen-SS* divisions have been attributed the latter.

176 The *1. Panzergruppe* was renamed *1. Panzerarmee* on 25 October 1941.

177 Krivosheev, *Soviet Casualties and Combat Losses in the 20th Century*, pp. 94

spent. True, personnel losses had not entirely been replaced and the lack of specific information concerning replacements precludes much beyond a general conclusion. However, the injection of personnel replacements should have meant that average battalion strengths remained high. In general terms, by early October the combat battalions of *Heeresgruppe Nord* should have hovered around 78-82 percent of their *Sollstärke*, and those of *Heeresgruppe Mitte* around 92-93 percent. A month later, the respective figures for the battalions belonging to *Heeresgruppe Süd* should have been 75-80 percent. Admittedly speculative, this assumes that all casualties and replacements were concentrated within combat units and distributed equally; nor does it take into account casualties due to sickness. Nonetheless, these projections indicate that, until this point, the German Army at least had the *potential* to maintain its combat formations at levels that rendered them capable of offensive operations. The issue may not have been the availability of sufficient manpower, but its proper distribution. Even if the true figures were closer to those illustrated in Table 3.9, this would not have meant that the offensive potential of the *Ostheer* had been exhausted. However, given the Soviet ability to field new armies, the Germans own worsening supply situation and the increasing exhaustion of their troops, as well as the steadily deteriorating weather conditions, what remained to be seen was if this offensive potential would be sufficient to knock out the Soviet Union and end the war before all these issues reached their culmination point.

Table 3.1 Expansion of the Red Army 1938 to June 1941[1]

Formation	June 1938	September 1939	December 1940	June 1941
Armies	1	2	20	27
Rifle Corps	27	25	30	62
Rifle Divisions (regular)	71	96	152	196
Rifle Divisions (cadre)	35	0	0	0
Motorised rifle and Mechanized Divisions	0	1	10	31
Cavalry Corps	7	7	4	4
Cavalry Divisions	32	30	26	13
Rifle Brigades	0	5	5	5
Tank Divisions	0	0	18	61
Tank Corps	4	4	0	0
Fortified Regions	13	21	21	57
Airborne Brigades	6	6	12	16
Airborne Corps	0	0	0	5
Total Personnel	1,513,000	1,520,000	4,207,000	5,373,000

1 Glantz, *Stumbling Colossus*, p. 107.

Table 3.2 German Armoured Strength during the Advance upon Leningrad, September 1941.[1]

	Initial Strength	Total Available/Total Operational							Percentage of Initial Strength
		Pz I	Pz II	Pz III	Pz 35/38(t)	Pz IV	Befpz.	Total	
1. PD	156	10/9	35/28	56/43	–	13/10	9/9	123/99	79
6. PD	256	9/9	42/38	–	110/102	24/21	11/11	196/181	77
8. PD	223	8/8	42/36	–	98/78	24/17	15/15	187/154	84
12. PD	232	9/7	30/25	–	62/42	22/14	8/8	131/96	56
Total	867							637/530	73

1 Strength figures for the *12. Panzer Division* date to 26 August, while those of the remaining divisions refer to their strength on 10 September. Jentz, *Panzertruppen, Vol. One*, p. 206.

Table 3.3 Second Panzer Group Personnel Losses, 22 June – 4 July 1941[1]

	Killed	Wounded	Missing	Total	Feldersatz Battalion	Deficit/ Surplus
3. Panzer Div.	196	629	35	860	Yes	-70
4. Panzer Div.	119	234	16	369	Yes	+421
10. (Mot.) Inf. Div.	52	24	5	81	Yes	+709
1. Kavallerie Div.	93	354	17	464	No	-464
10. Panzer Div.	322	576	37	935	Yes	-146
SS-Reich Div.	157	406	4	567	Yes	+223
17. Panzer Div.	295	690	66	1,051	Yes	-261
18. Panzer Div.	331	1,018	165	1,514	Yes	-724
29. (Mot.) Inf. Div.	268	680	78	1,026	Yes	-236
Division Totals	1,833	4,611	423	6,867		-537

1 The corps- and army-level troops belonging to the panzer group sustained an additional 74 killed, 143 wounded, and 5 missing. See *Anlagenband Nr. 2b zum KTB, PzAOK 2 Ia/IIa., Vom 22.7.1941. Verlustenmeldungen: Zahlmassige Verluste 5.7.1941 – 25.3.1942.*

Table 3.4 Losses Among the Divisions belonging to *Heeresgruppe Mitte*, 22 June to 10 August 1941[1]

	Killed	Wounded	Missing	Total
3. Panzer Division	673	2,161	90	2,924
4. Panzer Division	448	1,263	39	1,750
7. Panzer Division	886	2,271	108	3,265
10. Panzer Division	674	1,785	112	2,571
12. Panzer Division	704	1,351	59	2,114
17. Panzer Division	690	2,095	201	2,986
18. Panzer Division	662	2,167	582	3,411
19. Panzer Division	709	1,192	49	1,950
20. Panzer Division	724	1,754	60	2,538
(Mot.) SS-Div. 'Reich'	854	2,596	86	3,536
10. (Mot.) Inf. Div.	671	1,720	70	2,461
14. (Mot.) Inf. Div.	621	1,528	93	2,242
18. (Mot.) Inf. Div.	322	1,125	52	1,499
20. (Mot.) Inf. Div.	417	1,011	19	1,447
29. (Mot.) Inf. Div.	731	2,469	90	3,290
7. Infanterie Division	380	1,479	135	1,994
15. Infanterie Division	332	1,046	34	1,412
23. Infanterie Division	442	1,615	97	2,151
78. Infanterie Division	287	794	57	1,138
137. Infanterie Division	615	1,626	188	2,429
263. Infanterie Division	445	1,328	195	1,968
268. Infanterie Division	421	1,254	35	1,710
292. Infanterie Division	571	1,145	84	1,800

1 *Anlagenband Nr. 2b zum KTB, PzAOK 2 Ia/IIa., Vom 22.6.1941. Verlustenmeldungen: Zahlmassige Verluste 5.7.1941 – 25.3.1942. BA-MA RH 21-2/757* and *Tatigkeitsbericht (25 May – 31 August 1941), Pz Gr. 3, IIa.* NARA T313 Roll 231, Frame 7496139.

Table 3.5 Armoured Status of *Heeresgruppe Mitte*, Late August/Early September 1941[1]

	Initial Strength	Date	Pz I/ Pz II	Pz III	Pz 35/ 38(t)	Pz IV	Befpz.	Total	% of Initial Strength
			Total Available/Total Operational						
2. Panzergruppe									
3. PD	229	4.9.1941	51/35	75/6	–	22/5	11/8	161/54	70.3
4. PD	212	9.9.1941	42/29	83/24	–	16/11	21/19	162/83	76.4
10. PD	200	4.9.1941	55/47	86/75	–	19/18	15/13	175/153	87.5
17. PD	216	10.9.1941	35/23	67/20	–	19/4	7/5	128/52	59.2
18. PD	229	9.9.1941	53/39	113/30	–	31/16	10/8	207/93	90.4
Total	1,086							833/435	76.7
3. Panzergruppe									
7. PD	278	6.9.1941	54/46	-	129/62	21/14	13/8	217/130	78.0
12. PD	232	26.8.1941	39/32	-	62/42	22/14	8/8	131/96	56.5
19. PD	239	25.8.1941	30/26	-	89/57	20/9	10/10	149/102	62.3
20. PD	240	25.8.1941	27/23	-	98/52	23/11	2/2	150/88	62.5
Total	989							647/416	65.4
Overall	2,075							1,480/851	71.3

1 Jentz, *Panzertruppen, Vol. One*, p. 206.

Table 3.6 Estimated Total Armoured Strength of *Heeresgruppe Mitte* for Operation Typhoon, 30 September 1941[1]

	Date	Total Available
Already with *Heeresgruppe Mitte*		
7. PD	6.9.1941	217
10. PD	4.9.1941	175
19. PD	25.8.1941	149
20. PD	25.8.1941	150
From *Heeresgruppe Nord*		
1. PD	10.9.1941	123
6. PD	10.9.1941	196
From *Heeresgruppe Süd*		
11. PD[2]	30.9.1941	130
From OKH Reserve		
2. PD	30.9.1941	194
5. PD	30.9.1941	186
Replacements[3]	Sept.-Oct.	316
12 StuG battalions	30.9.1941	216
2. Panzergruppe		
3., 4., 9., 17. & 18. PD	1.10.1941	520
Grand Total		2,572

1 Unless otherwise noted, figures derived from Jentz, *Panzertruppen, Vol. One*, p. 206.

2 Reinhardt, *Die Wende vor Moskau*, p. 317.

3 This represents the total number dispatched to the *Ostfront* during September and October, and presumes that all were sent to *Heeresgruppe Mitte*. Boog, et. al. *GSWW. Vol. IV*, pp. 1120-1122.

Table 3.7 Initial Personnel Strength and Combat Losses Sustained by *1. Panzergruppe* as of 11 September 1941[1]

	Iststarke 15.6.41	Losses by 11.9.41	Estimated Replacements[2]	Estimated Shortage	Per Combat Battalion
9. PD	16,295	2,849	1,892	957	160
13. PD	16,811	3,292	1,102	2,190	365
14. PD	16,811	3,012	1,102	1,910	318
16. PD	17,133	3,575	1,892	1,693	282
SS-Wiking	19,155	2,873	1,892	981	98
16. Mot. ID	15,266	2,747	1,892	855	107
25. Mot. ID	15,079	1,957	1,892	65	8
60. Mot. ID	14,617	2,969	1,892	1,077	135

1 *Kriegstagebuch der Oberquartiermeisterabteilung der 1. Panzerarmee O.Qu. Panzergruppe 1 O.Qu. 2.5-31.10.1941.* NARA T313 Roll 15, Frame 7241682.

2 Replacements compiled by dividing the number of replacements dispatched from Germany with the number of combat divisions with *Heeresgruppe Süd* on 1 September (54,000 divided by 49 = 1,102 per division). Replacement personnel held within Feldersatz battalions (790) have been included in the replacement totals for those divisions known to have contained such units.

Table 3.8 Armoured Strength of *1. Panzergruppe*, Early September 1941[1]

	Initial Strength	Date	Operational	In Repair	Total	Percentage Remaining
9. PD	154	5.9.1941	62	67	129/62	84
11. PD	166	5.9.1941	60	75	135/60	81
13. PD	157	28.8.1941	93	34	127/93	81
14. PD	158	6.9.1941	112	24	136/112	86
16. PD	157	22.8.1941	61	26	87/61	55
Total	792				614/388	78

1 By this time, these divisions had received 20 replacement panzers from Germany. Jentz, *Panzertruppen, Vol. One*, p. 206.

Table 3.9 Estimated Manpower Status of the *1. Panzerarmee*, 1 November 1941[1]

	Losses 22.6-1.11.41	Ersatz	Shortages	Combat Battalions	Strength per Battalion	Shortage per Battalion	% Remaining
13. PD	4,736	2,145	2,591	6	1,089	432	60
14. PD	3,850	1,247	2,603	6	1,089	434	60
16. PD	4,693	2.470*	2,223	6	1,089	371	66
60. Mot. ID	4,044	3,684*	360	8	1,089	45	96
198. ID	4,746	1,740*	3,006	10	861	301	65
SS-Wiking Div.	4,182	1,863*	2,319	10	1,089	232	79
SS-LSSAH	3,340	1,664	1,676	5	1,089	335	69
1. Geb. Div.	5,228	3,099*	2,129	6	861	355	59
4. Geb. Div.	5,027	3,702*	1,325	7	861	189	78
Army & Corps Troops	1,195	1,119	76				
Totals	41,071	22,733	18,338				

* Includes 790 men belonging to organic Feldersatz battalion.

1 *Kriegstagebuch der Oberquartiermeisterabteilung der 1. Panzerarmee O.Qu. Panzergruppe 1 O.Qu. 2.5-31.10.1941.* NARA T313 Roll 15, Frame 7241682. Where applicable, assumed number of personnel held within *Feldersatz* battalions has been added to the actual number of received replacement personnel.

4

Requiem for a Kriegsspiel: The Failure of Barbarossa and the Rebuilding of the Ostheer, November 1941 to June 1942

In this situation there is only one answer...plug the gaps and hold on!

Adolf Hitler

16 December 1941[1]

In late 1941, the German Army appeared to be on the verge of successfully concluding its difficult campaign against the Soviet Union. Although halted by a combination of inclement weather, logistical difficulties, and persistently fierce Soviet resistance, the early stages of Operation Typhoon had nonetheless swept *Heeresgruppe Mitte* to the outskirts of Moscow. Elsewhere, the capitulation of Leningrad appeared inevitable after Heeresgruppe Nord had captured Tikhvin on 8 November and stood posed to link up with Finnish forces along the Svir River.[2] To the south, the *11. Armee* had cleared Soviet forces from the Crimea and laid siege to Sevastopol by 16 November. The *1. Panzerarmee* took Rostov four days later, whereupon it was expected to push on into the Caucasus and its coveted oilfields. The optimism these events generated amongst Hitler and the senior officers at OKH had already resulted in the decision to begin transferring resources out of theatre. In consequence, seven Army divisions were transferred westwards between mid-October and early November.[3] Concurrently, the

---

1 Irving, *Hitler's War*, p. 444.
2 For the best examinations of this operation, see Gerald R. Kleinfeld, "Hitler's Strike for Tikhvin." *Military Affairs*, Vol. 47, No. 3 (October 1983), pp. 122-128, and Glantz, *The Battle for Leningrad, 1941-1944*, pp. 94-116.
3 The *1. Kavallerie, 8.*, and *28. Infanterie Divisions* departed *Heeresgruppe Mitte* in October, followed the next month by the *5. Infanterie Division*. From *Heeresgruppe Süd*, the *71.* and *113. Infanterie Divisions* also left in October, while the *99. Leichte Infanterie Division* was shipped out in early November. In contrast, *Heeresgruppe Mitte* had received the *339.* and *707. Infanterie Divisions* in August, and the *2.* and *5. Panzer Divisions* in late September. This army group also received the *638. Infanterie Regiment* (*Legion des Voluntaires Francais*, or LVF) consisting of French volunteers in October. The *212.* and *250. Infanterie Divisions* (the latter made up of Spanish volunteers) arrived at *Heeresgruppe Nord* in November,

headquarters of *Luftflotte 2* and nine air groups were also withdrawn from the Moscow sector for redeployment elsewhere.[4] Finally, once the ground had frozen, *Heeresgruppe Mitte* resumed its advance upon Moscow on 15 November. Despite fierce resistance, falling temperatures, and continuing supply difficulties, the advance steadily ground forward, inflicting heavy losses upon the Red Army.[5] By 28 November, the *7. Panzer Division* had established a bridgehead across the Moscow-Volga Canal, while the neighbouring *2. Panzer Division* stood 20 kilometres northwest of Moscow. On 2 December, elements of the *258. Infanterie Division* reached the town of Khimki, a mere eight kilometres from the Soviet capital. The following day *Generalfeldmarschall* von Bock, still hopeful that his army group would prevail, wrote in his diary: "Despite

followed by the *215. Infanterie Division* by mid-December. For more regarding Spain's involvement with the Axis, see Donald S. Detwiler, "Spain and the Axis during World War II." *Review of Politics*, Vol. 33, No. 1 (January 1971), pp. 36-53, Arnold Krammer, "Spanish Volunteers against Bolshevism: The Blue Division." *Russian Review*, Vol. 32, No. 4 (October 1973), pp. 388-402, Wayne H. Bowen, "The Ghost Battalion: Spaniards in the Waffen-SS, 1944-1945." *The Historian*, Vol. 63, No. 2 (2001), pp. 373-385, and Juan-Carlos Escalonilla, "The Spanish Blue Division." MA. Thesis (Carlisle, PA: U.S. Army War College, 2005). In terms of French participation on the Eastern Front, see Owen A. Davey, "Origins of the Legion des Volontaires Francais contre le Bolchevisime." *Journal of Contemporary History*, Vol. 6, No. 4 (1971), pp. 29-45.

4   These included four fighter (I. & III./JG.3, III./JG. 27, III./JG. 53), one twin-engine fighter (I./ZG. 26), two dive-bomber (III./StG. 1 & I./StG. 2), and two bomber groups (I./KG. 2 & KGr. 100), which joined a further five fighter (II./JG. 27, I. & II./JG. 53, II./JG. 52, II./JG. 54), one ground-attack (I./SKG. 210) and nine bomber groups (II. & III./KG. 51, II. & III./KG. 55, I. & II./KG. 54, I. & II./KG. 77, KGr. 806) that had already been withdrawn or would be before the end of the year. See Bergstrom, *Barbarossa: The Air Battle, July – December 1941.*

5   The *4. Panzergruppe* alone claimed to have taken 21,860 prisoners between 16 November and 3 December, and captured or destroyed 449 tanks and 264 artillery pieces. Jacobsen, (Ed.) *KTB OKW. Band I,* p. 793. Another report from *Heeresgruppe Mitte* claimed that between 15 November and 1 December the army group had captured 71,827 men, and captured or destroyed 939 tanks, 299 artillery pieces, 232 anti-tank and 166 anti-aircraft pieces. See *Ia Anlagen zum Kriegstagebuch Nr.1 (Band Dezember 1941) des Oberkommando der Heeresgruppe Mitte (1-16. Dezember 1941),* NARA T311 Roll 288, Frame 000450. Such claims appear supported by the woeful condition of many Soviet units; by 18 November, the Soviet 58th Tank Division was reduced to only 350 men, 15 light tanks, and five artillery pieces, while five tank brigades had to be withdrawn from the front on 5 December for rebuilding. Even before the Germans had resumed their advance on 15 November, the Soviet 50th Army reported that six of its seven rifle divisions averaged between 600 and 2,000 men and two or three artillery batteries each, all of which had to occupy a 70-kilometre sector of front. Klaus Reinhardt, *Moscow – The Turning Point: The Failure of Hitler's Strategy in the Winter of 1941-42.* (Providence, RI: 1992), pp. 212, 229 & 286.

the adverse circumstances I have not given up hope. There remains the remote possibility of conquering the city of Moscow. The last battalion will decide the issue!"[6]

Whatever hopes Bock and other senior German leaders may still have entertained, by 4 December German offensive operations along the Moscow axis had sputtered to a halt. Local Soviet counterattacks the next day forced the Germans to relinquish some of their hard-won gains and in some sectors even achieved dangerous penetrations that threatened the panzer spearheads. On 6 December, these local Soviet attacks evolved into a general counteroffensive that rippled across the Moscow front, penetrating its weak points and threatening German forces with encirclement. For the first time in the war, large numbers of German troops faced the prospect of being surrounded and annihilated on the battlefield. They had little choice but to retreat.[7]

The German Army's woes opposite Moscow were exacerbated by the worsening situations that had arisen with equal rapidity along other portions of the front. Across the northern sector, *Heeresgruppe Nord*'s grip on Tikhvin was jeopardized by incessant Soviet counterattacks. By striking at its long flanks, these attacks threatened the *XXXIX. (Mot.) Armee Korps* holding the city with encirclement and on 8 December the Germans were forced to evacuate, beginning an agonizing withdrawal back to the Volkhov River. This was completed by 30 December, but not before the forces involved had sustained heavy losses of men and equipment.[8] Similarly, the *1. Panzerarmee* had held Rostov for only two days before Soviet attacks crumpled its exposed left flank

6   Alfred W. Turney, *Disaster at Moscow: Von Bock's Campaigns, 1941-1942*. (Albuquerque: 1970), p. 150.

7   The most detailed study concerning the Soviet counteroffensive around Moscow can be found in Reinhardt, *Moscow – The Turning Point*. For operations from a Russian perspective, see Parrish, (Ed.) *Battle for Moscow*, Rodric Braithwaite, *Moscow 1941*. (New York: 2006), and Glantz, *Forgotten Battles of the German-Soviet War, 1941-1945. Vol. Two*. Also see, Ronald Seth, *Operation Barbarossa: The Battle for Moscow*. (London: 1964), Geoffrey Jukes, *The Defence of Moscow*. (London: 1969), Turney, *Disaster at Moscow*, Albert Seaton, *The Battle for Moscow, 1941-1942*. (London: 1971), Janusz Piekalliewicz, *Moscow 1941: The Frozen Offensive*. (Novato, CA: 1981), and David M. Glantz, *Operation Barbarossa: Hitler's Invasion of Russia 1941*. (Gloucestershire, UK: 2011), pp. 175-192.

8   The *12. Panzer Division* had been reduced to 33 operational panzers by 11 December. Gerd Niepold, *Die Geschichte der 12. Panzer Division – 2. Infanterie Division (Mot.) 1921-45*. (Self-Published, 1988), p. 40. According to the Heeresarzt 10-Day Casualty Reports for *Heeresgruppe Nord* in BA-MA RW 6/556 and 6/558, between 11 October and 31 December the army group lost 9,550 killed, 36,861 wounded, and 975 missing, for a total of 47,386 casualties. Note that this represents the casualties for the entire army group and not just for the fighting around Tikhvin. Boog, et. al. *GSWW. Vol. VI*, p. 865, notes that 35,400 men departed the army group during December 1941. This includes killed and missing as well as wounded and sick transported out of theatre. Since the 10-day reports (which do not include those listed as sick) indicate that the number of killed, wounded, and missing during December only totalled 14,808, it would appear that the army group lost 20,592 to sickness or frostbite during the month. In contrast, about 27,000 replacement personnel arrived.

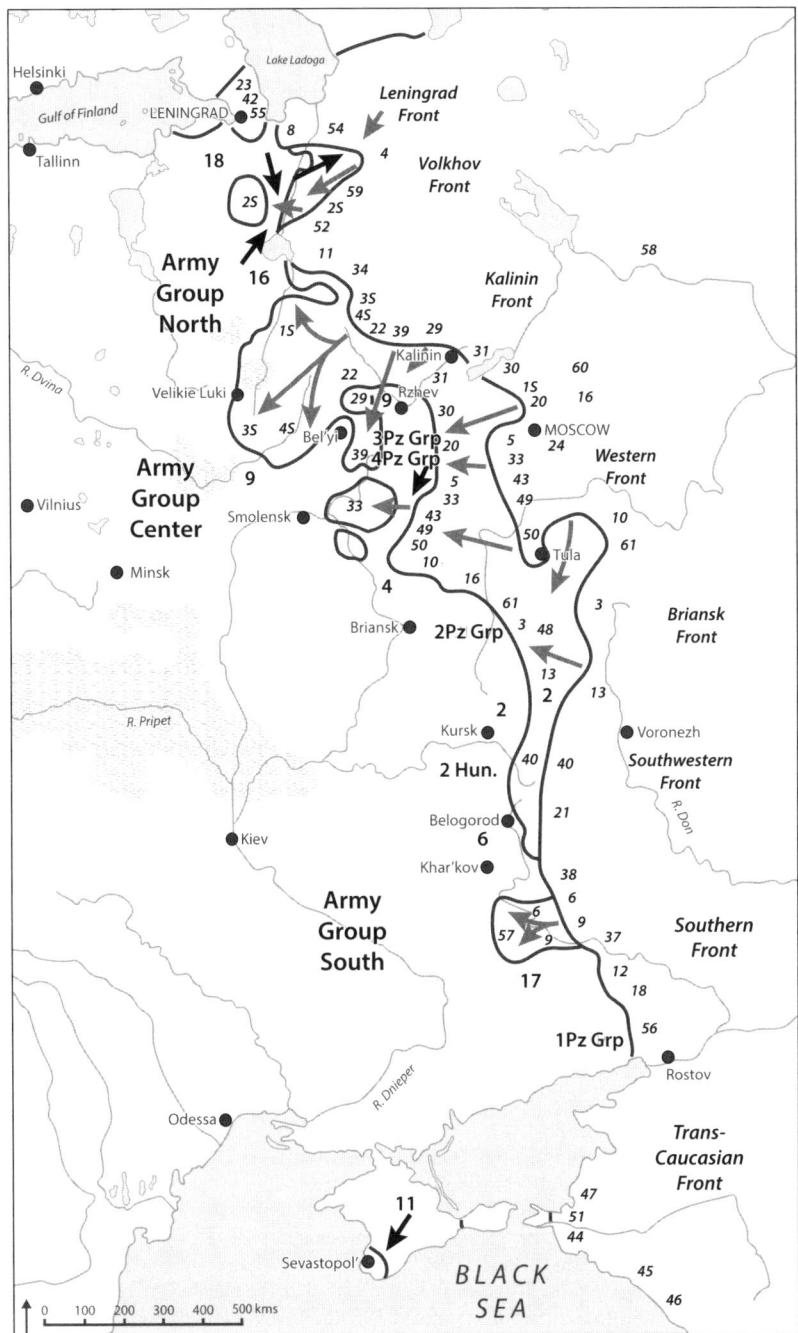

Map 4.1 The Winter Campaign, December 1941 to April 1942.

and threatened to encircle it. Bowing to the inevitable, the Germans were compelled to relinquish their tenuous hold of Rostov on 28 November and retreat to a more secure position along the Mius River.[9] Soon after, further Soviet offensives erupted across the entire length of the Eastern Front, engulfing the *Ostheer* in a life or death struggle that lasted until late April 1942.

As foretold in a series of war games conducted by the German General Staff in late 1940, Operation Barbarossa had proven abortive.[10] Its momentous failure has been attributed to a litany of causes, including the size and resistance of the Red Army, terrain and climatic conditions, the inadequacies of the German logistics, a catastrophic disconnect between Germany's senior leadership and the realities of events at the front, and Hitler's own misguided strategy and obstinate interference in military operations. To be certain, all of these issues played some role in the ultimate failure of Barbarossa. Yet amongst the post-war writings of senior German officers, Hitler's leadership and the numerical weakness of the German Army during this period tend to receive a particularly scathing emphasis. In consequence these aspects have received prominence within the historiography to the marginalization of everything else. However, one must tread carefully when navigating such accounts; given the scope of Barbarossa's failure, the fact that it dramatically ended a three-year winning streak for the *Wehrmacht*, and the damage it did to the German Army's image of infallibility, reputations had to be protected, both in terms of senior individuals and the German officer corps as a whole. At the time and consequently, the authors of the memoir material tended to blame almost everything for the defeat around Moscow, except of course their own leadership.[11] Interestingly, *General der Infanterie* Georg Thomas, the man responsible for organizing and co-ordinating the Wehrmacht's armament production as head of OKW's Defence Economy and Armament Office (*Wehrwirtschafts- und Rustungsamt*), noted in a conversation in early January 1942 that, "We must now present a completely clear picture since some day somebody will be held responsible."[12]

This is not to say that manpower and equipment shortages were not a significant problem. The formations of *Heeresgruppe Mitte* were doubtlessly nearing the end of their endurance by December 1941. Its logistics had reached a culmination point and those supplies that did make it to the frontlines were invariably inadequate. Battlefield casualties in the preceding two months had been heavy, totalling no fewer than 111,944

9   For more detail, see Ewald Klapder, *Der Ostfeldzug 1941 – Eine Vorprogrammierte Niederlage: Die Panzergruppe 1 zwischen Bug und Don.* (Siek: 1989), and Boog, et. al. *GSWW. Vol. IV,* pp. 613-627.
10   See Walter Görlitz, *Paulus and Stalingrad.* (London: 1963), pp. 99-120, Fugate, *Operation Barbarossa,* pp. 80-82, Leach, *German Strategy against Russia,* pp. 105-106, and Stahel, *Operation Barbarossa and Germany's Defeat in the East,* pp. 55-59. For war games concerning the logistical component, see Schuler, *Logistik im Russlandfeldzug,* pp. 160-167.
11   In particular, see Guderian, *Panzer Leader.*
12   Tooze, *The Wages of Destruction,* pp. 506-507.

killed, wounded, and missing.[13] Continuous operations and a dire lack of spare parts had also blunted its offensive edge: by early December, six of its available panzer divisions mustered only 142 operational panzers between them.[14] Lacking proper winter equipment and clothing, troops froze to death as the temperature suddenly plunged to -25°F, and then further to -40°F.

While such statistics seem to validate assertions within the historiography that the German units involved were simply too numerically depleted to take Moscow, it should be noted that some evidence suggests that this was not universally the case, or at least that the emphasis upon this factor may have been overblown *ex post facto*. For instance, the 6. *Panzer Division* reported that it possessed 142 panzers, of which 66 were operational, on 31 October.[15] Similarly, the 5. *Panzer Division* still retained 101 of its tanks on 29 November and two days later the 7. *Panzer Division* reported that 52 of its tanks were still operational with a further 142 in repair.[16] Thus is appears that serviceability was the foremost problem faced by the panzer divisions instead of a general lack of tanks.[17] In terms of personnel, overall German losses in the East by the end of November, including sick transported back to Germany for treatment, amounted to 926,100 men. During this same period 410,000 replacements had arrived to join the 90,000 already present within divisional replacement battalions, meaning that the *Ostheer* would have been short 426,221 men by December.[18] With the 130 field divisions and two brigades then present containing a total of 1,201 combat battalions, evenly dividing the shortages produces an average of 355 per battalion.[19] As noted

13 Casualties compiled from Heeresarzt 10-Day Casualty Reports for *Heeresgruppe Mitte* (1.10-30.11.41) in BA-MA RW 6/556 and 6/558.
14 On 30 November, the 1. *Panzer Division* possessed 37 operational panzers, while the 10. *Panzer Division* reported 40 operational the following day. Jentz, *Panzertruppen, Vol. One*, pp. 210-211. According to Paul, *Geschichte der 18. Panzer Division 1940-1943*, p. 135, the 18. *Panzer Division* retained 22 operational tanks on 6 December. The number of operational panzers with the remaining divisions was as follows: 3. *Panzer Division* (6 December) with 22 tanks, 6. *Panzer Division* (30 November) with only four, and the 17. *Panzer Division* (24 November) had 17. See Reinhardt, *Die Wende vor Moskau*, p. 317.
15 Jentz, *Panzertruppen, Vol. One*, p. 208.
16 See Plato, *Die Geschichte der 5. Panzer Division, 1938-1945*, p. 177, and 7. *Panzer Division. Ia., Anlagen zum Kriegstagebuch Nr. 3, Teil II (28.9.1941-5.5.1942)*. NARA T315 Roll 407, Frame 000239.
17 On 22 December, the 16 panzer divisions of *Heeresgruppe Nord* and *Heeresgruppe Mitte* possessed 1,185 tanks (excluding Pz I and command tanks), averaging 74 per division. However, only 405 were operational that day, or approximately 25 for each division. Jentz, *Panzertruppen, Vol. One*, p. 209.
18 Kroener, et. al. *GSWW. Vol. V: Part One*, p. 1,020.
19 The number of divisions cited here does not include those formations that had been withdrawn from Russia at this point, or those that had arrived after August aside from the 2. and 5. *Panzer Divisions*. It also excludes the security divisions and brigades located in the German rear areas. The number of divisional and brigade combat battalions (infantry, reconnaissance and motorcycle units only) may therefore be derived as follows:

in the previous chapter, the *Sollstärke* of German infantry and motorised infantry battalions at this stage of the war amounted to 861 and 1,089 men, respectively. One could thereby conclude that, even by early December, the average German infantry battalion should have retained 58.8 percent of its authorized manpower strength. For an average motorised infantry battalion, the figure would have been 67.4 percent. Although the methodology for this estimate is admittedly problematic, it is interesting to note that as late as 31 December the *6. Schützen Regiment* of the *7. Panzer Division* reported a shortage of 551 men; when divided amongst its two battalions this produces a figure (275) that is close to the battalion average conjectured above. Similarly, the division's *37. Panzeraufklärungs Battalion* noted a shortfall of only 102 men.[20] Lacking a more systematic manpower review, one certainly cannot conclude that German frontline battalions were in an optimal condition by early December. However, given their wide range of strengths and circumstances, it would likewise be premature to deduce that the failure of these battalions before Moscow was primarily due to their lacking sufficient manpower to achieve their objective.

Alternatively, the physical and psychological exhaustion of all the personnel involved, and the effect this had upon strategic and operational decision-making as well as the behaviour of the troops in the field, was invariably a major factor – perhaps even the most important – in the German defeat outside Moscow. Faced by the shock of the sudden onset of brutal winter temperatures and large-scale attacks by an opponent who had seemed all but defeated just days before, the already-depleted physical and mental state of many personnel may have been pushed over the edge. Though frequently unacknowledged by many historians, references to this are scattered throughout the literature. For example, Guderian provides insight into the behaviour of one of his foremost officers: "For the first time during this exacting campaign Colonel Eberbach gave the impression of being exhausted, and the exhaustion that was now noticeable was less physical than spiritual. It was indeed startling to see how deeply our best officers had been affected by these latest battles."[21] On 6 December, the commander of the *XXXIX. (Mot.) Armee Korps* noted, "They have already gone beyond the bounds of physical endurance…the troops…are becoming listless and indifferent…danger of panic…" By 12 December, the morale in the *2. Armee* had sunk

---

19 panzer divisions (x6)	= 114	93 infantry divisions (x10)	= 930
Ten mot. infantry divisions (x8)	= 80	Mot. Inf. Regt. 'GD'	= 4
Three *Waffen-SS* divs. plus one brigade	= 36	900. Lehr Brigade	= 2
Five mountain or light inf. divs. (x7)	= 35	Total	= 1,201

In this instance combat battalions refers to all infantry, motorized infantry, motorcycle, mountain, light infantry, and reconnaissance battalions. Divisional engineer battalions are not included.

20   To be sure, its *7. Schützen Regiment* reported a deficit of 964 men, or 482 for each of its two battalions. *7. Panzer Division. Ia., Anlagen zum Kriegstagebuch Nr. 3, Teil II (28.9.1941-5.5.1942).* NARA T315 Roll 407, Frames 000310, 000320, & 000337.

21   Guderian, *Panzer Leader*, p. 235.

to the point that its commander ordered, "individuals who make defeatist remarks to be singled out and shot as an example." In a conversation with Halder that same day, von Bock remarked, "We cannot stop our troops from running away as soon as they see a Russian tank!"[22] In his post-war recollection of this time, *General der Panzertruppen* Ferdinand Schaal bluntly remembered that, "Discipline began to crack."[23] One colonel reported to his superior that, "Our soldiers are in such a state that some, through sheer desperation, may turn their guns on their own officers. They are going out of their minds."[24] The implications of this physical and psychological strain had already been apparent on 17 November when parts of the *112. Infanterie Division* had fled the battlefield in panic. A similar event of smaller proportions may also have occurred among the *29. (Mot.) Infanterie Division* on the night of 24-25 November.[25] At more senior levels, Hitler himself fell ill as early as August and increasingly exhibited signs of nervous exhaustion.[26] On 10 November the Commander-in-Chief of the German Army, *Generalfeldmarschall* Walther von Brauchitsch, suffered a heart attack, while on 16 December von Bock requested that he be relieved of his command because of his poor health and exhaustion.[27] *Generalfeldmarschall* Walter von Reichenau, the recently appointed commander of *Heeresgruppe Süd*, had a stroke on 15 January 1942 and died of a heart attack two days later.

While more research is required in terms of its precise dimensions and impact, the physical and psychological exhaustion of the German troops would undeniably have undermined their combat performance and resolve on the battlefield. Even more fatefully, one can only speculate how this stress and exhaustion impacted leadership, and command and control, at all levels and just what the ramifications of this may have been. It certainly would also have exacerbated the abandonment of equipment during any retreat. As noted in one landmark study of German operations around Moscow, "...everywhere the troops pulled back they left equipment standing."[28] In discussing its retreat from the area around the city of Klin, the former Chief-of-Staff of *4. Panzergruppe*, *Generalleutnant* Walter Chales de Beaulieu, later recounted that on 18-19 December alone two of its corps had to abandon a combined total of 111 10.5 cm and 44 15 cm field howitzers, 40 anti-tank guns, 100 8.1 cm mortars, and 300 machine-guns. Although the loss of equipment is usually attributed to the combination of a lack of fuel, insufficient towing vehicles, or impassable roads, the growing

---

22   Reinhardt, *Moscow – The Turning Point*, pp. 236, 246 & 299.

23   As quoted in Carell, *Hitler Moves East, 1941-1943*, p. 318.

24   As quoted in Michael Jones, *The Retreat: Hitler's First Defeat*. (New York: 2009), p. 132.

25   See Clark, *Barbarossa*, pp. 173-174, and Seaton, *The Battle for Moscow, 1941-1942*, p. 159.

26   Irving, *Hitler's War*, pp. 402-404. Also see Ellen Gibbels, "Hitler's Nervenkrankheit: Eine neurologisch-psychiatrische Studie." *Vierteljahrshefte für Zeitgeschichte*, Vol. 42, No. 2 (1994), pp. 155-220.

27   Turney, *Disaster at Moscow*, p. 159.

28   Earl Ziemke & Magna E. Bauer, *Moscow to Stalingrad: Decision in the East*. (Washington, D.C: 1987), p. 75.

apathy and demoralization amongst German soldiers caused by their physical and mental exhaustion likely played a key factor in such circumstances.[29] That many front-line officers and men may have been less than inclined to fight it out in the face of the Soviets unexpected counteroffensive could also be indicated by curious tendencies within their casualty rates. Considering that the collapse of a part of its front precipitated the need to abandon Klin and the copious quantities of equipment noted above, it is interesting to note that the casualties sustained by the *3. Panzergruppe* were rather modest, especially within the first two decades of the month (see Table 4.1). Since this period encompassed the final German attacks, the onset of the Soviet counteroffensive, and the eventual abandonment of Klin, and is thereby assumed to have been a time of extremely desperate fighting, one would presume the consequence would have been very heavy casualties. However, this does not appear to be the case.[30] Similarly, the combat losses sustained by most of the divisions belonging to the *4. Armee* are relatively small during December, during which they too had been staging their final assaults around Moscow, absorbing the initial attacks of the Soviet counteroffensive, and conducting retreats to the west. Significantly, their losses increased dramatically during January (see Table 4.2), by then having reached the line demarcated by Hitler as the point of no retreat, which forced them to stand and fight. In either of these instances, the lack of greater casualties during December appears to suggest that the scale and intensity of the fighting was not nearly as substantial as one would presuppose given that the period involved a Soviet counteroffensive that produced the first major German defeat, and subsequent retreat, of the war. While far from conclusive, when this lack of sizeable numbers of casualties is conjoined with the abandonment

---

29   Walter Chales de Beulieu, "Sturm bis vor Moskaus Tore. Der Einsatz der Panzergruppe 4. Teil II: November 1941 – Januar 1942." *Wehrwissenschaftliche Rundschau*, Vol. 6, No. 8 (1956), p. 431.

30   Figures for both the *3. Panzergruppe* and the *4. Armee* have been drawn from the *Armeearzt* reports submitted every ten days by their respective medical authorities. Because not all casualties may have been known at the time of the report, these tended to be lower than the Army-wide *Heeresarzt* reports. Weekly losses should also be handled with care since losses not known one week were frequently added (in post-script reports or *Nachtragmeldungen*) to later weeks. There are also instances where casualties for some formations are missing entirely. For a more detailed explanation, see Burkhart Müller-Hillebrand, "Statistics Systems." (March 1949). NARA FMS P-011. For example, the *Armeearzt* reports of the *4. Armee* note that its total losses for December 1941 included 1,884 killed, 6,779 wounded, and 872 missing, for a total of 9,501 casualties. See *4. AOK. Oberquartiermeisterabteilung O.Qu. Anlagen zum Kriegstagebuch O.Qu.-Besondere Anordnungen für die Versorgung, Verluste, Einsatz, Meldungen, Transportlage. Band 8. (9-31. Dezember 1941)* BA-MA RH 20-4/889, and *Band 9. (1-15. Januar 1942)* BA-MA RH 20-4/890. However, because parts of the original documents were lost, these figures are incomplete. In contrast, the figures found in the Heeresarzt 10-Day Casualty Reports for *4. Armee* (1-31.12.41) in BA-MA RW 6/556 and 6/558 cite the army's losses for the month as being 2,130 killed, 8,316 wounded, and 786 missing, for a total of 11,232 casualties.

of substantial quantities of equipment, all within the context of a major defeat, the resulting impression is that the formations involved, already weakened, exhausted, and facing a number of adverse circumstances, may very well have been inclined to retreat rather than stand their ground. Whether this was due to leaders at various levels losing their equilibrium in a moment of unexpected crisis, the troops panicking and giving way, or some combination of both, remains to be determined.

In such an atmosphere, accurate reporting regarding the condition of individual formations and the German Army writ large does appear to have become problematic. To be sure, the precise reporting of circumstances would have been extremely difficult for frontline German officers given the dire situation in which they found themselves during the winter of 1941-1942. With the front seemingly collapsing around them, little time or inclination would have remained to compile precise reports. And yet, as Rolf-Dieter Müller has noted, "it was not in the interests of a unit to provide details of surplus materials. On the other hand, there must often have been a temptation to manipulate the figures on losses, repairs, and combat-readiness, in order to secure as large a share of supplies as possible, or to justify the failure to carry out orders to hold on or attack…"[31] While probably not widespread, such tendencies were also probably not entirely rare, especially during that first calamitous winter in Russia. At least to some extent, they do appear to have partially motivated Hitler in the substance of his first basic order issued to the Army on 26 December 1941. Having recently assumed direct command of the Army himself, Hitler's first act as its new Commander-in-Chief was to demand and stress the importance of honest, accurate reports.[32]

Admittedly, the fact that the *Ostheer* did sustain heavy losses is incontrovertible: total German Army casualties in the East amounted to 1,094,251 men by 31 December, including 167,354 killed, 600,584 wounded, 34,514 missing, and at least 291,799 sick who had to be repatriated to Germany.[33] In addition, an estimated 2,735 tanks and 104 assault guns had been listed as *Totalausfälle* by this point, with a further 415 being permanently lost in January.[34] Other equipment and vehicle losses were equally heavy, the largest proportion of which were lost during the retreats of December and

---

31   Boog, et. al. *GSWW. Vol. IV,* p. 1130.

32   Ibid, p. 724. Also see "Fuhrer Directives and other Top-Level Directives of the German Armed Forces, 1939-1941." (U.S. Army Historical Division, 1948), p. 239.

33   Kroener, et. al. *GSWW. Vol. V: Part One,* p. 1020. Additionally, during the same period German forces fighting in Finland sustained 28,445 casualties (6,375 killed, 20,724 wounded, and 1,346 missing). See Heeresarzt 10-Day Casualty Reports for *Armee Norwegen* (22.6-31.12.1941) in BA/MA RW 6/556 & 6/558. Note that sick includes those suffering from frostbite. Jacobsen, (Ed.) *KTB OKW. Band I,* pp. 1120-1121, indicates that the *Ostheer* (excluding the forces in Finland) lost 173,722 killed, 621,308 wounded, and 35,875 missing, but provides no information regarding the sick.

34   Boog, et. al. *GSWW. Vol. IV,* p. 1120-1122. Hahn, *Waffen und Geheimwaffen des deutschen Heeres, 1933-1945, Band II,* p. 220 concurs with these numbers except in terms of assault guns. Smaller alternate figures can also be found in Burkhart Müller-Hillebrand, "German Tank Strength and Loss Statistics." (December 1950), FMS P-059, Appendix 3.

January (see Table 4.3). By the end of January some 179,132 horses had died and a further 27,811 were listed as sick, a devastating number considering the Army's reliance upon horse transport.[35] The situation in the air was equally grim: *Luftwaffe* losses in Russia amounted to 2,505 aircraft destroyed and 1,895 damaged to all causes by the end of 1941.[36] Although as many as 1,700 aircraft were still deployed in Russia at the outset of 1942, these were plagued by serviceability rates as low as 43 percent, further hampering the *Luftwaffe*'s ability to provide the Army with appropriate amounts of ground support and air cover.[37] Moreover, bitter fighting continued to rage across the Eastern Front throughout the first half of 1942, producing another 501,029 killed, wounded, and missing, and a staggering 423,601 sick.[38] By the time the German Army resumed large-scale offensive operations in late June, overall losses during its operations against the Soviet Union had climbed to 1,303,481 combat casualties and 715,400 sick, for a total of 2,018,881 men.

At first glance, losses on such a scale would appear to have incontrovertibly sealed Germany's fate by inflicting a mortal wound upon its military might, thereby rendering null its prospects of successfully concluding the war. The effect of these losses upon many of the divisions deployed on the *Ostfront* was indeed devastating.

35   Since the *Ostheer* had marched into Russia with an estimated 625,000 horses, this represents a 33 percent loss rate. Reinhardt, *Moscow – The Turning Point*, p. 372. For the importance of horses in the German Army, see Richard DiNardo & Austin Ray, "Horse-Drawn Transport in the German Army." *Journal of Contemporary History*, Vol. 23 (1988), pp. 129-142.

36   *Luftwaffe* personnel losses in Russia during this period totaled 20,221 men (6,232 killed, 11,425 wounded, and 2,564 missing), including 4,404 flying personnel. Kroener, et. al. *GSWW. Vol. V: Part One*, pp. 817-818. The *Luftwaffe* also lost 645 flak guns (250 8.8 cm, 144 3.7 cm and 251 2 cm) during this timeframe, although some of these were actually lost in North Africa. Ibid, p. 731. Bergstrom, *Barbarossa: The Air Battle, July – December 1941*, pp. 117-118 cites *Luftwaffe* aircraft losses in the East till 6 December as being 2,093 destroyed and 1,362 damaged to all causes.

37   The intense pace of operations, poor weather conditions, supply problems, and generally inadequate airfields and maintenance facilities all contributed to the low serviceability rate. Supply difficulties and the subsequent lack of spare parts and materials were exacerbated by the fact that only 15 percent of the 100,000 vehicles the *Luftwaffe* committed to the East were still operational by January 1942. Matthew Cooper, *The German Air Force, 1933-1945: An Anatomy of Failure*. (New York: 1981), pp. 239-240.

38   Boog, et. al. *GSWW. Vol. VI*, pp. 865-867, appears to incorrectly list combat casualties as 'killed'. The sick have thereby been derived by deducting 'killed' (ie. combat casualties) from the total given as 'losses'. The Heeresarzt 10-Day reports for the armies operating on the Eastern Front (1.1-30.6.1942) in BA/MA 6/556 & 6/558 indicate a slightly lower combined tally of 490,138 casualties (98,274 killed, 366,483 wounded, and 25,381 missing). Reinhardt, *Die Wende vor Moskau*, p. 247, records that losses to frostbite in January 1942 totaled 92,563 men (including at least 1,856 requiring amputations), with a further 58,934 men reported as sick. Kroener, et. al. *GSWW. Vol. V: Part One*, p. 1020 indicates a smaller combined total of 127,718 sick and frostbitten for the month, although this only includes personnel transferred out of theatre.

By late November, the *(Mot.) SS-Division Reich* had been forced to disband five of its eleven combat battalions to maintain the combat strengths of the remainder. Losses continued and on 13 February 1942 the *Gefechtsstärke* of its *SS-Regiment Der Fuhrer* had been reduced to a mere eight officers and 104 men.[39] The *10. Panzer Division* faced similar circumstances. On 22 June the *Sollstärke* of its two *schützen* regiments had amounted to 2,243 men each, but by 2 December these regiments reported that their number of "fully-fit fighters" (*einsatzfahige kämpfer*) only amounted to a combined 725 men.[40] As exemplified in the condition report of the *2. Panzerarmee* on 15 December (see Table 4.4), such woeful *Gefechtsstärke* levels appear to have been commonplace throughout the *Ostheer* during the winter of 1941-1942.[41] In consequence, by the late spring of 1942 numerous infantry divisions deployed with *Heeresgruppe Nord* and *Mitte* had been forced to disband three of their nine infantry battalions, reduce artillery batteries from twelve to nine guns, and fold their *Panzerjäger* and *Aufklärungs* battalions into single mixed *Schnelle* battalions. Many panzer divisions were also badly damaged, being reduced to a single panzer battalion and having to make considerable use of the ubiquitous horse-drawn *Panje* wagon native to Eastern Europe in lieu of motor vehicles.[42]

And yet, before any conclusions can be reached regarding the *Wehrmacht*'s long-term prospects, one must take into consideration the fact, frequently overlooked within the historiography, that by the spring of 1942 the Soviet Union found itself struggling with the same dire circumstances that now confronted Germany. Despite the final outcome of Barbarossa, the *Ostheer* had inflicted massive damage and dislocation upon the armed forces of the Soviet Union and its supporting infrastructure. Even by the most conservative estimates, the losses inflicted upon the Red Army had been staggering.[43] At the end of 1941, personnel losses totalled at least 802,191

---

39   Weidinger, *Division Das Reich. Band III*, pp. 169, 240 & 378.
40   Schick, *Die 10. Panzer Division 1939-1943*, p. 444.
41   A report from the *XXXIX. (Mot.) Armee Korps* dated to 8 December indicates similar circumstances. The *Kampfstärke* available to the *61. Infanterie Division* was listed as follows:

	I. Battalion	II. Battalion	III. Battalion
151. Infanterie Regiment	164	185	178
162. Infanterie Regiment	209	207	197
176. Infanterie Regiment	287	212	294

Likewise, the *12. Panzer Division* reported that its *5.* and *25. Schützen Regiments* possessed a combined *Kampfstärke* of 396 and 331 men, respectively. See *Heeresgruppe Nord. Besprechungs und Vortragsnotizen Nr. 2 (19.9.1941 – 12.1.1942)*, NARA T311 Roll 51, Frame 7064625.

42   By early 1943 the *18. Panzer Division* began referring to itself as the 'Panje Division' because of its heavy reliance upon this form of transport. Paul, *Geschichte der 18. Panzer Division 1940-1943*, p. 237.

43   Considerable variations exist within most references concerning Soviet losses. For example, in terms of service personnel killed during the war, Krivosheev cites 8,668,400,

dead, 1,336,147 wounded or sick, and 2,335,482 missing, a total of 4,473,820 casualties. Equipment losses included 5.5 million rifles, 190,800 machine-guns, 4,100 anti-aircraft and 12,100 anti-tank guns, 24,400 field artillery pieces, 60,500 mortars, 20,500 tanks, and between 10,600 and 21,200 aircraft.[44] Roughly 159,000 motor vehicles were also lost.[45] Soviet losses during the first half of 1942 amounted to a further 3,404,313 casualties, including 1,518,209 dead and missing, and 1,886,104 wounded or sick.[46] Specific equipment losses during this period are unknown, but even a partial accounting amounts to an additional 3,048 tanks and 11,351 guns and mortars.[47] Further aircraft losses totalled at least 2,037.[48] With overall manpower losses between June 1941 and June 1942 amounting to at least 7,878,137 men, the ration between Soviet and German casualties was almost four to one. In all probability the actual ratio was even more in the German favour since the Soviet personnel losses

while Sokolov maintains that the true figure is likely in the region of 26.4 million. Krivosheev, *Soviet Casualties and Combat Losses in the 20th Century*, p. 84, and Sokolov, "The Cost of War: Human Losses for the USSR and Germany, 1941-1945.", p. 12. Wherever possible, Krisvosheev's figures have been cited in the text because of his information concerning specific battles and periods. However, as the most conservative of estimates, they should be considered a minimal number. In this respect, actual Soviet losses were probably much greater, especially in terms of personnel. For insight into the inherent problems found within Soviet accounting procedures and post-1990 Russian estimates, see Zetterling & Frankson, "Analyzing World War II Eastern Front Battles.", pp. 176-188.

44   Krivosheev, *Soviet Casualties and Combat Losses in the 20th Century*, pp. 94, 246-255. OKH estimated that its forces had captured 214,379 rifles, 29,113 machine-guns, 4,439 mortars, 4,164 anti-tank and 1,927 anti-aircraft guns, 19,605 field artillery pieces, 55,753 motor vehicles, 13,935 tanks, and 980 aircraft by 20 December 1941. Considering the penchant of German formations to equip themselves with captured weaponry and concerns that these might be taken away when reported, these figures are probably incomplete and the actual totals may have been higher. Jacobsen, (Ed.) *KTB OKW. Band I*, pp. 1107-1108.

45   Mawdsley, *Thunder in the East*, p. 47.

46   Krivosheev, *Soviet Casualties and Combat Losses in the 20th Century*, pp. 94.

47   These figures are the combined totals of German claims of Soviet losses during Operations Trappenjagd (8-19 May), Bruckenschlag (21 March-30 April), Wilhelm (10-15 June), the Second Battle of Kharkov (12-28 May), and during their encirclement of the Soviet 2nd Shock Army around Liuban (31 May-28 June), and Russian estimates of their own losses during the Rzhev-Viazma Offensive (8 January-20 April). Figures for the German claims are taken from Andreas Hillgruber, (Ed.) *Kriegstagebuch der Oberkommandos der Wehrmacht (Wehrmachtfuhrungsstab). Band II: 1 Januar 1942 – 31 Dezember 1942.* (Frankfurt am Main: 1963), pp. 49, 77, 340, 391 & 429. For Soviet losses around Rzhev-Viazma, see Krivosheev, *Soviet Casualties and Combat Losses in the 20th Century*, p. 261.

48   This represents the combined total of Soviet aircraft losses noted in Bergstrom, *Stalingrad: The Air Battle, 1942 through January 1943*, pp. 23, 30-31, & 35, and those mentioned as having occurred during the Soviet Rzhev-Viazma Offensive in Krivosheev, *Soviet Casualties and Combat Losses in the 20th Century*, p. 261.

cited here are conservative estimates.[49] By the spring of 1942 these losses prompted senior Soviet officials to issue warnings to their subordinates about the need to minimize the casualties their units were suffering, since even the Soviet Union's manpower were not limitless, and the issue of manpower losses appears to have become a major factor in subsequent Soviet planning for the duration of the conflict.[50] To find more manpower, the Red Army discarded previous restrictions regarding the use of problematic ethnic and political groups, began the mass recruitment of women, trimmed personnel from the Soviet Navy, the NKVD, and training establishments, and even drew upon workers vital to industry.[51] Despite these measures, many Soviet rifle divisions remained chronically short of personnel for the duration of the war and the occasions when they were not became increasingly few and far between.

In terms of equipment, throughout 1942 Soviet industry was able to manufacture prodigious quantities of new armaments to replace losses, but this was no easy task. Aside from having to cope with the daunting prospect of re-establishing the factories that had been evacuated, the regions now occupied by the Germans had supplied 58 percent of all Soviet steel, 71 percent of pig iron, 92 percent of manganese, 63 percent of coal, and a large proportion of all food supplies. To make good the resources now controlled by the Germans, production elsewhere had to be expanded and new industries, mines, power stations, and farms established from scratch, usually under the harshest of conditions. New sources of labour had to be found too – by late 1941 the industrial workforce had declined to 60 percent of its pre-war level – and in April 1942 new compulsory labour decrees were issued in which all able-bodied males and females between 14 and 55 were to be mobilized for the duration of the conflict.[52]

In these circumstances and despite increases in production, during the first half of 1942 the Red Army had to endure considerable shortages, forcing it to lower both the manpower and equipment establishments of its subordinate units. In contrast to the prolific expansion in the number of field formations, most stocks of equipment remained badly depleted (see Table 4.5), meaning that less equipment was now spread even more thinly. Significant resources also had to be retained by training

49   Note that, in contrast to the number of missing personnel admitted to by the Red Army, by the end of 1941 the Germans claimed they had taken 3.8 million prisoners. Boog, et. al. *GSWW. Vol. IV*, p. 849. Referring to other Soviet-era documents, Sokolov, "The Cost of War: Human Losses for the USSR and Germany, 1941-1945.", p. 159, argues that the actual number of irreversible losses (ie. dead and missing) during the first half of 1942 totalled approximately 3,152,000 men.
50   See Ibid, pp. 166-167, and Glantz, *Zhukov's Greatest Defeat*, p. 14. For the role of intelligence estimates of Soviet manpower availability and their influence upon German planning, see Boog, et. al. *GSWW. Vol. VI*, pp. 884-889.
51   Mawdsley, *Thunder in the East*, pp. 213-214.
52   Ibid, p. 49, and Boog, et. al. *GSWW. Vol. IV*, pp. 854-857. Also see Harrison, *Accounting for War: Soviet Production, Employment, and Defence Burden, 1940-1945* and Mark Kragh, "Soviet Labour Law during the Second World War." *War in History*, Vol. 18, No. 4 (2011), pp. 531-546.

establishments, deployed on garrison duties within Russia, or stationed in the Soviet Far East to keep a wary eye on the forces of Imperial Japan (see Table 4.6).[53] Especially in terms of tanks, the dire need for equipment compelled the Soviet Union to make use of the generally inferior models it had received from its Western allies, as well as maintain the production of indigenous types that had proved wanting, so that its armoured formations were at least provided with something.[54] Of the 11,178 tanks manufactured by Soviet industry in the first half of 1942, as many as one-third were of the inadequate light T-60 and T-70 variety. By July 1942, the new TOE for tank brigades established that 21 out of 53 (40 percent) of its tanks were to be T-70s, meaning that the combat performance of these units was less than might first appear because of the low-survivability and high maintenance requirements of the numerous lighter models.[55] Moreover, the increased production of T-34 tanks in early 1942 was mitigated by the introduction of improved armoured vehicles and anti-tank guns by the Germans, which meant that even the T-34 was no longer quite as formidable as it had been in 1941.[56] For the Soviet Union in early 1942 the prospects for victory would have appeared remote while those of defeat may have seemed all too apparent.

Aside from overstating Soviet strength, the historiographical focus upon the many military and economic problems confronting Germany in early 1942 also tends to

53   Significant numbers of troops were maintained in the Far East despite the signing of the Soviet-Japanese Neutrality Pact on 13 April 1941.
54   During the first year of the Russo-German War, British tank deliveries to the Soviet Union amounted to 1,442 vehicles, the preponderance of which were Matilda and Valentine models. Though these represented the best British tanks in large-scale production at the time, they proved ill suited to operations in Russia. American deliveries are unknown, but assumedly included numbers of Stuart light tanks that were no match for the improved armour assigned to the Panzer divisions by 1942. Alexander Hill, "British Lend-Lease Aid and the Soviet War Effort, June 1941-June 1942", pp. 783-785. For arguably the Western Allies greatest contribution to the Soviet war effort, see Roger Munting, "Soviet Food Supply and Allied Aid in the War, 1941-1945." *Soviet Studies*, Vol. 36, No. 4 (October 1984), pp. 582-593. Among other studies regarding Anglo-American support for Russia, see Stanislav Gribanov, "The Role of US Lend-Lease Aircraft in Russia in World War II." *Journal of Slavic Military Studies*, Vol. 11, No. 1 (March 1998), pp. 96-115, and V.F. Vorsin, "Motor Vehicle Transport Deliveries through 'Lend-Lease." *Journal of Slavic Military Studies*, Vol. 10, No. 2 (1997), pp. 153-175.
55   Goff, "Evolving Soviet Force Structure, 1941-1945: Process and Impact", pp. 387-389. In terms of size, main armament, and armour, the T-60 was approximately the equivalent of the German Pz II. The T-70 was already outclassed by the models of Pz III being produced in late 1941, and was little match for the up-gunned and up-armoured versions of the Pz III that entered service by the spring of 1942.
56   These German vehicles included the Pz IV F2 and G models equipped with the 7.5 cm L/43 gun and (eventually) up to 80 millimetres of frontal armour, the 5 cm L/60 gun of the Pz III J model, and the StuG III now equipped with the long-barrelled 7.5 cm L/43. Various makes of 7.5 cm anti-tank guns also became increasingly available. The L/43 could penetrate the frontal armour of opposing T-34s at ranges up to 1,600 metres; the L/60 was effective under 500 metres.

distract attention from the fact that it still retained formidable capabilities to reinforce and regenerate its armies deployed on the *Ostfront*. When crises exploded across the length of the front in December, Hitler and the OKH responded energetically.[57] That month, using returned convalescents and by combing personnel out of its training and administrative establishments, the *Ersatzheer* rapidly formed four new infantry divisions that constituted the *17. Welle*. These were followed by two further waves with another nine infantry divisions during January and February. Together with three new panzer divisions and the Spanish-manned *250. Infanterie Division* that had been formed during the preceding months, a total of 17 new divisions were created by the spring of 1942.[58] All of these formations were dispatched to the Eastern Front as reinforcements. They were joined by many of the divisions that had remained behind in Western Europe on garrison duty, and who received considerable injections of younger personnel and modern equipment to increase their combat worth. Between October 1941 and June 1942, a total of 44 divisions (including the three new panzer divisions), parts of two others, and a number of smaller ancillary units had been shipped east (see Appendix Five).[59]

Germany also tapped its European allies, who dispatched an additional ten Hungarian, two Slovak, seven Italian, and 25 Romanian divisions. Of these formations, some 24 (twelve Romanian, two Slovak, three Italian, and seven Hungarian) had arrived, or were in the process of arriving, by late June 1942. Romania also

---

57 For directives related to this response, see Jacobsen, (Ed.) *KTB OKW. Band I*, pp. 1083-1086.

58 This includes the *328.*, *329.*, *330.*, and *331. Infanterie Divisions* of the *17. Welle*, the *383.*, *384.*, *385.*, *387.*, and *389. Infanterie Divisions* constituting the *18. Welle*, and the *370.*, *371.*, *376.*, and *377. Infanterie Divisions* belonging to the *19. Welle*. The panzer divisions were numbered *22.*, *23.*, and *24.*, the latter having been formed from the disbanded *1. Kavallerie Division*. Two *sicherungs* brigades (*201.* and *203.*) were expanded into divisions, but have not been included here because they were not considered frontline combat formations.

59 Significant portions of the *7. Gebirgs* and *7. Flieger Divisions* were also dispatched, primarily to *Heeresgruppe Nord*. The smaller units included at least two new *Sturmgeschütz* battalions, the regiment-sized *9. SS-Standarte*, two Estonian *Schützmannschaft* battalions, and various 'legions' composed of Dutch, Flemish, and Scandinavian volunteers. The most significant of these smaller units was the *203. Panzer Regiment* equipped with 142 panzers, which arrived at *Heeresgruppe Nord* in late December 1941. Jentz, *Panzertruppen, Vol. One*, p. 212. Aside from ad hoc *Alarmeinheiten* created on an emergency basis, in order to assist the hard-pressed Army during the winter of 1941-1942 the *Luftwaffe* formed *Luftwaffe Infanterie Regiment Moskau* (of two battalions) and the *1.* to *5. Luftwaffe Feld Regiments* (each with four battalions) from its own personnel. Each battalion consisted of three rifle companies and a heavy weapons support company equipped with two 8.8 cm and 12 2 cm flak guns. For the best treatments of the *Luftwaffe's* ground forces, see E. Denzel, *Die Luftwaffen Felddivisionen 1942-1945 sowie die Sonderverbande der Luftwaffe 1939/1945.* (Neckargemund: 1976), Werner Haupt, *Die deutsche Luftwaffe Felddivisionen, 1941-1945.* (Eggolsheim: 1993), Kevin C. Ruffner, *Luftwaffe Field Division, 1941-1945.* (London: 1990), and Werner Stang, "Zur Geschichte der Luftwaffefelddivisionen der faschistischen Wehrmacht." *Zeitschift fur Militargeschichte*, Vol. 8 (1969), pp. 196-207.

expanded its two mountain and three cavalry brigades already in Russia to full division status and provided additional security forces to garrison the western Ukraine.[60] Although frequently derided in most accounts because of their shortcomings in terms of leadership, motivation, morale, training, and equipment, these allied Axis formations performed competently enough on most occasions, and sometimes with considerable distinction.[61] It is significant to remember that much of their poor reputation originated from early post-war German accounts, which tend to reveal more about the

60   The Italian forces alone numbered 229,005 men, 4,399 machine-guns, 1,297 mortars, 297 anti-tank and 366 anti-aircraft guns, and 946 field artillery pieces. For the foremost study of Italy's participation on the Eastern Front, see Stato Maggiore Dell'esercito, *La Operazioni delle Unita Italiane al Fronte Russo, 1941-1943.* (Rome: 1977). For studies concerning Germany's European allies, see Peter Abbott & Nigel Thomas, *Germany's Eastern Front Allies, 1941-1945.* (London: 1982), Truman Anderson, "A Hungarian Vernichtungskrieg? Hungarian Troops and the Soviet Partisan War in the Ukraine, 1942." *Militargeschichtliche Mitteilungen,* Vol. 58 (1999), pp. 345-366, Axworthy, et. al. *Third Axis, Fourth Ally,* Mark Axworthy, *Axis Slovakia: Hitler's Slavic Wedge, 1938-1945.* (Bayside, NY: 2002), Richard L. DiNardo, *Germany and the Axis Powers: From Coalition to Collapse.* (Lawrence, KS: 2005), Richard L. DiNardo, "The Dysfunctional Coalition: The Axis Powers and the Eastern Front in World War II." *Journal of Military History,* Vol. 60, No. 4 (October 1996), pp. 711-730, Waldemar Erfurth, *Der Finnische Krieg, 1941-1944.* (Munich, 1977), Mario Fenyo, "The Axis Allied Armies and Stalingrad." *Military Affairs,* Vol. 29, No. 2 (Summer 1965), pp. 57-72, Mario Fenyo, *Hitler, Horthy, & Hungary: German-Hungarian Relations, 1941-1944.* (New Haven, CT: 1972), Mihai T. Filipescu, *Reluctant Allies: The Romanian Army in Russia, 1941-1944.* (Chapultepeq: 2006), Dinu C. Giurescu, *Romania in the Second World War, 1939-1945.* (Boulder, CO: 2000), Andreas Hillgruber, "Der Einbau der verbundeten Armeen in die deutsche Ostfront, 1941-1944." *Wehrwissenschaftliche Rundschau,* Vol. 10, No. 12 (1960), pp. 659-682, Charles Kliment & B. Nakladal, *Germany's First Ally: Armed Forces of the Slovak State, 1939-1945.* (Atglen, PA: 1998), MacGregor Knox, *Hitler's Italian Allies: Royal Armed Forces, Fascist Regime, and the War of 1940-1943.* (Cambridge: 2000), Andris J. Kursietis, *Hungarian Army and Its Leadership in World War II.* (Bayside, NY: 1996), Alexander Lopaisc, "Italian Military Performance in the Second World War: Some Considerations." *Journal of Strategic Studies,* Vol. 5, No. 2 (1982), pp. 270-275, Leo Niehorster, *The Royal Hungarian Army, 1920-1945.* (Bayside, NY: 1999), Jozef Pecina & Michael Tkacik, "Eastern Front Operational Constraints on Slovak Artillery, 1941-1943." *Journal of Slavic Military Studies,* Vol. 18, No. 1 (2005), pp. 75-107, J. Lee Ready, *Forgotten Axis.* (Jefferson, NC: 1967), Thomas Schlemmer, *Die Italiener an der Ostfront 1942/1943: Dokumente zu Mussolinis Krieg gegen die Sowjetunion.* (Munchen: 2005), and Alexander Statiev, "The Ugly Duckling of the Armed Forces: Romanian Armour 1919-1941." *Journal of Slavic Military Studies,* Vol. 12, No. 2 (June 1999), pp. 220-244. For perhaps one of the least known aspects of the Axis alliance, see David Alvarez, "Axis Sigint Collaboration: A Limited Partnership." *Intelligence & National Security,* Vol. 14, No. 1 (1999), pp. 1-17.

61   Although usually critical (sometimes overly so) of their overall performance, Manstein notes in his memoirs that the common Romanian soldier was, "a capable, brave fighter". Manstein, *Lost Victories,* pp. 206-207. Similarly, in 1942 members of the Slovak Mobile Division were praised by the Germans for being "brave soldiers with very good discipline." Abbott & Thomas, *Germany's Eastern Front Allies, 1941-1945,* p. 26.

bias and perceived stereotypes of their authors than they do about the actual fighting prowess of the Axis formations involved.[62] There is also the matter of the Germans using their allies as convenient scapegoats whenever something went horribly wrong.[63] This is not to say that Axis divisions did not have their problems, but one must guard against the unwarranted notion that these formations were practically useless and therefore a source of perpetual weakness. At the very least, in terms of manpower and equipment establishments, as well as general combat capabilities, the allied Axis divisions should be considered the equals of their Soviet counterparts.[64] Furthermore, by occupying relatively quiet secondary sectors or being employed on security duties, these formations allowed the Germans to concentrate their resources at decisive points along the front. Their arrival on the *Ostfront* thereby constituted a very real and positive reinforcement.

Overall, a total of 68 Axis divisions arrived in time for Germany's 1942 summer offensive, codenamed Operation Blue, and a further 20 Hungarian, Romanian, and Italian divisions would arrive shortly after its commencement. Moreover, despite the heavy losses sustained during Barbarossa, and by including those formations employed in Finland and on internal security duties, the total German forces deployed against Russia increased by 33 divisions. These reinforcements surpassed the 18 German divisions that by June 1942 were withdrawn from the *Ostheer* for rebuilding or else had been disbanded.[65] Although scholars have frequently pointed to the increased use of allied formations during the 1942 offensive as proof of the German Army's mounting

62   See Grant Harward, "First among Un-Equals: Challenging German Stereotypes of the Romanian Army during the Second World War." *Journal of Slavic Military Studies*, Vol. 24, No. 3 (2011), pp. 439-480.

63   More recent tomes have noted that when German formations were confronted in 1943-1945 by circumstances comparable to those experienced earlier by their Axis comrades-in-arms, the results were not altogether dissimilar. For a reasonable discussion of comparative Axis performances, see Axworthy, et. al. *Third Axis, Fourth Ally*, pp. 115-118.

64   For example, most of the Romanian formations committed to the 1942 campaign spent the previous winter undergoing considerable re-training, especially in anti-tank tactics, and received new infusions of equipment, including 15,600 Italian- and German-made submachine guns, 1,860 French 6 cm and 8.1 cm mortars, and 1,600 German trucks. Large numbers of captured Soviet 4.5 cm anti-tank guns were also issued, as were 1,700 captured Soviet trucks. Ibid, pp. 76-81.

65   As mentioned previously, seven divisions had been withdrawn by the end of 1941. The *239. Infanterie Division* was disbanded in January 1942, while in May the *162. Infanterie Division* was reduced to its divisional staff, which was transferred to Poland to supervise the creation of *Ostbataillone*; the remaining elements of these two divisions were distributed to other formations. The other formations that departed the Eastern Front in the first half of 1942 were the *6., 7.,* and *10. Panzer, (Mot.) SS-Division Reich* and the *15., 17., 23., 106.,* and *167. Infanterie Divisions*. See Kroener, et. al. *GSWW. Vol. V: Part One*, p. 1066.

weakness, such a conclusion appears largely gratuitous.[66] First, as illustrated in Table 4.7, the number of allied Axis divisions only moderately increased and, as explained above, their arrival was generally a positive occurrence. Secondly, in terms of the overall number of Axis divisions committed against the Soviet Union, the preponderance remained German. At the outset of Barbarossa, German formations had constituted 82 percent of the Axis divisions employed; in late June 1942 they still amounted to 81 percent. Not including the Axis forces arrayed in Finland, the proportion of German divisions on the *Ostfront* in mid-1942 rises to 86 percent.

For Hitler and his subordinates at OKH, the dispatch of reinforcements to Russia was the most expedient means of bolstering the strength of the *Ostheer* during the first half of 1942, but the far more challenging task was to procure the massive quantities of replacement manpower and equipment needed to replenish its depleted ranks. This already formidable task was exacerbated by the strategic situation the Third Reich faced in early 1942.[67] The entry of the United States into the war in December 1941 meant that an Anglo-American return to continental Europe was only a matter of time, thereby dictating that increased quantities of the German Army's resources be assigned to the defence of Western Europe. Similarly, given what German intelligence knew of the prodigious size and capacity of the American aeronautical industry, the *Luftwaffe* warned that the inevitable intensification of the air war in the West required more air defence assets. This in turn demanded increased allocations of labour, raw materials, fuel, and manufacturing capacity, as well as the expansion of existing pilot training programmes and aircraft production facilities.[68] In addition, these demands hastened the need to defeat the Soviet Union so that resources could be shifted westwards; German intelligence anticipated that the Anglo-Americans could mount a landing in Europe by late 1942 and the bombing of German cities had already commenced in earnest that spring.[69] At a bare minimum, the oilfields of the Caucasus had to be secured. On the one hand, their capture would deny them to the Soviets, greatly diminishing the Red Army's offensive capabilities and possibly precipitating the collapse of the Soviet economy, thereby forcing Russia into a negotiated peace. On the other hand, Germany's own precarious fuel situation had already resulted in dire shortages during the winter of 1941-1942. Without new sources of

---

66   For examples of this assertion, see Seaton, *The Russo-German War, 1941-1945,* pp. 270-271, and V.E. Tarrant, *Stalingrad: Anatomy of an Agony.* (London: 1992), p. 26.

67   For a further summary of Germany's broader position and strategic considerations in early 1942, see Boog, et. al. *GSWW. Vol. VI,* pp. 110-130.

68   See Tooze, *The Wages of Destruction,* pp. 404-410, and Boog, et. al. *GSWW. Vol. IV,* pp. 826-832.

69   The city of Mannheim had been heavily bombed on the night of 16-17 December 1941, followed by Lübeck on 28-29 March and Rostock between 24-27 April. On the night of 30-31 May, Cologne was subjected to the first thousand-plane raid. Cooper, *The German Air Force, 1933-1945,* p. 185.

supply the *Wehrmacht*'s prospects of successfully defending Europe were grim.[70] This imperative, to create "an economically viable and militarily and politically defendable power-sphere", was apparent to Halder, who in early 1942 noted, "[the] war will be decided in the east."[71] Hitler was even more emphatic when, during a conference with his senior commanders in the spring of 1942, he declared, "If I do not get the oil of Maikop and Grozny, then I must end this war."[72]

Concurrent with Germany's two-front military crisis was the equally dire situation in regards to its industrial war effort. Throughout the second half of 1941, the productivity of most sectors of the economy had steadily declined because of mounting shortages of labour and raw materials. These two factors were closely linked. As noted in previous chapters, the availability of labour in Germany had been constricting even before the war began and had only worsened with the call-up of millions of males into the *Wehrmacht*. During the first years of the war, rationalization of production, the closing of non-essential industries, and the increased use of women and foreign labour had made the situation manageable, but only just. During the preparatory phase of Barbarossa, a further 1.4 million workers were drafted for what was hoped would be a short, victorious campaign, after which most would be discharged back into the economy.[73] The resulting gaps were to some extent filled by foreign workers, but the preponderance of shortfalls was not, and, by the end of June 1941, Germany was already short one million workers – a figure that would rise by another one-half a million within two months.[74] In consequence, the productivity of Germany's industries declined, but the worst effects were felt in the mining sectors where the lack of labour quickly translated into the decreasing production of raw materials, especially coal.[75] Since coal was vital for 84 percent of all electricity generation, various industrial processes, and the harvesting of other resources, the effects were soon rippling throughout the economy and by July iron and steel production had already fallen

---

70   For the fuel crisis of 1941/1942, see Reinhardt, *Moscow – The Turning Point*, pp. 149-153, 270-272, & 412-413. Germany's thin margin of oil security can be found in Kroener, et. al. *GSWW. Vol. V: Part Two*, pp. 472-477, Tooze, *The Wages of Destruction*, pp. 411-412, and Krammer, "Fueling the Third Reich.", pp. 394-422. A solid synopsis of the role oil played in Germany's actions during 1942 can be found in Joel Hayward, "Hitler's Quest for Oil: The Impact of Economic Considerations on Military Strategy, 1941-1942." *Journal of Strategic Studies*, Vol. 18, No. 4 (1995), pp. 94-135.

71   Boog, et. al. *GSWW. Vol. VI*, p. 844.

72   Ibid, p. 869.

73   Tooze, *The Wages of Destruction*, p. 436.

74   Reinhardt, *Moscow – The Turning Point*, p. 28, and Boog, et. al. *GSWW. Vol. IV*, p. 1097. Aside from prisoners of war, some 2,139,553 foreign civilians were employed within Germany by September 1941. Herbert, *Hitler's Foreign Workers*, p. 98.

75   This was exacerbated in May 1941 when 50,000 Belgian coal miners went on strike; this affected 26 percent of all coal production within the German sphere of power, and thereby greatly constricted the supply of coal throughout the early summer. Reinhardt, *Moscow – The Turning Point*, p. 190.

by 350,000 tons from the previous month.[76] The catastrophic reverses suffered by the *Wehrmacht* in Russia during the winter of 1941-1942 only deepened the crisis by forcing the conscription of fresh cohorts of German workers, many of whom were drawn from the armaments industry.[77]

Concurrently, this disastrous situation was aggravated by another crisis brought on by the limitations of the Reich's long-neglected railway transport resources. With priority allotted to other sectors of the economy, during the interwar period the *Reichsbahn* had struggled to receive meagre resources with which to acquire increased quantities of rolling stock and to maintain and expand its rail network and service facilities. While the economy grew substantially, transport capacity did not, and though the system usually managed to keep the flow of goods and materials going by slender margins, it was highly susceptible to disruptions.[78] Bad weather frequently created extensive backlogs within the rail network, while the demands placed upon the Reichsbahn forced it to increase the intensity of its operations that, in turn, worsened the wear on equipment and increased the amount of rolling stock that had to be taken out of service for maintenance.[79] However, the greatest disruptions stemmed primarily from the demands periodically placed upon it by the military authorities. Specifically, this relates to the mobilization and deployment of the *Wehrmacht* in late August 1939, its movement to the west in late 1939, and later the assembly of forces in Poland and East Prussia for Barbarossa, all of which required the use of prodigious quantities of rolling stock.[80] The occasional removal of large consignments of rolling stock from the normal transportation requirements of the economy resulted in major disruptions in the flow of goods and raw materials, especially coal. As noted above, the availability of coal was *the* key component within the German economy, and by mid-1940 some 81,000 of the average 152,747 freight cars that the *Reichsbahn* operated on a daily basis were used for its transport.[81] Therefore, any disruption to the normal operations of the *Reichsbahn* had cascading effects upon the delivery of coal and, thereby, the smooth running of the German economy and its armaments industries.

76   Ibid, p. 28. For the key role of coal in the production of electricity in Germany, see Tooze, *The Wages of Destruction*, pp. 413-48, and Kroener, et. al. *GSWW. Vol. V: Part Two*, p. 494.

77   A further 1,270,000 German males were inducted into the *Wehrmacht* during the first half of 1942, including at least 168,400 from the armaments industry. Ibid, p. 850.

78   Between 1938 and 1939, the *Reichsbahn's* stock of locomotives increased by 20 percent, that of freight cars by 26.6 percent, and passenger cars by only 4.8 percent. Mierzejewski, *The Most Valuable Asset of the Reich*, p. 165. However, during this period the length of track it had to manage grew by 42 percent. Boog, et. al. *GSWW. Vol. VI*, p. 879.

79   By late 1940, the general backlog of trains amounted to 200 per day, though on some days this climbed to 1,000-1,200. Mierzejewski, *The Most Valuable Asset of the Reich*, p. 90.

80   Mobilization in August 1939 had required the use of at least 14,857 locomotives and 185,400 passenger and freight wagons, while the assembly of forces for Barbarossa had preoccupied as many as 2,500 trains per day. Ibid, pp. 78 & 97.

81   Ibid, p. 90 & 92.

The rapid victories during the first years of the war allowed these periodic disruptions to be managed and the precarious state of Germany's railways to be glossed over, but the invasion of Russia brought the matter to a head. The vastness of the eastern theatre and the pressing need to keep the *Ostheer* supplied posed massive demands upon a transport system that was already creaking under the strain. Although much-touted within the literature as being a fundamental problem in the smooth running of German logistics, the conversion of Russian rail lines was a relatively quick and easy affair – by December 1941 German engineers had converted some 15,000 kilometres of track, and their total rose to 21,000 kilometres by May 1942.[82] The real problems were the repair of existing rail yards and maintenance facilities, the need to construct new ones from scratch, and bureaucratic rivalry and mismanagement on the part of both civilian and military railway authorities. Contrary to the hopes of planners at OKH, rail facilities in the newly captured territories had been extensively damaged, and since this development had been unexpected, the assignment of personnel, equipment and vehicles to the Army's *Eisenbahntruppen* (railway construction troops) had received a low priority.[83] Additionally, only small quantities of Russian rolling stock were captured, requiring the employment of German models designed for use in the dense rail networks of Western and Central Europe. With their limited operating range, the use of German designed trains meant the need to construct new service centres in the intervals between existing facilities.[84] Subsequently, the simultaneous requirements to repair old facilities and construct new ones overwhelmed the limited quantities of men and material initially assigned the task, which therefore could only be addressed at an agonizingly slow pace. At the same time, communications systems vital to the efficient management of the railways had to be repaired and expanded, and German administrative personnel brought in to replace their Russian counterparts who had fled.[85]

Even when lines were opened, the low-density rail network in European Russia, most of it single track, had to meet the competing needs of the Army, the *Luftwaffe*, various civilian and military administrations, and the work crews of the *Reichsbahn* and *Eisenbahntruppen*.[86] During operations in Western Europe this had not been a

82 Ibid, p. 99, and Boog, et. al. *GSWW. Vol. VI*, p. 879.

83 Only one-sixth of the units belonging to the *Eisenbahntruppen* were fully motorized, with a mere 1,000 vehicles being assigned before the onset of operations. Since most of these were captured French and British models, serviceability quickly became a major problem. Stahl, *Operation Barbarossa and Germany's Defeat in the East*, p. 135.

84 Ibid, p. 136. By 31 December 1941 the Germans had captured 2,173 Russian locomotives, of which 1,223 were operational, along with 53,850 passenger and freight wagons. Schuler, *Logistik im Russlandfeldzug*, p. 257.

85 Kriedler, *Die Eisenbahnen im Machtbericht der Achsenmachte wahrend des Zweiten Weltkrieg*, p. 127.

86 For example, during August 1941 *Heeresgruppe Sud* reported that of the 843 trains that had arrived in its area of operations, 224 carried munitions, 172 fuel, 122 supplies, 112 were for the railway authorities, and 213 carried various goods and materials. See

problem since every individual German army had its own dedicated double-track, high-capacity rail line. But, in Russia, there existed only one such main rail line per army group.[87] Overall, this meant that the number of supply trains arriving in the forward area proved inadequate to meet all the needs of the army groups, which were increasingly forced to conduct their operations on a hand-to-mouth supply basis.[88] In response, German transport authorities endeavoured to push through larger numbers of trains along a finite amount of track. Inevitably, accidents or acts of sabotage along the track rendered the entire line temporarily unserviceable. Even worse was the piling up of trains at stations where the lack of personnel, equipment, and most importantly leadership and organization, translated into increasingly lengthy wait times before trains could be unloaded.[89] With the entire rail net becoming ever more congested and chaos mounting, relations between the civilian authorities of the *Reichsbahn* and their military counterparts in the *Eisenbahntruppen* deteriorated in an atmosphere of bitter recriminations, jurisdictional jealousy, and acrimonious debate as to who was to blame. Some trains simply became lost within the system, army commanders began to complain that "their" trains had been "hijacked" by other authorities, and the *Luftwaffe* even began putting armed officers on "its" trains to ensure they arrived at their proper destinations.[90]

Although the system never entirely collapsed, the transport situation continued to fester throughout the summer and autumn with the optimism generated by the *Wehrmacht*'s victories once again allowing the relevant authorities to muddle through the crisis and literally hope for the best. This already lamentable situation dramatically changed for the worse when winter arrived in earnest during the latter days of November. Heavy snows blocked rail lines, bridges were damaged by ice, and by early December as may as 70 percent of the German-made trains in the area of *Heeresgruppe Mitte* had been damaged or rendered unserviceable by the bitter cold as temperatures dropped to minus 40 degrees Celsius.[91] At one point, 1,100 backlogged trains

Transportlagemeldungen zum Kriegstagebuch Heeresgruppe Süd/General der Transportwesens Sud, 7.9.1941 bis 31.5.1942. NARA T311 Roll 296, Frame 254.

87   Tooze, *The Wages of Destruction*, p. 454.

88   Between 16 August and 30 September, *Heeresgruppe Süd* reported that it had received an average of 14.5 supply trains per day when its requirements were 24 per day. During November, an average of only 16 of the needed 31 supply trains had arrived for *Heeresgruppe Mitte*. Boog, et. al. *GSWW. Vol. IV*, pp. 1119 & 1138.

89   Instead of the regulation three hours, anywhere from 12 to 80 hours were needed before a train could be unloaded. Martin van Crevald, *Supplying War: Logistics from Wallenstein to Patton.* (New York: 1977), p. 160. Van Crevald's study of German logistics in the summer of 1941 remains one of the best short summaries yet produced on the subject. See Ibid, pp. 142-180.

90   Ibid, p. 161.

91   Reinhardt, *Moscow – The Turning Point*, p. 245. For the best source regarding weather conditions around Moscow and their impact upon German operations, see Russel Stolfi,

were stalled along damaged rail lines and hopelessly congested stations.[92] The effect upon the supply of frontline units, already precarious at best, was immediate: rations had to be curtailed, and only the barest allocations of ammunition and fuel could be moved forward. Men also began freezing to death because they lacked proper winter clothing, even though the Army Quartermaster had planned to conduct a major transport operation to provide the front with such supplies in late October. Although 130 trains had been organized and loaded by that point, the congestion along the rail lines kept most of them in the area around Warsaw, waiting for a chance to slip in between ammunition and fuel trains that had priority.[93] As a result, winter equipment and clothing arrived at the front slowly and sporadically.

Initially, the burden placed upon the *Reichsbahn* by the *Wehrmacht*'s new campaign in the East appears to have been mitigated by the Army's heavy use of motorised transport during the first stages of the campaign, the few fully operational rail lines that were available that restricted the use of (and therefore demand upon) rail transport, and the short distances the trains initially had to travel to reach the forward railheads. Although most rail traffic within the Reich continued to function satisfactorily during the summer, by August the *Reichsbahn* was already incapable of moving all the coal demanded by industry and problems increased as the front pushed further east.[94] Desperate to solve the Army's mounting supply problems, in late November the chief of *Wehrmacht* Transport (*Wehrmachttransportchef*) and head of the Army's Transport Branch (*Chef des Feldtransportwesens*), *Generalleutnant* Rudolf Gercke, insisted that the head of the *Reichsbahn*, Julius Dorpmüller, dispatch more resources to Russia regardless of other considerations.[95] Dorpmüller responded by committing extra personnel and 1,000 additional locomotives to the support of the *Ostfront*; consequently, the number of trains dispatched eastwards increased from 600 to 900 per day. The reassignment of these resources immediately disrupted rail movements within the Reich, where car traffic decreased 16.4 percent versus the number achieved in November 1940.[96] As already noted, even this considerable reallocation of resources did little to alleviate the Army's supply crisis in the face of the brutal Russian winter. The *Reichsbahn* reacted by dispatching even more trains and by mid-January 1942 some 4,280 locomotives had been deployed to the East.[97] Although this measure temporarily added to the congestion, the supply situation of the *Ostheer* slowly began

---

"Chance in History: The Russian Winter of 1941-1942." *History*, Vol. 65, No. 214 (June 1980), pp. 214-228.

92   Schuler, *Logistik im Russlandfeldzug*, p. 523.
93   Ibid, p. 459, and Boog, et. al. *GSWW. Vol. IV*, p. 1136.
94   Mierzejewski, *The Most Valuable Asset of the Reich*, p. 99.
95   Julius Dorpmüller was also Reich Transport Minister.
96   Mierzejewski, *The Most Valuable Asset of the Reich*, pp. 99-101.
97   Ibid, p. 102. By April this figure had grown to 5,716 locomotives. Schuler, *Logistik im Russlandfeldzug*, p. 613.

to improve with the arrival of more resources and improved management.[98] In the interval, however, the crisis rippled westwards as rail transport within the Reich was gripped by increasing shortages of rolling stock and scheduling disruptions. In February 1942, railcar traffic was 25.4 percent lower than in the previous year. From this low point rail transport within Germany began to improve, but it was May before the situation returned to normal.[99]

Struck simultaneously by labour shortages and the disruption of rail transport, German manufacturing was thrown into crisis. Production of raw materials plummeted, and by spring 1942 *Wehrmacht* requirements far outstripped availability (see Table 4.8). The torrent German economic planners had hoped would pour from captured Russian mines and resource areas was initially only a trickle because of transport problems and damage to production facilities.[100] By the end of February, power shortages because of the lack of coal brought production at 134 armaments factories to a standstill, of which 34 had to be partially shut down.[101] The situation became so dire that Dr. Fritz Todt, the Minister for Armaments and Munitions (*Reichsminister für Bewaffnung und Munition*), told Hitler that only a political solution could end the war since, "Militarily and in terms of the war economy the war has already been lost."[102]

Early efforts by Germany's leaders to deal with the crisis were marred by official vacillation, inter-service and bureaucratic rivalry, and the premature euphoria created by the initial victories in Russia that convinced authorities to shift priorities in war manufacturing, all of which threw German industry into further disarray by

---

98   Between September and December 1941, an average of 1,162 trains per month arrived at *Heeresgruppe Süd*. In the first months of 1942, this increased to the following monthly totals:

  January   1,346   March 2,447
  February   1,576   April 3,139

  See *Transportlagemeldungen zum Kriegstagebuch Heeresgruppe Süd/General der Transportwesens Sud, 7.9.1941 bis 31.5.1942*. NARA T311 Roll 296, Frames 254, 315, & 317.

99   For measures undertaken to rectify the problems within the *Reichsbahn*, see Mierzejewski, *The Most Valuable Asset of the Reich*, pp. 100-113, and Schuler, *Logistik im Russlandfeldzug*, pp. 606-636.

100 The crucial exception being manganese ore imports from the Krivoi Rog area of the Ukraine; in the second half of 1941, the 25,500 tons of ore imported from here already constituted 40 percent of total German consumption. During the first half of 1942, the 39,000 tons mined grew to 70 percent of consumption. Kroener, et. al. *GSWW. Vol. V: Part Two*, p. 463.

101 Reinhardt, *Moscow – The Turning Point*, pp. 401-402.

102 Comment made during a conference on 29 November 1941. Ibid, p. 262. Four days prior, *Generaloberst* Friedrich Fromm, the Chief of Army Armaments and Commander of the *Ersatzheer*, had made the same recommendation to Hitler. Boog, et. al. *GSWW. Vol. IV*, p. 1180.

dislocating production and scattering available resources.[103] Effective countermeasures, such as the massive importation of forced labour, and the rationalization and prioritization of production, were only enacted in early 1942 when they could no longer be avoided and it became clear that the struggle against Russia would be a protracted one.[104] In consequence, the manufacture of armaments fluctuated wildly. As noted in Table 4.9, production levels of some types of Army equipment remained generally stable, but most witnessed significant declines before increasing again in the spring of 1942.

Given the host of seemingly insurmountable challenges noted above, one might be excused for thinking that Germany's prospects by the summer of 1942 were hopeless. This is certainly the tenor of many of the post-war historical accounts. With their emphasis upon various shortages and deficiencies, most argue that Germany was simply incapable of replacing the equipment lost during Barbarossa and that the subordinate formations of the *Wehrmacht* were thereby irretrievably weakened.[105] In actuality, the material state of the German Army appears to have been less dire than has usually been portrayed, at least in terms of the overall numbers. Remarkably, despite all its problems, the German armaments sector still managed to provide the Army with extensive quantities of new equipment by the time Operation Blue commenced in late June 1942.[106] Moreover, as illustrated in Table 4.10, in most instances new production not only replaced the equipment lost to that point, but also permitted existing stocks to be increased by a considerable degree.

How well did the German manufacturing sector meet the material needs of the German Army in time for the 1942 summer campaign? By employing the figures derived from the methodology outlined in previous chapters as a base, and by adjusting for divisions created, reorganized, or disbanded by 1 July 1942, a rough estimate of the German Army's material requirements can be made. These are outlined in Table 4.11. Admittedly, this does not account for changes in the requirements for non-divisional support units or the *Ersatzheer*. Moreover, assessing material needs based upon pre-Barbarossa tables of organization and equipment means the indicated requirements are actually greater than they really were, since alterations and reductions, such as the disbandment of divisional sub-components, have not been taken into account. Still, these figures indicate that large stocks of machine-guns, mortars, light flak and anti-tank guns still existed that were superfluous to the Army's needs. Surpluses are

---

103 Boog, et. al. *GSWW. Vol. IV*, pp. 1081-1099, Tooze, *The Wages of Destruction*, pp. 440-452 & 493-499, and Overy, "Mobilization for Total War in Germany 1939-1941.", pp. 630-636.
104 See Tooze, *The Wages of Destruction*, pp. 552-584.
105 For example, see Cooper, *The German Army, 1933-1945*, pp. 407-409, Ellis, *Brute Force*, pp. 80-83 and Glantz & House, *When Titans Clashed*, pp. 103-104.
106 From the start of the campaign until 15 March 1942, the *Ostheer* was supplied with 27,100 replacement machine-guns, 2,715 anti-tank guns, and 537 10.5 cm and 350 15 cm field howitzers. No specific figures for what was provided after this date could be found. Müller-Hillebrand, *Das Heer 1933-1945, Band III*, p. 53.

also indicated for heavy 15 cm field howitzers, but many of these would have been required by the training establishments of the *Ersatzheer*, the needs of which would also increase the shortages noted for 10.5 cm howitzers.

Undoubtedly, serious shortfalls of anti-tank and infantry guns, and light and heavy field artillery are also evident. However, even these gaps were not as perilous as they appear, nor were they unmanageable. The majority of the anti-tank guns lost to date had been the now obsolete 3.7 cm Pak, the production of which had ceased in December 1941. The overall decline in the number of 3.7 cm Pak available would not have been detrimental to the anti-tank abilities of the divisions in the field, as these were instead being replaced by increasing quantities of heavier guns whose improved performance against Soviet T-34 and KV tanks made them far more valuable than their more numerous, but now quite inadequate predecessors.[107] Indeed, by 10 June 1942 some 1,671 7.5 cm or 7.62 cm Pak had already been assigned to units deployed on the *Ostfront*.[108] Similarly, shortages of infantry guns were compensated by increased allocations of mortars or else their replacement by 15 cm rocket launchers. Coping with deficiencies of field artillery was more difficult. Slated to participate in Operation Blue, the formations of *Heeresgruppe Süd* received priority in terms of the allocation of German-made guns; even then, some of its infantry divisions were given two batteries of *Nebelwerfer* in lieu of conventional artillery. Anticipating that Soviet offensive activity in their sectors would be limited, and since they would largely be confined to a defensive posture anyway, OKH assigned a lower priority to the divisions within *Heeresgruppe Nord* and *Mitte* to focus upon the crucial offensive into the Caucasus. Consequently, the artillery batteries of many of the divisions of *Heeresgruppe Nord* and *Mitte* were reduced from four guns to three; this reduction was one of the most serious aspects related to production shortfalls since this reduced the amount of available heavy fire support for the divisions affected by 25 percent. In partial recompense for the reductions, numerous divisions were assigned captured French or Russian artillery whose performance characteristics were roughly equal or even superior to their

107 These heavier anti-tank guns included the 5 cm Pak 38 and 7.5 cm Pak 40/41. Complementing these were large numbers of 7.5 cm Pak 97/38 (based on captured French-made 7.5 cm 1897 model field guns) and 7.62 cm Pak 38(r) (converted from captured Soviet 7.6 cm M1936 divisional guns).

108 According to *Generalstab des Heeres, Org. Abt. Gruppe III., Beitrag zum Kriegstagebuch für die Zeit vom 1-10.6.1942*, NARA T78 R414, Frame 6382408, these were divided amongst the army groups as follows:

Army Group	Pak 40	Pak 41	Pak 36(r)	Pak 97/38(f)	Total
South	360	–	–	425	785
Centre	–	141	150	295	586
North	–	–	150	150	300

German counterparts.[109] In terms of other weaponry, during the course of 1942 the conditions found within the formations deployed in central and northern Russia seem to have gradually improved from the nadir they had experienced the previous winter and early spring. Indeed, by the summer most of these divisions appear to have largely regained their authorized *Sollstärke*, although it should be remembered that in many instances these had been significantly reduced.[110] The weapon holdings of the divisions of *Heeresgruppe Süd*, however, had been restored to roughly what they had possessed the previous year.[111]

But if the Reich was to have any chance of capturing the oilfields of the Caucasus and thereby establishing its "economically viable and militarily and politically defendable power-sphere", the foremost task was the restoration of the Army's mobility and its armoured offensive capabilities. This would prove no easy task. Between June 1941 and the end of June 1942, the *Wehrmacht* had lost at least 127,731 motor vehicles and even larger numbers were in various stages of disrepair.[112] On 20 February 1942 *Heeresgruppe Süd* reported that it had suffered the *Totalausfalle* of 23,526 of its motor vehicles since the start of operations in the East: even more disconcertingly, out of the 86,757 it still possessed, some 70,969 (81.8 percent) were not operational because

---

109 For one example, the following pieces could be found within the heavy divisional artillery batteries of *Heeresgruppe Nord* by late summer 1942:

	German 15 cm sFH 18	French Cannon de 155 mm GPE	Russian 152 mm M1937 ML-20 howitzer-gun
Weight of Shell	96 lb	95 lb	97 lb
Range	13,250 m	19,500 m	17,230 m

110 For example, the condition report from the *2. Panzer Division* dated to 11 July 1942 notes the following situation:

	MG	8 cm GrW	3.7 cm Pak	5 cm Pak	7.5 cm Pak	7.5 cm IG	15 cm IG	2 cm Flak	le. FH	s. FH	10 cmK
TOE	579	30	12	39	10	18	14	13	18	6	3
Short	70	2	3	28	none	none	none	none	none	none	none

See *XLIII. Armee Korps. Kriegstagebuch Anlagen, Unternehmen Kreml, Ia., Feldzug gegen die Sowjet Union (3.6-11.7.1942)*, NARA T314 Roll 1008, Frames 000600-000601.

111 For the condition of the divisions within the *2. Armee* just prior to Operation Blue, see *2. AOK. O. Qu. Anlage z. Kriegstagebuch 5 und 6, Band 55, Auffrischung Fruhjahr 1942 (20.1-14.6.1942)*. NARA T312 Roll 1659, Frames 000275-000482. For those of the *4. Panzerarmee*, see *4. PzAOK. Operation II. zum Kriegstagebuch Nr. 5 (Teil III), PzAOK 4, Ia. (30.4-29.6.1942)*, NARA T313 Roll 355, Frames 8640096-8640167 & 8640493-8640497.

112 Compiled from Army motor vehicle losses for June to December 1941 found in Kroener, et. al. *GSWW. Vol. V: Part One*, p. 730 and those indicated as either lost or transferred by the entire *Wehrmacht* in January to June 1942 in Kroener, et. al. *GSWW. Vol. V: Part Two*, p. 684 & 687. Boog, et. al. *GSWW. Vol. VI*, p. 872 states that motor vehicle losses in the East until 20 March 1942 totalled 142,660, but this includes both *Totalausfalle* and vehicles not repairable within five days.

they required some kind of significant overhaul or repair. Of the three panzer divisions then serving with the army group, these alone required 6,147 new replacement motor vehicles, circumstances that appear to have been commonplace throughout the *Ostheer* during the first months of 1942.[113] Thousands of additional vehicles would also have been required for both the newly raised formations and those redeployed to the East. By the end of January 1942 a mere 19,768 new vehicles (including 6,584 captured Russian vehicles) had in fact been allotted to the *Ostheer*, and this figure rose to only 27,087 by 20 March.[114] For the German Army, the ruinous state of its motor park clearly had deleterious implications – a reduced ability to manoeuvre and supply its forces with food, fuel and ammunition on the battlefield, infantry divisions that were even more closely bound to horse-drawn transport and railheads, and motorised formations that could only move their components in a piecemeal fashion, all of which made the prospects of conducting rapid, highly-mobile offensive operations problematic.[115]

In consequence, most sources expound on the German Army's motor vehicle shortages by early 1942. However, in recompense German industry managed to produce 127,918 new motor vehicles during the period of June 1941 and the end of June 1942. As well, at least 6,584 of the 52,238 vehicles captured by the *Ostheer* in Russia had been re-issued to its units by 31 January 1942 and many others were doubtlessly dragooned into service from the civilian sectors of both Germany and occupied Europe.[116] Greatly adding to the capabilities of the panzer divisions was the fact

---

113 *Heeresgruppe Süd/Ia, Kriegstagebuch Teil III Band 4, Anlagen Nr. 710-772. (19-28.2.1942)*, NARA T311 Roll 296, Frames 000096-000097, 000113. On 30 December 1941 the *7. Panzer Division* with *Heeresgruppe Mitte* reported that it was short 1,312 motor vehicles, and that of those it still retained some 2,276 were in repair. *7. Panzer Division. Ia., Anlagen zum Kriegstagebuch Nr. 3, Teil II. (28.9.1941 – 5.5.1942)*, NARA T315 Roll 307, Frame 000301.

114 See Boog, et. al. *GSWW. Vol. IV*, pp. 1120-1122, and Boog, et. al. *GSWW. Vol. VI*, p. 872.

115 Equally discomfiting was the tally of 264,854 dead and 38,967 wounded or sick horses between the start of the campaign and 20 March 1942. Ibid, p. 872. According to Müller-Hillebrand, *Das Heer 1933-1945, Band III*, p. 59, these losses were partially mitigated by the dispatch of 109,000 horses from Germany, and the requisition of 118,000 more from the occupied eastern territories.

116 Total vehicle production compiled from figures of new manufacturing for both the Army and the *Luftwaffe* during June to December 1941 indicated in Kroener, et. al. *GSWW. Vol. V: Part One*, pp. 742-743 and new production for the entire *Wehrmacht* between January and June 1942 found in Kroener, et. al. *GSWW. Vol. V: Part Two*, pp. 684 & 687. For the allocation of captured Russian vehicles till 31 January 1942, see Boog, et. al. *GSWW. Vol. IV*, pp. 1120-1122. Of the increase in the motor vehicle stock of the Army between January and July 1942, only 57,724 can be accounted for from new production, meaning that the balance (137,982) must either have been damaged vehicles previously stricken off strength but then repaired within Germany and returned to service, transfers from other branches of the *Wehrmacht*, or requisitions from the civilian sectors of Germany and occupied Europe.

that production of valuable SPW during the first half of 1942 greatly outstripped losses, with 1,146 being produced versus only 123 being lost.[117] Despite the terrible losses it had sustained the German Army's stock of motor vehicles actually grew from 664,522 in January 1942 to some 860,228 by July, an impressive increase of almost 30 percent.[118] This growth in stock alone indicates that the Army's vehicle problems did not reside with manufacturing or procurement, at least not to the degree that scholars have usually maintained.

Instead, it is significant to recall that most German military planners, from Hitler to the senior officers at OKH, had gambled on the expectation that the campaign would conclude by the late fall of 1941, after which time the bulk of the armoured and motorised divisions would return to Germany for a comprehensive refit. In the heady days of that summer, sending large numbers of replacement vehicles to the *Ostfront* did not make sense, since it was expected that most would shortly have to be shipped back to Germany anyway. Moreover, even if the inclination to send out more vehicles had actually existed, it is unlikely that larger numbers could have been dispatched during that time. Considering the restrictions on rail transport noted previously, the dispatch of additional vehicles would only have exacerbated the already precarious supply problems confronting the *Ostheer* by consuming vital freight space. Given the pressing need to defeat the Soviet Union before it fully mobilized its resources, the dispatch of more fuel, ammunition, and food to keep the panzer spearheads rolling simply took priority. Once the campaign had clearly failed by late December, the necessity of restoring the combat strength of the formations in the field became paramount in order to halt the incessant Soviet counterattacks and prevent an outright collapse of the Army in the East. But the rail transport situation – which had meanwhile gone from bad to catastrophic – prevented the shipment of all but the most essential material and equipment.[119] With men literally freezing to death in the thousands, the dispatch of large consignments of new vehicles would not have been a priority. New vehicles could therefore only arrive at a laboriously slow pace and it was only when the transportation mess was finally rectified in March 1942 that matters gradually improved. Even then priority had to be given to the divisions of *Heeresgruppe Süd* and

---

117 Kroener, et. al. *GSWW. Vol. V: Part Two*, p. 688.

118 These figures represent the combined total of trucks, staff cars, and motorcycles illustrated in Ibid, p. 700.

119 The near collapse of rail transport during the winter of 1941-1942 forced the *Luftwaffe* to employ an increased amount of its air transport assets in order to fill the breach. From 18 December 1941 to 31 May 1942, these conducted 24,115 sorties and flew 75,675 men and 38,111 tons of material to *Heeresgruppe Nord* and *Mitte*, and ferried 57,082 wounded and other personnel back to Germany. *Heeresgruppe Nord. Kriegstagebuch 1-30.6.1942*, NARA T311 Roll 55, Frame 7068168. At least 3,268 replacement personnel were also flown to *1. Panzerarmee* between 26 November and 5 December 1941. Boog, et. al. *GSWW. Vol. IV*, p. 752.

the feverish preparations for Operation Blue.[120] In essence, the availability of replacement vehicles for the *Ostheer* was not driven so much by their shortage, but instead by a complex web of shockingly-poor strategic planning, the failure of transport and logistics, and by the pace of events in the field.

Even though its circumstances still remained less-than-ideal, by the time Operation Blue commenced, the mobility of *Heeresgruppe Süd* had improved markedly. At the army group and army level, transport assets with 11,000 tons of lift capability had been marshalled for supply duties.[121] In a status report of the *2. Armee* dated to 1 June, five of the six divisions specified were assuredly listed as being fully mobile and ready for any offensive tasks once their allotted consignments of vehicles and horses arrived by the middle of the month.[122] The condition report of the *4. Panzerarmee* submitted on 28 June is even more illuminating. The *3. (Mot.) Infanterie Division* and the *9. Panzer Division* reported that they possessed 85 percent of their authorized number of motorcycles, trucks, and staff cars, but only 58 percent and 48 percent, respectively, of their vital towing vehicles. Nonetheless, both divisions were rated as being fully ready for all offensive operations. The *82. Infanterie Division* reported that it possessed 96 percent of its authorized motor vehicle *Sollstärke*, while the *385. Infanterie Division* noted its only shortages were 200 horses and vehicles for part of its anti-tank battalion. Similarly, both formations were rated as being ready for any offensive task. The *24. Panzer Division* and *(Mot.) Infanterie Division Grossdeutschland* both reported themselves as also being fully mobile and prepared for any assignments. In contrast, the *11. Panzer Division* noted that 25 percent of its vehicles were still in repair depots. While the remainder of the division was fully operational, the bulk of one of its two motorised infantry regiments and one of its three artillery battalions were immobile.

---

120 The number of trains arriving at *Heeresgruppe Süd* increased from 1,576 in February to 3,139 in April. *Transportlagenmeldungen zum Kriegstagebuch Heeresgruppe Süd/General der Transportwesens Süd (7.9.1941 – 31.5.1942)*, NARA T311 Roll 296, Frame 000254. The build-up for Operation Blue amounted to a formidable transportation and logistical feat. Aside from what was issued to the troops, the first two stages of operation required the creation of three large supply depots containing 68,000 tons of munitions, 39,600 tons of fuel and lubricants, and 55,000 tons of food. Grant, *Barbarossa*, p. 127. Further large quantities of supplies were probably also consumed during the heavy fighting in southern Russia in May and June, including 29,234 tons of munitions during the reduction of the Soviet fortress of Sevastopol (7 June to 4 July). Hahn, *Waffen und Geheimwaffen des deutschen Heeres, 1933-1945, Band II*, p. 225.

121 Grant, *Barbarossa*, p. 128. This was considerably below the tonnage of the *Grosstransportraum* mustered behind each army group in 1941, which had totalled 20,000 tons each. Van Crevald, *Supplying War*, p. 151.

122 These included the *16. (Mot.) Infanterie Division*, and the *45., 88., 95.*, and *340. Infanterie Divisions*. The *299. Infanterie Division* reported that it still needed a considerable period of time before it would be fully capable of offensive operations. *2. AOK. O. Qu. Anlage zum Kriegstagebuch 5 und 6, Band 55, Auffrischung Fruhjahr 1942 (20.1-14.6.1942)*, NARA T312 Roll 1659, Frames 000281-000318.

The division's supply columns also lacked 180 tons of their lift capability. Even so it too was reported as being fit for offensive operations.[123]

While *Heeresgruppe Süd* was ready to resume offensive operations by the summer of 1942, the balance of the *Ostheer* operating in central and northern Russia was to remain largely on the defensive during the course of the year. The formations posted in those regions were afforded lesser priority in terms of new equipment, especially in terms of motor vehicles. Consequently, these divisions do appear to have suffered from significant shortages of motor vehicles and horses well into 1942.[124] However, because of the lack of detailed information their specific overall circumstances remain unclear, especially for later in the year. No post-war scholarship has yet addressed if the formations of *Heeresgruppe Nord* and *Mitte* continued to suffer from a lack of vehicles, horses, and overall mobility after Operation Blue began. If this was in fact the case, such a state of affairs would be rather perplexing given the fact that the Army's overall stock of motor vehicles continued to grow until it totalled 998,564 by January 1942, an imposing 50 percent increase from the previous year.[125]

123 Conversely, though maintaining that it was fully mobile and short only 248 horses, the *377. Infanterie Division* was reported ready for only limited offensive tasks. *4. PzAOK. Operation II. zum Kriegstagebuch Nr. 5 (Teil III), PzAOK 4, Ia. (30.4.-29.6.1942)*, NARA T313 Roll 355, Frame 8640493.

124 "In general, the divisions which were to be rehabilitated…would have only limited mobility and reduced combat efficiency, the shortage of motor vehicles and horses being their greatest handicap." Grant, *Barbarossa*, p. 130. For similar assessments, see Glantz & House, *When Titans Clashed*, p. 104, Warlimont, *Inside Hitler's Headquarters, 1939-1945*, p. 240, and Ziemke & Bauer, *Moscow to Stalingrad*, p. 295. Information concerning actual conditions within the divisions of *Heeresgruppe Nord* and *Mitte* are scarce, but one report from the *331. Infanterie Division* dated to 15 May 1942 notes the shortage of 90 motor vehicles and 978 horses, while the *267. Infanterie Division* noted the lack of 92 trucks, staff cars and towing vehicles, and 1,419 horses on the same date. At the start of the war, the assigned TOE for the latter formation included the provision of 1,306 motor vehicles of all types (of which 977 were staff cars, trucks and towing vehicles) and 4,077 horses. *XLIII. Armee Korps. Kriegstagebuch Anlagen, Unternehmen Kreml, Ia., Feldzug gegen die Sowjet Union (3.6-11.7.1942)*, NARA T314 Roll 1008, Frame 000550. The *2. Panzer Division* reported on 11 July that it possessed 1,940 operational vehicles and had a deficit of 705. *XLIII. Armee Korps. Kriegstagebuch Anlagen, Ia., Unternehmen Wirbelwind, Feldzug gegen die Sowjet Union (5.7-9.8.1942)*, NARA T314 Roll 1008, Frame 000604.

125 The overall increase over the course of the year breaks down as follows:

	January 1942	January 1943	% increase
Trucks	250,061	425,174	70
Staff Cars	199,452	290,174	46
Motorcycles	215,009	282,112	31
Raupenschlepper Ost (Caterpillar Tractor East)	–	1,104	–
Total	664,522	998,564	50

Note that these figures do not include half-tracked towing vehicles (*Zugmaschine*). See Kroener, et. al. *GSWW. Vol. V: Part Two*, pp. 700-701.

Equally vital to the German Army's restoration of its offensive capabilities was the rebuilding of the panzer divisions. There is no question that these had been reduced to shadows of their former strength by early 1942. Many had been scattered into their subcomponents or ad hoc emergency units (*Alarmeinheiten*) that were strewn across the front, bolstering the lines of the conventional infantry formations or more usually serving as small, tactical *kampfgruppen* racing from one crisis to the next.[126] Following months of nearly continuous operations in atrocious climatic conditions, the operational armoured strengths of the panzer divisions crumbled to dismal levels. By 10 December the *14. Panzer Division* had been reduced to a mere five operational panzers; some eleven days later, the *1. Panzer Division* reported that only six of its panzers were still operational.[127] Although the *7. Panzer Division* still retained a total of 99 panzers on 30 December just eight were serviceable.[128] Overall, of 1,185 tanks reportedly in the possession of the 16 panzer divisions belonging to *Heeresgruppe Nord* and *Mitte* on 22 December, only 405 (34 percent) were operational.[129] Against the 3,903 tanks and assault guns that had started the campaign, some 2,839 had been listed as *Totalausfalle* by 1 January 1942.[130] Faced with the same strategic planning assumptions and transport circumstances that had constrained the delivery of motor vehicles, only 1,140 additional around vehicles had arrived in the interim. In consequence, no more that 2,354 tanks and assault guns remained with the *Ostheer* at the start of 1942 (see Table 4.12). Of these, as many as 1,015 panzers were listed as being non-operational and hundreds more may actually have been in Germany where they were being repaired in armaments factories or Army maintenance facilities.[131] Further heavy fighting during January resulted in the total loss of an additional 415 tanks and assault guns, for which only 159 replacements arrived.[132] On 1 February, the number of tanks in the East had fallen to 1,479, of which a mere 340 were operational.[133]

---

126 For example, on 30 March elements of the *10. Panzer Division* found themselves attached to seven different divisions and two corps commands, while still other portions were under the direct command of both the *4. Panzerarmee* and *Heeresgruppe Mitte*. Schick, *Die 10. Panzer Division 1939-1943*, p. 489. Similarly, following its retreat from Tikhvin, the remaining combat-ready units of the *8. Panzer Division* were consolidated into three *kampfgruppen* and assigned to three corps commands or infantry divisions. The remainder of the division was sent to locations in Estonia and Latvia to rest and rebuild. Haupt, *Die 8. Panzer Division im Zweiten Weltkrieg*, p. 198.

127 Jentz, *Panzertruppen, Vol. One*, pp. 210-211.

128 *7. Panzer Division. Ia., Anlagen zum Kriegstagebuch Nr. 3, Teil II (28.9.1941-5.5.1942)*. NARA T315, Roll 407, Frame 000301-000302.

129 Jentz, *Panzertruppen, Vol. One*, p. 209.

130 Boog, et. al. *GSWW. Vol. IV*, pp. 1120-1122.

131 Ibid, p. 252. For the practice of returning damaged vehicles to Germany, see Müller-Hillebrand, "The Tank Repair Service in the German Army."

132 Boog, et. al. *GSWW. Vol. IV*, pp. 1120-1122.

133 Jentz, *Panzertruppen, Vol. One*, p. 252.

From this nadir, the circumstances of the panzer divisions slowly began to improve. In total, the German Army lost or wrote-off 4,667 armoured vehicles between June 1941 and June 1942. Remarkably, during this period German industry, despite the difficulties it faced, still managed to produce 4,635 tanks and assault guns as well as 293 self-propelled anti-tank guns, for a grand total of 4,928 new vehicles. In fact, between 1 February and 1 July 1942 no less than 2,332 replacement panzers arrived on the Eastern Front, far surpassing the 642 that were in the meantime listed as *Totalausfalle*.[134] Consequently, on 1 July 1942 the Army's overall stock of tanks, assault guns, and self-propelled anti-tank guns totalled 6,854, an increase of 510 vehicles (eight percent) from the previous year (see Table 4.13). Moreover, at least 1,221 of these were improved models armed with long-barrelled, high-velocity guns and enhanced armour that vastly increased their performance against the T-34.[135] In broad terms, by the time Operation Blue commenced Germany was indeed able to replace the losses sustained by its fleet of armoured vehicles, achieve a small increase in their stock, and significantly improve its overall quality and effectiveness.

Favourable as Germany's overall armoured vehicle situation was, this did not translate into an immediate improvement for all panzer divisions. The formations allotted to Operation Blue had priority but most of these had to be extensively refurbished and reorganized in an active theatre of operations within a short timeframe. It should be remembered that the refurbishment of entire panzer divisions was a more complicated process than simply piling in numbers of new tanks, requiring as it did fresh consignments of men, vehicles and equipment, as well as extensive periods of time for unit training and personnel integration. However, of the nine panzer divisions assigned to participate in the main offensive, three were new formations transferred from the West but the remaining six were already serving on the *Ostfront* where time and transport constraints meant they had to be comprehensively rebuilt just behind the front. Even so, the unrelenting pace of operations in the East meant that most of the latter were only withdrawn into reserve during the course of April. With Operation Blue originally scheduled to commence on 15 June, this gave these formations between six to ten weeks to receive new equipment, incorporate replacement personnel, and work

---

134 Ibid, p. 252.
135 This includes 237 Pz IV Ausf. F2 and Ausf. G models armed with the 7.5 cm KwK L/43, 185 StuG III Ausf. F armed with the 7.5 cm StuK 40 L/43 and later the 7.5 cm StuK 40 L/48, and 293 Marder II and III self-propelled anti-tank guns (the former equipped with a 7.5 cm Pak 40 L/46 main gun, and the latter with captured Russian 7.62 cm anti-tank guns). See April to June 1942 production figures in Müller-Hillebrand, "German Tank Strength and Loss Statistics", p. 28. Actual production of Pz III Ausf. J equipped with the 5 cm KwK L/42 during this period in unknown, but one source shows 506 Pz III armed with long-barrelled 5 cm guns on strength with the panzer units deployed in Russia in late June and early July. Jentz, *Panzertruppen, Vol. One*, pp. 236-239. For technical details of German armoured vehicles, see Senger und Etterlin, *German Tanks of World War II*.

themselves up to full operational readiness.[136] During this time, they had to undergo extensive organizational changes as their panzer regiments were expanded from two battalions to three by the transfer of personnel from the panzer divisions stationed along the central sector of the front. The four motorised infantry divisions assigned to the offensive were likewise each assigned a panzer battalion whose personnel were also drawn from the same source.[137] Most of these additional panzer battalions only started arriving in mid-May and a number only did so shortly before the main offensive began in late June. Likewise, the majority of the armoured vehicles destined to stock these units only arrived shortly before Operation Blue commenced – indeed, some materialized only after the panzer divisions had actually left their start lines.[138] This is illustrated by the fact that of the 2,332 replacement panzers arriving on the *Ostfront* between 1 February and 1 July, some 1,554 (67 percent) arrived between

136 Initial orders specifying the measures to be taken for the rehabilitation of the *Ostheer*, especially the panzer and motorized divisions, were sent out as early as 12 February. For these formations to be ready in time for the commencement of operations, these insisted that the rehabilitation period begin no later than mid-March. See Jacobsen, (Ed.) *KTB OKW, Band I*, pp. 1096-1098. Formal orders for Operation Blue were issued via Hitler's extensive War Directive No. 41 on 5 April. Trevor-Roper (Ed.), *Hitler's War Directives, 1939-1945*, pp. 116-121. For the various planning and preparations for this operation, see Grant, *Barbarossa*, pp. 109-142. The specific formations referred to here are the *3., 9., 11., 13., 14.,* and *16. Panzer Divisions*, and the *3., 16., 29.* and *60. (Mot.) Infanterie Divisions*.
137 Other organizational changes for both the panzer and motorized divisions participating in Blue included the incorporation of army anti-aircraft battalions (*Heeres Flakartillerie Battalions*) each of two batteries with four 8.8 cm and three 2 cm Flak guns each, and one battery with 12 2 cm Flak guns, and the absorption within these divisions of the reconnaissance battalions into the motorcycle battalions. The *schützen* regiments of the panzer divisions (all of which were renamed *Panzergrenadier* on 1 July 1942) each received a company of 12 2 cm Flak guns (four of which were four-barreled *Vierlingsflak*) mounted on trucks. The increased availability of armoured half-tracks also meant that by the summer of 1942 eight of the panzer divisions on the *Ostfront* now had entire battalions mounted on SPW. For a succinct, but thorough, explanation of all these various organizational changes, see Pier P. Battistelli, *Panzer Divisions: The Eastern Front 1941-1943*. (Botley, Oxford: 2008). Also see Nafziger, *The German Order of Battle - Panzers and Artillery in World War II*.
138 The first of the additional panzer battalions was assigned to the *3. (Mot.) Infanterie Division* on 15 February, but the remainder seems to have arrived only from mid-May to late-June. Aside from the late arrival of these units, the shipment of additional panzers appears to have stretched on for longer than first anticipated. At least 328 of the panzers assigned to refurbish *Heeresgruppe Süd* only arrived between 16 May and 10 June, a number of which were replacements for losses that had been sustained in the meantime. In the case of the *16. Panzer Division*, its *III./2. Panzer Regiment* was held back from the initial phase of Operation Blue because it was still waiting for its tanks. Yet another report dated to 11 June notes that 48 tanks still had to be allotted to the *13., 14.* and *16. Panzer Divisions*. See *Generalstab des Heeres, Org. Abt. Gruppe III., Beitrag zum Kriegstagebuch für die Zeit vom 1-10.6.1942*, NARA T78 R414, Frames 6382404, 6382408 & 6382411.

April and June.[139] Interestingly, this latter period corresponds to both the time in which most of the armoured and motorised divisions were finally withdrawn from the front for rebuilding, and the point at which the railway net in the East was finally unsnarled.

Exacerbating this hasty period of refurbishment was the fact that in May and June many of the formations that should have been resting were actually involved in a series of large-scale and fiercely fought operations.[140] While these various engagements did not result in the destruction of many German tanks (only 140 being listed as *Totalausfälle* across the entire front in May and June), the strain of continuous operations produced considerable wear that kept operational ready rates low.[141] Consequently, the combined implications of the late start in rehabilitating the panzer and motorised divisions, followed by their prodigious use before Operation Blue even commenced, meant that fresh tanks had to continuously be dispatched to *Heeresgruppe Süd*, to the detriment of other sectors, until well past the start of the main offensive.

Further retarding the rebuilding process was the diversion of resources to formations and areas other than the Eastern Front that drew heavily upon Germany's available stock of armoured vehicles. The rehabilitation of the *2.* and *5. Panzer Divisions* in Germany during the summer of 1941 had required a considerable number of panzers, and the reconstitution of the *6.*, *7.* and *10. Panzer Divisions* in France, though only beginning in the late spring of 1942, required still more. Between 1 June 1941 and 1 July 1942, at least 369 panzers were shipped to the *Afrika Korps*, while a further 184 were given to Germany's European allies. Yet the greatest drain arose from the creation of new formations. These included four new panzer divisions, four Army and four *Waffen-SS* panzer battalions, seven assault gun battalions, and some smaller units.[142] Additionally, the *(Mot.) Infanterie Regiment Grossdeutschland* was expanded into a motorised division with its own panzer and assault gun battalions, and the *203. Panzer Regiment* was upgraded by having its captured French tanks replaced by German models. Overall, these various diversions siphoned off at least 2,375 tanks and assault guns by late June 1942 (see Table 4.14).[143]

---

139 Jentz, *Panzertruppen, Vol. One*, p. 252.

140 These included Operations Bustard Hunt (8-24 May), Wilhelm (10-15 June), and Fredericus II (22-25 June), together with the Second Battle of Kharkov (12-30 May). For more details concerning these engagements, see Glantz, *To the Gates of Stalingrad*, Ziemke & Bauer, *Moscow to Stalingrad*, Citino, *Death of the Wehrmacht*, and Glantz, *Kharkov 1942*.

141 Jentz, *Panzertruppen, Vol. One*, p. 252.

142 For a complete explanation regarding the creation of these formations and their organizational structure see Jentz, *Panzertruppen, Vol. One*, pp. 214-220.

143 Although usually attributed as being symptomatic of Hitler's fetish for creating new units instead of replenishing old ones, there was some rational behind the establishment of these new formations. Two of the new panzer divisions (specifically the *22.* and *23. Panzer*), established in September 1941, were created at a time when a German victory in Russia still appeared imminent. The apparent intention was to have these divisions ready for operations in 1942, whereby they would be used to lead a German offensive into the

With priority given to the belatedly refurbished armoured formations of *Heeresgruppe Süd*, and with large consignments of armour being used to establish new units or else being dispatched elsewhere, in early 1942 OKH decreed that the ten panzer divisions remaining along the central and northern stretches of the Eastern Front would largely have to make due with the resources already at their disposal, at least until later that summer.[144] Since they also had to give up the personnel of some of their panzer battalions to buttress the formations deployed in the south, the armoured contingent within

Middle East. Given their heavy engagement, the panzer divisions operating in Russia would have required an extensive refit, possibly precluding their use until well into 1942. For similar reasons the *24. Panzer Division* was created in November, before the disastrous winter campaign of 1941/1942 had unravelled Germany's long-term strategic plans. The *25. Panzer Division*, established in February 1942, constituted only a minor addition to replenishing the ranks of the armoured fleet, since it was purposely created in Norway from a hodgepodge of units already in country in order to provide some modicum of an offensive capability in the region, and because, for at least the first several months of its existence, it was almost entirely equipped with captured French tanks. The creation of the four Army and two of the *Waffen-SS* panzer battalions also made sense since these were assigned to motorised divisions allotted to Operation Blue and because their inclusion into these formations gave them a heavier offensive punch than had previously been then case. However, one of the two *Waffen-SS* battalions (that created for the *SS-(Mot.) Division Leibstandarte SS Adolf Hitler*) together with the remaining two actually sat out most of 1942 in France. Finally, the creation of additional assault gun battalions appears to been a response both to the increased availability of StuG III and growing demands of the German infantry divisions for more intimate armoured support.

144 See Jacobsen, (Ed.) *KTB OKW, Band I*, pp. 1096-1098. It should be recalled that these instructions were issued at a time when Germany's military fortunes had reached their lowest point yet experienced in the war – Soviet attacks continued to ripple across the Eastern Front, war production and the availability of raw materials appeared to be collapsing, and the rail transport situation was simply a disaster. Within the various constituents of the Army General Staff, the suddenness and monumentality of these events produced shock and in many cases a dejected sense that Germany no longer possessed the ability to win the war. At the very least, many viewed the possibility of staging a large-scale offensive in 1942 as impossible.

Significantly, this included Generals Friedrich Fromm (Chief of Army Armaments and Commander of the *Ersatzheer*), Eduard Wagner (Army Quartermaster General), Emil Leeb (Chief of the Army Ordnance Department), and Georg Thomas (head of OKW's Defence Economy and Armament Office). See Boog, et. al. *GSWW, Vol. VI*, pp. 861-862, and Megargee, *Inside Hitler's High Command*, p. 175. Given that these were the individuals responsible for the procurement of the various means with which the Army needed to be resupplied, their now very pessimistic assessments would have formed the basis for the OKH order of 12 February. In turn, this order, based upon *projections* that major shortages of armoured vehicles would exist in four months time, resulted in reduced tank establishments for all the panzer divisions on the *Ostfront* except those slated to participate in Operation Blue. Put succinctly, one of the reasons why the panzer divisions of *Heeresgruppe Nord* and *Mitte* may have had so few vehicles was simply because that was what they were authorized to have, not necessarily because actual overall shortages of tanks existed by the summer of 1942.

seven of these divisions was reduced to a single panzer battalion. Even though these panzer divisions would be crucial in fending off Soviet assaults against the circuitous fronts held by *Heeresgruppe Nord* and *Mitte* and were also expected to play the leading role in a number of limited-objective attacks OKH planned to stage in these sectors, their armoured strengths – and hence their offensive punch – remained far below that of the previous year or even of their compatriots campaigning in southern Russia. As detailed in Appendix Six, at the beginning of July 1942, the strongest of these divisions possessed 103 panzers, the weakest a mere 48, and the median average was 67. In contrast, the panzer divisions committed to Operation Blue possessed an average strength of 145 tanks. Even more disconcerting for these formations was the fact that the armour on hand consisted of older models of the Pz III and Pz IV, and that even these had to be bolstered by a large number of increasingly obsolescent Pz 38(t). Only in August would consignments of improved models arrive in significant numbers.[145]

Despite the priority given them, even the favoured panzer divisions of *Heeresgruppe Süd* did not have all the tanks that they were authorized by the time Operation Blue commenced. As illustrated in Table 4.15, the worst off possessed only 43 percent of its *Sollstärke*, and even the strongest only managed 79 percent. Overall, these divisions possessed only 64 percent of the armour they should have. However, these percentages need to be understood with a considerable degree of caution. First, they only refer to German tank models and thereby exclude the 140 Pz 38(t) operating with the *22. Panzer Division*. When these are included, this produces a modest increase in actual holdings to 71 percent of *Sollstärke*. Secondly, of the 230 panzers that eight of these divisions were authorized, a large proportion (32 percent) were Pz II whose characteristics were of increasingly limited utility on the battlefields of the Eastern Front. Significantly, the strength requirements of the *Sollstärke* were the result of a new series of KStN for panzer units that were published on 1 November 1941.[146] Coming shortly before Germany's catastrophic military reverses and the near economic collapse in the winter of 1941-1942, these KStN were the product of the heady optimism that pervaded throughout the *Wehrmacht* at the time and which anticipated huge increases in armoured vehicle production and extended periods of refit for the panzer divisions in the near future. In reality, because of its mounting obsolescence on the battlefield and in order to switch manufacturing resources to the production of more capable vehicles, early in 1942 the decision was made to halt production of the standard version of the Pz II and the final examples rolled off assembly lines that July. With shortages of Pz II amounting to 441 (66 percent) of the 671 tanks that the panzer

---

145 One report notes the dispatch of 57 Pz III, 15 Pz IV, 25 StuG, and 72 self-propelled anti-tank guns to *Heeresgruppe Mitte* between 11 and 20 August 1942. *Generalstab des Heeres, Org. Abt. Gruppe III., Beitrag zum Kriegstagebuch für August 1942*, NARA T78 R414, Frame 6382425. The *2. Panzer Division* received its first five Pz IV equipped with long-barreled 7.5 cm L/43 guns on 11 August. Hilary Doyle & Thomas Jentz, *Panzerkampfwagen IV Ausf. G, H and J, 1942-1945*. (Oxford: 2001), p. 34.
146 Jentz, *Panzertruppen, Vol. One*, p. 215.

divisions of *Heeresgruppe Süd* lacked, it needs to be recognized that this was largely the result of a bureaucratic decision, made almost eight months before Operation Blue, that did not conform to the realities of manufacturing or battlefield transitions that had occurred in the meantime. Finally, it should also be noted that these panzer divisions did possess 83 percent of their authorized number of Pz III and Pz IV, a factor of some significance given that these models were the mainstay of the panzer divisions and their abilities on the battlefield.

At first glance, the lamentable tank state of the panzer divisions, especially those with *Heeresgruppe Nord* and *Mitte*, appears to representative of an overall shortage of armoured vehicles within the German Army. Certainly, this is the conclusion presented within the post-war literature, even though most provide scant details, if any.[147] The problem with this assumption is that the whereabouts of a large number of the 6,558 panzers and StuG in stock with the German Army on 1 July 1942 are unknown. Of these, an estimated 2,836 can reasonably be accounted for as being present with the *Ostheer*, while a further 1,613 were preoccupied elsewhere (see Table 4.16). This leaves 2,109 tanks and assault guns unaccounted for. Evidently, more armoured vehicles were either on the Eastern Front, or at least should have been, than the diminutive figures cited with the panzer divisions have led scholars to believe. Admittedly, because of severe shortages of spare parts, a number of these may actually have been in long-term repair.[148] Consequently, they might have been located at maintenance facilities within Germany or at the major tank repair centres established within the occupied eastern territories. However, they also may have been with formations in the field but went unreported by these units since they were not expected to become operational for an extended period of time.[149] The temptation and benefits of exacerbating deficiencies and the German Army's shambolic reporting methods at this time may also have played a role.[150]

147　For example, Evan Mawdsley limits his comments to the armoured status of *Heeresgruppe Mitte*, saying, "The 'panzer' armies were now tank formations in name only..." but only elaborates that they "suffered from a lack of troops and equipment..." Mawdsley, *Thunder in the East*, p. 153. In his study of the *Panzertruppen*, Richard DiNardo simply asserts that, during 1942, "German industry... could not make good the losses in equipment suffered during the previous year." Richard DiNardo, *Germany's Panzer Arm*. (Westport, CT: 1997). Boog, et. al. *GSWW, Vol. VI*, pp. 871, notes the dire circumstances of the first months of 1942, but then leaves the reader with this impression, providing no statistics regarding the circumstances once Operation Blue commenced. Alan Clark provides a similarly gloomy picture, but likewise provides no specific details. See Clark, *Barbarossa*, pp. 194-195.

148　See Müller-Hillebrand, "The Tank Repair Service in the German Army." According to Müller-Hillebrand, "German Tank Strength and Loss Statistics", p. 26, of the 5,663 tanks with the German Army on 1 July, some 2,192 (39 percent) were in repair. Jentz, *Panzertruppen, Vol. One*, p. 252 notes that 723 (35 percent) of the 2,060 tanks in the East at the beginning of July were non-operational.

149　See Zetterling & Frankson, "Analyzing World War II Eastern Front Battles", pp. 188-192.

150　For either issue, see Boog, et. al. *GSWW. Vol. IV*, pp. 1128-1132. The style and substance of reports concerning manpower and equipment strengths during this period vary almost

Given all these varied complexities and inconsistencies, historians could perhaps be forgiven for never having solidly ascertained what the circumstances of the *Panzertruppen* actually were by the summer of 1942. On the one hand, Germany's overall production of armoured vehicles surpassed known losses and, even with the addition of new formations, this should have translated into the panzer divisions being largely restocked with the tanks they needed. On the other hand, the detailed figures we have for the actual strength of the panzer divisions reveal significant shortages. A final conclusion awaits a more thorough study. However, even the detailed reports, representing a minimal estimate, still indicate that the German Army was able to muster a considerable number of armoured vehicles in time for Operation Blue. Overall, *Heeresgruppe Süd* began its operations with around 1,934 tanks and assault guns (see Appendix Six), against which the Red Army was able to deploy 2,959 tanks.[151] Meanwhile, the armoured formations deployed along the central and northern portions of the German front, despite having been denied resources in preference of their colleagues in the south, still managed to muster approximately 902 panzers and StuG. Given the circumstances and challenges that had confronted the Germans in the previous months, the assembly of 2,836 armoured vehicles is still an impressive feat. As will be explored in the next chapter, this assignment of armoured resources proved sufficiently adequate to both propel the German Army deep into the Caucasus and to the Volga River, and to hold the remainder of the front against a series of formidable Soviet offensives.

New formations, equipment, vehicles, and tanks were all key elements of the rebuilding process that the German Army found itself feverishly engaged in during the first half of 1942, but the most crucial would be replenishing its vital human resources. Based upon the expectation that the campaign in the East would have concluded by the winter of 1941, no substantive planning or preparations were made for the supply of personnel replacements beyond that point, the assumption being that a number of infantry divisions would simply be broken up, both to bring the remainder up to strength and to release personnel back to the German economy. Once the original consignments of men held within the *Ersatzheer* were expended, the immediate pool of replacements was then largely confined to returning convalescents; the 19-year olds of the 1922 age group were inducted into the *Wehrmacht* on 15 October, but their four-month training period meant that these would only become available starting in February 1942.[152] By November, these circumstances meant that only 55,000 replace-

from one report to the next. Although this generally continued throughout the war, reporting did become more uniform starting in late 1942.

151 Glantz, *To the Gates of Stalingrad*, pp. 117-120.

152 This class numbered a potential 689,401 men, but the actual total available was considerably smaller because of occupational deferments, or because their physical or mental status made them unsuitable for military service. Of the remainder, these had to be divided amongst the entire *Wehrmacht*. Kroener, et. al. *GSWW. Vol. V: Part One*, pp. 831-832 & 1024.

ments were dispatched to the East even though losses that month totalled 157,143.[153] This situation went from bad to calamitous when the already under-strength forma-tions of the *Ostheer* were confronted by the Soviet winter counteroffensive around Moscow, which proceeded to expand across the entire breadth of the front and that continued until April 1942. As the front wavered upon the point of collapse, German units were almost continuously engaged in combat that produced hefty numbers of casualties at a relentless pace. The unrelenting pace of the fighting, conducted within the brutal operating environment of a Russian winter for which the *Ostheer* was virtu-ally unprepared for, also created tremendous quantities of sick and frostbitten.[154]

A precise determination of the overall personnel shortages afflicting the *Ostheer* at this time remains frustratingly abstruse because of conflicting reports, a lack of specific details, and variable accounting practices. After the war Burkhart Müller-Hillebrand, who was Chief of the Organization Department of the Army General Staff from 15 April to 22 October 1942, noted the deficiencies in the methodologies employed by his department, summarized as follows:

> In actual practice the exact authorized strength of the wartime army could no longer be ascertained at short notice, for at any time it meant several weeks of calculation. [I]n order not to burden the army with further reports, no attempt was made to ascertain replacement requirements by obtaining and comparing the authorized strengths with the actual strengths. The forwarding of replacements was regulated approximately in accordance with incoming casualty figures. The [casualty] reports listed only those losses sustained through enemy action, and losses through sickness, transfer, etc., did not appear. Since in any case available replacements were not sufficient to meet the existing deficit, the less accurate method used was considered adequate.[155]

---

153 This included 84,051 combat casualties and 73,143 sick. Ibid., p. 1020. According to the monthly casualty figures compiled by OKW, the number of Army combat casualties on the Eastern Front during November actually totaled 87,139. See BA MA RH 6/543.
154 Between 1 December 1941 and 1 May 1942, combat casualties in the East amounted to an approximate 418,322. In contrast, during this timeframe some 414,028 men were listed as sick or frostbitten, but this only includes those whose treatment required their transfer back to Germany. The actual number of the sick and frostbitten was probably much greater. Boog, et. al. *GSWW, Vol. VI*, p. 865. According to casualty statistics later compiled by OKW, the number of frostbite cases totaled 141,957 by 31 March 1942, of whom 1,424 had required amputations. See BA MA RH 6/543. In contrast, Reinhardt, *Die Wende vor Moskau*, p. 247, states the number of amputations by the end of January already amounted to 1,856.
155 Müller-Hillebrand, "Statistics Systems", pp. 10,12, 40 & 43. As one comprehensive study of the German Army's replacement system has determined, "There is no possibility of arriving at a precise statistical picture of German losses and replacements. Aside from the fact that not all records have survived or are readily available, those that are available covering the same or overlapping periods of time often vary widely both in types or categories of coverage and in actual figures. Prepared by different offices, from different

As Müller-Hillebrand admits, the ability of the reporting system adopted by the Organization Department in terms of gauging actual personnel shortages was at best problematic since it was based on an automatic supposition that the availability of replacements could never compensate for losses, and that shortages were thereby inevitable. It also made no effort to account for personnel transfers or losses through sickness, the latter being especially notable given that the *Ostheer* had been forced to repatriate an estimated 715,400 sick to Germany by 1 July 1942.[156] In essence, such assessments represented little more than a guess. By the spring of 1942 it would appear that nobody within OKH actually knew what the exact personnel requirements and shortages of the *Ostheer* really constituted.

And yet, as vague as these accounting procedures were, that the cumulative effect of the winter campaign upon the *Ostheer* had been ruinous should have been blatantly obvious. Losses consistently outpaced replacements whose arrival was retarded by the chaos afflicting the transportation system.[157] Personnel strengths plummeted, especially amongst combat battalions. Desperate to maintain at least some of their units at an effective strength, many divisional commanders were forced to disband some of their infantry battalions, consolidating their remnants into those that remained. Men skimmed from the rear echelons and headquarters establishments, together with artillerymen and other troops who had lost their equipment, were amalgamated into the remaining combat battalions or else formed into emergency *Alarmeinheiten* with depressing frequency. A report from the *VII. Armee Korps* dated to 3 April, which notes that its three infantry divisions had disbanded a total of 11 (out of 27) infantry battalions, nine artillery batteries and two anti-tank companies, appears fairly typical.[158] By the time operations finally began to subside copious gaps existed in the ranks of most divisions. A cursory look at the divisions present with *Heeresgruppe Nord* (displayed in Table 4.17) on 1 April reveals that each division was short an average of at least 3,648 men. For *Heeresgruppe Mitte*, information for the same period could

sources, for different purposes, they are impossible to reconcile." Trevor Dupuy, *German and Soviet Replacement Systems in World War II*. (Maclean, VA: 1980), p. 48.

156 Compiled from Kroener, et. al. *GSWW. Vol. V: Part One*, p. 1020, and Boog, et. al. *GSWW. Vol. VI*, pp. 865-867. Note that the latter incorrectly lists combat casualties as 'killed'. The sick have thereby been derived by deducting 'killed' (ie. combat casualties) from the total given as 'losses'.

157 Significant numbers of replacements were moved to the front via air transport, but the majority moved by rail. Due to snarled rail lines and the subsequent congestion at major rail centres, many troop trains were waylaid while making their way towards the front. In a number of cases, personnel were forced to march hundreds of kilometers from stations far to the rear of the front line; since many had been hastily assembled and left ill equipped to confront the bitter winter conditions, these replacements sometimes sustained significant personnel losses to frostbite before they had even reached the front. See Jones, *The Retreat*, p. 242.

158 *VII. Armeekorps. Ia., Anlagen z. Kriegstagebuch 5d (March-April 1942)*, NARA T314 Roll 352, Frames 000769-000770.

only be found for four divisions, but these note an average shortfall of 4,551 men.[159] In overall terms, the situation appeared bleak. Statistics for the other army groups could not be found, but one incomplete report from *Heeresgruppe Nord* indicated that it was short 120,462 men of its *Sollstärke* on 1 May.[160] Although contentious given its methodology, a study compiled by the Organization Department concluded that as of 1 June 1942 some 740,000 personnel vacancies existed throughout the entire *Ostheer*.[161]

Although tardy in recognizing the full extent of the crisis, various Army authorities had instituted a number of remedial measures at an early stage. Mostly this involved finding replacements from within the Army itself. Commencing in mid-August 1941, Army establishments and training units within Germany were systematically scoured for younger, combat-fit men who were then exchanged with older, less-fit personnel manning the divisions garrisoning Western Europe, thereby raising the combat-readiness of these formations should the need arise for their deployment to Russia. By late October, this had garnered 250,000 men, a number of whom appear to have been injected directly into the *Ostheer* as replacements. Other measures included reductions in the manning requirements of various rear echelon posts throughout Germany and Europe, which freed a further 25,000 men for frontline service. The removal of one infantry battalion each from ten of the divisions stationed in the West also freed up more replacements. However, the ongoing scale of the losses sustained in Russia far outweighed the numbers generated by these measures and in early November the Organization Department demanded that at least 20 divisions be disbanded to provide the needed replacements. Although two divisions were ultimately disbanded, Hitler refused to allow such a wholesale reduction in the number of the Army's divisions because of the negative effects such an action might have upon the morale of the German public.[162]

Despite official disapproval, field commanders in the East had quietly taken matters into their own hands by late summer 1941 and had begun recruiting volunteers from among the range of ethnic groups that resided within the Soviet Union. Known as *Hiwis* (abbreviated from *Hilfswillige*, or volunteer helpers), these volunteers assumed a variety of rear echelon roles – cooks, drivers, medical orderlies or construction labourers – in order to free German personnel for combat duty. Initially unarmed, these

---

159 Ibid, Frame 000692. These divisions and their shortages were:

| 7. Infanterie Division | 3,615 | 258. Infanterie Division | 4,332 |
| 197. Infanterie Division | 5,802 | 267. Infanterie Division | 4,854 |

160 *Heeresgruppe Nord. Abt. IIa/IIb., Tatigkeitsberichte zum Kriegstagebuch vom 1.4.42 – 31.12.42. Dazu: Anlagenband 1. und 2.* NARA T311 Roll 105, Frames 7139583-7139594.
161 Boog, et. al. *GSWW. Vol. VI*, p. 864.
162 Kroener, et. al. *GSWW. Vol. V: Part One*, pp. 1022-1023. Also see Müller-Hillebrand, *Das Heer 1933-1945, Band III*, p. 19. For a greater explanation regarding Hitler's concerns, see Crouthamel, "Nervous Nazis: War Neurosis, National Socialism and the Memory of the First World War.", pp. 55-75, and Marlis G. Steinert, *Hitler's War and the Germans: Public Mood and Attitude during the Second World War.* (Athens, OH: 1977).

Hiwis were gradually incorporated into frontline units where many found themselves in combat against their countrymen. To police the vast swaths of occupied Russia, German security officials had also recruited from amongst the indigenous population to establish a series of home guard and police organizations. Starting in November, many of these were merged to create *Schutzmannschaft* (auxiliary police) battalions; originally intended for anti-partisan duties, many were committed to combat and held sections of the front line during the winter of 1941-1942. Also formed around this time were a variety of (usually) ethnically homogenous units grouped together under the rubric *Osttruppen* (Eastern Troops); these included everything from detachments of Cossacks and companies of Crimean Tartars, to battalions of Russians, Balts, Ukrainians and *Ostlegionen* (Eastern Legions) from the Caucasus.[163] At least 310,000 of these volunteers were already serving in the *Ostheer* and the various German security organizations by the early summer of 1942.[164] In such numbers, they played a major role by boosting German personnel strengths and, hence, military capabilities.

Ultimately, it took the disastrous winter reverses to jar Hitler and the rest of Germany's military and civilian leadership out of their complacency. Further personnel exchanges and strenuous reductions in home front establishments allowed the *Ersatzheer* to generate another 141,000 men for the *Feldheer* by the end of December. This was at least partly facilitated by the passing of new laws that made military service for women aged 18-40 compulsory; subsequently, more men were

---

163 A rich literature exists regarding the Eastern volunteers of the *Wehrmacht*. For just a few useful examples, see Wladyslaw Anders, *Russian Volunteers in Hitler's Army*. (Bayside, NY: 1998), Rolf-Dieter Muller, *The Unknown Eastern Front: The Wehrmacht and Hitler's Foreign Soldiers*. (New York, NY: 2012), Joachim Hoffmann, *Die Geschichte der Wlassow Armee*. (Freiburg: 1983), Joachim Hoffmann, *Die Ostlegionen 1941-1943: Turkotataren, Kaukasier, und Wolgafinnen im Deutschen Heer*. (Freiburg: 1986), Carlos C. Jurado, *Foreign Volunteers of the Wehrmacht, 1941-1945*. (London: 1983), Erich Kerne, *General von Pannwitz und seine Kosaken*. (Oldendorf: 1971), Antonio J. Munoz, *The Kaminski Brigade, 1941-1945*. (Bayside, NY: 1996), J. Lee Ready, *Forgotten Axis*. (Jefferson, NC: 1967), and Heike Wolf-Dietrich, *Sie Wollten die Freiheit. Geschichte der Ukrainische Division, 1943-1945*. (Dorheim: 1974). Also see Ruth B. Birn, "Collaboration with Nazi Germany in Eastern Europe: the Case of the Estonian Security Police." *Contemporary European History*, Vol. 10, No. 2 (2001), pp. 181-198, Alexander A. Maslov, "Tried for Treason Against the Motherland: Soviet Generals Condemned after Release from German Captivity." *Journal of Slavic Military Studies*, Vol. 13, No. 2 (June 2000), pp. 86-138, Timothy Mulligan, "Escape from Stalingrad: Soviet Nationals with the German Sixth Army." *Journal of Slavic Military Studies*, Vol. 20, No. 4 (2007), pp. 739-748, Leonid Rein, "Untermenschen in SS Uniform: 30th Waffen-Grenadier Division of Waffen-SS." *Journal of Slavic Military Studies*, Vol. 20, No. 2 (April 2007), pp. 329-345, and Oleg Zarubinsky, "Collaboration of the Population in Occupied Ukrainian Territory: Some Aspects of the Overall Picture." *Journal of Slavic Military Studies*, Vol. 10, No. 2 (1997), pp. 138-152.

164 Some 60,421 Soviet citizens had been enlisted as security police by December 1941, while a possible 250,000 *Hiwis* may have been serving throughout the *Ostheer* by the following summer. Kroener, et. al. *GSWW. Vol. V: Part One*, p. 1028, and Rolf-Dieter Muller, *The Unknown Eastern Front*, p. 223.

released from administrative and service tasks through the creation of various corps of female auxiliaries.[165] At the same time, the decision was made to curtail the generous deferment system that by the end of 1941 had excluded 5.5 million able-bodied males from military service. From amongst these, it was decided to call-up 473,000 deferred reservists who had already completed their military training and who it was hoped could quickly be deployed following a brief refresher course.[166] By mid-February the first cohorts of the 1922 class had completed training and the 270,000 allotted to the Army were quickly fed into the replacement system; even though they would not become available until the late summer at the earliest, the 1923 class also began their training that April.[167] Finally, one OKW study noted that by mid-July some 150,000 17-year olds of the 1925 class had already volunteered for service in the *Wehrmacht*, of whom 70,000 were in the Army.[168]

The overall impression is that huge numbers of men (and some women) were in fact made available for military service. According to one source, a total of 3,098,400 men and women were inducted into the *Wehrmacht* between 1 June 1941 and 31 May 1942. Other figures indicate that at least 1.07 million of these occurred during the first five months of 1942.[169] For reasons that have already been noted, the problem is determining just how many of these actually found their way into the ranks of the *Ostheer*. As stated by one document, the number of departures (combat casualties and sick requiring treatment in Germany) from the armies in the East totalled 2,018,881 men by 1 July 1942; the corresponding number of replacements arriving from Germany was 1,252,000. Adding a further 240,000 convalescents who had been treated and recuperated within the army group rear areas, and who were then directly sent back

---

165 The *Nachrichtenhelferinnen der Heeres* (Army Signal Auxiliaries) had already been established on 1 October 1940, and, amongst others, the *Stabshelferinnen* (Female Staff Auxiliaries) was created in January 1942. Ultimately, all female auxiliaries of the *Wehrmacht* would be combined into the *Wehrmachthelferinnen* (Corps of Female Auxiliaries) on 29 November 1944. An estimated 450,000 women were in uniform by November 1943, and these are believed to have freed up 300,000 men during the war by taking over their duties. See Blank, et. al. *GSWW. Vol. IX: Part One*, pp. 41-49. For more elaborate accounts, see Rosmarie Killius, *Frauen für die Front: Gespräche mit Wehrmachthelferinnen*. (Leipzig: 2003) and Gordon Williamson, *World War II German's Women Auxiliary Services*. (Botley, Oxford: 2003).
166 For the background of this decision, see Kroener, et. al. *GSWW. Vol. V: Part One*, pp. 1050-1067. During the first half of 1942, an actual total of 558,100 men working in the armaments industry were conscripted into the *Wehrmacht*. Kroener, et. al. *GSWW. Vol. V, Part Two*, p. 850.
167 Müller-Hillebrand, *Das Heer 1933-1945, Band III*, p. 51. The 1923 class totalled a potential 657,692 men. Kroener, et. al. *GSWW. Vol. V: Part One*, p. 832.
168 Müller-Hillebrand, *Das Heer 1933-1945, Band III*, p. 53.
169 Total inductions found in Müller-Hillebrand, "Statistics Systems", p. 76. The number of inductees during the first months of 1942 has been deducted from figures noted in Kroener, et. al. *GSWW. Vol. V: Part Two*, p. 850.

to the front, produces a total of 1,492,000 replacements.[170] This indicates an overall shortfall of 526,881 men, but even this figure needs to be scaled back because replacements for the 18 divisions that had in the meantime been disbanded or withdrawn from the Eastern Front would no longer have been required. Even so, it is clear that significant gaps still existed by the summer of 1942 despite the arrival of substantial numbers of personnel replacements.

However, a more detailed appreciation reveals that the manpower situation within the individual divisions of the *Ostheer* had indeed improved significantly. As illustrated in Table 4.18, within almost all of the divisions of *Heeresgruppe Nord* shortages fell markedly between 1 April and 1 July.[171] This was despite the fact that OKH records indicate that the army group lost 108,530 men to all causes during this period, but received only 101,200 replacements; at best, shortages should have remained roughly even with those in April.[172] In a number of instances, divisions disbanding a number of their battalions could explain the reduction in shortages – the deficiencies within the disbanded units being eliminated altogether, while shortages in the remaining battalions were alleviated by the transfer of personnel from the units that had been broken up. And yet, this cannot account for all the reductions, since a significant number of divisions are recorded as having retained all of their original battalions. Either *Heeresgruppe Nord* was reporting fewer shortages than in fact existed (an unlikely possibility given that its circumstances at this time would have inclined it to present a bleaker picture rather than the opposite) or it sustained fewer losses or received more replacements than are recorded in the OKH records (a more plausible explanation given the difficulties with record keeping noted above).[173]

---

170 Losses and replacements compiled from statistics illustrated in Kroener, et. al. *GSWW. Vol. V: Part One*, p. 1020, and Boog, et. al. *GSWW. Vol. VI*, pp. 865-866.
171 Interestingly, although usually attributed within the historiography as being favored in terms of allocations of manpower and equipment, some of the worst shortages noted herein reside with the two divisions of the *Waffen-SS*. According to summaries found within BA MA 19/1520, the initial strength of the formations of the *Waffen-SS* committed to Operation Barbarossa totaled 115,841 men. By 20 March 1942, these had sustained 12,562 killed, 186 deaths through accidents, 39,902 wounded, 1,548 missing, and 21,503 sick, for a total loss of 75,701 men. In compensation, they had received only 29,818 replacements. The strengths, casualties and replacements mentioned here can be found listed under 'SS Losses' on the website "Human Losses in World War II: German Statistics and Documents" at ww2stats.com/index.html
172 Statistics regarding these months found in Boog, et. al. *GSWW. Vol. VI*, pp. 865-866.
173 For details concerning operations along the army group's front, see Glantz, *Forgotten Battles of the German-Soviet War, 1941-1945. Vol. Two*, pp. 47-117, and Ziemke & Bauer, *Moscow to Stalingrad*, pp. 254-260. The discrepancies between the records of *Heeresgruppe Nord* and OKH continue until at least the late spring of 1944. While those concerning losses may be reconcilable given that the army group records do not include the sick, it is interesting that these also report the arrival of significantly more replacements than noted in the OKH summary. Overall, the records of *Heeresgruppe Nord* indicate the arrival of 711,352 replacement personnel between June 1942 and May 1944; the relevant

Whatever the exact circumstances, the personnel strengths of the majority of the divisions belonging to *Heeresgruppe Nord* clearly reveal that their manpower situation had been ameliorated to a considerable degree.

The overall personnel condition of the divisions with *Heeresgruppe Mitte* is more difficult to ascertain because no summary concerning the status of its formations could be located. To be sure, it had taken a worse beating than its sister army groups during the previous months and its divisions thereby required considerably more rebuilding. Between 1 December 1941 and 1 July 1942 the army group endured the loss of 560,200 men, representing 51 percent of all the losses sustained by the *Ostheer* during this period; in compensation, it had received 344,300 replacements (42 percent of the total number).[174] As a result, most of its infantry divisions had been reduced to six infantry battalions, and in a few instances four.[175] Yet even here matters appear to have improved significantly by the summer. For instance, on 11 July the *2. Panzer Division* reported that it was short only 22 officers and 760 men.[176] A detailed look at the evolution of the *260. Infanterie Division* is even more revealing. During the winter fighting, the division had been badly mauled and was forced to disband three of its infantry battalions. By 25 April the division noted a *Verpflegungsstärke* of only 6,817 men, and a lamentable *Kampfstärke* of 1,386. On the 15 May, even after the three disbanded infantry battalions had been removed from its personnel requirements, the division was still short 6,044 men, but during the course of the next 30 days it received 1,497 replacements. Though still short 4,805 men, by 15 June the *Verpflegungsstärke* had improved to 8,478 men and the *Kampfstärke* to 2,457. Yet the greatest improvement occurred during July, when a total of 4,355 replacements arrived. As a result, on 1 August the division was able to report its *Verpflegungsstärke* as being 11,561 men and *Kampfstärke* as 5,110; personnel shortages had fallen to 1,446 men (a 70 percent decline since 15 June).[177]

OKH figures total only 517,270, a difference of 194,082 men. Compare figures on losses and replacements found in NARA T311 Roll 105, and departure and arrival statistics illustrated in the document entitled '*Ubersicht uber personelle Abgange und Zugange des Ostheeres ab 1.12.41*' in *Generalstab des Heeres/Org. Abt./II.*, NARA T78 Roll 415, Frames 6384069-6384073. That latter may also be found in Kroener, et. al. *GSWW. Vol. V: Part One*, p. 1020, and Boog, et. al. *GSWW. Vol. VI*, pp. 865-867. Possibly, the army group records are including wounded men who remained in the army group rear areas and then returned to their units outside the normal replacement system, which the OKH records do not cite.

174 Ibid, pp. 865-867.
175 For example, the *267. Infanterie Division* possessed only four infantry battalions on 1 June 1942. *XLIII. Armee Korps. Kriegstagebuch Anlagen Unternehmen Kreml, Ia., Feldzug gegen die Sowjet Union (3.6-11.7.1942)*, NARA T314 Roll 1008, Frame 000552.
176 *XLIII. Armee Korps. Kriegstagebuch Anlagen, Ia., Unternehmen Wirbelwind, Feldzug gegen die Sowjet Union (5.7-9.8.1942)*, NARA T314 Roll 1008, Frame 000600.
177 *260. Infanterie Division. Ia., Anlagenband 2 zum Kriegstagebuch (1.5-31.10.1942)*, NARA T315 Roll 1823, between Frames 000570-000903.

Although the lack of information precludes one from reaching the conclusion that the circumstances of all its divisions improved to this degree, perhaps the most illustrative testament to the improved strength of *Heeresgruppe Mitte* was its combat record during the summer of 1942. Despite being delegated a secondary front because of the priority given Operation Blue, it nonetheless managed to launch three offensive operations of its own: Operations Hannover (21 May-21 June), Seydlitz (2-27 July), and Whirlwind (11-24 August), the former two being complete successes. It also effectively endured four major Soviet offensives: Zhizdra-Bolkhov (5-14 July), Rzhev-Sychevka (30 July-23 August), Gzhatsk-Viazma (14-23 August), and Bolkhov (23-29 August).[178] A partial listing of German claims of the losses incurred by the Red Army includes 77,000 prisoners, and 720 tanks, 975 artillery pieces, and 749 mortars destroyed or captured.[179] Although Russian sources were available for only three of these engagements, they do admit to at least 395,837 casualties and the loss of 500 tanks.[180] Clearly the army group was strong enough to attack and defend on an operational scale.

As one would expect considering the priority given them by their participation in Operation Blue, the majority of the divisions with *Heeresgruppe Süd* appear to have been relatively well off in terms of manpower. According to reports submitted by the *2. Armee* shortly before the offensive commenced, the *9. Panzer Division* and *16. (Mot.) Infanterie Division* possessed their full *Sollstärke*, and even had 1,000 and 750 men, respectively, within their integral *Feldersatz* battalions to serve as ready

---

178 For details concerning these engagements, see Glantz, *Forgotten Battles of the German-Soviet War, 1941-1945. Vol. Three*, Ziemke & Bauer, *Moscow to Stalingrad*, pp. 240-254 & 398-408, and Boog, et. al. *GSWW. Vol. VI*, pp. 954-957 & 1001-1005.

179 See Hillgruber, (Ed.) *KTB OKW. Band II*, pp. 74, 492 & 639. These figures relate to the German offensives only, and are broken down as follows:
Operation Hannover   = 10,000 prisoners, 250 artillery pieces.
Operation Seydlitz   = 50,000 prisoners, 170 tanks, 340 artillery pieces, 749 mortars.
Operation Whirlwind   = 17,000 prisoners, 550 tanks, 385 artillery pieces.

180 According to Russian sources, the Soviet Kalinin Front sustained 61,722 casualties (including 4,376 killed and 47,072 missing) during June and July, most of which would have occurred during the course of Operation Seydlitz. See Aleksei Isaev, *Kratkii Kurs Istorii Velikoi Otechestvennoi Voiny: Nastupleniie Marshala Shaposhnikova* [Short course in the Great Patriotic War: The Offensive of Marshal Shaposhnikov] (Moscow: 2005). During the Bolkhov Offensive (23-29 August), the Soviet Western Front sustained 34,549 casualties (12,134 killed or missing and 22,415 sick or wounded) among the 218,412 men it engaged, and lost 500 of its 700 tanks. Glantz, *Forgotten Battles of the German-Soviet War, 1941-1945. Vol. Three*, p. 129. The Soviet forces committed to the Rzhev-Sychevka Offensive (30 July-23 August) sustained 223,967 casualties (including 48,815 killed and 8,883 missing). While the main offensive had concluded, heavy local fighting continued throughout most of September during which Soviet forces endured a further 75,599 casualties (including 16,941 killed and 4,280 missing). See Ministry of Defence, TsAMO RF, Shelf 208, Drawer 2579, Folder 16, Vol. II, pp. 150-158 & 163-166, quoted in Aleksei Isaev, "Soviet Casualties during the War at the Rzhev Salient." *Modern History Magazine* (July 2012).

replacements.[181] Another from the *4. Panzerarmee* noted that the average battalion *Gefechtsstärke* of its divisions ranged from being described as "full" for the *24. Panzer Division* and *(Mot.) Infanterie Division Grossdeutschland*, to a more specific 660 men for the *11. Panzer Division*, which was also the weakest.[182] In general, the divisions with the *2. Armee* and *4. Panzerarmee* were probably in the best shape, while those of the *1. Panzerarmee* and the *17. Armee* had seen relatively little fighting after February and the constant injection of replacements since then should have brought them close to full strength.[183] Given that its formations had been heavily engaged in the fighting around Kharkov in May, and then played the leading role in the preliminary operations staged in June, one could reasonably assume that some shortages did exist within the *6. Armee*.[184] Worst off were the divisions of the *11. Armee*. By late June these were in the process of completing their reduction of the Soviet fortress of Sevastopol, during which they had sustained very heavy casualties.[185] On balance, *Heeresgruppe Süd* appears to have received 219,400 replacements between 1 March and 1 July:

181 *2. AOK. O. Qu. Anlage zum Kriegstagebuch 5 und 6, Band 55, Auffrischung Fruhjahr 1942 (20.1.-14.6.1942)*, NARA T312 Roll 1659 Frames 000279-000282.

182 *4. PzAOK. Operation II. zum Kriegstagebuch Nr. 5 (Teil III), PzAOK 4, Ia. (30.4-29.6.1942)*, NARA T313 Roll 355, Frames 8640493-8640497.

183 The casualties sustained by these two armies between 1 March and 1 July amounted to 15,712 for the *1. Panzerarmee*, and 17,510 for the *17. Armee*. See Heeresarzt 10-Day casualty reports in BA MA RW 6/556 & 6/558. For example, the *76. Infanterie Division* received 2,000 replacements on 11 March alone and was not heavily engaged until the start of Operation Blue. Jochen Loser, *Bittere Pflicht: Kampf und Untergang der 76. Berlin-Brandenburgischen Infanterie Division.* (Osnabruck: 1988), p. 163. The *125. Infanterie Division* possessed its full *Sollstärke* of 16,940 men on 21 June. Breymayer, *Das Wiesel*, p. 190. Both these divisions were subordinate to the *17. Armee*.

184 The *6. Armee* sustained 16,583 casualties in May and a further 16,641 in June. See Heeresarzt 10-Day casualty reports in BA MA RW 6/556 & 6/558. According to its divisional history, the *62. Infanterie Division* received 2,405 replacements by the end of May to compensate for the 3,121 casualties it suffered during the Battle of Kharkov. While participating in Operation Fredericus, the division's *190. Infanterie Regiment* lost one battalion and eight company commanders in a single day (22 June). H.G. Hermann, et. al., *Die 62. Infanterie Division 1938-1944, Die 62. Volksgrenadier Division 1944-1945.* (Munchen: 1968), pp. 286-287 & 290. Though possessing a *Gefechtsstärke* of 12,422 men on 11 May, the *305. Infanterie Division's* participation in Operation Wilhelm cost it dear: between 10-15 June, the division had 1,838 casualties (333 killed, 1,169 wounded, and 83 missing), of whom 1,072 were suffered by its *578. Infanterie Regiment*. Friedrich W. Hauck, *Eine Deutsche Division in Russland und Italien. 305. Infanterie Division, 1941-1945.* (Dorheim: 1975), pp. 29-31 & 50.

185 The *11. Armee* sustained 25,020 casualties during June; a further 3,590 casualties occurred in July, the majority during the first days of month. See Heeresarzt 10-Day casualty reports in BA MA RW 6/556 & 6/558. Additionally, the participating formations of the Romanian Mountain Corps suffered 8,454 casualties. Axworthy, et. al. *Third Axis, Fourth Ally*, p. 70.

excluding those sustained by the *11. Armee* during its fighting around Sevastopol in June, combat losses during this period totalled 93,641.[186]

It is clear that the manpower situation found within the *Ostheer* underwent a major improvement by the summer of 1942, an impressive achievement considering what it had endured the previous winter and the circumstances in which this improvement had occurred. What is perhaps more significant is that even this state of affairs fell far short of its potential. Typically, historians have pointed to the expansion of the Army by 22 divisions between June 1941 and June 1942 as representing a prime example of how manpower within the Third Reich was squandered or misallocated, since the personnel going into these formations should instead have been allocated towards the restoration of those that already existed.[187] But the problem was that the *Ostheer* needed both. The existing personnel strengths certainly had to be maintained, but the vastly expanded length of the front – some 3,000 kilometres including the twists and turns of the actual front lines – also needed more divisions both just to simply man it and maintain operational reserves. In fact, far worse excesses illustrating Germany's misuse of its manpower exist. Regardless of the heavy losses sustained over the previous year, the *Wehrmacht* as a whole had witnessed a net increase of about 1.1 million personnel by 1 July 1942. However, despite the urgency of defeating the Soviet Union as quickly as possible, which should have resulted in a ruthless prioritization towards meeting the needs of the Army, large consignments of personnel were still allocated to the *Luftwaffe* and the *Kriegsmarine* (see Table 4.19). Indeed, the bulk of the personnel increases enjoyed by these two services seem to have actually occurred after the beginning of January 1942, the point at which it was both obvious that Operation Barbarossa had failed and during which time the Army endured its darkest hour.[188] In addition, Hitler and other Nazi Party leaders squandered opportunities when they stubbornly resisted the idea of employing Soviet prisoners within German industry for ideological reasons. At a time when the Army was being denied access to the pool of 5.5 million able-bodied German males who had been deferred from military service, millions of Russian prisoners were left to die through executions, starvation, disease or simple neglect.[189] Suggestions from within the Army and the German Foreign Office to tap into anti-communist and nationalist sentiments

---

186 Combat losses compiled from Heeresarzt 10-Day casualty reports in BA MA RW 6/556 & 6/558. Figure on replacements drawn from totals indicated in Boog, et. al. *GSWW. Vol. VI*, pp. 865-866. Conversely, the latter notes that the overall *Abgänge* (total departures) during this period amounted to 172,500 men.

187 For example, see Tarrant, *Stalingrad*, p. 26.

188 Between 4 January and 1 July 1942, the strength of the *Luftwaffe* increased by 300,000 personnel; that of the *Kriegsmarine*, 119,000. The increases in these services during the preceding six months had been, respectively, 55,000 and 46,000. Kroener, et. al. *GSWW. Vol. V: Part One*, p. 1103.

189 Of the 3,355,499 Soviet prisoners taken during 1941, nearly 60 percent had perished by 1 February 1942, including 600,000 since the start of December. Boog, et. al. *GSWW. Vol. IV*, p. 1176.

among the populations in the East and recruit them for military purposes were likewise rejected. Only when faced with the incontrovertible disasters at both the front and within German industry during the winter of 1941-1942 did Hitler acquiesce to demands for the mass employment of Eastern workers or the official recruitment of military units, and even then only gradually.[190] German political and military authorities did a dismal job of managing available manpower resources. Ultimately this meant that the *Ostheer* was deprived of hundreds of thousands of additional replacements at a time when Germany's last real chance to avert a complete defeat was about to begin.

As Army Chief of Staff Franz Halder had already concluded in November 1941, the German Army would never again possess the strength and capabilities that it had mustered during the summer of 1941.[191] Then again, those forces had been assembled over the course of a year of relative peace and quiet, and they were supported by an armaments industry that, for all its problems, managed to produce adequate quantities of equipment at a steady pace. The contrast with the Army's circumstances a year later could not have been greater. Even though it had survived the disastrous failure of Operation Barbarossa, tremendous quantities of men and equipment had been lost. Efforts to rebuild the *Ostheer* were handicapped by the near-collapse of both the war economy and the transportation system, vacillation amongst Germany's political and military leaders regarding the future conduct of the war, and by the relentless cost of continuous operations on the Eastern Front itself. Time was also short, with only a few months to prepare before large-scale offensive operations were set to resume. In these circumstances, shortages seem hardly surprising. Instead, what is truly astonishing was the ability of Germany to regenerate its forces in such circumstances and within such a short timeframe. Prodigious quantities of men and equipment were shipped east. Although only those forces committed with *Heeresgruppe Süd* had more or less been restored to their former strengths by 1 July 1942, given the aims of the summer campaign, these were the ones that mattered the most. The formations deployed along the central and northern portions of the front were also rehabilitated to a considerable degree – at least far more than historians have usually alluded to.[192] The *Ostheer* had come a long way from the nadir of the winter. What remained to be seen was whether it was enough to achieve its ambitious, and desperate, set of objectives.

---

190 By 31 October Hitler had issued a degree ordering the mass employment of both Soviet prisoners and civilians as workers within the Reich, but for a variety of reasons its implementation was haphazard and unsystematic. Till the end of March 1942, only 166,881 Red Army prisoners (five percent of the total taken) were employed as workers within Germany. Herbert, *Hitler's Foreign Workers*, p. 98. Hitler officially authorized the establishment of the first *Ostlegionen* on 22 December 1941; even then, they were not to be deployed in groups larger than a battalion.

191 Quoted in Kroener, et. al. *GSWW. Vol. V: Part One*, p. 1022.

192 For instance, Albert Seaton noted that many of the divisions with *Heeresgruppe Nord* and *Mitte* were, "so under strength that they were little more than regiments." Seaton, *The Russo-German War, 1941-1945*, p. 270. As illustrated previously, this was clearly an exaggeration.

Table 4.1 Ten-Day Divisional Losses Reported by *3. Panzergruppe*, December 1941[1]

	Losses per decade			
	1-10.12.41	**11-20.12.41**	**21-31.12.41**	**Division Total**
1. Panzer Division	155	126	71	352
2. Panzer Division	306	358	482	1,146
36. (Mot.) Infanterie Div.	307	293	197	797
6. Panzer Division	397	203	735	1,335
7. Panzer Division	442	184	452	1,078
14. (Mot.) Infanterie Div.	270	403	206	879
Total	1,877	1,567	2,143	

1 *3. PzAOK. Quartiermeister bzw. Oberquartiermeister Abt. Kriegstagebuch O.Qu., (10 Juni-31. Dezember 1941).* BA-MA RH 21-3/611.

Table 4.2 Combat and Non-Combat Losses sustained by the *4. Armee*, December 1941 and January 1942[1]

	Losses December 1941			Losses January 1942		
	Combat	Non[2]	Total	Combat	Non[3]	Total
19. Panzer Division	622	380	1,002	896	1,079	1,975
10. (Mot.) Infantry Division	680	67	747	1,258	842	2,100
17. Infanterie Division	95	259	354	823	507	1,330
31. Infanterie Division	393	245	638	1,478	1,820	3,298
34. Infanterie Division	590	390	980	970	725	1,695
52. Infanterie Division	483	143	626	1,680	848	2,528
98. Infanterie Division	564	496	1,060	880	1,347	2,227
131. Infanterie Division	281	342	623	638	631	1,269
137. Infanterie Division	340	168	508	714	746	1,460
260. Infanterie Division	1,272	297	1,569	641	673	1,314
263. Infanterie Division	86	528	614	2,297	822	3,119
268. Infanterie Division	1,176	378	1,554	954	1,087	2,041
Army/Corps Troops	282	4,371	4,653	835	17,671	18,506
Total	6,864	8,064	14,928	14,064	28,798	42,862

1 See *4. AOK. Oberquartiermeisterabteilung O.Qu. Anlagen zum Kriegstagebuch O.Qu.- Besondere Anordnungen fur die Versorgung, Verluste, Einsatz, Meldungen, Transportlage. Band 8 (9-31 Dezember 1941)*. BA-MA RH 20-4/889, *Band 9 (1-15 Januar 1942)*. BA-MA RH 20-4/890, *Band 10 (15-31 Januar 1942)*. BA-MA RH 20-4/891, and *Band 11 (1-14 Februar 1942)*. BA-MA RH 20-4/892. Note that for some divisions their December losses are incomplete because of a lack of reports.

2 The term 'Non' in this case refers to non-combat losses. For December, this includes only those personnel reported sick.

3 Non-combat losses for January include both those reported sick and those with frostbite sufficient to require treatment in Germany.

Table 4.3 German Army Equipment Losses on *Ostfront*, 22 June 1941 to 31 January 1942

	Total Losses 22.6.1941-31.1.1942[1]	Losses Dec 1941 & Jan 1942[2]	December/January Percentage
MG	24,362	6,686	27.4
Mortars	6,001	1,852	31.0
3.7 cm Pak	3,714	1,089	29.3
5 cm Pak	475	184	38.7
7.5 cm le. IG	1,047	346	33.0
15 cm s. IG	352	124	35.2
2 cm/3.7 cm Flak	210	87	41.4
8.8 cm Flak	17	5	29.4
10.5 cm le. FH 18	1,300	649	49.9
15 cm s. FH 18	642	288	44.8
10 cm K18	132	57	43.1
SPW	305	62	20.3
PSW	645	110	17.0
Zugmaschine	2,946	970	32.9
Trucks	39,870	11,165	28.0
Other vehicles	74,794	15,965	21.3

1   Total losses for all motor vehicles (including SPW and PSW), field artillery, infantry and anti-tank guns taken from Boog, et. al. *GSWW. Vol. IV*, pp. 1120-1122. Figures for small arms, machine-guns, mortars, and flak guns compiled from numbers listed in Hahn, *Waffen und Geheimwaffen des deutschen Heeres, 1933-1945, Band II*, p. 216-217 and the losses for these weapons during January 1942 indicated in Kroener, et. al. *GSWW. Vol. V: Part Two*, pp. 636, 668 & 670.

2   Compiled by combining December losses found in Jacobsen, (Ed.) *KTB OKW. Band I*, pp. 1115-1116, and January losses found in Boog, et. al. *GSWW. Vol. IV*, pp. 1120-1122, and Kroener, et. al. *GSWW. Vol. V: Part Two*, pp. 636, 668 & 670.

Table 4.4 Condition of *2. Panzerarmee*, 15 December 1941[1]

	Number of Combat Battalions	Average Gefechtsstärke	Operational Artillery	
			10.5 cm	15 cm
31. Infanterie Div.	9	71	38	8
131. Infanterie Div.	9	102	26	8
112. Infanterie Div.	7	130	26	2
167. Infanterie Div.	9	150	29	4
296. Infanterie Div.	9	235	36	9
10. (Mot.) Inf. Div.	5	180	8	3
25. (Mot.) Inf. Div.	7	120	16	3
17. Panzer Division	4	270	9	12
18. Panzer Division	4	300	13	6
3. Panzer Division	5	206	16	9
4. Panzer Division	4	350	10	8
(Mot.) Inf. Regt. 'GD'	3	235	5	1

1 *Ia Anlagen zum Kriegstagebuch Nr.1 (Band Dezember 1941) des Oberkommando der Heeresgruppe Mitte (1-16. Dezember 1941),* NARA T311 Roll 288, Frames 000787-000789.

Table 4.5 Comparison of the Strength of the Soviet Armed Forces, 22 June 1941 and 1 May 1942

	Strength 22.6.1941[1]	Strength 1.5.1942[2]
Personnel	**5,700,000**	**10,936,631**
Formations		
Armies	20	63
Mech./Tank Corps	29	14
Rifle Divisions	196	426
Tank Divisions	61	2
Motorised Divisions	31	6
Cavalry Divisions	13	60
Tank Brigades	-	191
Rifle Brigades	5	148
Mot. Rifle Brigades	-	17
Airborne Brigades	16	36
Artillery & Mortars	112,800	107,795
Rocket launchers	-	1,544
Tanks		
Heavy	500	944
Medium (T-34)	900	1,956
Light & Specialized	21,200	6,395
Total	22,600	9,325
Aircraft		
Fighters	11,500	7,634
Ground-Attack	100	553
Bombers	8,400	4,819
Recon	?	1,961
Total	20,000	14,967
Motor Vehicles	273,000	364,029

1 Glantz, *Stumbling Colossus*, pp. 11 & 107, and Mawdsley, *Thunder in the East*, p. 47.

2 Glantz, *To the Gates of Stalingrad*, p. 47.

Table 4.6 Strength and Deployment of the Soviet Armed Forces, 1 May 1942[1]

	Deployments			
	Russo-German Front	STAVKA Reserves	Internal/Far East	Total
Personnel	5,677,915	218,276	5,040,440	10,936,631
Artillery & Mortars	71,476	2,591	33,728	107,795
Rocket launchers	1,339	53	152	1,544
Tanks				
Heavy	660	47	237	944
Medium (T-34)	1,291	88	577	1,956
Light	2,025	42	4,299	6,366
Specialized	44	-	15	59
Grand Total	4,020	177	5,128	9,325
Aircraft				
Fighters	3,468	93	4,073	7,634
Ground-Attack	331	95	127	553
Bombers	1,170	59	3,590	4,819
Recon	544	-	1,417	1,961
Grand Total	5,513	247	9,207	14,967
Motor Vehicles	239,227	3,765	121,037	364,029
Tractors	22,250	214	17,443	39,907
Horses	751,399	49,261	474,663	1,275,323

1 Glantz, *To the Gates of Stalingrad*, p. 47.

Table 4.7 Comparison of Axis Formations deployed on *Ostfront* (including Finland), June 1941 and June 1942

	22.6.1941[1]	24.6.1942[2]	24.6.1942 (excl. Finland)
Divisions			
Panzer	19	19	19
Mot. Infantry	13	14	14
Cavalry	1	–	–
Mountain	5	7	3
Light Infantry	4	6	6
Infantry	100	127	125
Axis Divisions	33	39	26
Combat Division Total	175	212	193
German Security Divisions	9	11	11
Axis Security Divisions	–	4	4
Division Grand Total	184	227	208
Brigades			
German	6	4	4
Axis	12	4	–

1 Axis formations include two Slovak infantry divisions and one mobile brigade, 15 Romanian divisions and eight brigades, and 16 Finnish divisions and three brigades.

2 Axis formations include one Slovak security division and one mobile division, 12 Romanian divisions, six Italian divisions, seven Hungarian combat and three security divisions, and 13 Finnish divisions and four brigades.

Table 4.8 Monthly Raw Material Requirements of the *Wehrmacht* versus Actual Allocation, First Quarter of 1942 (tons)[1]

	Monthly Requirements	Actual Allocation	Shortage (%)
Iron	1,570,000	1,143,000	27.2
Copper	34,450	12,000	65.2
Aluminium	44,700	26,500	40.8
Pewter	1,500	650	56.7
Lead	22,150	11,000	50.4
Chrome	3,050	1,850	39.4
Rubber	6,500	4,450	31.6

1 Reinhardt, *Die Wende vor Moskau*, p. 257.

Table 4.9 Monthly Production of Army Equipment, 1941-1942[1]

	June 1941	Sept. 1941	Dec. 1941	April 1942
Rifles	123,959	106,647	76,565	97,606
MG	6,620	5,733	3,424	5,960
Mortars	1,073	413	207	1,276
3.7 cm/5 cm Pak	372	255	222	450
Infantry Guns	163	89	72	160
Light Artillery	89	79	21	106
Heavy Artillery	50	45	15	110
Motor Vehicles	9,917	9,998	9,004	10,060

1 Kroener, et. al. *GSWW. Vol. V: Part One*, pp. 725-727 & 742-743, and Kroener, et. al. *GSWW. Vol. V: Part Two*, pp. 668-679 & 684.

Table 4.10 German Armaments Production versus Total Losses on All Fronts, 1 June 1941 to 1 July 1942

	Army Stock 1.6.1941	Production 1.6.41-1.7.42[1]	Total Losses 1.6.41-1.7.42[2]	Increase/ Decrease	Change in Stock (%)
Rifles	4,372,800	1,249,158	127,402	+1,121,756	+25.7
MG	203,250	71,440	39,851	+31,589	+15.5
Mortars	27,896	11,312	9,897	+1,415	+5.0
2 cm Flak	2,153	1,462[3]	402	+1,060	+49.2
Light Pak[4]	17,354	4,327	6,586	-2,259	-13.0
7.5 cm Pak	–	1,743	124	+1,619	
Infantry Guns	5,043	1,688	2,195	-507	-10.0
10.5 cm &15 cm FH	10,875	1,296	2,744	-1,448	-13.3

1 Figure compiled from monthly production statistics found in Kroener, et. al. *GSWW. Vol. V: Part One*, pp. 725-727 & 742-743, and Kroener, et. al. *GSWW. Vol. V: Part Two*, pp. 668-679.

2 Compiled from Ibid, pp. 668-679 and Jacobsen, (Ed.) *KTB OKW. Band I*, pp. 1115-1118.

3 Note that this only represents Army production for the period January to June 1942. See Kroener, et. al. *GSWW. Vol. V: Part Two*, p. 636. A further 3,690 2 cm Flak were manufactured between June and December 1941, but what portion of these were allotted to the Army is unknown. Kroener, et. al. *GSWW. Vol. V: Part One*, pp. 725-727.

4 This figure refers to the combined total of available 3.7 cm, 4.7 cm, and 5 cm Pak.

Table 4.11 Estimated Material Requirements of the German Army, 1 July 1942

	Army Stock 1.7.1942[1]	Army Requirements 1.7.1942[2]	Ersatzheer Requirements	Total Army Requirements	Surplus/ Deficit
MG	218,264	116,128	15,144	131,272	+86,992
Mortars	29,800	23,909	1,002	24,911	+4,889
Infantry Guns	4,571	4,195	728	4,923	-352
Pak	15,202	11,938	1,860	13,798	+1,404
2 cm Flak	3,712	1,557	?	1,557	+2,155
10.5 cm FH	6,317	6,348	?	6,348	-31
15 cm FH	3,410	2,524	?	2,524	+886

1 Kroener, et. al. *GSWW. Vol. V: Part Two*, p. 700.

2 These figures have been derived by using the estimated divisional equipment requirements of the German Army on 1 June 1941 (see pages 99-102) as a baseline. From this total have been deducted the equipment of those formations that were converted (*5., 8.,* and *28. Infanterie Divisions, 1. Kavallerie Division, 99. Leichte Infanterie Division, 201.* and *203. Ersatz Brigades,* and *(Motorisierte) Infanterie Regiment Grossdeutschland*), disbanded (*161.* and *239. Infanterie Divisions*), or upgraded for frontline service (*81., 82., 83., 88., 205., 208., 211., 212., 215., 216., 218., 223., 225., 227., 246., 305., 323., 336., 340.,* and *342. Infanterie Divisions*). This amounted to 14,775 machine-guns, 1,926 5 cm and 617 8.1 cm mortars, 1,302 Pak, 414 light and 28 heavy infantry guns, 57 2 cm Flak, and 916 10.5 cm and 252 15 cm field howitzers. The revised equipment requirements of the converted or upgraded formations listed above were then added together with those divisions that had been newly created between 1 July 1941 and 1 July 1942. Altogether, the material needs of these divisions were:

24,257 MG	138 s. IG	64 Mountain guns	36 8.8 cm Flak
3,212 5 cm GrW	1,878 Pak	16 10 cm K	
2,314 8.1 cm GrW	1,140 10.5 cm FH	225 15 cm NbW	
570 le. IG	416 15 cm FH	203 2 cm Flak	

These revised requirements were then added to the remaining baseline figure to establish the estimate illustrated in the table. For the specific divisional requirements of the formations modified or created by 1 July 1942, see *Kriegsgliederung des Feldheeres. Stand: 15. Okt. 1942 bis Sommer 1943, Band II.* NARA T78 Roll 406.

Table 4.12 Estimated German Tank Strength on the *Ostfront*, 1 January 1942

	Initial Complement[1]	Replacements to 30.12.1941[2]	Reinforce-ments to 30.12.1941[3]	Total	Losses by 30.12.1941[4]	Remaining Total
Pz I	337	12	–	349	428	-79[5]
Pz II	890	38	163	1,091	424	667
Pz 35/38(t)	780	108	–	888	796	92
Pz III	973	277	281	1,581	660	921
Pz IV	439	80	60	579	348	231
Befelpz.	225	7	18	250	79	171
StuG	259	12	105	376	104	272
Total	3,903	534	627	5,114	2,839	2,354

1   For tank strengths, see Jentz, *Panzertruppen, Vol. One*, pp. 193 & 206. Number of StuG based upon authorized strengths of assault gun battalions and those attached to divisions.

2   See June to December 1941 allocations, Boog, et. al. *GSWW. Vol. IV*, pp. 1120-1122.

3   These included the *2.* and *5. Panzer Divisions* and the *203. Panzer Regiment*. For their strengths upon arrival in the East, see Jentz, *Panzertruppen, Vol. One*, p. 212. Also included are the *177., 189., 202., 244.*, and *245. Sturmgeschütz Abteilung*, each of which should have possessed a full complement of 21 StuG III.

4   Losses from June to December 1941 in Boog, et. al. *GSWW. Vol. IV*, pp. 1120-1122.

5   The reason for this discrepancy is unclear but the figure given for losses may include lost self-propelled guns mounted on Pz I chassis. There also exists the possibility that the panzer divisions may have possessed more Pz I than were actually reported.

Table 4.13 Overall Development of German Armoured Strength by 1 July 1942

	Stock 1.7.1941[1]	Total Losses June 1941 to June 1942[2]	New Production July 1941 to June 1942[3]	Estimated Stock	Actual Stock 1 July 1942[4]
Pz I	1,122	506	15	631	692
Pz II	1,219	633	440	1,026	1,021
Pz 35/38(t)	1,042	995	553	600	471
Pz III	1,562	1,570	2,364	2,356	2,604
Pz IV	651	556	654	749	723
Tiger	–	–	1	1	1
Befelpz.	335	172	45	208	266
StuG	433	235	563	761	780
Sfl. Pak	–	–	293	293	306
Total	6,354	4,667	4,928	6,625	6,864

1 Hahn, *Waffen und Geheimwaffen des deutschen Heeres, 1933-1945, Band II*, p. 211. This figure does not include 38 self-propelled heavy infantry guns (15 cm s.IG mounted on a Pz I chassis) and 202 Panzerjager I self-propelled anti-tank guns (Czech 4.7 cm Pak on a Pz I chassis). Of the latter, at least 162 were deployed in Africa and Russia during the summer of 1941. Both vehicles were produced in small numbers in 1940-1941. See Senger und Etterlin, *German Tanks of World War II*, p. 23.

2 Compiled from panzer losses of all types noted in Jentz, *Panzertruppen, Vol. One*, pp. 254-271, and StuG losses from Müller-Hillebrand, "German Tank Strength and Loss Statistics.", p. 27. Müller-Hillebrand cites a lower total of 4,081 armoured vehicles lost for this same period.

3 Composite of panzer production of all types found in Jentz, *Panzertruppen, Vol. One*, pp. 254-271, and StuG and self-propelled anti-tank gun production from Müller-Hillebrand, "German Tank Strength and Loss Statistics", p. 28.

4 See panzer inventories in Jentz, *Panzertruppen, Vol. One*, pp. 254-271, and StuG and self-propelled anti-tank gun holdings listed in Müller-Hillebrand, "German Tank Strength and Loss Statistics", p. 26. Note that the holdings listed here include 122 Pz III armed with 3.7 cm guns that had been pulled from frontline service and regulated to training duties, or were slated for decommissioning or conversion. No overt reason could be found explaining the differences between the estimated and actual stocks, but one possibility is that vehicles previously written-off were actually rebuilt and kept on strength. The figures found in Jentz indicate that 948 tanks (306 Pz I, 99 Pz II, 195 Pz 35/38t, 195 Pz III, 92 Pz IV and 61 command tanks) were rebuilt in Germany and available for reissue between June 1941 and July 1942, but how these have been factored into various strength returns could not be ascertained.

Table 4.14 German Armour Requirements for New Formations, Replacements Dispatched to North Africa, and Allotments to Axis Allies, 1 July 1941 to 30 June 1942[1]

	Pz I	Pz II	Pz 38t	Pz III	Pz IV	Befpz.	StuG	Total
2. Panzer Division	–	63	–	105	20	6	–	194
5. Panzer Division	–	55	–	105	20	6	–	186
22. Panzer Division	–	60	114	–	20	–	–	194
23. Panzer Division	–	34	–	112	32	3	–	181
24. Panzer Division	–	32	–	111	32	7	–	182
203. Panzer Regiment	–	45	–	71	20	6	–	142
Mot. ID Grossdeutschland	–	12	–	2	30	1	21	66
6. & 10. Pz Div. (rebuilding)	–	–	–	77	–	–	–	77
103. Pz Btl. (3. Mot. ID)	–	10	–	35	8	1	–	54
116. Pz Btl. (16. Mot. ID)	–	10	–	35	8	1	–	54
129. Pz Btl. (29. Mot. ID)	–	12	–	36	8	2	–	58
160. Pz Btl. (60. Mot. ID)	–	17	–	35	4	1	–	57
1. SS-Pz Btl. (SS-Div. LSSAH)	–	12	–	32	–	1	–	45
2. SS-Pz Btl. (SS-Div. Das Reich)	–	10	–	35	–	–	–	45
3. SS-Pz Btl. (SS-Div. Totenkopf)	–	6	–	36	10	1	–	53
5. SS-Pz Btl. (SS-Div. Wiking)	–	12	–	36	4	1	–	53
Seven StuG Btls.[2]	–	–	–	–	–	–	147	147
Pz Kp./Fuhrer Begleit Btl.	–	5	–	17	–	–	–	22
Pz Kp./Regt. Hermann Göring	–	–	–	12	–	–	–	12
Replacements to Africa 1.6.1941-30.6.1942	–	22	–	298	49	–	–	369
Deliveries to Axis Allies[3]	8	–	128	10	32	6	–	184
Totals	8	417	242	1,200	297	43	168	2,375

1 Figures are derived from Jentz, *Panzertruppen, Vol. One*, pp. 212-220 & 239.

2 These were the *177., 189., 202., 209., 244., 245.*, and *249. Sturmgeschütz Abteilung*, each equipped with 21 StuG.

3 Of these, six command tanks, eight Pz I, ten Pz III, 32 Pz IV, and 102 Pz 38(t) were delivered to the Hungarians, and 26 Pz 38(t) sold to Romania.

Table 4.15 Authorized versus Actual Strength of the Panzer Divisions with
Heeresgruppe Süd, 1 July 1942[1]

	Pz II		Pz III		Pz IV		Befelpz.		Total		% of Soll
	Soll	Ist	Soll	Ist	Soll	Ist	Soll	Ist	Soll	Ist	
3. PD	74	25	106	106	42	33	8	-	230	164	71
9. PD	74	22	106	99	42	21	8	2	230	144	63
11. PD	74	15	106	124	42	13	8	3	230	155	67
13. PD	74	15	106	71	42	12	8	5	230	103	45
14. PD	74	14	106	60	42	24	8	4	230	102	44
16. PD	74	13	106	57	42	27	8	3	230	100	43
22. PD*	51	39	71	13	28	30	6	-	156	82	53
23. PD	74	27	106	84	42	27	8	-	230	138	60
24. PD	74	32	106	110	42	32	8	7	230	181	79

* Plus 140 Pz 38(t).

1 *Iststärke* taken from Jentz, *Panzertruppen, Vol. One,* pp. 236-239. Note that the *Iststärke* figures given for the *22. Panzer Division* includes its *III./204. Panzer Regiment* that was detached from the division at this time. For the figures given as *Sollstärke*, see Battistelli, *Panzer Divisions*, pp. 19 & 64.

Table 4.16 Estimated German Armour Distribution and Surplus, 1 July 1942

	Stock 1 July 1942[1]	Ersatzheer/ Africa/Other[2]	Ostfront (Est.) 1 July 1942[3]	Remaining Available
Pz I	692	460	–	232
Pz II	1,021	189	410	422
Pz 38t	471	–	322	149
Pz III	2,604	713	1,271	620
Pz IV	723	177	369	177
Tiger	1	1	–	–
Befelpz.	266	10	65	191
StuG	780	63	399	318
Total	6,558	1,613	2,836	2,109

1 Composite of panzer production of all types found in Jentz, *Panzertruppen, Vol. One*, pp. 254-271, and StuG production from Müller-Hillebrand, "German Tank Strength and Loss Statistics", p. 28.

2 This includes 363 panzers that were with the *Afrika Korps* on 25 May 1942, 122 Pz III armed with 3.7 cm guns that had been withdrawn from frontline service, and 226 tanks that equipped various panzer formations then stationed in France (including the *6.* and *10. Panzer Divisions*, the *1.*, *2.* and *3. SS-Panzer Battalions*, and one company each from the *Fuhrer Begleit Battalion* and *Flak Regiment General Göring*). Jentz, *Panzertruppen, Vol. One*, pp. 178, 214-220, & 262. Also included are 901 panzers and StuG that are estimated to have been with the *Ersatzheer* at this time. The single Tiger tank was a prototype produced in June 1942.

3 See Appendix Six.

Table 4.17 Personnel Shortages among Divisions with *Heeresgruppe Nord*, 1 April 1942[1]

1. ID	3,503	93. ID*	895	227. ID*	3,816
5. le. ID	4,732	96. ID*	3,044	250. ID	3,183
8. le. ID	3,630	121. ID*	2,617	254. ID	5,838
11. ID	5,582	122. ID*	1,058	269. ID	5,074
12. ID	3,486	123. ID*	5,188	290. ID	6,295
18. Mot. ID	4,131	126. ID	5,102	291. ID	4,461
21. ID	4,069	212. ID*	1,020	329. ID	3,025
30. ID	4,221	215. ID	4,391	8. Pz Div.	3,748
32. ID	3,731	217. ID*	392	SS-Pol. Div.	3,379
58. ID*	1,391	218. ID*	1,497	SS-Totenkopf	6,800
61. ID	2,757	223. ID*	1,737		
81. ID	5,567	225. ID	4,676		

*Incomplete figure. Reports of some divisional units are missing.

1 *Heeresgruppe Nord. Abt. IIa/IIb., Tatigkeitsberichte zum Kriegstagebuch vom 1.4.42 – 31.12.42. Dazu: Anlagenband 1. und 2.* NARA T311 Roll 105, Frames 7139513-7139514. Note that many of the figures given here are incomplete because of a lack of reports from some divisional components, and that figures for the *12. Panzer Division* and *20. (Mot.) Infanterie Division* are lacking entirely.

Table 4.18 Personnel Shortages within the Divisions of *Heeresgruppe Nord*, 1 April and 1 July 1942

Division	Shortage 1 April 1942[1]	Shortage 1 July 1942[2]	Difference	Battalions Disbanded by 1 July 1942[3]	during July
1. ID	3,503	1,890	-1,613	3	None
5. le. ID	4,732	3,519	-1,213	None	None
8. le. ID	3,630	4,268	+638	None	None
11. ID	5,582	715	-4,867	3 (2 inf./1 rec.)	None
12. ID	3,486	2,761	-725	None	None
21. ID	4,069	789	-3,280	3	None
30. ID	4,221	3,717	-504	None	None
32. ID	3,731	1,437	-2,294	None	None
58. ID	1,391*	1,968	?	None	3
61. ID	2,757	1,120	-1,637	3 (2 inf./1 rec.)	1
81. ID	5,567	2,797	-2,770	3	None
93. ID	895*	1,268	?	1	None
121. ID	2,617*	1,376	?	1	2
122. ID	1,058*	1,998	?	4 (3 inf./1 rec.)	None
123. ID	5,188*	2,934	?	None	None
126. ID	5,102	3,286	-1,816	1 (1 rec.)	None
212. ID	1,020*	22	?	2	None
215. ID	4,391	2,057	-2,334	1	1
217. ID	392*	520	?	None	None
218. ID	1,497*	1,636	?	1	1
223. ID	1,737*	1,649	?	2	None
225. ID	4,676	3,247	-1,429	None	None
227. ID	3,816*	1,528	?	2	None
250. ID	3,183	?	?	Unknown	Unknown
254. ID	5,838	3,840	-1,998	None	None
269. ID	5,074	1,130	-3,944	4 (3 inf./1 rec.)	None
290. ID	6,295	3,591	-2,704	None	None
291. ID	4,461	949	-3,512	None	None
329. ID	3,025	4,062	+1,037	Unknown	Unknown
8. PD	3,748	1,783	-1,965	None	None
18. (Mot.) ID	4,131	2,296	-1,835	None	None
20. (Mot.) ID	?	1,771	?	None	None
SS-Pol. Div.	3,379	5,477	+2,098	None	None
SS-Div. 'Totenkopf'	6,800	7,053	+253	Unknown	Unknown

1 *Heeresgruppe Nord. Abt. IIa/IIb., Tatigkeitsberichte zum Kriegstagebuch vom 1.4.42 – 31.12.42. Dazu: Anlagenband 1. und 2.* NARA T311 Roll 105, Frames 7139513-7139514.

2 *Heeresgruppe Nord. Abt. IIa/IIb, Anlagenband 1 zu den Tatigkeitsberichten zu KTB vom 1.4.42-31.12.42.* NARA T311 Roll 105, Frame 7139749.

3 What battalions were disbanded has been determined through an examination of the relevant divisional and regimental histories detailed on the website "Lexikon der Wehrmacht" found at http://lexikon-der-wehrmacht.de/ and the orders of battle in *Kriegsgliederung des Feldheeres. Stand: 15. Okt. 1942 bis Sommer 1943, Band II.* NARA T78 Roll 406.

Table 4.19 Estimated Personnel Changes within the *Wehrmacht*, June 1941 to July 1942[1]

	Strength 15 June 1941	Strength 1 July 1942	Increase	(%)
Army	5,200,000	5,750,000	550,000	(11)
Navy	404,000	569,000	165,000	(41)
Luftwaffe	1,545,000	1,900,000	355,000	(23)
Waffen-SS	160,000	190,000	30,000	(19)
Total	7,309,000	8,409,000	1,100,000	(15)

1 Boog, et. al. *GSWW. Vol. IV*, p. 1176.

5

Resurgence. The Ostheer between June and November 1942

For whenever the anger of divine spirits harms someone it first does this: it steals away his mind and good sense, and turns his thought to foolishness, so that he should know nothing of his mistakes.

Oration Against Leocrates
Lycurgus of Athens (330 BCE)

When the first stage of Operation Blue commenced during the early morning of 28 June, an observer may easily have concluded that the German Army had indeed regained the strength and capabilities it had employed to such devastating effect the previous summer. A total of 72 German and 30 Axis divisions, equipped with at least 1,934 tanks and assault guns and supported by approximately 1,700 combat aircraft, were assembled.[1] The German armies committed to the offensive boasted an impressive *Iststärke* of at least 1,210,861 men, and were backed by 159,426 Romanian and tens of thousands of Hungarian, Italian, and Slovak troops.[2] Spearheaded by its *XLVIII. Panzer Korps* and lavishly supported by the *Luftwaffe*, the *4. Panzerarmee* smashed through Soviet defences and advanced 48 kilometres on the first day.

---

1   For German armoured strengths, see Appendix Six. Estimates regarding German air strength tend to vary. According to Boog, et. al. *GSWW. Vol. VI*, p. 965, on 20 June *Luftflotte 4* had mustered 1,593 aircraft, of which 1,155 were operational. Hayward, *Stopped at Stalingrad*, p. 129, pegs total German air strength at 1,610 planes, while Bergstrom, *Stalingrad: The Air Battle, 1942 through January 1943*, p. 49, cites 1,200 operational aircraft out of the 1,700 assembled. However, according to figures compiled by this author, the air units present with *Luftflotte 4* possessed an actual total of 2,035 aircraft of all types by 1 July. For specific air unit strengths and deployment, see *Flugzeugbestand und Bewegungsmeldungen* at the website "The Luftwaffe, 1933-1945" found at www.ww2.dk

2   The individual army personnel *Iststärke* for 1 July break down as follows:

2. Armee	280,482	1. Panzerarmee	226,688
6. Armee	317,896	4. Panzerarmee	85,643
11. Armee	164,648	Total	1,210,861
17. Armee	135,504		

Though delayed by heavy rains, when the *6. Armee* began its attack on 30 June it too brushed aside Soviet resistance and pushed 32 kilometres into the hinterland.[3] Despite offering fierce resistance and staging multiple counterattacks, the response of the Red Army was marred by poor co-ordination and, as a result, its front in this sector soon collapsed. By 5 July the *XLVIII. Panzer Korps* had already gained a number of bridge-heads across the Don River, and on the following day it captured the city of Voronezh. On 9 July both the *4. Panzerarmee* and *6. Armee* wheeled to the southeast and the first phase of Operation Blue was over. Two Soviet armies had been demolished, and German claims of enemy losses until 8 July included 73,000 prisoners, and the destruction or capture of 1,200 tanks and 1,200 artillery pieces. Simultaneously, the *Luftwaffe* claimed to have shot down 540 Soviet aircraft.[4] Victories elsewhere along the front added to German euphoria. The Soviet fortress at Sevastopol was finally declared secure on 4 July, resulting in the capture of a further 95,000 prisoners and 467 artillery pieces. In the sector of the *2. Panzerarmee*, the Soviet Zhizdra-Bolkov Operation was petering out after having made only miniscule gains for the cost of 289 tanks. In Operation Seydlitz, the converging pincers of the *9. Armee* met outside the town of Belyi on 5 July, trapping and eventually destroying the entire Soviet 39th Army. Near Leningrad, another 48,000 Soviet prisoners were taken by 28 June as the last embers of the Soviet 2nd Shock Army, completely cut off around Liuban since 31 May, were gradually extinguished.[5] In the series of victories it had achieved since the start of May, the *Ostheer* destroyed eight Soviet armies, badly damaged a number of others, and claimed to have taken an estimated 660,500 prisoners.[6] Equals portions of relief and elation swept the ranks of Germany's leaders and Hitler confidently declared, "The Russian is finished!"[7] Despite all the trials and hardships of the winter, the German Army seemed set to finish what it had started the year before.

Note that this does not include personnel under the direct command of *Heeresgruppe Süd*. See BA MA RW 6/535. A further 91,805 Romanian troops were on garrison duty in the Trans-Dniester region. Alesandru Dutu, et. al. *Armata romana in al doilea razboi mondial, 1941-1945.* [Romanian Army in the Second World War, 1941-1945] (Budapest: 1999)

3   Ziemke & Bauer, *Moscow to Stalingrad*, pp. 334-336.

4   See Philippi & Heim, *Der Feldzug gegen Sowjetrussland, 1941-1945*, p. 135, and Bergstrom, *Stalingrad: The Air Battle, 1942 through January 1943*, p. 55.

5   See Hillgruber, (Ed.) *KTB OKW. Band II*, p. 50, Halder, *Kriegstagebuch. Band II*, p. 1479, and Glantz, *Forgotten Battles of the German-Soviet War, 1941-1945. Vol. Three*, pp. 130-149. Including those among the forces attempting to relieve the pocket, overall Soviet losses around Liuban between 13 May and 10 July amounted to 94,751 casualties (54,774 killed or missing and 39,977 wounded or sick). Glantz, *The Battle for Leningrad, 1941-1944*, pp. 207-208.

6   Figure compiled from various German claims found in Philippi & Heim, *Der Feldzug gegen Sowjetrussland, 1941-1945*, p. 135, Hillgruber, (Ed.) *KTB OKW. Band II*, pp. 50, 74, 391, 429, 453, & 492, Glantz, *The Battle for Leningrad, 1941-1944*, p. 207, and Glantz, *To the Gates of Stalingrad*, p. 77.

7   See Citino, *Death of the Wehrmacht*, pp.167-168 & 172.

Traditionally, historians have pointed to this stage of the campaign as being the key moment at which Operation Blue was destined to fail because the bulk of the Red Army initially opposing it was allowed to escape. They argue that the fighting was comparatively light because, rather than stand and be destroyed, the STAVKA wisely ordered its forces to conduct a strategic withdrawal, thereby luring German forces deep into the Caucasus and to the Volga River. At Stalingrad, the Soviet forces that had escaped destruction in the Donets River Basin engaged their German opposites in vicious street fighting that bled the latter white. Judiciously conserving their resources, the STAVKA then launched its own offensive that ultimately resulted in the destruction of the *6. Armee* and irrevocably turned the tide of the Eastern Front in the Soviets favour.[8]

In reality, the first phases of Operation Blue did indeed sow the seeds for the eventual failure of German designs in 1942, but not for the reasons outlined above. According to the latest scholarship, there was no STAVKA order regarding a strategic retreat and this now appears to have been created *ex post facto* by post-war Soviet historians.[9] Instead, the Soviet fought doggedly, if ineffectively, to hold back the German advance. The initial Soviet forces lined up to oppose Operation Blue, who had already received considerable reinforcements, consisted of 1,715,000 troops, equipped with 2,959 tanks and 16,500 guns and mortars. When the attack commenced, further huge quantities of reinforcements poured in: the entire 5th Tank Army, five separate tank corps, 23 rifle divisions, and two brigades by 3 July, another 20 rifle divisions on 12 July, and nine additional rifle divisions on 28 July. During August, the Soviet forces deployed along the Stalingrad axis received another three tank corps, 37 rifle divisions and two tank brigades; to defend the Caucasus region, officials there raised a further 27 rifle divisions, and 13 various brigades.[10] Additional aircraft were also dispatched by the STAVKA, and the *Luftwaffe* found its operations in southern Russia ferociously challenged throughout the campaign.[11] If this wasn't proof enough of the Soviet determination to resist, on 29 July Stalin issued his now famous Order No. 227

8   The idea of the STAVKA ordering a strategic retreat is mainly advanced in Ziemke & Bauer, *Moscow to Stalingrad*, p. 343. Most sources were less convinced that this was a deliberate act, and instead maintain that Soviet soldiers took matters into their own hands in order to avoid German efforts to encircle them. They do tend to state that the fighting was relatively light and that most Soviet soldiers managed to slip away. For example, Alan Clark states that, "Russian resistance was negligible until the Germans reached the Chir River" while Tarrant simply notes, "the majority of the Soviet forces had fallen back over the Don." Clark, *Barbarossa*, p. 212, and Tarrant, *Stalingrad*, p. 39.

9   For a thorough refutation see Glantz, *To the Gates of Stalingrad*, pp. 485-486, Citino, *Death of the Wehrmacht*, pp. 172-173, and Mawdsley, *Thunder in the East*, pp. 170-172.

10   Regarding the strength of Soviet forces on 28 June, see Glantz, *To the Gates of Stalingrad*, p. 121. Of the reinforcements the Soviets committed, these have been compiled from their mention throughout the above work.

11   Bergstrom, *Stalingrad: The Air Battle, 1942 through January 1943*, pp. 54-65.

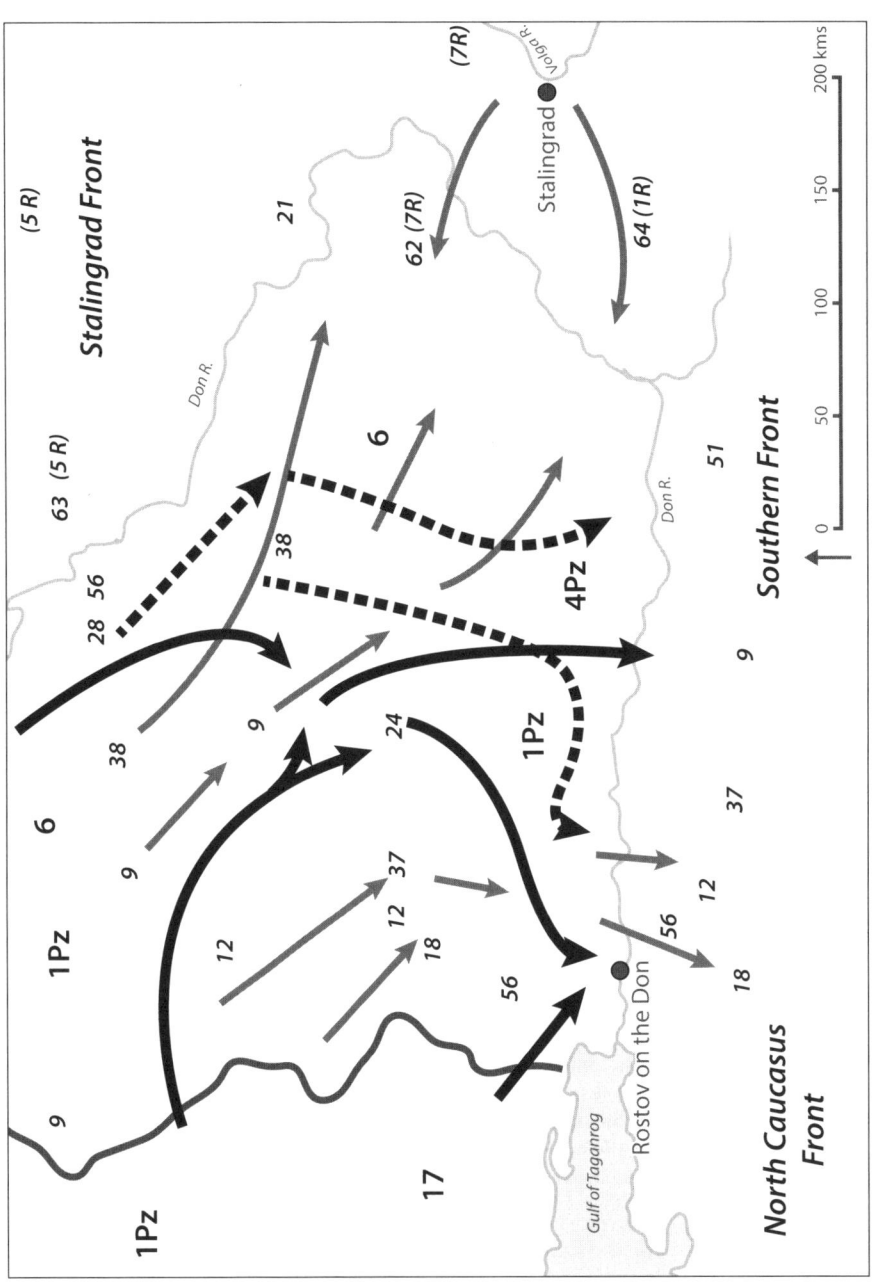

Map 5.1 Operation Blue Stage Two: Operations in the Donets River Basin, 10-24 July 1942.

that forbade any further retreats and committed the Red Army to fight for every foot of Soviet territory.[12]

For the first two phases of Operation Blue, the consequence of the Soviet response was extremely intense fighting and a steady toll of German losses. As soon as it began, Soviet tank corps persistently jabbed at the flanks of the advancing panzer spearheads. The arrival of the Soviet 5th Tank Army and other reinforcements around Voronezh led to the massing of an estimated 1,600 tanks and heralded a series of attacks against German lines east and northwest of the city, subsequently referred to as the First (4-15 July) and Second (15-26 July) Voronezh Counteroffensives.[13] Although these attacks were defeated and extremely heavy losses inflicted upon the attacking Soviet units, by 10 July casualties among many of the German formations had already reached dangerous proportions (see Table 5.1). The average battalion *Gefechtsstärke* within the *9. Panzer Division* declined from 905 men on 28 June, to 553 men by 6 July; those of the *82. Infanterie Division* went from 811 men to only 494 in the same period.[14] The decline of armour strengths was even more alarming. In only two days, the *23. Panzer Division*, fighting as the lead element of the *6. Armee*, had lost 20 tanks as *Totalausfälle*; of its initial complement of 138 panzers, only 35 remained fully operational by the end of the day on 1 July.[15] More favourable circumstances existed amongst the armoured formations of the *4. Panzerarmee*, but even here the number of operational tanks by 5 July constituted slightly less than 70 percent of the total it had available only a week before (see Table 5.2). Simultaneously struggling to control the skies of the Voronezh region while providing German ground forces with much-needed support, the air units of the *VIII. Fliegerkorps* lost 110 aircraft between 28 June and 10 July.[16]

Despite the scale of the losses already incurred, operations continued at a frenzied pace as German forces pushed south and southwest to commence the second stage of Operation Blue. Already heavily battered, Soviet armies persistently endeavoured to establish new defence lines but these successively collapsed under the weight and

---

12   For an interesting discussion of this order, see Mawdsley, *Thunder in the East*, pp. 167-169.
13   By 15 July the Soviet 5th Tank Army had sustained 7,929 casualties; of its initial complement of 641 tanks, 341 were listed as total losses with a further 158 in repair. Similarly, the strength of the supporting 16th Tank Corps declined from 181 tanks on 28 June to a mere 12 operational tanks (another 33 in repair) by 13 July. For the best study of these operations around Voronezh, see Glantz, *To the Gates of Stalingrad*, pp. 146-156.
14   *4. PzAOK. Ia., Kriegsrangliste, Verlustliste, Gefechts- und Verpflegungsstärken zum KTB. Nr. 5 (Teil III) UdSSR (28.4-31.12.1942)*, NARA T313 Roll 355, Frames 8640198-8640199.
15   Carl Wagener, "Der Vorstoss des XXXX. Panzerkorps von Charkow zum Kaukasus, July-August 1942." Part One. *Wehrwissenschaftliche Rundschau*, Vol. 5, No. 9 (September 1955), p. 399.
16   Bergstrom, *Stalingrad: The Air Battle, 1942 through January 1943*, p. 56.

speed of the German attack.[17] For the Germans, this stage of the campaign (10-24 July) nonetheless proved deeply frustrating: logistical problems kept mobile formations stalled for days on end, and disputes between Hitler, OKH, and the commanders in the field on how to proceed created a great deal of confusion in terms of command and control, further delaying the advance.[18] Although most of the Donets Basin was captured by the time this second stage ended, and German forces were now in a position to lunge toward Stalingrad and into the Caucasus, these delays hamstrung efforts to create large encirclements, and German officers at the time – and historians ever since – have concluded that most Soviet troops managed to make good their escape.

In reality, the Red Army sustained a disaster of staggering proportions. According to German claims, between 21 June and 31 July the offensive had already garnered a total of 309,998 prisoners (another 180,933 were reportedly taken during August).[19] As David Glantz has concluded, nine Soviet field armies were "either virtually destroyed or survived as mere shadows of their former selves."[20] And if the tally of prisoners had been less than expected, this "did not mean that the Soviet forces in the region escaped unscathed, ready to fight another day." Of the 1,715,000 personnel initially deployed to oppose the German offensive, total losses between 28 June and 24 July amounted to 568,347 men (370,522 killed or missing and 197,825 wounded or sick). Equipment losses included 2,436 tanks, 13,716 guns and mortars, and 783 aircraft.[21] The effect of these losses upon individual Soviet units was devastating. The 13th Guards Rifle Division, later to become famous for its participation in the fighting

---

17   According to Russian sources, the personnel strength of some of the Soviet divisions directly in the path of the German advance had already been reduced to the following by 11 July:

13th Guards Rifle Division	387 men	169th Rifle Division	786 men
15th Guards Rifle Division	325 men	175th Rifle Division	200 men
38th Rifle Division	60 men		

See Aleksei V. Isaev, *Stalingrad: Za Volgoi dlia nas zemli net* [Stalingrad – There is no land for us Beyond the Volga.] (Moscow: 2008), pp. 11-22.

18   Supply problems continued even though the *Luftwaffe* flew up to 200 tons of fuel to the panzer spearheads every day. Hayward, *Stopped at Stalingrad*, p. 142. For details concerning German decision-making and the problems therein, see Geoffrey Jukes, *Hitler's Stalingrad Decisions*. (Berkeley, CA: 1985), pp. 33-48, Buchheit, *Hitler der Feldheer*, pp. 291-296, and Boog, et. al. *GSWW. Vol. VI*, pp. 973-991.

19   This figure is based upon 10-day reports submitted by army intelligence officers to OKH and encompasses the number of prisoners taken by *Heeresgruppe Süd* (and its offshoots, *Heeresgruppe B* and *Heeresgruppe A*) during the period of 21 June and 31 July 1942. See BA-MA RH 2/2087, 2/2621, 2/2622K, 2/2633K, 2/2635K, 2/2636-2642, 2/2707 and 2/2773 quoted in "OKH 10-Day POW Reports – AOK/Ic Figures (East)" at ww2stats. com/index.html. These indicate that a total of 452,598 prisoners were in fact taken, but those taken at Sevastopol (95,000) or during Operations Wilhelm (24,800) and Fridericus II (22,800) have been deducted in order to derive the number related to Operation Blue.

20   Glantz, *To the Gates of Stalingrad*, p. 216.

21   Krivosheev, *Soviet Casualties and Combat Losses in the 20th Century*, pp. 123-124 & 261.

within Stalingrad, was reduced to a mere 387 men by 11 July and subsequently needed to be withdrawn for rebuilding. From its initial muster of 141 tanks on 28 June, the strength of the 24th Tank Corps dwindled to only 21 operational vehicles by 20 July.[22] This was not some shrewd Soviet strategy designed to lure the *Wehrmacht* deep into the Russian hinterland. Rather, as Evan Mawdsley has candidly observed: "This was a simple collapse rather than a cunning ruse."[23]

It had indeed been a magnificent operation-level German victory, but the strategic prospects of Operation Blue attaining what Germany required – the seizing of the oilfields and mineral resources of the Caucasus and the forcing of Russia to the peace table – were already fading. Many of the same problems that had proved so detrimental to the *Wehrmacht* the previous summer had already reappeared. The deployment of successive waves of reserves by the Red Army slowed and gradually blunted the strength of the advancing German armies. Incessant Soviet counterattacks around Voronezh produced a steady stream of casualties, and on 12 August the defending *2. Armee* reported that its formations were already short 55,032 men.[24] In fact, the situation in this sector was so tenuous that two of the nine panzer divisions committed to the summer offensive were tied down here for the remainder of July. Although the armoured strengths of the remaining panzer divisions were still at respectable levels (see Table 5.3), the hard campaigning in July had already produced 57,381 battlefield casualties and perhaps another 13,219 sick.[25] Losses amongst many divisions were already significant: the *111. Infanterie Division* noted 843 casualties during 11-26 July, while the *198. Infanterie Division* lost 522 personnel between 11 and 18 July. In the course of the entire month, the *24. Panzer Division* endured 1,674 casualties and the *29. (Mot.) Infanterie Division* sustained 1,553.[26] The *62. Infanterie Division* estimated that its *Kampfkraft* (fighting power) had been reduced to 60 percent by 23 July, while

22   Isaev, *Stalingrad*, pp. 11-22.
23   Mawdsley, *Thunder in the East*, p. 170.
24   *2. AOK. Ia., Kriegstagebuch Russland Teil 7 (1.8-30.9.1942)*, T312 Roll 1659, Frame 000697. On this day, the Russians commenced their Third Voronezh Counteroffensive (12-15 August). See Glantz, *Forgotten Battles of the German-Soviet War, 1941-1945. Vol. Three*, pp. 66-74, and Glantz, *To the Gates of Stalingrad*, pp. 453-456. Supported by 1,083 *Luftwaffe* sorties, during 11-17 August German claims of Soviet losses included 2,861 prisoners or deserters, 501 tanks, 31 artillery pieces, 164 machine-guns and 86 mortars. German casualties during this period totalled 165 officers and 5,555 men. *2. AOK. Ia., Kriegstagebuch Russland Teil 7 (1.8-30.9.1942)*, T312 Roll 1659, Frame 000708.
25   Combat losses derived from July figures for *Heeresgruppe Süd* indicated in Heeresarzt 10-Day Reports found in BA/MA RW 6/556 & 6/558. The estimated number of sick has been determined by deducting these combat casualties from the total number of personnel losses listed for *Heeresgruppe A* and *B* in Boog, et. al. *GSWW. Vol. VI*, p. 876
26   For the losses amongst the two infantry divisions see Musculus, *Geschichte der 111. Infanterie Division, 1940-1944*, pp. 431-433, and Graser, *Zwischen Kattegat und Kaukasus*, p. 164. For the casualties sustained by the *29. (Mot.) Infanterie Division*, see Note 51 in Glantz, *To the Gates of Stalingrad*, p. 556. The *24. Panzer Division* sustained a further 663 lightly wounded during this period who remained with their units. F.M. von

the *305. Infanterie Division* reported that its *Gefechtsstärke* had fallen from 12,422 men on 11 May to 9,462 on 11 July.[27] Such losses should have been made good by the arrival of 71,000 replacements.[28] However, as the Germans advanced into the eastern Donets region, and then towards Stalingrad and the Caucasus, they were entering a kind of transportation desert where even fewer rail lines existed than in the rest of European Russia. This low-density rail net, almost entirely single-track, proved incapable of meeting all the logistical needs of the advancing Axis forces: by October the *6. Armee* received a daily average of four supply trains even though its requirements were between eight and ten trains.[29] With Army truck columns and *Luftwaffe* transport groups already preoccupied trying to fill the logistical breaches caused by the inadequacies of the railways, the movement of personnel replacements to the formations that needed them became lengthy affairs. Upon arrival at established railheads, such as those at Kharkov or Stalino, the stark choice was to either wait for some kind of transport to become available or march the hundreds of kilometres to their intended destinations. The result was that the arrival of replacements became increasingly tardy and piecemeal the further the Germans advanced.

Yet what truly doomed the prospects of Operation Blue was Hitler's incessant dispersal of his available military strength. According to the original OKH plan (Directive No. 41), the German armies, having cleared the regions west of the Don River, were to make a concerted push on Stalingrad: only when the city and its environs had been secured was the drive into the Caucasus to begin. But Hitler, anxious to cut off Soviet armies retreating across the Don around the city of Rostov, issued new orders on 13 July. German forces now split into two separate army groups. In the north, *Heeresgruppe B* was reduced to the *2.* and *6. Armee* and the bulk of the Hungarian, Italian and Romanian forces. Whilst the remainder guarded the long flank running from Voronezh to the southeast along the Don River, its *6. Armee* would advance upon Stalingrad alone, destroy the Soviet forces accumulating there, and establish a solid defensive position. After trapping and destroying the Soviet armies around Rostov, *Heeresgruppe A*, consisting of most of the available mobile formations and now organized into the *1.* and *4. Panzerarmee* and the *17. Armee*, would immediately thrust into the Caucasus. These preliminary orders were formalized in Directive No. 45 on 23 July.[30] In effect, Hitler had scrapped the original intention to conduct the offensive in stages. Instead, he divided his forces and sent them off in two different

Senger u. Etterlin, *Die 24. Panzer Division vormals 1. Kavallerie Division, 1939-1945.* (Neckargemund: 1962), p. 101.

27   See, respectively, Hermann, et. al., *Die 62. Infanterie Division 1938-1944*, p. 294, and Hauck, *Eine Deutsche Division in Russland und Italien*, p. 50.

28   This represents the combined July arrivals for *Heeresgruppe A* and B in Boog, et. al. *GSWW. Vol. VI*, p. 876.

29   See Boog, et. al. *GSWW. Vol. VI*, pp. 985-986 & 1091-1095.

30   For the directives mentioned here, see Trevor-Roper (Ed.), *Hitler's War Directives, 1939-1945*, pp. 116-121 & 129-131.

directions, expecting that he could achieve two objectives simultaneously rather than consecutively. However, it soon became apparent to Hitler that the *6. Armee* was too weak to achieve its objectives. On 31 July the *4. Panzerarmee* had to be detached from *Heeresgruppe A* and sent backtracking to the northwest. This reorganization ultimately meant that neither army group was quite strong enough to achieve its objectives.

Concurrent with this large-scale regrouping was the removal of divisions for service elsewhere. Of the 72 German divisions initially deployed for Operation Blue, eleven of them (or 15 percent) had been withdrawn by mid-August; four divisions each were sent to *Heeresgruppe Nord* and *Mitte*, and three more were dispatched to either France or the Balkans.[31] In compensation, three Italian and four Romanian divisions had arrived and a further eight Romanian divisions were scheduled to by early September.[32] Although these Axis divisions had their uses, they certainly lacked the offensive capabilities of their German counterparts. Even more disconcerting was that the forces shifted away included four panzer or motorised divisions, or 25 percent of the mobile formations committed to the summer offensive. To be sure, the four divisions sent to *Heeresgruppe Nord* and two of those dispatched to *Heeresgruppe Mitte* played important roles there by helping to defeat powerful Soviet offensives.[33] Even so, this still dispersed scarce resources away from the main effort in southern Russia, upon which all of Germany's fortunes hinged, to what were secondary sectors. Less defensible were the decisions behind the shifting of other formations. The two panzer

---

31   Specifically, the *24., 132.* and *170. Infanterie Divisions* and the *28. Jäger Division* were sent to *Heeresgruppe Nord*; the *(Mot.) Infanterie Division Grossdeutschland*, *9.* and *11. Panzer Divisions*, and the *72. Infanterie Division* went to *Heeresgruppe Mitte*. The *SS (Mot.) Division LSSAH*, and the *22.* and *257. Infanterie Divisions* were dispatched to the West.

32   These included the Italian 'Julia', 'Cuneense' and 'Tridentina' *Alpini* Divisions, and the Romanian 2nd and 3rd Mountain, 9th Cavalry and 13th Infantry Divisions by mid-August. The Romanian 5th, 6th, 7th, 9th, 11th, 13th and 14th Infantry, 1st Cavalry and 1st Armoured Divisions began arriving in early September.

33   The four divisions dispatched to *Heeresgruppe Nord* were intended to spearhead the reduction of the Soviet armies besieged within Leningrad in an operation codenamed Northern Light. Scheduled to begin on 23 August, this was pre-empted by four days when the Red Army launched its own Second Siniavino Offensive (19 August–9 September). The forces assembled for Northern Light had to be committed to contain the assault and later to stage a counterattack (21 September-15 October) to eliminate the Soviet penetrations of the German lines. For a detailed treatment of Operation Northern Light and the Soviet attack at Siniavino, see Glantz, *The Battle for Leningrad, 1941-1944*, pp. 212-232. The *72. Infanterie Division* was initially allotted to participate in Northern Light, while the *(Mot.) Infanterie Division Grossdeutschland* was to go to France, but both had to be diverted to support *Heeresgruppe Mitte* after the Soviet Rzhev-Sychevka Offensive (30 July-23 August) came close to breaking the lines of the *9. Armee*. Details concerning this battle may be found in Ziemke & Bauer, *Moscow to Stalingrad*, pp. 400-408, Glantz, *To the Gates of Stalingrad*, pp. 456-461, and Boog, et. al. *GSWW. Vol. VI*, pp. 1001-1005.

divisions moved to *Heeresgruppe Mitte* took part in Operation Whirlwind (11-24 August), designed to eliminate the Soviet salient around the town of Sukhinichi. Although this was pre-empted by the Soviet Rzhev-Sychevka Offensive (30 July-23 August) that drew off approximately one-third of the forces assembled for the operation, the southern arm of Whirlwind was launched anyway. Lacking surprise and running straight into deeply echeloned Soviet defences backed by powerful reserves, the attack stalled after a short advance. Cancelled shortly thereafter, the operation produced little besides heavy German casualties and yet another useless dispersion of scarce resources from the main effort to the south.[34] Even more wasteful had been the dubious decisions that resulted in the dispatch of the three divisions to the West. The result of Hitler's growing concern regarding an Allied decent upon the coasts of Western Europe, this included the transfer of the *257. Infanterie Division* and the *SS (Mot.) Division LSSAH* to France, where these precious formations quietly sat out the remainder of the year waiting for an attack that never came. Stirred by a sudden premonition that the British were about to retake Crete, Hitler also moved the battle-hardened *22. Infanterie Division* to the Aegean island. Aside from having to deal with Cretan irregulars, this valuable formation languished in comfortable garrison duties until late 1944. While the number of divisions withdrawn initially may appear trivial given the scale of the fighting on the Eastern Front, for the German armies operating in southern Russia they were significant, particularly given that the outcome of the fighting was eventually decided by margins that were far narrower than most historians have appreciated.[35]

The adverse repercussions of such dispersions of German strength became readily apparent as the *6. Armee* pushed east into the great bend of the Don River in late July.

---

34   Under the command of the *2. Panzerarmee*, a total of five panzer, one motorized and six infantry divisions were still committed to Operation Whirlwind and initially possessed around 500 tanks and assault guns. At least three panzer and three infantry divisions were to constitute the northern prong under the command of the *4. Armee*, but these had to be employed to support the buckling German lines around Rzhev. From 11 August to 4 September the *2. Panzerarmee* sustained 26,894 casualties (4,571 killed, 21,264 wounded, and 1,069 missing). *2. PzAOK. Anlagen zum Kriegstagebuch, September 1942, Teil I, PzAOK 2, Ia. (1-15.9.1942)*, T313 Roll 115, Frame 7361600. The Germans claimed that by 25 August Soviet losses included 17,000 prisoners, 550 tanks, 385 artillery pieces and 204 aircraft. Hillgruber, (Ed.) *KTB OKW. Band II*, p. 639. For what little has been written about this battle and the subsequent Soviet Bolkhov counterattack (23-29 August), see Ziemke & Bauer, *Moscow to Stalingrad*, pp. 403-406, Glantz, *To the Gates of Stalingrad*, pp. 459-462, Glantz, *Forgotten Battles of the German-Soviet War, 1941-1945. Vol. Three*, pp. 114-129 and Boog, et. al. *GSWW. Vol. VI*, pp. 1003-1004. Small pieces of additional information may also be gleamed from the relative dates in Hillgruber, (Ed.) *KTB OKW. Band II*.

35   This was especially true regarding the fighting in the Caucasus. See the observations made in Citino, *Death of the Wehrmacht*, p. 243 and Showalter, *Hitler's Panzers*, p. 208. For the most detailed account of this nearly forgotten theatre, see Glantz, *Armageddon in Stalingrad*, pp. 544-595.

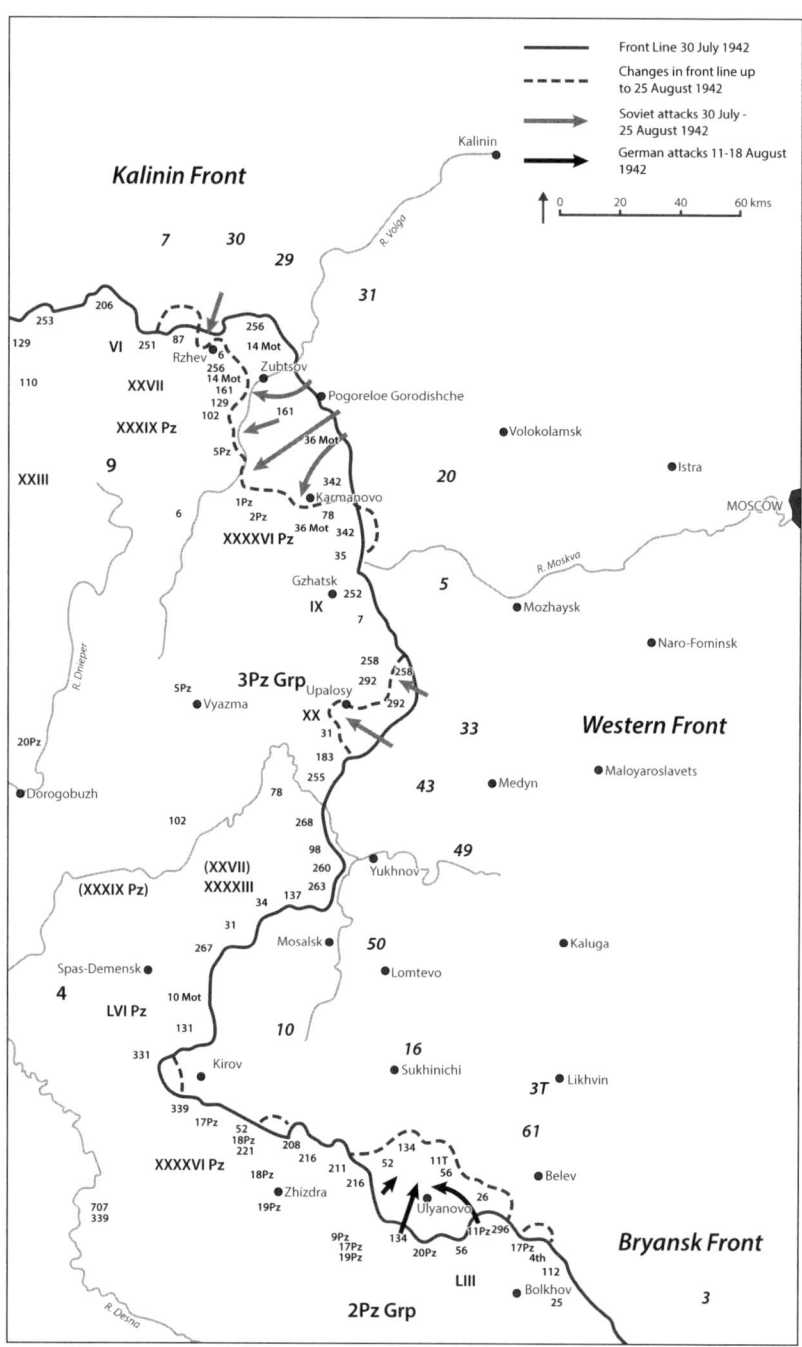

Map 5.2 Operation Whirlwind and the Soviet Offensive around Rzhev, August 1942.

Having given up a significant portion of its resources to the *4. Panzerarmee* pushing south with *Heeresgruppe A*, the advancing Germans ran headlong into two newly-arrived Soviet armies consisting of 12 full-strength rifle divisions.[36] Behind them, even more Soviet forces were assembling including two new tank armies. Organized into the recently activated Stalingrad Front, on 22 July these armies fielded 1,239 tanks against which the Germans could muster just 251 armoured vehicles.[37] Soviet forces resisted with stubborn ferocity and mounted numerous counterattacks. Lacking the resources to stage simultaneous assaults, the commander of the *6. Armee*, *General der Panzertruppen* Friedrich Paulus, was forced into a lengthy process of demolishing the opposing Soviet armies piecemeal, each time pausing to shift and regroup his own troops from one sector to the next. Even though Hitler ordered the *4. Panzerarmee* to turn around and advance on Stalingrad from the southwest, this was matched by the 37 rifle divisions, three tank corps and three tank brigades the STAVKA poured into the region as reinforcements during August. Instead of a lightning advance, progress was frustratingly slow. Not until 3 September did the Germans finally reach the western suburbs of Stalingrad, from where they could begin the direct assault upon the city in earnest.

Despite a number of anxious moments, the fighting along the approaches to Stalingrad between 22 July and 3 September had produced yet another array of German victories.[38] One Soviet army was destroyed and three more badly mauled. German claims of Soviet losses included 80,000 prisoners, 1,430 tanks, 930 artillery pieces and 703 aircraft.[39] Detailed Soviet casualties for this period have never been compiled, but many of the Red Army formations that participated were virtually destroyed.[40] Forced back within the confines of Stalingrad by 3 September, most of the formations with the Soviet 62nd and 64th Armies were reduced to similar circumstances.[41]

---

36 These were the Soviet 62nd and 64th Armies that between them fielded 609 guns, 1,760 mortars and 332 tanks. Glantz, *To the Gates of Stalingrad*, pp. 221-223. For the full order of battle of the Stalingrad Front on 23 July see Ibid, p. 541 note 77.

37 Ibid, pp. 268-269. Figure for German armour includes 202 panzers with the *16. Panzer Division* and the *3.* and *60. (Mot.) Infanterie Divisions*, as well as 37 StuG and 12 Marder with smaller units. *6. AOK. Ia/Ic Anlagenband z. KTB Nr. 13, Russland (20-24.7.1942)*, NARA T312 Roll 1685, Frames 000048 & 000102.

38 For the most comprehensive study yet produced regarding this stage of the fighting around Stalingrad, see Glantz, *To the Gates of Stalingrad*, pp. 217-395.

39 Boog, et. al. *GSWW. Vol. VI*, p. 1065-1066 & 1072.

40 Assigned to the Soviet 62nd Army, when the 184th and 196th Rifle Divisions arrived at the front on 22 July they had possessed 12,903 men and 11,428 men respectively. By 30 July the 184th Rifle Division was reduced to 1,196 men and two days later the 196th Rifle Division had already lost 2,159 killed, 2,894 wounded and 2,089 missing, for a total of 7,142 casualties. The fighting continued at a relentless pace, and on 20 August the strength of the 184th Rifle Division had dwindled to a mere 676 men. Glantz, *To the Gates of Stalingrad*, pp. 543 note 4, 545 note 43 & 561 note 107. Also Isaev, *Stalingrad*, pp. 23-79.

41 Glantz, *Armageddon in Stalingrad*, p. 85.

And yet, despite the series of tactical victories and the damage done to the Red Army, this period ultimately proved extremely detrimental to the outcome of the campaign. The shifting of *4. Panzerarmee* to the support the *6. Armee* meant that *Heeresgruppe A* had been denied the services of five German (including three mobile) and four Romanian divisions, which was the main reason why it failed to secure its objectives in the Caucasus. Even so, the struggle to clear the distant approaches to Stalingrad consumed six precious weeks during which the STAVKA was able to pour reinforcements into the region and prepare fresh reserves.[42] The effects of this were twofold. First, even as the *6. Armee* endeavoured to attack Stalingrad proper, the build-up and continuous injection of forces into the region allowed the Soviets to stage a number of counterstrokes against the long, over-extended German flank to the north. These included attacks at Serafimovich (20-28 August) along the juncture between the *6. Armee* and the newly inserted Italian Eighth Army, and at Kremenskaya (22-29 August): in both instances Russian troops managed to establish dangerous bridge-heads across the Don River that would later be used to great effect during the Soviet counteroffensive in November.[43] These attacks were followed by the First Kotuban Offensive (3-12 September), which took place between the Don and Volga Rivers just north of Stalingrad and involved 19 rifle divisions, three tank corps and five tank brigades fielding 400 tanks. Although this attack failed to breach the German defences and thereby make contact with the Soviet forces fighting in Stalingrad, it would prove to be the first of four offensives conducted in this area until late October; like the attacks at Serafimovich and Kremenskaya, these distracted German attention and resources at a time when all available forces were needed to capture Stalingrad.[44]

The second effect the steady injection of Soviet reinforcements into the Stalingrad region had was that this resulted in extremely intense and almost-continuous fighting that, in turn, produced large numbers of German casualties. As shown in Table 5.4, between 21 July and 31 August the *6. Armee* sustained 38,553 casualties and, during

---

42   On 31 August, Stalin ordered the strengthening of the strategic reserves available to STAVKA and the creation of five new reserve armies. Ibid, pp. 35-37.

43   For what little has been written of these engagements, see Glantz, *To the Gates of Stalingrad*, pp. 383-393. As Glantz has noted, "If the names of strange and remote places like Serafimovich and Kletskaia meant little to Hitler, OKH, or Army Group B in August and September, by year's end they would be rallying cries to every Soviet and curses to every German." Ibid, p. 394.

44   For the best account of the Soviet attacks north of Stalingrad, see Glantz, *Armageddon in Stalingrad*. The First Kotuban Offensive was followed by the Second (18 September-2 October), Third (9-11 October) and Fourth (20-26 October) Offensives. For the participating Soviet 1st Guards, 24th and 66th Armies, the result were 107,453 casualties (20,332 killed, 72,873 wounded, 13,518 missing and 730 other losses) during the period of 1-26 September alone. In mid-September these armies fielded 232,382 men and were supported by at least 611 artillery pieces and 1,956 mortars. Additionally, the armoured units assigned to the 1st Guards Army possessed 340 tanks on 18 September, having received 94 replacement T-34s by this point. Isaev, *Stalingrad*, pp. 181-216.

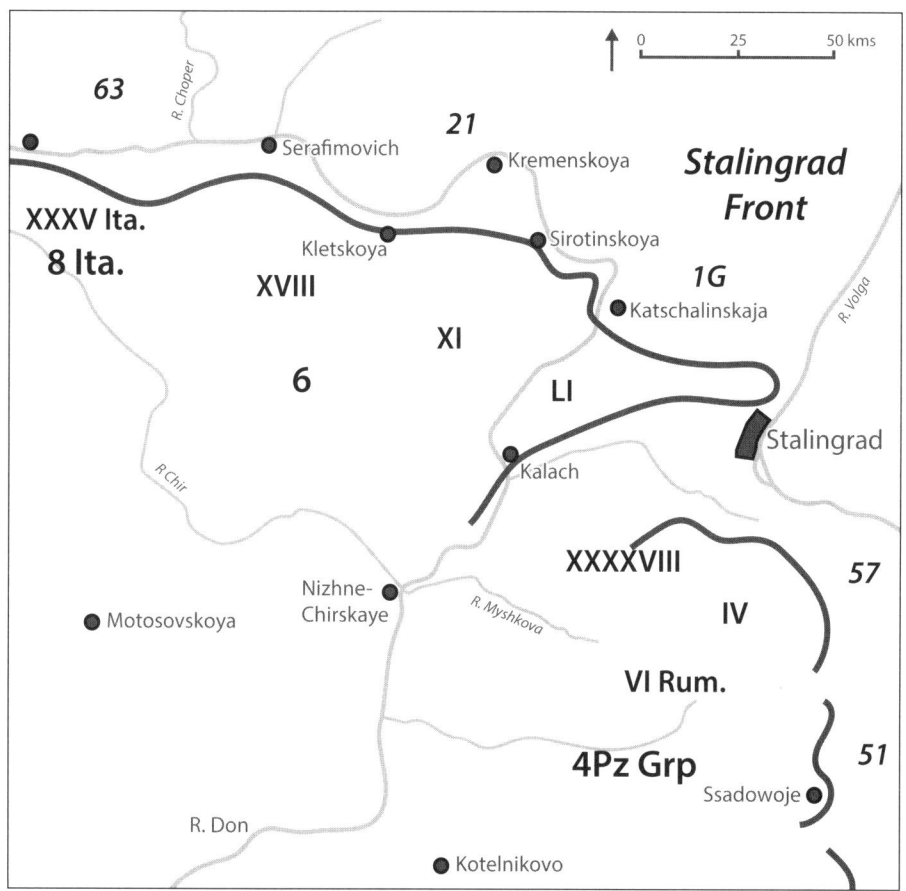

Map 5.3 The German Advance upon Stalingrad and the Soviet Bridgeheads at Serafimovich and Kremenskoya, late August 1942.

the first ten days of September, it would incur 8,695 more.[45] By 9 September its divisions were short 52,899 men (including 1,944 officers). Since the majority of these losses occurred within their combat units, especially amongst the infantry, the effect of such figures upon the divisions involved was devastating. Of the 103 infantry battalions with the 6. *Armee* on 31 August, some 73 (71 percent) possessed a *Grabenstärke* of less than 300 men each; of these, 27 (26 percent) were already categorized as being "weak" or "burnt-out" (see Table 5.5). Even these low strengths were only possible by disbanding a number of battalions and consolidating their remnants with those that remained – indeed, five of the divisions listed in the table appear to have already disbanded 10 (24 percent) of their original 42 infantry battalions.[46] Worst hit had been the *100. Jäger Division*. Its six *Jäger* battalions had dwindled to only three and the attached Croatians of the three-battalion *369. Infanterie Regiment* had to be consolidated into a single battalion. Circumstances were probably similar within the formations of the *4. Panzerarmee*, since it had sustained 11,186 casualties in the course during August.[47] Specifically, its *14. Panzer* and *29. (Mot.) Infanterie Divisions* lost 1,533 and 1,911 men respectively, and between 27 July and 15 September the supporting *94. Infanterie Division* endured 3,128 casualties.[48]

Losses such as these directly impacted the operational capabilities of the formations involved, limiting their ability to attack, defend, and how long they could sustain either. Having already endured heavy casualties and a consequential diminution of their operational abilities *before* that had even reached Stalingrad, and with persistent Soviet attacks requiring the dispersion of considerable resources to their increasingly vulnerable flanks, the Germans only real hope of capturing the city by early September was if it could be done swiftly, before the defenders organized themselves and received reinforcements. Yet when the attack upon the western suburbs commenced on 3 September the tenacity of the Soviet defenders quickly revealed that this would not be possible. The STAVKA had no intention of giving up the city. Instead, the struggle for Stalingrad would be used to draw in the maximum number of German troops who would then be worn down in a pitiless battle of attrition. Once German reserves had been consumed, a massive counterstroke would be launched against the weakly held and over-extended flanks of the German bulge protruding around Stalingrad.[49] The

---

45   Losses for this period given in the Heeresarzt 10-Day Casualty Reports indicate a slightly smaller number of casualties (35,178). See figures for *6. Armee* between 21 July and 10 September in BA-MA RW 6/556 & 6/558.

46   The particular formations referred to here are the *3. (Mot.), 113., 295., 376.* and *384. Infanterie Divisions*.

47   See August figures for *4. Panzerarmee* in Heeresarzt 10-Day Casualty Reports in BA-MA RW 6/556 & 6/558.

48   For the losses sustained by the *14. Panzer* and *29. (Mot.) Infanterie Divisions*, see Glantz, *To the Gates of Stalingrad*, p. 556 note 50.

49   The exact genealogy of Soviet planning concerning a large counterstroke around Stalingrad remains the subject of considerable historical debate, but most accounts agree that on 26 September Stalin ordered the STAVKA to beginning planning and

need to protect those flanks meant that by 12 September the Germans could commit only six divisions and elements of three more (out of the 27 divisions with *6. Armee* and the *4. Panzerarmee*) during their initial assault upon the city. In the next five weeks, only three more divisions were injected as reinforcements. By contrast, the Red Army reinforced their defending 62nd Army with nine more divisions, five tank or rifle brigades and tens of thousands of personnel replacements.[50] With their offensive capabilities already badly eroded by previous campaigning, the attacking German divisions lacked the strength to simply smash through and overwhelm the Soviet defences in a single operation. Instead, their weakened condition and the Soviet determination to resist compelled the Germans to adopt a more methodical approach, which meant a gruelling, house-by-house battle of attrition.[51]

What exacerbated these circumstances for the German forces involved was their dire lack of personnel replacements. Given the far more crucial need to safeguard the rear of the forces pushing deep into the Caucasus, one could assume that *Heeresgruppe B*, and especially its *6. Armee* should have received priority in terms of the allocation of new men. In fact, this was not the case. Although the army group sustained 30,827 casualties during July, it received only 19,400 replacements. The situation only worsened during the bitter fighting of August; as combat losses grew to 49,225 men, the number of replacements dwindled to a meagre 13,000. Remarkably, although *Heeresgruppe B* endured roughly one-third of all the casualties incurred by the entire

preparations for two major operations. These were Operation Uranus, designed to encircle the *6. Armee* within the environs of Stalingrad, and Operation Mars, which was to eliminate the German Rzhev salient. They were to be followed by the even more ambitious operations codenamed Jupiter and Saturn. See Geoffrey Roberts, *Stalin's Wars*, pp. 148-153, Glantz, *Zhukov's Greatest Defeat*, pp. 14-24, Ziemke & Bauer, *Moscow to Stalingrad*, p. 441-447, and Mawdsley, *Thunder in the East*, pp. 174-177. Also see Mark Harrison, *Soviet Planning in Peace and War, 1938-1945.* (Cambridge: 1985) and Louis Rotunda, (Ed.) *Battle for Stalingrad: The 1943 Soviet General Staff Study.* (Washington, DC: 1989).

50   Glantz, *Armageddon in Stalingrad*, pp. 102-104 & 135.
51   For German tactics regarding the reduction of Stalingrad, see Boog, et. al. *GSWW. Vol. VI*, p. 1087. The works by Glantz regarding the fighting in and around Stalingrad are the most authoritative, but other useful studies include Sabine R. Arnold, et. al. *Stalingrad: Mythos und Wirklichkeit einer Schlacht.* (Frankfurt a. Main: 1992), Jay W. Baird, "The Myth of Stalingrad." *Journal of Contemporary History*, Vol. 4, No. 3 (July 1969), pp. 187-204, Jukes, *Hitler's Stalingrad Decisions*, Chuikov, *The Battle for Stalingrad*, William Craig, *Enemy at the Gates*, Doerr, *Der Feldzug nach Stalingrad*, Frank Ellis, "10th Rifle Division of Internal Troops NKVD: Profile and Combat Performance at Stalingrad." *Journal of Slavic Military Studies*, Vol. 19, No. 3 (2006), pp. 601-618, Erickson, *The Road to Stalingrad*, Jurgen Forster, *Stalingrad: Risse im Bundnis, 1942-1943.* (Freiburg: 1975), Will Fowler, *Stalingrad: The Vital 7 Days. The Germans Last Desperate Attempt to Capture the City, October 1942.* (Staplehurst, UK: 2005), Joel Hayward, "Stalingrad: An Examination of Hitler's Decision to Airlift." *Airpower Journal*, Vol. 11, No. 1 (Spring 1997), pp. 21-38, Manfred Kehrig, *Stalingrad: Analyse und Dokumentation einer Schlacht.* (Stuttgart: 1974), Janusz Piekalkiewicz, *Stalingrad: Anatomie einer Schlacht.* (Munchen: 1977), Heinz Schroter, *Stalingrad.* (London: 1958), and Bernd Ulricht, *Stalingrad* (Munich: 2005).

Ostheer during July and August, it received only 11 percent and 14 percent, respectively, of the arriving replacements. While the allocation of replacements to the army group moderately improved during the next few months, its overall situation did not. As noted in Table 5.6, despite the fact that *Heeresgruppe B* endured the greatest proportion of the combat losses sustained by the entire *Ostheer* between July and November, it received the smallest number of replacements. The replacements that did arrive had to be spread throughout the entire army group and not simply concentrated within the *6. Armee*. For example, of the replacements that arrived during August, at least 7,589 (58 percent) were allotted to the *2. Armee* fighting around Voronezh. The remaining 5,411 men had to be parcelled out not only to the *6. Armee*, but to the *4. Panzerarmee* and the smaller German units supporting the Axis armies as well. Overall, at least 21,259 (31 percent) of the 68,100 replacements received by *Heeresgruppe B* between September and November went to *2. Armee* and the German divisions assigned to the Italian Eighth Army.[52]

The diminutive scale of the assigned personnel replacements, combined with the prolonged period of intense and costly combat in which they were engaged, steadily eroded the fighting strength of *Heeresgruppe B*, and especially its *6. Armee*, to catastrophic proportions. As illustrated in Appendix Seven, by early September the divisions constituting the army group already registered the highest average personnel shortages within the entire *Ostheer*. Divisions assigned to *Heeresgruppe Nord* were on average short 2,029 men and those with the *2. Panzerarmee* of *Heeresgruppe Mitte* lacked 2,120. In contrast, the personnel shortages of the formations with *Heeresgruppe B* already averaged 3,521. Within the latter's *6. Armee* the figure was even higher at 3,779 men per division. As heavy fighting in and around Stalingrad continued throughout the next two months, the situation only worsened. Deficiencies amongst the 22 divisions deployed there (noted in Appendix Eight) totalled an astounding 143,414 men by early November. Admittedly, the costly fighting during the summer and fall meant that large-scale personnel shortages had become endemic across the *Ostheer* by this point: *Heeresgruppe Nord* reported that on 1 November it lacked 125,909 personnel, while the 14 divisions of the *2. Armee* had a combined deficit of 54,288 men.[53] Still, shortages amongst the formations deployed around Stalingrad appear

---

52   Total number of arriving replacements derived from Boog, et. al. *GSWW. Vol. VI*, p. 866. Those consigned to the *2. Armee* have been determined by reviewing the monthly status reports of the formations under its control. See *2. AOK. Ia Anlage zum KTB Russland, Schriftwechsel, Zustandsberichte, Teil I-II (1.9-20.12.1942)*, NARA T312 Roll 1663, Frames 000001-000911. These included 4,466 replacements in September, 9,887 in October, and 6,626 in November. In addition, the *62. Infanterie Division* attached to the Italian Eighth Army received 280 replacements on 14 September 1942. Hermann, et. al. *Die 62. Infanterie Division 1938-1944*, p. 311.

53   *Heeresgruppe Nord. Abt. IIa/IIb, Anlagenband 1 zu dem Tatigkeitsberichten zum KTB vom 1.4.42-31.12.42 (April-December 1942)*, NARA T311 Roll 105, Frame 7139721. Shortages amongst the *2. Armee* have been determined by reviewing the monthly status reports of the formations under its control. See *2. AOK. Ia Anlage zum KTB Russland,*

grossly disproportionate to those in the rest of the *Ostheer*. Whereas the average deficit amounted to 2,737 men within the divisions of *Heeresgruppe Nord* and 3,878 for those of the *2. Armee*, the corresponding figures for the formations with the *6. Armee* and *4. Panzerarmee* totalled 6,519. In short, divisional personnel deficits within the latter two armies were 51 to 82 percent greater than those found elsewhere on the Eastern Front. Since their authorized personnel strengths potentially ranged from 18,724 to 13,484 men per division, this implies that in early September the formations arrayed along the Stalingrad sector lacked an average of 20 to 28 percent of their *Sollstärke*. By November, these figures had soared to between 35 and 48 percent, and in many individual cases the situation was even worse (see Table 5.7).

It has not been possible to determine why *Heeresgruppe B* was afforded such a disproportionately low priority despite its importance to the final outcome of the summer campaign. Admittedly, there was a need to refill the depleted ranks of *Heeresgruppe Nord* and *Mitte*, both of which had been neglected in the rush to prepare the forces assigned to Operation Blue. In their weakened condition, the replenishment of these army groups may reflect a concern by OKH that their sectors were on the verge of collapse, especially since these were subjected to a number of dangerous Soviet attacks throughout the summer and fall.[54] It may also mirror Hitler's insistence that their formations be prepared to undertake a series of limited offensive operations, even though all of these had been cancelled or indefinitely postponed by September.[55] Despite all the mounting difficulties, simple overconfidence may have also played a role. In their discussions with Hitler on 11-12 September, Paulus and the commander of *Heeresgruppe B*, *Generaloberst* Maximilian von Weichs, were confident that Stalingrad would be taken by the end of the month despite the weakened condition of their forces. This in turn may have lessened the apparent urgency for their

---

Schriftwechsel, Zustandsberichte, Teil I-II (1.9-20.12.1942), NARA T312 Roll 1663, Frames 000001-000911.

54   Between July and November, the army groups on the central and northern sectors of the front had to endure ten major Soviet offensive operations. Aside from those previously mentioned, these included the Second (17-24 July), Third (10-21 August), Fourth (15-16 September) and Fifth (28 November-26 December) Demyansk Operations, the Velikie-Luki Operation (20 November 1942-16 January 1943), and Operation Mars (24 November-26 December). Along with Operations Seydlitz and Whirlwind, the German forces also staged Operation *Schlingpflanze/Winkelreid* (27 September-9 October), which widened the corridor linking their forces within the Demyansk salient. For more concerning these engagements, see Ziemke & Bauer, *Moscow to Stalingrad*, and Glantz's, *Zhukov's Greatest Defeat*, *The Battle for Leningrad, 1941-1944*, and *Forgotten Battles of the German-Soviet War, 1941-1945. Vol. Three.*

55   As already noted, *Heeresgruppe Nord* was to stage Operation Northern Light to capture Leningrad, but this was preempted by a Soviet attack. In the sector of *Heeresgruppe Mitte*, Operation Whirlwind was actually a scaled down version of a more ambitious attack codenamed Orkan. This was to have been followed by Operation Derfflinger, whose goal was to eliminate the Soviet salient centered upon the town of Ostashkov. See Ziemke & Bauer, *Moscow to Stalingrad*, pp. 398-400.

replenishment. Such sentiments would have been augmented by Hitler's belief that the strength of the Red Army had been exhausted.[56] Finally, the schism that emerged between Hitler and Halder regarding the conduct of the war, which continued to mount until the dismissal of the latter on 24 September, likely increased the incredulity that Hitler expressed towards the pessimistic reports produced by OKH. Such scepticism was only reinforced by the outspoken criticism of the commander of the *Luftwaffe* forces supporting *Heeresgruppe B*, *Generaloberst* Wolfram von Richthofen, who felt that German difficulties around Stalingrad were the result of poor Army leadership and a lack of fighting spirit.[57] However, lacking specific details all that can be said with certainty is that the effect of these issues upon the actual distribution of personnel replacements was tertiary. After all, the allocation of replacements remained the purview of the Organizational Department of OKH and Hitler's direct involvement appears to have been limited to periodic general instructions.[58] Nonetheless, the skewered distribution of replacement personnel does indicate shockingly poor staff work, fault for which resides squarely upon the German General Staff and the various departments of OKH.

In the end, problematical distribution was a symptom of an even greater crisis – namely the overall lack of replacements that plagued the German Army during the second half of 1942. Total combat losses on the *Ostfront* between July and November numbered 498,786 men, but this was compensated by the arrival of 509,700 replacements. However, the records of the Organization Department of OKH indicate that the total number of departures from the *Ostheer* during this period amounted to 856,700 men, implying that 357,914 sick had to be repatriated to Germany.[59] Although the veracity of the number of sick suggested by the OKH records might be suspect because this is contradicted by other information (which also places the indicated total number of departures in doubt), it is clear from the divisional shortages noted previously that the quantity of arriving replacements were still insufficient.[60]

56 For German assessments of Soviet strength and capabilities, see Boog, et. al. *GSWW. Vol. VI*, pp. 882-903, and Hillgruber, (Ed.) *KTB OKW. Band II*, p. 592.
57 For more regarding the dismissal of Halder and the events leading up to it, see Irving, *Hitler's War*, pp. 478-44, Megargee, *Inside Hitler's High Command*, pp. 178-189 and Boog, et. al. *GSWW. Vol. VI*, pp. 1048-1059. Of Richthofen's scathing comments, see Ibid, p. 1086, and Görlitz, *Paulus and Stalingrad*, pp. 189-195.
58 Burkhart Müller-Hillebrand, "Personnel and Administration." (August 1948), NARA FMS P-005.
59 Combat losses compiled from Heeresarzt 10-Day Loss Reports found in BA-MA RW 6/556 & 6/558. Note that statistics compiled at a later date by OKW indicate a slightly higher number of combat casualties during this period (500,922). See OKW Eastern Front monthly casualty reports in BA-MA RW 6/543 & 6/544. Figures for replacements and total departures taken from Boog, et. al. *GSWW. Vol. VI*, p. 866.
60 Together with contradictory figures found elsewhere, the disproportionate number of sick versus combat casualties during some months makes this implied number of sick appear dubious. According to the summaries produced by the Organizational Department of

Given the scale and intensity of the fighting in the East some degree of personnel deficiencies within the German Army was inevitable, but the magnitude of the problem rested upon the efficient utilization of manpower resources rather than their actual availability. In this regard, Germany's military and political leaders are to blame because of their abysmal management of the situation. In response to the crisis that erupted during the winter of 1941-1942, the generous deferral qualifications that had exempted 5.5 million German males from military service were tightened and during the next three months the number of deferments declined by roughly 360,000. Through a series of rigorously applied rationalization measures, labour officials believed that at least one million German males could be released for military service.[61] Although the OKW anticipated that this change in policy would henceforth procure 100,000 to 200,000 previously deferred males per month, these hopes soon proved illusionary. Nazi Party officials at all levels of government strenuously resisted any measures that might jeopardize civilian morale, especially the drafting of workers producing consumer goods. They even stated to mobilization officers that any party members in reserved occupations were ineligible for call-up. The successive military victories in the East during the spring and summer, lavishly touted by propaganda officials who promised that this indicated the imminent defeat of the Soviet Union, created unjustified confidence within German leadership circles and the general public, which in turn reduced any sense of urgency. Even worse were the actions of Albert Speer, who had been appointed Minister of Armaments and Munitions on 8 February. A favourite of Hitler, Speer moved quickly to consolidate and then expand his powers within the Byzantine political and military hierarchy of the Third Reich. Principally this meant expanding his control over labour resources, and jealously guarding the manpower already under his authority. Exploiting concerns that the conscription of workers would threaten armaments production, Speer used his

---

OKH, *Heeresgruppe A* had a total *Abgange* of 158,300 men between 1 August and 31 October. See Ibid, p. 866. Deducting the combat losses of the Heeresarzt 10-Day Loss Reports for this army group (totaling 52,087) found in BA-MA RW 6/556 & 6/558, this leaves a difference of 106,213 who are presumed to have been sick personnel transferred back to Germany. However, according to Hillgruber, (Ed.) *KTB OKW. Band II*, p. 1011, the actual number of sick recorded in the army group war diary for the period between 7 July and 31 October was only 25,198. The OKW figures for the monthly number of Army sick also appear far more consistently stable than they should be according to the numbers produced by the Organizational Department of OKH. See *Armee Krankenbestand* in BA-MA RW 6/543 & 6/544. For example, while the latter indicates that 98,700 sick were repatriated from the *Ostheer* to Germany in August 1942, the OKW summary notes that the number of sick with the *Ersatzheer* (and thereby inside Germany) during the month increased by only 17,246. Significantly, the Heeresarzt, OKH and OKW records all seem to generally agree on the number of combat casualties. Although doubt remains because the methodology and statistics used by the Organizational Department to arrive at its figures is unknown, it is possible that the number of departures was purposely inflated in order to create an even bleaker picture than the one that already existed.

61   Kroener, et. al. *GSWW. Vol. V: Part One*, p. 1089.

influence with Hitler to stymie the demands of the military for more men. In late July, he had bluntly informed Hitler that the proposed release of 100,000 armaments workers per month was impossible, and demanded that the conscription of workers in August be limited to only 6,600 men. Buoyed by *Wehrmacht* victories in the East, Hitler readily assented. Gradually, exemption qualifications were again loosened, mainly by the redefinition of workers as "specialists" whom industry simply could not do without.[62] By the beginning of June, the number of deferrals had again risen to nearly 5.4 million.[63] Even though the *Ostheer* was increasingly starved of men, this tendency continued until late 1942.

Given the rich availability of foreign labour controlled by the Third Reich by 1942, any concerns that the withdrawal of German workers would threaten armaments production should have been mute. Remarkably, efforts to utilize fully this vital resource over the course of the year were obstructed by a combination of bureaucratic incompetence, and the implacable, murderous tendencies of Nazi ideology. After his appointment as General Plenipotentiary for Labour Deployment on 21 March 1942, Fritz Sauckel was given wide powers to procure foreign labour and, by the end of November, 1.5 million Soviet workers had been recruited or forcibly impressed. However, by that point their wretched treatment meant that only 1.125 million were actually registered as working in Germany. At least 80,000-100,000 that were no longer capable of work had been sent back to Russia, while the balance had died. Meagre rations and unhealthy living conditions meant that many of those who remained were either too sick or too weak to work at full proficiency.[64] Circumstances for the *Ostarbeiter* (Eastern workers) only improved by the end of the year when rations were increased, working and living conditions improved, and incentive programs introduced to promote greater productivity. Matters were much worse for the Jewish population as the SS intensified their extermination during the course of 1942. Initially this was limited to those considered useless mouths – mainly women, children and the elderly – who were deemed incapable of making any useful contribution to the German war effort. However, despite the persistent protests of German labour officials and industrialists who recognized their usefulness, even those considered valuable or essential workers were to be killed off gradually through starvation and over-work. By claiming the lives of a conservatively estimated 2.4 million potential workers, as Adam Tooze has remarked, "the

---

62   The most thorough discussion regarding the struggle between the military and civilian leadership over manpower during this period can be found in Kroener, et. al. *GSWW. Vol. V, Part Two*, pp. 835-884. For a persuasive argument that counters long-held notions regarding Speer's role in creating an "armaments miracle", see Tooze, *The Wages of Destruction*, pp. 552-589. For more information concerning Albert Speer and other civilian managers of Germany's war effort, see Speer, *Inside the Third Reich*, and Guido Knopp, *Hitlers Manager*. (Germany: 2006). Regarding German armaments production, also see Overy, *War and Economy in the Third Reich*.

63   Kroener, et. al. *GSWW. Vol. V: Part One*, p. 1089.

64   Herbert, *Hitler's Foreign Workers*, pp. 163-192.

Holocaust involved a catastrophic destruction of labour power." All told, at least 4.8 million workers died *after* the crisis of 1941-1942 because of the murderous ideologies of the Third Reich.[65]

Despite the unwillingness to draw upon the large number of exempted German males, pressure to find some new reservoirs of manpower for the Army steadily grew as the carnage in the East continued. At some point during August, the OKW submitted to Hitler a proposal whereby 20,000 naval and 50,000 air force personnel would be transferred to the Army. Göring vehemently resisted the idea, stating that he refused to allow his "Nationalist Socialist boys" to wear the field-gray of the reactionary Army, and instead offered that the *Luftwaffe* could provide even greater numbers of men if only it was allowed to create its own field formations.[66] Encouraged by Göring's insistence that he would create "a strong body capable of joining in the land battle", and since the *Luftwaffe* ground units already committed to the *Ostfront* had given a good account of themselves, on 9 September Hitler decreed that the existing units be expanded into brigades. Shortly thereafter, this was revised to 22 divisions comprising 200,000 men.[67] The first five divisions were established that month, followed by seven in October, five in November, and three in December. But their actual worth on the battlefield was marginal. Organized into four rifle battalions, and supported by single battalions of field, anti-tank and anti-aircraft artillery together with companies of engineers, reconnaissance and signal troops, these divisions were effectively brigades.[68] While generally well equipped, both officers and men usually lacked any appreciable combat training or battlefield experience. Although mustering only commenced on 19 September, the first divisions began their deployment to the front in early November.[69] It was intended that they be assigned to quiet sectors, but almost immediately many found themselves embroiled in heavy fighting, in which they were frequently given tasks that even fully-trained and fully-manned formations would have found challenging. On 25 November, having arrived only weeks before, the *2.*

---

65 Tooze, *The Wages of Destruction*, pp. 522-551.

66 Hillgruber, (Ed.) *KTB OKW. Band II*, p. 796.

67 Kroener, et. al. *GSWW. Vol. V, Part Two*, pp. 890-891.

68 Each rifle battalion was comprised of three rifle (each with 20 machine-guns and 11 mortars) and one heavy weapons companies (equipped with 12 machine-guns, three mortars, and four 2 cm Flak). The flak battalion possessed four 8.8 cm and 27 2 cm Flak guns organized into three batteries. The artillery battalion was equipped with a mixture of 7.5 cm Geb. K15 mountain guns and *Nebelwerfer* and some were assigned an assault gun battery with five StuG. Service and administrative services were minimal. Some divisions possessed two infantry regimental staffs that each controlled a pair of rifle battalions. Typical of the personnel strength of these formations was the *1. (Luftwaffe) Feld Division*; on 28 October 1943 it possessed an *Iststärke* of 6,429 men, and a *Kampfstärke* of 2,779. When taken over by the Army, an additional infantry regiment and two artillery battalions were added. Ruffner, *Luftwaffe Field Division, 1941-1945*, pp. 10-11. Also see Haupt, *Die deutsche Luftwaffe Felddivisionen, 1941-1945*.

69 Ruffner, *Luftwaffe Field Division, 1941-1945*, pp. 9-10.

(Luftwaffe) Feld Division found itself in the direct path of the latest Soviet offensive (Operation Mars) aimed at crushing the German salient around Rzhev. While acquitting itself well enough considering the circumstances, it nonetheless sustained heavy casualties.[70] In the aftermath of the encirclement of the *6. Armee* around Stalingrad, the *7.* and *8. (Luftwaffe) Feld Divisions* were thrown in to shore up the German front and participate in the effort to relieve the pocket. Both were shattered in short order, and their remnants attached to regular Army divisions. Subsequently, while some divisions performed with distinction, many were destroyed during their first major engagements.[71] In late 1943 the Army formally absorbed those divisions that still remained. By 1945 only four of the 21 divisions established were still in existence, the remainder having been destroyed and their survivors incorporated into other formations. Losses amongst the estimated 250,000 air force personnel these formations contained were disproportionately high. "Sacrificed in the name of personal egotism and inter-service rivalries," the establishment of the *Luftwaffe* field divisions constituted a gross waste of good troops that otherwise would have done much to refill the Army's ranks.[72]

Constantly denied the millions of German males deferred from military service by the machinations of Speer and other Nazi officials, and with the *Luftwaffe* having dodged the transfer of its personnel, the Army was forced to look elsewhere for replacements. By the early autumn of 1942, the bulk of the 1923 class of recruits who were inducted during the spring had already been assigned to field units. In desperation, the eighteen year-olds of the 1924 class were called up in mid-October. However, while this class totalled 654,057 men, the Army's allotment amounted to only 260,000 and these would not be ready for service until early 1943. Even then they would do little to dent the staggering shortages pervading the Army, which by the end of 1942 were forecast at around one million men.[73] Lacking alternatives, the Army was compelled to find the men it needed by scouring its own ranks through a series of additional reorganization and rationalization measures. These included the increased use of *Hiwis*

---

70   Glantz, *Zhukov's Greatest Defeat*, pp. 111-115. From 1 October to 31 December, the *2. (Luftwaffe) Feld Division* sustained 1,630 casualties, including 288 killed, 902 wounded, and 440 missing. *9. AOK. Anlagen zum Tatigkeitsbericht der Abt. IIa/b. (1.10-31.12.1942)*, NARA T312 Roll 307, Frame 7874417.

71   See Haupt, *Die deutsche Luftwaffe Felddivisionen, 1941-1945* for the histories of individual formations. On one notorious occasion that seemed to illustrate the unreliability of these divisions, when attacked by Soviet forces around Nevel in October 1943 significant portions of the *2. (Luftwaffe) Feld Division* broke and ran. While it sustained 722 personnel casualties on 6-12 October, its equipment losses included 2,648 rifles, 1,175 pistols, 552 machine-pistols, 26 anti-tank guns, 31 mortars, and 4 8.8 cm and 38 2 cm Flak guns. Ibid, p. 40. In consequence, the division was ordered disbanded on 15 October.

72   Ruffner, *Luftwaffe Field Division, 1941-1945*, p. 39.

73   Kroener, et. al. *GSWW. Vol. V: Part One*, pp. 831-832. For the number allotted to the Army, see Halder, *Kriegstagebuch. Band II*, p. 297. Figures regarding shortages can be found in Kroener, et. al. *GSWW. Vol. V, Part Two*, p. 881.

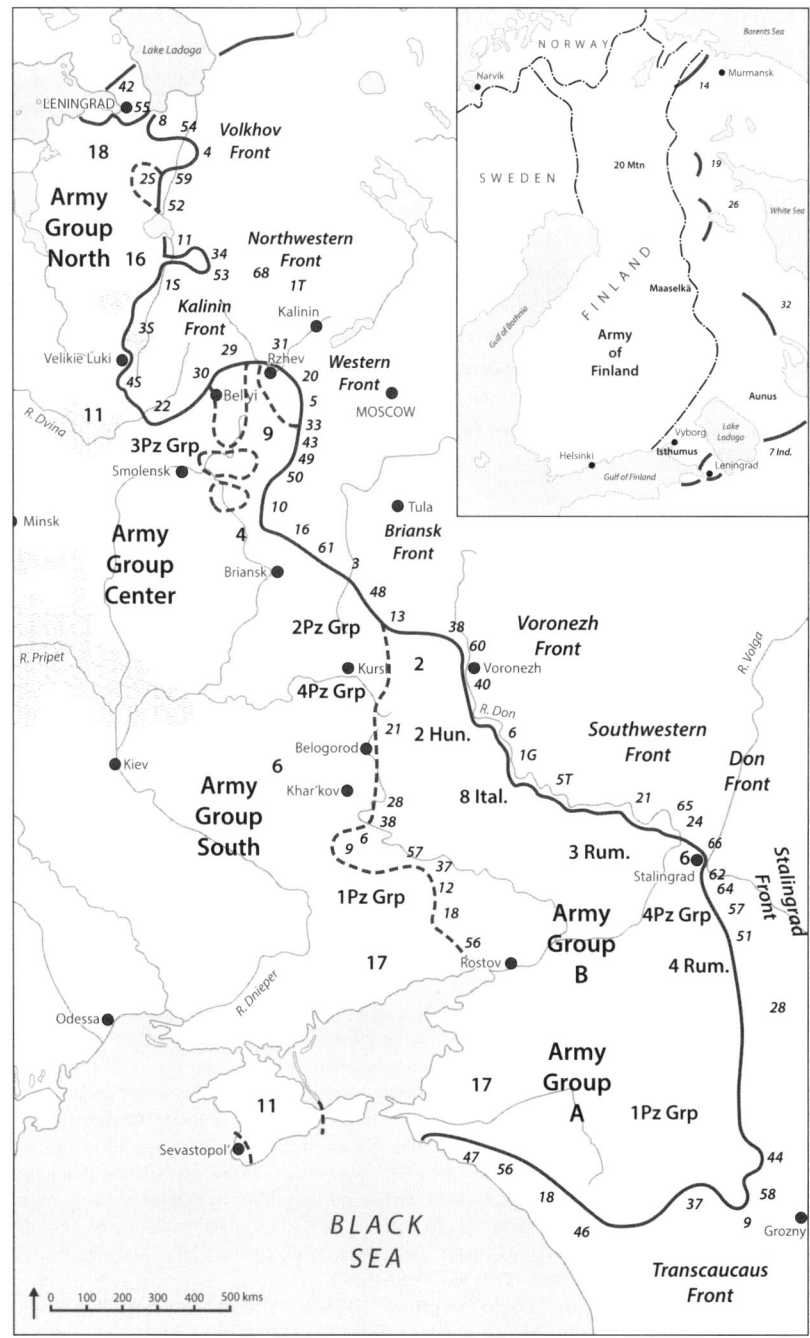

Map 5.4 The Extent of German Gains by 18 November 1942.

and the reduction and elimination of many staff positions. It also entailed the broad reorganization of the Army's field divisions; some intended for offensive operations were to be kept at full strength and maintain their old organization, but the majority of the infantry formations were to be scaled down from nine to six infantry battalions. The Organization Department of the OKH believed that these measures would release 860,000 men. In reality though, few men appear to have actually been re-mustered for front-line service. In most instances, all this reorganization did was formally acknowledge the changes that had already occurred in the field – most infantry divisions on the *Ostfront* had already been reduced to six infantry battalions and many of the positions earmarked for *Hiwis* had been filled by them long ago. Of the staff appointments, most of these had been vacant for some time, in some cases since the start of the war. In short, the real effect of these measures was on paper – shortages were reduced by the simple expedient of downsizing formations and eliminating various posts and offices, but few men were actually freed up for the front.[74]

Remarkably, even as the existing formations faced copious manpower shortages, the number of Army divisions continued to grow. Three new infantry divisions constituting the *20. Welle* were created in July to augment the forces guarding France; another division was created using pre-existing units, together with two more that were formed in a similar manner the following month.[75] Before the end of November, another two panzer and 11 infantry divisions had been established. The steady growth of insurgencies across German-occupied Europe resulted in the *Ersatzheer* creating six *Feldausbildung* (field training) and 18 reserve divisions; these would provide advance training to new recruits and simultaneously augment local security forces.[76] The *Waffen-SS* also expanded its cavalry brigade into a full division in August, and followed this by upgrading three other formations into full *Panzergrenadier* divisions during November.[77] Aside from establishing the 20 field divisions noted above (the

---

74   Ibid, pp. 884-890.
75   The *38., 39.* and *65. Infanterie Divisions* constituted the *20. Welle.* The *210. Division* was a headquarters staff created to control various fortress infantry battalions and coastal artillery batteries in Norway. During August the *325. Sicherungs Division* was established to control all German security units in occupied Paris, while the *164. Leichte Division* was converted from *Festungs Division Kreta* and then dispatched to Africa.
76   The *26. Panzer Division* was raised in September through the conversion of the *23. Infanterie Division*; the *27. Panzer Division* was established in the field by using components of the *22. Panzer Division* and various corps and army units. Between September and November, the *345.* and *386. (Mot.) Infanterie Divisions*, and the *23., 326., 334., 338., 343., 344., 346., 347.* and *348. Infanterie Divisions* were created, usually by drawing heavily upon the *Ersatzheer*. Of the training divisions created to augment the internal security forces, these were the *153., 381., 387., 388., 390.* and *391. Feldausbildung Divisions*, and the *141., 143., 147., 148., 151., 153., 154., 156., 157., 158., 159., 165., 171., 174., 182., 187., 189.* and *191. Reserve Divisions.*
77   The strength of the *Waffen-SS* increased from 198,364 men in December 1941 to over 230,000 a year later. Müller-Hillebrand, *Das Heer 1933-1945, Band III*, p. 80. On 5 July 1942 the motorized infantry (*Schützen*) regiments of the panzer divisions were re-titled as

other two were created in early 1943), the *Luftwaffe* also raised its *Regiment Göring* to divisional status. All told, 68 new field divisions were created during the latter half of 1942.

Arguably, at least some new formations would have been legitimately required by the end of 1942. The steady transformation of the insurgency in Yugoslavia into a full-blown conventional conflict and the mounting prospect of an Allied decent somewhere along the coast of Western Europe demanded that the garrisons in these regions be augmented. The gradual decline of its Italian ally, especially after the Allied land-ings in North Africa in November 1942 and the resulting collapse of Axis forces in Tunisia the following spring, meant that increasing amounts of German ground and air assets had to be dispatched to the Mediterranean.[78] Given the prodigious length of the frontline and the continual increases in the size and capabilities of the Red Army, the assignment of additional divisions to reinforce the initial forces allotted to the Eastern Front was also probably inevitable.

However, the expansion of the Army, when combined with the mismanagement and waste of manpower elsewhere, meant that across-the-board personnel shortages

panzergrenadier regiments. This was followed on 15 October by the renaming of infantry regiments as *grenadier* regiments. Although the motorized divisions were progressively renamed *panzergrenadier* divisions, their infantry regiments were called *(Mot.) Grenadier Regiments* until 1944 when they were gradually re-titled as *panzergrenadier* units. The motorized *Waffen-SS* divisions converted were the *Leibstandarte SS Adolf Hitler*, *Das Reich*, and *Totenkopf*, each of which was given, together with an array of support units, a two-battalion panzer regiment with a further company equipped with Tiger tanks, and two three-battalion *panzergrenadier* regiments. Lavishly equipped and effectively full panzer divisions, these formations, together with the Army's *(Mot.) Infanterie Division Grossdeutschland* that was upgraded in early 1943, were a attempt to create powerful mechanized formations that incorporated the latest military equipment and which endeavored to find the right mix of firepower, mobility, infantry and armour. This organization would remain unique to these particular formations; as the war continued a single panzer battalion usually equipped with assault guns supported the standard motorized infantry divisions of the Army.

78   The presence of the *Luftwaffe* in the Mediterranean steadily increased from 828 aircraft in August 1942, until it reached a peak strength of 1,158 aircraft in April 1943. Thereafter it precipitously declined. Karl Gundelach, *Die Deutsche Luftwaffe im Mittelmeer 1940-1945*, Vol. 1 & 2. (Frankfurt am Main: 1981), pp. 415 & 555. It should also be noted that its operations in the Mediterranean cost the *Luftwaffe* a heavy toll of lost aircraft: between November 1942 and May 1943 alone this amounted to at least 2,238 aircraft. Murray, *Strategy for Defeat*, p. 123. Following the Axis collapse in North Africa, the number of ground divisions deployed to Italy during 1943 increased from six divisions on 7 July to 21 divisions on 26 December. At the same time, German forces in the Balkans grew from 15 to 23 divisions. Walther Hubatsch, (Ed.) *Kriegstagebuch des Oberkommando der Wehrmacht (Wehrmachtführungsstab), Band III: 1 Januar 1943-31 Dezember 1943*. (Frankfurt am Main: 1963), pp. 735-736 & 1402. For the most comprehensive study regarding German policy in the Mediterranean until 1942, and especially the endeavor to keep the region quiet, see Gerhard Schreiber, et. al. *GSWW. Vol. III.*

were a forgone conclusion for the *Ostheer*. Between June 1941 and June 1943, Army personnel losses totalled nearly four million men; in contrast, the number of new recruits and returning convalescents amounted to roughly 4.5 million (see Table 5.8). As Müller-Hillebrand has argued, if the size of the Army had been kept to the 203 divisions that existed in June 1941, the available manpower would have been sufficient to cover losses, maintain the existing divisions at their original organization and personnel strengths, and still leave about one-half million men available as replacements. Instead, by 1 January 1943 the Army had expanded to 259 divisions and the number of formations belonging to other branches of the *Wehrmacht* grew from seven to 26 divisions.[79] During the next six months another 12 new Army and eight new *Waffen-SS* or *Luftwaffe* divisions would join them, while another 22 divisions would be raised to replace those destroyed at Stalingrad or lost when the Axis position in North Africa finally collapsed.[80] Although many were formed from pre-existing units, all still required large numbers of new recruits and returning convalescents, along with equipment, that otherwise would have been injected into older formations.[81] Of the roughly 4.5 million men made available to the Army between June 1941 and June 1943, the new formations created during this period consumed 1.1 million men. This left 3.27 million men available as replacements to cover losses that approached 4 million, producing a shortage of about three-quarters of a million men.[82]

Fundamentally, the widespread personnel shortages experienced by the German Army late in 1942 were largely self-inflicted, the result of a series of official policies (or lack thereof) rather than an actual lack of manpower. Clearly, if the Army had retained its pre-Barbarossa size, the allotted number of men would have been enough to cover its losses by a significant margin. Yet even with the expansion in the number of Army divisions, Germany still possessed sufficient manpower either to have kept its formations at full strength or very close to it. At the very least, shortages could have been less acute than they were. Large numbers of men could have been transferred

---

79   For the complete German order of battle on 1 January 1943, see Hubatsch, (Ed.) *KTB OKW. Band III*, pp. 3-9.

80   The new Army formations included the *264., 265., 266., 274., 282., 355., 356., 369.*, and *373. Infanterie Divisions*, the *999. Afrika Division*, *Sturm Division Rhodes*, and *Division Brandenburg*. Those of the *Waffen-SS* were its new *9., 10., 11., 12.*, and *13. SS-Divisions*, while the *Luftwaffe* created the *2. Fallschirm Division*, and the *19.* and *20. (Luftwaffe) Feld Divisions*.

81   When its formation was completed on 1 April 1943, the *282. Infanterie Division* possessed a *Verpflegungsstärke* of 12,311 men, and was equipped with 631 machine-guns, 150 mortars (90 5 cm & 60 8.1 cm), 18 5 cm and 9 7.5 cm Pak, 18 light infantry guns, 24 light and 12 heavy German-made howitzers, and 12 captured French artillery pieces. See Friedrich Kaufmann, *Die Vergessene Division. 282. Baden-Württembergische Infanterie Division*. (Germany: 1985).

82   Müller-Hillebrand, *Das Heer 1933-1945, Band III*, p. 110.

from the bloated ranks of the *Luftwaffe* and *Kriegsmarine* with relative ease.[83] The shifting of male workers who had been deferred from military service would have been more difficult, since this required a significant degree of foresight and efficient planning based upon realistic appraisals of Germany's circumstances. It would also have meant that the essential nature of Nazi policy, namely its prejudices and genocidal tendencies towards Jews, Slavs, and other undesirables, would need to be disregarded at least for the duration of the war. The huge number of foreign labourers brought in to replace German workers would have required sufficient housing, adequate food rations, constant medical care, and various incentive programs in order to maintain their productivity and keep incidents of industrial sabotage or worker absenteeism to a minimum. A comprehensive training program would also have been needed if skilled German workers drafted into the Army were to be replaced in a timely manner. Such measures would have been administratively challenging, but were neither impossible nor improbable. Given that such expedients were in fact enacted sporadically, at various times and to various degrees, it is quite clear that Germany had the *potential* to solve its manpower shortages within the *Wehrmacht*, while simultaneously maintaining its wartime economy and industrial output.

In contrast to the intractable manpower situation, Germany's production of weapons and equipment during this period was far rosier, though it too had its problems. As seen in Table 5.9, armaments production between July and November 1942 generally superseded equipment losses, frequently by considerable margins. As was the case earlier in the year, shortfalls continued in terms of heavy field artillery and most categories of motor vehicles. Compensation for the former was found by the increased use of captured foreign guns. By December, for example, a total of 2,447 Russian-made 12.2 cm and 15.2 cm field guns, amongst others, were in service, mostly with Army coastal artillery batteries.[84] Deficiencies of motor vehicles were far more serious since they jeopardized the mobility of the Army. However, Table 5.10 indicates that the actual number of motor vehicles with the Army increased by over one hundred thousand during this period, presumably through the requisition of civilian vehicles, the capture of foreign models, and possibly through the return of vehicles written-off, but then rebuilt by German factories.[85] Except for the number of German-made artil-

---

83   Despite the pressing needs of the Army, the size of both services continued to grow. Between 15 June 1941 and 1 July 1943, the *Luftwaffe* expanded from 1,545,000 to 2,011,000 personnel; simultaneously, *Kriegsmarine* went from 404,000 to 650,000 personnel. Kroener, et. al. *GSWW. Vol. V: Part One*, p. 1103, and Müller-Hillebrand, *Das Heer 1933-1945, Band III*, p. 111.

84   Hahn, *Waffen und Geheimwaffen des deutschen Heeres, 1933-1945, Band II*, p. 230. During the following year, German munitions factories produced nearly one million shells for these two particular types of guns. Ibid, *Band II*, pp. 161 & 170.

85   According to Kroener, et. al. *GSWW. Vol. V: Part One*, p. 737, the actual number of trucks produced in Germany and the occupied territories during 1942 totalled 126,706; initially allocated for other uses, some of these may have found their way into the Army instead. Specific figures concerning the importance of repaired vehicles to the overall number

lery pieces, the table also reveals that most equipment stocks significantly increased. Remarkably, this growth was achieved despite the generally unremarkable achievements of German industry during 1942. As illustrated in Table 5.11, the quarterly manufacture of most weapons and equipment tended to be uneven. Significant production increases were achieved for machine-guns, mortars, light artillery and flak, and assault guns, while the manufacture of staff cars and motorcycles actually declined. In most categories, production generally held steady or witnessed only modest increases. This appears to have been the ultimate product of the near collapse of the German war economy during the winter of 1941-1942. Despite the efforts of Speer and other German officials, recovery from this disaster was slow and made even more difficult by the near stagnation, or even decline, in the production of most kinds of raw materials.[86] By August, difficulties in the mining of sufficient quantities of coal had threatened the manufacture of steel to such an extent that, in a meeting with officials charged with coal production, Hitler bluntly declared that "if, due to the shortage of coking coal the output of the steel industry cannot be raised as planned, then the war is lost."[87] The introduction of increasingly strict rationalization measures designed to increase efficiency, and the gradual concentration of resources to meet the needs of the Army ameliorated the worst shortages, but it was only during the latter part of 1942 that armaments production began to show signs of real improvement.[88]

Despite the difficulties in manufacturing, stocks of equipment held by the Army on 1 October 1942 should theoretically have matched requirements even though its size had ballooned to 246 field divisions and a host of smaller units by this point. This circumstance is revealed via the figures illustrated in Table 5.12, which show calculations of the *Sollstärke* equipment requirements of the *Feldheer* and then compares these to what the entire Army actually possessed. Additionally, the material requirements of the *Ersatzheer* and the *Waffen-SS* must also be taken into account, but ascertaining just what these were is extremely difficult. The *Ersatzheer* had recently split its training and replacement functions, the result being a myriad of different sized units and organizational schematics. Lacking more detailed information, assumptions also need to be made regarding the requisite KStN. The result is a very rough guess at best. Even so, this indicates that the *Ersatzheer* required approximately 13,272 to

available during 1942 could not be found, but in the following year the number of vehicles refurbished for the *Wehrmacht* totalled 77,823, whereas those supplied via new production amounted to 108,585. Kroener, et. al. *GSWW. Vol. V: Part Two*, p. 685.

86   For a thorough discussion on the development of the German war economy and the production of raw materials during 1942, see Ibid, pp. 449-494. Also see figures in Tooze, *The Wages of Destruction*, pp. 680-683.

87   Ibid, pp. 571-575.

88   The allocation of iron and steel to meet the needs of the Army increased from a monthly average 180,000 tons during the fourth quarter of 1941, to 400,000 tons in the third quarter of 1942. At the same time, the combined allowance provided to the *Luftwaffe* and *Kriegsmarine* decreased from 530,000 tons to 300,000 tons. Kroener, et. al. *GSWW. Vol. V: Part Two*, p. 597.

20,994 machine-guns, 2,188 to 3,904 mortars, 537 infantry guns, 147 *Nebelwerfer*, 1,875 anti-tank guns (including 270 7.5 cm Pak), and 56 8.8 cm and 232 2 cm Flak guns (see Appendix Ten). As noted in previous chapters, the amount of field artillery needed is unknown. Determining the material requirements of the *Waffen-SS* is even more problematic; no specifics concerning the organization of its formations dated to this period were available, and it is unknown if the available statistics regarding total Army equipment stocks include those of the *Waffen-SS*. Assuming that they do, reliance must thereby be placed upon the *Sollstärke* material needs of the *Waffen-SS* of June 1941, which amounted to 4,204 machine-guns, 1,002 mortars, 150 infantry and 439 anti-tank guns, 274 10.5 cm and 15 cm field howitzers, and 138 2 cm Flak guns.[89] Although dated, these figures may not be that far from the mark since the expansion of the *Waffen-SS* by October 1942 had been very limited.[90] After subtracting these estimates, large surpluses remain in terms of machine-guns (62,464 to 54,742), mortars (4,855 to 3,139), 2 cm Flak (3,529), and rocket launchers (1,911), while shortages appear for infantry guns (232) and 8.8 cm Flak (56). Surpluses also continue for anti-tank guns (61) and artillery pieces (787), but the diminutive number of the former essentially constitutes an even break between requirements and availability, while it can be assumed that most of the latter were consumed by the training needs of the *Ersatzheer*.

The margin between equipment availability and requirements became increasingly thin. In many instances even this was achieved only through the employment of captured ordnance and reductions in authorized establishments. Stocks of infantry weapons remained ample, but the situation regarding heavier support weapons and artillery pieces was far more tenuous, as the once prodigious surpluses of anti-tank, infantry and artillery guns (see previous chapters) had virtually disappeared. Sufficient material clearly still existed to meet the needs of the *Feldheer* for one last effort, but only at the expense of the *Ersatzheer*. Though a seemingly reasonable measure considering Germany's strategic circumstances at this stage of the war, this would have meant the ruthless prioritization and organizational management of the available

89   See the 1941 German Army and Waffen-SS TOE schematics detailed on the website of Dr. Leo Niehorster, "World War II Armed Forces – Orders of Battle and Organizations" at http://niehorster.orbat.com

90   Already roughly the size of a full division, *SS-Kampfgruppe Nord* was renamed *SS-Division Nord* and in September 1942 it was reorganized into the *SS-Gebirgs Division Nord*. The reinforced *SS-Brigade Leibstandarte SS Adolf Hitler* (LSSAH) and the *SS-Kavallerie Brigade* were both expanded into divisions, respectively, in February and August. The only completely new formation was the *SS-Freiwilligen Gebirgs Division Prinz Eugen* which was created in February 1942, and that appears to have been mainly equipped from captured stocks. The remaining formations largely retained their previous organization until the conversion of *SS-Divisions LSSAH, Das Reich*, and *Totenkopf* into *panzergrenadier* divisions commenced in November. For more details concerning the organizational development of these divisions, see Roger Bender & Hugh Taylor, *Uniforms, Organization and History of the Waffen-SS. Volumes Two & Three*. (San Jose, CA: 1971-1972).

stock. However, this would have required levels of precision and efficiency that the organization and planning departments of OKH probably no longer possessed as a result of the gradual reduction in the size of their staffs and mounting shortages of fully trained staff officers.[91] Moreover, as the number of Army formations continued to grow and the specific manner in which they were organized became increasingly multifarious, the remaining staff personnel were hard pressed to provide accurate estimates in a timely manner. As Müller-Hillebrand has stated, these required several weeks of calculations by which point, depending upon the scale and circumstances of combat operations, they were already outdated.[92]

However, it should be understood that possessing sufficient stocks of equipment was one thing; transporting them in a timely manner to the field units that needed them was something else entirely. Under normal conditions, the turnaround time between a replacement request and when this request was actioned through OKH was several weeks. As noted previously, difficulties with rail transport had been the bane of the *Ostheer* during the winter of 1941-1942. By late 1942, the situation had markedly improved, but only to the point that the requirements of the field armies could just barely be met. Conversely, conditions in those parts of southern Russia conquered by the *Wehrmacht* during the summer were worse because of the dearth of existing rail lines and infrastructure. With priority given to the supply of food, ammunition, and fuel, the replacement of lost or damaged equipment simply had to be postponed. In consequence, the formations operating in these regions suffered from the most acute material and equipment shortages.[93] Elsewhere in the East, the provisioning of forces along a front that extended for 3,000 kilometres meant that transport resources were stretched thin, and the continuous use of the rail network at high capacity exacerbated maintenance problems that required considerable and constant attention. This rendered the system highly susceptible to disruption. Compounded by incidences of normal breakage and the occasional Soviet air attack upon rail stations, the main source of these disruptions were partisan attacks against rail lines and bridges. Though the damage caused could usually be repaired fairly quickly, such attacks did have an accumulative effect. In the sector of the *16. Armee* alone, partisans

---

91 Regarding the development of the German officer corps in 1942-1945, see Kroener, et. al. *GSWW. Vol. V: Part Two*, pp. 918-942.
92 Müller-Hillebrand, "Statistics Systems", p. 10.
93 For example, a comparison between the authorized and actual material holdings of the *389. Infanterie Division* on 25 September 1942 produces the following picture:

	MG	Mortars	3.7 cm/ 5 cm Pak	7.5 cm Pak	10.5 cm le. FH	15 cm s. FH	Nebelwerfer
Authorized	587	162	39	2	24	12	21
Actual	235	47	21	8	21	8	17

Authorized strength from *OKH Generalstab des Heeres, Org. Abt. Kriegsgliederung des Feldheeres, 15 Oktober 1942*. NARA T78 Roll 406, Frame 6375957. Actual strength derived from unspecified document.

conducted 114 attacks on rail lines and bridges between May and July 1942, during which 20 locomotives and 113 wagons were destroyed or damaged. More disconcertingly, the resulting disruption in rail movement delayed the scheduled re-provisioning of this army by a total of 47 days. Circumstances elsewhere were even worse.[94] Although German security measures ensured that communication links were never entirely severed, this problem continued to grow in tandem with the expansion of the partisan movement.[95] In the meantime, as the size, strength, and offensive capabilities of the Red Army continued to grow, so too did the frequency and intensity of its operations. For the Germans, the increasingly frequent battles this produced consumed ever-larger quantities of supplies and invariably required the replacement of more equipment; this placed even more pressure upon the already tenuous pace of resupply. When combined, disruptions in rail movement and the growing magnitude of the fighting meant that deliveries increasingly struggled to catch up to the needs of the frontline troops. Adequate stocks of equipment may indeed have existed in depots within Germany, but transporting them to divisions in the field in a timely manner steadily became a relentless, and perhaps insurmountable, challenge. Under these conditions, constant material shortages became almost unavoidable.

Much the same can be said of the condition by late 1942 of Germany's armoured forces, which also presented a mixed picture. On the one hand, while the monthly production of tanks remained constant, that of assault guns and self-propelled anti-tank guns had increased considerably. In compensation for the 1,708 armoured vehicles written-off between 1 July and 1 December 1942, German industry had managed to produce 2,730 replacements. As a result, the total number of armoured vehicles had swollen from 6,749 to 7,798 (see Table 5.13). Moreover, production now consisted almost entirely of the improved versions of the Pz III, Pz IV, and StuG III, which

---

94   Between June and December 1942, successful partisan attacks against railway installations in the rear areas of *Heeresgruppe Mitte* totaled 1,183, or an average of between five and six per day. Boog, et. al. *GSWW, Vol. VI*, pp. 1010-1011.

95   Statistics regarding the number of Soviet partisans at any given point tend to vary wildly, but it would seem the their numbers expanded from roughly 82,000 in July 1942, to 130,000 by the end of the year. The organization appears to have peaked in mid-1943, having reached about 200,000 men and women. Mawdsley, *Thunder in the East*, pp. 232-237, and Nigel Thomas & Peter Abbott, *Partisan Warfare, 1941-1945*. (London: 1983), pp. 12-13. According to German figures, partisan attacks throughout occupied Europe (including Russia) destroyed 5,079 locomotives and 12,400 railway wagons during 1943; in contrast, losses to Allied bombing amounted to 1,512 and 12,430, respectively. Kroener, et. al. *GSWW. Vol. V: Part Two*, p. 498. For additional works concerning the Soviet partisan movement, see Armstrong (Ed.), *Soviet Partisans in World War II*, Mathew Cooper, *The Phantom War: The German Struggle against Soviet Partisans, 1941-1944*. (London: 1979), Leonid Grenkevich, *The Soviet Partisan Movement, 1941-1944: A Critical Historiographical Analysis*. (Portland, OR: 1999), Alexander Hill, "The Partisan War in North-West Russia, 1941-1944: A Re-examination." *Journal of Strategic Studies*, Vol. 25, No. 3 (2002), pp. 37-55, and Ben Shepherd, *War in the Wild East: The German Army and Soviet Partisans*. (Cambridge, MA: 2004).

meant that more obsolescent versions were gradually being phased out. Production of the new Pz VI (or Tiger) tank, equipped with a high-velocity 8.8 cm gun and 100 mm of frontal armour, was already well underway and the first units equipped with these vehicles had already seen combat around Leningrad during September. Trials of the equally formidable Pz V (or Panther) tank had also commenced, with a monthly production of 600 vehicles set to begin in January 1943.[96] The development of a further array of improved assault gun, tank destroyer and self-propelled artillery designs was also well advanced, as were plans for the phasing out of production of the Pz III in favour of even greater numbers of Pz IV. Once these designs reached field units in considerable numbers, the superiority the Soviet T-34 had held over its German opposites in terms of armour protection and armament since the start of Operation Barbarossa would be gone, and German tankers would hold the advantage. The stage thus appeared set for an imminent, massive improvement of the *Panzerwaffe* in terms of overall numbers and quality.

But the circumstances for the panzer divisions operating deep within Russia were far less agreeable. As promising as the new designs were, it would still be several months before their presence was felt on the battlefield in any appreciable numbers. In the meantime, the *Panzertruppen* would have to soldier on with whatever was available. Arrivals of replacement panzers between July and November had exceeded losses, and during this time the overall number of tanks on the *Ostfront* increased from 2,060 to 2,677.[97] Moreover, the tanks lost had included many inferior models, and these had been replaced by substantially enhanced versions, resulting in a steady improvement in quality. Indeed, the number of now-almost-useless Pz II and Pz 38(t) had declined substantially, dropping from 732 in July to 271 by November. However, as had occurred during the course of Operation Barbarossa, the fundamental problem was not the availability of tanks, but in maintaining them at operational readiness. As illustrated in Table 5.14, the number of operational tanks with the panzer divi-

---

96   Despite the reputation and the characteristics of the Tiger, the Panther was actually the superior vehicle because of its sloped armour and the higher muzzle-velocity of its main gun. See comparison in Zetterling, *Normandy 1944*, pp. 58-62. The Tiger was never mass-produced, and only 1,303 were built before production ended in August 1944. Heavy, but equipped with an underpowered engine, the Tiger suffered from low serviceability rates. Actual mass production of the Panther did not commence until May 1943 because of shortages of machine parts. Rushed into service to participate in the Battle of Kursk, the Panther suffered from low serviceability rates and during the battle a number suffered spontaneous engine fires because of overheating. The various teething problems with the design would not be fully rectified until late 1943. For the specifics of these and other German armoured vehicles, see Senger und Etterlin, *German Tanks of World War II*.

97   See Jentz, *Panzertruppen, Vol. One*, p. 252, and *Panzertruppen, Vol. Two*, p. 43. It should be noted that the number of tanks Jentz cites herein as being repairable actually appear to have been the total number of tanks available. Compare his March 1943 figures from Ibid, p. 43, with those dated to 28 February 1943 in Müller-Hillebrand, *Das Heer 1933-1945, Band III*, p. 125.

sions of the *Ostheer* had plunged sharply, particularly among the divisions assigned to *Heeresgruppe A* and *B*. This is not surprising given the high operational tempo and the intensity of the combat in which they had been engaged since the onset of Operation Blue. Depending upon the specific circumstances, strengths could drop dramatically. For example, the *13. Panzer Division* mustered 130 operational tanks on 20 October, but after a month of heavy fighting this number had fallen to 27 by 20 November.[98] Although they likely possessed far more tanks than were listed as being operational in the table, residing deep in the Caucasus or along the Volga River meant the armoured formations of *Heeresgruppe A* and *B* were reliant upon a grossly inadequate rail system that struggled just to provide them with their minimum requirements of food, fuel and ammunition. The arrival of spare parts was at best erratic, forcing maintenance crews to cannibalize vehicles with only minor damage in order to keep the rest operational. The arrival of new tanks would have done little to arrest this trend; without a comprehensive improvement in the logistical tether, the ultimate result was simply a gradual increase in the number of machines accumulating in workshops. The crucial significance regarding this connection between adequate logistics and operational panzer strengths is further evidenced by the circumstances of the formations assigned the two other army groups. These too had been heavily engaged throughout the year, but the scope of their operations had been limited, meaning the degree of wear upon their vehicles was also less. Moreover, the panzer formations located in central and northern Russia could also rely upon a railway network that, whatever its problems, was considerably more proficient at meeting their needs than the one supplying their compatriots to the south. In consequence, the level of operational readiness had remained far more stable – the number of operational tanks declining in some divisions, but rising in others. Clearly, the overall increase in the number of tanks in the East did not translate into any appreciable improvement or impede a general decline. This illustrates that the effect of even substantial deliveries of new vehicles could be muted, and that German armoured strengths in Russia were mainly dependent upon the availability of spare parts, the amount of time maintenance personnel had to conduct repairs, and the pace and intensity of combat operations.

Back at the front, the accumulated impact of these various problems – for the most part the product of poor German decision-making and appalling management – together with the actions of the Red Army, meant that by mid-November the most important facets of Operation Blue had failed. To be sure, German armies had conducted a spectacular advance into southern Russia. Except for a handful of narrow bridgeheads still held by the Red Army, the city of Stalingrad was in German hands. A continuous front shielding the rear of *Heeresgruppe A* had also been established, permitting the latter to push deep into the Caucasus and occupy huge portions of the region. In the process, staggering losses had been inflicted upon the Soviets; according to post-war Russian estimates these totalled at least 1,586,100 personnel, 4,852 tanks,

---

98   Jentz, *Panzertruppen, Vol. One*, p. 251.

30,902 guns and mortars, and 3,490 aircraft. In contrast, combat casualties amongst the German armies participating in Operation Blue totalled 223,996 men between 1 July and 1 November.[99] However, regardless of its terrible losses, the Soviet Union was far from having been brought to the peace table. Along the Don front, ominous signs of an impending Soviet counteroffensive had been mounting since September. Most of Stalingrad had been captured, but the strength and capabilities of the German formations in the region had been left horribly debilitated in the process. With huge stretches of the front manned by allied Axis divisions, much would depend on how well these same German forces reacted to any Soviet attack. In the Caucasus, despite impressive territorial gains *Heeresgruppe A* had failed to capture any of the more sizeable oilfields. Even worse, the last of its offensive capability had finally been spent when its latest endeavour (25 October-11 November) to punch through the mountains at Ordzhonikidze had failed.[100] At the end of a grossly inadequate supply chain and with its badly depleted formations strung out across hundreds of kilometres of front, *Heeresgruppe A* was forced onto the defensive. The resumption of offensive operations to conquer the remainder of the Caucasus would have to wait until the spring of 1943. If this was to have any chance of success, the meandering front stretching from Voronezh to south of Stalingrad had to hold. But with a Soviet offensive in the region imminent, the question was, could it?

99   Soviet figures represent the combined losses sustained during the Voronezh-Voroshilovgrad Defensive Operation (28 June-24 July), the Stalingrad Defensive Operation (25 July-18 November), and the North Caucasus Defensive Operation (25 July-31 December). Glantz, *Armageddon in Stalingrad*, pp. 714-716. For German combat casualties, see Heeresarzt 10-Day Loss Reports for *Heeresgruppe Süd* (1-31.7.1942), *Heeresgruppe B* (1.8-31.10.1942), and *Heeresgruppe A* (1.8-31.10.1942) in BA-MA RW 6/556 & 6/558. Based upon the differences between these combat losses and the figures cited as the total *Abgänge* for these army groups during the same period, it may also be speculated that the number of sick that had to be transported back to Germany numbered around 128,804. See total departures for *Heeresgruppe Süd/A/B* for the period of July to October 1942 noted in Boog, et. al. *GSWW, Vol. VI*, p. 866. Personnel losses amongst the allied Axis formation during this period included 8,950 Italians (30.7-10.12.1942), 21,621 Hungarians (28.6-15.9.1942), and 39,089 Romanians (1 July-31 October 1942), for a rough total of at least 69,660 men. For Romanian losses, see Axworthy, et. al. *Third Axis, Fourth Ally*, pp. 86-87. Total Axis personnel losses may therefore be estimated at around 425,000 from all causes.
100 For the best descriptions of this operation, see Citino, *Death of the Wehrmacht*, pp. 240-243, and Glantz, *Armageddon in Stalingrad*, pp. 574-591.

Table 5.1 Personnel Losses amongst German Divisions committed to the First Stage of Operation Blue until 10 July 1942[1]

	Period	Killed	Wounded	Missing	Total
9. PD	4.6-10.7.42	243	965	24	1,232
11. PD	13.6-10.7.42	196	815	35	1,046
(Mot.) ID 'GD'	4.6-18.7.42	284	1,047	7	1,338
3. (Mot.) ID	13.6-10.7.42	181	612	11	804
82. ID	4.6-10.7.42	453	2,085	57	2,595
88. ID	1-10.7.42	172	635	81	888
377. ID	4.6-10.7.42	287	1,365	60	1,712
383. ID	29.6-2.7.42	51	231	6	288
385. ID	6.6-10.7.42	326	993	76	1,395

1 *4. PzAOK. Ia., Kriegsrangliste, Verlustliste, Gefechts- und Verpflegungsstarken zum KTN. Nr. 5 (Teil III) UdSSR (28.4-31.12.1942)*, NARA T313 Roll 355, Frame 8639941.

Table 5.2 Tank Strength of *4. Panzerarmee* in the Voronezh Sector, 28 June to 5 July 1942[1]

	Total Strength 28.6.1942	Operational 5.7.1942
9. Panzer Division	144	97
11. Panzer Division	155	78
24. Panzer Division	181	144
3. (Mot.) Infanterie Division	54	47
16. (Mot.) Infanterie Division	54	37
(Mot.) Inf. Div. 'GD'	45	32
Total	633	435

1 For strengths in late June, see Appendix Six. Figures for 5 July taken from *4. PzAOK. Ia., Kriegsrangliste, Verlustliste, Gefechts- und Verpflegungsstärken zum KTN. Nr. 5 (Teil III) UdSSR (28.4-31.12.1942)*, NARA T313 Roll 355, Frame 8640196.

Table 5.3 German Armoured Strengths, Late July 1942[1]

	Iststarke 28.6.1942[2]	Operational	
		Date	Strength
3. PD	164	27.7.	105
13. PD	103	29.7.	112
16. PD	100	21.7.	106
23. PD	138	27.7.	52
24. PD	181	30.7.	138
3. (Mot.) ID	54	21.7.	42
29. (Mot.) ID	58	27.7.	50
60. (Mot.) ID	57	21.7.	54
177. & 244. StuG Abt.	42 (est.)	21.7.	37
Total	897	696 (78%)	

1 Operational strengths dated 21 July taken from *6. AOK. Ia/Ic Anlagenband zum Kriegstagebuch Nr. 13, Russland (20-24.7.1942)*, NARA T312 Roll 1685, Frame 000102. Those cited 27 July are from *4. PzAOK. Ia., Kriegsrangliste, Verlustliste, Gefechts- und Verpflegungsstarken zum KTB. Nr. 5 (Teil III) UdSSR (28.4-31.12.1942)*, NARA T313 Roll 355, Frame 8640412. Figures for the *13.* and *24. Panzer Divisions* are noted in Jentz, *Panzertruppen, Vol. One*, pp. 248 & 251.

2 Ibid, pp. 236-239.

Table 5.4 Losses and Personnel Status of Divisions with *6. Armee* by 9 September 1942. (Figures for Officers in Brackets)[1]

	Personnel Losses 21.7-31.8.1942	Personnel Shortages by 9.9.1942
16. Panzer Div.	3,005 (75)	1,856 (51)
3. (Mot.) Inf. Div.	2,595 (62)	3,700 (111)
60. (Mot.) Inf. Div.	3,101 (84)	2,502 (96)
44. Inf. Div.	2,398 (84)	3,602 (147)
71. Inf. Div.	3,020 (110)	4,827 (170)
76. Inf. Div.	2,397 (113)	4,603 (182)
79. Inf. Div.	2,871 (58)	3,769 (148)
100. Jager Div.	2,886 (61)	3,310 (114)
113. Inf. Div.	1,128 (49)	3,019 (137)
295. Inf. Div.	2,854 (134)	5,702 (194)
305. Inf. Div.	2,643 (94)	4,313 (137)
376. Inf. Div.	2,539 (86)	4,696 (137)
384. Inf. Div.	3,551 (73)	3,570 (165)
389. Inf. Div.	3,565 (89)	3,430 (155)
Totals	38,553 (1,172)	52,899 (1,944)

1 *6. AOK. Ia/Ic Anlagenband z. KTB Nr. 13, Russland. (12-17.9.1942)* NARA T312 Roll 1685, Frame 000987.

Table 5.5 Status of Infantry Battalions with 6. *Armee* based upon available *Grabenstärke*, 31 August 1942[1]

| | Infantry Battalions (Rating | | | | |
	'Strong' +400 Men	'Medium Strength' 300-400 Men	'Average' 200-300 Men	'Weak' 100-200 Men	'Burnt Out' Less than 100 Men
16. PD	–	4	–	–	–
22. PD	–	2	–	1	–
3. (Mot.) ID	1	2	1	–	–
60. (Mot.) ID	–	4	2	–	–
44. ID	–	–	6	2	1
71. ID	–	2	5	2	–
76. ID	–	–	3	6	–
79. ID	–	4	3	2	–
100. JD	1	1	1	1	–
113. ID	1	5	1	–	–
295. ID	–	1	4	2	–
305. ID	2	–	6	1	–
376. ID	–	–	3	4	1
384. ID	–	–	5	–	1
389. ID	–	–	6	3	–
Totals	5	25	46	24	3

1 *6. AOK. Ia/Ic Anlagenband z. KTB Nr. 13, Russland. (30.8-3.9.1942)* NARA T312 Roll 1685, Frames 000388-000390.

Table 5.6 Distribution of Combat Losses and Replacements within the *Ostheer*, July to October 1942[1]

	Heeresgruppe Nord	%	Heeresgruppe Mitte	%	Heeresgruppe B	%	Heeresgruppe A	%	Total
Combat Losses									
July	14,767	15	23,765	25	30,827	32	26,554	28	95,913
August	25,508	16	70,655	45	49,225	31	12,774	8	158,162
September	37,824	29	27,889	21	43,378	33	21,573	17	130,644
October	16,545	24	11,965	18	21,925	32	17,740	26	68,175
November	10,013	22	12,136	26	10,910	24	12,813	28	45,872
Total	104,657	21	146,410	29	156,265	31	91,454	19	498,786
Replacements									
July	35,200	20	71,600	40	19,400	11	51,600	29	177,800
August	22,000	25	31,150	35	13,000	14	23,600	26	89,750
September	20,400	24	30,200	36	20,000	24	13,150	16	83,750
October	22,300	23	36,600	38	29,900	31	8,400	8	97,200
November	11,200	18	22,400	37	18,200	30	9,400	15	61,200
Total	111,100	22	191,950	38	100,500	19	106,150	21	509,700

1 Losses shown here compiled from Heeresarzt 10-Day Loss Reports found in BA-MA RW 6/556 & 6/558. Figures for replacements taken from Boog, et. al. *GSWW. Vol. VI*, p. 866.

Table 5.7 German Divisional Shortages along the Stalingrad axis as Percentage of Estimated *Sollstärke*, September and November 1942[1]

	Estimated Sollstärke	Shortages 9.9.1942	% of Soll	Shortages Nov. 1942	% of Soll
16. Pz. Div.	18,724	1,856	10	7,673	41
3. (Mot.) ID	13,484	3,700	27	4,831	36
60. (Mot.) ID	14,781	2,502	17	5,848	40
44. ID	14,839	3,602	24	4,238	29
71. ID	16,259	4,827	30	7,353	45
76. ID	15,004	4,603	31	6,981	47
79. ID	16,274	3,769	23	8,294	51
100. Jäger Div.	16,414	3,310	20	7,739	47
113. ID	15,315	3,019	20	5,854	38
295. ID	15,936	5,702	36	9,037	57
305. ID	15,203	4,313	28	8,520	56
376. ID	14,651	4,696	32	6,464	44
384. ID	14,758	3,570	24	5,937	40
389. ID	15,392	3,430	22	7,852	51
14. Pz. Div.	15,673	–	–	5,434	35
22. Pz. Div.	16,211	–	–	5,000	31
24. Pz. Div.	16,076	–	–	5,126	32
16. (Mot.) ID	16,000	–	–	6,000	37
29. (Mot.) ID	16,000	–	–	4,000	25
94. ID	15,702	–	–	8,233	52
297. ID	16,898	–	–	7,000	41
371. ID	16,317	–	–	6,000	37

1 The *Sollstärke* indicated here have been established by combining divisional ration strengths and deficits illustrated in Kehrig, *Stalingrad*, p. 668, and should be considered only a rough estimate. November shortages have been taken from same source. For those dated to September, see *6. AOK. Ia/Ic Anlagenband z. KTB Nr. 13, Russland. (12-17.9.1942)* NARA T312 Roll 1685, Frame 000987.

Table 5.8 Army Personnel Losses and Assigned Replacements, June 1941 to June 1943[1]

	Total Losses	Assigned Replacements	Balance
22 June 1941 – 30 June 1942	1,980,000	2,090,000	+110,000
1 July 1942 – 30 June 1943	1,985,000	2,350,000	+365,000
Total	3,965,000	4,440,000	+475,000

1 Note that total losses refer to combat casualties and sick. Figures indicated as available replacements constituted new recruits and returning wounded. Müller-Hillebrand, *Das Heer 1933-1945, Band III*, p. 110.

Table 5.9 German Armaments Production versus Losses, July to November 1942[1]

	New Production July-November 1942	Equipment Losses July-November 1942	Balance
MG	37,289	20,608	+16,681
Mortars	9,140	4,124	+5,016
3.7 cm/5 cm Pak	2,068	2,114	-46
7.5 cm Pak	2,133	715	+1,418
Infantry Guns	657	538	+119
Light Flak	4,640	1,770	+2,870
Heavy Flak	644	239	+405
Rocket Launchers	1,591	291	+1,300
Light field artillery	651	541	+110
Heavy Artillery	417	663	-246
Very Heavy Artillery	13	34	-21
Trucks	21,637	26,178	-4,541
Staff Cars	9,848	14,647	-4,799
Motorcycles	14,077	15,405	-1,328
Towing Vehicles	3,229	1,021	+2,208
SPW	1,131	199	+932

1 Figures for Flak includes all those produced and lost for the entire *Wehrmacht*. Kroener, et. al. *GSWW. Vol. V: Part Two*, pp. 636-688.

Table 5.10 Equipment in Stock with the German Army, 1 July and 1 December 1942[1]

	Stock 1.7.1942	Stock 1.12.1942	Difference
MG	218,264	234,617	+16,353
Mortars	29,800	36,773	+6,973
3.7 cm/5 cm Pak	12,975	12,969	-6
7.5 cm Pak	2,227	1,837	-390
Infantry Guns	4,571	4,697	+126
Light Flak	3,712	6,294	+2,582
Heavy Flak	227	231	+4
Light Field Artillery	6,317	6,160	-157
Heavy Field Artillery	3,410	3,310	-100
Very Heavy Artillery	470	450	-20
Trucks	341,759	403,178	+61,419
Staff Cars	262,655	285,919	+23,264
Motorcycles	255,814	276,525	+20,711

1 Kroener, et. al. *GSWW. Vol. V: Part Two*, p. 700.

Table 5.11 German Armaments Production 1942, per quarter[1]

	Jan.-March	April-June	July-Sept.	Oct.-Dec.
MG	14,221	18,975	19,811	28,192
Mortars	2,565	4,486	5,050	6,450
3.7 cm/5 cm Pak	1,112	1,118	1,194	1,374
7.5 cm Pak	13	1,730	1,536	1,065
Infantry Guns	434	396	374	483
Light Flak	2,922	3,738	4,294	4,573
Heavy Flak	?	?	?	1,028
Rocket Launchers	549	1,606	955	754
Light Artillery	301	270	347	558
Heavy Artillery	200	222	258	251
Trucks	10,487	13,539	12,981	12,700
Staff Cars	6,154	6,544	6,747	4,707
Motorcycles	8,394	8,975	8,857	7,791
Towing Vehicles	1,645	1,986	1,811	2,185
SPW	525	621	672	709
Tanks	1,027	1,140	1,028	1,083
Assault Guns	93	185	210	300
Self-propelled AT guns	–	293	459	371

1 Figures for Flak include all those produced for the entire *Wehrmacht*. Production of armoured vehicles taken from Müller-Hillebrand, "German Tank Strength and Loss Statistics", p. 28. Otherwise, see Kroener, et. al. *GSWW. Vol. V: Part Two*, pp. 636-688. Note that according to Hahn, *Waffen und Geheimwaffen des deutschen Heeres, 1933-1945, Band II*, pp. 26-80, actual armoured vehicle production during 1942 totaled 4,269 panzers, 824 assault guns, and 965 self-propelled anti-tank guns.

Table 5.12 Estimated Field Army Equipment Requirements versus Existing Stocks, 1 October 1942[1]

	Army Stock 1.10.1942	Actual Div. Requirements 1942 TOE	Army Troops Requirements 1942 TOE	Total Requirements	Surplus Stock
MG	226,581	117,284	29,357	146,641	79,940
Mortars	32,883	23,766	1,072	24,838	8,045
3.7 cm/5 cm Pak	12,722	10,140	512	10,652	2,070
7.5 cm Pak	1,316	890	121	1,011	305
Light Flak	5,839	956	984	1,940	3,899
Heavy Flak	200	124	78	202	-2
Infantry Guns	4,633	4,126	52	4,178	455
Nebelwerfer	2,667	303	306	609	2,058
Light Artillery	6,204	5,555	20	5,575	629
Heavy Artillery	3,395	1,940	1,038	2,978	417
Very Heavy Art.	454	–	439	439	15
Foreign Guns	?	272	1,769	2,041	?

1 For Army stock, see Kroener, et. al. *GSWW. Vol. V: Part Two*, p. 700. Division requirements determined from *OKH Generalstab des Heeres, Org. Abt. Kriegsgliederung des Feldheeres, 15 Oktober 1942*. NARA T78 Roll 406. For the needs of army troops, see Appendix Nine.

Table 5.13 Development of the German Armoured Vehicle Fleet, July to December 1942[1]

	Stock 1.7.1942	Stock 1.12.1942	Total Write-Offs	New Production
Tanks				
Pz I	692	692	15	–
Pz II	1,021	1,006	116	20
Pz 38t	479	334	111	–
Pz III	2,482	2,767	897	1,045
Pz IV	723	901	257	477
Tigers	–	16	3	38
Befelpz.	266	257	36	81
Total	5,663	5,973	1,435	1,661
Assault Guns and Self-propelled Anti-Tank Guns				
StuG	780	966	151	390
StuH	–	9	–	–
Marder	306	850	122	679
Total	1,086	1,825	273	1,069
Grand Total	6,749	7,798	1,708	2,730

1 Müller-Hillebrand, "German Tank Strength and Loss Statistics", p. 28. Citing different totals, Jentz, *Panzertruppen, Vol. One*, pp. 254-270, also notes that 393 tanks were rebuilt, which may account for some of the discrepancies within the table.

Table 5.14 Operational Readiness amongst the Panzer units of the *Ostheer*, 1 July and mid-November 1942[1]

	Pz II/38t		Pz III		Pz IV		Befelpz		Total	
	July	Nov.	July	Nov.	July	Nov.	July	Nov	July	Nov.
Heeresgruppe Nord & Mitte										
1. PD	12	10	27	30	7	11	4	4	50	55
2. PD	55	11	20	30	5	12	2	1	82	54
4. PD	13	2	28	12	5	5	2	0	49	19
5. PD	26	15	55	40	13	16	9	7	103	78
8. PD	66	14	0	0	2	0	0	1	68	15
9. PD	22	26	99	62	21	12	2	2	144	102
11. PD	15	14	124	88	13	9	3	4	155	115
12. PD	0	1	48	41	10	20	0	3	58	65
17. PD	17	9	36	30	16	18	2	3	71	60
18. PD	11	5	28	22	8	19	2	2	49	48
19. PD	41	44	12	8	4	13	0	3	57	68
20. PD	47	26	20	14	13	16	7	6	87	62
MD 'GD'	12	7	2	1	30	19	1	3	45	30
203. PR	29	0	63	7	5	2	6	0	103	9
1./502. Schwere Pz Btl.	0	0	0	16	6	Tigers	0	1	0	23
Heeresgruppe A & B										
3. PD	25	13	106	44	33	8	0	0	164	65
13. PD	15	4	71	21	12	4	5	0	103	29
14. PD	14	0	60	29	24	7	4	5	102	41
16. PD	13	0	57	21	27	10	3	0	100	31
22. PD	179	7	13	22	30	11	0	0	222	40
23. PD	37	5	84	27	27	8	0	0	138	40
24. PD	32	5	110	31	32	17	7	2	181	55
27. PD	0	31	0	27	0	7	0	0	0	65
3. MD	10	3	35	25	8	4	1	0	54	32
16. MD	10	8	35	23	8	11	1	1	54	43
29. MD	12	7	36	32	8	18	2	2	58	59
60. MD	17	4	35	14	4	3	1	0	57	21
SS-Div. 'Wiking'	12	0	36	18	4	8	1	0	53	26

1 Jentz, *Panzertruppen, Vol. One*, pp. 236-239, and *Vol. Two*, p. 24.

6

Catastrophe and Reconstitution on the Eastern Front, November 1942 to July 1943

Morally, the Germans seemed completely stunned, unable to understand what the devil had happened.

Russia at War
Alexander Werth[1]

By late autumn 1942, the German Army still appeared as indomitable as ever. Successive victories throughout the summer had rendered the setbacks of the previous winter a fading memory. Most of continental Europe remained firmly under German control. In Egypt, the vaunted *Afrika Korps* stood only 140 kilometres from Alexandria, gateway to the strategic oilfields of the Middle East. On the Eastern Front, German armies had swept aside superior numbers of Soviet troops before advancing hundreds of kilometres into the Caucasus, and to the city of Stalingrad along the Volga River. Admittedly, the struggle for Stalingrad had taken longer than the Germans had expected and the scope of their advance into the Caucasus necessitated a pause to consolidate overextended lines of communication. Moreover, despite its horrendous losses, the strength and resolve of the Soviet Union also appeared undiminished, and German intelligence officers had picked up signs of Soviet offensive preparations around both the Rzhev salient and along the Don front. Nevertheless, the OKH still remained confident. After all, the Red Army had conducted a series of offensive operations throughout the year and each had been bloodily repulsed. Surely any new attacks would meet a similar fate. The *Ostheer* simply had to hold out until spring when fresh operations would complete the conquest of the Caucasus, force Russia to the peace table, and ensure German dominance of Europe.

But in just over a single month, everything changed. The near destruction of the *Afrika Korps* during the Second Battle of El Alamein (23 October-11 November) and the Anglo-American landings in French North Africa (8 November) not only suddenly

---

1   Werth, *Russia at War, 1941-1945*, p. 500.

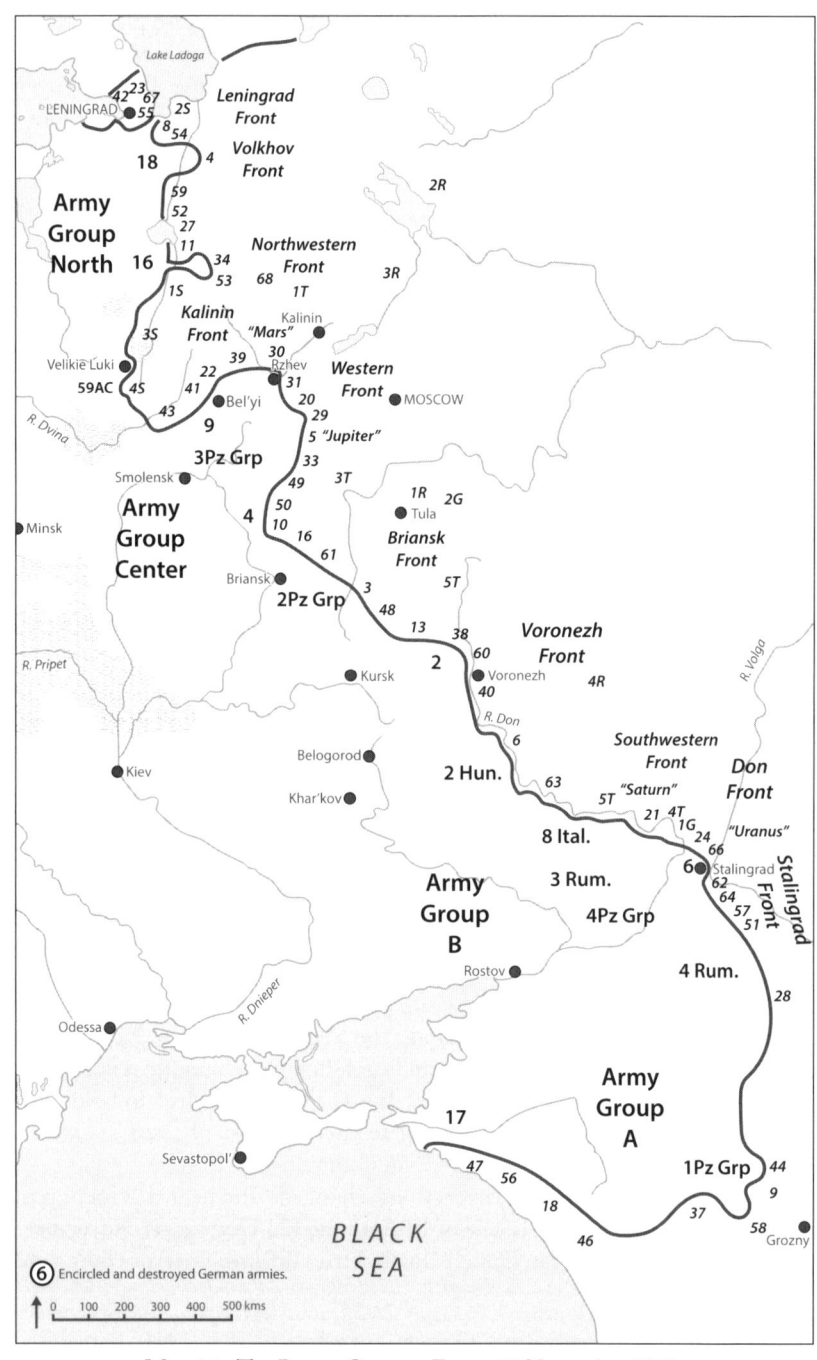

Map 6.1 The Russo-German Front, 18 November 1942.

threatened to eliminate the Axis presence in North Africa, they also placed the larger Axis strategic position in the Mediterranean in grave peril. Even worse, the Eastern Front abruptly appeared to be on the verge of a complete collapse. On 19 November the Red Army launched Operation Uranus around Stalingrad and within four days encircled the *6. Armee* and most of the *4. Panzerarmee*. Holding the Rzhev salient, the *9. Armee* faced a similar threat when Soviet forces commenced Operation Mars on 25 November. Additional Soviet attacks around Velikie Luki (25 November) and the Demyansk salient (28 November) added to German tribulations. The combined weight of these Soviet offensives not only threatened the specific German armies involved, but also jeopardized the fate of entire army groups and, therefore, the entire German position in the East. With astounding rapidity, Germany had regressively transitioned from dictating the course of events to haphazardly coping with one crisis after the other.

During the next seven months, the *Ostheer* experienced a series of devastating defeats even more calamitous than those experienced during the winter of 1941-1942. The desperate gamble to neutralize the Soviet Union and secure the resource areas upon which Germany's fortunes rested failed. All the hard-fought gains of the summer were irretrievably lost. In the process, entire armies were erased and personnel and material losses reached staggering new levels. Henceforth the *Ostheer* was confined to conducting a strategic defence – in retrospect, a gruelling rearguard action that lasted until the surrender of the Third Reich in 1945.

Conversely, these same seven months also witnessed a major regeneration of the *Ostheer*. Retaining its prowess for tactical and operational-level action and still capable of mustering formidable quantities of troops and equipment, the *Ostheer* managed to achieve a surprising number of battlefield victories. In fact, the majority of the Soviet attacks staged during this period were defeated outright or otherwise limited to modest gains.[2] Even the grand Soviet winter offensive that stampeded Axis forces back across southern Russia was eventually brought to a halt and the front reconstituted. Large numbers of fresh German divisions flooded into the East along with copious quantities of replacement personnel and new equipment. By early July 1943 the strength of the *Ostheer* was restored to a level that it hadn't enjoyed since the Russian campaign began. Even if the Soviet Union could no longer be defeated outright, this astounding resurgence allowed Germany's leaders to hope that the Red Army could be bled white, that vital resource areas already captured in the East could be retained, and even that some kind of compromise peace be negotiated.[3]

---

2   For the most comprehensive review of Soviet offensive operations during this period, see Glantz, *After Stalingrad.*

3   See Karl-Heinz Frieser, et. al. *Das Deutsche Reich und der Zweite Weltkrieg. Volume VIII: Die Ostfront 1943/44.* (Munchen: 2011), pp. 28-79, and H.W. Koch, "The Spectre of a Separate Peace in the East: Russo-German 'Peace Feelers', 1942-1944." *Journal of Contemporary History*, Vol. 10, No. 3 (July 1975), pp. 531-549. Also see Richard Breitman,

What spurred the crisis in the East in the first place were the massive German miscalculations of the size, capabilities, and offensive intentions of the Red Army in late 1942. Traditionally, historians have overwhelmingly placed the blame for this upon Hitler alone. Senior German Army officers, such as Halder or his replacement *General der Infanterie* Kurt Zeitzler, however, have been presented as having persistently warned Hitler that a massive Soviet offensive along the Don River threatened German forces around Stalingrad with encirclement. Because of his megalomania and self-delusion, Hitler simply refused to recognize the reality of the situation and take rational countermeasures. Rather than trust his military advisors, so the argument goes, Hitler instead relied upon his "intuition".[4] The problem with this narrative is that it too relied upon post-war accounts written by former German officers; as we have seen, these men may have been more interested in preserving their own reputations, and that of the wider German officer corps, than in producing a factual account. Thanks to the work of more scrupulous scholars, we now know that this description of events is largely false. The problem was not Hitler's refusal to heed the council of his military experts, but rather that in this particular case *he did*.

Specifically, this relates to the information Hitler received from the Army's eastern intelligence gathering organ, *Fremde Heere Ost* (Foreign Armies East, or FHO) led by *Oberstleutnant* Reinhard Gehlen.[5] On 19 August 1942, the FHO reported that the Red Army was still capable of mounting "attacks with operational objectives" and that these would likely be directed against *Heeresgruppe Mitte* and the deep flanks of *Heeresgruppe B*. Yet, during a lecture at the *Kriegsakademie* on 7 September, Gehlen seemed to backtrack somewhat, arguing "the Russian reserve of manpower...[was] not inexhaustible" and that the Soviets lacked reserves comparable to those they possessed the previous year.[6] By early October, the FHO was increasingly convinced that Soviet offensive activities would be focused along the central portion of the front.

"A Deal with the Nazi Dictatorship? Himmler's Alleged Peace Emissaries in Autumn 1943." *Journal of Contemporary History*, Vol. 30, No. 3 (July 1995), pp. 411-430.

4   For example, see Jukes, *Hitler's Stalingrad Decisions*, Tarrant, *Stalingrad*, pp. 87-93, Görlitz, *History of the German General Staff, 1657-1945*, pp. 418 & 424-426, and Shirer, *The Rise and Fall of the Third Reich*, pp. 917-919. For his part, Tarrant makes especially heavy use of Zeitzler's post-war recollections found in W. Richardson & S. Freidin, (Ed.) *The Fatal Decisions*. (London: 1956).

5   Information concerning the activities of the FHO and other German intelligence agencies in the East may be found in David Kahn, *Hitler's Spies: German Military Intelligence in World War II*. (New York: 1978), pp. 418-442, Oscar Reile, *Geheime Ostfront: Die deutsche Abwehr im Osten, 1921-1945*. (Munchen: 1992), David Thomas, "Foreign Armies East and German Military Intelligence in Russia, 1941-1945." *Journal of Contemporary History*, Vol. 22, No. 2 (April 1987), pp. 261-301, Magnus Pahl, *Fremde Heere Ost: Hitlers militarische Feindaufklarung*. (Berlin: 2012), and Perry Biddiscombe, "Unternehmen Zepplin: The Deployment of SS Saboteurs and Spies in the Soviet Union, 1942-1945." *Europa–Asia Studies*, Vol. 52, No. 6 (2000), pp. 1115-1142.

6   Boog, et. al. *GSWW, Vol. VI*, p. 1119.

During the middle of the month, it acknowledged that the Russians would eventually conduct some kind of offensive against the lines of *Heeresgruppe B*, but qualified this by insisting that its scale would be limited, since anything greater would force the Russians to take troops away from their main push against *Heeresgruppe Mitte*. On 31 October the FHO again reiterated that the main Soviet attack would fall along the central sector. Along the Don front, only local Soviet attacks seemed likely as "preparations for major attacks [were] not yet perceptible in any location."[7] This belief persisted throughout the first half of November despite mounting evidence to the contrary. Only on 18 November – the day before Operation Uranus commenced – did the FHO acknowledge that something more serious was brewing; for the first time, the FHO noted that the danger of a double encirclement seemed a possibility after Soviet attack preparations were observed south of Stalingrad. Even so, Gehlen continued to equivocate, admitting only "One may therefore reckon that the expected attacks – even if only with limited goals – may possibly exceed local proportions."[8] Distracted by the imminent Soviet offensive against *Heeresgruppe Mitte*, German intelligence still had no clear idea of the magnitude or timing of what was about to occur around Stalingrad.

Alongside the reassurances emanating from FHO were the attitudes of the Army Chiefs of Staff – namely Halder and later Zeitzler. Although sceptical of Germany's overall situation by late 1942, Halder viewed the Eastern Front with considerably more optimism. Throughout September, he doubted whether the Red Army still retained any sizeable reserves and thereby considered the possibility of a large-scale Soviet attack remote.[9] In addition to underestimating Soviet capabilities, Halder remained confident that the German Army was still more than a match for its Soviet adversary. In a letter to the commander of *Heeresgruppe Nord* on 21 September, Halder confidently wrote, "The numerical superiority of the Russians is a fact that we will continue to face, despite the lack of personnel on his side that is gradually becoming discernable. It will be balanced out through the high value of the German soldier."[10] He remained Panglossian despite his dismissal a few days later. According to the diary of Halder's close friend Ernst von Weizsäcker (State Secretary at the Foreign Office), "[Halder] says that above all he's leaving his post without worries for the army. The Russians are too far weakened to be the danger to us they were last winter."[11] Following his appointment as Army Chief of Staff, Zeitzler appears to have largely shared this sentiment. General instructions he issued to the Army on 23 October regarding the

7   Ibid, p. 1120. Also see Ziemke, *Stalingrad to Berlin*, p. 48.
8   Kahn, *Hitler's Spies*, pp. 437-438. Also see Boog, et. al. *GSWW, Vol. VI*, pp. 1120-1123 and Ziemke, *Stalingrad to Berlin*, p. 48.
9   See mention of Army Chief of Staff's assessment of Soviet reserves on 9 September in Hillgruber, (Ed.) *KTB OKW. Band II*, p. 703. Also noted in Boog, et. al. *GSWW, Vol. VI*, pp. 1118-1119.
10   Megargee, *Inside Hitler's High Command*, p. 181.
11   Irving, *Hitler's War*, p. 485.

forthcoming winter confidently asserted that, "the Russian is at this time hardly in a position to begin a large scale offensive with long range goals." At the daily briefing held at Hitler's headquarters four days later, Zeitzler reassuringly declared that he considered recent Soviet pronouncements about an imminent large-scale offensive a propaganda exercise rather than an indication of their true intentions.[12]

Despite the confident assertions of his senior advisors and intelligence experts, Hitler was less sanguine about the security of the German front along the Don River. As early as mid-August Hitler expressed concern that the Soviets might try to breech the Don front and advance on Rostov, thereby cutting off German forces to the east and south.[13] This anxiety only mounted and on 26 October he gave instructions that some of the newly formed *Luftwaffe* field divisions be dispatched to the Don front to stiffen the lines of the Axis armies deployed there. By the start of November, prisoner interrogations, radio intercepts and the increased pace of Soviet bridge building across the Don produced a more comprehensive picture of enemy activities and a sense of the growing Soviet readiness to attack. Alarmed, Hitler reacted quickly. On 2 November he directed the *Luftwaffe* to bomb the bridges and Soviet assembly areas, and the following day ordered one panzer and two infantry divisions be moved from France to serve as reserves behind the Italian Eighth and Romanian Third Armies. In the interim, blocking detachments and emergency units were to be formed throughout the rear areas of *Heeresgruppe B*.[14]

To the ultimate detriment of the German position around Stalingrad, the concordant views of FHO and the Army Chief of Staff swayed Hitler's decision-making for too long. Weighed against his own concerns was the fact that Hitler himself had always been incredulous towards assessments of Soviet strength and capabilities, believing them to be wildly exaggerated. He was also extremely reluctant to make any sweeping decisions, especially those he was inclined against, preferring instead to await developments in the hope that the problem would fix itself. With Army intelligence and his chief lieutenants repeatedly downplaying the Soviet threat along the Don, and essentially telling him what he wanted to hear, "it is obvious why Hitler, despite all anxieties, could see no cogent reason for truly drastic measures – such as the suspension of the attack in Stalingrad and the withdrawal of the front to a Don-Chir position."[15] Rather than make such unappealing decisions, throughout October Hitler placated

12   Megargee, *Inside Hitler's High Command*, p. 190 and Hillgruber, (Ed.) *KTB OKW. Band II*, p. 867.
13   According to Irving, *Hitler's War*, pp. 478 & 485, at this time Hitler ordered Halder to move the *22. Panzer Division* behind the Italian Eighth Army, but the division was not actually redeployed until late September.
14   Boog, et. al. *GSWW, Vol. VI*, pp. 1115-1121.
15   Ibid, p. 1120. For a more detailed study concerning the failure of German Army intelligence at this point, see Hans-Heinrich Wilhelm, "Die Prognosen der Abteilung Fremde Heere Ost 1942-1945" in Hans-Heinrich Wilhelm & Louis De Jong, *Zwei Legenden aus dem Dritten Reich*. (Stuttgart: 1974), pp. 47-48.

his own fears through a mixture of wishful thinking and some moderate measures designed to shore up the Don front. As we have seen, it was only during the first days of November that he ordered fresh reinforcements from France to the region.[16] But, even at this late hour, Hitler allowed himself to be lulled into a greater complacency than his own fears might have dictated. Reassured by his military chiefs, and still having no idea when the Soviet attack would actually occur, on 7 November Hitler departed his headquarters for an extended rest at the secluded Berghof. At the moment the Third Reich was about to reach the apex of its existence, Hitler went on vacation. Ultimately, the dispatch of reinforcements came too late – the first trains carrying the *6. Panzer Division* reached *Heeresgruppe B* on 26 November, three days after the *6. Armee* had been encircled at Stalingrad.[17]

In contrast to what Hitler and the German General Staff believed, the size and capabilities of the Red Army increased significantly during the course of 1942. True, the massive losses it endured since the spring produced a slight drop in the total number of overall military personnel by 1 November, and henceforth many Soviet formations would suffer endemic manpower shortages throughout the war. Indeed, the Soviet divisions committed to Operation Uranus possessed an average of only 75 to 79 percent of their assigned personnel. Circumstances were somewhat better amongst the formations allotted to Operation Mars, but even here personnel strengths ranged from 78 to 98 percent of authorized establishments.[18] Nonetheless, by marshalling fresh levies and drawing upon the large troop consignments stationed within the internal military districts and in the Far East, the number of personnel deployed across the Russo-German front actually increased by nearly one million (see Table 6.1).

While impressive, such figures alone represented neither an overwhelming Soviet numerical superiority nor an automatic guarantee of victory. After all, against the 6,605,498 troops deployed by the Soviet Union, Germany and its allies probably fielded around 4.1 million men in the East by November 1942.[19] Even excluding allied

16   Why this relatively simple measure was not adopted earlier is something of a mystery, but can probably be attributed to a combination of reasons including the logistical difficulties of supporting more troops in the region, the overall lack of urgency, fears of an Allied invasion of France, and the hope of preserving these troops for operations against Russia during the following spring.

17   The last transport trains moving the *6. Panzer Division* left France on this date, at which the first 11 trains of the *306. Infanterie Division* had also departed. Hillgruber, (Ed.) *KTB OKW. Band II*, p. 1029.

18   Glantz, *Colossus Reborn*, p. 209.

19   In regards to the Soviet figure, 5,781,229 personnel constituted the ground forces, the balance residing with the Soviet Army Air Force, the Air Defence force (PVO) and the Soviet Navy. The number of Axis personnel includes 2.9 million Germans with the *Ostheer* (on 1 October) and roughly 1.2 million allied Axis troops (including 229,005 Italians, 206,197 Hungarians, 380,103 Romanians, and 400,000 Finns). The actual total is probably considerably greater since the one shown here does not include German security personnel

Axis troops from the totals, the Red Army only outnumbered the *Ostheer* by little more than two to one, odds against which the Germans had managed to prevail in the past. Instead, it is crucial to recognize that the Red Army underwent a significant improvement in terms of its leadership, experience and capabilities. The relentless gristmill of the Eastern Front, combined with Stalin's own ruthless expectations, meant that poor commanders did not live long. Those Soviet officers who managed to survive learnt from their experiences, steadily improving their ability to plan and conduct complex large-scale operations. Similarly, enough of the rank and file survived to develop crucial battlefield skills and to pass these on to the fresh drafts of recruits. In short, the Red Army became an increasingly battle-hardened and well-led force.[20] Soviet commanders also became increasingly adept at conducting operational-level deception operations (*Maskirovka*); together with the refinement of internal security measures and counter-intelligence operations, this rendered German efforts to divine Soviet intentions increasingly difficult. This meant that the STAVKA could marshal superior forces along those sectors it chose to attack, while the Germans were forced to dissipate their resources across the entire breadth of the front.[21]

Between mid-1942 and early 1943, the Red Army also developed a considerably more complex and powerful force structure. This addressed four fundamental problems that had continuously plagued Soviet operations since the start of the Russo-German War: command and control, sufficient firepower, enough mobile reserves, and the regeneration of Soviet air power. Deficiencies in these areas were the combined product of the rapid expansion of the pre-war Red Army and the horrendous personnel and equipment losses the Soviets sustained during the first months of the German invasion. These in turn let to widespread shortages of both trained staff personnel and military equipment of all kinds. Since these were key components to successfully breeching German lines and exploiting the breakthrough, their resolution was vital to the ultimate victory of the Soviet Union. To alleviate the issue of command and control, the STAVKA expanded the number of rifle corps headquarters and increased the availability of communication units. To fill the burgeoning number of command and staff positions, Soviet military academies and training establishments created 564,000 officers during 1942.[22] Given the relentless pace at which vast

---

within those regions under German civil administration, the large number of *Luftwaffe* personnel in the East who were not under Army command, Hungarian security forces, or the 71,211 Romanian troops occupying the Trans-Dniester region. See Kroener, et. al. *GSWW. Vol. V: Part Two*, p. 1020, Dell'esercito, *La Operazioni delle Unita Italiane al Fronte Russo, 1941-1943*, and Dutu, et. al. *Armata romana in al doilea razboi mondial, 1941-1945.*

20 For the most thorough study charting the evolution of the Red Army during this period, see Glantz, *Colossus Reborn*. For the best insight into the experiences of the Soviet rank and file, see Roger R. Reese, *Why Stalin's Soldiers Fought: The Red Army's Military Effectiveness in World War II.* (Lawrence, KS: 2011).

21 See Glantz, *Soviet Military Deception in the Second World War*. Also, Glantz, *The Role of Intelligence in Soviet Military Strategy in World War II* and Stephan, *Stalin's Secret War.*

22 Glantz, *Colossus Reborn*, pp. 471-473.

amounts of material was lost, increasing the number of fire support units and mobile reserves were more challenging prospects. Nonetheless, thanks to the efforts of Soviet industry prodigious quantities of new equipment entered service (see Table 6.2).[23] This permitted the uninterrupted formation of new army support units and by the start of 1943 roughly 990 regiments and 245 separate battalions of field, anti-tank, and anti-aircraft artillery, mortars and rocket launchers stood at the disposal of the STAVKA. These would soon be joined by another 30 new regiments of self-propelled artillery.[24] To manage this host, the Soviets organized some units into 18 artillery and 27 anti-aircraft divisions, and began the process of establishing anti-tank, mortar and rocket launcher brigades. This development signified a fundamental shift in the nature of Soviet operations whereby the reliance upon sheer manpower – an increasingly scarce commodity as the war dragged on – was steadily replaced with one characterized by tremendous quantities of firepower and material. As noted in Table 6.3, the personnel strength of the Soviet armed forces would peak in mid-1943 but the accumulation of material continued at a relentless pace until the end of the war. Together with its more effective management, this steady accumulation of firepower and material played a key role in the Red Army's victory since it could now literally blast its way through German defences.

After near-annihilation during Operation Barbarossa, Soviet armoured forces staged a similar recovery. Thanks to the increased availability of armour, the number of tank corps (each with 146 to 180 tanks) grew from 14 on 1 May 1942, to 20 by 1 January 1943. This period also witnessed the formation of eight mechanized corps (containing 175 to 224 tanks apiece). Equally crucial was the creation of dedicated infantry-support tank units, which, by early 1943, totalled 181 brigades and regiments along with numerous independent battalions.[25] Previously, the dearth of armoured formations available for offensive operations meant that the same tank units had to support the infantry breaking into and through German defences, and then conduct the advance across the German rear areas. Achieving the former usually left these units too weak or disorganized to sustain the latter. Without the ability to press the

---

23   Significant amounts of weaponry arrived via Lend-Lease by the end of 1942, but these were still relatively small compared to Soviet production. The most important items supplied by the Western Allies were still raw materials and especially food. See Alexander Hill, "The Bear's New Wheels (and Tracks): US Armored and Other Vehicles and Soviet Military Effectiveness during the Great Patriotic War in Words and Photographs." *Journal of Slavic Military Studies*, Vol. 25, No. 2 (2012), pp. 204-219, Vorsin, "Motor Vehicle Transport Deliveries through 'Lend-Lease.'", Gribanov, "The Role of US Lend-Lease Aircraft in Russia in World War II.", and Munting, "Soviet Food Supply and Allied Aid in the War, 1941-1945."

24   This included 301 regiments (plus 23 separate battalions) of field artillery, 249 anti-tank artillery regiments, 231 anti-aircraft regiments (plus 109 separate battalions), 130 mortar regiments, and 79 rocket launcher regiments (plus 113 separate battalions). Glantz, *Colossus Reborn*, pp. 288-311.

25   Ibid, pp. 216-234.

advance deep into the German rear areas, few opportunities arose to encircle large bodies of German troops or, at least, disrupt significant portions of their defensive front to such an extent that it would compel the Germans to undertake a substantive withdrawal. Instead, most Soviet offensives during the first 18 months of the war rapidly degenerated into costly battles of attrition during which little territory was gained and Soviet losses tended to be disproportionately greater than those sustained by the Germans. But the increased availability of armour by late-1942 fundamentally altered this trend: separate infantry-support tank units now handled the penetration of German defences, leaving the tank and mechanized corps, increasingly organized into independent tank armies consisting of roughly 450-500 tanks and 46,000 men, fresh to exploit the breakthrough.[26] With powerful Soviet armoured forces now capable of conducting operations deep in their rear areas, German forces – who steadily became less mobile as the war progressed – became increasingly vulnerable to encirclement.

Paralleling the development of the ground forces, the Red Army Air Force (VVS) also experienced a massive transformation during 1942. In the aftermath of the horrendous losses sustained during Operation Barbarossa, the STAVKA endeavoured to regenerate the strength and capabilities of the VVS so that it would be capable of both shielding Soviet ground forces from *Luftwaffe* air attacks and of supporting them during offensive operations. As with the remainder of the Red Army, this development was impaired early in the war by the relentless pace of operations that produced heavy losses throughout 1942. At least 14,700 aircraft were lost and, according to German claims, 9,644 of these were destroyed during the last six months of the year.[27] Nonetheless, through its prodigious efforts Soviet industry manufactured 25,436 new aircraft and Lend-Lease deliveries provided thousands more.[28] Despite its heavy losses, the number of combat aircraft with the VVS increased from 14,967 on 1 May to 19,797 by 1 November, by which time 8,805 of these aircraft were actively engaged along the Russo-German front.[29] In contrast, *Luftwaffe* air strength on the *Ostfront* decreased from 2,635 aircraft on 20 June to 1,668 aircraft by 20 December.[30] By late 1942 each Soviet front was supported by at least one air army of 400-500 aircraft and when reinforced by STAVKA reserve formations this number could surge to 1,000 or more aircraft. Through its varied battlefield support roles – such as direct ground

---

26   For more details concerning the key role these new tank armies played in Soviet offensive operations, see David M. Glantz, "Action of the mobile group of the 5th Tank Army in the Penetration." *Journal of Slavic Military Studies*, Vol. 1, No. 4 (1988), pp. 547-564. Also see Goff, "Evolving Soviet Force Structure, 1941-1945: Process and Impact".

27   Krivosheev, *Soviet Casualties and Combat Losses in the 20th Century*, p. 254. For German claims, see Hillgruber, (Ed.) *KTB OKW. Band II.*

28   Glantz, *Colossus Reborn*, p. 323.

29   Glantz, *To the Gates of Stalingrad*, p. 47, and Institute of Military History at the Russian Defence Ministry, *Combat and Numerical Composition of the Armed Forces of the USSR in the period of the Great Patriotic War (1941-1945)*. Statistical Material No. 5 (1 November 1942).

30   Boog, et. al. *GSWW, Vol. VI*, p. 965.

attacks, suppression of German artillery batteries, or the interdiction of German reserves – the VVS played an increasingly vital role in Soviet offensive operations.[31] To facilitate coordination, the number of air-ground radio liaison stations was expanded from 180 in 1942 to 420 by 1943, ensuring near-continuous radio contact between every Soviet field army (and many of the mobile corps) and their supporting air contingents.[32] Although the *Luftwaffe* was never entirely defeated, henceforth its effect upon ground operations steadily diminished. Conversely, the impact of the VVS mounted as the skies over the Eastern Front filled with increasing numbers of Soviet aircraft.

It was this New Model Army that commenced Operation Uranus, the Soviet counteroffensive around Stalingrad, on 19 November 1942. Although the Romanian troops guarding the flanks of the *6. Armee* gave a far better account of themselves than they have usually been given credit for, they were nonetheless quickly overwhelmed and Soviet mobile units were soon racing deep into Axis rear areas.[33] A shortage of sizeable German reserves in the region, combined with the confusion produced by breakdowns in communications and a series of poor command decisions on the part of senior German officers, handicapped Axis efforts to stem the Soviet onslaught.[34] With Axis rear-echelons fleeing before them in panic-stricken rout, the converging Soviet spearheads made contact on 23 November and the encirclement of the *6. Armee* (together with most of the *4. Panzerarmee*) was complete.[35] Ordered by Hitler to hold their ground rather than escape westwards, the roughly 250,000 to 300,000 Axis troops of the *6. Armee* were now trapped in what for most would ultimately become their tomb.[36]

Yet as grave as the situation was around Stalingrad, it was not the only crisis that suddenly confronted the *Ostheer* – a fact routinely overlooked within the

31   The most detailed studies of air operations on the Eastern Front may be found in Bergstrom's, *Stalingrad: The Air Battle, 1942 through January 1943*, *Kursk: The Air Battle, July 1943*, and *Bagration to Berlin: The Final Air Battles in the East, 1944-1945*. For general studies concerning the VVS, consult Ray Wagner, (Ed.) *The Soviet Air Force in World War II: The Official History.* (Garden City, NY: 1973) and Von Hardesty, *Red Phoenix: The Rise of Soviet Air Power, 1941-1945.* (Washington, DC: 1982).

32   Glantz, *Colossus Reborn*, p. 318.

33   As Erickson recounted in his description of the Soviet breakthrough, "Romanian battalions, for all their pitiful equipment, were fighting it out manfully." Erickson, *The Road to Stalingrad*, p. 464. Also see Axworthy, et. al. *Third Axis, Fourth Ally*, pp. 89-105, and David M. Glantz, *Endgame at Stalingrad, Book One: November 1942. The Stalingrad Trilogy. Volume Three.* (Lawrence, KS: 2014).

34   See Axworthy, et. al. *Third Axis, Fourth Ally*, p. 93, Boog, et. al. *GSWW, Vol. VI*, p. 1123, and Ziemke & Bauer, *Moscow to Stalingrad*, p. 470.

35   For a description of this rout, see Wilhelm Adam, *Der schwere Entschluss: Wilhelm Adam, ehemaliger 1. Adjutant der 6. Armee.* (East Berlin: 1965), p. 175, quoted in Boog, et. al. *GSWW, Vol. VI*, p. 1126.

36   The process behind Hitler's decision to have the *6. Armee* stand its ground rather than escape to the west is too complex to relate here, but the best explanation yet produced may be found in Hayward, *Stopped at Stalingrad*, pp. 233-246.

historiography.[37] The long-awaited Soviet offensive against the Rzhev salient commenced on 25 November and immediately breached German lines in a number of locations. To the west, Soviet troops also attacked German positions around Velikie Luki and quickly surrounded its garrison. Three days later, yet another Soviet offensive was launched against the narrow corridor connecting the Demyansk salient with the main German front. In just a few short days dozens of German divisions were suddenly threatened with encirclement and destruction around Rzhev and Demyansk, presenting Hitler and the OKH with the prospect of having to contend with not just one, but three major encirclements of German forces at once. Equally worrisome was the Soviet attack around Velikie Luki which aimed at the weak boundary between *Heeresgruppe Nord* and *Mitte*. If the Soviets could exploit their success there, they could potentially plunge deep into the virtually undefended rear areas of either army group and possibly cause the entire German front to collapse. Fortunately for the *Ostheer*, these nightmare scenarios were avoided. In anticipation of the Soviet attack around Rzhev, *Heeresgruppe Mitte* assembled nine mobile divisions possessing roughly 500 operational tanks in and around the salient.[38] These reserves reacted quickly first to seal off, and then eliminate the Soviet penetrations. The participating Soviet units sustained horrendous losses and despite their persistent efforts, Operation Mars eventually petered out.[39] Around Demyansk, Soviet assaults made even less progress and here too their offensive gradually faded away.[40] Only around Velikie Luki did the Soviets register any success when they eventually recaptured the city and eliminated its garrison. However, the four German divisions moved into the region effectively barred the Red Army from exploiting even this modest triumph.[41]

37   No mention of the fighting around Rzhev, Velikie Luki and Demyansk are to be found in either Werth, *Russia at War, 1941-1945*, Clark, *Barbarossa*, or Seaton, *The Russo-German War, 1941-1945*. Interestingly, the much earlier account written by Wladyslaw Anders refers to all three. See Anders, *Hitler's Defeat in Russia*, pp. 147-148.

38   Together with the *41. (Mot.) Infanterie Regiment* belonging to the *10. (Mot.) Infanterie Division*, in *9. Armee* reserve when Operation Mars began were the *1.* and *5. Panzer Divisions*, the *14. (Mot.) Infanterie Division* and *(Mot.) Infanterie Division Grossdeutschland*. Arriving during the course of the battle from army group reserve were the *9., 12., 19.* and *20. Panzer Divisions* and the *SS-Kavallerie Division*. For the tank strengths of these formations, see *9. AOK. Tagesmeldungen. Anlagen z. KTB Nr. 6. AOK 9, Ia. (11.11-31.12.1942)* NARA T312 Roll 307, Frames 7873602-7873676.

39   According to Russian sources, Operation Mars cost the Red Army a total of 215,674 casualties (70,373 killed or missing and 145,301 wounded and sick). Glantz, *After Stalingrad*, p. 89. However, historian David Glantz has comprehensively argued that actual Soviet losses during the battle probably totalled around 335,000 casualties (100,000 killed or missing and 235,000 wounded or sick). See Glantz, *Zhukov's Greatest Defeat*, pp. 304-309 & 379-380, and Glantz, *After Stalingrad*, pp. 89-91.

40   For the best account of this battle, see Ibid, pp. 92-107.

41   These included the *8. Panzer Division, 20. (Mot.) Infanterie Division, 291.* and *331. Infanterie Divisions*. The *1. SS-(Mot.) Infanterie Brigade* and parts of the *205. Infanterie Division* also shifted to the region. For the very little has ever been written about this

These various Soviet operations achieved only miniscule gains at the cost of around 500,000 personnel casualties and as many as 2,000 destroyed tanks.[42] Nonetheless, while two of these three battles were clear German victories (the third amounting to only a minor defeat), their cumulative effect was still detrimental to the German Army's ability to cope with the overall crisis that gripped the *Ostfront* during the winter of 1942-1943. First, the German formations involved in these engagements suffered heavy casualties, ranging somewhere between 60,000 to 90,000 men.[43]

battle, see Franz Kurowski, *Die Heeresgruppe Mitte 1942/1943*. (Friedberg: 1989) and Carell, *Scorched Earth*.

42   As noted previously, the Red Army probably sustained around 335,000 casualties during Operation Mars (25 November to 16 December 1942). Soviet losses during the fighting around Velikie Luki (25 November 1942 to 20 January 1943) included 31,674 killed or missing and 72,348 wounded and sick. Glantz & House, *When Titans Clashed*, p. 296. Estimates of Soviet losses around Demyansk (28 November 1942 to 6 January 1943) range between 15,000 and 30,000, but these are probably too low. Glantz, *After Stalingrad*, p. 107. Soviet equipment losses during these engagements have never been compiled, but German claims during Operation Mars alone amounted to 1,847 tanks and 896 artillery pieces and mortars. These claims are probably not far from the mark: the Soviet 1st Mechanized and 6th Tank Corps lost virtually their entire complements of tanks during the course of the battle, while the 5th Tank Corps lost 97 of its 131 tanks in only three days of fighting. Glantz, *Zhukov's Greatest Defeat*, pp. 306-307.

43   According to the relevant 10-Day Heeresarzt Reports, the *9. Armee* sustained 28,771 casualties (6,025 killed, 21,070 wounded and 1,676 missing) between 21 November and 31 December 1942. See Heeresarzt 10-Day Casualty Reports for the *9. Armee* (21.11-31.12.1942) in BA-MA RW 6/556 and 6/558. However, actual German losses during the battle may have been significantly greater. According to one detailed report, the *9. Armee* sustained 53,542 casualties (11,349 killed, 38,332 wounded and 3,861 missing) between 1 October and 31 December. *9. AOK. Anlagen zum Tatigkeitsbericht der Abt. IIa/b. (1.10-31.12.1942)*, NARA T312 Roll 307, Frame 7874417. Given that this sector was relatively quiet prior to 25 November, the majority of these casualties were probably sustained during Operation Mars. Around Demyansk, the defending *16. Armee* endured roughly 17,780 casualties (3,606 killed, 13,220 wounded and 954 missing) between 21 November 1942 and 10 January 1943. Heeresarzt 10-Day Casualty Reports for the *16. Armee* (21.11.1942-10.1.1943) in BA-MA RW 6/556 and 6/558. No complete tally of German losses around Velikie Luki has ever been compiled, but a partial accounting includes the following:

	Time Period	Total Casualties
20. (Mot.) Inf. Div.	15.12.1942 – 18.1.1943	2,393
291. Infanterie Div.	15.12.1942 – 18.1.1943	2,880
331. Infanterie Div.	4-18.1.1943	2,916
205. Infanterie Div.	4-22.1.1943	3,220
8. Panzer Div.	20.11.1942 – 16.1.1943	2,532
3. Gebirgs Div.	24.11-25.12.1942	3,367
Total		17,308

Note that this does not include losses sustained by the *83. Infanterie Division* or any of the smaller German units present. For the casualties of the *3. Gebirgs Division*, see Klatt, *Die*

As additional Soviet offensives rippled across the front in the months to come, the German Army would be hard pressed to make up these losses in a timely manner. Secondly, these operations diverted crucial German ground and air assets at a time when all available forces were needed to shore up the Don sector and liberate the *6. Armee* trapped in Stalingrad.[44] By the end of December only five divisions could be shifted from *Heeresgruppe Mitte* to the crumbling southern front.[45]

Despite the host of crises elsewhere, Hitler and the OKH moved quickly to re-establish a continuous front along the Chir River and out into the featureless steppe east of the Don. In little more than a fortnight nine divisions (including four panzer divisions) were moved into the region and another was in the process of arriving.[46] Now organized into *Heeresgruppe Don* and commanded by *Generalfeldmarschall* Erich von Manstein, this force was also given the task of staging Operation Winter Storm, the rescue of the *6. Armee* trapped within Stalingrad. Illustrating the continuing ability of the *Ostheer* to assemble forces of formidable strength despite the challenges it faced, the troops under Manstein's command possessed an impressive total of roughly 471 tanks and self-propelled anti-tank guns by 12 December (see Table 6.4). Although Soviet pressure elsewhere along the front of the army group meant that only 263 of these vehicles (reinforced by another 48 tanks of the *17. Panzer Division* on 17 December) could be devoted to Winter Storm, these initially faced only the diminutive Soviet 51st Army of 34,000 men, 77 tanks, and 419 guns and mortars.[47] Not surprisingly, when the relief effort began on 12 December the attacking Germans smashed through the Soviet defences and, within a few days, advanced 50 kilometres. By 20 December, German spearheads had pushed to within 48 kilometres of their beleaguered comrades in Stalingrad.

3. Gebirgs Division, 1939-1945, p. 108. The losses of all the other divisions listed above can be found in Kurowski, *Die Heeresgruppe Mitte 1942/1943*.

44   Despite Zhukov's postwar claims that Operation Mars was solely intended to divert German resources from the Stalingrad sector, David Glantz and Jonathan House have pervasively argued that Mars was actually a major offensive in its own right and that it was in fact the centerpiece of Soviet strategic ambitions. Beyond the elimination of German forces in southern Russia, these "sought to collapse enemy defenses along virtually the entire Eastern Front." Glantz & House, *When Titans Clashed*, p. 143. Also see Glantz, *Zhukov's Greatest Defeat*. Most Western historians, such as Mawdsley, *Thunder in the East*, pp. 154-155 and Roberts, *Stalin's Wars*, pp. 151-153, now agree with this interpretation. For the arguments of one of the few who do not, see Anthony Beevor, *The Second World War*. (London: 2012).

45   These included the *11., 17.* and *19. Panzer Divisions, 3. Gebirgs Division* and the *26. Infanterie Division*.

46   These were the *6., 11., 17.* and *23. Panzer Divisions*, the *62., 294.,* and *.336. Infanterie Divisions*, and the *7.* and *8. Luftwaffe Feld Divisions*. On 12 December, the first elements of the *304. Infanterie Division* were also in the process of arriving in the Don region.

47   Initially only the *6.* and *23. Panzer Divisions*, supported by Romanian formations, were available to conduct Operation Winter Storm. For the initial strength of the Soviet 51st Army, see Erickson, *The Road to Berlin*, p. 11.

Yet, by this point, any prospect of actually reaching them quickly evaporated. The STAVKA rapidly redeployed strong forces to stop the German attack and, in a few days, the advance was effectively brought to a halt.[48] Even worse, on 16 December the Red Army unleashed Operation Little Saturn against both the Italian Eighth Army on the Don front and the German-Romanian forces stationed along the Chir River. Despite the best efforts of the defenders, by 19 December these sectors had started to collapse. Soviet tank units moved quickly to exploit emerging breeches in the line and were soon racing deep into Axis rear areas.[49] With Axis forces in the region completely disorganized, a rapid Soviet capture of the city of Rostov suddenly appeared imminent. Such an eventuality could effectively isolate any Axis forces deployed east and south of the city within the Caucasus. Although these troops might eventually be withdrawn via the Crimea, their immediate non-availability would have produced a disaster significantly greater than the one associated with the destruction of the 6. *Armee* around Stalingrad. With little or nothing to bar the main Soviet westward advance through the Donets region and into the eastern Ukraine, Soviet armies would have reached the Dnepr River faster than the Axis forces in the Caucasus could have been evacuated through the Crimea. At best, huge amounts of Axis troops and equipment would have been trapped in the Crimea from where they could do little to influence subsequent events along the main front. At worst these forces could potentially have been annihilated. Upon reaching the Dnepr, the Red Army would also have been in a position to wheel north into the deep rear of the German armies stationed in central Russia. Since the alternative was complete destruction, this would have forced the entire *Ostheer* into a hasty strategic retreat spanning hundreds of kilometres.[50] Faced with ramifications of such magnitude, Hitler and the OKH had little choice

---

48   Significantly, until 20 December losses amongst the formations conducting Operation Winter Storm had been relatively small. By this point, combat casualties amongst the three participating panzer divisions totaled only 1,613 men. Although they had collectively been reduced to 90 operational tanks, only 33 were listed as *Totalausfalle* with another 211 tanks in repair. See *Heeresgruppe Don. Kriegstagebuch Anlagen Band 4 (15-23.12.1942)*, NARA T311 Roll 269, Frames 000299-000300.

49   Very little has been written in English regarding this battle. Of the few that have, Hope Hamilton, *Sacrifice on the Steppe: The Italian Alpine Corps in the Stalingrad Campaign.* (Havertown, PA: 2011) provides little strategic context or operational detail, while Eugenio Corti, *Few Returned: Twenty-Eight Days on the Russian Front, Winter 1942-1943.* (Columbia, MO: 1997) is a memoir of limited value. The most detailed account may be found in David M. Glantz, *Endgame at Stalingrad, Book Two: December 1942 – February 1943. The Stalingrad Trilogy. Volume Three.* (Lawrence, KS: 2014), pp. 223-285, and Glantz, *From the Don to the Dnepr*, pp. 10-73. There is also the official Italian account in Stato Maggiore Dell'esercito, *La Operazioni delle Unita Italiane al Fronte Russo, 1941-1943.* For useful details concerning Romanian actions along the Chir River, see Axworthy, et. al. *Third Axis, Fourth Ally*, pp. 105-109.

50   As Erickson later wrote, "the prospects [of Operation Saturn] were dazzling indeed and loaded with intimations of decisive strategic success." Erickson, *The Road to Berlin*, p. 5.

but to allow Manstein to shift resources to deal with Little Saturn and abandon the *6. Armee* to its fate.

Despite the failure of Operation Winter Storm, the forces assembled by mid-December with *Heeresgruppe Don* nonetheless played a major role in the subsequent course of events on the Eastern Front. Initially, the STAVKA had intended to follow up Operation Uranus with Operation Saturn, the more ambitious forerunner of Little Saturn.[51] Scheduled to begin on 10 December, the goal of Saturn was to smash the Italian Eighth Army along the Don, press the advance south to capture Rostov, and thereby isolate *Heeresgruppe A* within the Caucasus. Along the lines already noted above, both Stalin and the STAVKA expected that Operation Saturn would produce a Soviet victory of strategic proportions. Anxious to free resources in order to fully exploit the opportunities he expected Saturn to produce, Stalin demanded that the seven Soviet armies besieging the *6. Armee* eliminate the trapped Germans immediately. Notwithstanding five days of heavy fighting (2-7 December), all Soviet assaults were repulsed. This made it clear to the STAVKA that it had badly underestimated the size and capabilities of the German force it had encircled. Increasingly frustrated, Stalin insisted that a renewed effort to destroy the Germans (codenamed Operation Ring) be made no later than 18 December. To ensure its success, he ordered the full-strength 2nd Guards Army to reinforce the attack. This army had been scheduled to lead the drive on Rostov, but, and at a stroke, its transfer to help with the reduction of the Stalingrad pocket reduced the number of troops that ultimately participated in Operation Saturn by almost one-fifth.[52]

With growing concern, the STAVKA also noted the steady build-up of *Heeresgruppe Don* and therefore created the 5th Shock Army to disrupt the concentration of German forces along the Chir River. Significantly, one of the two mobile corps assigned to the 5th Shock Army came from the forces allotted to Saturn and the other was transferred from the STAVKA reserve; its five rifle divisions originated from the reserves of the armies ringing Stalingrad.[53] While its attacks were successful in keeping the German troops deployed along the Chir from participating in Operation Winter Storm, the formation of this army entailed the weakening of the critical mobile forces available to conduct Saturn or exploit its subsequent success; it also appears to have contributed

---

51   For the full details concerning Soviet planning, see Ibid, pp. 5-16 and Glantz, *From the Don to the Dnepr*, pp. 10-23.

52   A total of 425,476 men and 1,030 tanks actually conducted Operation Little Saturn. Including the attached 2nd Guards Mechanized Corps, the Soviet 2nd Guards Army totaled 90,564 personnel and 195 tanks in late November 1942. This would indicate that the decision to shift the 2nd Guards Army reduced the number of Soviet personnel involved in Little Saturn by at least 18 percent and the number of tanks by 16 percent. For the number of troops actually committed to Little Saturn, see Ibid, p. 17. For the tank strength of the 2nd Guards Mechanized Corps, see Glantz, *Colossus Reborn*, p. 274.

53   The 3rd Guards Cavalry Corps was transferred from the Soviet Southwest Front, which was tasked with conducting Saturn. The fresh 7th Tank Corps had been in STAVKA reserve.

to the decision to postpone the operation until 16 December. Likewise, the transfer of reserve rifle divisions meant a significant weakening of the Soviet forces being marshalled for Operation Ring, a situation made even worse by the transfer of yet another four rifle divisions to the 5th Tank Army so that it too could join in the attacks along the Chir. All tolled, the effort to disrupt the assembly of German forces along the Chir River occupied the attention of at least 121,000 Soviet troops, 324 tanks, and 1,714 guns and mortars, many of which had originally been intended for Operations Saturn and Ring.[54]

Although the STAVKA still believed its operations could proceed as originally intended, the considerable success the Germans achieved during the first days of Operation Winter Storm necessitated a major revision of Soviet planning. On 14 December the STAVKA postponed Ring indefinitely and assigned the 2nd Guards Army, reinforced by a fresh mechanized corps previously allotted to Saturn, with the task of halting the German relief effort. In consequence, Soviet forces opposing Winter Storm swelled from an initial strength of 34,000 men and 77 tanks on 12 December, to 149,000 men supported by 635 tanks on 23 December.[55] Recognizing the changed circumstances and the lack of resources to conduct the operation as originally intended, the STAVKA also grudgingly scaled back Operation Saturn to Little Saturn. Instead of an all-out drive south to Rostov, Soviet armies would instead advance southeast into the deep rear areas of *Heeresgruppe Don*, thereby disrupting its operations and curtailing Winter Storm. In effect, the goal of the operation was watered down from one that held out the prospect of achieving a decisive strategic victory of almost incomprehensible proportions, to a vastly more modest objective of simply preventing the relief of the *6. Armee*.

Through the disruption and delay they imposed upon Soviet operations, the strength and size of the forces concentrated with *Heeresgruppe Don* ultimately produced two major consequences. The first was that the postponement of Operation Ring until 10 January 1943 meant that large numbers of Soviet troops were tied down around Stalingrad until the last remnants of the *6. Armee* finally capitulated on 2 February.[56] With the German front between Voronezh and Rostov having entirely collapsed by mid-January, these forces would have added significant weight to the Soviet advance westwards across the Donets region had they been available at that

---

54   Erickson, *The Road to Berlin*, pp. 10-11. On the basis of the alternate figures given for the 5th Tank Army found in Glantz, *From the Don to the Dnepr*, p. 15, the actual combined strength of the 5th Shock and 5th Tank Armies may have been 141,000 men, 434 tanks, and 2,037 guns and mortars.

55   Erickson, *The Road to Berlin*, pp. 11 & 23.

56   At the start of Ring, these still included seven armies consisting of 39 rifle divisions, 14 tank or rifle brigades, and 13 independent tanks regiments possessing a total strength of at least 281,000 men, 257 tanks, and 10,370 artillery pieces, rocket launchers and mortars. Tarrant, *Stalingrad*, pp. 196-197.

point.[57] Conceivably, their addition may have given the Red Army enough strength in the region to overwhelm arriving German reinforcements, ward off Manstein's famous counterstroke (19 February-18 March) and reach the Dnepr River, thereby isolating the large number of Axis troops still located in the Caucasus and the Crimea. Even after the elimination of the Stalingrad pocket, the STAVKA had still hoped to use these troops, first as part of the Sevsk-Truschevsk Offensive (25 February-6 March) and later in the expanded Smolensk Offensive (7-21 March), to exploit the now wide-open southern flank of *Heeresgruppe Mitte* and encircle the entire army group. However, the fierce fighting around Stalingrad had left many of the Soviet units there in dire need of rest and replenishment, meaning they were not immediately re-employable.[58] The relatively few troops that were dispatched arrived too late, as the German rapidly moved in powerful reinforcements to block the Soviet advance.[59] The chance to encircle *Heeresgruppe Mitte* or at least force it to conduct a major retreat was therefore lost.

The second major consequence relates to the Soviet force reductions and planning changes that influenced Operation Little Saturn. The shifting of the axis of the offensive, from a direct advance south on Rostov to a drive southeast into the rear area of *Heeresgruppe Don*, ultimately gave the Germans what they needed most – time. With Soviet intentions riveted upon *Heeresgruppe Don*, just enough German forces were assembled to hold the northern approaches to Rostov. By the thinnest of margins, this allowed 12 divisions of *Heeresgruppe Don* and another five from the Caucasus to slip through Rostov and redeploy into the eastern Donets region.[60] Here they joined six German divisions struggling to contain Little Saturn and a further seven that arrived during January as reinforcements. Within a month, this assemblage of forces would form the basis of a dramatic reversal of fortune.[61] While the Red Army was still able

57 Following Little Saturn, the Red Army conducted the Ostrogozhzk-Rossosh Offensive (12-27 January 1943) against the Hungarian Second Army and the Voronezh-Kastornoe Offensive (24 January-2 February 1943) against the *2. Armee.* These smashed the defending Axis forces and created a 325-kilometre hole in the German lines between Voronezh and Voroshilovgrad. See Ziemke, *Stalingrad to Berlin*, p. 81.

58 According to Glantz, *Endgame at Stalingrad, Book Two*, p. 579, by the time the battle ended most of the participating Soviet divisions had been reduced to an average strength of 3,900 to 4,900 men.

59 For a complete explanation of STAVKA intentions and subsequent operations, see Glantz, *After Stalingrad*, pp. 252-388.

60 On 28 December Hitler had finally given his consent for a withdrawal from the Caucasus. As noted in Boog, et. al. *GSWW, Vol. VI*, p. 1174, "Hitler's decision came too late to save the situation in Stalingrad, but it may have been just in time to save Army Group A from a similar fate." Together with the headquarters of the *1. Panzerarmee*, the divisions transferred from the Caucasus included *SS-Panzergrenadier Division Wiking* and the *3. Panzer, 111. Infanterie, 15. Luftwaffe Feld*, and *454. Sicherungs Divisions.*

61 Deployed with the Italian Eighth Army or in the process of arriving when the Soviet offensive began were the *27. Panzer Division*, and *298., 385.* and *387. Infanterie Divisions.* The *19. Panzer* and *3. Gebirgs Divisions* arrived as the attack developed. Of the formations

to smash what was left of *Heeresgruppe B* during the Ostrogozhsk-Rossosh (13-27 January) and Voronezh-Kastornoe (24 January-17 February) Offensives, the reallocation of resources to cope with the initial assembly of *Heeresgruppe Don* meant that the Soviets lacked sufficient quantities of fresh troops to fully exploit their successes. Instead, the STAVKA was compelled to employ the same troops – which had already sustained heavy losses in their initial operations – in one relentless non-stop drive from the Don to the Dnepr Rivers.[62] Suffering from a continuously high casualty rate, increasing troop exhaustion, lengthening supply lines, and the gradual wearing out of equipment, the strength and effectiveness of these Soviet formations steadily declined the further west the Red Army advanced. For example, the Soviet 3rd Tank Army, tasked with leading the advance across the northern Donets region, had fielded 479 tanks on 10 January, but, by 14 February, this number had declined to 100. Two weeks later, only 39 of these tanks still remained. Similarly, in the wake of Operation Little Saturn, the STAVKA ordered its Southwest Front to continue its advance into the Donets region on 29 January, even though its four tank corps retained only 212 of the 680 tanks they were authorized. By 19 February these units had been further reduced to only 40 tanks.[63] By 10 March the Southwest Front reported that shortages amongst its formations totalled 256,000 personnel, 1,013 tanks, and 1,041 artillery pieces.[64] Many Soviet rifle divisions were reduced to between one-half and one-third of their authorized strength of 11,000 men.[65]

Now reorganized into *Heeresgruppe Süd* and commanded by *Generalfeldmarschall* Manstein, German forces in southern Russia – the divisions that had escaped through Rostov and bolstered by the steady arrival of fresh troops from Western Europe – were able to slow, and then eventually halt the Soviet advance, particularly along the Mius River sector. This gave Manstein the chance to pull a number of panzer divisions out of the line and concentrate them against the flanks of those Soviet troops who had nearly reached the Dnepr River. With Soviet forces overextended and their strength waning, Manstein was then able to orchestrate a series of counterattacks between 19 February and 18 March to destroy the leading Soviet armies, force the remainder to retreat behind the Donets River and re-establish a continuous German front.[66] The

---

arriving during January, *SS-Panzergrenadier Division Das Reich* and the *7. Panzer, 302., 304., 320.* and *335. Infanterie Divisions* were transferred from France while the *(Mot.) Infanterie Division Grossdeutschland* was redeployed from *Heeresgruppe Mitte.*

62   See Glantz, *After Stalingrad*, pp. 110-226 and Glantz, *From the Don to the Dnepr*, pp. 82-214. Additional information may be found in Ziemke, *Stalingrad to Berlin*, pp. 66-90 and Erickson, *The Road to Berlin*, pp. 45-55.

63   Glantz, *Colossus Reborn*, pp. 274-275.

64   Steven D. Mercatante, *Why the Germany Nearly Won: A New History of the Second World War in Europe.* (Santa Barbara, CA: 2012), p. 176, Note 46.

65   Glantz, *Colossus Reborn*, p. 210.

66   For more details concerning the German counterstroke, see George M. Nipe, *Last Victory in Russia: The SS-Panzerkorps and Manstein's Kharkov Counteroffensive, February-March 1943.* (Atglen, PA: 2000), Friedrich W. Hauck, "Der Gegenangriff der Heeresgruppe

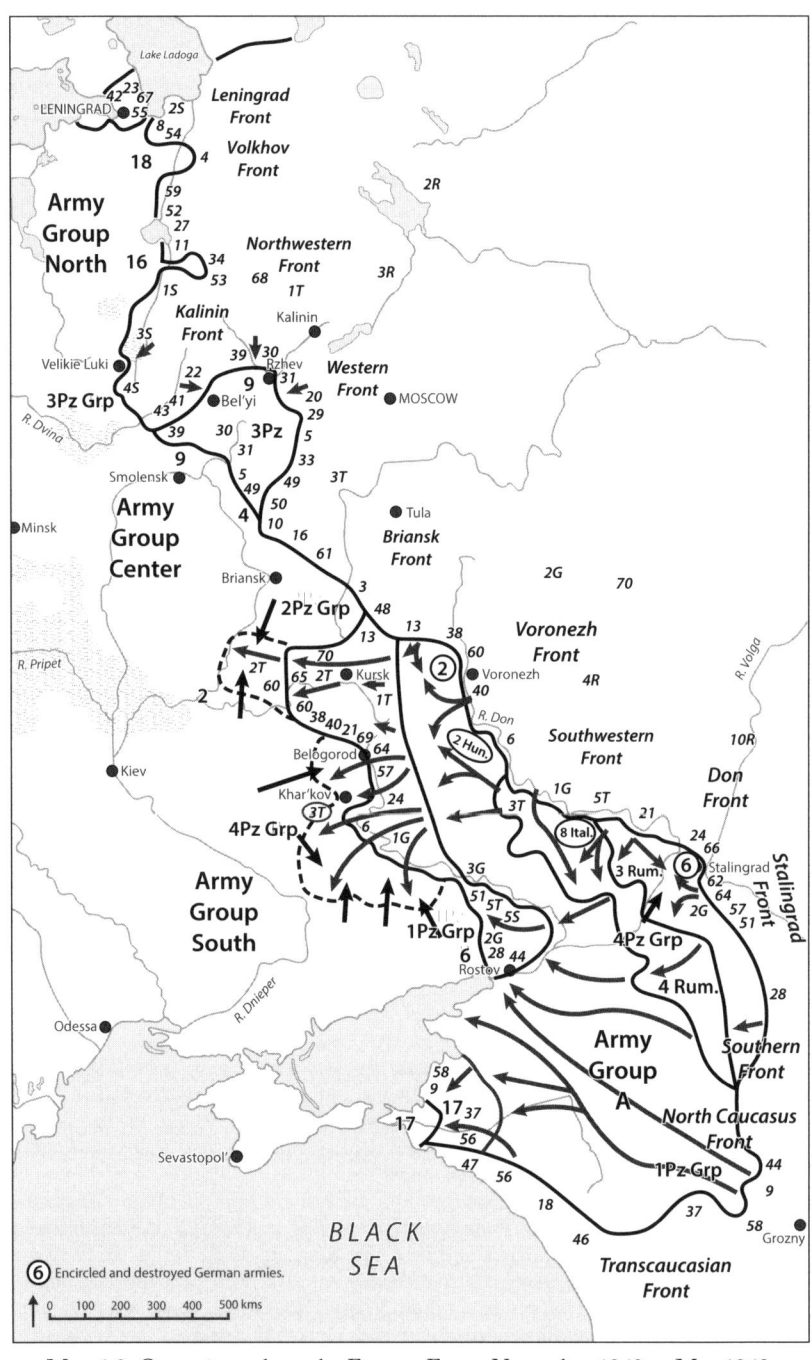

Map 6.2 Operations along the Eastern Front, November 1942 to May 1943.

ambitious attempt by the STAVKA to reach the Dnepr River and collapse the entire German front in Russia had failed.

Endeavouring to explain the sudden and dramatic turn of events along the southern portion of the Eastern Front during February and March 1943, many historians have long attributed the German success almost exclusively to the brilliance and prowess of Manstein as a military commander. Indeed, many accounts refer to this episode as "Manstein's Miracle".[67] But this overlooks the significant reinforcements Hitler and the OKH poured into southern Russia to stem the Soviet onslaught.[68] Between 1 December 1942 and 1 March 1943 at least 1,934 tanks, assault guns, and self-propelled anti-tank guns were dispatched to the region (see Table 6.5), and since this does not account for all the vehicles allotted as replacements, the actual figure was probably greater still.[69] To fill the gaping holes torn in the front, 26 divisions, including 12 panzer or motorised ones, arrived between December and February. Half of these were fresh, full-strength formations transferred from France. Another 13 infantry divisions, including ten from Western Europe, arrived over the next four months, for a total of 39 by June (see Appendix Eleven). Manstein's counterstroke was also well supported by the *Luftwaffe* whose average sortie rate increased from 350 per day in January to 1,000 per day in February.[70]

Admittedly, many of the arriving divisions sustained heavy personnel and equipment losses as they hastily deployed to stem the Soviet advance, although the lack of detailed information makes any estimate of actual German strength at the start of their counterattack problematic. According to one document, Manstein's army group possessed 1,021 tanks (of which 529 were operational) on 28 February, but the number

Sud im Fruhjahr 1943: Die Entwicklung der Lage vor Beginn des Gegenangriffs." *Wehrwissenschaftliche Rundschau*, Vol. 12, No. 8 (1962), pp. 452-481 and "Der Gegenangriff der Heeresgruppe Sud in Fruhjahr 1943: Die Fortsetzung der Angriffs nach Norden – Schlacht um Charkov und Einnahme von Bjelgorod." *Wehrwissenschaftliche Rundschau*, Vol. 12, No. 9 (1962), pp. 520-549, Carl Wagener, "Der Gegenangriff des XXXX. Panzerkorps gegen den Durchbruch der Panzergruppe Popow im Donezbecken, Februar 1943." *Wehrwissenschaftliche Rundschau*, Vol. 7, No. 1 (1957), pp. 21-36, and Boog, et. al. *GSWW, Vol. VI*, pp. 1184-1193.

67   For example, Chapter 19 of Bob Carruthers, *The Wehrmacht Experience in Russia*. (Great Britain: 2012) is titled "Von Manstein's Miracle". Also see Clark, *Barbarossa*, p. 419 and Walter Dunn, *Kursk: Hitler's Gamble, 1943*. (Westport, CT: 1997), pp. 15-16.

68   Indeed, while listing reasons for the German success, Boog, et. al. *GSWW, Vol. VI*, p. 1192 makes no mention of arriving reinforcements.

69   A total of 982 replacement panzers arrived on the Eastern Front between 1 December 1942 and 1 March 1943. Jentz, *Panzertruppen, Vol. Two*, p. 43. Some 115 replacement assault guns also arrived in January and February according to Zetterling & Frankson, *Kursk 1943*, p. 147. Given the circumstances, most of these were probably dispatched to the panzer divisions deployed in southern Russia. No information could be found regarding the number of self-propelled anti-tank guns that arrived.

70   Hooten, *Eagle in Flames*, pp. 188-190.

of available assault guns and self-propelled anti-tank guns is unknown.[71] However, it is interesting to note that Table 6.6, though an incomplete summary, shows that well into the counterattack (6-10 March) at least 461 operational panzers and assault guns were still available. It also illustrates that the strength of most of the formations listed was actually *increasing*. This suggests that either significant numbers of replacement tanks had arrived, that maintenance teams had performed prodigious feats in repairing damaged vehicles, or that initial German armoured strengths had in fact been greater than reported. Without more specific information, one can only conclude that, depending upon the specific formation, all three may have been prevalent.

Similarly, German personnel losses in southern Russia (excluding the *6. Armee* destroyed at Stalingrad) between 1 December 1942 and 1 March 1943 included 83,233 combat casualties and perhaps as many as 120,153 sick or frostbitten who were repatriated to Germany. In contrast, 74,300 men arrived as replacements.[72] At first glance this would seem to be a clear illustration of Germany's inability to maintain the strength of the *Feldheer* and replace its losses. Yet here too the actual circumstances may have been less egregious than a cursory review of such figures would suggest. First, the number of evacuated sick and frostbitten appears suspect. According to figures maintained by OKW, the total number of sick soldiers recuperating in Germany with the *Ersatzheer* increased by only 61,951 men between 30 November 1942 and 28 February 1943. This included all sick men from throughout the entire German Army stationed outside of Germany and not just those coming from southern Russia. It is also offset by the decrease in the number of sick registered with the *Feldheer*, so that the real increase in the overall number of sick was only 40,273.[73] Secondly, the number of arriving replacements only refers to those dispatched directly by the *Ersatzheer* and thereby excludes the large number of men injected into German formations by less official channels. As noted previously, significant numbers of sick and wounded recuperated in army group rear areas and thousands of these were returned to their units every month. Also available were tens of thousands of men belonging to the *6. Armee* who had either evaded encirclement during Operation Uranus or who were returning

---

71   See the Ostfront Panzerlage dated to 28 February 1943, in BA-MA RH 10-60. It should also be noted that another 157 replacement panzers were in the process of arriving.
72   The figures shown here relate to *Heeresgruppe B, Don*, and *Süd*. The number of sick has been determined by deducting combat casualties found in the Heeresarzt 10-Day Loss Reports within BA- MA RW 6/556 and 6/558 from the figures listed as total losses in Boog, et. al. *GSWW, Vol. VI*, pp. 866-867. The number of replacements has also been taken from the latter source.
73   According to the OKW Eastern Front Monthly Casualty Reports for these months in BA MA RW 6/544 and 6/545, the number of sick in hospital break-down as follows:

	30 November 1942	28 February 1943	Difference
With the *Feldheer*	114,153	92,475	-21,678
With the *Ersatzheer*	281,893	343,844	+61,951
Total	396,046	436,319	+40,273

from a period of convalescence and leave.[74] With the German front buckling under Soviet pressure, these were formed into a series of *ad hoc* emergency units, attached to a particular division or higher headquarters, and pitched into combat. As the campaign progressed, some of these men were eventually pulled out of the front and sent to rejoin their old units, which were being rebuilt in France, but many others were incorporated directly into the ranks of the divisions to which they had been attached. The remnants of the seven divisions destroyed outside of Stalingrad in the wake of Operation Little Saturn constituted another source of manpower.[75] Having suffered very heavy losses, and in some cases having performed poorly in combat, OKH seems to have judged that these formations were not worth rebuilding and ordered them disbanded. Whatever men and equipment they still possessed was redistributed to other units.[76] The disbandment of these divisions not only meant a reduction in the replacement requirements of the specific formations to which their remnants were assigned. It also meant that fewer overall replacements were needed, since the casualties sustained by the disbanded divisions no longer needed to be replaced.

Just how well the injection of personnel replacements through both normal and extraordinary means managed to maintain the strength of German units is difficult to gauge, but some indication may be gleaned from the reports of two of the German armies deployed in southern Russia: *1. Panzerarmee* and *Armee Abteilung Hollidt*. These show that, at the start of Manstein's counterstroke, some 60 (45.4 percent) of their combined total of 132 infantry battalions were still rated as "strong" or "medium strong", meaning they possessed a *Grabenstärke* of more than 300 men (see Appendix Twelve). More specifically, given its vital role in the success of Manstein's operation, 33 of the 59 combat battalions of the *1. Panzerarmee* belonged to these two categories. Given the debilitated state of many of the formations leading the Soviet advance, this would suggest that many German units might in fact have been numerically stronger than their Soviet adversaries at the start of the German counterstroke. Though their condition was still far from ideal, these German forces were nonetheless strong enough to inflict a major setback upon the Red Army – and the ambitions of the STAVKA.

---

74   According to its divisional history at least 2,000 men belonging to the *16. Panzer Division* in late November avoided the encirclement of the rest of their division in Stalingrad. Wolfgang Werthen, *Geschichte der 16. Panzer Division 1939-1945.* (Bad Nauheim: 1958), p. 138. Likewise, some 2,000 men of the *44. Infanterie Division* assembled outside the pocket. Schimak, et. al., *Die 44. Infanterie Division*, p. 257. By mid-December, *Heeresgruppe Don* reported that its reception centres had collected 6,622 returning convalescents and 6,098 men back from leave who belonged to the formations trapped in Stalingrad. *Heeresgruppe Don. Kriegstagebuch Anlagen Band 3 (7-14.12.1942)*, NARA T311 Roll 268, Frames 000937 & 001055.

75   This includes the *22.* and *27. Panzer Divisions*, the *298., 377.* and *385. Infanterie Divisions*, and the *7.* and *8. Luftwaffe Feld Divisions*.

76   For example, according to Ernst Rebentisch, *The Combat History of the 23rd Panzer Division in World War II.* (Mechanicsburg, PA: 2012), p. 259, on 10 April the *23. Panzer Division* received 2,203 men from the disbanded *22. Panzer Division*.

The *Ostheer* survived the tumultuous winter of 1942-1943 but only by the slimmest of margins and even the belated success of Manstein's counterstroke could not obscure the fact that Germany had sustained a near catastrophic strategic setback. Virtually all the hard-fought gains of the previous summer had been lost, as had any realistic chance of seizing the oilfields of the Caucasus. In the process, 27 German and 38 allied Axis divisions had been destroyed and many others had been badly mauled. Approximations of German losses on the *Ostfront* between 1 December 1942 and 1 July 1943 tend to vary wildly but certainly included 664,632 combat casualties. Estimating the number of sick and frostbitten is problematic for reasons noted previously, but these may have amounted to 336,551 men. Total losses may therefore have amounted to just over one million men (Table 6.7).[77] Germany's allies also endured at least 378,459 casualties during this period.[78] The material losses of the German Army during these seven months were equally staggering: a total of 4,505 tanks, assault guns and self-propelled anti-tank guns were listed as *Totalausfälle* (Table 6.8). Other equipment losses included 3,883 artillery pieces, 3,307 anti-tank and 6,017 anti-aircraft guns, 9,012 mortars and 258,703 motor vehicle (see Table 6.9).[79] Although a proportion of these figures can be associated with the collapse of the Axis forces in North Africa, the vast majority were lost on the Eastern Front.[80]

Alarmed at the dramatic turn in Germany's fortunes, Hitler promulgated a series of decrees designed to increase armaments production and restore the tattered strength of the German Army. These included his order of 13 January 1943 that called for the complete conversion of German society and the economy to meet the needs of the armed forces. Industries and businesses not directly engaged in war work would be

---

77   In contrast, conservative Russian sources note that the Red Army sustained 2,834,947 casualties (including 918,618 killed or missing) between 1 January and 30 June 1943. An incomplete accounting of material losses during this period includes at least 6,368 tanks, 11,294 guns and mortars, and 1,520 aircraft. See Krivosheev, *Soviet Casualties and Combat Losses in the 20th Century*, pp. 94 & 261-262, and Glantz & House, *When Titans Clashed*, pp. 295-296.

78   Losses amongst the allied Axis forces included 158,854 Romanians, 105,085 Hungarians, and 114,520 Italians. Axworthy, et. al. *Third Axis, Fourth Ally*, p. 114, Nigel Thomas & Laszlo Szabo, *The Royal Hungarian Army in World War II*. (London: 2008), p. 18, and Stato Maggiore Dell'esercito, *La Operazioni delle Unita Italiane al Fronte Russo, 1941-1943*, p. 487.

79   Added to these were the material losses of the four allied Axis armies destroyed along the Don River and at Stalingrad who lost virtually their entire complement of heavy weapons. The Hungarians alone appear to have lost 780 guns and mortars, 460 anti-tank guns, and 6,600 motor vehicles.

80   A concise accounting of German equipment losses in North Africa between 1 December 1942 and 13 May 1943 has never been published, but based upon the remaining tank strength of the *Afrika Korps* on 2 December and equipment deliveries in November 1942 to May 1943 these would have included at least 504 tanks, 523 artillery pieces and 5,958 motor vehicles. Gundelach, *Die Deutsche Luftwaffe im Mittelmeer 1940-1945*, pp. 474 & 570-574, and Jentz, *Panzertruppen, Vol. Two*, p. 13.

ruthlessly screened and any deemed superfluous would be closed for the duration of the war. The construction of public works and new factories not slated for completion in the immediate future, or non-essential to the war effort were to cease immediately and the assigned labour and material resources reallocated to the armaments industry. Most dramatically, all German males (aged 16-65) and females (aged 17-50) now had to register with labour authorities that could reassign them to priority sectors of the economy. In effect, this signalled the official conversion of the German economy to a total war footing.[81] Alongside the more stringent mobilization of German manpower, even greater numbers of foreign labourers would also be recruited or conscripted for work within Germany.[82] The announcement of the Adolf Hitler Tank Programme followed nine days later. Considered to be of "decisive importance for the outcome of the war" the goal was to increase the production of armoured vehicles, with the ultimate target being the manufacture of 900 tanks and 2,000 assault guns and tank destroyers per month by late 1944.[83] To achieve this, the programme was to receive priority allocations of labour, raw materials and industrial plant; all other sectors of the war economy were made subservient to its needs.

While the full impact of Hitler's decrees would not be felt until late-1943, German armaments production had already been steadily increasing since its nadir of the previous spring. Overall armaments production had increased 120 percent since then and in contrast to the 629 vehicles built in May 1942, the production of tanks, assault guns and self-propelled anti-tank guns had almost doubled to 1,205 by May 1943. The manufacture of 2,200 combat aircraft during the latter month also represented a new peak.[84]

Just how well these increases managed to compensate for Germany's heavy material losses is difficult to ascertain given the discrepancies between the available statistics. At first sight, one could be excused for concluding that the circumstances of the German Army had taken a catastrophic turn for the worse. But these statistics can be misleading and require a thorough understanding of their nuances and particulars. For example, Table 6.8 indicates that the total stock of armoured vehicles declined by almost 300 between 1 December 1942 and 1 July 1943. Yet it must be noted that the composition of this stock had undergone a substantial improvement. Whereas the number for December includes 2,032 obsolete Pz I, Pz II and Pz 38(t) tanks (26 percent of total stock), by the beginning of July these had declined to only

---

81   See Martin Moll, *Führer Erlasse 1939-1945*. (Germany: 1997), pp. 311-313. For more details, including the overall effectiveness of the program, see Kroener, et. al. *GSWW. Vol. V, Part Two*, pp. 905-918.

82   According to Herbert, *Hitler's Foreign Workers*, pp. 275 & 279, between November 1942 and December 1943 the number of French, Dutch and Belgian workers in Germany increased by 744,621; simultaneously, the number of Russian civilians employed in the Reich also grew by almost 700,000.

83   Tooze, *The Wages of Destruction*, pp. 594-595.

84   Ibid, p. 596 and Müller-Hillebrand, "German Tank Strength and Loss Statistics", p. 28.

440 (roughly 6 percent of total stock). Although some had been lost in combat, the majority had been stricken off strength. These were scrapped, converted into a variety of self-propelled guns, or simply no longer registered in strength returns.[85] The first half of 1943 also witnessed the phasing out of the Pz III. With the design having reached the end of its ability to be up-gunned and up-armoured, the factories manufacturing the Pz III were gradually shifted to the production of more powerful assault guns and the final Pz III rolled off the assembly lines in June.[86] Henceforth the main German battle tanks would be the Pz IV, Panther and Tiger models. This shift is illustrated by the fact that their numbers grew from the 917 (15 percent of tank stock) available in December, to 2,140 (47 percent of tank stock) by July and that their overall strength had increased by 133 percent.[87] The number of assault guns, tank destroyers and self-propelled anti-tank guns also grew by 63 percent. This in turn improved the lot of the infantry since it resulted in the creation of additional infantry-support *Sturmgeschütz Abteilungen*. It even allowed for the gradual distribution of vehicles to individual infantry divisions so that each would have its own company of StuG or Marders (occasionally even one of each), thereby expanding both their offensive and defensive capabilities. Despite the minor reduction in the overall number of armoured vehicles, increasing numbers of superior models meant that the German Army of July 1943, and particularly its *Panzerwaffe*, was considerably more formidable that it had been just seven months earlier.

Comprehending the statistics for other kinds of military hardware dated to this period is equally challenging. As noted in Table 6.9, production tended to exceed losses in most categories – occasionally by surprisingly large margins. The exceptions to this were very-heavy artillery pieces (20.3 cm and above) and especially motor vehicles, the production of which lagged far behind the number lost or written-off. Yet the generally rosy picture presented by these figures is seemingly contradicted by the development of the German Army's overall equipment stocks illustrated in Table 6.10. This shows the actual stock in hand on 1 December 1942 and 1 July 1943 and how these had changed. It also estimates what the stock on 1 July *should* have been given the balances shown in Table 6.9, as well as the differences between the actual and estimated stocks for the latter date. Some categories of actual stock witnessed growth, while others actually declined. It also suggests that, while new production of motor vehicles fell far behind losses, this gap was compensated largely by the diversion of

---

85   The chassis of the Pz II and Pz 38(t) were used for Marder II/III self-propelled anti-tank guns, and the Wespe and Grille self-propelled artillery pieces. Throughout 1943 some 1,030 Marders and 742 Wespe or Grille were built. See Hahn, *Waffen und Geheimwaffen des deutschen Heeres, 1933-1945, Band II*, pp. 26-30 & 66-73.

86   The Pz III chassis was used at the basis of the StuG III (equipped with a 7.5 cm gun) and StuH (mounting a 10.5 cm howitzer) assault guns. Some of the sub-components of the Pz III were also used in the manufacture of the Hummel self-propelled artillery piece.

87   From April 1943 production of the Pz IV shifted entirely to its latest version, the Ausf H that featured 80 millimeters of frontal armour and mounted a 7.5 cm L/48 main gun.

vehicles from the civilian sector and other branches of the *Wehrmacht*.[88] But the most striking revelation is that, despite production exceeding losses, the actual equipment stocks by 1 July had not experienced a more comprehensive and universal growth. The probable reasons for this are varied. Potentially, it could be the result of incomplete reports or changes in the accounting system. Losses could have been somewhat higher than what was previously reported, older and worn-out weapons may have been scrapped, or some equipment may have been delivered to Germany's allies to help compensate for the disastrous losses they had suffered during the winter. The most significant reason could simply be that some types of equipment were no longer being recorded because they were regarded as obsolete or were being phased out. This may particularly be the case for the large discrepancies shown for mortars and 3.7 cm Pak. The 5 cm mortar had long been considered inadequate in terms of range and shell weight. In fact, by early 1943, the decision had been made that they be replaced by 8.1 cm mortars, and their production ended around this time. Numbers were allowed to gradually run down through attrition and henceforth they were usually no longer reported in unit strength returns. Even so, as late as 1 March 1945 some 2,820 were still in service and another 1,133 resided within ordnance depots.[89] Likewise, production of 3.7 cm Pak ceased in 1942 and their presence with the *Feldheer* gradually dissipated in favour of more powerful models of anti-tank guns. By late 1943 most unit reports no longer included them in summaries of their equipment holdings except as occasional side notes. Nonetheless, 4,477 were still in service that December.[90] Aside from explaining how stock could drop so precipitously, this also complicates any analysis since equipment could still exist even though it wasn't officially registered. Clearly, without further research or more details, analysis of these inventories will continue to be a speculative exercise.

Fortunately, a great deal of other information is available so that a determination of how well the material requirements of the *Ostheer* were met is still possible. Thanks to Hitler's order early in the year to devote three full months of armaments production exclusively to the East, the number of panzers and assault guns with the *Ostheer* grew from 2,103 on 10 April to 3,087 by 10 July (a 46.8 percent increase).[91] What the influx of new equipment meant for the formations involved can be seen in an array of monthly divisional status reports dated to 1 July (see Appendix Thirteen).

---

88   As noted in figures given for potential change in Table 6.10, it would seem that as many as 123,771 motor vehicles were reallocated to the Army in this way. See Moll, *Fuhrer Erlasse 1939-1945*, pp. 323-324 for Hitler's orders of 3 March 1943 concerning the more stringent use of motor vehicles.

89   Hahn, *Waffen und Geheimwaffen des deutschen Heeres, 1933-1945, Band I*, p. 70.

90   Ibid, *Band II*, p. 252.

91   Zetterling & Frankson, *Kursk 1943*, p. 195. Note that these numbers do not include hundreds of Marder self-propelled anti-tank guns. For Hitler's orders giving the Eastern Front priority, see Jak P. Mallmann Showell, *Fuhrer Conferences on Naval Affairs, 1939-1945*. (London: 1990), pp. 306-308.

Specifically, this entails comparing their authorized *Sollstärke* with what they actually had available (*Iststärke*). Although these are confined to formations that were deployed on the *Ostfront*, the picture they present – given all of Germany's varied problems and the fact that it was well into its fourth year of war – is remarkable. Of the 17 panzer or *SS-panzergrenadier* divisions for which reports could be found, these formations possessed 86 percent of their authorized number of tanks, assault guns and self-propelled anti-tank guns. Stocks of other equipment are comparable: 91 percent of machine-guns, 99.5 percent of artillery, 87 percent of heavy anti-tank guns, and 82 percent of motor vehicles. The lowest figures relate to armoured half-tracks (SPW), for which only 70 percent were on hand. Although one could explain this by arguing that prized mobile formations received priority, a surprisingly similar picture presents itself in the reports for the seven infantry or *panzergrenadier* divisions for which reliable reports have been found. These had 87 percent of their required machine-guns, 94 percent of artillery, and 82 percent of motor vehicles. The worst category was heavy anti-tank guns, where only 68 percent of needs were met. While not comprehensive, given the sample size, it nonetheless shows that many German divisions were in very good condition in terms of equipment by 1 July 1943.

A similar picture presents itself in terms of manpower. As noted previously, the German Army faced a severe manpower crisis even before the disaster at Stalingrad. Starting in late 1942, this spurred a series of measures designed to arrest mounting shortages. On 19 December, Hitler ordered that 200,000 previously exempt men working in industry, but eligible for military service, be inducted into the *Wehrmacht*. Some 50,000 were to be drafted immediately while the remainder would eventually be made available to the field army through an exchange program whereby older service personnel would be released back into the industrial sector. Another 200,000 combat-fit men were to be squeezed out of the *Ersatzheer* by replacing them with women and men of the older age classes.[92] In late December, the first of the 475,560 men of the 1924 age class that had been drafted in mid-October also became available as they finished their training. These were followed in May 1943 by the call-up of a further 485,505 men of the 1925 class.[93] At least half of these were assigned to the Army. Even more use was to be made of Hiwis to release German personnel for combat and the OKW anticipated that 610,000 Russian auxiliaries would be recruited during the course of 1943.[94] Despite fierce opposition from Speer and other Nazi Party officials, the tally of 5.4 million men exempt from military service on 1 June 1942 was trimmed down to 4.6 million by 1 June 1943. Thanks to these varied measures, the total strength of the *Wehrmacht* grew from 8 million in mid-1942, to 9.6

---

92   Moll, *Fuhrer Erlasse 1939-1945*, pp. 305-307; Kroener, et. al. *GSWW. Vol. V, Part Two*, p. 911.
93   Ibid, p. 895.
94   By late 1942 some 400,000 *Hiwis* were already attached to the *Ostheer* and 150,000 more were with the *Luftwaffe*. Ibid, p. 896.

million a year later.[95] This also allowed 20 of the 27 divisions destroyed on the Eastern Front during the winter to be reconstituted by May. Five of the seven divisions annihilated when the Axis position in Tunisia collapsed that month could also be reformed within weeks.

For the *Ostheer* these fresh levies translated into a real improvement of personnel strength. As noted previously in Table 6.7, the Germans sustained 664,632 combat casualties between 1 December 1942 and 1 July 1943. In contrast, 782,100 replacements arrived. But the figure for combat casualties includes at least 200,000 sustained during the destruction of the *6. Armee* and at least several thousand more could be attributed to the seven divisions disbanded outside the pocket. Since these losses belonged to formations that no longer existed or else were being rebuilt in France, their portion of the combat casualties did not need replacing. If we assume that these numbered about 250,000, this would mean that the arriving replacements, at the very least, managed to cover the remaining combat casualties and a large portion of those listed as sick. Yet by looking at the divisional level it becomes apparent that, not only did this stream of replacements cover ongoing losses, in many cases it rolled back the large personnel deficits many divisions had been accumulating since the war in the East began. For example, of 62 divisions for which strength reports could be located, some 40 (65 percent) had shortages of less than 500 German personnel on 1 July 1943 (see Appendix Fourteen). Many divisions actually had personnel surpluses. Moreover, whereas divisional shortages averaged 4,378 men in November 1942 (as noted in Appendix Eight), these had now fallen to an average of only 864 (425 German and 439 Russian auxiliaries per division).[96]

Considering the unrelenting pace at which operations in the East had continued since the start of hostilities in 1941, together with the scale of the disaster that occurred around Stalingrad, the regeneration of the *Ostheer* by July 1943 was astonishing. From a low point of roughly 2.7 million men on 1 April, the strength of the German Army on the Eastern Front was increased to 3.14 million by the injection of hundreds of thousands of personnel replacements and the arrival of 33 new divisions.[97] Although it may still have been short an overall total of 197,000 men, this represented only six percent of its *Sollstärke*.[98] Equipment holdings, while not having been completely refilled, were certainly much greater than either the circumstances, or the

---

95   Ibid, p. 914.
96   Although some of this decline could be attributed to structural changes such as the reduction of the number of infantry battalions from nine to six, this was by no means universal; indeed, many infantry divisions on the *Ostfront*, particularly those assigned to *Heeresgruppe Süd*, still retained their old nine-battalion structure. For examples, see Zetterling & Frankson, *Kursk 1943*, pp. 226-237.
97   While mostly confined to security or coastal defence duties, 121,000 Hungarian and 188,933 Romanian troops were still in the East. Additionally, the Finns still fielded 230,000 men. Ibid, p. 5.
98   Kroener, et. al. *GSWW. Vol. V, Part Two*, p. 1013.

usual historiographical narrative, would lead one to believe. Now fielding 187 divisions (plus another seven in Finland) and perhaps as many as 3,500 tanks, assault guns and self-propelled anti-tank guns, many of which were considerably superior to their Soviet opposites, by early July 1943 the *Ostheer* could look forward to the future with at least some confidence. Although Germany was now clearly on the strategic defence, Hitler and many senior German officers believed that a powerful attack against the Soviet-held salient around the city of Kursk (codenamed Operation Citadel) might destroy just enough of the Red Army to blunt its offensive capabilities for most of the remainder of 1943, and maybe even into 1944.[99] If things went well, this might give Germany time to build up its strength and perhaps complete a host of new weapon designs with which it could turn the tide of the war back in its favour. Its strength and capabilities restored, the *Ostheer* prepared for yet another throw of the dice.

99   The literature devoted to this battle is too voluminous to list here, but the best studies include David Glantz & Jonathan House, *The Battle of Kursk*. (Lawrence, KS: 1999), Zetterling & Frankson, *Kursk 1943*, and Valeriy Zamulin, *Demolishing the Myth: The Tank Battle at Prokhorovka – Kursk, July 1943: An Operational Narrative*. (Solihull: 2011).

Table 6.1 Comparison of the Strength of the Soviet Armed Forces, 1 May and 1 November 1942[1]

	Strength 1.5.1942	Strength 1.11.1942
Personnel		
Russo-German Front	5,677,915	6,605,498
STAVKA Reserves	218,276	202,965
Internal/Far East	5,040,440	3,800,620
Total	10,936,631	10,609,083
Artillery & Mortars	107,795	168,812
Rocket Launchers	1,544	2,493
Tanks		
Heavy	944	1,310
Medium (T-34)	1,956	3,878
Light & Specialized	6,425	8,609
Total	9,325	13,798
Aircraft		
Fighters	7,634	11,016
Ground-Attack	553	4,089
Bombers	4,819	3,496
Recon	1,961	1,196
Total	14,967	19,797
Motor Vehicles	364,029	377,438

1 Glantz, *To the Gates of Stalingrad*, p. 47, and Institute of Military History at the Russian Defence Ministry, *Combat and Numerical Composition of the Armed Forces of the USSR in the period of the Great Patriotic War (1941-1945)*. Statistical Material No. 5 (1 November 1942).

Table 6.2 Expansion of Soviet Equipment Stocks – Production versus Losses, 1942[1]

	Available 1.1.1942	Entered Service	Lost 1942	Available 1.1.1943
MG	113,200	238,200	106,100	245,300
Mortars	38,000	230,000	82,000	186,100
Anti-Tank Artillery	5,300	20,500	11,500	14,300
Anti-Aircraft Art.	7,900	6,800	1,600	13,100
Field Artillery	18,900	30,100	12,300	36,700
Rocket Launchers	1,000	3,300	700	3,600
Tanks				
Heavy	600	2,600	1,200	2,000
Medium (T-34)	800	13,400	6,600	7,600
Light	6,300	11,900	7,200	11,000
Total	7,700	27,900	15,000	20,600
Aircraft				
Fighters	7,900	10,700	7,000	11,600
Ground-Attack	400	7,200	2,600	5,000
Bombers	3,700	4,100	2,500	5,300
Motor Vehicles	318,000	153,000	66,000	404,000

1   Mawdsley, *Thunder in the East*, p. 47.

Table 6.3 Strength of the Soviet Armed Forces, 1942 to 1945[1]

	1.11.1942	1.7.1943	1.6.1944	1.1.1945
Personnel	10,609,083	11,936,777	11,204,474	11,408,363
MG	222,519	343,776	309,961	321,937
Artillery				
Field guns	30,712	40,820	44,330	49,724
45-57 mm AT guns	15,449	24,649	20,222	20,158
Anti-Aircraft guns	13,163	17,132	25,376	30,392
Mortars	109,488	118,394	82,339[2]	83,262
Total	168,812	200,995	172,267	183,536
Rocket Launchers	2,493	3,530	2,884	3,092
Tanks & SPG				
Heavy	1,310	990	1,022	1,306
Medium	3,878	6,981	6,991	8,245
Light	8,609	12,429	6,156	5,072
SPG	-	664	3,460	6,047
Total	13,798	21,064	17,629	20,670
Combat Aircraft				
Fighters	11,016	13,586	16,872	18,969
Ground-Attack	4,089	7,089	8,875	8,814
Bombers	3,496	5,174	6,132	8,774
Recon	1,196	1,186	1,218	1,445
Total	19,797	27,035	33,097	38,002
Motor Vehicles[3]	413,960	456,873	512,522	588,672

1 See Institute of Military History at the Russian Defence Ministry, *Combat and Numerical Composition of the Armed Forces of the USSR in the period of the Great Patriotic War (1941–1945)*. Statistical Material No. 5 (1 November 1942), Statistical Material No. 7 (1 July 1943), Statistical Material No. 9 (1 June 1944), and Statistical Material No. 10 (1 January 1945).

2 This drop in the number of mortars is probably due to the phasing out of 50 mm mortars, which may no longer have been included in subsequent strength reports.

3 These figures include tractors and other towing vehicles.

Table 6.4 Estimated Armoured Strength of *Heeresgruppe Don* **– mid December 1942**[1]

	Date	Pz II	Pz III	Pz IV	Befpz.	Pz 38t	Marder	Total
6. PD[2]	1.12.42	21	105	24	9	–	9	168
11. PD	8.12.42	–	64	9	3	–	–	76
23. PD	10.12.42	13	44	38	–	–	–	95
17. PD	15.12.42	4	26	16	2	–	–	48
22. PD	12.12.42	1	9	3	–	3	–	16
16. Mot. ID	10.12.42	10	13	2	–	–	–	25
1st Rom. Armd. Div.	12.12.42	–	1	–	–	5	–	6
KG 'Sauvant'[3]	15.12.42	?	?	?	?	?	?	26
1./301. (FKL) Pz. Abt.	26.11.42	–	11	–	–	–	–	11
Total		49	273	92	14	8	9	471

1 Unless otherwise noted, these figures represent operational strengths and have been taken from *Heeresgruppe Don. Kriegstagebuch Anlagen Band 3 (7-14.12.1942)*, NARA T311 Roll 268, Frame 001052 and *Heeresgruppe Don. Kriegstagebuch Anlagen Band 4 (15-23.12.1942)*, NARA T311 Roll 269, Frames 000298 and 000675. Based upon a report dated to 20 December 1942 concerning the status of the *17.* and *23. Panzer Divisions*, these two formations may originally have possessed a total strength of, respectively, 59 and 116 tanks. Ibid, Frame 000300.

2 The figures for this division represent its *Iststärke* when it arrived in Russia. Thomas L. Jentz, *Panzertruppen: The Complete Guide to the Creation and Combat Employment of Germany's Tank Force, 1943-1945.* (Atglen, PA: 1996), p. 26. Henceforth cited as Jentz, *Panzertruppen, Vol. Two.*

3 This unit was comprised of various elements of the *14. Panzer Division* that had not been trapped within Stalingrad. See Grams, *Die 14. Panzer Division, 1940-1945*, pp. 90-92.

Table 6.5 German Armoured Reinforcements sent to Southern Russia, 1 December 1942 to 1 March 1943[1]

	Arrival	Pz II	Pz III	Pz IV	Befpz.	Tiger	StuG	Marder	Total
3. PD	27.2.43	?	?	?	?	?	?	?	38[2]
6. PD	1.12.42	21	105	24	9	–	–	9	168
7. PD	5.1.43	21	105	20	9	–	–	9	164
11. PD	8.12.42	–	64	9	3	–	–	–	76
17. PD	15.12.42	4	26	16	2	–	–	–	48
19. PD	25.12.42	8	37	14	3	–	–	11	73
23. PD	12.12.42	13	44	38	–	–	–	–	95
Mot. ID 'GD'	1.3.43	5	46	85	2	9	32	–	179
LSSAH	22.1.43	12	10	52	9	9	22	27	141
Das Reich	4.2.43	10	81	21	9	10	20	9	160
Totenkopf	6.2.43	–	81	22	9	9	21	9	151
Wiking	3.1.43	6	26	7	1	–	–	–	40[3]
Replacements	12.42-1.43	–	162	40	–	–	52	151	405[4]
138. Pz Btl.	12.42	–	8	30	–	–	–	–	38
5./FuhBegl. Btl.	12.42	–	4	7	–	–	–	–	11
503. sPz Btl.	5.1.43	–	25	–	–	20	–	–	45
203. Stug Btl.	3.1.43	–	–	–	–	–	29	–	29[5]
Three Stug Btls.	12.42-1.43	–	–	–	–	–	63	–	63[6]
393. Stug Bty.	1.43	–	–	–	–	–	10	–	10
Total		100	824	385	56	57	249	225	1,934

1   Unless otherwise noted, strengths are taken from Jentz, *Panzertruppen, Vol. Two*, pp. 26-37, *Heeresgruppe Don. Kriegstagebuch Anlagen Band 3 (7-14.12.1942)*, NARA T311 Roll 268, Frame 001052 and *Heeresgruppe Don. Kriegstagebuch Anlagen Band 4 (15-23.12.1942)*, NARA T311 Roll 269, Frames 000298 and 000675.

2   Hauck, "Der Gegenangriff der Heeresgruppe Sud im Fruhjahr 1943: Die Entwicklung der Lage vor Beginn des Gegenangriffs", p. 481.

3   *Heeresgruppe Don. Kriegstagebuch Anlagen Band 6 (4-12.11943)*, NARA T311 Roll 270, Frame 000939.

4   *OKH. Generalstab des Heeres, Org. Abt. III. Kriegstagebuch August 1941 bis December 1943*, NARA T78 Roll 414, Frame 6382448.

5   *Heeresgruppe Don. Kriegstagebuch Anlagen Band 6 (4-12.11943)*, NARA T311 Roll 270, Frame 000939.

6   These were the *209., 228.* and *232. Sturmgeschütz Abteilungen* that arrived in December and January; it is presumed that they possessed their full *Sollstärke* of 21 StuG when they arrived.

Table 6.6 German Armoured Strengths in Southern Russia, February to March 1943

	19 February[1]		27 February[2]	28 February[3]	4–10 March[4]
	Operational	Total	Operational	Operational	Operational
3. Panzer Div.	–	38	25	–	–
6. Panzer Div.	–	–	–	6	30
7. Panzer Div.	–	76	18	–	–
11. Panzer Div.	–	99	20	55	71
17. Panzer Div	–	–	–	13	19
19. Panzer Div.	–	24	12	–	30
Div. 'GD'	–	–	–	–	147
LSSAH	110	–	–	–	90
Das Reich	56	–	–	–	8
Totenkopf	–	–	–	–	80
503. s.Pz Btl.	–	–	–	14	16

1 Nipe, *Last Victory in Russia*, p. 149.

2 Hauck, "Der Gegenangriff der Heeresgruppe Sud im Fruhjahr 1943: Die Entwicklung der Lage vor Beginn des Gegenangriffs", p. 481.

3 Jentz, *Panzertruppen, Vol. Two*, pp. 29-34, and 17. Panzer Division. *Ia, Kriegstagebuch IX (4.2-15.5.1943)*, NARA T315 Roll 692, Frame 000058. Note that the figure given for the *17. Panzer Division* includes nine Marder self-propelled anti-tank guns.

4 Jentz, *Panzertruppen, Vol. Two*, pp. 29-36, and Nipe, *Last Victory in Russia*, p. 257.

Table 6.7 German Personnel Losses and Replacements on the Eastern Front, 1 December 1942 to 1 July 1943

	Combat Losses[1]	Estimated Sick[2]	Estimated Total Losses	Personnel Replacements
Heeresgruppe A	49,467	63,427	112,894	78,600
Heeresgruppe Don/Süd	122,701	91,091	213,792	221,200
Heeresgruppe B	7,219	29,394	36,613	19,800
Heeresgruppe Mitte	170,513	143,399	313,912	272,500
Heeresgruppe Nord	136,227	9,240	145,467	190,000
Total	486,127	336,551	822,678	782,100
6. Armee Losses				
12.1-2.2.1943	178,505			
Grand Total	664,632	336,551	1,001,183	782,100

1 See Heeresarzt 10-Day Reports in BA-MA RW 6/556 and 6/558. Note that the OKW casualty figures (excluding the final losses of the *6. Armee*) total 490,971 men. BA-MA RW 6/543 and 6/546.

2 The number of sick has been determined by deducting combat casualties found in the Heeresarzt 10-Day Loss Reports within BA- MA RW 6/556 and 6/558 from the figures listed as total losses in Boog, et. al. *GSWW, Vol. VI*, pp. 866-867. The number of replacements is also taken from the latter source.

Table 6.8 The Development of German Army Armoured Vehicle Stocks, 1 December 1942 to 1 July 1943[1]

	Stock 1.12.1942	Stock 1.7.1943	Total Write–Offs	New Production 1.12.1942–30.6.1943
Tanks				
Pz I	692	–	–	–
Pz II	1,006	236	378	–
Flammpz.	–	109	1	100
Pz 38(t)	334	204	97	–
Pz III	2,767	1,423	1,871	436
Pz IV	901	1,472	926	1,432
Panthers	–	428	–	561
Tigers	16	240	51	308
Befelpz.	257	412	95	49
Total	5,973	4,524	3,419	2,886
Assault Guns and Self-propelled Anti-Tank Guns				
StuG	966	1,594	543	1,350
StuH	9	136	8	119
Sturmpanzer IV	–	60	–	60
Elephant	–	89	–	90
Marder	850	971	530	612
Nashorn	–	131	5	155
Total	1,825	2,981	1,086	2,386
Grand Total	7,798	7,505	4,505	5,272

1   See Müller-Hillebrand, "German Tank Strength and Loss Statistics", pp. 26-28.

Table 6.9 German Equipment Losses and New Production, 1 December 1942 to 30 June 1943[1]

	1 December 1942 – 30 June 1943		
	Losses	Production	Balance
MG	48,974	80,156	+31,182
Mortars	9,012	17,751	+8,739
Infantry Guns	1,014	1,507	+493
3.7 cm/5 cm Pak	1,669	2,457	+788
7.5 cm Pak	1,633	4,231	+2,598
8.8 cm Pak	5	670	+665
Light Flak	4,576	8,981	+4,405
Heavy Flak	1,441	3,192	+1,751
Rocket Launchers	672	1,005	+333
Light Artillery	1,410	2,039	+629
Heavy Artillery	733	746	+13
Very-Heavy Artillery	54	37	-17
Trucks	119,838	32,057	-87,781
Staff Cars	66,480	15,368	-51,112
Motorcycles	63,202	20,149	-43,053
Towing vehicles	7,513	6,218	-1,295
SPW	1,670	2,826	+1,156

1 Kroener, et. al. *GSWW. Vol. V, Part Two*, pp. 636-688. Figures for flak include all services.

Table 6.10 Development of German Army Equipment Stocks, 1 December 1942 and 1 July 1943[1]

	Actual Stock		Actual Change	Estimated Potential[2]	
	1.12.1942	1.7.1943		Stock 1.7.43	Change
MG	234,617	194,234	-40,383	265,799	-71,565
Mortars	36,773	37,126	+353	45,512	-8,386
Infantry Guns	4,697	5,084	+387	5,190	-106
3.7 cm/5 cm Pak	12,969	4,007	-8,962	13,757	-9,750
7.5 cm Pak	1,837	4,409	+2,572	4,435	-29
8.8 cm Pak	–	592	+592	665	-73
Light Flak	6,294	6,281	-13		
Heavy Flak	231	549	+318		
Rocket Launchers	2,749	2,284	-465	3,082	-798
Light Artillery	6,160	6,813	+653	6,789	+24
Heavy Artillery	3,310	3,094	-216	3,323	-229
Very-Heavy Artillery	450	425	-25	433	-8
Trucks	403,178	391,027	-12,151	315,397	+75,630
Staff Cars	285,919	273,613	-12,306	234,807	+38,806
Motorcycles	276,144	242,426	-33,718	233,091	+9,335

1   Kroener, et. al. *GSWW. Vol. V, Part Two*, pp. 700-701. Note that figures for flak include only Army stock.

2   Estimated potential stock based upon addition of balances shown in Table 6.9 with total stock available on 1 December 1942. Estimated potential change represents difference between figures shown for estimated potential stock and actual stock for 1 July 1943.

Conclusion

The problem of generating military strength, and then maintaining that strength during the course of a long and difficult campaign, has challenged nations and their armies since the dawn of civilization. This was especially the case for Germany during the first two years of its war against the Soviet Union. Rather than a quick victory that would secure its domination of Europe, the campaign in the East shackled Germany to an enemy whose leaders were as ruthless and implacable as its own. As armies of millions fought a seemingly endless series of battles across a vast area of operations, losses of men and equipment reached staggering proportions. With mounting desperation, in the summer of 1942 Hitler gambled that the *Ostheer* could still seize the oilfields of the Caucasus and force the Russians to the peace table. The gamble failed. Instead, an increasingly competent and powerful Red Army inflicted a devastating defeat upon Axis forces around Stalingrad.

In their explanations of the German failure, the historiography of the Russo-German War has long-argued that Germany was incapable of replacing its losses and that its field armies simply became too weak to win. But to what extent, between June 1941 and June 1943, was Germany able to provide the reinforcements and replacements needed to maintain the strength of the *Ostheer*? As this study has illustrated, Germany's ability to regenerate its forces was far greater than is usually believed.

Indeed, equipment availability was the least of the German Army's problems well into this period. Despite the hurried pace of its pre-war expansion, and intense competition with the other branches of the *Wehrmacht* over resources, the German Army started the Second World War in 1939 with significant surpluses of most kinds of material. During the next two years, armaments production steadily increased and equipment availability kept pace as the Army expanded. As Germany prepared to invade the Soviet Union in June 1941, not only had the immediate needs of the Army been met, but existing surpluses also grew by considerable margins. Given the expectations amongst Germany's senior leadership that the campaign in the East would be short, available equipment stocks seemed more than sufficient. Then came the disastrous winter of 1941-1942. German equipment losses in the first six months of the Russo-German War were heavy, but these only became significant because of the near collapse of German manufacturing and rail transport. The drop in armaments production meant that losses bit deep into existing equipment stocks. Even so, these stocks still remained considerable – because of interruptions within the rail network, equipment shortages at the front had more to do with their transport than their actual availability. During the course of 1942, armaments production gradually recovered and even reached new levels. However, this was countered by the steady expansion of the Army together with the continued pace of losses. It was only in the aftermath of the Stalingrad debacle that equipment availability became an increasingly serious problem. By the early summer of 1943, the majority of the formations belonging to the *Ostheer* had most of the equipment they required, but the previously substantial surpluses that had existed were largely gone.

Maintaining the strength of the *Panzerwaffe* was more problematic. There was a clear upward trend in the overall numbers of armoured vehicles with the German Army. Large numbers of replacement vehicles were continuously dispatched eastwards. Time and again, the *Ostheer* was able to assemble large concentrations of tanks – for Operation Barbarossa (June 1941), the attack upon Moscow (October 1941), Operation Blue (June 1942), and during the prelude to the great battle at Kursk (July 1943). But the *Panzerwaffe* was confronted by two major problems that persistently undermined its numerical strength. The first involved the unrelenting pace of armoured vehicle development. Having started the Second World War with tanks that were already inferior to their Anglo-French counterparts, the panzer divisions were then confronted by the even more formidable Soviet T-34. The result was an arms race that continued until the end of the war. Constantly having to re-tool production lines every time an improved tank model was developed meant that German armoured production rarely reached its potential. As older vehicles were phased out, it also meant that the panzer divisions were constantly engaged in a game of catch-up. This was particularly the case during the second half of 1942, when the *Panzerwaffe* was shedding off its series of obsolete light tanks in favour of improved versions of Pz III and Pz IV, and again from the summer of 1943, when the introduction of the Panther tank heralded the retirement of the Pz III. In cases where strength reports lamented a shortage of tanks, such as those dated to just before Operation Blue, these were frequently the product of outdated tables of organization and equipment that had yet to be adjusted to reflect new production realities.

The second major problem involved fluctuating levels of operational readiness. German panzer divisions usually possessed large numbers of armoured vehicles. But with the outcome of the summer campaigns of 1941 and 1942 hinging upon the speed of the German advance, Hitler and his military commanders drove the panzers onward at an unforgiving pace. The intensity of combat operations, together with the harsh nature of the operating environment in the East, and the unpredictable availability of spare parts (a problem only made worse by the introduction of new models), had the number of operational tanks oscillating widely. Given sufficient time between operations to conduct maintenance and repairs, operational readiness could, and frequently did, increase dramatically. Yet time was something Germany never had in abundance, especially when it was on the offensive and the need to crush the Red Army before it regained its strength and equilibrium was paramount. However, because of miscalculations regarding the strength and resolve of the Soviet Union, together with poor logistical planning on the part of OKH, the German offensives of 1941 and 1942 eventually came to a halt. At the end of long logistical tethers barely able to meet their basic needs, on both occasions the now run-down panzer divisions were left exposed to the counterstrokes of an increasingly powerful Red Army. Whenever the *Ostheer* was forced to conduct a major retreat, such as occurred outside Moscow or in the aftermath of the disaster around Stalingrad, large numbers of non-operational tanks had to be abandoned. Substantial consignments of replacement vehicles were dispatched from Germany, but the effort to restore the strength of the panzer divisions was counterbalanced by the unrelenting pace of operations that kept operational ready-rates low and frequently led to the abandonment of even more tanks. It was only when the Soviet counteroffensives were brought to a halt, and the *Ostheer* had fallen back upon more reliable lines of communication, that the condition of the panzer divisions could really be improved. It is in this context that a comprehensive understanding of the specific battles and engagements that constituted the Russo-German War becomes crucial in understanding how and why the armoured strength of the *Ostheer* fluctuated as it did. If German panzer divisions lacked their required number of armoured vehicles, the problem usually had more to do with the pace of events rather than an overall shortage of tanks.

Finding sufficient manpower to keep the formations of the *Ostheer* up-to-strength was perhaps Germany's greatest challenge. The labour requirements of the German economy meant that the availability of manpower was already constricted well before the Second World War began, and the personnel requirements of the *Wehrmacht* had to be constantly balanced against the needs of industry throughout the conflict. But the actual flow of men from the economic sector into the *Wehrmacht* was always determined by how Hitler and his advisors viewed Germany's strategic situation. Initially perceiving that the war with Great Britain and France would be a long, desperate, and costly venture, between September 1939 and May 1940, Hitler authorized the call-up of millions of men at the expense of the German economy. When the campaign in the West ended far more quickly, and cheaply, than expected, Hitler downsized the Army and discharged hundreds of thousands of men back to civilian life.

The invasion of the Soviet Union reversed this decision. By June 1941, the ranks of the newly expanded Army were full and nearly one-half million replacements stood by to replace casualties. During the first few months of the Russo-German War, the availability of these replacements generally managed to cope with the casualty rate. Despite the heavy losses they sustained, and considering the circumstances in which they operated, most of the field divisions maintained respectable force levels. Aside from seriously miscalculating its will to resist and ability to continuously muster fresh forces, the problem was that Hitler and his military chiefs believed that the Soviet Union could be defeated in a short campaign. No provision was made if this assumption turned out to be false. Even though the pool of replacements had been depleted by October 1941, German hubris meant that the problem of providing the *Ostheer* with new men was dealt with by a series of temporary, stopgap measures instead of an effective, comprehensive effort. Frontline unit strengths atrophied. It was only when the *Ostheer* was brought to the brink of destruction by a series of Soviet counteroffensives in December that the situation became serious enough to shake Hitler and his advisors out of their complacency. Although the series of measures enacted during the winter of 1941-1942 garnered large numbers of new men, they were too late to arrest the disastrous decline in unit strengths. As heavy fighting continued into the early spring of 1942, the persistently high number of combat casualties and sick nullified the impact of arriving replacements. By the time the intensity of operations finally declined, German field units faced huge personnel shortages.

The sudden realization that the war in the East would continue for the foreseeable future, together with the entry of the United States on the side of the Allies, forced a wholesale re-evaluation of Germany's strategic position. Confronted by the seriousness of their predicament – an implacable struggle with an increasingly powerful and unyielding Soviet Union, chronic shortages of raw materials, and the eventual Anglo-American return to continental Europe – Hitler and his advisors determined that the best chance of securing Germany's position was another offensive in the East to seize the oilfields of the Caucasus and thereby perhaps force the Soviets to make peace. But time was short – Operation Blue had to begin by June if its objectives were to be reached before the onset of winter brought operations to a halt. Equally problematic, the entire *Ostheer* required a comprehensive rebuilding; although the formations partaking in the offensive would receive priority, since the Red Army was expected to stage diversionary attacks, large resources would also have to be diverted to those that were not.

Remarkably, Germany managed to win this race. The tap controlling the flow of manpower from the German economy was opened and large numbers of personnel replacements and fresh divisions flooded the *Ostfront*. The formations assigned to Operation Blue were restored to full-strength and during the summer of 1942 were able to advance deep into the Caucasus and to the Volga River. Although most of the divisions deployed to other sectors of the front never completely regained their former strengths, they were nonetheless sufficiently rebuilt to successfully repel numerous Soviet attacks and even stage a number of their own. Thanks to the revitalization of its strength, between May and July 1942 the *Ostheer* achieved a remarkable number of stunning operational-level victories.

And yet, the very success achieved by the *Ostheer* ultimately led to yet another catastrophic manpower crisis. Buoyed by his victories, Hitler became over-confident. For the sake of maintaining production levels and civilian morale, his economic and political advisors convinced him to drastically curtail the number of German males being called-up for military service. The manpower tap was once more turned down and, by the late summer of 1942, the flow of personnel replacements to the *Ostfront* was once again unable to cope with the rate of loss. With heavy fighting raging unabated across the front, German unit strengths plummeted and shortages began to mount. The over-confidence that permeated all levels of Germany's leadership also produced a series of abysmal decisions that wasted the potential of the human resources that were available. Rather than transfer its surplus personnel to the Army where they were desperately needed, the *Luftwaffe* was allowed to create its own ill-fated divisions, and millions of Jews, Russians, and other undesirables were killed off instead of using them to replace German males in the armaments factories. Once again it would take yet another stunning reversal, this time during the winter of 1942-1943, to convince Hitler and his advisors to re-introduce rational manpower policies.

Shortages did exist at various times and to various degrees, and given the scale and intensity of the Russo-German War, these were probably inevitable. But in this context it is worth noting the significance of the periods witnessing the worst unit deficits, specifically November 1941 to April 1942 and August to November 1942; the former encompassed the final collapse, and subsequent repercussions, of German pre-invasion assumptions regarding how a war with the Soviet Union would unfold, while the latter relates to a period of mounting over-confidence among senior German leadership circles that permitted a faltering of Germany's war effort. In either period, declining unit strengths were a symptom, not of an abject shortage of men and material, but rather a comprehensive failure of German strategy and planning.

In the final analysis, Germany certainly had the ability to replace most, if not all, of the staggering human and material losses it sustained on the *Ostfront* between June 1941 and July 1943. As a result, German field formations were frequently far stronger than the tenor within the historiography would have one believe. This is most clearly illustrated in the condition of the *Ostheer* at the end of this period. Despite the scale of the Stalingrad disaster, by early July 1943, nearly all of the German divisions in the East had been brought back to full-strength. The previously large manpower deficits of late 1942 had been reduced to marginal levels or eliminated entirely, and equipment stocks largely matched requirements. Indeed, there was even enough manpower to permit the reconstitution of most of the divisions that were destroyed at Stalingrad or in Tunisia. Notably, this period had already been proceeded by Germany's initial gathering of its forces for the invasion of Russia in June 1941, and by the first comprehensive rebuilding of the *Ostheer* during the first half of 1942. In short, the German Army was able to generate forces of prodigious strength three times in the space of two and one-half years. If these efforts were ultimately insufficient to produce victory between June 1941 and July 1943, the root causes of Germany's failure during the Russo-German War reside elsewhere.

Appendix I

Equipment Requirements of Independent Units belonging to the German Army on 1 October 1939[1]

Two reconnaissance (*Aufklärungs*) battalions:
* Each with 18 MG, 3 5 cm GrW, 2 le. IG, 3 Pak, and 50 PSW.

Infanterie Regiment Grossdeutschland:
* 144 MG, 27 5 cm GrW, and 18 8.1 cm GrW.

57 mixed artillery battalions (each with two batteries 15 cm s.FH and one battery 10 cm K):
* 456 15 cm s.FH and 228 10 cm K.

Eight independent light artillery battalions and the *161. Landwehr Artillerie Regiment* with three light artillery battalions:
* 132 10.5 cm le.FH.

Two gun (10 cm K) artillery battalions:
* 24 10 cm K

Six heavy field artillery battalions:
* 72 15 cm s.FH

One heavy gun (15 cm K) battalion:
* 9 15 cm K.

Eight various artillery battalions:
* 12 15 cm K, 27 21 cm K, 6 24 cm K3, 8 30.5 cm (t), and six various pieces.

Three *Nebelwerfer* battalions:
* 54 *Nebelwerfer.*

14 machine-gun battalions (each with 38 MG, 9 5 cm GrW, 6 8.1 cm GrW, and 6 Pak):

1   See *Kriegsgliederung des Feldheeres, Stand: 15.1.1940*, NARA T78 Rolls 402 and 403.

- 532 MG, 126 5 cm GrW, 84 8.1 cm GrW, and 84 Pak.

29 pioneer (25 *Heeres*, 2 *Landwehr*, 2 *Grenzpionier*) battalions (each with 27 MG):
- 783 MG.

25 border guard (*Grenzwacht*) regimental headquarters and 10 independent border guard battalions controlling 263 rifle companies (with 16 MG each) and 15 anti-tank companies (with 12 Pak each):
- 4,208 MG and 180 Pak.

125. Grenzwacht Regiment organized as an infantry regiment belonging to the *1. Welle*:
- 125 MG, 12 Pak, 2 s. and 6 le. IG, 25 5 cm GrW, and 18 8.1 cm GrW.

Four *Landwehr* infantry regimental headquarters controlling 13 *Landwehr* battalions:
- 507 MG, 24 Pak, and 32 le. IG.

128. Stellungs Abschnitt controlling six guard (*Wacht*) companies and one machine-gun company:
- 66 MG.

19 *Panzerjäger* battalions:
- 684 Pak and 342 MG.

308 local defence (*Landesschützen*) battalions (each of four companies with 3 MG each):
- 3,696 MG.

21 *Wacht* battalions (each of three companies of 12 MG apiece):
- 756 MG.

Appendix II

Equipment Requirements of Independent Units of the German Army on 1 May 1940[1]

---

11. Schützen Brigade:
- 216 MG, 36 5 cm GrW, 24 8.1 cm GrW, 8 le.IG, 12 Pak, and 11 PSW.

(Mot.) Infanterie Regiment Grossdeutschland:
- 144 MG, 27 5 cm GrW, 18 8.1 cm GrW, 12 Pak, 6 le. and 4 s.IG.

Aufklärungs Lehr Bataillon:
- 18 MG, 1 2 cm Flak, 2 le.IG, 2 5 cm GrW, 2 8.1 cm GrW, 3 Pak, and 14 PSW.

Six light field artillery battalions:[2]
- 72 10.5 cm le.FH 16 and 18.

31 gun (10 cm K) artillery battalions, plus three independent batteries:
- 384 10 cm K.

37 heavy field artillery battalions:[3]
- 444 15 cm s.FH.

20 mixed field artillery battalions (each with two batteries 15 cm s.FH and one battery 10 cm K):
- 160 15 cm s.FH and 80 10 cm K.

Four heavy gun (15 cm K) artillery battalions (each of three batteries with three guns each), plus one independent battery:
- 36 15 cm K.

---

1   See *Kriegsgliederung des Feldheeres, Stand: 15.1.1940*, NARA T78 Rolls 402 and 403.
2   The *729. Schwere Artillerie Bataillon* was equipped with Czech-made 10.5 cm K pieces and is therefore not included.
3   The *I./77. Artillerie Regiment* was equipped with Czech-made 15 cm s.FH and is therefore not included.

Ten very heavy artillery battalions:
- Three 15 cm K 18, 15 21 cm H, eight 24 cm H, six 24 cm K3, six 24 cm K M16 (Czech), ten 30.5 cm (Czech), one 35.5 cm M1, one 42 cm (Czech), and one 42 cm artillery pieces.

Six heavy artillery (21 cm M 18) battalions (each of three batteries with three guns each):
- 54 21 cm M.

30 *Heeres Pionier* battalions (each of three companies with nine MG each):
- 810 MG.

Six *Fla* battalions, and 37 independent *Fla* companies:
- 684 2 cm Flak.

14 machine-gun battalions:
- 544 MG, 126 5 cm GrW, 84 8.1 cm GrW, and 102 Pak.

11 *Panzerjäger* battalions (both towed and self-propelled):
- 384 Pak and 198 MG.

Nine *Nebelwerfer* battalions (each of three batteries with six 10 cm/15 cm NbW apiece):
- 162 *Nebelwerfer*.

21 *Wacht* battalions (each of three companies with 12 MG each):
- 756 MG.

Two security *(Sicherungs)* regiments:
- 132 MG and 36 5 cm GrW.

Four bicycle guard (*Radfahr Wacht*) battalions (each of three companies with 9 MG each):
- 108 MG.

269 *Landesschützen* battalions (each of four companies with 3 MG each):
- 3,216 MG.

Static defence areas (*Bodenständige Abschnitt Eifel* and *Niederrhein*; *526. Division Stab (Grenzwacht)*:
- 1,506 MG, 16 Pak, and 22 le.IG.

Appendix III

Equipment Requirements of Independent Units of the German Army on 1 June 1941[1]

---

125. Infanterie Regiment:
- 148 MG, 27 5 cm and 18 8.1 cm GrW, 12 Pak, 6 le. and 2 s. IG.

100. Infanterie Bataillon Z.b.V.:
- 48 MG, 3 5 cm and 6 8.1 cm GrW, 4 Pak.

Four *Ersatz* brigades (each with 288 MG and 24 5 cm GrW):
- 1,152 MG and 96 5 cm GrW.

Lehr Aufklärungs Bataillon:
- 43 MG, 3 5 cm GrW, 2 le. IG, and 2 Pak.

900. Lehr Brigade:
- 152 MG, 18 5 cm and 12 8.1 cm GrW, 42 Pak, 4 le. and 2 s. IG, 7 StuG

(Mot.) Infanterie Regiment Grossdeutschland:
- 280 MG, 39 5 cm and 18 8.1 cm GrW, 27 Pak, 6 le. and 4 s. IG, 21 le. Flak, 8 10.5 cm and 4 15 cm FH, and 7 StuG.

11 *Sturmgeschütz* battalions (each of three batteries with 7 StuG each):
- 231 StuG.

30 gun (10 cm K) artillery battalions:
- 360 10 cm K.

12 mixed field artillery battalions (each with two batteries 15 cm s.FH and one battery 10 cm K):
- 96 15 cm s.FH and 48 10 cm K.

---

1   See *Kriegsgliederung des Feldheeres, Stand: 15.5.1941*. NARA T78 Roll 404.

35 heavy field artillery battalions:[2]
- 404 15 cm s.FH.

Seven heavy gun (15 cm K16/18/39) artillery battalions (six of three batteries with three guns each; one with two batteries with three guns, and one battery of two 15 cm K (SKC 28) guns):
- 60 15 cm K16/18/39 and 2 15 cm K (SKC 28).

30 heavy artillery (21 cm M18) battalions (each of three batteries with three 21 cm M18 each):
- 270 21 cm M18.

Two heavy gun (21 cm K 38/39) battalions (each of three batteries of two guns apiece):
- 12 21 cm K 38/39.

Seven very heavy artillery battalions:
- 6 24 cm K3, 6 24 cm K M16 (Czech), 8 24 cm H39 (Czech), 16 30.5 cm H (Czech), and one 35.5 cm M1.

17 *Nebelwerfer* battalions (each of three batteries with six 10 cm/15 cm NbW each):[3]
- 306 10 cm/15 cm NbW.

Ten *Heeres Flakartillerie* battalions (five battalions with two batteries of 4 8.8 cm Flak each and one battery of 12 2 cm Flak; five battalions with three batteries of 4 8.8 cm Flak each):
- 100 8.8 cm Flak and 60 2 cm Flak.

Ten *Fla* battalions and 29 independent *Fla* companies:
- 708 2 cm Flak.

14 *Panzerjäger* battalions (Eight equipped with 36 3.7 cm Pak and 18 MG each; Six equipped with 27 4.7 cm SP Pak (t) and 6 MG each):
- 450 Pak and 180 MG.

31 army coastal artillery (*Heeres Küstenartillerie*) batteries equipped with German-made guns (Eight with 4 10 cm K18 each; 12 with 3 21 cm M18 each; Ten with 4 10 cm K17 each; one with 3 15 cm K39):
- 32 10 cm K18, 36 21 cm M18, 40 10 cm K17, and 3 15 cm K39.

---

2   Of these, the *III./111. Artillerie Regiment* consisted of only two batteries. Not included are an additional three battalions (*I./77. Artillerie Regiment, 154.*, and *737.*), each equipped with 12 15 cm FH 37(t).

3   One additional battalion, excluded from these totals, was equipped with 24 of the newly designed 28/32 cm NbW.

239 *Landesschützen* battalions (averaging four companies per battalion, with 3 MG per company):
• 2,868 MG.

50 *Wacht* battalions (29 with 27 MG each; 15 with 36 MG each; Three with 44 MG each; Three with 48 MG each):
• 1,599 MG.

54 *Pionier* battalions (each with 27 machine-guns):
• 1,458 MG.

Two *Radfahr* battalions (each with 40 machine-guns, 12 8.1 cm GrW, and 3 Pak):
• 80 MG, 24 8.1 cm GrW, and 6 Pak.

Eight *Machinegewehr* battalions (Six with 46 MG, 9 5 cm and 6 8.1 cm GrW, and 6 Pak each; One with 42 MG and 3 Pak; One with 51 MG and 9 Pak):
• 369 MG, 54 5 cm and 36 8.1 cm GrW, and 48 Pak.

Appendix IV

Estimated Strength of German Infantry and Motorised Infantry Battalions, 1941[1]

Infantry Battalion: 22 Officers and 839 men (861 Total)

Battalion HQ:	5 Officers and 81 men	KStN 111, dated 1.10.1937.
Rifle Company:	4 Officers and 187 men	KStN 131c, dated 1.2.1941.
(X3:	12 Officers and 561 men)	
Machine-Gun Company:	5 Officers and 197 men	KStN 151c, dated 1.2.1941.

Motorised Infantry Battalion: 28 Officers, 3 Officials and 1,058 men (1,089 Total)

Battalion HQ:	5 Officers, 3 Officials and 68 men	KStN 1108, dated 1.10.1937.
Rifle Company:	5 Officers and 223 men	KStN 1114, dated 1.11.1941.
(X3	15 Officers and 669 men)	
Machine-Gun Company:	4 Officers and 177 men	KStN 1116, dated 1.2.1941.
HQ, Heavy Company:	1 Officer and 27 men	KStN 1121, dated 1.10.1937.
Anti-Tank Platoon:	1 Officer and 29 men	KStN 1122, dated 1.10.1937.
Infantry Gun Platoon:	1 Officer and 32 men	KStN 1123, dated 1.10.1937.
Pioneer Platoon:	1 Officer and 56 men	KStN 1124, dated 1.10.1937.

1   The specific KStN noted here can be found at the website www.wwiidaybyday.com

Appendix V

German Reinforcements to the *Ostfront*, October 1941 – June 1942[1]

	Arrival
Heeresgruppe Nord (Total: 11 divisions)	
5. Leichte Infanterie Division	February 1942
8. Leichte Infanterie Division	February 1942
5. Gebirgs Division	March 1942
212. Infanterie Division	November 1941
215. Infanterie Division	December 1941
218. Infanterie Division	January 1942
223. Infanterie Division	December 1942
225. Infanterie Division	January 1942
227. Infanterie Division	October 1941
250. Infanterie Division	October 1941
329. Infanterie Division	February 1942
Heeresgruppe Mitte (Total: 13 divisions)	
81. Infanterie Division	January 1942
83. Infanterie Division	February 1942
88. Infanterie Division	January 1942
205. Infanterie Division	February 1942
208. Infanterie Division	February 1942
211. Infanterie Division	February 1942
216. Infanterie Division	February 1942
246. Infanterie Division	February 1942
328. Infanterie Division	February 1942

---

1   Kroener, et. al. *GSWW. Vol. V: Part One*, p. 1006.

329. Infanterie Division	February 1942
330. Infanterie Division	January 1942
331. Infanterie Division	February 1942
342. Infanterie Division	February 1942

Heeresgruppe Süd (Total: 20 divisions)

22. Panzer Division	March 1942
23. Panzer Division	April 1942
24. Panzer Division	April 1942
28. Leichte Infanterie Division	February 1942
71. Infanterie Division	April 1942
82. Infanterie Division	May 1942
113. Infanterie Division	January 1942
305. Infanterie Division	May 1942
323. Infanterie Division	May 1942
336. Infanterie Division	May 1942
340. Infanterie Division	June 1942
370. Infanterie Division	June 1942
371. Infanterie Division	June 1942
376. Infanterie Division	May 1942
377. Infanterie Division	May 1942
383. Infanterie Division	April 1942
384. Infanterie Division	February 1942
385. Infanterie Division	March 1942
387. Infanterie Division	March 1942
389. Infanterie Division	April 1942

Appendix VI

Estimated German Armour Strength on the Eastern Front, 1 July 1942[1]

	Date	Pz II	Pz 38t	Pz III	Pz IV	Befpz	StuG	Total
Heeresgruppe Nord:								
8. Panzer Division	28.6.1942	1	65	–	2	–	–	68
12. Panzer Division	1.7.1942	–	–	48	10	–	–	58
203. Panzer Regt.	30.4.1942	29	–	63	5	6	–	103
Two StuG Btls.		–	–	–	–	–	42	42
Total		30	65	111	17	6	42	271
Heeresgruppe Mitte:								
1. Panzer Division	15.7.1942	2	10	27	7	4	–	50
2. Panzer Division	20.6.1942	22	33	20	5	2	–	82
4. Panzer Division	1.7.1942	13	–	28	5	2	–	48
5. Panzer Division	25.6.1942	26	–	55	13	9	–	103
17. Panzer Division	29.6.1942	17	–	36	16	2	–	71
18. Panzer Division	29.6.1942	11	–	28	8	2	–	49
19. Panzer Division	15.7.1942	6	35	12	4	–	–	57
20. Panzer Division	30.6.1942	8	39	20	13	7	–	87
Four StuG Btls.		–	–	–	– –		84	84
Total		105	117	226	71	28	84	631
Heeresgruppe Süd:								
3. Panzer Division	27.6.1942	25	–	106	33	–	–	164
9. Panzer Division	22.6.1942	22	–	99	21	2	–	144
11. Panzer Division	25.6.1942	15	–	124	13	3	–	155

1   Jentz, *Panzertruppen, Vol. One*, pp. 236-239. The strength of the *Sturmgeschütz* battalions has been estimated by assuming that all of them possessed their full *Sollstärke* of 21 guns each.

	Date	Pz II	Pz 38t	Pz III	Pz IV	Befpz	StuG	Total
13. Panzer Division	22.6.1942	15	–	71	12	5	–	103
14. Panzer division	20.6.1942	14	–	60	24	4	–	102
16. Panzer Division	1.7.1942	13	–	57	27	3	–	100
22. Panzer Division	1.7.1942	39	140	13	30	–	–	222
23. Panzer Division	28.6.1942	27	–	84	27	–	–	138
24. Panzer Division	28.6.1942	32	–	110	32	7	–	181
3. (Mot.) Inf. Div.	28.6.1942	10	–	35	8	1	–	54
16. (Mot.) Inf. Div.	28.6.1942	10	–	35	8	1	–	54
29. (Mot.) Inf. Div.	28.6.1942	12	–	36	8	2	–	58
60. (Mot.) Inf. Div.	7.7.1942	17	–	35	4	1	–	57
(Mot.) Inf. Div. GD	1.7.1942	12	–	2	30	1	21	66
SS-Div. Wiking	27.6.1942	12	–	36	4	1	–	53
300. Panzer Btl.	1.5.1942	–	–	31	–	–	–	31
Twelve StuG Btls.		–	–	–	–	–	252	252
Total		275	140	934	281	31	273	1,934
Grand Total		410	322	1,271	369	65	399	2,836

Appendix VII

Divisional Personnel Shortages among the *Ostheer*, early September 1942

Heeresgruppe Nord (1.9.1942) – Average: 2,029[1]

8. PD	1,396	30. ID	2,597	212. ID	1,435
18. (Mot.) ID	2,124	32. ID	1,894	217. ID	888
20. (Mot.) ID	1,297	61. ID	922	218. ID	2,494
5. Jäger Div.	4,357	81. ID	2,773	254. ID	2,484
8. Jäger Div.	5,437	93. ID	729	269. ID	1,102
1. ID	1,163	96. ID	871	290. ID	3,664
11. ID	494	122. ID	2,063	291. ID	760
12. ID	1,997	123. ID	2,783	329. ID	2,358
21. ID	2,320	126. ID	2,355		

Heeresgruppe Mitte:
2. *Panzerarmee* (1.9.1942) – Average: 2,120[2]

4. PD	115	26. ID	4,886	216. ID	2,251
9. PD	2,442	52. ID	3,640	262. ID	1,206
11. PD	2,271	56. ID	2,803	293. ID	821
17. PD	2,090	112. ID	2,084	296. ID	2,536
18. PD	1,717	134. ID	2,081	339. ID	1,411
19. PD	2,122	208. ID	2,096	707. ID	740
20. PD	2,694	211. ID	2,713	25. (Mot.) ID	1,799

Heeresgruppe B – Average: 3,521
2. *Armee* (1.9.1942) – Average: 3,280[3]

27. PD	826	82. ID	3,134	340. ID	4,601
45. ID	2,642	88. ID	3,145	377. ID	5,066
57. ID	4,172	95. ID	3,012	383. ID	2,600
68. ID	1,156	299. ID	2,550	385. ID	3,492
75. ID	4,492	323. ID	3,007	387. ID	5,311

6. Armee (9.9.1942) – Average: 3,779[4]

16. PD	1,856	76. ID	4,603	305. ID	4,313
3. (Mot.) ID	3,700	79. ID	3,769	376. ID	4,696
60. (Mot.) ID	2,502	100. Jäger Div.	3,310	384. ID	3,570
44. ID	3,602	113. ID	3,019	389. ID	3,420
71. ID	4,827	295. ID	5,702		

Notes

1   *HG Nord. Abt IIa/IIb, Anlagenband 1 zu den Tatigkeitsberichten zum KTB vom 1.4.1942 – 31.12.42.* NARA T311 Roll 105, Frames 7139734-7139735.
2   *2. PzAOK. Anlagen z. KTB, Sept. 1942, Teil I, Pz AOK 2 Ia.* NARA T313 Roll 115, Frame 7362013.
3   *2. AOK. Ia Anlage z. KTB Russland, Schriftwechsel "Zustandsberichte, Teil I-II. (1.9-20.12.1942),* NARA T312 Roll 1663, Frames 000252-000282.
4   *6. AOK. Ia/Ic Anlagenband z. KTB Nr. 13, Russland. (12-17.9.1942),* NARA T312 Roll 1685, Frame 000987.

Appendix VIII

Divisional Personnel Shortages among the *Ostheer*, early November 1942

Heeresgruppe Nord (1.11.1942) – Average: 2,737[1]

8. PD	1,335	30. ID	3,266	212. ID	2,328
18. (Mot.) ID	2,018	32. ID	2,886	215. ID	3,135
20. (Mot.) ID	1,487	58. ID	1,166	217. ID	998
5. Gebirgs Div.	3,336	61. ID	913	218. ID	3,742
5. Jäger Div.	4,330	81. ID	3,736	223. ID	3,763
8. Jäger Div.	3,368	96. ID	1,658	225. ID	912
28. Jäger Div.	4,552	121. ID	2,798	227. ID	4,063
1. ID	827	122. ID	3,168	254. ID	2,044
11. ID	875	123. ID	2,274	290. ID	3,636
12. ID	2,282	126. ID	4,226	291. ID	820
21. ID	2,003	132. ID	4,673	329. ID	3,666
24. ID	6,832	170. ID	2,695		

Heeresgruppe B
2. Armee (1.11.1942) – Average: 3,878[2]

27. PD	1,211	82. ID	3,834	377. ID	6,363
45. ID	2,636	88. ID	2,866	383. ID	4,187
57. ID	4,226	299. ID	2,559	385. ID	3,095
68. ID	2,626	323. ID	6,224	387. ID	5,045
75. ID	5,027	340. ID	4,289		

6. Armee/4. Panzerarmee (mid-November 1942) – Average: 6,519[3]

14. PD	5,434	44. ID	4,238	295. ID	9,037
16. PD	7,673	71. ID	7,353	297. ID	7,000
22. PD	5,000	76. ID	6,981	305. ID	8,520
24. PD	5,126	79. ID	8,294	371. ID	6,000

3. (Mot.) ID	4,831	94. ID	8,233	376. ID	6,464
16. (Mot.) ID	6,000	100. Jäger Div.	7,739	384. ID	5,937
29. (Mot.) ID	4,000	113. ID	5,854	389. ID	7,852
60. (Mot.) ID	5,848				

Notes

1   *HG Nord. Abt IIa/IIb, Anlagenband 1 zu den Tatigkeitsberichten zum KTB vom 1.4.1942 – 31.12.42.* NARA T311 Roll 105, Frames 7139726-7139727.
2   *2. AOK. Ia Anlage z. KTB Russland, Schriftwechsel "Zustandsberichte, Teil I-II. (1.9-20.12.1942),* NARA T312 Roll 1663, Frames 000721-000758.
3   Glantz, *Armageddon in Stalingrad*, pp. 719-722.

Appendix IX

Equipment Requirements of Independent Units belonging to the German Army, 1 October 1942[1]

Stab Panzerarmee Afrika
- 56 MG, 10 5 cm Pak, 8 2 cm Flak.

Panzerarmee Afrika Truppen
(606., 609., 612., & 617. Fla Btls., 605. Panzerjäger Btl., 1. & 2. Afrika Artillerie Regiments)
- 18 MG, 24 (Sfl.) 5 cm Pak, 6 Marders, 144 2 cm Flak, 20 10 cm K18, 9 15 cm K16, 6 21 cm M18.

Kommanduer der Sicherungsdienst/Befehlshaber der Heeresgebeit Mitte
- 190 MG, 29 5 cm GrW, 12 3.7 cm Pak.

Kdr. d. S./Befh. d. Heeresgebeit Nord
- 142 MG, 21 5 cm GrW, 12 3.7 cm Pak.

Kdr. d. S./Befh. d. Heeresgebeit 'B'
- 136 MG, 24 5 cm & 6 8.1 cm GrW, 6 3.7 cm Pak.

Kdr. d. S./Befh. d. Heeresgebeit 'A'
- 126 MG, 21 5 cm GrW, 12 3.7 cm Pak.

Festungs Brigade Kreta
- 163 MG, 27 5 cm & 18 8.1 cm GrW, 9 7.5 cm Pak, 12 le. FH, 8 10.5 cm GebH 40.

139. Gebirgsjager Regiment
- 175 MG, 27 5 cm & 18 8.1 cm GrW, 6 le. IG, 12 3.7 cm Pak, 8 7.5 cm GebK 15, 4 10.5 cm GebH 16.

5. Jägdkommando
- 44 MG, 12 5 cm GrW.

---

1   See *Kriegsgliederung des Feldheeres, Stand: 15.10.1942*. NARA T78 Roll 406.

Feldschulen
- 88 MG, 6 5 cm & 16 8.1 cm GrW, 15 3.7 cm, 7 5 cm & 4 7.5 cm Pak, 6 le. & 6 s. IG.

288. Sonderverband
- 186 MG, 19 8.1 cm GrW, 51 5 cm Pak, 4 le. & 2 s. IG, 12 2 cm Flak.

Two *Hoch Gebirgsjäger* battalions
- 112 MG, 16 5 cm & 24 8.1 cm GrW.

13 *Jäger* battalions
- 559 MG, 78 8.1 cm GrW, 26 le. IG, 52 2 cm Flak.

Four *Infanterie Bataillon Z.b.V. (Bewährungs)*
- 186 MG, 27 5 cm & 22 8.1 cm GrW.

776. Radfahr Bataillon
- 46 MG, 9 5 cm & 6 8.1 cm GrW, 3 5 cm Pak.

Kradschützen Lehr Bataillon
- 76 MG, 6 8.1 cm GrW, 3 3.7 cm & 3 5 cm Pak, 2 le. IG.

Eight *(Mot.) Machinegewehr* battalions
- 364 MG, 63 5 cm & 36 8.1 cm GrW, 48 3.7 cm Pak.

26 *Festungs* battalions
- 1,222 MG, 423 5 cm & 156 8.1 cm GrW, 78 3.7 cm Pak.

Four *(Mot.) Panzerjäger* battalions plus one independent company
- 66 MG, 93 3.7 cm, 18 5 cm & 42 7.5 cm Pak.

Six *(Sfl.) Panzerjäger* battalions
- 108 MG, 54 5 cm Pak (Sfl.), 60 Marders, 9 7.5 cm Pak (mot.).

Nine *Heeres Flakartillerie* battalions
- 72 8.8 cm & 162 2 cm Flak

13 *Fla* battalions
- 490 2 cm Flak or *Vierlingsflak*.

26 gun (10 cm K) artillery battalions (of three batteries each with four guns & six MG) plus three independent batteries equipped with Czech guns
- 312 10 cm K guns, 12 10 cm Czech guns, 156 MG

11 mixed field artillery battalions (each with two batteries 15 cm s.FH and one battery 10 cm K; each battery with six MG)
- 44 10 cm K, 88 15 cm s.FH, 66 MG

32 heavy field artillery battalions (most of three batteries 15 cm s.FH, each with 6 MG)[2]
* 344 15 cm s.FH, 190 MG

Two heavy (24 cm) howitzer battalions (each equipped with 5 24 cm M39 and four MG)
* 10 24 cm M39, 8 MG

25 heavy artillery (21 cm M18) battalions (20 of three batteries with three 21 cm M18 each; 5 of three batteries of four 21 cm M18 each)
* 240 21 cm M18, 150 MG

Eight heavy gun (15 cm K18/39) artillery battalions (seven of three batteries with three guns each; one with two batteries with three guns apiece)
* 69 15 cm K18/39, 46 MG

One heavy gun (17 cm K) artillery battalion and one independent battery
* 11 17 cm K, 8 MG

Six very heavy artillery battalions
* 18 21 cm K, 15 24 cm K, 16 30.5 cm (t), 2 35.5 cm M1, 42 MG

19 *Sturmgeschütz* battalions (each of three batteries with seven guns apiece)
* 399 StuGs

26 railway artillery batteries
* 64 various railway guns, 46 2 cm Flak

Four railway artillery batteries equipped with French guns
* 2 24 cm guns, 6 40 cm guns

19 army coastal artillery (10 cm) battalions
* 20 10 cm K, 12 10 cm K18, 18 15 cm K18, 236 foreign guns, 124 MG

23 army coastal artillery (15 cm/17 cm) battalions
* 402 foreign guns, 140 MG

322 independent army coastal artillery batteries
* 8 10.5 cm le.FH, 40 10 cm K17, 12 15 cm s.FH, 33 15 cm K16/18, 8 17 cm K, 5 21 cm K38, 63 21 cm M18, 1,123 foreign guns, 70 2 cm Flak, 644 MG

49 artillery observation (*Beobachtungs*) battalions
* 329 MG

---

2   Of these, the *III./111. Artillerie Regiment* consisted of only two batteries. Three battalions (*I./77. Artillerie Regiment, 154.*, and *737.*) were each equipped with 12 15 cm FH 37(t); one (716.) possessed French howitzers.

Six *Werfer* regimental staffs
- 12 MG

17 *Werfer* battalions
- 306 Nebelwerfer, 51 3.7 cm Pak, 187 MG

29 *Pionier* battalions (each with 27 MG) plus three independent companies (each with 9 MG)
- 810 MG

37 *Wacht* battalions plus one independent company
- 1,197 MG, 3 5 cm GrW

499 *Landesschützen* battalions (each with four companies equipped with 9 MG apiece)
- 17,964 MG

54 *Sicherungs* battalions (each with four companies equipped with 12 MG apiece)
- 2,592 MG

22 *Transport Sicherungs* battalions (each with four companies equipped with 9 MG apiece)
- 792 MG

Appendix X

Estimated Material Requirements of the *Ersatzheer*, October 1942[1]

---

286 *Infanterie/Jäger/Gebirgsjäger Ersatz* Battalions
- Three *schützen ersatz* companies (KStN. 6021), each with six MG and one GrW.
- One *machinegewehr ausbildungs* company (KStN. 6025), with nine MG and three GrW.
- Total: 7,722 MG, 1,716 GrW

Initially, *Ersatz* battalions were responsible for the training of all new recruits and their subsequent dispatch to units in the field. During the period between August and October 1942, this function was split between the old *Ersatz* battalions and newly established *Ausbildungs* battalions. While the latter assumed all training functions, the former became a replacement-holding unit consisting of a variable number of companies of new recruits that had completed their training and convalescents who were ready to be sent back to their units. Given their reduced function, it would seem probable that previous weapons-holdings had been given over to the *Ausbildungs* units, and that the *Ersatz* battalions now possessed only small arms (rifles, SMG, etc.). However, this could not be confirmed. Moreover, many *Ersatz* battalions still retained their old functions and organization and thereby would still have had their previous quantities of equipment. The above therefore indicates the general organization and equipment allotments of *Ersatz* battalions as they initially were before reorganization, and assumes that all were still organized this way. It is this opaque circumstance that is responsible for the wide variances in the estimated equipment holdings of the *Ersatzheer*.

109 *Infanterie Ersatz Regiment Stabs*
- One *(mot.) infanterie panzerjäger ausbildungs* company (KStN. 6045), with eight Pak and four MG.

---

1   Existence of units determined by review of information concerning 'Ersatztruppenteile' found at http://lexikon-der-wehrmacht.de

- One *infanteriegeschütz ausbildungs* company (KStN. 6041), with four le. IG.
- Total: 436 MG, 872 Pak, 436 IG

283 *Infanterie/Jager/Gebirgsjager Ausbildung/Reserve* battalions
- Three *schutzen ersatz* companies (KStN. 6021), each with six MG and one GrW.
- One *machinegewehr ausbildungs* company (KStN. 6025), with nine MG and three GrW.
- Total: 7,641 MG, 1,698 GrW

Three *Machinegewehr Ersatz* battalions
- Three *(mot.) ersatz machinegewehr* companies (KStN. 6029), each with 16 MG and five GrW.
- Total: 144 MG, 45 GrW

17 *Fla Ersatz* battalions
- Three *(mot.) Fla ausbildungs* companies (KStN. 6031), each with 12 2 cm Flak and three MG.
- Total: 204 2 cm Flak, 153 MG

24 *Panzergrenadier Ersatz* battalions
- Three *panzergrenadier ausbildungs* companies (KStN. 6550), each with six MG.
- Total: 432 MG

22 *Panzergrenadier Ausbildungs* battalions
- Three *panzergrenadier ausbildungs* companies (KStN. 6550), each with six MG.
- One mixed *Panzergrenadier Ausbildungs* company (KStN. 6559), with four MG, two le. IG, and two 5 cm Pak.

30 *Panzerjäger Ersatz* battalions
- One *stab panzerjäger ausbildung* battalion (KStN. 6548), with two MG
- Three *panzerjäger ausbildung* companies (KStN. 6581), each with six MG, four 3.7 cm, three 5 cm & three 7.5 cm Pak.
- Total: 600 MG, 360 3.7 cm, 270 5 cm & 270 7.5 cm Pak

18 *Kradschützen Ausbildungs* battalions
- One *stab kradschützen ausbildung* battalion (KStN. 6544), with two MG and three GrW.
- Three *kradschützen ausbildungs* companies (KStN. 6551), each with six MG.
- One mixed *panzergrenadier ausbildungs* company (KStN. 6559), with four MG, two le. IG, and two 5 cm Pak.
- Total: 432 MG, 54 GrW, 36 le. IG, 36 5 cm Pak

29 *Kavallerie/Radfahr Ersatz* battalions
- Three *radfahr ausbildungs* companies (KStN. 6131), each with six MG and three GrW.
- One *(mot.) machinegewehr ausbildung* company (KStN. 6065), with nine MG and four GrW.

- Total: 783 MG, 377 GrW

86 *Artillerie Ersatz* battalions
- Three *leichte* or *schwere ausbildungs* batteries (KStN. 6226), each with two MG.
- Total: 516 MG

71 *Artillerie Ausbildungs* battalions
- Three *leichte* or *schwere ausbildungs* batteries (KStN. 6226), each with two MG.
- Total: 426 MG

14 *Heeres Flakartillerie Ersatz* battalions
- Two *Heeres flakartillerie (8.8 cm) ausbildungs* batteries (KStN. 6238), each with two 8.8 cm Flak and seven MG.
- One *Heeres flakartillerie (2 cm) ausbildungs* battery (KStN. 6239), with two 2 cm Flak and six MG.
- Total: 280 MG, 56 8.8 cm & 28 2 cm Flak

Eight *Werfer Ersatz* battalions
- Three *werfer ausbildungs* batteries (KStN. 6227), each with six *Nebelwerfer* and two MG.
- Total: 144 *Nebelwerfer*, 48 MG

Two *Sturmgeschütz Ersatz* battalions
- One Battalion HQ (KStN. 6247), with 2 MG.
- Three *Sturmgeschütz* batteries (KStN. 6249), each with seven StuG and nine MG.
- Total: 58 MG, 42 StuG

77 *Pionier Ersatz/Ausbildungs* battalions
- Three *pionier ausbildungs* companies (KStN. 6321), each with six MG.
- Total: 462 MG

Five *Wehrkreis Unteroffizier Lehrgang* (that could be identified)[2]
- Total: 377 MG, 68 GrW, 21 IG, three *Nebelwerfer*, 23 Pak

2   See *Kriegsgliederung des Ersatzheeres, Stand Mitte November 1942*. NARA T78 Roll 410.

Appendix XI

German Reinforcements sent to Southern Russia, December 1942 to June 1943

From Western Europe:

6. Panzer Division	December
7. Panzer Division	January
SS-Panzergrenadier Division LSSAH	February
SS-Panzergrenadier Division Das Reich	January
SS-Panzergrenadier Division Totenkopf	February
15. Infanterie Division	February
17. Infanterie Division	March
38. Infanterie Division	March
39. Infanterie Division	March
106. Infanterie Division	April
161. Infanterie Division	May
167. Infanterie Division	March
257. Infanterie Division	April
282. Infanterie Division	April
302. Infanterie Division	January
304. Infanterie Division	January
306. Infanterie Division	December
320. Infanterie Division	January
328. Infanterie Division	June
332. Infanterie Division	March
333. Infanterie Division	February
335. Infanterie Division	January

From Germany:

7. Luftwaffe Feld Division	December
8. Luftwaffe Feld Division	December

From *Heeresgruppe Mitte*:

11. Panzer Division	December
17. Panzer Division	December
19. Panzer Division	December
(Mot.) Infanterie Division Grossdeutschland	January
3. Gebirgs Division	December
26. Infanterie Division	December
255. Infanterie Division	April

From *Heeresgruppe A*:

3. Panzer Division	January
23. Panzer Division	December
SS-Panzergrenadier Division Wiking	January
15. Luftwaffe Feld Division	January
46. Infanterie Division	April
111. Infanterie Division	January
198. Infanterie Division	April
454. Sicherungs Division	January

Appendix XII

Status of Infantry Battalions with the *1. Panzerarmee* and *Armee Abteilung Holidt*, Late February 1943[1]

	Infantry Battalions (Rating)				
	'Strong' +400 Men	'Medium Strength' 300–400 Men	'Average' 200–300 Men	'Weak' 100–200 Men	'Burnt Out' Less than 100 Men
1. Panzerarmee (20 February 1943)					
3. PD	–	3	3	1	–
7. PD	1	1	–	1	–
11. PD	–	1	1	1	–
19. PD	2	3	4	–	–
SS-Wiking	–	–	6	2	–
3. Gebirgs Div.	1	3	–	1	–
304. ID	–	1	–	3	–
333. ID	2	8	–	–	–
335. ID	–	7	3	–	–
Total	6	27	17	9	–
Armee Abteilung Holidt (23 February 1943)					
16. (Mot.) ID	2	3	2	–	–
15. LFD	2	3	–	–	–
79. ID	–	1	–	2	1

1   Hauck, "Der Gegenangriff der Heeresgruppe Sud im Fruhjahr 1943: Die Entwicklung der Lage vor Beginn des Gegenangriffs.", p. 481 and "Der Gegenangriff der Heeresgruppe Sud in Fruhjahr 1943: Die Fortsetzung der Angriffs nach Norden – Schlacht um Charkov und Einnahme von Bjelgorod.", p. 482.

	Infantry Battalions (Rating)				
	'Strong' +400 Men	'Medium Strength' 300–400 Men	'Average' 200–300 Men	'Weak' 100–200 Men	'Burnt Out' Less than 100 Men
111. ID	–	–	4	–	–
294. ID/8. LFD	–	–	11	–	–
302. ID	9	–	–	–	–
306. ID	1	–	8	–	–
336. ID	–	1	3	1	–
384. ID	–	1	3	1	–
444. SD	2	–	–	3	–
454. SD	–	–	4	3	–
Regt. Z.b.V.	2	–	–	–	–
Total	18	9	35	10	1
Grand Total	24	36	52	19	1
Percentage	18.1	27.3	39.4	14.4	0.8

Appendix XIII

Authorized and Actual Divisional Equipment Holdings on the Eastern Front, 1 July 1943[1]

	Pz III	Pz IV	StuG	Marder	Tigers	SPW etc.	MG	Art	7.5 cm Pak	Motor Vehicles
Panzer and SS-Panzergrenadier Divisions:										
SS-Panzergrenadier Division "Leibstandarte SS Adolf Hitler"										
Sollstärke	13	87	35	27	14	205	1,506	48	20	7,135
Iststärke	13	80	34	22	12	163	1,310	47	20	5,785
SS-Panzergrenadier Division "Das Reich"										
Sollstärke	78	28	34	13	14	257	1,653	36	18	5,076
Iststärke	69	34	34	12	14	160	1,554	36	18	4,837
2. Panzer Division										
Sollstärke	36	28	–	30	–	307	1,105	21	3	3,125
Iststärke	37	63	–	30	–	316	1,093	22	4	2,564
3. Panzer Division										
Sollstärke	106	42	–	13	–	138	821	44	12	4,021
Iststärke	57	23	–	14	–	99	771	44	7	3,474
4. Panzer Division										
Sollstärke	– 96 –		–	27	–	204	953	43	52	3,631
Iststärke	– 96 –		–	25	–	204	820	41	47	2,115
5. Panzer Division										
Sollstärke	–	?	–	26	–	81	605	42	35	3,641
Iststärke	–	93	–	14	–	24	520	38	14	3,639
6. Panzer Division										
Sollstärke	120	20	–	13	–	252	552	42	22	3,912

1 Most of the monthly strength reports related to these figures can be found in NARA T78 Roll 616.

	Pz III	Pz IV	StuG	Marder	Tigers	SPW etc.	MG	Art	7.5 cm Pak	Motor Vehicles
Iststärke	65	28	–	14	–	144	513	41	22	2,399
7. Panzer Division										
Sollstärke	105	20	–	10	–	182	865	37	9	3,572
Iststärke	55	38	–	6	–	164	774	48	9	3,475
8. Panzer Division										
Sollstärke	57	14	–	20	–	64	560	27	20	3,278
Iststärke	49	20	–	18	–	42	526	29	18	3,012
9. Panzer Division										
Sollstärke	53	14	–	18	–	324	739	50	32	3,492
Iststärke	28	36	–	16	–	288	702	46	30	3,258
11. Panzer Division										
Sollstärke	85	28	31	20	–	154	786	42	3	3,723
Iststärke	75	26	31	13	–	101	786	40	5	3,476
12. Panzer Division										
Sollstärke	43	29	–	13	–	70	652	28	–	3,370
Iststärke	21	43	–	16	–	40	652	28	5	3,339
13. Panzer Division										
Sollstärke	– 96 –		–	25	–	224	702	44	30	3,715
Iststärke	– 53 –		–	25	–	29	470	43	30	1,078
18. Panzer Division										
Sollstärke	53	14	–	9	–	66	593	27	27	3,419
Iststärke	31	38	–	8	–	23	564	29	20	1,883
19. Panzer Division										
Sollstärke	61	44	–	20	–	60	629	36	–	3,734
Iststärke	38	38	–	12	–	53	607	32	–	3,279
20. Panzer Division										
Sollstärke	52	14	–	30	–	57	612	27	–	3,160
Iststärke	15	35	–	30	–	34	612	27	–	2,631
23. Panzer Division										
Sollstärke	36	28	–	26	–	159	946	36	35	3,518
Iststärke	28	30	–	16	–	72	785	36	26	3,385
Overall Totals:										
Sollstärke	– 1,594 –		100	340	28	2,804	14,279	630	318	65,522
Iststärke	– 1,355 –		99	291	28	1,956	13,059	627	275	53,629
		85%	99%	86%	100%	70%	91%	99.5%	87%	82%

	Pz III	Pz IV	StuG	Marder	Tigers	SPW etc.	MG	Art	7.5 cm Pak	Motor Vehicles
Panzergrenadier and Infantry Divisions:										
15. Infanterie Division										
Sollstärke	–	–	–	13	–	–	653	48	25	1,200
Iststärke	–	–	–	13	–	–	565	45	25	1,189
25. Panzergrenadier Division										
Sollstärke	–	–	–	10	–	27	676	36	14	3,146
Iststärke	–	–	–	10	–	20	676	33	7	1,957
198. Infanterie Division										
Sollstärke	–	–	–	–	–	–	664	48	27	1,240
Iststärke	–	–	–	–	–	–	591	48	27	1,199
294. Infanterie Division										
Sollstärke	–	–	–	–	–	–	598	48	54	970
Iststärke	–	–	–	–	–	–	478	36	19	867
302. Infanterie Division										
Sollstärke	–	–	–	–	–	–	645	36	28	601
Iststärke	–	–	–	–	–	–	432	32	16	625
306. Infanterie Division										
Sollstärke	–	–	–	10	–	–	607	36	43	594
Iststärke	–	–	–	13	–	–	595	41	28	407
328. Infanterie Division										
Sollstärke	–	–	–	–	–	–	594	39	21	899
Iststärke	–	–	–	–	–	–	517	39	21	839
Overall Totals:										
Sollstärke	–	–	–	33	–	27	4,437	291	212	8,650
Iststärke	–	–	–	36	–	20	3,854	274	143	7,083
				109%		74%	87%	94%	68%	82%

Appendix XIV

Arrival of Replacements and Divisional Shortages by 1 July 1943[1]

| | Replacements per Month | | | | | | Shortages 1.7.1943 | |
	2.1943	3.1943	4.1943	5.1943	6.1943	Total	Germans	Hiwis
Heeresgruppe Nord								
18. PGD	324	1,113	2,721	708	1,357	**6,223**	7	603
1. ID	1,667	1,712	663	893	503	**5,438**	+781	711
11. ID	401	1,479	859	678	527	**3,944**	9	967
12. ID	185	220	2,168	1,087	259	**3,919**	91	673
21. ID	1,710	2,639	1,629	825	1,024	**7,827**	+1,549	831
23. ID	227	408	406	492	423	**1,956**	+723	732
30. ID	522	929	1,874	1,543	444	**5,312**	715	765
32. ID	40	1,509	1,129	1,251	605	**4,534**	812	710
58. ID	1,364	480	1,298	1,712	569	**5,423**	+635	517
61. ID	2,138	388	401	482	464	**3,873**	+255	861
69. ID	155	139	1,321	347	341	**2,303**	1,211	957
81. ID	287	1,235	1,143	490	328	**3,483**	349	824
93. ID	341	1,270	2,017	159	278	**4,065**	368	193
96. ID	1,241	1,498	399	1,402	371	**4,911**	483	469
121. ID	713	2,559	1,815	688	813	**6,588**	35	404
122. ID	0	971	1,535	1,023	430	**3,959**	1,191	406
123. ID	19	480	861	1,314	286	**2,960**	383	350
126. ID	547	2,016	1,500	1,652	614	**6,329**	331	880
132. ID	1,372	2,251	774	1,620	505	**6,522**	1,041	535
170. ID	982	2,941	645	1,668	691	**6,927**	493	488

1   These figures originate from a series of monthly reports found in NARA T78 Roll 616, T311 Roll 105, T314 Roll 1493, T314 Roll 583, and T314 Roll 1218.

	Replacements per Month						Shortages 1.7.1943	
	2.1943	3.1943	4.1943	5.1943	6.1943	Total	Germans	Hiwis
212. ID	1,730	889	1,857	1,459	745	**6,680**	937	563
215. ID	388	1,209	805	616	427	**3,445**	801	547
217. ID	81	1,072	336	1,284	224	**2,997**	+181	186
218. ID	253	391	88	807	181	**1,720**	887	564
223. ID	427	360	1,330	1,419	393	**3,929**	787	688
225. ID	420	1,634	1,340	791	438	**4,623**	312	419
227. ID	1,807	1,486	646	1,728	318	**5,985**	198	4
254. ID	602	1,095	1,142	3,579	984	**7,402**	+341	536
290. ID	466	2,310	607	761	330	**4,474**	1,286	659
329. ID	489	1,559	981	2,339	262	**5,630**	809	479
331. ID		—	417	541	527	**1,485**	998	490
5. Jäger Div.	1,238	957	2,329	2,019	794	**7,337**	270	1,227
8. Jäger Div.	789	1,675	2,098	1,910	601	**7,073**	47	1,422
28. Jäger Div.	4,584	1,121	1,796	911	1,231	**9,643**	244	712
5. Gebirgs Div.	571	1,655	1,159	722	699	**4,806**	388	2,132
Heeresgruppe Mitte								
2. PD	–	–	–	–	142		172	85
4. PD	1,484	–	–	–	954		559	64
5. PD	–	–	–	–	592		10	199
8. PD	–	–	–	–	303		170	342
9. PD	–	–	2,307	949	709	**3,965**	238	–
12. PD	–	–	–	–	382		+434	145
18. PD	–	–	–	–	562		14	112
20. PD	–	–	–	–	300		+114	240
25. PGD	–	–	–	–	253		1,432	+399
Heeresgruppe Süd								
3. PD	–	–	–	–	144		16	–
6. PD	–	–	–	–	629		–None–	
7. PD	–	–	–	–	481		3	–
11. PD	–	1,753	1,269	951	739	**4,712**	24	644
17. PD	968	3,136	656	–	–	**4,750**	?	?
19. PD	–	–	–	–	308		248	–
23. PD	–	–	4,242	–	709	**4,951**	6	69
1. SS–PGD	–	–	–	–	2,392		1,691	629

| | Replacements per Month | | | | | | Shortages 1.7.1943 | |
	2.1943	3.1943	4.1943	5.1943	6.1943	Total	Germans	Hiwis
2. SS–PGD	–	–	–	–	1,259		+362	–
3. SS–PGD	–	–	–	–	1,287		1,482	–
15. ID	–	–	–	–	894		1,382	147
161. ID	–	–	–	–	165		268	695
198. ID	–	–	–	–	728		460	–
294. ID	–	–	–	2,003	667		833	195
302. ID	–	–	–	920	468		2,479	–
306. ID	–	–	–	361	430		1,290	–
328. ID	–	–	–	–	180		1,451	–
336. ID	–	3,078	3,625	1,532	1,382	**9,617**	+67	+202
Heeresgruppe A								
13. PD	–	201	–	–	1,812		1,604	97
50. ID	–	1,199	443	–	–		?	?
125. ID[1]	–	664	725	3,437	277	**5,103**	?	?
370. ID	–	270	544	–	–		?	?

Note

1   Replacement figures for April taken from NARA T314 Roll 1218. The remainder may be found in Breymayer, *Das Wiesel*, p. 295. Note that the latter source provides no figures for the number of replacement officers that arrived in these months.

Bibliography

Archival Materials

Bundesarchiv-Militärarchiv (Freiburg, Germany)
RW 6/535, 6/543, 6/546, 6/544, 6/556, 6/558
RH 6/543, 10-60, 20-4/889, 20-4/890, 20-4/891, 20-4/892, 21-2/757, 21-3/611

National Archives and Records Administration (Washington, D.C.)
T78 Rolls 391, 392, 393, 394, 395, 396, 397, 402, 403, 404, 406, 410, 414, 415, 616
T311 Rolls 51, 55, 105, 268, 269, 270, 288, 296
T312 Rolls 44, 307, 1249, 1659, 1663, 1685
T313 Rolls 15, 115, 225, 231, 352, 355
T314 Rolls 568, 583, 594, 761, 1008, 1218, 1493
T315 Rolls 307, 323, 407, 692, 1823

Manuscripts

Escalonilla, Juan-Carlos. "The Spanish Blue Division." MA. Thesis. Carlisle, PA: U.S. Army War College, 2005.

Gore, Brett. "Blitzkrieg under Fire: German Rearmament, Total Economic Mobilization, and the Myth of the 'Blitzkrieg' Strategy, 1933-1942." M.A. Thesis. Calgary, Alberta: University of Calgary, 2000.

Institute of Military History at the Russian Defence Ministry, *Combat and Numerical Composition of the Armed Forces of the USSR in the period of the Great Patriotic War (1941-1945)*. Statistical Material No. 5 (1 November 1942), Statistical Material No. 7 (1 July 1943), Statistical Material No. 9 (1 June 1944), and Statistical Material No. 10 (1 January 1945).

Müller-Hillebrand, Burkhart. "Personnel and Administration." (August 1948), NARA FMS P-005.

—— "Statistics Systems." (March 1949). NARA FMS P-011.

—— "German Tank Strength and Loss Statistics." (December 1950), FMS P-059.

—— "The Tank Repair Service in the German Army." (March 1951), NARA FMS P-040.

Academic Articles

Alexander, Martin S. "After Dunkirk: The French Army's Performance against 'Case Red', 25 May to 25 June 1940." *War in History*, Vol. 14, No. 2 (2007), pp. 219-264.

Alvarez, David. "Axis Sigint Collaboration: A Limited Partnership." *Intelligence and National Security*, Vol. 14, No. 1 (March 1999), pp. 1-17.

Anderson, Truman. "A Hungarian Vernichtungskrieg? Hungarian Troops and the Soviet Partisan War in the Ukraine, 1942." *Militärgeschichtliche Mitteilungen*, Vol. 58 (1999), pp. 345-366.

Aptekar, Pavel & Olga Dudorova. "The Unheeded Warning and the Winter War 1939-1940." *Journal of Slavic Military Studies*, Vol. 10, No. 1 (March 1997), pp. 200-209.

Bacon, Edwin. "Soviet Military Losses in World War II." *Journal of Slavic Military Studies*, Vol. 6, No. 4 (1993), pp. 613-633.

Baird, Jay W. "The Myth of Stalingrad." *Journal of Contemporary History*, Vol. 4, No. 3 (July 1969), pp. 187-204.

Beaulieu, Walter Chales de. "Sturm bis vor Moskaus Tore. Der Einsatz der Panzergruppe 4. Teile II: November 1941—Januar 1942." *Wehrwissenschaftliche Rundschau*, Vol. 6, No. 8 (1956), pp. 423-439.

Beaumont, Roger A. "On the Wehrmacht Mystique." *Military Review*, Vol. 66, No. 7 (July 1986).

Biddiscombe, Perry. "Unternehmen Zepplin: The Deployment of SS Saboteurs and Spies in the Soviet Union, 1942-1943." *Europe-Asia Studies*, Vol. 52, No. 6 (September 2000), pp. 1115-1142.

Birn, Ruth B. "Collaboration with Nazi Germany in Eastern Europe: the Case of the Estonian Security Police." *Contemporary European History*, Vol. 10, No. 2 (2001), pp. 181-198

Bowen, Wayne H. "The Ghost Battalion: Spaniards in the Waffen-SS, 1944-1945." *The Historian*, Vol. 63, No. 2 (2001), pp. 373-385.

Breitmann, Richard. "A Deal with the Nazi Dictatorship? Himmler's Alleged Peace Emissaries in Autumn 1943." *Journal of Contemporary History*, Vol. 30 (1995), pp. 411-430.

Browder, George C. "Captured German and Other Nations' Documents in the Osoby (Special) Archive, Moscow." *Central European History*, Vol. 24, No. 4 (1991), pp. 424-445.

Carston, F.L. "A Bolshevik Conspiracy in the Wehrmacht." *The Slavonic and East European Review*, Vol. 47, No. 109 (April 1974), pp. 483-509.

Citino, Robert. "Beyond Fire and Movement: Command, Control, and Information in the German Blitzkrieg." *Journal of Strategic Studies*, Vol. 27, No. 2 (2004), pp. 324-344.

Corum, James S. "The Luftwaffe's Army Support Doctrine, 1918-1941." *Journal of Military History*, Vol. 59, No. 1 (January 1995), pp. 53-76.

—— "The Luftwaffe and Its Allied Air Forces in World War II: Parallel War and the Failure of Strategic and Economic Cooperation." *Air Power History*, Vol. 51, No. 2 (Summer 2004), pp. 4-19

Crevald, Martin van. "On Learning from the Wehrmacht and Other Things." *Military Review*, Vol. 68, No. 1 (January 1988).

Crouthamel, Jason. "Nervous Nazis: War Neurosis, National Socialism and the Memory of the First World War." *War & Society*, Vol. 21, No. 2 (October 2003), pp. 55-75.

Davey, Owen Anthony. "The Origins of the legion des Voluntaires Francais contre le Bolchvisme." *Journal of Contemporary History*, Vol. 6, No. 4 (1971), pp. 29-45.

Detwiler, Donald S. "Spain and the Axis during the World War II." *Review of Politics*, Vol. 33, No. 1 (January 1971), pp. 36-55.

Deutsch, Harold C. "The German Resistance: Answered and Unanswered Questions." *Central European History*, Vol. 14, No. 4 (December 1981), pp. 322-331.

Dickson, Gary A. "The Counterattack of the 7th Mechanized Corps, 5-9 July 1941." *Journal of Slavic Military Studies*, Vol. 26, No. 2 (June 2013), pp. 310-340.

DiNardo, Richard L. "The Dysfunctional Coalition: The Axis Powers and the Eastern Front in World War II." *Journal of Military History*, Vol. 60, No. 4 (October 1996), pp. 711-730.

DiNardo, R.L. & Austin Bay. "Horse-Drawn Transport in the German Army." *Journal of Contemporary History*, Vol. 23 (1988), pp. 129-142.

Ellis, Frank. "10th Rifle Division of Internal Troops NKVD: Profile and Combat Performance at Stalingrad." *Journal of Slavic Military Studies*, Vol. 19, No. 3 (2006), pp. 601-618.

—— "The Great Fatherland War in Soviet and Post-Soviet Literature." *Journal of Slavic Military Studies*, Vol. 20, No. 4 (2007), pp. 609-632.

Erickson, John. "The Soviet Response to Surprise Attack: Three Directives, 22 June 1941." *Soviet Studies*, Vol. 23, No. 4 (April 1972), pp. 519-553.

Fenyo, Mario. "The Allied Axis Armies and Stalingrad." *Military Affairs*, Vol. 29, No. 2 (Summer 1965), pp. 57-72.

Forster, Stig. "Facing 'People's War': Moltke the Elder and Germany's Military Options after 1871." *Journal of Strategic Studies*, Vol. 10, No. 2 (1987), pp. 209-230.

Gatzke, Hans W. "Russo-German Military Collaboration during the Weimar Republic." *American Historical Review*, Vol. 63, No. 3 (1958), pp. 565-597.

Geyr, Michael. "Insurrectionary Warfare: The German Debate about a Levee en Masse in October 1918." *Journal of Modern History*, Vol. 73, No. 3 (September 2001), pp. 459-527.

Gibbels, Ellen. "Hitlers Nervenkrankheit: Eine neurologisch-psychiatrische Studie." *Vierteljahrshefte für Zeitgeschichte*, Vol. 42, No. 2 (1994), pp. 155-220.

Glantz, David M. "Action of the mobile group of the 5th Tank Army in the Penetration." *Journal of Slavic Military Studies*, Vol. 1, No. 4 (1988), pp. 547-564.

—— "Soviet Mobilization in Peace and War, 1924-1942: A Survey." *Journal of Slavic Military Studies*, Vol. 5, No. 3 (September 1992), pp. 323-362.

—— "American Perspectives on Eastern Front Operations in the Second World War with Soviet Commentary." *Journal of Slavic Military Studies*, Vol. 1, No. 1 (1995), pp. 108-132.

—— "The Failures of Historiography: The Forgotten Battles of the German-Soviet War." *Journal of Slavic Military Studies*, Vol. 8, No. 4 (1995), pp. 768-808.

—— "Forgotten Battles of the German-Soviet War (1941-1945), Part One." *Journal of Slavic Military Studies*, Vol. 12, No. 4 (1999), pp. 149-197.

—— "Forgotten Battles of the German-Soviet War (1941-1945), Part Two." *Journal of Slavic Military Studies*, Vol. 13, No. 1 (2000), pp. 172-237.

Goff, James M. "Evolving Soviet Force Structure, 1941-1945: Process and Impact." *Journal of Soviet Military Studies*, Vol. 5, No. 3 (September 1992), pp. 363-404.

Gorlow, Sergej A. "Geheimsache Moskau-Berlin: Die militarpolitische Zusammenarbeit zwischen der Sowjetunion und dem Deutschen Reich, 1920-1933." *Vierteljahrshefte für Zeitgeschichte*, Vol. 44, No. 1 (1996), pp. 133-165.

Gribanov, Stanislav. "The Role of US Lend-Lease Aircraft in Russia in World War II." *Journal of Slavic Military Studies*, Vol. 11, No. 1 (March 1998), pp. 96-115.

Gunsburg, Jeffrey A. "The Battle of the Belgian Plain, 12-14 May 1940: The First Great Tank Battle." *Journal of Military History*, Vol. 56, No. 2 (April 1992), pp. 207-244.

—— "The Battle of Gembloux, 14-15 May 1940: The 'Blitzkrieg' Checked." *Journal of Military History*, Vol. 64, No. 1 (January 2000), pp. 97-140.

Harward, Grant. "First among Un-Equals: Challenging German Stereotypes of the Romanian Army during the Second World War." *Journal of Slavic Military Studies*, Vol. 24, No. 3 (2011), pp. 439-480.

Hauck, Friedrich Wilhelm. "Der Gegenangriff der Heersgruppe Sud im Fruhjahr 1943: Die Entwicklung der Lage vor Beginn des Gegenangriffs." *Wehrwissenschaftliche Rundschau*, Vol. 12, No. 8 (1962), pp. 452-481.

—— "Der Gegenangriff der Heeresgruppe Sud im Fruhjahr 1943: Die Fortsetzung des Angriffs nach Norden—Schlacht um Charkow und Einnahme von Bjelgorod." *Wehrwissenschaftliche Rundschau*, Vol. 12, No. 9 (1962), pp. 520-549.

Hayward, Joel. "Hitler's Quest for Oil: The Impact of Economic Considerations on Military Strategy, 1941-1942." *Journal of Strategic Studies*, Vol. 18, No. 4 (1995), pp. 94-135.

—— "Stalingrad: An Examination of Hitler's Decision to Airlift." *Airpower Journal*, Vol. 11, No. 1 (Spring 1997), pp. 21-38

Herwig, Holger H. "Prelude to Weltblitzkrieg: Germany's Naval Policy toward the United States of America, 1939-1941." *Journal of Modern History*, Vol. 43, No. 4 (December 1971), pp. 649-668.

Heuser, Beatrice. "Small War in the Age of Clausewitz: The Watershed Between Partisan War and People's War." *Journal of Strategic Studies*, Vol. 33, No. 1 (2010), pp. 139-162.

Hill, Alexander. "The Partisan War in North-West Russia, 1941-1944: A Re-examination." *Journal of Strategic Studies*, Vol. 25, No. 3 (2002), pp. 37-55.

—— "British Lend-Lease Aid and the Soviet War Effort, June 1941-June 1942." *Journal of Military History*, Vol. 17, No. 3 (July 2007), pp. 773-808.

—— "The Bear's New Wheels (and Tracks): US Armored and Other Vehicles and Soviet Military Effectiveness during the Great Patriotic War in Words and Photographs." *Journal of Slavic Military Studies*, Vol. 25, No. 2 (2012), pp. 204-219

Hillgruber, Andreas. "Der Einbau der verbundeten Armeen in die deutsche Ostfront 1941-1944." *Wehrwissenschaftliche Rundschau*, Vol. 10, No. 12 (1960), pp. 659-682.

—— "Noch einmal: Hitler's Wendung gegen die Sowjetunion 1940." *Geschichte in Wissenshaft und Unterricht*, Vol. 33, No. 4 (1982), pp. 214-226.

Hoffmann, J.H. "German Field Marshals as War Criminals? A British Embarrassment." *Journal of Contemporary History*, Vol. 23 (1988), pp. 17-35

Howard, N.P. "The Social and Political Consequences of the Allied Food Blockade of Germany 1918-19." *German History*, Vol. 11, No. 2 (June 1993), pp. 161-188.

Il'Enkow, S.A. "Concerning the Registration of Soviet Armed Forces' Wartime Irrecoverable Losses, 1941-1945." *Journal of Slavic Military Studies*, Vol. 9, No. 2 (1996), pp. 440-442.

Isaev, Aleksei. "Soviet Casualties during the War at the Rzhev Salient." *Modern History Magazine* (July 2012).

Kagan, Frederick. "The Evacuation of Soviet Industry in the wake of 'Barbarossa': A Key to the Soviet Victory." *Journal of Slavic Military Studies*, Vol. 8, No. 2 (June 1995), pp. 387-414.

Kleinfeld, Gerald R. "Hitler's Strike for Tikhvin." *Military Affairs*, Vol. 47, No. 3 (October 1983), pp. 122-128.

Koch, H. "The Spectre of a Separate Peace in the East: Russo-German 'Peace Feelers', 1942-1944." *Journal of Contemporary History*, Vol. 10, No. 3 (1975), pp. 531-549.

—— "Hitler's 'Programme' and the Genesis of Operation 'Barbarossa'." *Historical Journal*, Vol. 26, No. 4 (December 1983), pp. 891-920.

—— "Operation Barbarossa: The Current State of the Debate." *Historical Journal*, Vol. 31, No. 2 (June 1988), pp. 377-390.

Korol, V.E. "The Price of Victory: Myths and Realities." *Journal of Slavic Military Studies*, Vol. 9, No. 2 (1996), pp. 417-426.

Kragh, Mark. "Soviet Labour Law during the Second World War." *War in History*, Vol. 18, No. 4 (2011), pp. 531-546.

Krammer, Arnold. "Spanish Volunteers Against 'Bolshevism': The Blue Division." *Russian Review*, Vol. 32, No. 4 (October 1973), pp. 388-402.

—— "Fueling the Third Reich." *Technology & Culture*, Vol. 19, No. 3 (July 1978), pp. 394-422.

—— "American Treatment of German Generals during World War II." *Journal of Military History*, Vol. 54, No. 1 (January 1990), pp. 27-46.

Leonard, Raymond W. "Studying the Kremlin's Secret Soldiers: A Historiographical Essay on the GRU, 1918-1945." *Journal of Military History*, Vol. 56, No. 3 (July 1992), pp. 403-422.

Lockenour, Jay. "'The Rift in Our Ranks': The German Officer Corps, the Twentieth of July and the Path to Democracy." *German Studies Review*, Vol. 21, No. 3 (October 1998), pp. 469-506.

Lopaisc, Aexander. "Italian Military Performance in the Second World War: Some Considerations." *Journal of Strategic Studies*, Vol. 5, No. 2 (1982), pp. 270-275.

Major, Patrick. "'Our Friend Rommel': The Wehrmacht as 'Worthy Enemy' in Postwar British Culture." *German History*, Vol. 26, No. 4 (2008), pp. 520-535.

Marina, Christina. "Vernichtungskrieg, Kalter Krieg und Politisches Gedachtnis: Zum Umgang mit dem Krieg gegen die Sowjetunion in geteilten Deutschland." *Geschichte und Gessellschaft*, Vol. 34, No. 2 (2008), pp. 252-291.

Maslov, Alexander A. "Tried for Treason Against the Motherland: Soviet Generals Condemned after Release from German Captivity." *Journal of Slavic Military Studies*, Vol. 13, No. 2 (June 2000), pp. 86-138

Megargee, Geoffrey P. "Triumph of the Null: Structure and Conflict in the Command of German Land, 1939-1945." *War in History*, Vol. 4, No. 1 (1997), pp. 60-80.

Miller Jr., Jesse W. "Forest Fighting on the Eastern Front in World War II." *Geographical Review*, Vol. 62, No. 2 (April 1972), pp. 186-202.

Mulligan, Timothy. "Escape from Stalingrad: Soviet Nationals with the German Sixth Army." *Journal of Slavic Military Studies*, Vol. 20, No. 4 (2007), pp. 739-748.

Munting, Roger. "Soviet Food Supply and Allied Aid in the War, 1941-1945." *Soviet Studies*, Vol. 36, No. 4 (October 1984), pp. 582-593.

Murray, Williamson. "Munich 1938: The Military Confrontation." *Journal of Strategic Studies*, Vol. 2, No. 3 (1979), pp. 282-302.

—— "The German Response to Victory in Poland: A Case Study in Professionalism." *Armed Forces & Society*, Vol. 7, No. 2 (Winter 1981), pp. 285-298.

Overy, Richard J. "The German Pre-War Aircraft Production Plans: November 1936 – April 1939." *English Historical Review*, Vol. 90, No. 357 (1975), pp. 778-797.

—— "Hitler and Air Strategy." *Journal of Contemporary History*, Vol. 15, No. 3 (July 1980), pp. 405-421.

—— "German Air Strength, 1933 to 1939: A Note." *Historical Journal*, Vol. 27, No. 2

—— "'Blitzkriegwirtschaft'? Finanzpolitik, Lebensstandard und Arbeitseinsatz in Deutschland, 1939-1942." *Vierteljahrshefte für Zeitgeschichte*, Vol. 36, No. 3 (1988), pp. 379-435.

—— "Mobilization for Total War in Germany 1939-1941." *English Historical Review*, Vol. 103, No. 408 (July 1988), pp. 613-639.

Parrish, Michael. "Formation and Leadership of the Soviet Mechanized Corps in 1941." *Military Affairs*, Vol. 47, No. 2 (April 1983), pp. 63-66.

Pecina, Jozef & Michael Tkacik. "Eastern Front Operational Constraints on Slovak Artillery, 1941-1943." *Journal of Slavic Military Studies*, Vol. 18, No. 1 (2005), pp. 75-107.

Penter, Tanja. "Zwangsarbeit – Arbeit fur den Feind. Der Donbass unter deutscher Okkupation (1941-1943)", *Geschichte und Gesellschaft*, Vol. 31, No. 1 (2005), pp. 68-100.

Peszke, Michael. "Poland's Preparation for World War Two." *Military Affairs*, Vol. 43, No. 1 (February 1979), pp. 18-25.

Reese, Roger R. "Red Army Professionalism and the Communist Party, 1918-1941." *Journal of Military History*, Vol. 66, No. 1 (January 2002), pp. 71-102.

—— "Lessons of the Winter War: A Study in the Effectiveness of the Red Army, 1939-1940." *Journal of Military History*, Vol. 72 (July 2008), pp. 825-852.

Rein, Leonid. "Untermenschen in SS Uniform: 30th Waffen-Grenadier Division of Waffen-SS." *Journal of Slavic Military Studies*, Vol. 20, No. 2 (April 2007), pp. 329-345

Rotundo, Louis. "The Creation of Soviet Reserves and the 1941 Campaign." *Military Affairs*, Vol. 50, No. 1 (January 1986), pp. 21-28.

Searle, Alaric. "A Very Special Relationship: Basil Liddell Hart, Wehrmacht Generals and the Debate on West German Rearmament, 1945-1953." *War in History*, Vol. 5, No. 3 (1998), pp. 327-357.

—— "Revising the 'Myth' of a 'Clean Wehrmacht': Generals Trials, Public Opinion, and the Dynamics of Vergangenheitsbewaltung in West Germany, 1948-1960." *German Historical Institute London*, Vol. 25, No. 2 (November 2003), pp. 17-48.

Sella, Amnon. "'Barbarossa': Surprise Attack and Communication." *Journal of Contemporary History*, Vol. 13, No. 3 (July 1978), pp. 555-583.

Showalter, Denis E. "The Prussian Landwehr and Its Critics, 1813-1819." *Central European History*, Vol. 14, No. 1 (March 1971), pp. 3-33.

Sokolov, Boris V. "The Cost of War: Human Losses for the USSR and Germany, 1941-1945." *Journal of Slavic Military Studies*, Vol. 9, No. 1 (1999), pp. 152-193.

Souter, Kevin. "To Stem the Red Tide: The German Report Series and Its Effect on American Defense Doctrine, 1948-1954." *Journal of Military History*, Vol. 57, No. 4 (October 1993), pp. 653-688.

Stang, Werner. "Zur Geschichte der Luftwaffenfelddivisionen der faschistischen Wehrmacht." *Zeitschrift für Militärgeschichte*, Vol. 8 (1969), pp. 196-207.

Statiev, Alexander. "The Ugly Duckling of the Armed Forces: Romanian Armour 1919-1941." *Journal of Slavic Military Studies*, Vol. 12, No. 2 (June 1999), pp. 220-244.

—— "Antonescu's Eagles against Stalin's Falcons: The Romanian Air Force, 1920-1941." *Journal of Military History*, Vol. 66, No. 4 (October 2002), pp. 1085-1113.

Steinberg, Jonathan. "The Third Reich Reflected: German Civil Administration in the Occupied Soviet Union, 1941-1944." *English Historical Review*, Vol. 110, No. 437 (June 1995), pp. 620-651.

Stolfi, Russel. "Chance in History: The Russian Winter of 1941-1942." *History*, Vol. 65, No. 214 (June 1980), pp. 214-228.

—— "The Greatest Encirclement in History: Link up of the German 3rd and 9th Panzer Divisions on 15 September 1941 in the Central Ukraine." *Royal United Services Institute Journal*, Vol. 141, No. 6 (December 1996), pp. 63-72.

Strohn, Matthias. "Hans von Seeckt and His Vision of a 'Modern Army'." *War in History*, Vol. 12, No. 3 (2005), pp. 318-337.

Sydnor Jr., Charles W. "The History of the SS Totenkopfdivision and the Postwar Mythology of the Waffen-SS." *Central European History*, Vol. 6, No. 4 (December 1973), pp. 339-362.

Thomas, David. "Foreign Armies East and German Military Intelligence in Russia, 1941-1945." *Journal of Contemporary History*, Vol. 22, No. 2 (1987), pp. 261-301.

Tver, Tatiana. "The Battle for Rzhev: Ideology Instead of Statistics." *Journal of Slavic Military Studies*, Vol. 18, No. 3 (2005), pp. 359-368.

Vardi, Gil-li. "Joachim von Stulpnagel's Military Thought and Planning." *War in History*, Vol. 17, No. 2 (2010), pp. 193-216.

Volz, Arthur G. "A Soviet Estimate of German Tank Production." *Journal of Slavic Military Studies*, Vol. 21, No. 3 (2008), pp. 588-590.

Vorsin, V.F. "Motor Vehicle Transport Deliveries through 'Lend-Lease." *Journal of Slavic Military Studies*, Vol. 10, No. 2 (1997), pp. 153-175.

Wagener, Carl. "Der Vorstoss des XXXX. Panzerkorps von Charkow zum Kaukasus, Juli—August 1942. Part One." *Wehrwissenschaftliche Rundschau*, Vol. 5, No. 9 (1955), pp. 397-407.

—— "Der Gegenangriff des XXXX. Panzerkorps gegen den Durchbruch der Panzergruppe Popow im Donezbecken, Februar 1943." *Wehrwissenschaftliche Rundschau*, Vol. 7, No. 1 (1957), pp. 21-36.

Walter, Dierk. "Roon, the Prussian Landwehr and the Reorganization of 1859-1860." *War in History*, Vol. 16, No. 3 (2009), pp. 269-297.

Weinberg, Gerhard L. "Some Thoughts on World War II." *Journal of Military History*, Vol. 56, No. 4 (October 1992), pp. 659-668.

Wood, James A. "Captive Historians, Captivated Audience: The German Military History Program, 1945-1961." *Journal of Military History*, Vol. 69 (January 2005), pp. 123-147.

Zaloga, Steven J. "Technological Surprise and the Initial Period of War: The Case of the T-34 Tank in 1941." *Journal of Slavic Military Studies*, Vol. 6, No. 4 (1993), pp. 634-646.

Zarubinsky, Oleg. "Collaboration of the Population in Occupied Ukrainian Territory: Some Aspects of the Overall Picture." *Journal of Slavic Military Studies*, Vol. 10, No. 2 (1997), pp. 138-152.

Zegenhagen, Evelyn. "German Women Pilots at War, 1939 to 1945." *Air Power History*, Vol. 10, No. 4 (Winter 2009), pp. 11-27.

Zetterling, Niklas & Anders Frankson. "Analyzing World War II Eastern Front Battles." *Journal of Slavic Military Studies*, Vol. 11, No. 1 (March 1998), pp. 176-203.

Published Monographs

Abbott, Peter & Nigel Thomas. *Germany's Eastern Front Allies, 1941-1945*. London: Osprey Pub., 1982.

Achlasov, V.I. & N.B. Pavlovich. *Soviet Naval Operations in the Great Patriotic War, 1941-1945*. Annapolis, MD: Naval Institute Press, 1973.

Adair, Paul. *Hitler's Greatest Defeat*. London: Arms & Armour Press, 1994.

Adam, Wilhelm. *Der schwere Entschluss: Wilhelm Adam, ehemaliger 1. Adjutant der 6. Armee*. East Berlin: Verlag der Nation, 1965.

Ahlfen, Hans von. *Der Kampf um Schlesien*. Munchen: Grafe & Unzer Verlag, 1961.

Ahlfen, Hans von & Hermann Niehoff. *So Kämpfte Breslau*. Stuttgart: Motorbuch Verlag, 1960.

Allen, W.E.D. & Paul Muratoff. *The Russian Campaigns of 1944-1945*. New York: Penguin Books, 1946.

Allmayer-Beck, Christoph Freiherr von. *Die Geschichte des 21. Infanterie Division*. Munchen: Schild-Verlag, 1990.

Anders, Wladyslaw. *Hitler's Defeat in Russia*. Chicago: Regency, 1953.

—— *Russian Volunteers in Hitler's Army*. Bayside, NY: Axis Europa, 1998.

Arbeitsgemeinschaft "Das Kleeblatt". *Die 71. Infanterie-Division im Zweiten Weltkrieg 1939-1945. Gefechts- und Erlebnisberichte aus den Kämpfen der "Glückhaften Division" von Verdun bis Stalingrad, von Monte Cassino bis zum Plattensee*. Hildesheim: Arbeitsgemeinschaft "Das Kleeblatt" (Hrsg.), 1973.

Armstrong, John A. (Ed.) *Soviet Partisans in World War II*. Madison, WS: University of Wisconsin Press, 1964.

Armstrong, Richard N. *Red Army Tank Commanders: The Armoured Guards*. Atglen, PA: Schiffer Pub., 1994.

Arnold, Sabine R., Wolfram Wette, Gerd R. Ueberschar. *Stalingrad: Mythos und Wirklichkeit einer Schlacht*. Frankfurt a. M: Fischer Taschenbuch Verlag, 1992.

Axworthy, Mark. *Third Axis – Fourth Ally: Romanian Armed Forces in the European War, 1941-1944*. London: Arms & Armour Press, 1995.

—— *Axis Slovakia: Hitler's Slavic Wedge, 1938-1945*. Bayside, NY: Axis Europa Books, 2002.

Battistelli, Pier P. *Panzer Divisions: The Eastern Front 1941-1943*. Botley, Oxford: Osprey Pub., 2008.

Bauer, Josef. *290. Infanterie Division 1940-1945*. Delmenhorst: Selbstverlag Kameradenhilfswerk 290. Inf. Div., 1960.

Beaulieu, Walter Chales de. *Der Vorstoss der Panzergruppe 4 auf Leningrad*. Neckargemund: Kurt Vowinckel Verlag, 1961.

Beevor, Anthony. *The Second World War*. London: Little, Brown & Coy., 2012.

Bekker, Cajus. *Ostsee – Deutsches schicksal 1944/1945: Der Authentische Bericht von letzten Einsatz der Kriegsmarine*. Oldenburg: G. Stalling, 1959.

—— *The Luftwaffe War Diaries*. London: Macdonald & Co., 1966.

Benary, Albert. *Die Berliner Bäran-Division: Geschichte der 257. Infanterie Division, 1939-1945*. Bad Nauheim: Verlag Hans-Henning Podzun, 1955.

Bender, Roger & Hugh Taylor, *Uniforms, Organization and History of the Waffen-SS. Volumes Two & Three*. San Jose, CA: R. J. Bender Pub., 1971-1972.

Benz, Wigbert. *Paul Carell: Ribbentrop's Presschef Paul Karl Schmidt vor und Nach 1945.* Berlin: Wissenschaftlich Verlag, 2005.

Bergstrom, Christer. *Barbarossa: The Air Battle, July – December 1941.* Surrey, UK: Ian Allen Pub. Ltd., 2007.

—— *Stalingrad: The Air Battle, 1942 through January 1943.* Surrey, UK: Ian Allen Pub. Ltd, 2007.

—— *Kursk: The Air Battle, July 1943.* Surrey, UK: Ian Allen Pub. Ltd., 2007.

—— *Bagration to Berlin: The Final Air Battles in the East, 1944-1945.* Surrey, UK: Ian Allen Pub. Ltd., 2008.

Bidermann, Gottlob H. *In Deadly Combat: A German Soldier's Memoir of the Eastern Front.* Lawrence, KS: University Press of Kansas, 2000.

Blank, Ralf, et. al. *Germany and the Second World War. Volume IX/1: German Wartime Society 1939-1945: Politicization, Disintegration, and the Struggle for Society.* Oxford: Clarendon Press, 2008.

Blumentritt, Gunther. *Von Rundstedt: The Soldier and the Man.* London: Oldham's, 1952.

Boncsein, Heinrich. *Halten oder Sterben: Die hessisch-thüringische 129. Infanterie Division im Russland und Ostpreussen.* Potsdam: Kurt-Vominckel Verlag, 1999.

Bond, Brian & Ian Roy, (Ed.) *War and Society, Volume Two.* London: Croom Helm Ltd., 1977.

Boog, Horst, et. al. *Germany and the Second World War. Volume IV: The Attack on the Soviet Union.* Oxford: Clarendon Press, 1998.

—— *Germany and the Second World War. Volume VI: The Global War.* Oxford: Clarendon Press, 2003.

Bracher, K.D. (Ed.), *Deutschland zwischen Krieg und Frieden.* Dusseldorf: Droste Verlag, 1991

Bradley, Dermont. et. al. *Generale des Heeres, 1921-1945. Band 1-7.* Osnabruck: Biblio Verlag, 1993-2002.

Braithwaite, Rodric. *Moscow 1941.* New York: Knopf, 2006.

Braun, Julian. *Enzian und Edelweiss: Die 4. Gebirgs Division 1940-1945.* Bad Nauheim: Verlag Hans-Hening Podzun, 1955.

Breithaupt, Hans. *Die Geschichte der 30. Infanterie Division, 1939-1945.* Bad Nauheim: H.H. Podzun, 1956.

Breymayer, Helmut. *Das Wiesel: Geschichte der 125. Infanterie Division, 1940-1944.* Boblingen: Armin Vaas Verlag, 1983.

Buchheit, Gert. *Hitler der Feldheer: Die Zerstörung einer Legende.* Rastatt/Baden: Grote Verlag, 1958.

Burgmaier, Friedrich. *Der Ostfeldzug, 1941-1945. Band I-III.* Munich: Deutsches Rotes Kreuz, Suchdienst Munchen, 1969.

Caiden, Martin. *The Tigers are Burning.* New York: Hawthorn Books, 1973.

Carell, Paul. *Hitler Moves East.* New York: Little, Brown, & Coy., 1965.

—— *Scorched Earth: The Russo-German War, 1943-1944.* Toronto: Little, Brown, & Coy., 1966.

Carr, Edward H. *German-Soviet Relations between the Two World Wars, 1919-1939*. Baltimore, MD: John Hopkins University Press, 1951.

Carruthers, Bob. *The Wehrmacht Experience in Russia*. Great Britain: Coda Books Ltd., 2012.

Carsten, F.L. *The Reichswehr and Politics 1918-1933*. Oxford: Oxford University Press, 1996.

Chuikov, Vasily I. *The Battle for Stalingrad*. New York: Holt, Rinehart & Winston, 1964.

Citino, Robert M. *The German Way of War: From the Thirty Years War to the Third Reich*. Lawrence, KS: University Press of Kansas, 2005.

—— *Death of the Wehrmacht: The German Campaigns of 1942*. Lawrence, KS: University Press of Kansas, 2007.

Clark, Alan. *Barbarossa: The Russo-German Conflict, 1941-1945*. London: Hutchinson & Coy., 1965.

Command Magazine, (Ed.) *Hitler's Army: The Evolution and Structure of German Forces*. Conshohocken, PA: Combined Books, Inc., 1996.

Conze, Werner. *Die Geschichte der 291. Infanterie Division, 1940-1945*. Bad Nauheim: Verlag Hans-Henning Podzun, 1953.

Cooper, Mathew. *The German Army, 1933-1945: Its Political and Military Failure*. London: Macdonald & James, 1978.

—— *The Phantom War: The German Struggle against Soviet Partisans, 1941-1944*. London: Macdonald & James, 1979.

—— *The German Air Force, 1933-1945: An Anatomy of Failure*. New York: Jane's Pub., 1981.

Corti, Eugenio. *Few Returned: Twenty-Eight Days on the Russian Front, Winter 1942-1943*. Columbia, MO: University of Missouri Press, 1997.

Corum, James S. *The Roots of Blitzkrieg: Hans von Seeckt and German Military Reform*. Lawrence, KS: University Press of Kansas, 1992.

—— *The Luftwaffe: Creating the Operational Air War, 1918-1940*. Lawrence, KS: University Press of Kansas, 1997.

Craig, Gordon A. *Politics of the Prussian Army, 1640-1945*. London: Oxford University Press, 1975.

Craig, William. *Enemy at the Gates: The Battle for Stalingrad*. New York: Readers' Digest Press, 1973.

Crevald, Martin van. *Supplying War: Logistics from Wallenstein to Patton*. New York: Cambridge University Press, 1977.

—— *Fighting Power: German and U.S. Army Performance, 1939-1945*. Westport, CT: Greenwood Press, 1982.

Dallin, Alexander. *German Rule in Russia, 1941-1945: A Study of Occupation Policies*. New York: Octagon Books, 1980.

Davis, W.J.K. *Panzer Regiments: Equipment and Organization*. New Malden, Surrey: Almark Pub. Co. Ltd., 1978.

Deist, William. (Ed.) *The German Military in the Age of Total War.* Dover, NH: Berg Pub. Ltd., 1985.

Dell'esercito, Stato Maggiore. *La Operazioni delle Unita Italiane al Fronte Russo, 1941-1943.* Rome: Ufficio Storico SME, 1977.

Denzel, E. *Die Luftwaffen Felddivisionen 1942-1945 sowie die Sonderverbande der Luftwaffe 1939/1945.* Neckargemund: Vowinckel, 1976.

Detwiler, Donald S. (Ed.) *World War II German Military Studies.* New York: Garland Pub., 1979.

Dieckert, Kurt & Horst Grossmann. *Der Kampf um Ostpreussen.* Stuttgart: Motorbuch Verlag, 1960.

DiNardo, Richard L. *Germany's Panzer Arm.* Westport, CT: Greenwood Press, 1997.

—— *Germany and the Axis Powers: From Coalition to Collapse.* Lawrence, KS: University Press of Kansas, 2005.

Doerr, Hans. *Der Feldzug nach Stalingrad: Versuch eines Operativen Uberblickes.* Darmstadt: E.S. Mittler u. Sohn, 1955.

Donnhauser, Anton. *Der Weg der 11. Panzer Division, 1939-1945.* Germany: Traditiongemeinschaft der 11. PD, 1982.

Doyle, Hilary & Thomas Jentz, *Panzerkampfwagen IV Ausf. G, H and J, 1942-1945.* Oxford: Osprey Pub., 2001.

Duffy, Christopher. *Red Storm on the Reich.* London: Routledge Coy., 1997.

Dunn, Walter. *Hitler's Nemesis: The Red Army, 1930-1945.* New York: Greenwood Press, 1994.

—— *Kursk: Hitler's Gamble, 1943.* Westport, CT: Praeger Pub., 1997.

—— *Soviet Blitzkrieg: The Battle for White Russia, 1944.* Boulder, CO: Lynne Rienner Pub., 2000.

—— *Heroes or Traitors: The German Replacement Army, the July Plot, and Adolf Hitler.* Westport, CT: Praeger Pub., 2003.

Dunnigan, James F. *The Russian Front: Germany's War in the East, 1941-1945.* London: Arms & Armour Press, 1978.

Dupuy, Trevor. *A Genius for War: The German Army and the General Staff, 1807-1945.* London: Macdonald & Jane's, 1977.

—— *German and Soviet Replacement Systems in World War II.* Maclean, VA: NOVA Pub., 1980.

Dutu, Alesandru. et. al. *Armata romana in al doilea razboi mondial, 1941-1945.* Bucharest: Dicţionar enciclopedic, Ed. enciclopedică, 1999.

Dyakov, Yuri. *The Red Army and the Wehrmacht: How the Soviets Militarized Germany, 1922-33, and Paved the Way for Fascism.* Amherst: Prometheus, 1994.

Dyke, Carl van. *The Soviet Invasion of Finland.* London: Frank Cass, 1997.

Ellis, John. *Brute Force: Allied Strategy and Tactics in the Second World War.* New York: Penguin Books, 1990.

Engel, Gerhard. *Heeresadjutant bei Hitler 1938-1943: Aufzeichnungen des Majors Engel.* Stuttgart: Deutsche Verlags-Anstalt, 1974.

Eremenko, A. *The Arduous Beginning.* Moscow: Progress Pub., 1966.

Erfurth, Waldemar. *Der Finnische Krieg 1941-1944*. Munich, 1977.

Erickson, John. *The Soviet High Command: A Military-Political History, 1918-1941*. Boulder, CO: Westview Press, 1962.

—— *The Road to Stalingrad: Stalin's War with Germany*. New York: Harper & Row, 1975.

—— *The Road to Berlin: Stalin's War with Germany*. London: Weidenfeld & Nicolson, 1983.

Ericson, Edward E. *Feeding the German Eagle: Soviet Economic Aid to Nazi Germany, 1933-1941*. Westport, CT: Praeger Pub., 1999.

Erlau, Peter. *Flucht aus der Weissen Hölle: Errinerungen an die Grosse Kesselschlacht der 1. Panzerarmee Hube in Raum um Kamenz-Podolsk von 8. Marz bis 9. April 1944*. Stuttgart: Kulturhistorischer Verlag Dr. Reigler, 1968.

Fenyo, Mario. *Hitler, Horthy & Hungary: German-Hungarian Relations 1941-1944*. New Haven, CT: Yale University Press, 1972.

Filipescu, Mihai Tone. *Reluctant Axis: The Romanian Army in Russia 1941-1944*. Chapultepeq: 2006.

Foerster, Wolfgang. *Ein General Kampft gegen den Krieg: Aus nachgelassenen Papieren des Generalstabschefs Ludwig Beck*. Munchen: Munchener Don-Verlg, 1949.

Forster, Jurgen. *Stalingrad: Risse im Bundnis, 1942-1943*. Freiburg: Rombach, 1975.

Fowler, Will. *Stalingrad: The Vital 7 Days: The Germans Last Desperate Attempt to Capture the City, October 1942*. Staplehurst, UK: Spellmount, 2005.

Fretter-Pico, Maximilian. *Missbrauchte Infanterie: Deutsche Infanteriedivisionen in Osteuropäischen Grossraum, 1941-1944*. Frankfurt am Main: Bernard u. Graefe Verlag fur Wehrwesen, 1957.

Fricke, Gert. *'Fester Platz' Tarnopol 1944*. Freiburg: Verlag Rombach, 1969.

Friedli, Lukas. *Die Panzer-Instandsetzung der Wehrmacht*. Uelzen, Germany: Verlag Wolfgang Schneider, 2005.

Frieser, Karl-Heinz. *The Blitzkrieg Legend: The 1940 Campaign in the West*. Annapolis, MD: Naval Institute Press, 2005.

—— et. al. *Das Deutsche Reich und der Zweite Weltkrieg. Volume VIII: Die Ostfront 1943/44*. Munchen: Deutsche Verlags-Anstalt München, 2011.

Friessner, Hans. *Verratene Schlachten: Die Tragödie der Deutschen Wehrmacht in Rumänien und Ungarn*. Hamburg: Holsten-Verlag, 1956.

Fugate, Brian. *Operation Barbarossa: Strategy and Tactics on the Eastern Front, 1941*. Novato, CA: Presidio Press, 1984.

Fugate, Brian & Lev Dvoretsky. *Thunder on the Dnepr: Zhukov-Stalin and the Defeat of Blitzkrieg*. Novato, CA: Presidio Press, 1997.

Galante, Pierre. *Operation Valkyrie: The German Generals Plot Against Hitler*. New York: Harper & Row, 1981.

Gallagher, Matthew P. *The Soviet History of World War II: Myths, Memories, and Realities*. New York: Praeger, 1963.

Gatzke, Hans W. *Stresemann and the Rearmament of Germany*. Baltimore, MD: John Hopkins University Press, 1954.

Gebhardt, James F. *The Petsamo-Kirkenes Operation: Soviet Breakthrough and Pursuit in the Arctic, October 1944*. Leavenworth, KS: Combat Studies Institute, 1990.

Geyr, Hermann. *Das IX. Armeekorps in Ostfeldzug, 1941*. Neckargemund: Scharnhorst Buch Kameradschaft, 1969.

Giurescu, Dinu C. *Romania in the Second World War, 1939-1945*. Boulder, CO: East European Monographs, 2000.

Glantz, David M. *August Storm: The Soviet 1945 Strategic Offensive in Manchuria*. Leavenworth, KS: Combat Studies Institute, 1983.

—— (Ed) *From the Dnepr to the Vistula: Soviet Offensive Operations – November 1943-August 1944. The 1985 Art of War Symposium*. Carlisle, PA: U.S. Army War College, 1985.

—— *Soviet Military Deception in the Second World War*. Totowa, NJ: Frank Cass & Coy. Ltd., 1989.

—— *The Role of Intelligence in Soviet Military Strategy in World War II*. Novato, CA: Presidio Press, 1990.

—— *From the Don to the Dnepr: Soviet Offensive Operations, December 1942 – August 1943*. Portland, OR: Frank Cass Pub., 1991.

—— *The Initial Period of War on the Eastern Front, 22nd June – August 1941*. London: Frank Cass & Coy., 1993.

—— *A History of Soviet Airborne Forces*. London: Frank Cass & Coy., 1994.

—— *Kharkov 1942: Anatomy of a Military Disaster*. Rockville Centre, NY: Sarpedon Press, 1998.

—— *Stumbling Colossus: The Red Army on the Eve of World War II*. Lawrence, KS: University Press of Kansas, 1998.

—— *Zhukov's Greatest Defeat: The Red Army's Epic Disaster in Operation Mars, 1942*. Lawrence, KS: University Press of Kansas, 1999.

—— *Forgotten Battles of German-Soviet War, 1941-1945. Volume One: The Summer Fall Campaign, 22 June - 4 December 1941*. Carlisle, PA: Self-published, 1999.

—— *Forgotten Battles of the German-Soviet War, 1941-1945. Volume Two: The Winter Campaign, 5 December 1941 – April 1942*. Carlisle, PA: Self-published, 1999.

—— *Forgotten Battles of the German-Soviet War, 1941-1945. Volume Three: The Summer Campaign, 12 May – 18 November 1942*. Carlisle, PA: Self-published, 1999.

—— *Forgotten Battles of the German-Soviet War, 1941-1945. Volume Four: The Winter Campaign, 19 November 1942 – 21 March 1943*. Carlisle, PA: Self-published, 1999.

—— *Forgotten Battles of the German-Soviet War, 1941-1945. Volume Five: The Summer-Fall Campaign, 1 July – 31 December 1943, Parts One & Two*. Carlisle, PA: Self-published, 2000.

—— *Barbarossa: Hitler's Invasion of Russia*. Charleston, SC: Tempus Pub., 2001.

—— *The Battle for Leningrad, 1941-1944*. Lawrence, KS: University Press of Kansas, 2002.

—— *Forgotten Battles of the German-Soviet War, 1941-1945. Volume Six: The Winter Campaign, 24 December 1943 – April 1944. Parts One to Three*. Carlisle, PA: Self-published, 2004.

—— *Colossus Reborn: The Red Army at War, 1941-1943.* Lawrence, KS: University Press of Kansas, 2005.

—— *Red Storm over the Balkans: The Failed Soviet Invasion of Romania, Spring 1944.* Lawrence, KS: University Press of Kansas, 2007.

—— *After Stalingrad: The Red Army's Winter Offensive 1942-1943.* Solihull, UK: Helion & Coy., 2008.

—— *To the Gates of Stalingrad: Soviet-German Combat Operations, April–August 1942. The Stalingrad Trilogy. Volume One.* Lawrence, KS: University Press of Kansas, 2009.

—— *Armageddon in Stalingrad, September–November 1942. The Stalingrad Trilogy. Volume Two.* Lawrence, KS: University Press of Kansas, 2009.

—— *Barbarossa Derailed: The Battle for Smolensk, 10 July – 10 September 1941. Volume One.* Solihull, UK: Helion & Coy., 2010.

—— *Operation Barbarossa: Hitler's Invasion of Russia 1941.* Gloucestershire, UK: The History Press, 2011.

—— *Endgame at Stalingrad, Book One: November 1942. The Stalingrad Trilogy. Volume Three.* Lawrence, KS: University of Kansas Press, 2014.

—— *Endgame at Stalingrad, Book Two: December 1942 – February 1943. The Stalingrad Trilogy. Volume Three.* Lawrence, KS: University of Kansas Press, 2014.

Glantz, David M. & Jonathan M. House, *When Titans Clashed: How the Red Army Stopped Hitler.* Lawrence, KS: University Press of Kansas, 1995.

—— *The Battle of Kursk.* Lawrence, KS: University Press of Kansas, 1999.

Görlitz, Walter. *Der Zweite Weltkrieg, 1939-1945.* Two volumes. Stuttgart: Steingruben Verlag, 1951-1952.

—— *Paulus and Stalingrad.* London: 1963.

—— *History of the German General Staff, 1657-1945.* New York: Praeger Pub., 1966.

Grams, Rolf. *Die 14. Panzer Division 1940-1945.* Bad Nauheim: Verlag Hans-Henning Podzun, 1957.

Grant, Gordon. *Barbarossa: The German Campaign in Russia. Planning and Operations, 1940-1942.* Victoria, BC: Trafford Pub., 2006.

Graser, Gerhard. *Zwischen Kattegat und Kaukasus: Weg und Kämpfe der 198. Infanterie Division, 1939-1945.* Tubingen: Herausgegeben von Kameradenhilfswerk und Traditionsverband der ehemaligen 198. Infanterie Division, 1961.

Greiner, Christian. "'Operational History (German) Section' und 'Naval Historical Team.' Deutsches militarstrategisches Denken im Dienst der amerikanischen Streitkrafte von 1946 bis 1950." in Manfred Messerschmidt, et. al. (Ed.), *Militargeschichte. Problem-Thesen-Wege.* Stuttgart: Deutsche Verlags-Anstalt, 1982, pp. 409-435.

Grenkevich, Leonid D. *The Soviet Partisan Movement, 1941-1944 – A Critical Historiographical Analysis.* Portland, OR: Frank Cass Pub., 1999.

Groner, E. *Die Schiffe der deutschen Kriegsmarine.* Munchen: Lehmanns, 1976.

Grossmann, Horst. *Geschichte der Rheinisch-Westfälischen 6. Infanterie Division, 1939-1945.* Bad Nauheim: Verlag Hans-Henning Podzun, 1958.

Gschopf, Rudolf. *Mein Weg mit der 45. Infanterie Division*. Linz: Pberosterreichischer Landesverlag, 1955.

Guderian, Heinz. *Erinnerungen eines Soldaten*. Heidelberg: K. Vowinckel, 1951.

—— *Panzer Leader*. London: Michael Joseph Pub., 1952.

Guillaume, A. *The German Russian War, 1941-1945*. London: The War Office, 1956.

Gundelach, Karl. *Die Deutsche Luftwaffe im Mittelmeer 1940-1945, Vol. 1 & 2*. Frankfurt am Main: Lang, 1981.

Hagen, Mark von. *Soldiers in the Proletarian Dictatorship: The Red Army and the Soviet Socialist State, 1917-1930*. Ithaca, NY: Cornell University Press, 1996.

Hahn, Fritz. *Waffen und Geheimwaffen des deutschen Heeres, 1933-1945. Band I & II*. Bonn: Bernard & Gaefe, 1998.

Halder, Franz. *Hitler als Feldheer*. Munich: Munchener-Dom Verlag, 1949.

—— *Gesprache mit Halder*. Wiesbaden: Limes Verlag, 1950.

—— *Kriegstagebuch: Tägliche Aufzeichnungen des Chefs des Generalstabes des Heeres 1939-1942. Band II*. (Ed.) Hans-Adolf Jacobsen & Alfred Philippi. Stuttgart: Arbeitskreis fur Wehrforschung, 1962.

Hamilton, Hope. *Sacrifice on the Steppe: The Italian Alpine Corps in the Stalingrad Campaign*. Havertown, PA: Casemate, 2011.

Hardesty, Von. *Red Phoenix: The Rise of Soviet Air Power, 1941-1945*. Washington, DC: Smithsonian Institution Press, 1982.

Harrison, Mark. *Soviet Planning in Peace and War, 1938-1945*. Cambridge: Cambridge University Press, 1985.

—— *Accounting for War: Soviet Production, Employment, and Defence Burden, 1940-1945*. Cambridge: Cambridge University Press, 1996.

Hart, Russell A. *Guderian: Panzer Pioneer or Myth Maker?* Washington, DC: Potomac Books Inc., 2006.

Hauck, Friedrich W. *Eine Deutsche Division in Russland und Italien, 305. Infanterie Division, 1941-1945*. Dorheim: Podzun-Verlag, 1975.

Haupt, Werner. *Demjansk 1942: Ein Bollwerk im Osten*. Bad Nauheim: Verlag Hans-Henning Podzun, 1963.

—— *Kiew: Die Grösste Kesselschlacht*. Bad Nauheim: Podzun Verlag, 1964.

—— *Die 260. Infanterie Division, 1939-1944*. Bad Nauheim: Verlag Hans-Henning Podzun, 1970.

—— *Die 8. Panzer Division im Zweiten Weltkrieg*. Friedberg: Podzun-Pallas Verlag, 1987.

—— *Die deutschen Luftwaffe Felddivisionen 1941-1945*. Eggolsheim: Nebel Verlag GmbH, 1993.

—— *Army Group North: The Wehrmacht in Russia, 1941-1945*. Atglen, PA: Schiffer Military History, 1997.

—— *Army Group Centre: The Wehrmacht in Russia, 1941-1945*. Atglen, PA: Schiffer Military History, 1998.

Hayward, Joel S.A. *Stopped at Stalingrad: The Luftwaffe and Hitler's Defeat in the East, 1942-1943*. Lawrence, KS: University Press of Kansas, 1998.

Heidenkampfer, Otto. *Witebsk: Kampf und Untergang der 3. Panzerarmee.* Heidelberg: Kurt Vowinckel, 1954.

Herbert, Ulrich. *Hitler's Foreign Workers: Enforced Foreign Labour in Germany under the Third Reich.* Cambridge: Cambridge University Press1997.

Hermann, H.G., F. Kittel & A. Reinicke. *Der 62. Infanterie Division 1938-1944, Die 62. Volksgrenadier Division 1944-1945.* Munchen: Kameradenhilfswerk der ehemaligen 62. Division, 1968.

Hertlein, Wilhelm. *Chronik der 7. Infanterie Division.* Munchen: Bruckmann Verlag, 1984.

Heusinger, Adolf. *Befel im Widerstreit: Schicksalsstunden der deutschen Armee, 1923-1945.* Tubingen: Rainer Wunderlich Verlag, 1950.

Hillgruber, Andreas. (Ed.) *Kriegstagebuch der Oberkommandos der Wehrmacht (Wehrmachtfuhrungsstab). Band II: 1 Januar 1942 – 31 Dezember 1942.* Frankfurt am Main: Bernard & Graefe Verlag, 1963.

—— *Hitlers Strategie: Politik und Kriegfuhrung, 1940-1941.* Frankfurt am Main: Bernard & Graefe Verlag fur Wehrwesen, 1965.

Hinze, Rolf. *East Front Drama – 1944: The Withdrawal Battle of Army Group Center.* Winnipeg: J.J. Fedorowicz Pub., 1996.

—— *To the Bitter End: The Final Battles of Army Groups North Ukraine, A, Centre, Eastern Front, 1944-45.* Solihull, UK: Helion & Coy., 2005.

Hoffmann, Dieter. *Die Magdeburger Division: Zur Geschichte der 13. Infanterie und 13. Panzer Division, 1935-1945.* Magdeburg: Buch u. Offsetdrunkerei Max Schlutis, 1999.

Hoffmann, Joachim. *Die Geschichte der Wlassow-Armee.* Freiburg im Breisgau: Rombach, 1984.

—— *Die Ostlegionen 1941-1943: Turkotataren, Kaukasier und Wolgafinnen im Deutchen Heer.* Freiburg: Verlag Rombach, 1986.

Hoffmann, Peter. *The History of the German Resistance, 1933-1945.* Cambridge, MA: MIT Press, 1977.

Homze, Edward L. *Arming the Luftwaffe: The Reich Air Ministry and the German Aircraft Industry, 1919-1939.* Lincoln, NE: University of Nebraska Press, 1976.

Hooten, E.R. *Phoenix Triumphant: The Rise and Rise of the Luftwaffe.* London: Arms & Armour Press, 1994.

—— *Eagle in Flames: The Fall of the Luftwaffe.* London: Brockhampton Press, 1997.

Hossbach, Friedrich. *Zwischen Wehrmacht und Hitler, 1934-1938.* Wolfenbuttel: Wolfenbutteler Verlagsanstalt, 1949.

—— *Die Schlacht um Ostpreussen. Aus der kampfender deutschen 4. Armee um Ostpreussen in der zeit von 19.7.1944 – 30.1.1945.* Uberlingen/Bodensee: O. Dikreiter, 1951.

Hoth, Hermann. *Panzer-Operationen: Die Panzergruppe 3 und der Operative Gedanke der Deutschen Fuhrung, Sommer 1941.* Heidelberg: Kurt Vowinckel Verlag, 1956.

Hubatsch, Walther (Ed.) *Kriegstagebuch des Oberkommando der Wehrmacht (Wehrmachtfuhrungsstab), Band III: 1 Januar 1943-31 Dezember 1943.* Frankfurt am Main: Bernard & Graefe Verlag, 1963.

Husemann, Friedrich. *Die Guten Glaubens Waren: Geschichte der 4. SS-Polizei Panzergrenadier Division, Teile I.* Osnabruck: Munin Verlag, 1971.

Irving, David. *Hitler's War.* New York: Avon Books, 1990.

Isaev, Aleksei V. *Kratkii Kurs Istorii Velikoi Otechestvennoi Voiny: Nastupleniie Marshala Shaposhnikova.* [Short course in the Great Patriotic War: The Offensive of Marshal Shaposhnikov] Moscow: Iauza, Eksmo, 2005.

―― *Stalingrad: Za Volgoi dlia nas zemli net* [Stalingrad – There is no land for us Beyond the Volga.] Moscow: 2008.

Jacobsen, Hans-Adolf, (Ed.) *Kriegstagebuch des Oberkommandos der Wehrmacht (Wehrmachtfuhrungsstab). Band I: 1 August 1940 – 31 Dezember 1941.* Frankfurt am Main: Bernard & Graefe Verlag, 1965

Jacobsen, Hans-Adolf & Jurgen Rohwer (Ed.), *Entschiedungsschlachten des Zweiten Weltkrieg.* Frankfurt: Bernard & Graefe, 1960.

Jentz, Thomas L. *Panzertruppen: The Complete Guide to Creation and Employment of Germany's Tank Force, 1933-1942.* Atglen, PA: Schiffer Military History, 1996.

Jones, Michael. *The Retreat: Hitler's First Defeat.* New York: St. Martin's Press, 2009.

Jukes, Geoffrey. *The Defence of Moscow.* London: 1969.

―― *Hitler's Stalingrad Decisions.* Los Angeles, CA: University of California Press, 1985.

Jurado, Carlos Caballero. *Foreign Volunteers of the Wehrmacht, 1941-1945.* London: Osprey Pub. Ltd., 1983.

Kahn, David. *Hitler's Spies: German Military Intelligence in World War II.* New York: Da Capo Press, 1978.

Kalteneggar, Roland. *Die Stammdivision der deutsche Gebirgstruppe: Weg und Kampf der 1. Gebirgs Division, 1935-1945.* Graz: L. Stocker, 1981.

Kamenir, Victor. *The Bloody Triangle: The Defeat of Soviet Armour in the Ukraine, June 1941.* Minneapolis, MN: Zenith Press, 2008.

Kardel, Hennecke. *Die Geschichte der 170. Infanterie Division, 1939-1945.* Bad Nauheim: Verlag Hans-Henning Podzun, 1953.

Kaufmann, Friedrich. *Die Vergessene Division. 282. Baden-Württembergische Infanterie Division.* Germany: Kameradschaft ehem. Angehoriger der 282. Inf.Div., 1985.

Kaufmann, J.E. & H.W. Kaufmann, *Hitler's Blitzkrieg Campaigns: The Invasion and Defense of Western Europe, 1939-1940.* Conshohocken, PA: Combined Books, Inc., 1993.

Kehrig, Manfred. *Stalingrad: Analyse und Dokumentation einer Schlacht.* Stuttgart: Deutsche Verlags, 1974.

Kerne, Erich. *General von Pannwitz und seine Kosaken.* 3rd Ed. Oldendorf: Schutz, 1971.

Killius, Rosmarie. *Frauen für die Front: Gespräche mit Wehrmachthelferinnen.* Leipzig: Militzke Verlag, 2003.

Kliment, Charles & B. Nakladal, *Germany's First Ally: Armed Forces of the Slovak State, 1939-1945.* Atglen, PA: Schiffer Military History, 1998.

Klapder, Ewald. *Der Ostfeldzug 1941—Eine Vorprogrammierte Niederlage: Die Panzergruppe 1 zwischen Bug und Don*. Siek: Ewald Klapdor, 1989.

Klatt, Paul. *Die 3. Gebirgs Division 1939-1945*. Bad Nauheim: Hans-Henning Podzun Verlag, 1958.

Knobelsdorf, Otto von. *Geschichte der niedersächsischen 19. Panzer Division*. Bad Nauheim: Verlag Hans-Henning Podzun, 1958.

Knopp, Guido. *Hitlers Manager*. Germany: Goldmann Verlag, 2006.

Knox, MacGregor. *Hitler's Italian Allies: Royal Armed Forces, Fascist Regime and the War of 1940-1943*. Cambridge: Cambridge University Press, 2000.

Kocham, Lionel. *Russia and the Weimar Republic*. Cambridge: Bowes & Bowes, 1954.

Konev, Ivan S. *Year of Victory*. Moscow: Progress Pub., 1969.

—— *The Great March of Liberation*. Moscow: Progress Pub., 1972).

Koschorrek, Gunter K. *Blood Red Snow: The Memoirs of a German Soldier on the Eastern Front*. London: Greenhill Books, 2002.

Kriedler, Eugen. *Die Eisenbahnen im Machtbericht der Achsenmächte während des Zweiten Weltkrieg*. Gottingen: Musterschmidt, 1975.

Krivosheev, G.F. *Soviet Casualties and Combat Losses in the 20th Century*. Mechanicsburg, PA: Stackpole Books, 1997.

Kroener, Bernhard, et. al. *Germany and the Second World War. Volume V: Organization and Mobilization of the German Sphere of Power, Part One – Wartime Administration, Economy, and Manpower Resources, 1939-1941*. Oxford: Clarendon Press, 2000.

—— et. al. *Germany and the Second World War. Volume V: Organization and Mobilization of the German Sphere of Power, Part Two - Wartime Administration, Economy, and Manpower Resources, 1942-1944/45*. Oxford: Clarendon Press, 2003.

Kurowski, Franz. *Die Heeresgruppe Mitte 1942/1943*. Friedberg: Podzun-Pallas, 1989.

Kursietis, Andris J. *Hungarian Army and Its Leadership in World War II*. Bayside, NY: Axis Europa Books, 1996.

Leach, Barry A. *German Strategy against Russia, 1939-1941*. Oxford: Clarendon Press, 1973.

Lederrey, E. *Germany's Defeat in the East: The Soviet Armies at War, 1941-1945*. London: The War Office, 1955.

Le Tissier, Tony. *Zhukov at the Oder*. Westport, CA: Praeger Pub., 1996.

—— *Race for the Reichstag*. London: Frank Cass, 1999.

Liddell Hart, Basil H. *The Other Side of the Hill*. London: Cassell & Coy. Ltd., 1948.

—— *The German Generals Talk*. New York: William Morrow & Co., 1948

Lohse, Gerhardt. *Geschichte der Rheinisch-Westfälischen 126. Infanterie Division, 1940-1945*. Bad Nauheim: Verlag Hans-Henning Podzun, 1957.

Loser, Jochen. *Bittere Pflicht: Kampf und Untergang der 76. Berlin-Brandenburgischen Infanterie Division*. Osnabruck: Biblio Verlag, 1988.

Lossberg, Bernhard von. *Im Wehrmachtführungsstab: Bericht eines Generalstabsoffiziers*. Hamburg: H.H. Noelke Verlag, 1949.

Lucas, James. *Battlegroup! German Kampfgruppen Action of World War Two*. London: Arms & Armour Press, 1993.

Maier, Klaus, et. al. *Germany and the Second World War. Volume II: Germany's Initial Conquests in Europe.* Oxford: Oxford University Press, 1991.

Mann, Martin & Hermann Oehmichen, *Der Weg der 87. Infanterie Division.* Germany: Selbstverlag der Division, 1969.

Manstein, Erich von. *Verlorene Sieg.* Bonn: Athenaum Verlag, 1955.

—— *Aus einem Soldatenleben.* Bonn: Athenaum-Verlag, 1958.

—— *Lost Victories.* Novato, CA: Presidio Press, 1982.

Manteuffel, Hasso von. *Die 7. Panzer Division im Zweiten Weltkrieg: Einsatz und Kampf der 'Gespenster Division', 1939-1945.* Friedberg: Podzun-Pallas Verlag, 1986.

Mearsheimer, John J. *Liddell Hart and the Weight of History.* Ithaca, NY: Cornell University Press, 1988.

Megargee, Geoffrey. *Inside Hitler's High Command.* Lawrence, KS: University Press of Kansas, 2005.

—— *War of Annihilation: Combat and Genocide on the Eastern Front, 1941.* New York: Rowan & Littlefield, 2006

Meier-Welcker, Hans. (Ed.) *Abwehrkämpfe am Nordflugel der Ostfront, 1944-1945.* Stuttgart: Deutsche Verlag, 1961.

Mellenthin, Friedrich von. *Panzer Battles: A Study of the Employment of Armour in the Second World War.* New York: Cassel & Coy. Ltd., 1971.

Mercatante, Steven D. *Why the Germany Nearly Won: A New History of the Second World War in Europe.* Santa Barbara, CA: Praeger Pub., 2012.

Meretskov, Kirill A. *City Invincible.* Moscow: Progress Pub., 1970.

—— *Serving the People.* Moscow: Progress Pub., 1971.

Merker, Ludwig. *Das Buch der 78. Sturmdivision.* Tubingen: Kameradenhilfswerk der 78. Sturmdivision, 1955.

Merridale, Catherine. *Ivan's War: The Red Army 1939-1945.* London: Faber & Faber, 2005.

Messerschmidt, Manfred. *Die Wehrmacht im NS-Staat: Zeit der Indoktrination.* Hamburg: R. von Decker, 1969.

Meyer-Detring, Wilhelm. *Die 137. Infanterie Division im Mittelabschnitt der Ostfront.* Niederosterreich: Kameradschaft der Division, 1962.

Middeldorf, Eike. *Taktik im Russlandfeldzug: Erfahrungen und Folgerungen.* Darmstadt: E.S. Mittler, 1956.

Mierzejewski, Alfred A. *The Most Valuable Asset of the Reich: A History of the German National Railway, Vol. Two – 1933-1945.* Chapel Hill, NC: University of North Carolina Press, 2000.

Militargeschichtliches Forschungamt. (Ed.). *Operationsgebiet östliche Ostsee und der finnischbaltische Raum, 1944.* Stuttgart: Deutsche Verlags-Anstalt, 1961.

Mitcham Jr., Samuel W. *Crumbling Empire: The German Defeat in the East, 1944.* Westport, CT: Praeger Pub., 2001.

Mitcham Jr., Samuel W. & Gene Mueller, *Hitler's Commanders: Officers of the Wehrmacht, the Luftwaffe, the Kriegsmarine, and the Waffen-SS*. New York: Cooper Square Press, 2000.

Moll, Martin. *Fuhrer Erlasse 1939-1945*. Germany: Franz Steiner Verlag, 1997.

Müller-Hillebrand, Burkhart. *Das Heer 1933-1945, Band I-III*. Darmstadt/Frankfurt: E.S. Mittler & Sohn, 1954-1969.

Müller, Klaus Jürgen. *Das Heer und Hitler: Armee und nationalsozialistisches Regime, 1933-1940*. Stuttgart: Deutsche Verlags-Anstalt, 1969.

Muller, Richard. *The German Air War in Russia*. Baltimore, MD: The Nautical & Aviation Pub. Coy. of America, 1992.

Muller, Rolf-Dieter. *The Unknown Eastern Front: The Wehrmacht and Hitler's Foreign Soldiers*. New York, NY: I.B. Tauris & Co. Ltd., 2012.

Munoz, Antonio J. *The Kaminski Brigade: A History, 1941-1945*. Bayside, NY: Axis Europa, 1996.

Munzel, Oscar. *Panzer Taktik: Raids gepanzerter Verbände im Ostfeldzug, 1941/1942*. Neckargemund: Vowinckel Verlag, 1959.

Murray, Williamson, *Strategy for Defeat: The Luftwaffe, 1933-1945*. Secaucus, NJ: Chartwell Books, 1986.

—— et. al. *The Making of Strategy: Rulers, States, and War*. New York: Cambridge University Press, 1994.

Musculus, Friedrich. *Geschichte der 111. Infanterie Division, 1940-1944*. Hamburg: Herausgegeben von Traditionsverband der 111. Infanterie Division, 1980.

Myles, Bruce. *Night Witches: The Untold Story of Soviet Women in Combat*. Novato, CA: Presidio Press, 1981.

Nafziger, George F. *The German Order of Battle - Panzers and Artillery in World War II*. Mechanicsburg, PA: Stackpole Books, 1999.

—— *The German Order of Battle – Infantry in World War II*. Mechanicsburg, PA: Stackpole Books, 2000.

Nash, Douglas E. *Hell's Gate: The Battle of the Cherkassy Pocket, January to February 1944*. Southbury, CT: RZM, 2002.

Neumann, Joachim. *Die 4. Panzer Division, 1938-1943: Bericht und Betrachtung zu zwei Blitzfeldzugen und zwei Jahren Krieg in Russland*. Bonn: Selbtsverlag der Verfassers, 1989.

Nevenkin, Kamen. *Fire Brigades: The Panzer Divisions, 1943-1945*. Winnipeg: J.J. Fedorowicz Pub., 2008.

Newton, Steven. *Retreat from Leningrad: Army Group North, 1944-1945*. Atglen, PA: Schiffer Military History, 1995.

—— *Kursk: The German View*. Cambridge, MA: Da Capo Press, 2002.

Niehorster, Leo W.G. *The Royal Hungarian Army, 1920-1945*. Bayside, NY: Axis Europa Books, 1999.

Niepold, Gerd. *Die Geschichte der 12. Panzer Division – 2. Infanterie Division (Mot.) 1921-45*. Self-Published, 1988.

Nipe, George M. *Last Victory in Russia: The SS-Panzerkorps and Manstein's Kharkov Counteroffensive February-March 1943*. Atglen, PA: Schiffer Pub., 2000.

Nitz, Gunther. *Die 292. Infanterie Division*. Berlin: Verlag Bernard & Graefe, 1957.

Overy. Richard. *The Nazi Economic Recovery, 1932-1938*. London: Macmilan, 1982.

—— *War and Economy in the Third Reich*. Oxford: Clarendon Press, 1994.

—— *Russia's War: A History of the Soviet War Effort, 1941-1945*. London: Penguin Pub., 1997.

Pahl, Magnus. *Fremde Heere Ost: Hitlers militärische Feindaufklärung*. Berlin: Christoph Links Verlag, 2012.

Paget, Reginald T. *Manstein: His Campaigns and His Trials*. London: Collins, 1951.

Paret, Peter. *The Cognitive Challenge of War: Prussia 1806*. Princeton, NJ: Princeton University Press, 2009.

Parrish, Michael. (Ed.) *Battle for Moscow: The 1942 Soviet General Staff Study*. Toronto: Pergamon Press Canada Ltd., 1989.

Patzold, Kurt. *Ihr waren die besten Soldaten: Ursprung und Geschichte einer Legende*. Leipzig: Militzke, 2000.

Paul, Wolfgang. *Erfrorener Sieg: Die Schlacht um Moskau 1941/1942*. Esslingen: Bechtle Verlag, 1975.

—— *Geschichte der 18. Panzer Division 1940-1943, mit Geschichte der 18. Artillerie Division 1943-1944, anhang Heeresartillerie Brigade 88, 1944-1945*. Germany: Preussischer Militar-Verlag, 1989.

Pennington, Reina. *Wings, Women, and War: Soviet Airwomen in World War II Combat*. Lawrence, KS: University Press of Kansas, 2001.

Pflanz, Hans-Jochen. *Geschichte der 258. Infanterie Division, Band I-III*. Hamburg: Kameradenkries der 258. Division, 1979.

Philippi, Alfred & Ferdinand Heim. *Der Feldzug gegen Sowjetrussland, 1941-1945*. Stuttgart: W. Kohlhammer Verlag, 1962.

Piekalkiewicz, Janusz. *Stalingrad: Anatomie einer Schlacht*. Munchen: Sudwest Verlag, 1977.

—— *Moscow 1941: The Frozen Offensive*. Novato, CA: Presidio Press, 1981.

Plato, Anton von. *Die Geschichte der 5. Panzer Division, 1938-1945*. Regensburg: Walhala & Praetoria Verlag, 1978.

Polhman, Hartwig. *Geschichte der 96. Infanterie Division, 1939-1945*. Bad Nauheim: Verlag Hans-Henning Podzun, 1959.

Pottgiesser, Hans. *Die Deutsche Reichsbahn im Ostfeldzug, 1939-1944*. Neckargemund: Kurt Vowinckel Verlag, 1960.

Raus, Erhard. *Panzer Operations: The Eastern Front Memoir of Erhard Raus, 1941-1945*. New York: Da Capo Press, 2003.

Ready, J. Lee. *Forgotten Axis*. Jefferson, NC: McFarland & Coy., 1967.

Rebentisch, Ernst. *The Combat History of the 23rd Panzer Division in World War II*. Mechanicsburg, PA: Stackpole Books, 2012.

Reese, Roger R. *Stalin's Reluctant Soldiers: A Social History of the Red Army, 1925-1941*. Lawrence, KS: University Press of Kansas, 1996.

—— *Why Stalin's Soldiers Fought: The Red Army's Military Effectiveness in World War II.* Lawrence, KS: University Press of Kansas, 2011.

Reile, Oscar. *Geheime Ostfront: Die deutsche Abwehr im Osten 1921-1945.* Munchen: Welsermuhl Verlag, 1992.

Reincke, Adolf. *Die 5. Jäger Division 1939-1945.* Friedberg: Podzun-Pallas Verlag, 1980.

Reinhardt, Klaus. *Die Wende vor Moskau: Das Scheitern der Strategie Hitlers im Winter 1941/42.* Stuttgart: Deutsche Verlags-Anstalt, 1972.

—— *Moscow – the Turning Point: The Failure of Hitler's Strategy in the Winter of 1941-1942.* Oxford: Providence, 1992.

Reitlinger, Gerald. *The House Built on Sand: Conflicts of German Policy in Russia, 1939-1945.* New York: Viking, 1960.

Rich, Norman. *Hitler's War Aims, Volume One: Ideology, the Nazi State, and the Course of Expansion.* New York: Norton, 1973.

Richardson, W. & S. Freidin. (Ed.) *The Fatal Decisions.* London: Joseph, 1956.

Roberts, Geoffrey. *Stalin's Wars: From World War to Cold War, 1939-1953.* New Haven, CT: Yale University Press, 2006.

Robertson, E.M. *Hitler's Pre-War Policy and Military Plans, 1933-1939.* London: Longmans, 1963.

Rohde, Horst. *Das deutsche Wehrmachttrasnportwesen im Zweiten Weltkrieg: Entstehung, Organisation, Aufgaben.* Stuttgart: Deutsche Verlags-Anstalt, 1971.

Rohricht, Edgar. *Probleme der Kesselschlacht. Dargestellt an Einkreisungs-Operationen im Zweiten Weltkrieg.* Karlsruhe: Condor Verlag, 1958.

Rokossovskii, Konstantin K. *A Soldier's Duty.* Moscow: Progress Pub., 1970.

Romhild, Helmut. *Geschichte der 269. Infanterie Division.* Bad Nauheim: Podzun-Verlag, 1967.

Rotunda, Louis. (Ed.) *Soviet Planning in Peace and War, 1938-1945.* Cambridge: Cambridge University Press, 1985.

Samuelson, Lennart. *Plans for Stalin's War Machine: Tukhachevski and Military-Economic Planning, 1925-1941.* Basingstoke: Palgrave Pub., 2000.

Sanger, Hans. *Die 79. Infanterie Division.* Friedberg: Podzun-Pallas Verlag, 1979.

Scheibert, Horst. *Nach Stalingrad – 48 Kilometer! Der Entsatzvorstoss der 6. Panzerdivision, Dezember 1942.* Heidelberg: Kurt Vowinckel, 1956.

—— *Die Gespenster Division: Eine deutsche Panzer Division im Zweiten Weltkrieg.* Friedberg: Podzun Pallas Verlag, 1981.

Schelm, Walter & Hans Mehrle. *Von den Kämpfen der 215. württembergisch-badenischen Infanterie Division.* Kameradenhilfswerk und Traditionsverband der ehemaligen 215. ID, 1955.

Schick, Albert. *Die 10. Panzer Division 1939-1943.* Koln: J. Pohle Verlag, 1993.

Schimak, Anton, et. al. *Die 44. Infanterie Division: Tagebuch der Hoch und Deutschmeister.* Wien: Verlag Austria Press, 1969.

Schlabrendorff, Fabian von. *Offiziere gegen Hitler.* Zurich: Europa Verlag, 1946.

Schlemmer, Thomas. *Die Italiener an der Ostfront 1942/1943: Dukumente zu Mussolinis Krieg gegen die Sowjetunion*. Munchen: R. Oldenburg, 2005.

Schmidt, August. *Geschichte der 10. Division, 10. (Mot.) Infanterie Division, 10. Panzergrenadier Division, 1933-1945*. Bad Nauheim: Podzun-Verlag, 1963.

Schröder, Jürgen & Joachim Schultz-Naumann. *Die Geschichte der Pommerschen 32. Infanterie Division, 1935-1945*. Bad Nauheim: Verlag Hans-Henning Podzun, 1956.

Schuler, Klaus A. Friedrich. *Logistik im Russlandfeldzug: Die Rolle der Eisenbahn bei Planung, Vorbereitung und Durchführung des deutschen Angriffs auf die Sowjetunion bis zur Krise vor Moskau im Winter, 1941-1942*. Frankfurt: Peter Lang, 1987.

Seaton, Albert. *The Russo-German War, 1941-1945*. London: Arthur Baker Ltd., 1971.

—— *The Battle for Moscow, 1941-1942*. London: Rupert Hart-Davis, 1971.

Seeckt, Hans von. *Gedanken eines Soldaten*. Leipzig: K.F. Koehler, 1935.

Senger und Etterlin, F.M. von. *Der Gegenschlag*. Neckargemund: Kurt Vowinckel, 1959.

—— *Die 24. Panzer Division vormals 1. Kavallerie Division 1939-1945*. Neckargemund: Kurt Vorwinckel Verlag, 1962.

—— *German Tanks of World War II: The Complete Illustrated History of German Armoured Fighting Vehicles, 1926-1945*. New York: Galahad Books, 1969.

Seth, Ronald. *Stalingrad. Point of No Return: The Story of the Battle, August 1942-February 1943*. New York: Coward-Mckann, 1959.

—— *Operation Barbarossa: The Battle for Moscow*. London: A. Blond, 1964.

Shepherd, Ben. *War in the Wild East: The German Army and Soviet Partisans*. Cambridge, MA: Harvard University Press, 2004.

Shirer, William L. *The Rise and Fall of the Third Reich*. New York: Simon & Schuster, 1960.

Shores, Christopher, et. al. *Air War for Yugoslavia, Greece, and Crete 1940-1941*. London: Grub Street, 1987.

Showalter, Dennis. *Hitler's Panzers: The Lightning Attacks that Revolutionized Warfare*. New York: Berkley Pub., 2009.

Showell, Jak P. Mallmann. *Fuhrer Conferences on Naval Affairs, 1939-1945*. London: Greenhill Books, 1990.

Shtemenko, Sergei M. *The Soviet General Staff at War, 1941-1945*. Moscow: Progress Pub., 1970.

—— *The Last Six Months: Russia's Final Battles with Hitler's Armies in World War II*. New York: Penguin Books, 1977.

Smelser, Ronald & Edward Davies II, *The Myth of the Eastern Front: The Nazi-Soviet War in American Popular Culture*. Cambridge, MA: Cambridge University Press, 2007.

Spaeter, Hellmuth. *Die Geschichte des Panzerkorps Grossdeutschland. Volumes One to Three*. Bielefeld : Eiler-Werke Fritz Eilers, 1958.

Speer, Albert. *Inside the Third Reich*. New York: The Macmillan Coy., 1970.

Schreiber, Gerhard, et. al. *Germany and the Second World War. Volume III: The Mediterranean, South-East Europe, and North Africa, 1939-1941*. Oxford: Clarendon Press, 1995.

Schroter, Heinz. *Stalingrad*. London: Michael Joseph, 1958.

Stahl, David. *Operation Barbarossa and Germany's Defeat in the East*. Cambridge: Cambridge University Press, 2009.

—— *Kiev 1941: Hitler's Battle for Supremacy in the East*. Cambridge, UK: Cambridge University Press, 2012.

Steets, Hans. *Gebirgsjäger bei Uman: Die Korpsschlacht des XXXXIX. Gebirgs-Armeekorps bei Podwyssokoje, 1941*. Heidelberg: Kurt Vowinckel, 1955.

—— *Gebirgsjäger in der nogaischen Steppe: Von Dnjepr zum Asowschen Meer, August-October 1941*. Heidelberg: Kurt Vowinckel, 1956.

—— *Gebirgsjäger zwischen Dnjepr und Don: Von Tschernigowka zum Mius, October-Dezember 1941*. Heidelberg: Kurt Vowinckel, 1957.

Stein, Marcel. *Field Marshal von Manstein, A Portrait: The Janus Head*. West Midlands, UK: Helion & Coy. Ltd., 2006.

Steinert, Marlis G. *Hitler's War and the Germans: Public Mood and Attitude during the Second World War*. Athens, OH: Ohio University Press, 1977.

Stephan, Robert W. *Stalin's Secret War: Soviet Counterintelligence Against the Nazi, 1941-1945*. Lawrence, KS: University Press of Kansas, 2004.

Stolfi, Russel. *Hitler's Panzers East: World War II Reinterpreted*. Norman, OK: University of Oklahoma Press, 1991.

Stone, David R. *Hammer and Rifle – The Militarization of the Soviet Union, 1926-1933*. Lawrence, KS: University Press of Kansas, 2000.

—— *Fighting for the Fatherland: The Story of the German Soldier from 1648 to the Present Day*. Washington, DC: Potomac Books, Inc., 2006.

Stoves, Rolf. *Die 1. Panzer Division, 1935-1945*. Bad Nauheim: Verlag Hans-Henning Podzun, 1961.

Streim, Alfred. *Behandlung Sowjetischer Krieggefangenen im 'Fall Barbarossa'*. Heidelberg: Muller Jurisitischer Verlag, 1981.

Streit, Christian. *Keine Kameraden: Die Wehrmacht und die Sowjetischen Kriegsgefangen, 1941-1945*. Stuttgart: Deutsches Verlag-Anstalt, 1978.

Suvorov, Victor. *Icebreaker: Who Started the Second World War*. London: Hamish Hamilton, 1990.

Tarrant, V.E. *Stalingrad: Anatomy of an Agony*. London: Leo Cooper, 1992.

Taylor, A.J.P. *The Origins of the Second World War*. London: Hamilton Pub., 1961.

Tessin, Georg. *Verbände und Truppen der Deutschen Wehrmacht und Waffen-SS im Zweiten Weltkrieg, 1933-1945. Bande 1-17*. Frankfurt am Main: Mittler & Sohn, 1966-2002.

Tettau, Hans von. *Geschichte der 24. Infanterie Division, 1935-1945*. Stolberg: J. Leufgens, 1956.

Thomas, Nigel & Peter Abbott. *Partisan Warfare, 1941-1945*. London: Osprey Pub., 1983.

Thomas, Nigel & Laszlo Szabo. *The Royal Hungarian Army in World War II*. London: Osprey Pub., 2008.

Thurston, Robert W. & Berd Bonwetsch. (Ed.) *The People's War: Responses to World War II in the Soviet Union*. Chicago: University Of Illinois Press, 2000.

Tippelskirch, Kurt von. *Geschichte des Zweiten Weltkrieg*. Bonn: Athenaum Verlag, 1951.

Tooze, Adam. *The Wages of Destruction: The Making and Breaking of the Nazi Economy*. London: Penguin Books Ltd., 2006.

Traditionsverband der Division. *Geschichte der 121. Ostpreussischen Infanterie Division 1940-1945*. Berlin: Selbstverlag der Traditionsverbandes, 1970.

Trevor-Roper, H.R. (Ed.) *Hitler's War Directives, 1939-1945*. London: Sidgwick & Jackson, 1964.

Tsouras, Peter G. (Ed.) *Fighting in Hell: The German Ordeal on the Eastern Front*. Mechanicsburg, PA: Stackpole Books, 1994.

—— *The Anvil of War: German Generalship in Defense on the Eastern Front*. Mechanicsburg, PA: Stackpole Books, 1994.

Tumarkin, Nina. *The Living and the Dead: The Rise and Fall of the Cult of World War II in Russia*. New York: Basic Books, 1994.

Turney, Alfred W. *Disaster at Moscow: Von Bock's Campaigns, 1941-1942*. Albuquerque: University of New Mexico Press, 1970.

Ueberschar, Gerd R. & Wolfram Wette. (Ed.) *'Unternehmen Barbarossa': Der deutsche Uberfall auf die Sowjetunion 1941*. Paderborn: F. Schoningh, 1984.

Ulrich, Bernd. *Stalingrad*. Munich: C.H. Beck, 2005.

United States Army. *The War in Eastern Europe*. West Point, NY: Dept. of Military Art and Engineering, U.S. Military Academy, 1949.

Vasilevsky, Aleksandr M. *The Matter of My Whole Life*. Moscow: Progress Pub., 1978.

Wagner, Ray. *The Soviet Air Force in World War II: The Official History*. Garden City, NY: Doubleday & Coy., 1973.

Warlimont, Walter. *Inside Hitler's Headquarters, 1939-1945*. Novato, CA: Presidio Press, 1964.

Wawro, Geoffrey. *The Austro-Prussian War: Austria's War with Prussia and Italy in 1866*. New York: Cambridge University Press, 1996.

Weeks, Albert L. *Stalin's Other War: Soviet Grand Strategy, 1941-1945*. Lauham, MD: Rowman & Littlefield, 2002.

Wegener, Bernd. "Erschriebene Siege. Franz Halder, die 'Historical Division' und die Rekonstruktion des Zweiten Weltkrieges im Geiste des deutschen Generalstabs." in Ernst Willi Hansen, et. al. (Ed.), *Politischer Wandel, organisierte Gewalt und nationale Sicherheit. Beitrage zur neuren Geschichte Deutschlands und Frankreich*. Munich: R. Oldenbourg, 1995, pp. 287-302,

Weidinger, Otto. *Division Das Reich. Der Weg der 2. SS-Panzer Division 'Das Reich'. Die Geschichte der Stammdivision der Waffen-SS. Band II & III*. Osnabruck: Munin Verlag BMGH, 1972.

Werth, Alexander. *The Year of Stalingrad*. New York: Alfred A. Knopf, 1947.

—— *Russia at War, 1941-1945*. New York: E.P. Dutton Coy., 1964.

Werthen, Wolfgang. *Geschichte der 16. Panzer Division 1939-1945*. Bad Nauheim: Verlag Hans-Henning Podzun, 1958.

Wette, Wolfram. *The Wehrmacht: History, Myth, Reality*. Cambridge, MA: Harvard University Press, 2006.

Whaley, Barton. *Covert German Rearmament, 1919-1939: Deception and Perception*. Frederick, MD: University Publications of America, 1984.

Wilhelm, Hans-Heinrich & Louis De Jong, *Zwei Legenden aus dem Dritten Reich*. Stuttgart: Deutsche Verlags-Anstalt, 1974.

Williamson, Gordon. *World War II German's Women Auxiliary Services*. Botley, Oxford: Osprey Pub., 2003.

Wolf-Dietrich, Heike. *Sie Wollten die Freiheit. Geschichte der Ukrainische Division 1943-1945*. Dorheim: Podzun, 1974.

Wray, Timothy A. *Standing Fast: German Defensive Doctrine on the Russian Front during World War II – Prewar to March 1943*. Fort Leavenworth, KS: U.S. Army Command and General Staff College, 1986.

Zamulin, Valeriy. *Demolishing the Myth: The Tank Battle at Prokhorovka – Kursk, July 1943: An Operational Narrative*. Solihull: Helion & Coy. Ltd., 2011.

Zetterling, Niklas. *Normandy 1944: German Military Organization, Combat Power and Organization*. Winnipeg: J.J. Fedorowicz Pub., 2000.

Zetterling, Niklas & Anders Frankson, *Kursk 1943: A Statistical Analysis*. Portland, OR: Frank Cass Pub., 2000.

—— *The Korsun Pocket: The Encirclement and Breakout of a German Army in the East, 1944*. Philadelphia, PA: Casemate Pub., 2008.

Ziemke, Earl. *Stalingrad to Berlin: The German Defeat in the East*. Washington, DC: US Army Centre of Military History, 1968.

Ziemke, Earl & Magna E. Bauer. *Moscow to Stalingrad: Decision in the East*. Washington, DC: US Army Centre ofMilitary History, 1987.

Zubkova, Elena. *Russia After the War: Hopes, Illusions and Disappointments*. Armonk, NY: M.E. Sharpe, 1998.

Internet Sources

"Human Losses in World War II: German Statistics and Documents" at ww2stats. com/index.html

"Lexikon der Wehrmacht" at http://lexikon-der-wehrmacht.de/

"RKKA in World War II." at http://www.armchairgeneral.com

"The Luftwaffe, 1933-1945" found at www.ww2.dk

"World War II Armed Forces – Orders of Battle and Organizations." at http://niehorster.orbat.com

Index

INDEX OF PEOPLE

INDEX OF PLACES

INDEX OF GERMAN MILITARY FORMATIONS & UNITS

INDEX OF SOVIET MILITARY FORMATIONS & UNITS

INDEX OF GENERAL & MISCELLANEOUS TERMS

Submissions

The publishers would be pleased to receive submissions for this series. Please contact us via email (info@helion.co.uk), or in writing to Helion & Company Limited, 26 Willow Road, Solihull, West Midlands, B91 1UE.

Titles